A Modern Legal History of England

A Modern Legal History of England and Wales 1750-1950

by A.H.Manchester, MA, LLM

Senior Lecturer in Law,
University of Birmingham

London
Butterworths
1980

| England | Butterworth & Co (Publishers) Ltd |
| London | 88 Kingsway, WC2B 6AB |

Australia Butterworths Pty Ltd
Sydney 586 Pacific Highway, Chatswood, NSW 2067
Also at Melbourne, Brisbane, Adelaide and Perth

Canada Butterworth & Co (Canada) Ltd
Toronto 2265 Midland Avenue, Scarborough, M1P 4S1

New Zealand Butterworths of New Zealand Ltd
Wellington 77 – 85 Customhouse Quay

South Africa Butterworth & Co (South Africa) (Pty) Ltd
Durban 152 – 154 Gale Street

USA Butterworth (Publishers) Inc
Boston 10 Tower Office Park, Woburn, Mass. 01801

ISBN Casebound 0 406 62263 9
Limp 0 406 62264 7

Reproduced from copy supplied
printed in Great Britain
by Billing and Sons Limited
Guildford, London, Oxford, Worcester

Preface

The period 1750 – 1950 was one of tremendous change in all spheres of the national life. In this book I have attempted both to describe those legal institutions and those areas of law which were of major significance and which experienced change during that period and also to comment upon them. In addition I have attempted to discuss the process of law reform. Of course no single volume can offer a really comprehensive treatment of the whole of the legal system and of the law. However, I do hope that my book captures the essence of that system and of its law: we can take considerable pride in both.

Although much of the book is based upon original work, I have written it as an introductory work for a general audience rather than for lawyers and law students alone.

The book is based upon a series of lectures which I first offered to students in my Faculty at the University of Birmingham in 1968. I am obliged to all those students who offered encouragement over the years. Long may our Brougham Club flourish! I am obliged also to those of my colleagues who were kind enough to comment upon draft chapters. In particular I am obliged to my friend and former colleague, Dr. Harry Smith, who read several chapters in draft and who offered me a number of valuable suggestions. Finally, I would like to thank my wife, Anne, and my children Anneliese, David and Graham for the tolerance which they showed during the long period when this History dominated my life.

Faculty of Law,   A.H. Manchester
University of Birmingham   September, 1979

Contents

Chapter 2

Law

Chapter 3

Lawyers and judges

Chapter 4

The courts: an introduction

Chapter 5

Inferior civil courts

Chapter 6

Superior courts of civil jurisdiction

Chapter 7

Courts of criminal jurisdiction

Chapter 8

Review and appeal

Chapter 9

The substantive criminal law

Chapter 10

The enforcement of the criminal law

Chapter 11

The criminal and punishment

Chapter 12

Civil liability

Chapter 13

Property

Chapter 14

Labour and capital

Chapter 15

The family and the law

Chapter 16

Conclusion

Table of Statutes

References in this Table to '*Statutes*' are to Halsbury's Statutes of England (Third Edition) showing the volume and page where the annotated text of the Act will be found.

PAGE

PAGE

List of Cases

Chapter 1

Introduction

1 The challenge

'It was the boast of Augustus — it formed part of the glare in which the
perfidies of his earlier years were lost — that he found Rome of brick and
left it of marble, — a praise not unworthy of a great prince and to which
the present reign also has its claims. But how much nobler will be the
Sovereign's boast when he shall have it to say that he found law dear, and
left it cheap; found it a sealed book — left it a living letter; found it the
patrimony of the rich — left it the inheritance of the poor; found it the
two-edged sword of craft and oppression — left it the staff of honesty and
the shield of innocence.'

Such was the hope which Henry Brougham, a powerful Whig politician and
distinguished lawyer who was soon to be Lord Chancellor expressed to the House
of Commons in 1828.[1] Such seemed to be the hope also of Brougham's fellow
Whigs and of a considerable portion of public opinion generally, including more
liberal Tories such as Robert Peel. There was about to be, it seemed, a deliberate
attempt to reform the age-old institutions of the law, a conscious effort to meet
the challenge of dramatically changed social conditions, of new commercial and
financial techniques, of quite staggering technological advances, and of new
philosophies which sought to define afresh the relationship between the state and
the individual. Would the law, the lawyers and the political system be able to
meet such a challenge?

2 The legal system in 1750

In 1750 the law and the legal system bore rather the marks of its feudal past than
the signs of any visible reaction as yet to the demands of a new and changing
world. At Westminster Hall a mere 12 common law judges presided over the law,
a number which was not to be increased until well into the nineteenth century.

---

1   18 Official Report (2nd series: 1828) cols. 127ff.

The Lord Chancellor, who was also a considerable political figure, presided over the Court of Chancery with the aid of the Master of the Rolls. It is true that there were numerous other minor judges and courts. For example, the justices of the peace were of considerable importance in criminal cases: local courts of various kinds also exercised jurisdiction over a variety of civil matters. To the population as a whole, however, those 14 judges personified the law.

The law which they administered was concerned primarily with land. Blackstone's *Commentaries on the Laws of England*, which were published in the 1760s, make that perfectly clear by devoting the whole of one of the four volumes to a discussion of land law. Further, that land law still bore very clearly the marks of its feudal origins. It was altogether a mysterious science. Commercial law and the principles of civil liability i.e. of contract and tort received relatively brief treatment. The substantive criminal law and criminal procedure, by way of contrast, were in a relatively modern state, despite the fact that the great number of offences which were then subject to the punishment of death caused the former to be dubbed the 'Bloody Code'. The law itself was very largely common law i.e. judge-made or case law, rather than the Act of Parliament or statute which was to become so popular during the nineteenth century. Further, the archaic procedures which the courts followed, had been fashioned over the years. All too often these procedures led to undue delay and expense. Up to a point such delay and expense was tolerable in a society which was relatively static. It was less likely that a more dynamic commercial and industrial world would be content with such a system. New and changing social and economic factors would clearly place all aspects of the law and of the legal system under considerable strain over the coming years.

3 Social and economic factors 1750-1850

a) *Introduction*
During this period England and Wales underwent a social and economic revolution. The population grew considerably. A primarily agricultural society was transformed into the commercial and industrial leader of the world. A largely paternalistic society was transformed into the world's most vigorous advocate of laissez-faire economics. The provision of better roads, of canals, and of railways meant that for the first time people might travel with relative ease into areas beyond their immediate parish or township. Aspects of those changes deserve further mention.

b) *Population*
In 1746 the population was 6 millions; in 1811 it was 12 millions and by 1851 it was 18 millions. New cities were created. For example, whereas in 1801 the populations of Liverpool and of Leeds were 82000 and 52000 respectively, their respective populations in 1831 were 202000 and 123000. Similarly, Birmingham more than quadrupled its population between 1675 and 1760; by the end of the century the city's population had doubled again. Such rapid change left a number of anomalies in its wake. Until well into Victoria's reign the bustling and important city of Birmingham, one of the birthplaces of the Industrial

Revolution, had no Assize i.e. court of superior jurisdiction, of its own; citizens were required instead to travel 15 miles, no inconsiderable journey in those days, to the far less populous and commercially significant county town of Warwick. Policing of the great new industrial cities was clearly an even more difficult task in the absence of new methods. During London's infamous Gordon riots of 1780, even the house of the Lord Chief Justice, Lord Mansfield, was not safe from attack. In 1791 a loyalist mob in Birmingham burned down the house and laboratory of Dr. Joseph Priestley, a dissenter, who happened also to be the father of modern chemistry. Even as late as 1839 the Birmingham magistrates felt that they were incapable of maintaining public order in the city at the time of a Chartist gathering there. Numerous other examples could be given. Moreover, the drift from the country into the large, impersonal, urban areas, and into the massed ranks of workers in the great, new factories meant that the patterns of social control which had existed in tightly-knit rural communities no longer existed. Contemporaries believed that conditions in the factories had led to a deterioration in family life, that parents were no longer able to supervise their children adequately, and that this led to an increase in juvenile crime.

Above all the growth of the new industrial cities was to present a series of unique and complex general problems; the manner of their solution was relevant in terms of the method employed to questions of law reform. Public health was the crucial issue. Thousands lived in overcrowded and insanitary conditions. Cholera had struck in 1831 and London's poor sanitation was a national disgrace. A number of Commissions inspired by Edwin Chadwick, a disciple of Bentham, educated the public in the need for change. Finally, despite the vested interests and other opposition, legislation was passed. Indeed, of the Public Health Act 1848 it has been said that 'no moment in the world's history has been more significant'.[2] The method of reform through the medium of the initial inquiry, the report of the Commission, and subsequent legislation was typically Benthamite, typically Victorian. Equally typical was the fact that the Act was only a permissive measure and that it lacked fully efficient means of enforcement. Yet the country had been edging gingerly towards more efficient methods of enforcing social legislation ever since the enactment of the first Factory Act, the Health and Morals Act 1802. Subsequent legislation was to provide for the appointment of an inspectorate. Other legislation, and not least the new Poor Law of 1834, began to accustom society to the merits of scientific inquiry into society's ills, to the regular appearance of numerous 'Blue Books' which set out the results of such inquiries, to the role of legislation and to the necessity of enforcing that legislation adequately. There was substantial opposition to such processes and to the values which they appeared to embody. Both the county gentlemen, who regretted the loss of some of their former powers, and the poor, who regretted its inhuman face, were hostile during the 1830s to the Poor Law and to all that was associated with it. Further, a country which had coped up to that time with a remarkably small civil service found that many citizens were opposed strongly to any extension of government which meant an increase in public taxation. As early as the 1820s the *Quarterly Review* had complained of a flood of legislation. By mid-nineteenth century such a complaint was even more

2   E.C Midwinter *Victorian Social Reform* p. 34.

justified.[3] By that time, however, a spirit of scientific reform seemed apparent on all sides and with it an acceptance of, or at all events a resignation to, increased intervention by both central and local authorities.

c) *The changing agricultural scene*

Improvements in agricultural techniques made it possible both to reclaim land e.g. by drainage, and to use existing land more profitably e.g. by using new equipment. In addition discoveries of minerals were made and, as the new towns grew rapidly, the value of land adjacent to them also rose dramatically. Not surprisingly, perhaps, the manorial lords sought to claim much waste or common land for their personal ownership. The position in law at that time was that certain persons called commoners had rights, in common with the lord himself, in such lands. Not all such commoners were willing to surrender those rights. Accordingly, many private enclosure Acts were passed whose object was to deprive the commoners of their rights. Indeed, Watson writes[4] that before 1760 the yeomen of England had ceased to exist as an important class in the community.

The contemporary face of rural England and Wales owes much to the success of the enclosure movement. Farming standards improved and so benefited the community as a whole. Yet there were social costs also. Whereas in 1700 as much as half the arable land in England had been in open fields, by 1830 the enclosure movement had succeeded almost everywhere.[5] By 1887 only some 12 per cent of the occupiers of agricultural land owned it. Marx interpreted the enclosure movement as 'robbery of communal lands by the landlords in order to create large capitalist farms and, by throwing large numbers off the land, to set free a proletarian labour force for manufacturing industry'. Some economic historians also interpreted the movement as one by which the wealthy deprived small men of their rights. A more recent generation of economic historians sees the enclosure movement as neither the force which drove the unemployed agricultural labourer into the factories nor as the destroyer of the small farmer. Further, the fairness of the enclosure commissioners was so impressive that, in the view of Chambers and Mingay, 'parliamentary enclosure represented a major advance in the recognition of the rights of the small man'.[6]

Probably the enclosure movement was a factor in the impoverishment of the agricultural labourer during this period. There were many other factors. What is impressive in legal terms, however, irrespective of the merits of enclosure, is the speed with which the legislature reacted to the demand for enclosure. Within the space of just a few generations traditional legal rights which many had cherished had been swept away. Clearly radical change within the system was possible. Almost as interesting is the manner in which any further encroachment upon common land was restricted after 1866. Now it had become important to preserve such land for recreational use by the swollen populations of the new cities.

3   J. Toulmin Smith *Government by Commissions.*
4   S. Watson *The Reign of George III 1760-1815* p. 35.
5   R. K. Webb *Modern England from the Eighteenth Century to the Present.*
6   T. May *The Economy 1815-1914*, J. D. Chambers and G. E. Mingay *The Agricultural Revolution, 1750-1880.*

d) *Industrial change*
In the mid-eighteenth century there were three great manufactures — those based on wool, iron and leather. But the large factory, such as the Darby works at Coalbrookdale in Shropshire, was exceptional. Often traditional methods survived for many years, especially in craft centres such as Birmingham and Sheffield. However, new methods, a new technology were coming into use, even if slowly. The cotton trade was the first to develop in this way. As never before the work of the 'hands' in the factories was integrated: workpeople were subjected to a new and largely impersonal form of discipline. Often children were recruited to carry out the routine yet laborious tasks. Here, then, were the beginnings of a social and industrial revolution. The new 'masters' were above all successful individuals, living proof of the validity of an individualist philosophy. Their capital requirements posed unprecedented problems for the law. Eventually the new workers were to believe that their best interests would be furthered by the collective action of fellow workmen or trade unions. The law was also required to cope with that action.

The process of industrialisation was gradual. Even as late as 1851 more than a quarter of all men over the age of 20 were still employed in agriculture while twice as many men and women worked in domestic service as in the cotton trade, the largest industrial employer.[7] By then, however, industry dominated the national life and extended in scope far beyond the three great manufactures of 100 years before.

e) *Roads, canals, railways*
Contemporaries were keenly aware of the social effects of the dramatic improvements in communications which were implemented during those years. New roads and canals meant that for the first time it had become relatively easy by the beginning of the nineteenth century for people to travel and for goods to be moved long distances. During the period 1830 to 1846 there was an equally dramatic provision of fresh railway track. Changed methods of organisation and of financing, together with novel problems such as deaths caused by the new machines, posed unprecedented problems for the lawyers of the day,

f) *Capital and commerce*
The City of London already exercised a worldwide influence, as a financial institution, in commercial, monetary and insurance matters. The City served commerce rather than industry. However, during the second half of the eighteenth century the country banks expanded rapidly. Whereas in 1750 there were about a dozen such banks, there were around 700 by 1815. It is scarcely surprising, therefore, that it was during this period that Lord Mansfield played a major part through case law in developing a rational system of commercial law. Similarly, it was during this period that the judges and the legislature modernised the law of theft as offences such as embezzlement and false pretences were created.

The railways apart, the capital sums required to finance the new undertakings were not dramatically high. If a family company could not itself raise the capital required, the formation of a partnership was the answer. Joint-stock

7 *Webb* pp. 112-13.

organisation was regarded as being particularly susceptible to fraudulent practices. However, after the repeal of the Bubble Act in 1825 there was considerable pressure for change. In 1856 statute granted limited liability to all companies, except banks, which met certain conditions. That legislation, to which the practice and experience of railway investment had contributed, demonstrated a remarkable change in public attitudes. Would the new companies be less honest than their predecessors?

4 Public attitudes and beliefs 1750-1850

a) *Status, paternalism, protectionism*

The England and Wales of 1750 was a paternalistic and protective society. It was governed by the aristocracy and the gentry. Because society as a whole conceded some degree of respect to that rank, they could usually afford to be relatively easygoing in the exercise of their influence. Everybody knew his station but there was nevertheless a certain degree of social mobility. Indeed, the recklessly feckless and extravagant might cause a rapid decline in even a great family's rank and authority by dissipating its fortune. In the eighteenth century the lawyers devised the strict settlement which prevented the nominal owner of land from alienating land for any period beyond his own life. The settlement might also provide a dowry for a daughter or a portion for a son. During the eighteenth century the familiar device of the strict settlement controlled the inheritance of about half the land in the country. Henceforth the status and influence within society of both the aristocrat and the gentleman was reasonably secure.

The practices of paying customary wages, restrictive apprenticeship laws, and vagrancy and poor laws which provided for some supervision of the poor were further marks of a paternalistic society which was based on status. At a national level, too, there was a belief in protectionist policies. Mercantilist theories, in addition to providing 'nurseries of seamen' for use in time of war, added up in practice to a complex system of protectionist trading regulations.

At the same time as individual fortunes were being made in industry and in commerce British explorers such as that great Yorkshireman, Captain Cook, were opening up whole new worlds. Such factors called for a changed philosophy which stressed the value of individual effort and which preached a correspondingly reduced role for the state. An outstanding advocate of such a philosophy was Adam Smith.

b) *Adam Smith*

Adam Smith's *Wealth of Nations* was first published in 1776. The essence of Smith's philosophy was his belief in the force of the individual's self-interest so that 'in general, if any branch of trade, or any division of labour be advantageous to the public, the freer and more general the competition, it will always be the more so'; he held also that 'the national effort of every individual to better his own condition when suffered to exert itself with freedom and security, is so powerful a principle, that it is alone and without any assistance, not only capable of carrying on the society to wealth and prosperity, but of surmounting a hundred impertinent obstructions with which the folly of human laws too often incumbers its operations'.[8] In similar fashion he argued for a limited role only for government. In his view the state had but three functions. These were to defend the realm, to administer public justice and to carry out those public works which it was impossible for private individuals to undertake.

Based upon liberty, argued lucidly and apparently based upon contemporary successful business experience, Smith's views soon became both widely known and influential. Unlike Smith himself, his advocates subsequently tended to ignore much of the social cost which was implicit in an unqualified application of Smith's general principles. Although he himself was no revolutionary, Smith's views were to influence not only radical economic change but also changing social attitudes which rejected paternalism on the part of the state. Other economists, such as Ricardo, were to exercise a very considerable influence, yet it was Smith who first captured his countrymen's imagination.

c) *Other factors*

Of course many other influences were also at work. A general reaction against what were seen as the excesses of the French Revolution first stifled the enthusiasm which many had felt for the exciting ideas of the French philosophers and then effectively thwarted most attempts at reform during the first quarter of the nineteenth century. There was, too, the influence of evangelical Christians, of Non-conformists and of a whole generation of economists. Above all there was the stark reality of life in the great, new cities and their teeming factories. In one such city, Manchester, a German manufacturer named Engels was making observations upon the condition of the people which would contribute to a new communist philosophy. By mid-nineteenth century the country as a whole was committed to individualism. In the space of 100 years there had been, in Maine's famous phrase, a transition from status to contract.

5 England and Wales 1850-1950

a) *Prosperity*

The Great Exhibition of 1851 symbolised the rapid growth during the previous century of the country's commercial and industrial wealth and of its hopes for the future. Years of peace with neighbours abroad, the peaceful passing of the great Chartist demonstration of 1848, together with a steadily increasing domestic prosperity appeared to herald a period of stability at home. Of all decades, wrote G. M. Young, one should choose the 1850s in which to be young. At home the country's agriculture and industry advanced and expanded by leaps and bounds, throughout the 1860s. By 1870 the foreign trade of the United Kingdom was more than that of France, Germany, and Italy together and nearly four times that of the United States and foreign investment was substantial. But this period of expansion was now drawing to a close: a new era was dawning. The so-called 'Great Depression' of 1873-96 marked not only a crisis of confidence in the business community but also a period of relative decline, which perhaps was inevitable, as foreign industries grew and began to compete with British

---

8 W. S. Holdsworth *A History of English Law* vol 11, p. 501.

industries even in Britain. German imports were the occasion of considerable concern: in the 1890s British output of steel was less than that of either the United States or Germany.[9] It was possibly in response to such competition that the size of industrial enterprises began to grow. There was an increasing recourse by companies to limited liability and an increasing unionisation, even amongst the unskilled, for the first time. Nevertheless, thanks largely to the returns on massive overseas investments, the standard of life remained pleasant for many people. Since Mayhew's dramatic newspaper articles in mid-century on the conditions of some working people, much had been done to improve standards of both public health and work. Despite the trauma of the First World War a rise in living standards continued. Indeed, according to R. K. Webb, it is probable that 'at no time before in English history had the quality of life changed so rapidly, and generally so much for the better, as in the decades between the wars'.[10] Even so, the generation which had fought the Second World War was determined that peace should bring with it a greater measure of social justice.

b) *Assumptions*

Free trade, individualism, progress were the country's guiding beliefs in mid-nineteenth century. Yet we can see, with hindsight at least, that even in mid-nineteenth century there was a recognition of the fact that, irrespective of the merits of individualism, the state had a special role to play in an industrial society. Protective factory legislation and public health legislation illustrate some aspects of that role.[11] Other legislation recognised that by no means all parties to contracts were able to bargain upon an equal footing. For example, railway commissioners were appointed in 1873 especially to ensure that the railways treated all business concerns fairly. Such legislative concern was not of general application. For example, in a mass producing, industrialised society the standard form contract became increasingly popular. Such contracts were offered, often by large companies which might even have a virtual monopoly, upon a take it or leave it basis. Many years were to pass, however, before the courts and the legislature began to protect the individual customer in such cases. Even so, from mid-nineteenth century on there was an increasing public belief, among workmen at all events, in the justice of collective rights. Increasing unionisation, first amongst craftsmen and by the end of the century amongst semi-skilled and unskilled workmen led to a belief, however inadequately it was articulated, in the justice of their combining together to secure their economic self-interest. The principle of state intervention in areas outside the traditional governmental fields of defence and public justice was being established with remarkable speed. Reference has already been made to protective legislation which had been born out of sheer necessity and also out of concern for the moral wellbeing of the community as well as a degree of humanitarianism. In addition Mill and others had long believed that education could not be left to the demands of the market with the result that he was a fervent supporter of compulsory education.[12] By the close of the nineteenth century the growth of a host of

9   *Webb* p. 375.
10   *Webb* p. 546.
11   W. C. Lubenow *The Politics of Government Growth.*
12   M. Cowling *Mill and Liberalism*, M. Ginsberg 'The Growth of Social Responsibility' in *Law and Opinion in England in the Twentieth Century* p. 3.

state and municipal enterprises had eroded the pure individualist ethic. England and Wales were set firmly on the path to what Dicey was to dub 'collectivism'. For Dicey collectivism meant socialism, 'which favours the intervention of the state, even at some sacrifice of individual freedom, for the purpose of conferring benefit upon the mass of the people'. Dicey identified collectivism especially with the labour laws and with laws 'intended to regulate the conduct of trade and business in the interest of the working classes, and, as collectivists believe, for the benefit of the nation'.[13] No government of any political persuasion sought to reverse that trend, although as the Liberal Industrial Inquiry pointed out in 1928 'there has hardly been one of the forms of state action...proved by experience to have been beneficent, which was not hotly opposed at its inception as an unwarrantable invasion of individual liberty'.[14] It was the desire to do justice in the individual case, the desire to achieve a greater measure of social justice which was largely responsible for the erosion of the individualistic ethic. Certainly some sturdy individualists had sought to apply that ethic with due rigour. This is clear from the country's enthusiasm for the pamphlets of Dr. Samuel Smiles such as *Self Help* (1859) and *Thrift* (1875). No doubt it was just such an attitude which in Victorian London compelled Octavia Hill to restrain a kindly gentleman from offering a coin to a beggar. There were relatively few Octavia Hills. Theorists also noted that it was possible to hedge individualism about with so many limitations in the public interest that it would be possible to argue on such grounds even for the complete abolition of private property in land, as Sidgwick suggested in 1891. Few theorists took the fertile concept of equality as far as that during the nineteenth century. Individuals were to be regarded as equal before the law. Little effort was expended in seeking to use the concept of equality as a means of achieving a more egalitarian distribution of property. In that sense a certain inequality even appeared inevitable in the general public interest to some. Naturally such views coloured the approach of the lawyers to questions such as public access to the courts in terms of legal aid.

The gradual extension of democracy to the working classes, an ever-increasing humanitarianism or social conscience, the radical approach of the Liberal Party and of the newly created Labour Party, which was formed only at the beginning of the twentieth century, were to ensure the further extension of collectivist measures. Within the spirit of such measures we may include an Act such as the Children and Young Persons Act 1908, the Children's Charter, which even abrogated to a certain extent traditional parental rights. To some extent the state, rather than the parent, was to determine what was best for the family. The state soon undertook further obligations in the field of social insurance. Measures taken during the First World War and the spirit of national unity which had been aroused during that emergency also served to encourage a collectivist approach. Disappointment of the social and economic expectations of a generation of soldiers who survived the holocaust of that War, led to a degree of disillusionment during the period between the two World Wars. Political stability was maintained yet those who sought a greater degree of social and

---

13 A. V. Dicey *Law and Public Opinion in England during the Nineteenth Century* pp. 64-5.
14 *Ginsberg* (above) p. 21.

economic justice became more convinced than ever of the merits of state intervention. The generation which fought the Second World War, or at least a great
majority of it, was determined that it would not be deprived, as it felt that its
parents had been, of such an increased measure of social and economic justice.
In 1945 a Labour Government was returned with a substantial majority. An
unprecedented degree of state intervention was planned which included schemes
of nationalisation. Clearly the spirit of such legislation had implications for the
future interpretation of rights in property at common law which had insisted so
sharply upon strict observance of such rights.

   To attempt to sketch the relevant history of 200 years within so brief a compass is a difficult, if not impossible, task. Concepts have been mentioned which
will need considerable further examination in order to arrive at a proper understanding of their significance. What exactly do we mean by laissez-faire, collectivism or the welfare state? Other possibly influential factors have not been considered at all. For example, to what extent may religious beliefs have coloured
approaches to law reform before the twentieth century? Surely the approach of
James Fitzjames Stephen to criminal punishments, his emphasis on retribution,
was coloured by his distinctive Christian beliefs? The variety of factors which
have contributed over the years to legislative change and law reform cannot be
over-estimated.

6 Law reform

a) *Public opinion*

Such social, economic and philosophic change meant that change was inevitable
within the law and the legal system. The pace at which any such developments
occurred would reflect how receptive a powerful legal profession would be to
suggestions for change, how insistent public opinion would be in demanding
change, and how adequate the machinery for reform would prove itself to be in
the light of the demands which were to be thrust upon it.

   The England and Wales of the mid-eighteenth century was a land of vested
interests in which the leaders of the legal profession played a considerable constitutional and political role which conferred a certain prestige upon the profession
as a whole. Since the constitutional settlement of the late seventeenth century
had emphasised a certain respect for property, it was inevitable that as the interpreters of that constitution, the lawyers would respect vested proprietary
interests. Such a society was unlikely to welcome change. Further, a country
which had only vanquished the motley forces of Prince Charles Edward with
some difficulty at Culloden as recently as 1746 and whose commercial prosperity
was increasing rapidly tended rather to welcome, even to insist upon, the status
quo than to favour suggestions for change. That does not mean that society was
totally blind to its faults. Contemporary novelists such as Richardson, Smollett
and Fielding demonstrated an awareness of the faults of their society: philanth-
ropists sought to remedy some of the faults of that society. Much opinion,
however, found little, if any, fault with contemporary society.

   It was also a land in which there was a strong libertarian instinct. The powers
of central government were strictly limited in practice, the idea of a standing

army was anathema, administration — even policing, such as it was — was on a local basis. Its criminal procedure was to be admired in revolutionary France. Englishmen and Welshmen might be subjects rather than citizens in constitutional theory yet they believed that theirs was a free country. Public opinion counted, therefore. To minister to that budding public opinion there were in London alone in 1782 some 18 daily newspapers with an average readership of up to 500 per copy.

b) *William Blackstone*

Any critic who wished to achieve a broadly based measure of public support for his proposals was well advised to couch his language in measured terms which made clear his support for the constitution as a whole. The legal commentator and judge, Sir William Blackstone, chose just such an approach.[15] He wrote:

> 'the fundamental maxims and rules of the law, which regard the rights of persons, and the rights of things, the private injuries that may be offered to both, and the crimes which affect the public, have been and are every day improving, and are now fraught with the accumulated wisdom of ages: that the forms of administering justice came to perfection under Edward the first; and have not been much varied, nor always for the better, since....Of a constitution so wisely contrived, so strongly raised and so highly finished, it is hard to speak with that praise, which is justly and severely its due:- the thorough and attentive contemplation of it will furnish its best panegyric....Nor have its faults been concealed from view; for faults it has, lest we should be tempted to think of it more than human structure; defects, chiefly arising from the decays of time, or the rage of unskilful improvement in later ages. To sustain, to repair, to beautify this noble pile, is a charge intrusted principally to the nobility, and such gentlemen of the kindgom, as are delegated by their country to parliament.'[16]

Accordingly, Blackstone's four volume *Commentaries on the Laws of England* are of interest to us at the present day not only because they formed an important statement of contemporary rules of law but because they express a contemporary attitude towards law reform.

William Blackstone was born in London in 1723. After graduating from Oxford at the age of 18, he became a member of the Middle Temple with a view to practising at the Bar. He practised in London, albeit with little success, until 1753. However, in 1743 he was elected a Fellow of All Souls, Oxford and thereafter spent a considerable portion of his time in Oxford. Disappointed in his hopes of the Regius Chair, apparently upon the grounds of 'political unreliability', he took the advice of friends that he should retire to his Fellowship and complete a series of lectures upon the laws of England. Although Blackstone was later to serve both as a Member of Parliament and as a judge of Common Pleas, his lasting and deserved fame rests upon those lectures for they formed the basis of his *Commentaries*. Blackstone was elected to the Vinerian Chair at Oxford in

---

15 On Blackstone see: D. J. Boorstin *The Mysterious Science of Law*, H.G. Hansbury 'Blackstone in Retrospect' (1950) 66 LQR 318, G. Jones *The Sovereignty of the Law*, R. Cross 'Blackstone v Bentham' (1976) 92 LQR 516.

16 4 Bl Com (5th edn) 435-6.

1758. He held that Chair until 1766 when the demands of his practice compelled him to resign. He died in 1780.

The first edition of his *Commentaries* was published in four volumes between 1765 and 1769. In those four volumes he set out in a lively and articulate manner the leading principles of the law and of the legal system. It was a remarkable achievement which can be appreciated fully only when it is contrasted with the dreary manuals which had preceded Blackstone and, sadly, were to be produced subsequently. It was just such an appeal to the educated, general reader which had been Blackstone's principal aim. They do not pretend to be, nor within their relatively brief compass could they have been, a comprehensive digest of the law. Yet here, virtually for the first time, we have a lucid, principled statement of the law. Moreover, it was accurately stated law. Despite the abundant criticism, even abuse, which has been levelled at various aspects of the *Commentaries* — often, it seems, by those who have read them either inattentively or not at all — there has been no serious criticism of Blackstone upon that score. Accordingly, the *Commentaries* offer us a precise statement of the law as it appeared to an intelligent and able lawyer in the second half of the eighteenth century.

Blackstone's alleged complacency, of which the passage cited above is often said to be an example, has infuriated many critics, of whom Gibbon and Bentham were among the first and the most virulent. Such criticism is frequently unfair to Blackstone. By the standards of his day Blackstone offered a considerable amount of useful criticism. Indeed, his overall tone of reasoned exposition leavened by restrained, reformist criticism was not only representative of the culture of his day but was also more likely to yield tangible, political results, a lesson which Bentham was never to learn even to the end of his long life. Moreover, Blackstone wrote at a time when legal change appeared to be in the air. The great Lord Chief Justice, Lord Mansfield,[17] was in the process of creating through judicial decisions a body of commercial law suited to the rapidly increasing commercial needs of a great commercial country. At the same time he was seeking also to streamline the procedure of his court with a view to reducing unnecessary delay and expense. Other judges were creating a modern law of theft, virtually within the span of half a century, which the country was to use until 1968. The work of the magistrates, especially the Fieldings, at Bow Street appeared to herald still more widespread improvements in both summary justice and in policing. Public debate on criminal punishments was beginning. Of course more conservative views were advanced as well. Although we can point to Romilly and Eden as protagonists of a liberal point of view in criminal matters, we must point also to Madan and to Paley as popular exponents of a much more conservative approach. Paley's *Principles of Political and Moral Philosophy*, which was published in 1785, was an especially influential work, yet to a rational, contemporary observer the existence of such public debate might well have suggested the view that some change at least was possible. He would have been encouraged in such views later in the century by the popularity of the views of those who, like Shelburne, favoured administrative reform, and of those who, like Pitt, frowned upon nepotism and sinecures in government. No doubt an

17 C. H. S. Fifoot *Lord Mansfield*.

awareness also of more radical views still, such as those of the London Corresponding Society or of Jeremy Bentham might have encouraged even more the view that some change at least was imminent. In fact it did not happen. Bentham was an especially significant figure.

c) *Jeremy Bentham*

Jeremy Bentham, like Adam Smith, argued persuasively against legal restraints. A notable example of his approach is in his *Truth v Ashurst*, which was written in 1792 as a comment on a charge to a grand jury by Ashurst J on 17 November 1792, but which was not published until 1823. By way of reply to Ashurst J's basic position that 'the law of this country only lays such restraints on the actions of individuals as are necessary for the safety and good order of the community at large', Bentham has Truth point out instances of restraint which Bentham suggests do not fall within Ashurst J's proviso:

> 'The trade I was born to is overstocked; hands are wanting in another. If I offer to work at that other, I may be sent to gaol for it. Why? Because I have not been working at it as an apprentice for seven years. What's the consequence? That, as there is no work for me in my original trade, I must either come upon the parish or starve.'

Clearly Bentham has his place in the pantheon of the uniquely nineteenth century concept of freedom. Yet his life's work was the promotion of law reform.[18] Indeed, so distinguished a jurist as Maine wrote in mid-nineteenth century that he did not know of a single law reform which had been effected since Bentham's day which could not be traced back to his influence. Others, too, have written in generous terms of Bentham's influence.

Jeremy Bentham was born in 1748, the son of a well-to-do father whose fortune supported Jeremy throughout a long life. After Oxford he settled down in London at the age of 19 to the study of law. There he was an early admirer of Lord Mansfield: 'Days and weeks together have I made my morning pilgrimage to the chief seat of the living idol', and was called to the Bar in 1769. However, he did not practise but instead he gave his life to the study of law and, in particular, to the advancement of law reform.

Initially, he worked upon an analysis of theories and punishments. The work remained unpublished until Dumont published it some 40 years later in the *Théorie des Peines*. Next came Bentham's *Comment on the Commentaries*, his comment on Blackstone's *Commentaries* which was not published until 1928. His principal work during this period was *Principles of Morals and Legislation* which was printed in 1780 but was not published until 1789. It was the publication of the *Fragment on Government* which led to his friendship with the Earl of Shelburne, whose country seat at Bowood he was to visit frequently during the following ten years. It was also during this period that he came to know Samuel Romilly, who was to work so hard for the mitigation of capital punishment. Then followed years of work upon his scheme for the Panopticon which was to be

18 There is a considerable literature upon all aspects of Bentham's work. By way of
   introduction see: A. V. Dicey *Law and Public Opinion in England during the Nineteenth Century* (2nd edn, 1914) pp. 126 ff., W. S. Holdsworth *A History of English Law* vol 13, p. 40, H. A. Holland 'Jeremy Bentham, 1748-1832' (1948) 10 CLJ 3, G. Keeton and G. Schwarzenberger *Jeremy Bentham and the Law*.

a circular prison building with cells on every storey of the circumference and a lodge in the centre for the inspector who would be able to see all the prisoners without himself being seen. Despite some initial official encouragement and some 20 years of effort, however, the scheme was finally rejected in this country. It was the publication in 1802 of the *Traités de la Législation Civile et Pénale* which established his reputation. In 1808 he began his long friendship with James Mill. The *Rationale of Judicial Evidence* was finally published in 1827 and he wrote on many other matters, including codification. He died in 1832.

The mainspring of his views was the doctrine of utility, that is, that the proper end of every law was the promotion of the greatest happiness of the greatest number. It was not an original principle by any means: it was a principle, more-over, which could be interpreted and applied in quite different ways. Yet it did provide a basic premise upon which the whole machinery of the administration of government might be reformed — a cutting edge which would sweep away the whole mass of out-dated practice and a theory which would suggest what should be put in its place. According to Mill, Bentham's novelty of method lay in his remorseless insistence on the criticism of existing law and institutions, and in his schemes of reform on 'treating wholes by breaking them down into parts, abstractions by resolving them into things and generalisations by distinguishing them into the individuals of which they are made up'.[19] It was a scientific method — 'What's the use of it?' became a common test.

It is over-simple, however, to talk of 'Benthamism' and of 'Benthamites' as though there were one accepted body of doctrine, one group of devoted adherents. It can be argued, for example, that the culmination of the first period of Benthamism was marked by the enactment of the Reform Bill of 1832. Subsequently, Benthamites were very much concerned with the problems of their own period, and, as they faced up to the daunting task of translating theory into practice, some modifications to, and adjustments of, the theory were made. This was true of the work of both J. S. Mill and of Chadwick — indeed, at an earlier date neither Romilly nor Brougham had been prepared to accept the word of the master in toto. Brougham, who freely acknowledged his debt to Bentham, was criticised severely by both Bentham and by that distinguished Benthamite organ, the *Westminster Review*. Yet can one really deny that he was influenced by Bentham and by Bentham's writings?

How influential was Bentham?[20] On the one hand extravagant claims have been made on his behalf. It is possible to point to a considerable number of reforms which Bentham suggested and to note that reformers were able to imple-ment such or similar reforms later in the nineteenth century. Certainly, Romilly

---

19   H. L. A. Hart *Bentham* (British Academy Lecture, 1962) p. 299. *Dicey* pp. 134 ff. summarises Bentham's views as to the principles of law reform as: (1) legislation is a science (2) the right aim of legislation is the carrying out of the principle of utility (3) every person is in the main the best judge of his own happiness.

20   E. Halevy *The Growth of Philosophic Radicalism*, O. MacDonagh 'Nineteenth Century Revolution in Government' (1958) 1 Historical Journal 52, J. Hart 'Nineteenth Century Social Reform: A Tory Interpretation of History' (1965) 31 Past Present 39, D. Roberts 'Jeremy Bentham and the Victorian Administrative State' (1959) 2 Victorian Studies 193, H. Parris 'The Nineteenth Century Revolution in Government: A Re-appraisal Re-appraised' (1960) 3 Historical Journal 17.

and Brougham were among the distinguished parliamentarians who spread his ideas; the Mills and Austin also promulgated Benthamite ideas. Yet the old positions did not fall in the light of Benthamite theory alone, although the reformers often used, or purported to use, that theory to achieve reform. It has been claimed that, although Bentham was important, 'a great deal of administrative and legislative development was the result of the empirical actions and hard-bought experience of a number of officials, many of whom had probably never heard of Bentham, but on whom public demand had imposed novel and very difficult tasks'. This thesis is supported in general terms by a number of distinguished historians and may be dubbed as the 'Tory interpretation of history'. Other historians disagree. Hart, for instance, argues that ideas can influence people who are unconscious of their origin by becoming part of the general climate of opinion. Accordingly, the criteria of 'reading the works' or of 'hearing the name' are improper criteria by which to assess influence. Hart also emphasises the point that 'the Benthamites did not confine themselves to stating a principle. They made empirical studies, often of a novel kind, and found out what actually happened, and then proposed specific remedies for what they considered evils.' Finally Hart points out that the 'Benthamites were not doctrinaire advocates of laissez-faire. The main principle of utilitarianism was that the test of policy should be its effect on human happiness.'

Those arguments were not framed with reference to the law and to the legal system, yet they are easily applicable to them. In fact, no conclusive verdict upon Bentham's influence upon law reform can safely be arrived at. On the one hand, numerous contemporary reformers, such as practising politicians, acknowledged their debt to Bentham and some credit is therefore due. On the other hand, it can be argued that many changes within the system — for example, within the courts and even with regard to the institution of new police forces in 1856 — owed far more to the pragmatic forces of the day than to any wish to implement basic theory.

d) *Henry Brougham*
Conservative attitudes prevailed during the 1790s. A reaction against the excessess of the French Revolution ensured that those attitudes were to prevail for several years. A more liberal approach only became evident in the 1820s and was personified in the major changes which Robert Peel, a great Tory Home Secretary, introduced. Consolidation of statutes, prison reform and police all benefited from his administrative skill and political genius in piloting potentially contentious measures through parliament with little fuss. By contrast Henry Brougham was the very personification of a new class of crusading Whig.[1] Unlike Peel, he achieved relatively little, although he did inspire legal reformers virtually from the time when he helped to found the *Edinburgh Review* in the early years of the nineteenth century to the time of his death in 1868. Henry Peter Brougham, who was born in Edinburgh on 19 September 1778, was a distinguished advocate who just possibly might have become Prime Minister. Instead he became a reforming Lord Chancellor who lent his name and active support to a wide variety of causes throughout his long life. He may be associated especially,

1 C. New *Life of Henry Brougham to 1830*, F. Hawes *Henry Brougham*.

however, with his work for the anti-slavery movement, for education and for law reform. Much of the credit for the passage of the great Reform Act of 1832 may also be attributed to the legal and political skills of Henry Brougham.

In the field of law reform his famous six hour speech in 1828 upon the state of the common law led to the appointment of two Royal Commissions. As Lord Chancellor during the period 1830-34 he spared no effort, despite the constant pressure of his other duties, in seeking to press the cause of law reform. Certainly his admirers held high expectations of him. At the time when he became Lord Chancellor, he may well have been the most popular public man in England — a unique situation, surely, for any lawyer. Even Campbell, whose judgment as a biographer was often less than charitable (it was said of his *Lives of the Chancellors* that he had added a sting to dying) wrote of this period in Brougham's life that: 'People came to town to see the Tower, the lions and Brougham in the Court of Chancery.' Sidney Smith had fewer inhibitions still:

> 'Look at the gigantic Brougham, sworn in at twelve-o-clock and before six p.m. he has a bill on the table abolishing the abuses of a court which has been the curse of England for centuries...in an instant the iron mace of Brougham shivered to atoms the House of Fraud and Delay.'

In fact Brougham's 'iron mace' had achieved no such thing. Yet the extravagance of the language illustrates both the very real measure of public enthusiasm for legal reform which did exist as well as the absurd over-expectation which was entertained of what any one man, however able and distinguished, might achieve — at all events when he faced the influence of vested interests. Perhaps it was a recognition of this fact which persuaded Brougham in 1844 to help to found the Law Amendment Society and, some years later, the Association for the Promotion of Social Science.

Although Brougham's direct influences were relatively few, therefore, his indirect influence was considerable. Sir John Eardley Wilmot produced a total of 112 bills which he said that Brougham had either inspired or introduced. There was some truth even in that extravagant claim. For example, the creation of the new County Court in 1846 may not be attributable directly to Brougham yet there can surely be little doubt that it was his pioneering work in the 1830s which had paved the way for that new venture. In truth, although the personal qualities of the would-be reformer would always be of importance, personal qualities alone could rarely conquer the opposition of vested interests and the cumbersome parliamentary machinery of reform. By the time of Brougham's death the 'great man' approach to successful reform was outdated: the mark of the reforming new age was the committee and the commission.

e) *The ebb and flow of law reform*

The use of select committees and royal commissions reached its peak in mid-nineteenth century.[2] Naturally, they included several important inquiries of a legal nature. *The Times* warned the lawyers not to impede legal reform. A legal magazine proclaimed that we were all reformers now. Even the government of the day appeared to be taking law reform seriously. It seemed that at a time when a proud and rich country was displaying its engineering and commercial genius

---

2   H. Clokie and J. W. Robinson *Royal Commissions of Inquiry* pp. 78-9.

to the world at the Great Exhibition of 1851, it was at long last also about to undertake radical reforms of its legal system and its law. By the mid-seventies that spirit had virtually disappeared: the Judicature Acts of that period, which reshaped the structure of the superior courts, were its final manifestation.

Of course, there were to be many subsequent inquiries, a certain amount of piecemeal reform, a considerable continuing concern at the apparent inability of the legal system to meet the old bogeys of undue delay and expense and of the law itself to meet changing social needs. Commercial men turned with increasing frequency to arbitration rather than to the courts; many liberal politicians especially tended to feel that the courts had mishandled the great labour disputes of the nineties and of the first decade of the twentieth century. When Lloyd George introduced an important measure of social insurance in 1911, he turned — perhaps inevitably in the light of the great numbers of persons involved — to a specially created administrative tribunal rather than to the courts for the settlement of any subsequent disputes. For the most part such factors occasioned little lasting concern among the majority of lawyers. When one distinguished professor raised the subject of law reform in his inaugural lecture in 1928, there was litttle that was radical, or even original, in his proposals.[3] The fire had long departed from the reformers. Proposals which were made during and after the Second World War regarding the law and the legal system sounded a note of rather greater urgency yet were still far from radical, despite the fact that radical concepts such as the nationalisation of large sectors of industry were being discussed with some enthusiasm.[4] For the most part law reform was no longer a question of general concern. For example, commercial men in 1950 no longer sought the reform of the law as their counterparts had done in 1850; instead they sought to bypass it. By and large, after 1914 law reform was in the main a technical question for lawyers alone. To what extent this was because there was general satisfaction with the law and the legal system or because many citizens had followed other means of solving their disputes, remains an open question.

7 The machinery of law reform

a) *Judicial reform*
The judges coped well, through the medium of an evolving case law, with many new situations. Although older origins exist, it is true to say that the judges created virtually the whole of the modern commercial law, and the law of contract and tort during this period. Similarly, almost the whole of the modern law of theft was developed, much of it by the judges, during the latter half of the eighteenth century. Yet to develop new principles of law is one thing: to eradicate long-established abuses is quite different. On the latter score a determined judge might do something, as Mansfield did in the matter of the procedure of his court. Generally speaking, however, the judge who was

3 P. H. Winfield 'Law Reform' (1928) 44 LQR 289.
4 G. W. Keeton 'The Problem of Law Reform after the War' (1942) 58 LQR 247, G. Williams *The Reform of the Law*, and cf. (1952) 68 LQR 114 and (1952) 15 MLR 378. H. Hart *The Way to Justice, a Primer of Legal Reform*, and cf. (1941-3) 5-6 MLR 156.

necessarily immersed in the day-to-day duties of his office lacked the time, quite apart from the vision, will or capacity, to tackle long-established practices and abuses, especially those which were of an administrative nature. Moreover, what one judge might accomplish, a more conservative judge might later reverse. Much of Mansfield's work was to suffer that fate. As a result Bentham condemned judicial reform in characteristically forthright terms:

> 'Should there be a judge who enlightened by genius, stimulated by honest zeal to the work of reformation, sick of the caprice, the delays, the prejudices, the ignorance, the malice, the fickleness, the suspicious ingratitude of popular assemblies, should seek with his sole hand to expunge the effusions of traditionary imbecility, and wrote down in their room the dictates of pure and native justice, let him but reflect that partial amendment is bought at the expense of universal uncertainty; that partial good thus purchased is universal evil; and that amendment from the judgment seat is confusion.'[5]

b) *Legislative reform*

Legislation was to be the reforming tool of the future. Indeed, it was already clear at the beginning of the nineteenth century in the context of the developing law of theft that there were limits beyond which the judges, bound by precedent, were not prepared to take the law in order to achieve what they may have felt was a socially desirable result. In such cases, too, legislation was necessary. During the second quarter of the nineteenth century the increased flow of all kinds of legislation had accustomed both the public and the lawyer to the growing importance of legislation as a source of law and to its value as a tool of reform.

Now the aim of all reformers, including law reformers, was to secure the enactment of legislation which would be sympathetic to their cause. To that end it was necessary to appeal to the public opinion of the day. Newspapers such as *The Times* and *The Morning Chronicle* gave a platform to such causes. A would-be reformer might publish his own newpaper, as Francis Place, the arch-opponent of the combination laws, did or he might publish pamphlets. Throughout the nineteenth century the intellectual periodicals gave a certain amount of coverage of legal matters. The Whig-inclined *Edinburgh Review*, the Benthamite *Westminster Review*, and the Tory *Quarterly Review* are especially worthy of note. Taken as a whole these nineteenth-century journals offer a remarkably high standard of public debate upon serious issues and demonstrate a powerful belief in the capacity of reason to overcome obstacles. The law magazines are also worthy of note. The high quality *Law Magazine* and professional journals such as *The Jurist*, the *Law Times* and *Solicitors' Journal* contributed to, and at times sought to stimulate, the debate upon law reform. The prestigious *Law Quarterly Review*, perhaps because it was founded only in the latter years of the nineteenth century, concerned itself primarily with analyses, albeit of a generally high quality, of black letter law rather than with any real concern for the promotion of law reform.

c) *Pressure groups*

The rise of Statistical Societies in the 1830s, contributed to society's growing

---

5 J. Bentham *A Comment on the Commentaries* (Oxford edn, 1928) p. 214.

interest in itself: they took a special interest in crime. Nor should we discount the influence of a novelist such as Dickens. Pressure groups also were of some importance in the field of law reform as they were in other areas of national life. The Law Amendment Society which later merged into the National Association for the Promotion of Social Science is especially worthy of note. Each year at its congress, which the host city invariably regarded as an important civic occasion, the Association brought together a large number of participants from various professional disciplines and interests with a view to discussing the leading social issues of the day. What concerned them were issues such as law reform, education, penal organisation, public health and social and economic conditions. Many lawyers were members — indeed, the General Secretary, G. W. Hastings, was a barrister. The Association was a middle-class reformist organisation[6] whose influence it is difficult to assess. In the view of one writer its most important successes were 'the appointment of the Royal Commission on Sanitary Legislation in 1869, an important stage in the history of the Public Health Act of 1875, and the passage of the Married Women's Property Act of 1870'. Quite possibly its debates influenced a wider discussion still of reform issues.

d) *Inquiries*

Subsequently, a royal commission or a select committee of the House of Commons or of the House of Lords might be appointed to investigate the particular issue. They were not a new device. Royal commissions of inquiry had sat during the latter years of the eighteenth century. Yet some 60 or more were appointed during the years 1800-1831. There was also a wide and increasing use during those years of select committees. Their use reached a peak during the mid-nineteenth century yet they remained popular throughout this period. It was the Benthamites who had found a particular use for them, yet it was the anti-slavery movement which first pointed out the way in which a reform movement might succeed eventually in securing the enactment of legislation which was sympathetic to its cause.

The Benthamites believed strongly in the efficacy of rational argument supported, where appropriate, by a sound knowledge of the relevant facts. For them the process of inquiry, report and legislation was both logical and inevitable. They were scientific observers of, and investigators into, society. Once diligent inquiries had possessed them of the relevant facts, they would be able to suggest a fitting solution to the social problem in question. Legislation based upon such scientific investigation was a step on the way to viewing legislation as a science in the Benthamite tradition. Chadwick's investigations of the 1840s in the public health field provide the classic example,[7] but there was no shortage of diligent inquiries in the legal field.

In practice royal commissions did enjoy a certain government favour for in reality their members were appointed by the Cabinet. Indeed, the royal commission could be seen as the natural weapon by which the Crown acted for investigative purposes. By contrast governments on occasion might feel hindered, or even

6 B. Rodgers 'The Social Association 1857-1886' in *The Manchester School* p. 283.
7 S. E. Finer *The Life and Times of Sir Edwin Chadwick.*

offended by select committees. Yet the recommendations of neither were assured of being translated into legislation — parliament had the final word. Undoubtedly, such bodies collected a great deal of useful information, much of it from overseas, which casts valuable light upon many aspects of the legal system. Faith in royal commissions continued in the twentieth century. 'We are unanimous', declared the Balfour Report in 1910, 'in believing that the appointment of royal commissions is useful for the elucidation of difficult subjects which are attracting public attention, but in regard to which the public information is not sufficiently accurate to form a preliminary to legislation.' Even so, the twentieth century saw increasing use being made of the report of a departmental committee.

e) *Parliament and law reform*

Nor was parliament always willing to find the time for legislation upon a particular subject. Despite the growth of delegated legislation in the twentieth century, parliament was unwilling also to give up its rights to discuss and to amend even measures which were largely technical and made little or no change in the law. It was apparent, therefore, that certain delays were inherent in a democratic parliamentary procedure which complemented both the country's natural conservatism and the apathy felt by much of public opinion with regard to most questions of legal reform. Clearly the lot of the legal reformer was far from being a happy one.

Bibliography

In touching upon questions of social, economic and political history in this introductory chapter, I have been indebted to a number of works which I list below.

R. K. Webb	*Modern England from the Eighteenth Century to the Present*
A. Briggs	*Victorian Cities*
G. D. H. Cole and R. Postgate	*The Common People*
A. V. Dicey	*Law and Public Opinion in England during the Nineteenth Century* (2nd edn, 1962)
R. C. K. Ensor	*England 1870-1914*
G. Kitson Clark	*The Making of Victorian England*
C. L. Mowat	*Britain between the Wars 1918-1940*
J. H. Plumb	*England in the Eighteenth Century*
D. Thomson	*England in the Nineteenth Century*

E. P. Thompson   *The Making of the English Working Class*

G. M. Young   *Portrait of an Age: Victorian England*

S. Watson   *The Reign of George III 1760-1815*

L. Woodward   *The Age of Reform 1815-1870*

T. May   *The Economy 1815-1914*

Chapter 2

Law

1 Common law and statute

Blackstone divided the law into two categories. On the one hand there was the *lex non scripta*, the unwritten or common law. On the other hand there was the *lex scripta* which was the written or statute law.[1] Statutes might be classified as being either declaratory of the common law or remedial of some defects therein.[2] Of course, statute was paramount. However, that classification expressed the lawyers' view of the all embracing, comprehensive nature of the common law and of its fundamentally important role. It both reflected and shaped lawyers' attitudes over the years towards the respective roles and relative importance of the common law and of statute. Statute was to be seen primarily as no more than complementary to the common law.

It followed that lawyers tended to oppose any scheme, even if its aim was to simplify the sources of the law, which appeared to strike at this fundamental concept of the common law. For example, in mid-nineteenth century a would-be reformer sought to consolidate the entire statute and common law. Of his attempt a legal magazine commented:

'He could only have made it in forgetfulness of the essential difference between the common law and the statute. The operation is impossible. A code of common law is a contradiction in terms. The function of a statute is to correct and supply the deficiencies of the common law, but not to replace it; and every statute becomes in the course of time the nucleus of a group of common law precedents, by which it is construed and applied.'[3]

That and other like attempts at such reform failed.

---

1 1 Bl Com (5th edn) 63. The common law may also be contrasted with equity i.e. the principles followed by the Court of Chancery, or with the principles which were followed in other courts such as the ecclesiastical courts. In this chapter the phrase 'common law' is used primarily to indicate the volumes of judicial precedents known as case law, irrespective of the court in which those precedents may have originated.
2 1 Bl Com (5th edn) 86.
3 (1853) 17 Jur 458 at 459. Cf. (1858) 5 Sol Jo 122.

It was scarcely surprising that the judicially developed rules of statutory interpretation also reflected the lawyers' reverence for the common law. Accordingly, a presumption existed that no statute was intended in the absence of clear words to take away a common law right. As such rights tended to have been formulated during periods when a high value had been placed upon the right to private property and upon individualism, it was clear that there was to be a conflict of values in a society which placed increasing faith in collectivist approaches and social legislation. How restrictively such measures were to be interpreted and how well the common law faced up to that situation in general was to provide a test of the capacity of the common law to adapt itself to meet a new situation.

The reality was that in Blackstone's day parliament played a relatively minor legislative role with the result that the common law was of correspondingly greater importance. After 1832, however, a steadily increasing volume of legislation reversed that situation quite decisively. Lawyers often found it difficult to concede the implications of that reversal. In 1908 the great American jurist, Roscoe Pound, wrote of the 'indifference, if not contempt' with which American courts and lawyers regarded the contemporary 'excessive output of legislation'.[4] It was a verdict which was equally true of courts and lawyers in England and Wales, despite the fact that legislation such as the Workmen's Compensation Acts brought them much work. For such courts and lawyers it remained true even in the twentieth century that the function of statute was simply to supply the deficiencies in an all embracing common law. That approach had a considerable influence upon the judicial interpretation of statutes.

2 The common law

a) *Introduction*
Blackstone wrote that general customs, 'or the common law, properly so called' was that law by which proceedings and determinations in the king's ordinary courts of justice were guided and directed.[5] Such customs were known by the judges of the several courts of justice:

> 'They are the depositary of the laws; the living oracles, who must decide in all cases of doubt, and who are bound by an oath to decide according to the law of the land. Their knowledge of the law is derived from experience and study...and from being long personally accustomed to the judicial decisions of their predecessors.... The reports which furnish the lawyers library serve as indexes to, and also to explain, the records.'[6]

The nature of those reports and the manner in which they were used, together with other sources used, will therefore be of some interest.

b) *The law reports*
Burrow, whose reports began to be published in 1756, set new standards in law reporting in terms of the accuracy and the detail of his reports. By the turn of the century it was common practice for reports to be published quite speedily after

---

4   R. Pound 'Common Law and Legislation' (1908) 21 HLR 383.
5   1 Bl Com (5th edn) 68.
6   1 Bl Com (5th edn) 69.

the case: the common law courts also began to appoint authorised reporters. We should not underestimate the importance of these changes. Now a court whose decisions were not reported adequately might be subjected to some professional ridicule. There was now also a general belief that the public interest required that the principles according to which the law was administered should be made known. For example, the common lawyers were ready to allege at the turn of the century that a failure on the part of the civilians who practised in the ecclesiastical and admiralty courts to publish adequate reports was due to a jealousy of the common lawyers and a wish to conceal what passed in the courts of the civilians.[7] Clearly professional and public expectations of the law reports at the beginning of the nineteenth century were higher than ever before. The days when Lord Holt had complained wryly of 'these scrambling reports which will make us to appear to posterity for a parcel of blockheads' or when Lord Mansfield might refuse quite curtly even to have certain reports cited in his court on the grounds that they were unreliable appeared increasingly to belong to a past age.[8] Of course, the relics of that age remained in the form of numerous reports of varying degrees of accuracy and antiquity, yet a new age appeared to have set more demanding standards.

That new age was an era during which laissez-faire principles were dominant. Accordingly, when complaints of undue expense and of unreasonable delay in publication were levelled at the authorised reports, the public interest was held to require the restoration of free competition. Once again numerous reports of varying degrees of quality began to appear. Now the newly created and competitive weekly law magazines for the profession felt compelled to contribute to the publication of a mass of law reports. This free trade in law reporting, which was rife in the middle years of the nineteenth century, led to a multiplicity of law reports, many of which were unreliable. The *Law Times* gave eloquent testimony on both counts in 1843 when it stated that there were few more serious grievances affecting the profession than the multiplicity of reports; the practitioner was not safe if he did not consult each one of the multitude to the exhaustion alike of his pocket and of his patience. The *Law Times* then referred to a recent case in which Baron Alderson had rejected a case which was directly in point because 'the statement of facts in the report is imperfect': it asserted that this was a common judicial practice.[9] In 1863 Daniel, a barrister who was to achieve a measure of reform in this area, claimed that the evils of the existing system were its enormous expense, its prolixity, delay and irregularity in publication, and imperfection as a record because of both a lack of continuity and because cases were reported indiscriminately without reference to their fitness or usefulness as precedents but merely because their omission might prejudice circulation and consequently diminish profit. The Attorney-General therefore summoned a meeting of the Bar in December 1863 which affirmed its belief that

7 Preface to *Decisions in the High Court of Admiralty: During the Time of Sir George Hay and Sir James Marriott* (1801) vol 1. Cf. A. H. Manchester 'The Principles and Rules of Ecclesiastical Law and Matrimonial Relief' (1968) 6 Sydney Law Review 25.

8 *Slater v May* (1790) 2 Ld Raym 1071. See generally C. K. Allen *Law in the Making* (7th edn) pp. 187 ff, V. Veeder 'English Reports 1537-1865' in *Select Essays in Anglo-American History* vol 2, p. 123, J. W. Wallace *The Reporters* (4th edn, 1882), L. Fox *A Handbook of English Law Reports*.

9 (1843) 1 LT 325, 347. Cf. (1848) 9 Law Magazine 1, (1853) 17 Jur 97.

the system of reporting needed amendment. There was some opposition from those who felt that compensation should be paid to those reporters who, it was feared, would soon be put out of work by the new reports. Moreover, some solicitors — solicitors were not represented at the meeting summoned by the Attorney-General — were well satisfied with the existing arrangements. Eventually, however, Daniel triumphed and the Council of Law Reporting, which was later incorporated by Royal Charter, published its first issue in November 1865. Their *Law Reports* proved successful and were priced initially at five guineas and in 1885 at four guineas per annum.[10] No doubt their success was very largely responsible for the shift in the latter part of the century to the strict view of the binding force of judicial precedent which had simply not been possible, even if it were desirable, at a time when both the quality and the continuity of the reports had been so lacking. The new reports did not secure that monopoly within the profession for which some had hoped and so did relatively little either to lessen the multiplicity of reports or to ensure uniformity of quality, but they were of benefit in setting standards for their rivals. A further difficulty was that even these reports were unofficial in the sense that they were not published by the state: the essence of the scheme had been simply that the profession itself should co-operate to produce reliable reports rather than rely upon the efforts of individuals acting with a view to thir own interests. However, the judges appear to have been rather more prepared than they had been in Burrows' day to assist actively in ensuring the accuracy of the reports. Under Daniel's scheme they were not asked to put all their judgments in writing — an argument for this being that such a requirement would mean that the judges could not possibly get through their work. They were asked to review the reports of their unwritten judgments before they were published and it seems that they did do this.

Although higher standards of reporting had been set and there was now a quasi-official set of reliable law reports, little else changed. The question of improving the existing arrangements for recording case law again came to the fore in 1940. The criticisms of the existing system were familiar enough i.e expense, the library space required, repetition, the difficulty of tracing cases, and incompleteness for there was still no guarantee that an important case would be reported. On that final point it was difficult to justify the system, remarked a critic, until it was remembered that 'the Emperor Caligula, whose sanity has been doubted, was severely criticised for placing the only copies of his statutes on top of a high pillar where the ordinary citizen could not read them'.[11] Was it impossible for a modern system of law reporting to meet the desiderata of accuracy, speed of publication and completeness? In 1939 the Lord Chancellor appointed a committee to consider the question. To a large extent the committee acknowledged the validity of the criticisms which had been made of the existing system, but it offered no real solutions. It even rejected a suggestion that the publication of wholly unofficial law reports should either be restricted or eliminated on the ground that such an innovation would strike at 'one of the

10   W. T. S. Daniel *The History and Origin of the Law Reports,* J. P. Dawson *The Oracles of the Law.*
11   (1939) 55 LQR 31.

pillars of freedom, that the administration of justice must be public'.[12] In its essentials the system of law reporting remained very much the system which had been criticised so convincingly over the years.

c) *Treatises*

Treatises by authors 'to whom great veneration and respect is paid by the students of the common law' might also be cited as authority.[13] Invariably, such authors were long dead. Perhaps the most authoritative of such writers in Blackstone's day was Coke.[14] Usually such treatises were regarded as evidence that cases had formerly happened in which such and such points were determined, which had since become settled and first principles. Accordingly, no such respect could be accorded to a treatise of more modern origin.

For the most part, therefore, a treatise or text of modern origin could exercise no direct influence upon the law. It was accepted, not as evidence of the law, but either as a manual for practitioners or as a text for students and as such it could not be cited in court. At most, therefore, its influence could only be indirect. In fact the majority of contemporary treatises were unsatisfactory on all counts. Brougham put the point pithily in 1846. Not only had lawyers 'no teachers, but what might prove a substitute for them — no books.... Not only are we deficient in productions of...higher character, but the greatest difficulty is found from the want even of good elementary works....At present we are indebted both in our public institutions, and in the profession, for whatever works of eminence we use, either to the schools of the Continent or to those of America.'[15] It was a view for which there was a considerable amount of support.[16] Still later in the century Stephen spoke disparagingly of the existing texts in the field of criminal law.[17] It was the expansion of law teaching within the universities during the final quarter of the nineteenth century which led to a great improvement in both the quality and quantity of legal writing: that improvement continued during the first half of the twentieth century.

At least the twentieth century law student now faced no lack of texts which expounded the law in a systematic and literate manner.[18] Within the bounds of orthodox professionalism, which were common both to the great majority of the academic lawyers and to the practitioners, such writing often attempted a critical analysis of particular decisions of the courts or of particular legal doctrines. By and large, however, the new legal writing was largely orthodox in its approach. It was not necessarily the worse for that. The contribution which Anson, Pollock, Dicey[19] and their successors made during the twentieth century was valuable

12   Report of the Committee on Law Reporting (Lord Chancellor's Office, 1940).
13   1 Bl Com (5th edn) 72-3.
14   Sir Edward Coke (1552-1634) *Institutes of the Laws of England.*
15   Report from the Select Committee on Legal Education no. 686 (1846) p. x.
16   R. Bethell in Select Committee Report no. 686 (1846) who later became both Attorney-General (1856) and Lord Chancellor (1861).
17   (1872) 18 Fortnightly Review 644.
18   O. Hood-Phillips 'Authors — Legal Authors since 1800' in P. Allsop (ed) *Then and Now 1799-1974* p. 3, cf. A. W. B. Simpson 'The Survival of the Common Law System' in P. Allsop (ed) *Then and Now 1799-1974* pp. 51, 63.
19   W. Anson *Law of Contract* (1st edn, 1879), F. Pollock *Principles of Contract* (4th edn, 1885), A. V. Dicey *The Conflict of Laws* (1st edn, 1896).

enough. The text-book had come of age but the writing of an influential class of jurists had not yet appeared, with the result that even such texts continued to be of no more than educational value. As yet the courts were not prepared to acknowledge expressly that such works might help to shape the law.

d) *Custom*

The common law or general customs formed the most important category of the unwritten or cómmon law. Two additional categories existed. There were particular customs which for the most part affected only the inhabitants of particular districts. Finally, there were certain particular laws which by custom were adopted and used by some particular courts of rather general and extensive jurisdiction. Within the former category was included the custom of gavelkind in Kent.[20] Most important of all, however, was the custom of merchants. Lord Mansfield made the most creative use of such customs as a source of the commercial law which he began to develop as part of the general common law during the second half of the eighteenth century.[1] Thereafter, perhaps inevitably in a small unified country with good communications, there was little recourse to the creative use of such custom.[2] Within the third category of custom Blackstone included the civil and canon laws. Such foreign laws were accorded respect:

> 'Only because they have been admitted and received by immemorial usage and custom in some particular cases, and some particular courts; and then they form a branch of the *leges non scriptae*, or customary law; or else, because they are in some other cases introduced by consent of parliament, and then they owe their validity to the *leges scriptae*, or statute law'.[3]

The civilians who practised in the ecclesiastical and admiralty courts at Doctor's Commons made ample use of such authorities. Even they appeared to be unclear on occasion as to the degree of respect which should be accorded to such authorities. For example, what was the precise authority of the pre-Reformation canon law? The greatest of all the ecclesiastical judges was Sir William Scott, a brother of Lord Eldon. In his view the canon law, as the ancient general law, was to be followed unless some variation in practice in this country could be shown.[4] Some years later another distinguished judge, Sir John Nicholl, placed rather more emphasis upon the necessity for a positive reception of such principles.[5]. With the passing of the civilians' jurisdiction in 1857 there was less reason for reference to such sources as authorities, although it has been necessary to do so in a number of modern cases.[6]

e) *Principle and precedent*

Blackstone saw law as a rational science. His avowed purpose was that of

---

20 1 Bl Com (5th edn) 74 ff.
1 See chap. 14.
2 *Crouch v Crédit Foncier of England* (1873) LR 8 QB 374. Contrast *Goodwin v Robarts* (1875) LR 10 Exch 337. The rules which governed the proof of custom are set out in 1 Bl Com (5th edn) 68, they are discussed by C. K. Allen in *Law in the Making* (7th edn) pp. 129 ff.
3 1 Bl Com (5th edn) 80.
4 *Dalrymple v Dalrymple* (1811) 2 Hag Con 54 at 81. Admittedly this was a case with a Scottish i.e. foreign, element.
5 *Norton v Seton* (1819) 3 Phillim 147 at 164.
6 *Harthan v Harthan* [1949] P 115, [1948] 2 All ER 639; *Padolecchia v Padolecchia* [1968] P 314, [1967] 3 All ER 863. See generally A. H. Manchester 'The Principles and Rules of Ecclesiastical Law and Matrimonial Relief' (1968) 6 Sydney Law Review 25.

'examining the great outlines of the English law, and tracing them up to their principles'.[7] Such an approach was typical of eighteenth century rationalism, of a belief in natural law and in discoverable general principles.

Thus it was scarcely possible to do more than accord respect to previous authorities or precedents rather as evidence of what the law was than as in themselves constituting good law. It was a characteristic common law approach. At a time when standards of law reporting were remarkably lax, it could hardly have been otherwise. Yet even in Blackstone's day the lawyers' respect for previous authorities, or precedent, was of long standing. It was:

> 'an established rule to abide by former precedents, where the same points come again in litigation; as well to keep the scale of justice even and steady, and not liable to waver with every new judge's opinion.... Yet this rule admits of exception where the former determination is most evidently contrary to reason.... Precedents and rules must be followed, unless flatly absurd and unjust.'[8]

It was an approach which ensured a high degree of certainty — receding from authorities unsettled property, Lord Hardwicke had pointed out in 1756. It also made possible that degree of flexibility in which lawyers took some pride and which gave them the opportunity to attempt to ensure that the common law kept pace with social change.[9] It was a method which gave some, albeit a limited, scope for creativity for, although the method of the common law approximated rather to an art than to science, the innovating judge was required in practice to pay due respect to the legal profession's understanding of the bounds within which the common law might properly be extended. Lord Mansfield's career illustrates such points admirably.[10]

A strong and able Lord Chief Justice, he presided over his court at a time of considerable economic change. To him in particular can be attributed the creation of a modern system of commercial law. With the commercial world in a state of some ferment as, for example, new forms of credit appeared, lawyers faced a novel situation. In such circumstances it was possible for Mansfield creatively to interpret such precedents as were available and to mould them into a coherent whole. In less fluid areas in which the law was already settled, like innovations were rejected. This was the case in Lord Mansfield's brush with the conveyancers. In a less settled, more contentious area of the law, the question of consideration in the law of contract, Mansfield's views were not rejected until many years after his death at a time when the profession was being invited to adopt what it considered to be a more traditional approach to the question of consideration. Even in Mansfield's day, therefore, the existence of relevant authorities or precedents could be decisive.

By the beginning of the nineteenth century an increasing respect appears to have been accorded to previous authorities. That coincided with the appearance of more authoritative reports. We cannot be sure whether such increased respect led to a demand for better reports or vice versa.[11] Yet the increased respect for

---

7   D. J. Boorstin *The Mysterious Science of Law.*
8   1 Bl Com (5th edn) 63-70.
9   Yet in *Earl of Chesterfield v Janssen* (1750) 1 Atk 301 at 353 Lord Hardwicke said that he was under 'an indispensable obligation' of following his predecessors.
10   C. H. S. Fifoot *Lord Mansfield.*
11   J. P. Dawson *The Oracles of the Law* p. 79.

authority and higher standards of law reporting went hand in hand until the high water mark of the doctrine of precedent was reached in 1898 with the decision of the House of Lords in *London Street Tramways Co v LCC*,[12] which decided that the House of Lords was bound by its own decisions. Of course the House of Lords had long respected precedent. So distinguished a judge as Lord Blackburn had even felt himself to be bound by precedent, despite apparently having doubts as to the wisdom of the legal principle embodied in that precedent.[13] A reformed House of Lords made it possible to accord to its decisions at the apex of a hierarchy of courts a respect which could not be given to the decisions of that House 100 years before. At the same time a more mechanistic, less creative and self-confident approach to the use of the common law had been growing. It was an approach which mirrored the general professional reluctance, evident since mid-nineteenth century, to rely on general principle rather than upon a highly technical approach to the use of authority. Further, such an approach had the added advantage of apparently being of a scientific, apolitical character in a world in which some decisions at least, in the field of trade union law, for example, were cast inevitably in a political mould.

A highly developed approach to the study and use of precedent was formulated. It was an extreme and mechanistic view of precedent which was far removed both from Blackstone's principled approach and from that degree of flexibility which admirers of the common law claimed for the common law system. Yet despite the effort which was spent upon explaining how to determine the principle of law, or *ratio decidendi*, which might be deduced from a particular case, it was recognised that another court would often be able subsequently to distinguish a previous case on its facts with little difficulty.[14] Many jurists, especially American jurists, began to question the validity of such an exercise.

What was especially important was the legal profession's, or rather the Bar's, understanding of the law. Blackburn J acknowledged the importance of such an understanding. James Fitzjames Stephen had insisted that the criminal law could not be understood without an understanding of the practice of the courts.[15] Accordingly, professional opinion was very much a force to be reckoned with in any judicial assessment of whether the time was ripe for any extension of the existing law.

f) The contribution of the common law

'My Lady Common Law' was the lawyers' unique contribution to society. It was a contribution of which they were immensely proud. Held to be at once both flexible and certain, the common law was said to allow the lawyers to keep pace with social change within the context of legal principles and rules which were yet held to be reasonably certain. For a judge to determine both whether change was

12 [1898] AC 489.
13 *Foakes v Beer* (1884) 9 App Cas 605.
14 C. K. Allen summarises much of the literature in *Law in the Making* (7th edn) pp. 219 ff.; B. Abel-Smith and R. Stevens *Lawyers and the Courts* p. 123, Lord Halsbury LC is there offered as an example of a judge who was highly skilled at distinguishing decisions for which he had little liking.
15 Judicature Commission: Second Report of the Commissioners no. C-631 (1869) vol 1, p. 26, Special Report from the Select Committee on the Homicide Law Amendment Bill no. 315 (1874), minutes of evidence p. 2, q. 10.

desirable and also whether it was possible within the existing system of precedent
was difficult. Inevitably, all legal change tended to lag behind public opinion.
When change did come, it was often based upon a strong judge's view of justice.
Sir William Erle, a distinguished nineteenth-century judge, who had a particular interest in trade union matters, wrote:

> 'the Chancellors who originated equitable rules overruling law saw by their
> intuitive perception the iniquity of the law to be overruled, and introduced
> the remedy; and amongst the judges at common law, Hale, Holt, and
> Mansfield may be taken as examples of men who by the exercise of the
> same intuitive perception became eminent. They were masters of the
> learning of their predecessors; their commissions ran then as now, to do
> what to justice appertained, according to the laws and customs of
> England; and although they maintained, in accordance with those laws
> and customs, some of the feudal principles established after the Conquest,
> which had survived to their time, yet when new relations in social progress
> raised new questions, and feudality had either expired or was irrelevant,
> they decided according to their own intuition of justice; and they have
> their eminence because their intuitions have accorded with those of the
> strong men in the generations that have succeeded. Mansfield takes rank as
> a benefactor of mankind; and the recommendation of Junius, that he
> should be impeached for introducing notions of substantial justice to
> modify some supposed rules of common law which worked iniquity is
> evidence of his title to that rank.'[16]

It was surely no accident that in mid-twentieth century another innovating
judge, Sir Alfred Denning, also sought his inspiration in the judge's commission
to do justice[17] nor that, like Mansfield, a number of his innovations were to be
thwarted or frowned upon by the conservatism of some of his colleagues. Such
tension between creative genius on the one hand and professional conservatism
with its understandable emphasis on certainty on the other hand is ever present.

By and large the common law coped well with the remarkable new demands
which were thrust upon it. During the latter half of the eighteenth century Lord
Mansfield shaped a modern commercial law and the judges generally played a
major role in developing a modern law of theft. During the nineteenth century
the judges fashioned a modern law of civil liability — the law of contract and of
tort. Within the established restraints of precedent and of constitutional
propriety, they were prepared on occasion to be bold. For example, in 1932 a
decision of the House of Lords in the law of tort effectively heralded the dawn of a
new age for the consumer in a mass-producing society.[18] More controversially, as
late as 1933 the courts found for the first time that an offence of public mischief
existed.[19] It was a decision which presumably would have caused some surprise to
those Commissioners on the Criminal Law who wrote in 1879:

> 'In by-gone ages, when legislation was scanty and rare, the powers referred

16   Sir W. Erle 'Memorandum on the Law relating to Trade Unions in Eleventh and Final
      Report of the Royal Commissioners...into the Organisation and Rules of Trades Unions and
      Other Associations' no. 4123 (1869) vol 1, p. lxxxix.
17   Sir A. Denning *Freedom Under the Law.*
18   *Donoghue v Stevenson* [1932] AC 562.
19   *R v Manley* [1933] 1 KB 529.

to may have been useful and even necessary; but that is not the case at the present day. Parliament is regular in its sittings and active in its labours; and if the protection of society requires the enactment of additional penal laws, parliament will soon supply them. If parliament is not disposed to provide punishments for acts which are upon any ground objectionable or dangerous, the presumption is that they belong to that class of misconduct against which the moral feeling and good sense of the community are the best protection.'[20]

In fact the judges were often unwilling to sanction any dramatic innovation, as Lord Mansfield had found. As the flood of statutes increased, judicial innovation more often found expression in reinterpreting the mass of case law which had developed upon a statute in such a way as to keep the law abreast of public opinion. In practice over the years they did liberalise the grounds of divorce by reinterpreting the concept of cruelty as a ground of divorce and also by developing the concept of constructive desertion as a ground of divorce. To assess the state of public opinion in more contentious areas still was a notoriously difficult and controversial task. For example, much of nineteenth-century labour law was concerned with judicial development of the common law concept of conspiracy. That concept had a long, albeit shadowy, history. The extent to which it might be applied properly in the troubled field of labour relations, in the absence of a public consensus upon that topic, was an issue upon which both the public and the judiciary itself was divided.[1] Inevitably a new political atmosphere of collectivism which did not harmonise readily with a common law based largely upon individualism meant that there was less scope than ever for judicial innovation. Nor did Victorian judges take readily to the idea that workmen injured in the course of their employment might be compensated in the absence of fault on the part of the employer as the Workmen's Compensation Acts required.[2] On the other hand they had been prepared themselves to introduce liability without fault into the common law in terms of both civil and also of criminal liability.[3] Such inconsistency reflected both a degree of judicial uncertainty as to the policy of certain statutes as well as a genuine and principled conviction of the merits of the common law, however dated such a conviction may have begun to appear to many critics, even at the beginning of the twentieth century. Yet values of considerable worth had been implicit in the common law system. It was only in the mid-twentieth century that the great judge, Sir Alfred Denning, sought to reassert them with any conviction, especially in his insistence that by his oath the judge had sworn to do justice.[4] Even so during the period 1750-1950 the common law had never been a truly innovating force or an instrument of social change as it had been for a time in the USA during the nineteenth century.[5] Nevertheless its contribution had been valuable, and its approach through the cases and the use

---

20 Report of the Royal Commission appointed to consider the law relating to Indictable Offences no. C-2345 (1879) pp. 9-10.
1 See chap. 14.
2 See chap. 12.
3 The modern law on strict liability in tort dates from *Rylands v Fletcher* (1868) LR 3 HL 330. The modern law on strict liability at criminal law dates from *R v Woodrow* (1846) 15 M & W 404.
4 Sir A. Denning *Freedom Under the Law.*
5 On the position in the USA see M. Horwitz *The Transformation of American Law.*

of precedent was as popular with lawyers in 1950 as it had been in 1750, although it was now recognised that it might be necessary for statute, rather than the judges, to dispense with outmoded common law doctrines such as that of common employment.

3 Statute

a) *Meaning and classification*

The *leges scriptae* or written laws of the kingdom were the 'statutes, acts or edicts, made by the king's majesty, by and with the advice and consent of the lords spiritual and temporal and commons in parliament assembled'.[6] At least that was the position in Blackstone's day and thereafter. In earlier days there was less certainty with regard to what measures might be accepted as statutes. For example, the important medieval statute, Quia Emptores, would not have satisfied Blackstone's criteria. Accordingly, Plucknett wrote that in the reign of Edward I a statute

> 'simply means something established by royal authority: whether it is established by the King in Council, or a Parliament of nobles and commons as well, is completely immaterial. It is equally immaterial what form the statute takes, whether it be a charter or a statute enrolled and proclaimed, or merely an administrative expression of the royal will notified to the judicial authorities...'[7]

As a result there was some uncertainty as to exactly which measures should be regarded as statutes. Accordingly, in 1800 a select committee recommended that a complete and authoritative edition of all the statutes should be published.[8] This led to the publication during the period 1810-22 in nine volumes of the Statutes of the Realm which covered the period up to 1713. For the subsequent period profession and public alike relied upon private enterprise. However, in 1870 the first volume of the Statutes Revised appeared. Each volume contained a chronological list of the Acts passed in the period covered by the volume and explained the extent to which each had been repealed. A further innovation was that from 1887 just one authoritative edition of the statutes was published annually.

Over the years the statutes were classified in various ways. Following recommendations made by Select Committees of the House of Commons in 1796, Parliament resolved that statutes enacted in 1798 and thereafter were to be classified as: (1) Public and General Acts; (2) Local and Personal Acts declared public and to be judicially noticed; (3) Private and Personal Acts — such Acts were not ordered to be printed. Finally, in 1868 it was determined that statutes were to be classified into the following three groups: (1) Public General Acts; (2) Local Acts; (3) Private Acts.[9]

6 1 Bl Com (5th edn) 85.
7 T. F. T. Plucknett *A Concise History of the Common Law* (5th edn, 1956) p. 322.
8 See generally C. Ilbert *Legislative Methods and Forms*, C. K. Allen *Law in the Making* (7th edn) pp. 436 ff.
9 Ilbert *Legislative Methods* pp. 49-50. Other changes were made during the century. Yet it was only in 1796 that it had been decided to promulgate statutes throughout the realm as soon as possible after their enactment. See F. Clifford *A History of Private Bill Legislation*.

An Act of Parliament was 'the exercise of the highest authority that this king-dom acknowledges upon earth', wrote Blackstone. A century earlier a chief justice had asserted that the common law might control a statute which was 'against common right and reason, or repugnant, or impossible to be performed'. Blackstone does make some reference to that doctrine.[10] However, it was now clear that in the event of a conflict between statute and common law, statute would prevail. Of course, it was for the judges to interpret the statutes.

b) *Statutory interpretation*
Blackstone wrote that there were three points to be considered in the construc-tion of remedial statutes;

> 'the old law, the mischief, and the remedy: that is, how the common law stood at the making of the act; what the mischief was, for which the common law did not provide; and what remedy the parliament hath provided to cure this mischief. And it is the business of the judges so to construe the act, as to suppress the mischief and advance the remedy.'[11]

It was a traditional approach which emphasised the all-pervasiveness, in a sense even the dominance, of the common law. It contributed to a judicial tendency to construe statutes narrowly, and to view them in much the same manner as any other document which required interpretation. The history of the statute was irrelevant. Its purpose was to be gleaned only from a careful reading of the statute alone. It followed that the plain or literal meaning of a statute, or of a particular statutory provision, was to be applied even if that ran counter to the general belief as to the real purpose of the statute. It is true that the so-called golden rule of interpretation allowed a judge some latitude. A distinguished common law judge, Baron Parke, expressed that rule as follows:

> 'It is a very useful rule in the construction of a statute to adhere to the ordinary meaning of the words used, and to the grammatical construction, unless that is at variance with the intention of the legislature to be collected from the statute itself, or leads to any manifest absurdity of repugnance, in which case the language may be varied or modified so as to avoid such inconvenience, but no further.'[12]

In fact much depended upon the approach of the individual judge. Different judges might use the literal, the golden or the mischief approach and yet arrive at the same result. Above all, however, the judges sought to adopt a strictly literal approach.

Such a position could be understood in Blackstone's England when there was relatively little legislation and the common law really was dominant. There was less conviction in the use of such a literal approach in nineteenth-century England as parliament legislated increasingly upon a multitude of diverse topics. Some critics believed that such a highly technical, literal approach to inter-pretation was simply a manifestation of the judiciary's lack of a sound legal education which would allow the judges to think in terms of principle. Many

---

10   1 Bl Com (5th edn) 91, Coke C J in *Bonham's case* (1610) 8 Co Rep 114 at 118. Cf. Lord Holt *City of London v Wood* (1701) 12 Mod Rep 669 at 687. Note also the old doctrine of the special equity which controlled statutes — *Eyston v Studd* (1574) 2 Plow 459 at 465. See Allen *Law in the Making* pp. 446 ff.
11   1 Bl Com (5th edn) 87. See R. Cross 'Blackstone v Bentham' (1976) 92 LQR 516.
12   *Becke v Smith* (1836) 2 M & W 191 at 195.

critics were convinced that a literal interpretation was required if the will of parliament were to be implemented adequately. There has been a tendency to suggest that this strict, literal interpretation of penal statutes was an instance of judicial humanitarianism during the period of the Bloody Code when so many criminal offences were subject to capital punishment. That was probably the case.[13] Yet similar interpretations were made in civil matters long after the Bloody Code was no more.[14]

In 1835 commissioners reported that such overtechnical rules of interpretation had led to the law becoming indefinite and uncertain. One of the commissioners later pointed out that in New York it appeared that the idea of a code was welcomed by both Bench and Bar, as a consequence of which the code was probably construed in a liberal way and with disregard for minute objections founded on the letter of the text, provided the general intention of the enactment could be ascertained. He thought that in this country there would be a desire rather to find a defect in a code than to assist it by broad and liberal interpretation. As he put it on a later occasion: '…I am quite convinced that the code of New York or the code of Boston, would not satisfy our courts here; I think there is hardly a line of the code of New York that would not employ the Court of Queen's Bench or the Court of Common Pleas for weeks.'[15] He then went on to suggest that the verboseness and minute enumeration of particular cases which 'are characteristic of our statutes, and are so contrary to all abstract principles of scientific expression, have been to a great extent caused by the tendency of the courts to narrow and technical rules of construction. That is, our draftsmen have felt obliged to provide specially for every contingency.' Certainly, he claimed

> 'when a draftsman finds that it has been gravely questioned by a court of law whether a dead turkey can be properly described as "a turkey", and whether an Act relating to convictions for stealing "horses" includes a conviction for stealing one horse, one can hardly wonder that he should give up all attempts at doing more than enumerating to the best of his ability all the particular instances he can think of, and stopping by express enactment all the misconstructions which it seems to him possible that perverse ingenuity may apply to the language which he employs'.

It was a line of thought to which this critic returned some years later:

> 'Those really are the rocks which we have. We are induced, on the one hand, to make our Acts of Parliament extremely verbose and extremely precise, to fit them to the principles of judicial decisions, when we have a judge who decides that a duck in an Act of Parliament does not mean a dead duck, and that ox, cow, calf and other cattle of any kind whatsoever does not mean a bull. A man having all those principles before him, and being employed to draw an Act of Parliament, always draws his Act of Parliament with reference to those principles of construction, and hence in a great degree arises that verbosity which those who frame Acts of

13 J. Hall *Theft, Law and Society*.

14 See Report from the Select Committee 99 Sess. 1 (1857) on the Second Report of the Statute Law Commissioners p. 461.

15 Third Report of Mr. Bellenden Ker to the Lord Chancellor on the Proceedings of the Board for the Revision of the Statute Law no. 302-T (1854) p. 40. See A. H. Manchester 'Simplifying the Sources of the Law An Essay in Law Reform' (1973) 2 Anglo-American Law Review 395.

Parliament are found fault with for employing. But if you take merely general principles to be worked out by the judges, you then find that it takes some half a century before the meaning of your abstract law is ascertained. That is the real difficulty of all persons who have either to prepare a code or even to prepare an Act of Parliament.'

Such a judicial approach made it less likely that the judges would be willing to implement sympathetically any statutory policy which was not expressed in the clearest and most unequivocal terms. In 1875 a distinguished Victorian judge, Sir George Jessel MR, conceded:

'undoubtedly judges vary in their practice:…I recollect in times past…that there were one or two judges who rather delighted in pulling an Act of Parliament to pieces, while others, on the contrary, simply endeavoured to find out what it meant.'[16]

At the same time a parliamentary draftsman commented that it was 'obvious that there is a sort of traditional antagonism between the courts and the legislature, and that the judges are not unwilling to exercise their critical faculty, and sometimes very severely'.[17] Yet even Sir George Jessel did not favour the judges giving a liberal interpretation to an Act as 'that would impose a great responsibility upon the judicature'.[18]

Thring, the first parliamentary draftsman, had believed that if any great reform in the law were to take place, the judges should favour that reform by interpreting the statutes liberally. Thring denied that there was any essential difference between common law with its general principles and statute with its certain words as 'the common law is really and truly old statute law, which is embedded in books instead of in statutes'. If the common law could be interpreted in a flexible manner, as the judges had always claimed, surely it was possible for the judges to discover and to apply the spirit of a statute in an equally flexible manner?[19] In fact, as we have noted already, even in their interpretation of the common law the judges were adopting an increasingly mechanistic role, a professional rampart which would shelter them from allegations of personal prejudice. It was scarcely likely that they would adopt a more liberal stance in the interpretation of statutes.

In a number of admittedly contentious areas the judges were less than successful in interpreting the will of parliament and the mood of the country. An outstanding example is in the field of labour relations during the period 1875-1914. Other examples are not lacking. The great property reform of 1925[20] appeared to be in jeopardy for a time. Similarly, when a radical interpretation was offered it appeared to be closer in spirit to a bygone age than to the spirit of contemporary legislation. For example in *Roberts v Hopwood*[1] the facts were that local authorities were empowered by statute to offer such wages to their employees as they 'may think fit'. However, the House of Lords quashed the action of one local authority in offering a minimum wage of £4 per week to its

16 Report from the Select Committee on Acts of Parliament no. 280 (1875) p. 85, q. 1175 and p. 90, q. 1226.
17 Report from the Select Committee no. 280 (1875) p. 47, q. 588.
18 Report from the Select Committee no. 280 (1875) p. 90, q. 1222-3.
19 Report from the Select Committee no. 280 (1875) p. 124, q. 1668 and p. 125, q. 1679-81.
20 For a general critique see J. Willis 'Statute Interpretation in a Nutshell' (1938) 16 CBR 1.
1   [1925] AC 578.

employees upon the grounds that such an offer was 'unreasonable'. It was inspired, said Lord Atkinson, by 'eccentric principles of socialistic philanthropy'. On the other hand critics of this decision of the House of Lords believed that it contravened the spirit of the statute.

A possible answer to overtechnical and illiberal rules of interpretation is that in constitutional terms nineteenth-century society saw the legislative and judicial roles as being quite properly distinct. On this view the judges were quite right not to don a legislative mantle. Their function, it could be argued, was not to create but to interpret the law. Yet really the question was often one of how far the judges were prepared to go beyond the literal interpretation of a particular statutory provision or statute in implementing what was known to have been parliament's intention in enacting the statute. It is possible to point out also both that the literal approach reflected the strong oral tradition of the courts and also that the fault finding approach of the judges was expressed not only with regard to statutes but also with regard to what they might see as slackly drawn pleadings. Baron Parke was more likely to frown upon loosely drawn pleadings than upon a badly drafted statute.

There was little conscious change even in the twentieth century. Yet there was an increasing tendency for detail to be supplied, usually in the form of ministerial regulations rather than in the Act itself. There was a tendency also to seek to reduce the extent to which judges were called upon to interpret legislation of an avowedly social nature by transferring a great part of such work to specially created tribunals.[2]

c) *Drafting: the office of the parliamentary draftsman*

The problems which arose with regard to statutory interpretation clearly indicated that greater care in the drafting of statutes was necessary. Yet there was little consistency in the method by which the increasing volume of statutes was enacted over the years. Until well into the nineteenth century bills were often introduced by a member of parliament in the most casual manner. Romilly told the story[3] of how in parliament one day he passed by a pleasant enough member who was writing busily. Upon Romilly asking him what he was doing, he replied that he was simply drafting a bill to provide that the stealing of turnips should be a capital offence. It is true that by mid-nineteenth century government support for a measure was often sought, even though this period is regarded as the golden age of the influence of the backbench member of parliament. Indeed, by this time government departments were themselves responsible for the drafting of a considerable number of bills. Yet there was little uniformity of method. Instead, as Brougham pointed out in 1849, there was 'an almost entire disregard, not only of general principles, but of former statutory provisions'. Further parliamentary amendments might introduce 'gross blunders'. For example, in 1834 one Commons amendment would have had the effect of suspending all criminal justice in the country.[4] In addition legislators complained of the 'vicious draftsmanship' of bills, and judges criticised, unjustly on occasion, it is true, the

---

2 See chap. 6.
3 P. Medd *Romilly*, L. Radzinowicz *History of English Criminal Law* vol 1.
4 Third Report of Mr. Bellenden Ker to the Lord Chancellor on the Proceedings of the Board for the Revision of the Statute Law no. 302-I (1854) p. 15.

'hopeless unintelligibility' of many of the Acts which they were called upon to interpret.[5] In 1857 the objections to the existing system were summarised as being:

> 'want of uniformity in the style, the language, and the arrangement of the different bills introduced: and occasionally also, a conflict may be observed in the provisions of different bills brought in upon analogous subjects and incidentally conflicting with one another'.[6]

Opinions differed as to the appropriate remedy. Some favoured the creation of a general board or of a joint committee of both Houses whose task it would be to satisfy itself of the formal correctness of all public general measures before they were introduced to parliament. On the other hand no less a person than Thomas Erskine May believed that, so far as government bills were concerned, the existing system of preparing bills in different departments was 'very superior to any which could be suggested, either for their preparation or preliminary revision by one General Board'.[7] The trend of reforming opinion went very much the other way. Yet when reform finally came, its immediate cause was not so much the cumulative effect of years of reforming efforts but of decisive administrative action on the part of an economy minded Chancellor of the Exchequer.

In 1869 Robert Lowe created the office of the parliamentary draftsman by means of the twin expedients of a Treasury minute and securing the agreement of the Commons to provide the necessary funds. Apparently the reason the Treasury took this initiative was that under the existing system any minister might introduce a bill whose enactment would require the government to spend considerable sums of money. Out of the understandable Treasury wish to be aware of such a situation came a solution to a problem of which mere law reformers had been aware for some time. The new office was soon recognised as a success. Yet even in the twentieth century the number of parliamentary counsel remained remarkably small. In 1919 there were just three parliamentary counsel and one assistant. In 1951 just seven parliamentary counsel, one deputy parliamentary counsel, and ten barristers, who were employed as assistants, dealt with a mass of legislation which the birth of the modern welfare state had increased considerably. Familiar complaints were still made regarding the intelligibility of statutes.[8] There had also been a considerable increase in the volume of delegated legislation in the form of the statutory instrument. By and large, however, the small band of parliamentary draftsmen had effected a quiet revolution, within the constraints imposed by their numbers and the rules of statutory interpretation in the improvement of the standards of parliamentary draftsmanship.

d) *Delegated legislation*

Up to mid-nineteenth century considerable use was made of the Private Act of Parliament. Such Acts were statutes. Their use accustomed the public to the fact that special rules might be made for special groups. Parliament approved such Acts in their entirety, but this was not the case with delegated legislation.

5 Sir F. Herschell *Transactions of the Social Science Association* (1873) p. 159.
6 T. Erskine May in Report from the Select Committee on the Statute Law Commission no. 99 (1857) p. 50, q. 435.
7 Erskine May in Report no. 99 (1857).
8 Sir W. Graham Harrison 'Criticisms of the Statute Book' (1935) JSPTL 9, Sir G. Ram 'The Improvement of the Statute Book' (1951) 1 JSPTL (n.s.) 442.

Instances of parliamentary delegation of legislative powers go back a considerable number of years. However, after the Reform Act 1832 a new spirit of governmental intervention, coupled with the necessities of the age, led to a considerable and increasing use of such delegated powers. Acts concerning the Poor Law, public health, factories and numerous other Acts permitted others to fill in the detail of the Act in question or even to alter or dispense with some existing statutory provisions. By the end of the nineteenth century some 1000 such statutory orders were made annually: after the First World War there were well over 2000 orders annually and during the inter-war period the average annual figure was of the order of 1500.[9] After 1890 such delegated legislation was published annually in the Statutory Rules and Orders.

Such an important shift in constitutional practice did not go completely unnoticed. Maitland commented upon it with some unease in 1887. By and large, however, there was little concern.[10] The rule of law was believed to prevail: this country was held neither to have, nor to need, any system of administrative law. After the First World War the national mood was rather different. The Lord Chief Justice, Lord Hewart, was a particularly vociferous opponent of the growth of delegated powers. In 1927 he spoke out against what he called the 'New Despotism'. A committee was appointed, yet there was little change. World War Two led to a vast increase in the use of delegated legislation. The advent in 1945 of a Labour Government with a philosophy of state intervention and a distrust of 'judicial interference', together with the inherent difficulties of the post war economic situation, meant that it was unlikely that the coming of peace would diminish the governmental appetite for the use of such legislation. As yet the courts had shown but little inclination to intervene.[11]

4 Simplifying the sources of the law

a) *Introduction*

That the body of the law should be made more simple, more certain, more easily available to all the people, had been the constant cry of the law reformer over the years. The young King Edward VI is said to have written to that effect in 1551:[12] the Law Commission is working to that end at the present day. Yet progress in this vital area of law reform has been desperately slow.

Neither the statute law nor the common law was satisfactory as a source of law in the second half of the eighteenth century. One of Blackstone's contemporaries, Barrington, another distinguished lawyer, wrote that the reformation of the statutes 'so far as to repeal obsolete and sometimes dangerous laws, as well as reducing the different acts of parliament, which relate to the same subject, into one consistent statute, would be a salutary, nay, is almost become a necessary work'.[13] Successive individuals and authoritative commissions and

---

9   C. K. Allen *Law and Orders* p. 31.
10 F. W. Maitland *Constitutional History of England* p. 415, cited by Allen *Law in the Making* pp. 533-4.
11 Sir A. Denning *Freedom Under the Law.*
12 In his *Discourse on the Reformation of Abuses*, cited by C. Ilbert *The Mechanics of Law Making* p. 25, cf. C. Ilbert *Legislative Methods and Forms* pp. 43-51.
13 W. Barrington *Observations on the Statutes.*

committees expressed similar opinions throughout the nineteenth and twentieth centuries. How could the people understand the law, demanded the radical author of the *Black Book*,[14] 'when even the judges, whose whole lives are devoted to the subject, are in the most pitiable state of perplexity, uncertainty and contradiction?' In 1867 a royal commission commented adversely upon the 'great bulk' of the statute law, upon the lack of systematic arrangement of the statutes, and upon the numerous obsolete and unrepealed provisions which might well trap the most experienced practitioner.[15] In 1879 a royal commission recommended unsuccessfully the codification of a substantial part of the criminal law.[16] Over the years useful work was achieved in tidying up the statutes by means of the expurgation of obsolete statutes and by consolidating numerous statutes upon a particular topic into just one statute. Yet lawyers shrank from the more radical solution of the codification of both the statute and the common law. Bentham did not, and he argued from first principles.

Law, Bentham wrote,[17] should be notorious for 'only in proportion as the conception a man has of it is clear, correct and complete, can the ordinances of the law be conformed to...' The law, too, should be complete: as the common law of its nature could never be complete, so was it necessarily uncertain. The aim, although it could not be attained in every case, should be that every man should be his own lawyer. Thirdly, the law should be concise. Fourthly, it should be clear in its language and fifthly, it should be compact in its form. In Bentham's view the object of a code was

> 'that every one may consult the law of which he stands in need, in the least possible time. "Citizen", says the legislator, "what is your condition? Are you a father? Open the chapter 'Of Fathers'. Are you an agriculturist? Consult the chapter 'Of Agriculture' "…. A complete digest, such is the first rule. Whatever is not in the code of laws ought not to be law…. The great utility of a code of laws is to cause the debates of lawyers and the bad laws of former times to be forgotten…'[18]

It was an extreme position. Bentham recognised that not every man would have the capacity to act as his own lawyer. Moreover, it would be extremely difficult to codify in a complete form in stages in view of the connection between the various branches of the law. Could you really define theft, for example, without a knowledge of the law relating to property, which was itself connected intimately with the law of contract, and so on? Considerations such as these persuaded James Fitzjames Stephen, who made such a valiant attempt to codify much of the criminal law in the late nineteenth century, to adopt a far more pragmatic approach. In particular, he believed that at that time it was possible only to codify a part of the criminal law i.e. his code was not complete in Bentham's sense, and even that part was not self-sufficient. Yet Stephen was just as clear as

14   J. Wade *The Black Book* (1835).
15   First Report of the Commissioners appointed to inquire into the Expediency of a Digest of Law no. 3849 (1867).
16   Report of the Royal Commission…on the Law relating to Indictable Offences…no. C-2345 (1879).
17   Jeremy Bentham 'An Englishman, to the Citizens of the several American United States', Letters II to IV in *Papers Relative to Codification and Public Instruction*.
18   *General View of a Complete Code of Law*, cited by C. Ilbert *The Mechanics of Law Making* p. 151.

Bentham on the merits of codification:

> 'To compare the Indian Penal Code with English criminal law is like comparing cosmos with chaos. Any intelligent person interested in the subject could get a very distinct and correct notion of Indian criminal law in a few hours from the Penal Code. I appeal to you to imagine the state of mind of a man who should try to read straight through the very best of English books on criminal law, say, for instance, Mr. Greaves' edition of *Russell on Crimes*.'[19]

Essentially, therefore, the distinction between the differing approaches to codification of Bentham and of Stephen is that between the idealist and the more pragmatic man of affairs: both differed from the French, and at the end of the nineteenth century, German views which allowed for a full statement of legislative principle but which on the whole laid down precise rules rather sparingly.

Despite Bentham's efforts his hopes for codification made little progress in his own country. The Benthamites did succeed in incorporating in the Charter Act of 1833 a number of clauses which were designed to promote the codification of the law in India. As a result the Indian Penal Code was inaugurated in 1862.[20] However, during the first part of the nineteenth century the reformers placed far more emphasis upon the rather less glamorous task of the consolidation of the statutes.

Consolidation was understood to be the 'process of throwing several statutes into one' whereas a code generally implies 'that a large and important part of the subject codified is then for the first time reduced to writing in an authoritative manner'. Stephen went on to point out that every code will 'always include more or less consolidation, as upon every subject there is a greater or less amount of statute law. On the other hand consolidation will be of very little use unless the person who consolidates feels at liberty to remodel and rearrange the statutes which he throws together, and to mould their language so as to give the effect of judicial decisions on their meaning.'[1] The latter point was of considerable importance in affecting questions of reform; just how far was it proper for the would be consolidators to amend the language of the statutes to be consolidated?

b) *Consolidation of the statutes*

In 1824 a select committee resolved that it was expedient that the statutes relating to the criminal law should be consolidated under their several heads.[2] It was left to Peel in March 1826 to introduce such a measure to parliament. Peel adopted Bacon's views as to the principles upon which a simplification of the statute law should be based. First, the books should be discharged of those statutes made redundant by passage of time e.g. regarding Jews, Lombards and Gauls. Secondly, all statutes which were sleeping and not of use should either be repealed or replaced by some more reasonable law. Thirdly, the grievousness of the penalty might be mitigated in many statutes, although the ordinance remained. Finally, consolidation might reduce concurrent statutes heaped one

---

19   (1872) 18 Fortnightly Review 644 at 654.
20   M. P. Jain *Outlines of Indian Legal History* pp. 452 ff.
 1   (1872) 18 Fortnightly Review 644 at 657.
 2   Report on the Consolidation of the Criminal Laws, and the Simplification of their Enactments no. 205 (1824).

upon another to one clear and uniform law. Peel said that he had selected the laws relating to theft in the first instance because he considered theft to constitute the most important class of crime, since committals and convictions for theft so far exceeded the committals and convictions for any other species of offence. He commented especially upon the fact that criminal legislation had been left 'to the desultory and unconcerted speculations of every man who had a fancy to legislate', while the 'new enactment too was frequently stuck into the middle of a statute passed probably at the end of a session'. One such example which he gave was as follows:

> 'An Act for the better securing the duties of customs upon certain goods removed from the outports and other places to London; for regulating the fees of his majesty's customs in the province of Senegambia in Africa; for allowing to the receivers general of the duties on offices and employment in Scotland a proper compensation; for the better preservation of hollis, thorns, and quicksets in forests, chases and private grounds, and of trees and underwoods in forests and chases; and for authorising the exportation of a limited quantity of an inferior sort of bailey called bigg from the port of Kirkwall in the island of Orkney.'

Peel commented that what he proposed was 'not to throw open the holly or thorn to wanton depredation, but merely to transplant them to a more congenial soil than the province of Senegambia'.[3]

Peel went on to secure the enactment of the consolidating Criminal Law Amendment Acts of 1826-32. Although they were themselves soon amended, their enactment was recognised generally as representing a useful and considerable achievement.[4] Peel had demonstrated that useful, non-revolutionary reforms might be achieved in this area of law. How did Peel achieve this? Above all, Peel stressed a common sense, non-revolutionary approach:

> 'I presume that I shall not have to combat at the outset any objections...to the principle of an attempt to consolidate and simplify the criminal law....
> It appears so conformable to the dictate of common sense, that the law, of which all men are supposed to have cognizance — and which all are bound under heavy penalties to obey, should be as precise and intelligible as it can be made — that it is almost needless to fortify by reasoning or authority, the first impressions of the understanding.'

He prepared carefully and he secured the co-operation of the judges. According to Gash, it was of greater consequence to Peel 'to create an agreed maximum of consent over a wide field of legal reform than to risk obstruction and defeat by pressing forward immediately to the furthest visible objective'.[5] The measure of Peel's pioneering success in the field of consolidation was that no other reformer surpassed it throughout the remainder of the nineteenth century.

In 1833 Brougham, as Lord Chancellor, secured the appointment of a Royal Commission[6] whose terms of reference were rather more ambitious than those which Peel had set himself. The whole of the criminal law was to be digested in

---

3 N. Gash *Mr. Secretary Peel* pp. 335 ff.
4 C. Ilbert *Legislative Methods and Forms* pp. 43-51, L. Radzinowicz *A History of English Criminal Law* vol 1, p. 574.
5 N. Gash *Mr. Secretary Peel*.
6 Report of the Commissioners on the consolidation of the Statute Law no. 406 (1835).

the form of two statutes: one statute would deal with the statutory criminal law, the other would deal with crimes at common law. Secondly, the Commissioners were to report as to how far it might be expedient to combine both those statutes into one body of criminal law. Finally, the Commissioners were to report and inquire how far it might be expedient to consolidate the other branches of the law. The Commissioners, who originally had included the distinguished jurist, Austin, prepared a considerable number of reports, which are valuable for their analysis of the problems of consolidation, of the contemporary criminal law and for the draft bills which they produced. No action was taken upon those reports. It was in 1853 that a new Lord Chancellor, Lord Cranworth, took up the same challenge. He undertook to bring forward a Criminal Law Bill which was based upon the earlier reports. He announced also, not only that he was about to attempt a consolidation of the statute law but that he hoped that such consolidation would amount to a Code Victoria.[7] Yet Cranworth failed in both ventures.[8] Cranworth had felt that it was desirable to seek judicial approval for the Criminal Law Bill, which was regarded at the time as a codifying measure. Each of the judges rejected the measure.[9] Accordingly, Cranworth felt compelled to abandon the Bill. For the most part the judges had objected to the Bill on the ground that it substituted written rules for the unwritten doctrines of the common law. Talfourd J did concede that to 'reduce the statute law into a narrow compass is an object entirely free from objection, and which if accomplished with care, can produce nothing but good'. However, he then went on to state that 'to reduce unwritten law to statute is to discard one of the greatest blessings we have for ages enjoyed in rules capable of flexible application'. Similarly, Baron Parke maintained that '...the rules of the common law,...are clear and well understood, and have the incalculable advantage of being capable of application to new combinations of circumstances perpetually occurring....' It was a common attitude among contemporary lawyers. Whatever reforms were introduced, the traditional role of the common law was to be left untrammelled.

Despite this early failure, Cranworth went on to instigate a determined attempt to consolidate the statutes. In 1853 a Statute Law Board was appointed for a 12 month period. Bellenden Ker, a distinguished Chancery lawyer and the only signatory to the 1835 Report who was still available, was appointed as the Board's part-time head commissioner. He had a staff of four full-time barristers. During the year which followed they produced no fewer than three reports which amounted in all to over 600 folio pages in length.[10] Yet those reports reveal a well nigh total lack of combination between the members of the Board in their efforts. Nor did they offer any legislative guide to a Lord Chancellor who had hoped 'to get something really done'.[11] Even their suggestion that a permanent

7   124 Official Report (3rd series) col. 4.

8   A. H. Manchester 'Simplifying the Sources of the Law: An Essay in Law Reform — 1. Lord Cranworth's Attempt to Consolidate the Statute Law of England and Wales' (1973) 2 Anglo-American Law Review 395.

9   Copies of the Lord Chancellor's Letters to the Judges and of their Answers respecting the Criminal Law Bills of the last session no. 303 (1854).

10 Reports of Mr. Bellenden Ker to the Lord Chancellor on the proceedings of the Board for the revision of the Statute Law: First no. 301 (1854), Second no. 302 (1854), Third no. 302-T (1854).

11 125 Official Report (3rd series) col. 294.

officer or Board be appointed to advise on current legislation was not new. On the lapsing of this Board, Cranworth secured the appointment in 1854 of a royal commission whose members were eminent lawyers and men of affairs. Unfortunately, their four Reports, which were published before the commission's extinction in 1859, display a similar want of purpose and method which was surely remarkable in such a distinguished body of which so much had been hoped.[12] As a pungent contemporary critic put it in 1857:

> 'If the [Third] Report lately issued had been the first instead of the sixth, he could readily believe all the promises that were made: but seeing that upon every occasion a fresh plan was propounded and fresh promises were made, he did not see how they could place any reliance upon it.'[13]

There had been a quite spectacular lack of method in the commission's approach to its task. In particular, the commission was unable to agree on the most fundamental point of all, the meaning of consolidation. George Coode, an adviser to the original Statute Law Board, had advised strongly that only statute law was to be consolidated for to attempt to consolidate the common law would be to alter altogether its existing flexible character. Nor was the substance of the law to be altered. These are consciously modest aims which smack of the recipe for success which Chalmers was to give at the end of the century after the successful enactment of the codification measures which he had proposed. In view both of the legal profession's respect for the common law and of parliament's concern for its exclusive legislative role, there can be no doubt that it was good advice: it was vital to the reformer that he should enjoy the co-operation of both the profession and of parliament.

Yet it really was not possible to consolidate without altering the language of the statutes to some extent: how could it be otherwise when the consolidator might be faced with the problem not only of consolidating several statutes but of harmonising in a single statute, statutory provisions from the ages of Chaucer, Wycliff, Shakespeare, Congreve and Dickens?[14] Was this to amend the substance of the law, then? The inclusion of conscious amendments of the law, of course, was a far more delicate matter. Moreover many, especially amongst the legal profession, felt strongly that the common law must be left untouched. Accordingly, when one of Ker's assistants attempted to consolidate both statute law and common law, a legal journal claimed that he must have forgotten the essential difference between the common law and statute, the function of a statute being merely to correct and supply the deficiencies of the common law but not to replace it.[15] Such difficulties were real enough. Unfortunately, the Royal Commission never considered them in depth. Indeed, like Lord Cranworth in 1853, the commissioners took the view that if their task were not to be commenced until a comprehensive plan had been matured in all its details, there was a considerable risk that nothing might be achieved. They suggested that by producing some useful bills but without making their acceptance dependent

12 Reports from the Commissioners appointed for the purpose of consolidating the Statute Laws of the realm: First no. 1963 (1854-55), Second no. 2045 (1856), Third no. 2219 Sess. 2 (1857) Fourth no. 78 Sess. 2 (1859).
13 146 Official Report (3rd series) cols. 777, 115.
14 C. Ilbert *The Mechanics of Law Making* p. 38.
15 (1853) 17 Jur 458, 459, cf. (1858) 5 Sol Jo 122.

upon the acceptance in all its details of any large scheme of change, the subject might be made familiar and popular, and so prepare the way for future measures on a more comprehensive scale. On the other hand the Law Officers, Cockburn — who as Lord Chief Justice was later to damage Stephen's hope of codifying part of the criminal law — and Bethell — who, as Lord Westbury, was later to propose a digest of the law — favoured a quite different approach. Such differences cannot have helped the Commission in its work. The Commission faced other difficulties, too. Government departments were reluctant to proceed with the consolidation of statutes when this might be made a pretext for re-opening political arguments concerning the merits of such statutes. It may be, however, that just as important a factor in the Commission's failure was Cranworth's amiable character as reflected both in the tentative nature of his initial proposals and in his persistence with Ker as his chief agent despite the contemporary awareness that Ker was failing in his work. This, after all, was a time for boldness and for decisive action, if Cranworth's hopes of a Code Victoria were to be achieved.

c) *Miscellaneous reforms*
So much, then, for the hoped for Code Victoria. Cranworth himself was later to claim no more than that he and Ker had cleared the ground for further reform. Indeed, a long line of Statute Law Revision Acts may be traced back to the first such Act in 1856. In 1861 seven Criminal Law Consolidation Acts were enacted.[16] Other useful, albeit less dramatic, reforms were undertaken in the years which followed. The work of indexing, expurgation and of statute law revision were highly successful, albeit unglamorous, tasks. The Statute Law Committee, which was first appointed in 1868, did excellent work in this field. The work of consolidation also continued intermittently, although a parliamentary storm, which erupted in 1897 when it was realised that what had purported to be a technical consolidating statute which introduced no changes in law in fact did amount to a change in the law, showed clearly enough that parliament was as jealous as ever of its legislative role. Criticism of the existing system continued. Lord Westbury, who as Bethell, the Solicitor-General in 1855, had advocated a digest of the existing statutory provisions, renewed his criticism of the body of the law in the following decade with the result that a Royal Commission on a Digest of the Law was appointed, which reported in 1867.[17] Nothing came of that Commission's report, despite its strong criticism of the 'great chaos of judicial legislation'. In 1870 a professional magazine, the *Law Times*, even proclaimed that codification was both practicable and desirable: it demanded that the profession 'urge on the work'.[18] It was in the field of codification that a considerable further reforming effort was to be made. That effort was due almost wholly to the work of James Fitzjames Stephen.

d) *Codification*
James Fitzjames Stephen[19] was called to the Bar in 1854 and, although he never

---

16   24, 25 Vict, cc. 94-100.
17   C. Ilbert *The Mechanics of Law Making*.
18   (1870) 48 LT 469, 470, (1870) 49 LT 401, 429. Cf. (1872) 53 LT 310, 312.
19   L. Stephen *Life of Sir James Fitzjames Stephen*, L. Radzinowics, *Sir James Fitzjames Stephen*.

achieved any particular success in practice, he took silk in 1868. He was a man of considerable personal distinction who was well known in the legal, political and literary circles of his day. From 1869-72 he was Law Member in India where he was impressed most favourably by the success of the Indian Penal Code and where he himself had codified with some enthusiasm. Upon his return to England he was soon involved in drafting a Homicide Bill which had been inspired originally by the dislike of John Bright, who had been a member of the Royal Commission on Capital Punishment which reported in 1866,[20] for the existing concept of constructive murder, whereby a defendant might be found guilty of murder, even though he had not intended actually to kill. From the very beginning, therefore, there was a reforming element in Stephen's work. That Bill foundered on the lukewarm approach of a Select Committee and upon a lack of judicial enthusiasm[1] which was grounded in the lawyers' traditional view of the 'elasticity', as Blackburn J put it, of the common law. What Mr. Justice Blackburn saw as the common law's desirable elasticity, Stephen described as its 'uncertainty and vagueness'. The Select Committee believed that a redefinition of murder was 'urgently needed' but was of the opinion that the Homicide Bill before them should not be proceeded with. The *Law Times* described its decision as 'ingenious but cowardly.... If we must be slow, deliberate and careful in making changes, and then begin codification by little bits of unimportant law, proceeding onwards only after "numerous trials", what is the prospect of English law being codified?'[2]

Stephen went on to publish a Digest of the Criminal Law in 1877: it then occurred to him that this Digest would form the basis of a draft Penal Code. Accordingly, in 1877 the Lord Chancellor, Lord Cairns, instructed him to draw bills for a penal code, to which he was soon directed to add a code of criminal procedure. The Attorney-General, Sir John Holker, introduced Stephen's measure into Parliament on 14 May 1878 and Parliament referred the matter to a royal commission. That commission, which included a number of distinguished judges — of whom Blackburn J was one — among its members, was strongly in favour of present codification, despite the risks involved. It reported:

'we are...convinced that however carefully a code of criminal law may be framed, much risk of occasional miscarriage must at first be incurred. If codification is postponed until some proposed code has been pronounced perfect, or until desultory and irresponsible criticism had been exhausted, the accomplishment of the work will be indefinitely deferred. In fact the merits or defects of a well considered code can only be ascertained after it has become law, and has been interpreted under the sanction of judicial responsibility.'[3]

Not all criminal offences were included within the Code; that would have been

20 Report of the Capital Punishment Commission no. 10438 (1866).
1 Special Report from the [Select] Committee on Homicide Law Amendment Bill no. 315 (1874).
2 (1874) 57 LT 243. Cf. (1874) 18 Sol Jo 623. See generally: A. H. Manchester 'Simplifying the Sources of the Law: An Essay in Law Reform — 11: James Fitzjames Stephen and the Codification of the Criminal Law of England and Wales' (1973) 2 Anglo-American Law Review 527.
3 Report of the Royal Commission...on the Law relating to Indictable Offences no. C-2345 (1879) p. 41.

too ambitious an experiment. The commissioners wrote that their object had been rather to include as far as practicable all those crimes, whether at common law or created by statute, which in the ordinary course of affairs came to be tried in the courts of criminal justice. Yet the Code did incorporate amendments in the law: indeed, a summary of the principal changes in the law covered some six folio pages. The distinction between felony and misdemeanour was to be abolished on the ground that the classification was arbitrary and that the distinction was 'nearly if not altogether unmeaning'. Similarly, the Draft Code did not use the word 'malice' because 'there is a considerable difference between its popular and its legal meaning' and nowhere was this more true than in the use of the phrase 'malice aforethought' in the definition of murder. The Draft Code also proposed a considerable simplification of the highly technical and outdated law of larceny: it provided also for the institution of a court of appeal in criminal cases. The Draft Code might not only have simplified considerably the sources of the law, therefore: had it been enacted, it would have introduced reforms, many of which have only gradually been introduced in subsequent years. Yet it was not to be. Really it was a change of ministry in 1880 which put paid to Stephen's hope, although in 1882 the part of the Draft Code relating to procedure was announced as a government measure in the Queen's speech. That was to be the Draft Code's last sign of life.

The result was that by the turn of the century England had enacted only three codifying Acts. They were the Bills of Exchange Act 1882, drawn up by Chalmers; the Partnership Act 1890, drawn up by Pollock and the Sale of Goods Act 1893, drawn up by Chalmers.[4] Why, then, did Stephen fail? Why was Chalmers, relatively speaking, so successful?

One of Stephen's most powerful critics was Lord Cockburn, the Lord Chief Justice: he (shades of Bentham) objected to the incompleteness of the Draft Code. He pointed out, for example, that the Draft Code kept alive statutes, or parts of statutes, rather than incorporating the whole of the relevant law within the Draft Code. He was concerned also that the Draft Code did not include all criminal offences. The Lord Chief Justice voiced those criticisms in a letter to the Attorney-General, probably before he had had the opportunity of studying the commissioners' report on the Code, which was published as a Parliamentary Paper in June 1879. In reply to the charge of incompleteness, Stephen pointed out that some of the omitted statutes were historical monuments of the political and religious struggles of former times rather than parts of the ordinary criminal law: others were passed under circumstances which are seldom, if ever, enforced, and so on.[5] The Attorney-General also rejected the criticisms by the Lord Chief Justice. It is impossible to assess accurately the effect of the criticisms of the Lord Chief Justice: it was surely unfortunate for Stephen's hopes, however, that they had been published at that particular time. For on the whole there was no enthusiasm for codification among either the nation as a whole — although the Trades Union Congress was in favour of codification — or among the legal profession. In France, at the beginning of the century, the Napoleonic Codes

4   45 and 46 Vict, c. 61; 53 and 54 Vict, c. 39; 56 and 57 Vict, c. 71.
5   Copy of Letter from the Lord Chief Justice...containing Comments and Suggestions in relation to the Criminal Code (Indictable Offences) Bill no. 232 (1879). Contrast J. F. Stephen (1880) 7 Nineteenth Century 136.

had been inspired by a strong movement for national unity and for an equality between citizens which it was thought that the codes would help to promote. Moreover, Napoleon himself had taken a personal interest in the advancement of the codification measures. Equally, in Germany towards the end of the century, there was a strong desire for a unified system of law as an expression of national unity. Similar factors had been at work in India: public enthusiasm had been marked in the State of New York. However, Stephen's own country was a far different matter, a 'centre of indifference', as he put it. Parliament, too, had always been jealous of its legislative role and could reasonably have been expected, therefore, to scrutinise closely any reforming measure. There could be no doubt that the Draft Code sought to introduce considerable reforms: indeed, an element of reform had always lain at the basis of much of Stephen's thought on codification. Certainly Chalmers felt that was a lesson to be learned from the sad fate of Stephen's Code. Chalmers attributed the success of his Bills of Exchange Act largely to the insistence of Sir Farrer Herschell, later Lord Chancellor, who steered it through the House of Commons, that so far as possible the Bill should reproduce exactly the existing law 'whether it seemed good, bad, or indifferent in its effects'. The Bill, too, had been discussed thoroughly and approved by the 'commercial classes' who appear always to have favoured codification.[6]

On the other hand Stephen must be given due credit for the quality of his reasoned response to criticism. Not the least of his achievements appears to have been the conversion to codification of Mr. Justice Blackburn, one of the most distinguished of the Victorian judges. Indeed, the response of the commissioners as a whole to the oft repeated objection that a code would lack the flexibility of the common law is worth considering in some detail. The commissioners commented:

> 'There is some apparent force in this objection, but its importance has to say the least been largely exaggerated, and it is in our opinion certainly not sufficient to constitute (as some people regard it) a fatal objection to codification. In order to appreciate the objection it is necessary to consider the nature of this so-called discretion which is attributed to the judges.
>
> It seems to be assumed that when a judge is called on to deal with a new combination of circumstances, he is at liberty to decide according to his own views of justice and expediency; whereas on the contrary he is bound to decide in accordance with principles already established, which he can neither disregard nor alter, whether they are to be found in previous judicial decisions or in books of recognised authority. The consequences of this are first, that the elasticity of the common law is much smaller than it is often supposed to be; and secondly, that so far as a code represents the effect of decided cases and established principles, it takes from the judges nothing which they possess at present....In fact, the elasticity so often spoken of as a valuable quality would if it existed, be only another name for uncertainty. The great richness of the law of England in principles and rules, embodied in judicial decisions, no doubt involves the consequence that a code adequately representing it must be elaborate and detailed; but

such a code would not (except perhaps in the few cases in which the law is obscure) limit any discretion now possessed by the judges. It would simply change the form of the rules by which they are bound.

The truth is that the expression "elasticity" is altogether misused when it is applied to English law. The great characteristics of the law of this country, at all events of its criminal law, is, that it is extremely detailed and explicit, and leaves hardly any discretion to the judges.'[7]

Opinions regarding the quality of the Draft Code differ. On the whole later reforms have vindicated Stephen's judgment regarding the desirability of certain reforms. Further, his Code was influential overseas. Even if his drafting could well have been improved on occasion, such blemishes must be balanced against the breadth of his work and the considerable improvement upon existing practice which it represented.

e) *Further initiatives*

There were to be no further wide ranging initiatives. However, the first edition of Halsbury's Laws of England, which was published between 1907 and 1917, was an attempt to implement the main outlines of the scheme which the Digest of Law Commission had suggested some years earlier. The success of Halsbury bore witness to the very real need which it helped to satisfy. All that remained was to decide upon the manner in which the few existing codes should be interpreted. The point was especially relevant in Chalmers' Bills of Exchange Act 1882 which had provided at s. 97(2) that:

'The rules of the common law, including the law merchant, save in so far as they are inconsistent with the provisions of this Act...shall continue to apply to bills of exchange.'

To what extent was it necessary, then, after 1882 to consider the existing common law, including the principles upon which the pre-1882 cases were said to be based? Lord Herschell expressed a majority judicial opinion when he said:

'I think the proper course is in the first instance to examine the language of the statute and to ask what is its natural meaning, uninfluenced by any considerations derived from the previous state of the law, and not to start with inquiring how the law previously stood, and then, assuming that it was probably intended to leave it unaltered, to see if the words of the enactment will bear an interpretation in conformity with this view.'[8]

However, previous decisions could be considered if a provision were 'of doubtful import' and in practice the pre-1882 decisions occupy a prominent place, even in today's texts upon the sale of goods. In practice reformers would continue to fear, and with some reason, that in time the judicial interpretation of an Act would become of equal or greater importance than the Act itself, as had been the case with the old Statute of Frauds.

During the first half of the twentieth century there was little interest in the simplification of the sources of the law. However, after the Second World War there was a resurgence of interest. Between 1948 and 1951 some 20 consolidation

---

7   Report of the Royal Commission...on the Law relating to Indictable Offences...no. C-2345 (1879) pp. 7-8.
8   *Bank of England v Vagliano Bros* [1891] AC 107 at 144.

Acts were passed: attention was paid also to the work of statute law revision.[9] However, further codification appeared to be no more than an academic dream.[10] Few commentators would then have expected that, as soon as 1965, a government-backed law commission would be created with the task of furthering the codification of the law.

9 Viscount Jowitt *Statute Law Revision and Consolidation* (1951). Cf. L. C. B. Gower 'Here Lies the Common Law: Rest in Peace' (1967) 30 MLR 241.
10 D. Lloyd 'Codifying English Law' (1949) 2 Current Legal Problems 155.

Chapter 3

Lawyers and judges

1 Change and the professions

a) *Introducton*

During the Victorian period in particular, the concept of the profession was sharpened considerably — a process which had implications regarding admission to a profession, the discipline of members and education for that profession.[1] Being long established and already influential, the legal profession was especially well placed either to implement, or to thwart, reforms proposed in its own field.[2] Changes which had been implemented within the medical profession and the civil service had pointed out a path forward for the lawyers.

b) *The medical profession*

Like the lawyers the doctors were divided into groups, only one of which was socially prestigious. There were the physicians, the surgeons and the apothecaries. Only the physicians were regarded as members of a learned profession. The physicians were fellows and licentiates of the Royal College of Physicians of London or members of similar colleges in Dublin and Edinburgh. The Royal College was a very small body which usually refused admission to anybody who was not a graduate of Oxford or of Cambridge. Yet for many years those universities had offered little or no medical education. Inquiries into medical education during the 1830s allowed reformers to demonstrate the lack of any guarantee of competence in medical men generally. The medical profession did then begin to take steps over the years to provide such a public guarantee of their competence. Better educational facilities were provided,

1 V. H. H. Green *The Universities*, A. M. Carr-Saunders and P. A. Wilson *The Professions*, W. J. Reader *Professional Men*.
2 See generally: M. Birks *Gentlemen of the Law*, W. S. Holdsworth *History of English Law* vol 12 pp. 77-101 and *History of English Law* vol 15, pp. 231-47, R. Pound *The Lawyer from Antiquity to Modern Times* pp. 75-128, R. Robson *The Attorney in Eighteenth Century England*. Especially valuable for the modern period is B. Abel-Smith and R. Stevens *Lawyers and the Courts*.

apprenticeship was allowed to wither away and the Medical Act 1858 created the registered medical practitioner, who had satisfied one or more of 21 existing licensing bodies, after examinations, that he was fit to practise. Yet it was the socially inferior apothecary who provided a model of nineteenth-century professional organisation in the form of the Apothecaries Act 1815 which allowed the Society of Apothecaries to determine the conditions of entry to their profession and gave it the power to prevent unqualified persons from calling themselves apothecaries.[3]

c) *The civil service*

The civil service, too, was in the process of being reformed. Eventually the competitive examination was adopted as a means of ensuring sorely needed efficiency in the light both of the new administrative skills required to administer the rapidly grown cities and of the public outcry which was consequent upon the increasing public awareness of the incompetence revealed during the Crimean War. The first step was taken in 1833 when statute provided for competitive examinations for the Indian Civil Service. That scheme proved to be so successful that the important Northcote-Trevelyan Report in 1854 recommended, successfully, that competitive examinations should replace patronage as the method of recruitment for the home civil service.[4]

d) *Schools and universities*

The schools, however, remained remarkably loyal to the traditional, and predominantly classical, curriculum, despite the labours of the Schools Enquiry Commission of 1868. Nor were the universities quick to respond to change. Critics of the universities had attacked the universities, inter alia, both for their ineffective teaching and for their neglect of research. Finally a commission, opposed bitterly by many in the universities, was instituted in 1850. The commission made a number of useful reformist proposals regarding university teaching and government. It recommended also that more attention should be given to schools of law and medicine. By 1880 Oxford and Cambridge had been revitalised. Some doubt must remain, however, as to whether the universities had yet accommodated themselves to the teaching of professional or 'practical' subjects.[5]

e) *Conclusion*

Clearly, therefore, the educational system and the professions were under considerable public scrutiny during Queen Victoria's first quarter-century on the throne. The examination emerged as a public guarantee of competence; the medical profession in particular embraced the new public expectations with some enthusiasm. Yet the evidence of competence in the civil service tended to be that of a general intellectual proficiency. There remained a certain disdain for the wholly professional training, however liberal and humane it be. As Matthew

---

3 See W. J. Reader *Professional Men* pp. 51-2.
4 Report of the Commissioners on civil service organisation no. 1713 (1854).
5 V. H. H. Green *The Universities*; Report of Her Majesty's Commission...into the State, Discipline, Studies and Revenues of the University and Colleges of Oxford no. 1482 (1852), Report of Her Majesty's Commission...into the State, Discipline, Studies and Revenues of the University and Colleges of Cambridge no. 1559.1017 (1852).

Arnold noted, there was 'an aristocratic form of ideas in the upper professional plane which was characterised by its indisposition and incapacity for science, for systematic knowledge'. Accordingly, a short course at a crammer came into its own as the hallmark of the training of the Victorian professional man.[6] That was a situation which boded ill for more ambitious schemes of professional education: on the other hand professional ideals, forged in the rapidly changing Victorian world, served the public well by emphasising, inter alia, the requirements of professional competence and professional honour.

2 The structure of the legal profession

By the mid-eighteenth century the legal profession was established along lines which would be reasonably familiar to the modern lawyer.[7] On the one hand there were the advocates or counsel: on the other hand there were the attorneys and solicitors. There were two species of advocate or counsel, sergeants and barristers. By custom the judges of the courts of Westminster were admitted to the order of sergeants before they were raised to the Bench and the king's counsel learned in the law were also selected from their ranks. The two principal such counsel were called the King's Attorney-General and the King's Solicitor-General. Counsel were admitted to the Inns of Court and were subject to the discipline of the Benchers of those institutions. Attorneys were regarded as officers of the respective courts in which they were admitted and so were subject to judicial supervision. To practise in the court of Chancery it was necessary to be admitted as a solicitor. To be a solicitor was to be more socially respectable than to be an attorney and so by mid-nineteenth century lawyers preferred to call themselves solicitors rather than attornies. In the civilian courts at Doctors' Commons in London there was a small group of advocates and proctors who filled the roles of barristers and of attorneys respectively.

3 Admission to the legal profession

a) *Formal requirements for admission*

i) *Attorneys and solicitors.* An Act of 1729 provided quite comprehensively for 'the better regulation of attorneys and solicitors'.[8] Nobody was to be permitted to act as an attorney until he was enrolled in the court where he was to act as an attorney; the judges of such courts were required and authorised 'to examine and inquire by such ways and means as they shall think proper, touching his fitness and capacity to act as an attorney'; no person was to be called as an attorney until he had first served as a clerk for five years to an attorney duly and legally sworn and admitted. The 1729 Act amounted to a national recognition of the desirability that its attorneys and solicitors at least should be trained adequately.

The Solicitors Act 1843 entrusted to the Incorporated Law Society the office of registrar for the registration of all admitted attorneys and solicitors.[9] An

---

6   See generally W. J. Reader *The Professions* chap. 7.
7   3 Bl Com (5th edn) 22 ff.
8   Attorneys' and Solicitors' Act 1728.
9   Section 21.

appeal for admission as a solicitor could be made to the Master of the Rolls by any person who had obtained from the Society a certificate of having passed a final examination. There were few other rules regarding admission, although at one time some attorneys had favoured proof of the attainment of a certain standard of education as a prerequisite to obtaining articles and a certificate as to character had to be produced by every person who wished to be admitted to the effect that he had diligently and faithfully employed himself during clerkship. According to a witness before a Royal Commission of 1854, instances had occurred where, 'in consequence of representations made to them, the examiners had felt it to be their duty to make strict inquiry into the moral character of candidates with reference to particular transactions'.[10]

ii) *Barristers.* The control of admission to the Bar was vested effectively in the Benchers of the respective Inns of Court — Gray's Inn, Lincoln's Inn, Inner Temple, and Middle Temple. Other Inns, the Inns of Chancery, had been used mainly by attorneys and solicitors. Even in Blackstone's day, the intending Bar student rarely used them as they were 'neither commodious nor proper for the resort of gentlemen of any rank or figure' with the result that the Inns of Chancery played no role in the history of the modern Bar.[11] Prior to his admission as a student of an Inn of Court the candidate was required to furnish a statement signed either by a Bencher or by two barristers with regard principally to his 'respectability and fitness to be admitted'. Few persons were refused admission or call. During the 20 years previous to a Report of 1834, Lincoln's Inn, for example, had refused admission to four persons only. The criteria were want of competent education, or of moral character and fitness to be received into the society of gentlemen, the latter point presumably being one which went, as Gray's Inn put it, to the candidate's station in life.[12] Further, nobody could be called to the Bar while he was on the roll of attornies, solicitors or proctors. A student was required also to keep 12 terms at his Inn i.e. to dine in Hall at least three times each term. Just a handful of persons, the Benchers, were in effective control, therefore, of admission to the country's most prestigious profession. Despite a number of reformist recommendations which were made by Commissioners in 1834, it was a control which the Benchers retained largely undiminished. However, in 1837 the Inns agreed that they would allow any person refused admission to appeal to the judges and that they would be bound by the judicial decision.[13]

b) *Who wanted to be a lawyer?*

When he gave evidence to a Select Committee in 1846, Sir George Stephen, a distinguished attorney, pointed to three classes of person who wished to become an attorney. First, there was the son of the tradesman or the rather wealthier

10 Report of the Commissioners appointed to inquire into the Arrangements in the Inns of Court and Inns of Chancery for promoting the study of Law and Jurisprudence no. 1988 (1855) p. 128, q. 1550.
11 1 Bl Com (5th edn) 25. See also *Smith v Kerr* [1900] 2 Ch 511, [1902] 1 Ch 774.
12 Sixth Report of the Commissioners on the Practice and Proceedings of Superior Courts of Common Law no. 263 (1834) p. 6. Cf. Documents relating to D. W. Harvey's Application to be called to the Bar no. 349 (1834).
13 W. S. Holdsworth *History of English Law* vol 12, pp. 23 ff.

merchant whose father felt that he might well place legal business in the way of a solicitor son. Secondly, there was the son of the gentleman of modest means. Thirdly, there were a considerable number who were 'suckled and cradled as an attorney'. Sometimes introduced into the lawyer's office when they were as young as ten, these persons acquired a great deal of practical knowledge. Later they were retained at a very moderate salary.[14] It was with that third group especially in mind that efforts were made over the years to raise the social status of the attorney. Blackstone had referred disparagingly to the attorney: in 1821 Parliament had sought to raise the social status of the attorney by providing that a graduate of Oxford or Cambridge would be required to serve articles of three years only.[15] The attorney himself was keen to increase his social status during the remainder of this period. In this respect he achieved considerable success, even though his particular branch of the profession had numerous members carrying out a wide variety of work. A survey of the social background of law students in 1910, revealed a situation similar to that which Stephen had offered many years earlier.[16] As the number of graduate entrants to the profession increased after the First World War, the status of this branch of the profession as a whole tended to rise correspondingly.

In fact the practising barristers' social background was not particularly superior. The unremitting grind which faced the young man who was to succeed in this branch of the profession meant that few wealthy young men were likely to devote themselves to it. The Inns of Court required the nineteenth century barrister to be a gentleman. That did not necessarily mean more than that he originated from a reasonably modest middle-class background. To a large extent his prestige arose from the respect which society accorded to the relatively small number of judges of the superior courts who were recruited exclusively from the ranks of the barristers. Naturally, the Bar valued, and was ready to justify, this link with the judiciary.

4 Legal education

a) *Introduction*

During the whole of the eighteenth century and for the greater part of the first half of the nineteenth century the legal profession was almost totally indifferent to the question of education for the profession. Some small interest flickered in the light of the major, yet little heeded, inquiries of 1846 and 1855. There were continuing hopes, which lingered into the twentieth century, that some kind of Law University would be created, but little was achieved. Even during the twentieth century progress was painfully slow, although the greatly increased provision for legal studies within the universities was a hopeful sign for the future.

14　Report from the Select Committee on Legal Education no. 686 (1846) pp. 144-5. For a more flattering view of the role of some attornies at an earlier date see B. L. Anderson 'The Attorney and the Early Capital Market in Lancashire' in F. Crouzet *Capital Formation in the Industrial Revolution* pp. 223, 224. Cf. P. Lucas 'Blackstone and the Reform of the Legal Profession' (1962) 77 English Historical Review 477.

15　Report from Select Committee on Admission of Attornies and Solicitors no. 137 (1821), B. Abel-Smith and R. Stevens *Lawyers and the Courts* pp. 26-7.

16　H. D. Hazeltine 'The Present State of Legal Education in England' (1910) 26 LQR 17, 21-2.

b) *The Select Committee of 1846*[17]

It is a remarkable fact that in mid-nineteenth century, at a time when the country was at its most influential in terms of its industrial, commercial, and political power, there was virtually no provision for legal education. A Select Committee of 1846 was unanimous in its affirmation that all who were interested in legal education had 'a more or less modified recognition of the inefficiency of the present system, the injurious consequences which have resulted from its continuance, and the urgent necessity of immediate alteration, both in reference to extent and improvement'. This view was based upon an impressive review of provisions for legal education which were made in this country and overseas. The Ormrod Report could assert as late as 1971 of its recommendations that 'the history of legal education in England over the past 120 years is largely an account of the struggle to implement the recommendations of the 1846 Committee and the results of that struggle'.

Of the universities only University College, London offered even the elements of a course in law. There, over a period of four to five years, Amos gave an hour long lecture every day to audiences which varied between 50 and 150. There were conversation classes, monthly examinations and also a private class course in his own chambers for a fee of 100 guineas per person. At the same time Austin was offering his rather more abstract lectures, albeit to considerably fewer students. Legal studies at Oxford and at Cambridge were virtually non-existent. At Oxford there were two professors, one of whom offered no course at all: the other offered 24 lectures on the common law during the course of the year, although there were no examinations. There was no chair of canon law. The situation at Cambridge was on a par with that at Oxford.

The professional bodies showed an equal lack of zeal for legal education. The responsibility of the Inns of Court for the education of the intending barrister was purely nominal. Lord Campbell, a distinguished lawyer who was later to become Lord Chancellor, told the Committee:

> 'all that has been required has been that the candidate to be called to the Bar should be of fair character; that he should have been a certain number of years upon the books of the Society: that he should have kept a certain number of terms by eating a certain number of dinners in the Hall each term, and have gone through the form of performing what are still called exercises, but which consist of a mere farce of a case being stated, and a debate on each side...'

This total absence of provision for legal education in the Inns of Court, and the meagre amount provided in the universities, had the natural effect, commented the Committee, of throwing the student on such chance instruction or studies as might fall in his way. It was true that future practitioners might attend under special pleaders, draftsmen or conveyancers. However, such education was 'in a great measure technical, and its acquisition must very much depend upon the individual intelligence and exertion of the pupil'.

The potential solicitor was offered even less opportunity for legal education. The Committee pointed out that he had been:

> 'treated more as a mechanical agent for carrying out the practical

---

17 Select Committee on Legal Education no. 686 (1846). Report of the Committee on Legal Education (Cmnd. 4595) p. 8, para. 19.

processes of the profession; and as the future chemist and apothecary is bound an apprentice, so is the future solicitor articled as a clerk, for the purpose of learning what has been too much considered in both cases as matter of mere manual dexterity. Hence, whatever higher or more comprehensive instruction he has been enabled to acquire, he owes it almost exclusively to himself.'

Articled clerks complained that the solicitor paid very little attention to the direction of their studies: they simply did not have the time. There was no prescribed course of occupation during the day, no course of lectures was compulsory, attendance at the courts was purely formal. Even the final examination appeared 'to be altogether inadequate to the purposes for which...it was designed'.

The Committee's conclusion was inevitable. So far as the mass of solicitors was concerned 'no guarantee whatever exists for that competency which the public have a right to demand'. The work of voluntary associations of solicitors such as the Incorporated Law Society and the Manchester Law Society was noted, yet it was necessarily limited. The success of lecture courses varied. Those of the Manchester Law Association had been 'remarkably well attended' yet they had amounted to a course of only eight each year. The Incorporated Law Society's examination served 'merely as a guarantee against absolute incompetency'.

How different was the situation, the Committee noted, in the Faculty of a German university. The three characteristic features of Germany's university system were said to be: '(1) A high scale of preparatory study, previous to being even admitted to any of the Faculty courses. (2) The immense number of professors, and minute subdivision of subject and labour. (3) The compulsory character of attendance on lectures and examinations, and the reality and stringency given to them by the mode in which both are carried out.'

The Committee recognised that eminent lawyers had been produced even under the existing system, but they maintained, like Blackstone before them, that the superiority of the few was not conclusive as to the abilities, and character of the many. The public should be able to assure themselves, as they could in the professions of Church and Medicine, of how 'far the many as well as the few are qualified to perform satisfactorily their respective duties'. Further, the evils of the existing system were said to be discoverable on the Bench in a hypercritical attention to technicalities, in the lack of professors of law, and law texts and in the poor drafting of legislation.

What was to be done? In the Committee's view a system of legal education, to be of general advantage, ought to meet the wants not only of the professional but also of the unprofessional student. For the general unprofessional student legal education could not commence earlier than the period of university education. In order to increase efficiency, examinations should be instituted. With a view to providing for the more advanced students, especially those who wished to devote themselves to the legal or even to the clerical profession, it was essential that existing teaching arrangements should be made more efficient. Therefore, it was necessary that greater advantages should be attached to the law degrees, and a greater amount of study and knowledge be demanded for their acquisition. Certain situations limited to barristers of seven years standing might be extended to Bachelors of Law; others again, more valuable and important, to Doctors. A rigorous examination, preceded by certificates of attendance at lectures, and by minor periodical examinations at the close of each course, should be instituted.

A college of law was no less important to the intending lawyer, the Committee continued, than a college of surgery or medicine to the prospective surgeon or physician: it was the natural preparation for entering into practice. The Committee believed that to this end the Inns of Court should co-operate to form a 'Law University', entrance to which should be by examination. For attendance on term dinners in the several Inns would be substituted attendance on term lectures. Examinations, too, were of great importance.

In providing for the special legal education of the solicitor, there should be a stringent examination to ensure that the candidate possessed a sound general education. For the further education of the solicitor it was highly advisable that even as an articled clerk he should have the opportunity to attend certain classes of lectures in the Inns of Court and also others of a nature more special to his profession in the Law Society. Finally, the Committee recommended that should there be a failure to take active and efficient measures to carry into operation the reforms proposed, recourse should be had to a Commission.

c) *The Royal Commission of 1854*[18]

In 1854 a royal commission was appointed to inquire into the arrangements in the Inns of Court and Inns of Chancery for promoting the study of law and jurisprudence. The commissioners wrote that in providing for a professional education at the Inns, there were two relevant considerations. First, there was the duty which the several societies to whom the power of calling students to the Bar had been confided owed to the student who was required to make payments to them and to remain a definite number of years without liberty to practise. Secondly, in the light of the barristers' privileges — that he alone was allowed to plead for others in the superior courts of Westminster — the community was surely entitled to require some guarantee as to his personal character and professional qualifications. It was pointed out that the clergyman, physician, surgeon, apothecary, attorney and solicitor, were all required to pass an examination before they were permitted to practise. The system of practical study in a barrister's chambers was not disparaged, but that afforded no facilities for the study of the scientific branches of legal knowledge such as constitutional law, legal history, civil law and jurisprudence.

The commissioners believed that considerable advantage would result to the Bar as a liberal profession from a more clearly defined and permanent combination of the Inns of Court, with reference to legal education, than existed in respect of the recently created Council of Legal Education. The Inns might be united in a University, but still preserving their individual independence with respect to property and internal arrangements. Such a university might not only regulate the proposed examinations but might also confer degrees in law. The commissioners recognised that they were using the word 'university' in a new sense. They commented that it had been applied commonly 'to a course of general or universal instruction in letters and science; but the word in its earlier

18 Report of the Commissioners appointed to inquire into the Arrangements in the Inns of Court and Inns of Chancery for promoting the study of Law and Jurisprudence no. 1988 (1855).

import simply implies a corporate body, and, notwithstanding late usage, may not inaptly be applied to a course of instruction in every department of law'.

d) *Reaction to the Reports of 1846 and 1854*

The two Reports, especially that of 1846, are impressive yet little was done to implement their recommendations. When the Attorney-General was asked in 1848 whether the Inns had implemented the recommendations of the 1846 Committee to establish preliminary examinations and lectureships in law, he pointed merely to the lectureships which had been created and to their overall poor attendance.[19] Similarly, there was no action on the Report of 1854, although it was alleged that parliament had failed to act in this matter 'solely in consequence of there being at least a tacit understanding' that as far as possible the Benchers themselves would carry out the recommendations of the Report.[20] Foreign affairs also were said to have distracted parliament's attention from legal education. Finally in 1859 the Benchers of Lincoln's Inn vetoed a recommendation of a committee of the four Inns to the effect that there should be a preliminary examination and also a compulsory examination previous to being called to the Bar.[1]

However the Inns were not wholly inactive. In 1851 Sir Richard Bethell, the Solicitor-General, persuaded the Benchers of the four Inns of Court to form the Council of Legal Education. Reports of the four Inns were published in 1861 and 1863, as a result of which a body of consolidated regulations was agreed to whereby, inter alia, additional readerships were established and the voluntary examination of students was instituted. Yet the idea of a law university — commended once again in 1860 by a member of the Law Amendment Society — was rejected once again by the Inns in 1863.[2]

Many felt that the Bar was in an unhappy state. The *Pall Mall Gazette* maintained that the standard of some barristers was deplorable while the *Law Times* asserted that: 'A barrister is not necessarily either a lawyer or an advocate. The public have found it out. In plenty of English provincial towns barristers are settled who have no more right to be members of such a profession than they have to be clergymen.' By contrast the attorneys and solicitors felt quite satisfied with the progress which they had made in recent years.[3]

e) *The Legal Education Association and a Law University*

It was in such circumstances that a Legal Education Association, whose President was Sir Roundell Palmer, a Bencher of Lincoln's Inn and, as the Earl of Selborne, a future Lord Chancellor, returned to the subject of a Law University in 1870. Selborne explained the Association's aims to the House of Lords in 1874. After welcoming the fact that examinations had recently become compulsory — the examination for Bar students had been made compulsory in 1872 — he said that members of the Association believed that:

> 'there was no reason why all the available means of legal instruction should not be concentrated in one great public institution — call it a university,

---

19   (1849) 12 LT 505.
20   (1860) 6 Jur (n.s.) 247.
 1   (1875) 138 Quarterly Review 153.
 2   (1875) 138 Quarterly Review 153, (1860) 6 Jur (n.s.) 248.
 3   (1870) 48 LT 291, 323, (1865) 40 LT 621.

or a school of law, or what they would — and that all examinations which should be thought necessary for admission to either branch of the profession, and all instruction which it might be thought desirable to give to students seeking admission to either branch, should be conducted by that institution....The Inns of Court as places of legal discipline and education should be as broad and liberal as possible, and without any attempt being made at the earlier stages of that education to draw lines of demarcation between the different branches of the profession or to narrow the education to be given into a mere dry acquirement of legal rules.'[4]

Undoubtedly, this proposal was approved by those solicitors who sought to improve their profession's competence and status. The Law Society itself approved the initial proposals: the Birmingham Law Society voted a third of the year's income to the objects of the Association.[5] It was clear also that a substantial number of members of the Bar supported the objects of the Association. Yet there was some opposition. Some solicitors maintained that the education of attornies and solicitors should not be taken out of the hands of the Incorporated Law Society: every professional society, it was argued, should retain in its own hands, entire and undiminished, the conduct and function of its own members.

In assessing these, and later, proposals which implied to some degree a common education for both the potential barrister and the potential solicitor, it must be remembered that many members of the Bar felt very strongly that a small centralised Bar must continue in existence. There could be no common education for that might lead to a fusion of the two branches of the profession and there must be as clear a demarcation as possible between the role of the two branches.[6] Even the report of 1846 did not sanction a common education for both branches of the profession largely on the ground that such a proposition would not be acceptable to the Bar. Implicit in such arguments very often was the view that the barrister required a much higher degree of learning than the solicitor. Certainly fusion was to be resisted at all costs for that would mean that the 'great English Bar would exist no longer.... It is impossible that there can be this confusion of classes and functions, without loss of that fearless independence which is now characteristic of the English barrister.'[7]

The motives of some members of the Bar in supporting such arguments may have had rather more to do with maintaining their view of their social status than with preserving the public interest. Yet a strong case for the preservation of a small, centralised Bar could be made on the grounds of the public interest. Blackburn J did not sign the Second Report of the Judicature Commissioners on the grounds, inter alia, that:

'I have great doubts as to the expediency of establishing any such intermediate class of courts at all. I attach much importance to the keeping up of the great central Bar of England. The only practical check on the judges is the habitual respect which they all pay to what is called "the opinion of the profession", and the same powerful body forms, as I think, a real and

4 220 Official Report (3rd series) cols. 1457, 1463, (1874) 57 LT 208, (1871) 52 LT 76.
5 (1877) 52 Westminster Review 103, (1871) 52 LT 76.
6 (1875) 138 Quarterly Review 157.
7 Report from the Select Committee on Legal Education no. 686 (1846) p. liii, (1875) 138 Quarterly Review 173-4.

the principal check on the abuse of patronage by the government.'[8]

It was an argument which was accorded a great deal of respect. In the context of the current debate about local judicatures, *The Spectator* granted that the existing system was dilatory and costly. Yet it was fair to inquire, *The Spectator* suggested,

> 'whether in these circumstances so different from that glare of public discussion in which judicial promotions and judicial acts stand now, we could reasonably expect the same substantial guarantees that we have got at present against inefficiency, jobbery, favouritism and corruption.... The local Bench, so far inferior to the present class of judges, in professional standing, social position and fortune, would be open to suspicion at least, if not to temptations, which would weaken public confidence in the purity of justice.'[9]

It was probably a tactical mistake for Selborne to open two campaigns at once i.e. moves for both a law university and some common education. At all events a Joint Committee of the Inns resolved, albeit by only a small majority, against it, although they did recommend also that there should be a compulsory examination of students for the Bar before call and that the Council of Legal Education, increased in number and authority, should be responsible for it. So far as the universities were concerned, Oxford and Cambridge both demonstrated their readiness to consider the proposals of the Association. Yet it was the attitude of London University which was crucial: London expressed reservations at the proposal 'to assume the name of a university and to confer degrees'. In the event the opposition to Selborne's proposals, relatively modest as they were — the *Westminster Review* dubbed his Bill both narrow and professional — was too strong and nothing was achieved.[10]

f) *Legal education in the 1890s*

It 'was no secret', wrote the *Law Quarterly Review* in 1890, 'that the scheme of legal education existing in the Inns of Court has been felt by a considerable proportion of those Benchers who take any serious interest in the matter to be far from satisfactory'.[11] In fact the Inns appointed yet another Joint Committee in 1890. It too achieved nothing, despite the hope of some movers of the Committee that a legal university would result.[12] Indeed, in 1898 the Inns turned down quite curtly a proposal that the four Inns should be named Schools of the University or that the Council should be named a School on their behalf. It may be that the Inns, centuries old institutions, found it hard to welcome the proposal that they should be recognised merely as departments of a new teaching university.[13] Later more considered proposals were made to the Haldane Commission on London University which were no more successful. As a result the heartfelt desire felt by many students for a better scheme of legal education went largely unanswered. It is 'almost pathetic', wrote the *Law Times* in an echo of the student complaints of

---

8   Second Report of the Judicature Commissioners no. C-631 (1872) p. 26.
9   Cited in (1872) 53 LT 395.
10   (1907) 23 LQR 263, (1877) 52 Westminster Review 120.
11   (1890) 6 LQR 228.
12   (1891) 91 LT 172.
13   (1907) 23 LQR 264.

the 1840s, to see how anxious most articled clerks are to learn.[14] The verdict of a contributor to an American review in 1895 had about it the ring of truth regarding the system as a whole:

> 'Education under this system is no longer flagrantly insufficient, but it is far from satisfactory: and there is not, for either branch of the profession, anything like such efficient provision as may be found in Scotland, for example: and no law school so good as some of the larger law schools of America.'[15]

g) *The role of the universities*

Were the universities also inactive? The profession as a whole continued to look with little favour upon a university education in law. The kind of matter in which a lawyer was interested, Lord Halsbury LC told students in 1895, was 'the amount which will enable you to recover costs by the County Courts Acts'. Jenks, a distinguished academic of the day, later attributed such a view on the part of the profession to 'a feeling that scientific training is calculated in the long run to damage the interests of the profession and reduce its emoluments and influence...'[16]

Presumably, it was in that spirit that in 1904 Vaughan Williams LJ remarked that a school of law would lead to a code and so he was against it.[17] For their part the universities displayed a considerable uncertainty with regard to the choice of legal topics which were deemed suitable for study. Too often they shrank from the treatment of topics which had any contemporary relevance. It was with some justice that the *Law Times* asked of the Cambridge degree: 'What was the value of training a man as a lawyer in the time of Edward I?'[18]

In 1758, in his inaugural lecture as Oxford University's first Vinerian Professor of the Laws of England, Blackstone had delivered a persuasive plea for the improvement of law studies within the university.[19] Upon the question whether the study of law was 'regularly academical', a point similar to that which Dicey was to put to another Oxford audience over 100 years later,[20] he expressed 'astonishment and concern' that it should ever have been deemed unnecessary for a science like law to be studied in a university. Ethics were recognised as a branch of academic learning and law was the science which distinguished right from wrong. He went on to disparage the existing lack of system, to condemn the idea that all liberal education was of no use to law students, and to dismiss the belief that apprenticeship was enough. Blackstone continued:

> 'If practice be the whole he is taught, practice must also be the whole he will ever know; if he be uninstructed in the elements and first principles upon which the rule of practice is founded, the least variation from established precedents will totally distract and bewilder him...he must never aspire to form, and seldom expect to comprehend any arguments drawn a priori from the spirit of the laws and the natural foundations of justice.'

14 The *Law Times* had for many years expressed concern regarding the lack of a sound legal education.
15 See generally W. Hurst *The Growth of American Law*.
16 (1896) 100 LT 460.
17 (1904) 116 LT 494.
18 (1900) 109 LT 73.
19 1 Bl Com (5th edn) chap. 1, H. G. Hanbury *The Vinerian Chair and Legal Education*.
20 A. V. Dicey 'Can English Law be Taught at the Universities?' (1883).

Blackstone recommended that the law student should study the classical writers, logic, mathematical dispositions, experimental philosophy, the law of nature and Roman Law. Blackstone's course would trace the outlines of the law and make clear its origins. The primary rules and fundamental principles should be weighed and compared with the precepts of the law of nature, and the practice of other countries, explained by reason, illustrated by examples, and confirmed by undoubted authorities: their history should be deduced, their changes and revolutions observed, and it should be shown how far they were connected with, or had at any time been affected by, the civil transactions of the kingdom. Such studies might even lead to the introduction of law reforms.

In his learned, yet lucid and elegant, commentaries Blackstone showed his countrymen exactly what he had in mind. On the whole his was a practical vision which failed to inspire either his successors at Oxford or within the profession. Rote learning and later the crammer were the distinguishing features of education for the profession.

The emphasis which the 1846 Committee placed upon the role of the universities in furthering legal education was quite radical. They reported in the context of discontent among some lawyers and law students with existing arrangements, coupled with an awareness of educational advances in other professions. Such critics had suggested that the funds of the Inns, which were believed to be ample, should be used for the purposes of an organised system of legal education for the Bar. In like vein a deputation from the Metropolitan and Provincial Legal Association waited upon the Lord Chief Justice to suggest the foundation of a 'legal institution, which should meet the requirements of articled clerks desirous of improvement'.[1] In the Committee's view the province of the university was to teach the philosophy of the science, yet a general view of university study would see its 'chief end is not so much the acquirement of knowledge as the creating and maintaining of the habits of acquiring it; nor is it less true that a few subjects well mastered, outweigh in real utility many indifferently or partially attended to'. It was a call to which the existing universities paid little heed, despite further prompting from a commission in the early 1850s. Sadly, therefore, it was just as appropriate in 1883 for Dicey to entitle his inaugural lecture at Oxford, 'Can English Law be Taught at Universities?' as it had been for Blackstone to address himself to a similar question so many years earlier. Dicey's own university made some progress during the following years, as Bryce pointed out in a valedictory lecture in 1893. Bryce maintained that during the 23 years he had held a Chair the changes within the university had been many and momentous. Since 1870 the University had nearly doubled the number of its undergraduates and had greatly increased the number of its teachers: the examination system had been remodelled and the quality of work had improved. Bryce took particular pride in the law books which had been written by members of the Faculty. He granted that it would not be a long list for a German Faculty with its 25 or 30 teachers but compared with Oxford's small numbers and contrasted with the barrenness of Oxford in previous years it was encouraging. Of course, there were other, less welcome, points. He regretted that the professional authorities did not give full recognition to the Oxford law examinations and degree; the University had been outstripped in post-graduate studies by both

1   (1843) 7 Jur 373.

Germany and the United States; it was too exclusively occupied with the giving of a general liberal education to the detriment of professional studies. Yet overall Bryce's message was one of qualified hope. After all this was the age not only of Bryce and Dicey but of Maitland, Holland, Anson and Pollock. It may well have seemed natural to assume that a new generation of equally impressive legal academics would follow them. The growth of the new civic universities, too, was encouraging. By 1910 law was taught not only at the universities of Oxford, Cambridge and London but also at Manchester, Liverpool, Leeds and Sheffield. A Society of Public Teachers of Law had been founded in 1909 whose aim would surely be to develop within the universities a suitable philosophy and practice of legal education.

h) *Legal education 1914-1950*
Prior to the First World War, therefore, there were reasonable grounds for expecting that standards of legal education would improve. There was some accuracy in the assertion that in the Inns 'united action has been directed by men immersed in practice, indifferent to the intellectual and scholarly aspects of the law', but there were grounds for hope in the increased provision being made for legal education. Thus, it could reasonably be claimed in 1942 that the years between 1919 and 1939 had witnessed a minor revolution in legal education: reasonably well equipped law faculties were organised in the provincial universities, the young barrister usually had a degree while the value of a degree to the young solicitor was recognised increasingly widely.[2]

After the First World War there had been an abundance of law students. Public and private grants enabled London University to expand its staff with a view to meeting this demand.[3] Even more significant was the effect of the Solicitors Act 1922 which provided that, subject to certain exceptions, all intending solicitors were to attend at an approved law school for one year. In addition the Council of the Law Society was prepared to offer grants to such schools, with the result that several new law faculties were inaugurated. At long last it appeared that legal education was on the move. For that the solicitors, always more active than the barristers in this field, deserve some credit, especially as they were helping to finance the new scheme out of their own pockets.

As the new schools and faculties set about their task a fresh committee was appointed by the Lord Chancellor, under the chairmanship of Lord Atkin, to consider the whole question of the organisation of legal education with a view to:
1) closer co-ordination between the work done by the universities and the professional bodies, and
2) further provision for advanced research in legal studies.
The two most important recommendations which were made unanimously in the Report when it was published in July 1934 were that:
1) a permanent Advisory Committee on Legal Education should be established whose membership would be drawn from the universities and from the professional bodies, and
2) an Institute of Advanced Legal Studies should be established.[4]

2   (1942) 58 LQR 253.
3   (1935) 51 LQR 171.
4   Report of the Legal Education Committee (Cmd. 4663).

At the time the Report was received quite well. Laski, who had sat on the Committee, offered only mild criticism; the *Law Quarterly Review* commented that the Committee had been 'a particularly strong one' so that its recommendations carried special authority;[5] Jenks suggested that the Report was a document of great value.[6] In retrospect the Atkin Report seems an undistinguished and disappointing document which contrasts unfavourably with the outstanding Report of 1846. Its complacency was reflected in even the Attorney-General's utter lack of interest in implementing its two main recommendations as late as 1947,[7] although an Institute was established in 1948 under the auspices of London University. Such complacency was not shared by many members of the legal profession. In 1942 there was said to be 'anxiety and criticism' about the Law Society's system of education and the view was also taken that training for the Bar ought to be placed generally upon a basis similar to that of training for the profession of medicine.[8] Were the universities in reality not living up to their promise?

The long-established faculties at Oxford, Cambridge and London continued to dominate the teaching of law in the universities. Of 1879 academic students who were enrolled during the session 1933-34, 1317 were students of those universities while a further 70 were with the Law Society: not surprisingly, those institutions claimed 94 out of 175 teaching staff. What is surprising at this late date is that the Oxford Faculty had only 26 teaching staff, Cambridge a mere 15.[9] Such numbers appear especially inadequate when contrasted with the size of some of the faculties in the USA and Germany. The legal academic had little time for scholarship which was to be done, oddly enough, in the proposed new Institute. The primary role of the universities, and especially of the new schools and faculties, was to be that of teaching although they were aware from the start of their responsibility for research[10] and did produce a number of useful texts.

It is difficult to assess how well the legal academics fulfilled their important teaching role. The foundation of the Society of Public Teachers of Law in 1909 had been designed to further the progress of legal education within the universities. However, over the years there is an embarrassing lack of writing upon that subject, an omission which contrasts markedly with the debate in the USA. Significantly, there was often also a lack of imagination in the presentation of what was offered. When one distinguished academic recalled in 1951 the period 30 years before when he had begun to read law, he wrote of too many teachers who contributed little beyond the tedious annual dictation of notes and of a fantastic amount of cramming for examinations, nor was much attention paid to reform of the law for when 'we were on the point of achieving substantial reform of the law of real property...our teachers, if they mentioned the matter at all, did so with feelings of abhorrence'.[11] However, he believed that standards had risen considerably over the years.

5   (1934) 50 LQR 472.
6   (1935) 51 LQR 173.
7   (1950) 13 MLR 147. Cf. E. C. S. Wade 'Legal Education, the Changing Scene' (1951) 1 JSPTL (n.s.) 415 at 417.
8   (1942) 58 LQR 254.
9   E. Jenks 'English Legal Education' (1935) 51 LQR 162 at 179.
10 C. Grant Robertson 'A Birmingham School of Law' (1924) JSPTL 22.
11 E. C. S. Wade 'Legal Education: the Changing Scene' (1951) 1 JSPTL (n.s.) 415.

Standards of research were less encouraging overall, although little else could be expected since it was inevitable that such small schools and faculties would be hard-pressed to cope even with their teaching function. More disappointingly, the promise of Oxford's Faculty at the turn of the century was not to be fulfilled in a future generation of legal scholars. The only twentieth-century academic whose name was on a par with those early great names was Holdsworth, the historian. Why that early promise was not fulfilled is not clear. Was it, perhaps, yet another casualty of the First World War? Perhaps the fact that university salaries compared less than favourably with professional salaries may have deterred many able students from entering academic life. Others, again, may have been deterred by the fact that the status of the legal academic was relatively low in comparison with that of the professional lawyer, a situation which was in marked contrast with that which prevailed in the USA and Germany. When criticisms of the law were offered by academics they tended, in the words of an academic critic in 1950, 'to be so moderate and humble that it is sometimes difficult to be sure that they are criticisms at all'.[12] That humble, narrow vision was reflected also in a legalistic, albeit often very able, approach to the teaching of law which owed little to Blackstone's liberal approach to the potential of legal studies which might have offered the intending practitioner a more realistic vision of the complex and changing world in which he was to practise but which smacked all too familiarly of the mechanistic approach of the old-fashioned professional lawyer. In 1950 the academic lawyer had still to define his role.

i) *Conclusion*

The history of legal education is one of professional apathy and of the frustration of would-be reformers. Such a disappointing record was not inevitable. In the United States the great American law schools had set the tone for the whole profession with a new and demanding approach to the study of law from which the whole profession had benefited not only in terms of its education but in terms also of its standing in the community and its prosperity.[13] In Germany also the universities had set the pace. It was surely no accident that towards the close of the nineteenth century when the American law schools were establishing their characteristic features, the professional associations were markedly weak. By contrast in England and Wales the profession was dominant. Its internal divisions and the pressure of other work upon the leaders of the profession contributed to a continuing lack of any substantial achievement. Such failure was all the more marked since in the field of medicine there were close and valuable links between the profession and the medical faculties within the universities. The law faculties lacked the necessary capacity and self-confidence to develop any philosophy of legal education, despite the hopes of Blackstone and of the 1846 Committee. Instead there were unrealistic hopes of what might usefully be achieved e.g the Solicitors Act 1877 provided that the final examination should be a test of the candidate's fitness and capacity to act as a solicitor in all business and matters transacted by solicitors. Nor was there agreement as to the purpose of a legal education. A characteristic of the Victorian professional man's training was the time spent at the crammer. It was a feature of Victorian

12   L. C. B. Gower 'English Legal Training' (1950) 13 MLR 137.
13   W. Hurst *The Growth of American Law.*

life which the professional bodies continued to embrace with considerable enthusiasm throughout the first half of the twentieth century. Law students, and the public, deserved better.[14]

5 Organisation and discipline

a) *Attorneys and solicitors*

i) *Introduction.* On occasion the judges had acted to regulate the attorneys and solicitors. In the *Highwaymen's case*, for example, a highwayman had actually filed a bill in equity for an account against his partner in crime. Not surprisingly, the court held his solicitors to be in contempt of court, fined them and committed them to the Fleet prison until they had paid their fine.[15] The 1729 Act also made important provisions e.g. judges were to refer bills to be taxed and settled by the proper officer of court. Even more significant, however, were the attempts by attorneys and solicitors to regulate their own affairs.

ii) *The Society of Gentlemen Practisers.* In 1739 a small group of London lawyers met to form the Society of Gentlemen Practisers in the Courts of Law and Equity. The Society 'unanimously declared its utmost abhorrence of all male and unfair practice, and that it would do its utmost to detect and discountenance the same...and that 21 members should be appointed to meet once a month or oftener, if thought proper, to consider of such methods as might best answer the purposes aforesaid...'[16] In 1745 the Society considered the 'undue and irregular admission of attorneys and solicitors'. Informed also that one Landon Jones had suffered the punishment of the pillory and yet continued to practise as a solicitor in Chancery, the Society resolved that an application should be made to the High Court of Chancery to have his name struck off the Roll. The Society also studied pending legislation. In 1751 the Society thanked the author of a pamphlet written to assist the intending attorney. The Society's most notable victory was probably its successful resistance to the demand of the Scrivener's Company that all attorneys and solicitors who did conveyancing business in the City of London should join that company. Here, then, was an organisation which already met quite a few of Carr Saunders' and Wilson's classic criteria regarding the function of a professional association — to secure the competence and honour of members and to protect their material interests and public activities while retaining study functions. However, the Society was always relatively small in numbers and it would probably be unwise to claim too much for it, but the professional standards which it set lived on and the professional magazines such as the *Jurist*, the *Law Times*, and the *Solicitors' Journal* sought to enforce them. Touting for business was especially frowned upon. In 1843, for instance, the *Law Times* referred to an advertisement which had appeared in *The Times* — a solicitor undertook the recovery of debts (for a commission of 10 per cent) on the

14   For a modern appraisal see R. Ormrod 'Education and Training for the Professions' (1977) 30 Current Legal Problems 15.
15   See (1893) 9 LQR 197. Cf. *Frazer's case* (1757) 1 Burr 291.
16   E. Freshfield (ed) *The Records of the Society of Gentlemen Practisers* p. 11.

amount recovered free of costs to client — castigated it as 'an audacious specimen of those unprofessional practices which it is one of the objects of the *Law Times* to denounce and expose', and sought the help of its readers in tracing the identity of the solicitors in question.[17]

iii) *The growth of associations of lawyers.* Other local societies were formed from the late eighteenth century onwards. Indeed, by 1846 there may have been more than 30 such societies. One such was the Manchester Law Association which was said to be 'a society of solicitors formed for the purpose of maintaining the character of the profession, preventing improper practices, and watching over such legislative and other proceedings as affect the profession and the public...'[18] Similarly, members of the profession in Birmingham had resolved in 1810, some years before the actual formation of their local Society, that the practice of inserting in conditions of sale by auction a provision that the conveyance to the purchaser should be prepared by the vendor's attorney was 'highly improper and ought to be abolished'.[19] Despite the influence of such local societies — and of other societies formed later such as the Metropolitan and Provincial Law Society — it is clear that at a national level the dominant role was played by the Incorporated Law Society. Formed in 1825, probably as a quite separate body from the old Society of Gentlemen Practisers, the Law Society's special role was very soon recognised. The ultimate accolade was conferred when the Solicitors Act 1888 empowered the Society to hear any application to strike a solicitor off the roll of solicitors, although it was the Master of the Rolls who was to appoint the members of the committee from amongst the members of the Society's council. This committee was an investigative body only which simply reported its finding to the High Court. It was the duty of the Law Society to bring the matter to the attention of the High Court if it appeared that the facts as found disclosed prima facie a case of professional misconduct. The Court had a discretion either to order that a guilty solicitor's name be struck off the Roll, or to suspend him from practice or simply to pay the costs of the application and inquiry.

The Solicitors Act 1919 empowered the committee itself to exercise that disciplinary power. Moreover, the committee was composed wholly of lawyers, a remarkable contrast with the lay representation which existed on other comparable disciplinary bodies.[20] Subject to minor amendments that Act remained the basis of the committee's power. The most common matters with which it dealt were misappropriation of clients' money, conduct in the nature of touting or advertising for clients, or sharing costs with an unqualified person. However, the crux in every case was said to be whether the facts established constituted conduct unbecoming an officer of the court or a member of an honourable profession.[1] In *Re Weare*[2] the facts were that Weare, a solicitor, had been convicted of being unlawfully and wilfully a party to the continued use of certain premises as brothels. Upon Weare appealing from the Divisional Court's order

17 (1843) 1 LT 467.
18 Report of the Select Committee on Legal Education no. 686 (1846) p. 73.
19 G. Manning Butts 'A Short History of the Birmingham Law Society 1818-1968' (pamphlet) p. 13.
20 B. Abel-Smith and R. Stevens *Lawyers and the Courts* p. 192.
1 T. G. Lund 'The Professional Discipline of Solicitors' in R. S. W. Pollard (ed) *Administrative Tribunals at Work* p. 118.
2 [1893] 2 QB 439.

that he be struck off the roll of solicitors, the Court of Appeal held that a solicitor might be struck off for an offence which had no relation to his character as a solicitor, the question being whether it was such an offence as made a person guilty of it unfit to remain a member of the profession. Conviction for a criminal offence prima facie made a solicitor unfit to continue on the roll, although the court did have a discretion. In the case of Weare the court considered that the nature of the offence was such that he ought to be struck off the roll.

iv) *The achievement of the Law Society.* Over the years the Law Society played a distinguished and honourable role in raising the professional standards of its members and in securing public recognition of those standards. Not the least remarkable feature of its success was that it achieved these standards despite the fact that membership of the Law Society remained wholly voluntary. Standards of admission to the profession had been raised, minimum ethical standards were enforced, although the Society offered no remedy in respect of the negligent solicitor. Other professional standards were enforced, although some critics have suggested that in the public interest the rules which forbade touting for business, or ambulance-chasing, might have been relaxed. In return the Society had secured or maintained for the 'inferior' branch of the profession not only an enhanced social status but a certain protection of their livelihood and in particular their monopoly of conveyancing.[3] It was its success in such matters which conferred upon the Law Society an influence over solicitors as a whole in the achievement of professional standards.

b) *Barristers*

i) *The circuit messes.* In the case of the barristers it was the Benchers who had the power to disbar a member of their Society for dishonourable conduct, a category which, as in the case of the attorney and solicitor, did not include technical incompetence. In fact the most potent force for the maintenance of accepted standards was probably the professional spirit which was fostered by a relatively small centralised Bar and by the circuit messes.[4] All barristers who practised in the common law courts were required to choose a circuit and, by convention, to practise only on that circuit. When on circuit the barrister would dine frequently in the circuit mess and there can be little doubt that such close contacts fostered the professional ethic in a manner which served the public interest well. The less scrupulous barrister, for example, would be encouraged to mend his ways. On the other hand it could be alleged that some professional practices were unduly restrictive and so were not in the public interest:[5] that was surely a strong argument in a country in which so many people supported the doctrines of laissez-faire and of free trade.

ii) *Restrictive practices.* Was not the rule which prevented the barrister from either being an attorney or being partner with an attorney a rule against free

3   Abel-Smith and Stevens *Lawyers and the Courts* pp. 62, 196, 206. Note the Attorneys and
    Solicitors Act 1874.
4   R. Pound *The Lawyer from Antiquity to Modern Times* pp. 119 ff.
5   A. V. Dicey (1867) 8 Fortnightly Review 169.

trade? There were also the conventions or rules which prohibited a barrister from taking less than a guinea fee and limited their right of changing circuit or sessions. Some barristers maintained that as such rules were enforced simply by the penalty of being required to leave the circuit mess they were of little consequence. In fact they were supported quite unequivocally by the full strength of professional feeling, as the experience of Charles Rann Kennedy illustrates.[6]

In 1849 Kennedy was elected a professor of law at Queen's College, Birmingham. Believing that his efficiency as a lecturer would be increased if he kept up his knowledge of legal practice, he left the Home circuit where he had practised without success for the Midlands, in which Birmingham was situated, and immediately began to attend the sessions of the town. This gave rise to disputes with his fellow barristers who on 1 April 1850 passed a resolution that he should not be permitted to join them. Kennedy was informed that he was rejected because a Mr. Davison of the Welsh circuit who had proposed to change to the Midland was 'from his length of standing at the bar, and his having for several years been a member of another circuit held to be inadmissible'. Because a wrong had been done to Mr. Davison, commented Kennedy, a similar wrong was to be done to him. What right had 'a company of gentlemen sitting over their wine...to make precedents in their own favour and then to cite them as binding law?' Kennedy claimed that his professional existence was destroyed and that he had no redress. He explained that on circuit a barrister in his position suffered in every way. He was not invited to dine with the judges, on occasion associated members of a circuit combined not to hold briefs with him, and few solicitors would venture to give a brief to one whom his own profession had designated an outcast.

Practices such as that, or legal etiquette, as the lawyers chose to call them, were the subject of some discussion at a time when trade union practices were coming under the microscope. In 1867 a journeyman engineer maintained that the learned professions in general and the Bar in particular were unions 'which contained some of the worst features of the unions of mechanical trades'. By way of reply a barrister maintained that the Bar rules were simply nominal laws which were enforced by no real sanction and that 'there is not a single Bar rule which either does prevent or is meant to prevent the most unrestricted competition between man and man for business'. Dicey distinguished the Bar from the unions on the grounds that the Bar enforced its rules by professional opinion alone, that — although it insisted upon a minimum fee — it did not attempt to equalise the gains of its members, and that the Bar occupied an acknowledged public position, so incurring disabilities as well as privileges. Moreover, although legal etiquette did produce 'considerable evils', the rules were changing all the time.[7]

iii) *Critique of the circuit system.* Such changes did not necessarily work in the public interest. In 1893 a legal critic even suggested that although the circuit system may once have been justifiable at a time when railways and telegraphs were unknown, when the whole Bar resided in London and when practice on more than one circuit was practically impossible, the rule had lost its raison

6   C. R. Kennedy 'Circuit Leagues' (pamphlet).
7   A.V. Dicey (1867) 8 Fortnightly Review n. 5.

d'être in an age of free competition and rapid communication.[8] Such criticisms had little effect. The circuit system was reaffirmed after the reorganisation consequent upon the Judicature Acts. The old practice regarding choice of circuit was further strengthened; a barrister should not appear as an advocate on behalf of a client without the intervention of a solicitor and if a Queen's Counsel were retained to appear at a trial, a junior counsel also must be retained. To many critics such practices appeared to add substantially, and unnecessarily, to the cost of going to law.[9]

iv) *The Bar Council.* Some members of the Bar believed that they should exert themselves rather more in the disciplining of their members. It was argued that members of the Bar had a public as well as a private duty to perform; it was for this reason that they were granted immunity from actions for ignorance, negligence or mistake and that they had the privilege of an exclusive audience in the courts of law.[10] Surely, then, the Bar itself should have a power of disciplining its members? A Bar Committee was formed in 1883, but achieved little during the first ten years of its life. In 1893 a critic commented that the committee rarely met and that when it did, it did not do much. Its annual meeting was usually fixed for a spring or summer Saturday afternoon, and if possible upon Boat Race day.[11] At about this time the Bar Committee, or the Bar Council, as it had become, retreated in the face of the Benchers' opposition to its request that it should have powers regarding the discipline of members of the Bar and the etiquette of the profession. Subsequently the Inns granted the Council a certain recognition. Essentially, however, little had changed — real power still lay with the Benchers, but over the years the Bar Council exercised a growing influence, especially in matters of professional etiquette.

c) *Primarily a male profession*
Until 1919 one outstanding characteristic of the legal profession remained constant: its practitioners were male. The reluctance of the lawyers to admit women to their ranks is all the more surprising in the light of the fact that ever since 1881 women doctors appeared in steadily increasing numbers. In 1901 there were 212; in 1911 there were as many as 477 women doctors.[12] Further, women were admitted to the universities and could obtain degrees in law, yet the profession remained closed to them. In *Bebb v Law Society*[13] the plaintiff spinster brought an action against the Law Society, seeking a mandamus directing the Society to admit her to their preliminary examination. She maintained that unmarried women at least had the same legal rights as men. However, the Court of Appeal held that before the enactment of the Solicitors Act 1843 women were by the common law of England under a general disability, by reason of their sex, to become attornies or solicitors; that disability could not be removed by a mere interpretation clause, such as the Solicitors Act 1843, s. 48

---

8   (1893) 9 LQR 261 at 263.
9   Abel-Smith and Stevens *Lawyers and the Courts* pp. 220 ff.
10   (1863) 7 Sol Jo 265.
11   (1893) 96 LT 50 at 51.
12   N. St. John-Stevas 'Women in Public Law' in R. H. Graveson and F. R. Crane (eds) *A Century of Family Law* p. 256.
13   [1914] 1 Ch 286.

which provided that words importing the masculine gender should extend to a female. Therefore, the Law Society could not admit any woman to their preliminary examination with a view to her becoming a solicitor. After the First World War, and the dramatically changed role which women played during the course of that conflict, society began to take a radically different view of women's proper role in society. In 1919 the Law Society itself resolved that women might be admitted to the profession.[14] The Sex Disqualification (Removal) Act 1919 went on to provide that a person should not be disqualified by sex or marriage from entering or assuming or carrying on any civil profession or vocation. Gradually, women began to enter the profession.

d) *No fusion of the profession*

A major feature of the legal profession was the separation of functions between the barrister and the solicitor. Fusion of the two branches of the profession was possible until mid-seventeenth century for at that time the attorney or solicitor could be a member of an Inn of Court. However, separation became a fact, probably due to different methods of admission to the profession and to the different forms of work which each undertook. In Blackstone's day the attorney was so little regarded that Blackstone did not even include him among the ranks of the profession.[15] As the professional competence of the solicitor increased over the years and with it the complexity of the legal tasks which he was competent to undertake, as increasingly he began to come from much the same social background and to receive much the same type of legal education as the barrister, it became more difficult to justify the continuing separation of the two branches of the profession. Hesitant moves to render easier transfer from one branch of the profession to the other were made, yet the Bar opposed any suggestions for fusion with a fierce and emotional intensity based chiefly on the argument that as the judges were appointed from the Bar it was essential, if judicial quality were to be maintained, that there be a small, centralised Bar.

6 Numbers and public attitudes

As both population and commerce increased during the nineteenth century, there was a considerable rise in the number of lawyers. It was an increase which was regretted on occasion both by those lawyers who worried for the future prospects of the profession in view of the numbers entering it, although it had long been recognised that by no means all who qualified as barristers intended to practise, and also by those critics of the profession who saw lawyers as parasites upon society. Make the laws clearer, suggested one early nineteenth century critic, and there would be less call for 'dealers in the black art'.[16]

Colquhoun had estimated at the beginning of the nineteenth century that the number of judges, barristers, attornies and clerks, together with their families and domestics, amounted to 95000. This compared with a figure of 90000 who were employed in Physic (physicians, surgeons and apothecaries) and of 114500 persons employed under government.[17] For the author of the *Black Book* there

14 Abel-Smith and Stevens *Lawyers and the Courts* p. 193.
15 3 Bl Com (5th edn) 28, n. (a).
16 J. Wade (ed) *The Black Book* (1835) pp. 296-7. Cf. (1883) 74 LT 207.
17 Cited by J. Wade *The Black Book* (1820) p. 194.

were simply too many lawyers: his estimate in 1820 was that there were some 30000 counsel, attornies, clerks and assistants in England and Wales — he did not count the judges and their assistants. 'In the number and magnitude of Inns of Court, law institutions, and other buildings the legal classes rival the ancient religious houses', he proclaimed in 1835, and attributed to lawyers an influence equal to that of the old priesthood.[18] Of the other contemporary writers Henry Mayhew was to publish in his legal London a table showing the distribution of the professional classes throughout London, a map of the Inns of Court and their descriptions. Mayhew estimated London's legal establishment in 1862, inclusive of law clerks and law court officers, at 11112.[19] Perhaps a more reliable estimate is that in 1881 there were 4019 barristers and 13376 solicitors serving a population of almost 26 million people; in 1911, 4121 barristers and 17259 solicitors served a population of rather more than 36 million people.[20]

English and Welsh society has never loved the lawyer; nor has the lawyer been accorded the respect which the American lawyer has commanded in his society. Still over the years respect for the profession as a whole did increase. Now excluded from the Inns of Court the attorney was generally held in low public esteem in eighteenth century England. To many, the lawyers were 'vile pettifoggers'; Blackstone showed a concern for the social status of the profession and Dr. Johnson summed up the public attitude well enough when he commented that, although he disliked speaking ill of any man, he understood that an acquaintance was an attorney. Even as late as 1865 a correspondent commented in a legal magazine that 'attorney' was a current expression for the lowest term of 'Brummagem' intellect, a 'beauteous compound of cunning, vulgarity, and the self-confidence of ignorance'.[1] Accordingly, much of the attorney's professional history during this period was directed to removing such impressions. In commenting upon a proposition for better legal education, the *Law Times* wrote that it was 'a means to raise the respectability of the profession...it is of greater importance to society that the attorney should be a gentleman than that he should be a lawyer'.[2] It was an aim which the Solicitors Act 1860 sought to meet by establishing a preliminary examination in general knowledge with the aim of including within the profession only those who were gentlemen. Whatever the cause, it does appear that from about this time the stock of the solicitor began to rise, although it remained inferior to that of the barrister whose prestige was increased as the result of the glamour attached to just a handful of leading barristers in the eyes of a newspaper-reading public.

7 Income

Overall the nature of the average solicitor's practice had changed considerably by mid-nineteenth century. Once a general man of business who would refer virtually any point of law to counsel, he now dealt with many such points himself.

18   *The Black Book* pp. 296-7.
19   *Criminal Prisons of London* p. 70.
20   W. J. Reader *Professional Men* p. 211.
 1   See generally W. S. Holdsworth *Charles Dickens as a Legal Historian* p. 43, R. Robson *The Attorney in Eighteenth Century England* chap. 10. Cf. J. Wade *The Black Book* p. 213, 'Brummagem' was a disparaging reference to the city of Birmingham.
 2   (1845) 5 LT 104. Cf. (1853) 21 LT 198 at 209, 233.

Subsequent to the institution of the county court in 1846 he began on occasion to be seen as a potential competitor for certain kinds of business with the barrister, a prospect which filled many barristers with foreboding for the future of their branch of the profession. Clearly the commercial and industrial revolutions had opened up new areas of practice for lawyers generally. Yet there were great discrepancies between the nature of the practices enjoyed by different solicitors. Some lived almost solely by the solicitors' monopoly of conveyancing or, in mid-nineteenth century, even by debt-collecting. Others dealt almost exclusively with the more lucrative forms of commercial practice.

Other professions, especially accountancy, competed for areas of business which the lawyer could perhaps have made his own. Overall the British lawyer lacked the dynamic view of his own function and of that of the law which his North American colleague possessed in ample measure. Nevertheless, over the years both solicitor and barrister succeeded in establishing, subject to continuing criticism of the solicitors' monopoly of conveyancing, a recognised area of professional expertise. Accurate details regarding the income of the profession are very difficult to come by. Some had very high incomes, many others had correspondingly low incomes. The radical pamphleteer Wade, no friend of the lawyers, reflected this diversity when he wrote that one counsel earned £15000 annually but that:

> 'There are other counsel who, probably, make ten or twelve thousand a year; others, a half, a third, a fourth, or twentieth part of that sum; and others, again, who make nothing.... In the incomes of attorneys are great diversities. Some few, in London, make ten or eleven thousand pounds a year; a great many more about three or four thousand pounds; and some obscure practitioners do not clear more than £100 a year. Their clerks experience similar variety of fortune. Some are starving on a paltry £50; others living comfortably on £200; and others sumptuously on a £500 salary.'

Nevertheless Wade clearly distrusted the lawyers: 'Of all classes who prey on the community, the lawyers require to be most narrowly watched...they have contrived to have more sumptuous pickings than any other description of employees.... The claim for legal fees has been a principal obstacle to judicial reform, and it has only been by the most extravagant concessions this obstacle has been surmounted.'[3]

In fact accurate details of the average lawyer's earnings are hard to come by. In giving evidence to a Select Committee in 1850, Sir J. Jervis said: 'It is contrary not only to the etiquette, but, I am happy to say, to the universal practice at the Bar, ever to notice or talk of fees.' According to a distinguished solicitor who gave evidence before that same Select Committee, the large majority of barristers earned 'very few hundreds' while the average earnings of the barristers from whom the puisne judges were selected, not the 'topping practitioners', were estimated not to exceed £3000 per annum. At much the same time the income of the average solicitor was estimated at betwen £200 and £300.[4] Quite possibly incomes had risen over the years. At all events in 1860 one commentator believed that the standard of living of judges and barristers had increased considerably

3   J. Wade *The Black Book* (1835) pp. 297-8, 499-500.
4   (1860) 36 LT 106.

since 1824. In 1824 there were not, he wrote, 'the attempts at variety, fashion, and récherché cookery as now, or the number of livery servants which appear at the present day'. In 1874 one estimate suggested that 19 out of 20 of the men doing second or third rate business at the Bar were earning between £500 and £1500 per annum.[5] Reader has estimated that during this period £1000 per annum represented moderate prosperity and that few people earned as much as £5000 per annum.

Nor did lawyers' earnings increase dramatically over the years. Before the Second World War it continued to be true that a handful of leading barristers earned very large sums indeed but the average barrister probably earned rather less than £400 per annum. At much the same time the average net income to the solicitor was said to be no more than £400 per annum,[6] whilst the average wage earner was earning rather less than £200 per annum. Despite that differential, it appears that the enhanced social status of the lawyer was not matched to any marked extent by his salary.[7]

8 The judiciary: an introduction

A judge or judges presided over the administration of justice in all courts, superior and inferior, civil and criminal. By popular usage, however, it was only the small number of judges of the superior courts of common law who were known, by way of pre-eminence, as the judges of the land, or simply as the judges.[8] Because they enjoyed considerable prestige, their judicial standards guided their more numerous colleagues in the inferior courts in the maintenance of judicial standards. It was with just such a colleague that a member of the public was most likely to come into professional contact. It is therefore appropriate that in the first instance we should consider the most numerous of all such judges, the justice of the peace.

9 Justices of the peace

a) *Introduction*
We can trace the justices back at least as far as a statute in 1361.[9] The powers of the justice depended upon his commission and also upon the numerous individual statutes which, even in mid-eighteenth century, were said to have heaped such an 'infinite variety' of business upon him that 'few care to undertake, and fewer understand, the office'. The commission empowered a justice singly to conserve the peace. He might suppress riots and affrays, take securities for the peace, and apprehend and commit felons and other inferior criminals. Further, any two or more justices might hear and determine all felonies and other offences. This was the ground of their jurisdiction at sessions.[10] Such work

5   (1874) 56 LT 413.
6   Abel-Smith and Stevens *Lawyers and the Courts* pp. 242-3, 210.
7   P. Wilsher *The Pound in Your Pocket 1870-1970* p. 161.
8   H. J. Stephen *New Commentaries* vol 3 (4th edn, 1858) p. 396.
9   34 Edw III, c. 1.
10 1 Bl Com (5th edn) 353-4.

always remained of great importance, but it should be remembered that, during the first part of this period, it was often overshadowed, even at sessions, by their administrative work.

b) *Selection and appointment*

Justices were appointed by the King's special commission under the great seal. In practice the Lord-Lieutenant of the county nominated persons for the office for the approval of the Lord Chancellor. That practice conferred considerable power upon the Lord-Lieutenant to choose only those whom he considered to be suited to the office. It is likely that, especially during the eighteenth century, many appointments were made largely on the basis of political affiliation. Even as recently as the late nineteenth and early twentieth centuries there might be bias, or a suspicion of bias, on the part of a Lord-Lieutenant or of a Lord Chancellor in making an appointment to a judicial office. Liberals alleged that the Lord-Lieutenants were Conservative and that this was reflected over-whelmingly in their appointments to the Bench. Attitudes of the Lord Chancellors varied. Halsbury was alleged very seldom to have appointed to the Bench anyone who was not a Conservative. On the other hand Herschell and Loreburn preferred to adopt a more even-handed approach which stressed the suitability of the individual for the post. Considerable political pressure was put upon Loreburn to restore the political balance. Although anxious to do so, he refused in effect 'to job the judicial bench' and indicated that he would resign office rather than do that. In fact a royal commission in 1910 adopted proposals made by Loreburn, Loreburn immediately implemented those proposals and they form the basis of the existing system. The commissioners had stated that appointments influenced by considerations of political opinion and services were highly detrimental to public interests. Now an advisory committee was to be formed in each county and borough.[11] The Lord Chancellor was to appoint its members who were to report to him directly, although the Lord-Lieutenant might act as chairman of the committee. Subject only to minor changes, these reforms formed the basis of the modern system. Loreburn had established both a principle of political neutrality, although political parties would continue to be the most important source of nominations, and the appropriate machinery for its implementation. Of course, careful consideration had no doubt always been given to other personal factors. However, after 1910 selection and appointment was seen to be upon an institutional basis which offered far less scope for the implementation of personal whim, whether of Lord-Lieutenant or of Lord Chancellor. In 1918 women became eligible to serve as justices.

Within the boroughs the selection and appointment of justices was made on a completely different basis. In practice appointments went confined to those who were close to the corporation. They incurred strong criticism. To some extent that criticism may have been inspired by the fact that such justices were usually of a decidedly lower social class than the county justices, a fact which

11 1 Bl Com (5th edn) 353-4, Abel-Smith and Stevens *Lawyers and the Courts* pp. 132-3, R. F. V. Heuston *Lives of the Lord Chancellors 1885-1940* p. 156, E. Moir *The Justice of the Peace* pp. 184-5.

recommended them neither to the county justices nor to the growing class of merchants and of manufacturers. At all events a royal commission of 1833 found, however unfairly, that there was a distrust of the municipal magistracy, often accompanied by contempt of the magistrates. Change was inevitable. After 1835 the office of justice of the peace was severed from corporation office and the Lord Chancellor made appointments in just the same manner as he appointed other justices.

c) *Social class: independence: impartiality*

Throughout this period the justices as a whole were characterised by their honesty and by their integrity, although there were blemishes upon that proud record — the trading justices cast a shadow upon the justices as a whole, albeit during only a relatively brief period, for these justices, especially in eighteenth century London, indulged in corrupt practices. Further, especially during the first years of the nineteenth century, the justices over-enthusiastic enforcement of the game laws and their zeal in stopping up footpaths incurred considerable public disapproval. To many critics it appeared that they were acting less than impartially in the pursuit of their own class interest. In 1828 Brougham declared roundly that no worse tribunal existed than that of a brace of sporting magistrates.[12] Indeed, as justices appeared to be drawn almost exclusively from one social class, some workmen had long felt that some justices at least were partial in the manner in which they administered the law. That was true, for example, of the enforcement of the Combination Acts. Equally, it was suggested that some magistrates were slack in enforcing the Arbitration Acts, 'being more nearly allied to the masters by rank and fortune'.[13]

Certainly social class had been an important factor in the selection of justices. Statute had long required justices to be of the best reputation and the most worthy men in the county. Because, as Blackstone put it, contrary to these statutes 'men of small substance had crept into the commission, whose poverty made them both covetous and contemptible', statute provided that no justice should be put in commission if he had not lands to the value of £20 per annum. A later statute provided that, subject to certain exceptions, every justice should have £100 per annum clear of all deductions.[14] The property qualification was abolished only in 1906 after the return of a Liberal Government.

Criticism of the justices had reached a crescendo by the mid-1830s, yet they survived virtually unscathed. The Webbs explain that remarkable survival upon two grounds. First, even the Radicals were prepared neither for elections to the magistracy nor for the appointment of a vastly increased number of stipendiaries: 'To dislike of any increase of public expenditure, there was added the growth of the jealousy of a professional staff, and a rooted distrust of the central government, to which few were prepared to confide the making of so many appointments.' Secondly, the Webbs cite Sidney Smith as follows:

> 'What in truth could we substitute for the unpaid magistracy? We have no doubt but that a set of rural judges, in the pay of government, would very

12   18 Official Report (new series: 1828) col. 166, S. and B. Webb *The Parish and the County* vol 1, p. 597.
13   E. P. Thompson *The Making of the English Working Class* pp. 592, 221.
14   1 Bl Com (5th edn) 352-3.

soon become corrupt jobbers and odious tyrants, as they often are on the continent. But magistrates, as they now exist, really constitute a bulwark of some value against the supreme power of the state. They would not submit to be employed for base and criminal purposes. They are tools, perhaps, in some cases, but still tools that must be respected.'[15]

In fact, if we except the trading justices and others of relatively lowly rank, the social exclusiveness of the magistracy had already been breached by the addition of numerous clerical justices to the Bench during the late eighteenth and early nineteenth centuries. At their best they had brought a welcome efficiency to their judicial duties; at their worst they incurred considerable odium on occasion by their over-zealous enthusiasm for reforming the manners of the people. Even so, deference remained strong in the community as a whole. The result was that, despite the broadening of the social composition of the justices during the nineteenth century with the addition of the newly rich, few working-class people were represented on the Bench even at the beginning of the twentieth century. The Bench in the twentieth century remained middle class in its compositon. The fact that the post remained honorary probably ensured that. During the eighteenth and nineteenth centuries there had been some public advantage, quite apart from the financial, in the post remaining honorary for it ensured that persons of a relatively high social status would continue to serve out of a sense of public duty. Such persons tended to maintain a measure of independence from outside pressures and to exert a natural authority to an extent which others of more lowly rank found difficult. Indeed, the eighteenth-century experience of the trading justices appeared to suggest that it was positively dangerous to place men of low financial status on the Bench. Yet for many, especially amongst working-class people, the remaining traces of such social exclusiveness on the Bench became increasingly offensive. No solution to that problem was found during the first half of the twentieth century.

d) *Stipendiary magistrates*

Sheer necessity, together with respect for the work of the Fielding brothers at Bow Street, enabled statutory provision to be made in 1792 for the establishment in Middlesex of seven public offices with a salaried magistracy of 24. Fines and fees went to the Treasury. After 1835 a municipal borough might have a stipendiary magistrate if it chose to ask for one and to pay him. Stipendiaries were to be appointed from the ranks of the barristers, solicitors became eligible only in 1949. Like other justices of the peace, the stipendiaries held office only during good pleasure.

Relatively few stipendiaries were appointed throughout the country. The hostility of Fox and Sheridan to the original proposal, on the ground that it increased Crown patronage, lost little of its sting in subsequent years, despite the considerable quality of those who were actually appointed as stipendiaries. Indeed, a statutory accolade of a kind was conferred by the Metropolitan Police Courts Act of 1839 which established the office of Chief Metropolitan Magistrate and which provided also that the police offices should now be known as police courts, a change which confirmed the criminal nature of the work which the stipendiaries undertook. Even in the twentieth century there were relatively few

15   1 Bl Com (5th edn) n. 92, 606.

stipendiaries. There was little overt dissatisfaction with the stipendiary, rather was there a lack of enthusiasm for him. That his salary was chargeable to local funds, that dissatisfaction with one stipendiary may have led to not appointing a successor may have been among the reasons for this. It illustrated the country's enthusiasm for the unpaid lay magistracy.

e) *Immunity*

A number of statutes had offered some protection to the justice who was acting bona fide. He might not be sued for any oversights without notice beforehand and all suits begun might be stopped on tender made of sufficient amends. Such protection did not go very far. Attornies were not slow on occasion to bring actions in respect of unlawful use of power nor were the superior courts slow to punish any misuse of the summary jurisdiction. Indeed, all persons who recovered a verdict against a justice for any wilful or malicious injury were entitled to double costs. Accordingly, the Justices Protection Act 1848 offered rather more extensive protection. Now the justice was to be protected from liability for any action done by him in the execution of his duty unless that act was done maliciously and without reasonable and probable cause. Uncertainty as to the precise scope of that legal protection was to endure for over a century,[16] yet over the years it appeared in practice to afford reasonable protection to the justice of the peace.

f) *Numbers*

Originally there were few justices. The Webbs state that by 1796 there were 2656 justices, without counting those for Lancashire, and that in 1818 there were in all, excluding duplicates, about 4000. In 1832 the total number was 5371, of whom 1354 were clergymen, however, the number who habitually attended sessions was estimated at about 2200. By and large, therefore, there was an adequate number of justices, even though many of them were relatively inactive. The problem sometimes was that they were distributed unevenly which could lead to delay on the occasion, for example, of riots.

g) *Income*

In medieval days the justices of the peace had been allowed a daily payment for their services. In practice, such service had long been honorary, yet the justice was allowed to charge fees. Henry Fielding of Bow Street told of how a predecessor of his used to boast that he made one thousand pounds a year in his office. Fielding brought a new respectability to his office in this as in other matters. However, many justices, especially the so-called trading justices, made quite lucrative incomes by encouraging litigation, by charging improper fees and by other malpractices. Probably such justices were but a small minority, but they introduced a contempt for local justice, especially in London, which lasted for some years.

Impressed by the Fielding brothers' administration of the Bow Street office, the government made available from Secret Service funds a certain number of salaries of £200 per annum with a view to increasing the income derived from fees by certain magistrates, especially in Middlesex and Westminster. Such payments

16   14 MLR 267, 21 MLR 517, *Law v Llewellyn* [1906] 1 KB 487.

were regularised in 1792 when statute provided for the appointment and payment of stipendiary magistrates.[17]

h) *Training*

The Magistrates' Association, a voluntary association of justices formed in 1920, made some useful provision for the training of justices but it was only in 1949 that a statutory basis for the training of justices was established.[18]

i) *Tenure: removal*

As the office of justice was conferred by the King, so it subsisted only during his pleasure.[19] This power was exercised by the Lord Chancellor, although in practice the Lord Chancellor did not so remove a justice from the commission save for good cause. It appears to have been a power which was exercised relatively rarely.

10 Other judges

There were a substantial number of professional judges who occupied an intermediate position between the relatively small number of judges of the superior courts and the more numerous, and non-professional, justices of the peace. In particular there were the judges of the county courts. They were appointed in practice by the Lord Chancellor and might be removed by him for 'inability or misbehaviour'. The recorder, a part-time judge who presided over quarter session, was subject to similar conditions of appointment and removal.

11 The judges of the superior courts

a) *Selection and appointment*

As the fountain of justice, the Crown retained the power to appoint the judges, albeit on the advice of the Lord Chancellor. In his turn the Lord Chancellor might consult the Prime Minister. Especially since the later years of the nineteenth century, the Lord Chancellor was assisted in this task by his department, yet ultimately the decision was to be taken by the Lord Chancellor alone.

The professional and personal standards and standing of a candidate for judicial office — at one time no divorced man would be appointed — were obviously of the highest importance amongst the shifting criteria which the Lord Chancellor of the day adopted in deciding whom to recommend for appointment. In practice there was no sure way of determining whether a particular candidate was likely to be successful as a judge. For example, there was widespread professional condemnation of the appointment of Mr. Justice Blackburn, yet that particular judge emerged as one of the most distinguished of all the Victorian judges. On the other hand although the appointment over the years of men such as Crompton, Ridley and — as Lord Chief Justice — Hewart

17 1 Bl Com (5th edn) 352, S and B. Webb *The Parish and the County* vol 1, p. 383, contrast
     Moir *The Justice of the Peace* p. 89. W. S. Holdsworth *History of English Law* vol 1, p. 289,
     F. W. Maitland *The Constitutional History of England* p. 494, S. and B. Webb *The Parish
     and the County* vol 1, pp. 333, 340.
18 Justices of the Peace Act 1949.
19 1 Bl Com (5th edn) 353.

commanded considerable professional support, each was less than successful in some respects as a judge. Amongst the few sure criteria for selection of a judge were that he would be a member of the Bar — no solicitors or academic lawyers were to be appointed — and that in practice he would be male.

One other factor was common to a considerable number of appointments. This was the importance which seems to have been attached on occasion to political allegiance. In the light of the older concept of the judicial function, that is not surprising. Indeed, Lord Mansfield, although he was Chief Justice, served as a minister during the period 1757-65. Some 50 years later another Chief Justice, Lord Ellenborough, also served as a minister. Increasingly, however, such links between the judiciary and politics were subjected to considerable public criticism. The author of the *Black Book* suggested that it was very unfortunate that judges should be selected on the 'exclusive principle' that they were on the ministerial side in politics as:

> 'This tends to lower the character of the judges in public estimation, by clearly evincing that politics, as well as legal fitness, have a share in ministerial promotions. It also instils into the minds of both expectant judges, and of men already on the bench, a party feeling fatal to strict justice on political questions.'[20]

Yet many judges continued to have had a background in active party politics before they were raised to the Bench. Laski found that of 139 appointments which had been made to the High Court and the Appeal Court between 1832 and 1906, 80 had been MPs. Of those 80, 63 had been appointed by the party which they supported.[1] Even at the beginning of the twentieth century, it could be alleged of the Lord Chancellor, Lord Halsbury, that he 'had no hesitation in appointing to the High Court or county court judges whose claims rested more on their political or family ties than on their standing at the Bar'. That view was commonly held amongst the legal profession. Heuston has shown that such a judgment tends to be unfair to Halsbury, at least in so far as the 30 appointments to the High Court for which he was responsible are concerned. On occasion political belief may have been more significant in relation to the superior judicial offices. For example, in 1897 Salisbury, the Prime Minister, wrote to Halsbury suggesting that the office of the Master of the Rolls should be offered to one person 'on party grounds', despite the Lord Chancellor's 'unfavourable judgment' as to that person's judicial capacities. Indeed, there had long been a tradition that the Attorney-General of the day should be given first refusal of the office of Lord Chief Justice, should that office fall vacant. It was a tradition which the government of the day went to quite extraordinary lengths to preserve, on one occasion by appointing a caretaker Lord Chief Justice who was said to have signed on his appointment an undated letter of resignation. That Lord Chief Justice later learned of his resignation when he read his copy of *The Times* newspaper. The government went to such lengths in order to keep the position open for the then Attorney-General, Sir Gordon Hewart. However, when Lord Goddard was appointed Lord Chief Justice in 1946, he was a Law Lord — the Attorney-General's 'right' appeared to have been set aside and political

---

20   J. Wade (ed) *The Black Book* (1835) pp. 286-7.
1   H. J. Laski *Studies in Law and Politics* p. 168, Abel-Smith and Stevens *Lawyers and the Courts* p. 129.

background seemed to be of far less importance in judicial appointments generally. By this time also the Law Lords, at the very apex of the system of appeals, were appointed on professional grounds alone.[2]

b) *Social background*
Landed families made a substantial contribution to the Bench during the second half of the eighteenth century. By mid-nineteenth century, however, the Bench was recruited predominantly from families which belonged to the professional classes. Group loyalty was accorded to the ethic of a powerful, prestigious and proud profession and to the individual judge's view of his personal role. A certain social homogeneity occurred, however, in the light of the popularity from the late Victorian period of the public school. So in mid-twentieth century some three quarters of the judiciary had been educated at major public schools and at either Oxford or Cambridge. Conceivably such a background, followed swiftly by entry to a busy life at the Bar, might develop certain common attitudes and remoteness from the general public, but this is supposition.[3]

c) *Salaries*
The judges were paid a basic salary. A puisne judge of King's Bench received an annual salary of £2400, subject to certain deductions. The Chief Justice received an annual salary of £3500. In addition the judges received substantial fees. Indeed, Lord Ellenborough was said to have enjoyed an annual income of £16000. However, in 1825 it was decided to pay the judges inclusive salaries. A puisne judge was to receive £5500 per annum; in 1832 this sum was reduced to £5000 per annum. Court fees were now paid into the public revenues, and salaries stayed at that level. In 1873 Gladstone even sought — unsuccessfully — to reduce the latter to £4000 per annum. A similar question came to the fore in the 1930s when a government once again sought to reduce judicial salaries in line with similar cuts which were being implemented throughout the civil service as part of an emergency economic programme. Was this an attack, however unintentional, upon judicial independence? Was it constitutional? Judicial emphasis upon such points resulted in the proposal being withdrawn, yet judicial salaries were not increased over the years despite a steady increase in prices, although salaries had been increased on several occasions during the eighteenth century. The result was that in 1950 a puisne judge was being paid no more — £5000 per annum — than his predecessors were paid in 1832.[4]

d) *Numbers*
At the beginning of this period there were just 12 puisne common law judges. Their small numbers enhanced their prestige but even in the 1820s it was becoming apparent that their numbers were inadequate to deal with the workload, especially in King's Bench. Critics wanted to know if there were any

2   R. F. V. Heuston *Lives of the Lord Chancellors 1885-1940* pp. 36, 52 and 603. Cf. S. Shetreet *Judges on Trial.*
3   D. Duman 'A Social and Occupational Analysis of the English Judiciary: 1770-1790 and 1855-1875' (1973) 17 AJLH 353, Abel-Smith and Stevens *Lawyers and the Courts* pp. 299-300.
4   Report of the Commissioners for Examining into the Duties, Salaries and Emoluments, of the Officers, Clerks and Ministers, of the Several Courts of Justice as to the Court of King's Bench...no. 292 (1818) pp. 4, 6, Abel-Smith and Stevens *Lawyers and the Courts* p. 38, n. 1, W. S. Holdsworth 'The Constitutional Position of the Judges' (1932) 48 LQR 25.

religious significance in maintaining the number of judges at 12 only but the numbers rose slowly and in mid-nineteenth century there were only 15 such judges. In 1924 provision was made for 17 puisne judges in King's Bench alone, although there was still considerable reluctance further to increase the number on the ground that this would lead to a decline in judicial quality. By then, however, prestige was beginning to be accorded to the appellate judges rather than to the puisne judges in a manner which simply had not been possible before the creation of the new appellate courts in the late nineteenth and early twentieth centuries.

e) *Tenure: removal: independence*

In medieval days no clear distinction had been made between the legislative, executive and judicial functions of the state. Demarcation of activities and a concept of judicial independence were the result of a long process which reached a peak during the Civil War but which began to be adopted wholeheartedly only at the close of the eighteenth century. Bacon had expounded a popular view of the judicial function when he wrote that judges were lions 'but yet lions under the throne, being circumspect that they do not check or oppose any points of sovereignty'. By way of contrast Coke urged the supremacy of the common law. By and large it was Coke's view which won the day. Accordingly, it became necessary to secure the independence of the common law judges who alone were the living oracles of the common law.

The Act of Settlement provided that the judges were appointed during good behaviour i.e. a judge might be removed from office only on the ground of his misconduct. Later statutes provided that they should no longer lose office on the death of the Sovereign: it was lawful to remove them only upon an address of both Houses of Parliament. Now the dignity and independence of the judges was stressed. The King assured Parliament that he:

> 'looked upon the independence and uprightness of the judges, as essential to the impartial administration of justice; as one of the best securities of the rights and liberties of his subjects; and as most conducive to the honour of the Crown'.[5]

To secure that degree of security of tenure which would ensure independence, especially from the Crown, it was necessary also to guarantee immunity from both civil and criminal liability for things done or said while acting within the jurisdiction, even if done maliciously and without reasonable or probable cause.[6] It could be argued that both in theory and in practice, as the doctrine of the sovereignty of parliament became established, there might be a degree of judicial dependence upon parliament. Any conflict was avoided because to a large extent the judiciary adopted quite a restrictive view of their role and because for their part responsible parliamentarians recognised the independence of the judiciary as an established constitutional principle. Of course, to a certain extent the system could be manipulated and conventional pressure could be exerted. For example, the person who determined which judge should hear a particular case

---

5   S. Shetreet *Judges on Trial* pp. 6-7 and 251-2, T. P. Taswell-Langmead *English Constitutional History* (1960) p. 466, Commons Journal for 3 March 1761 cited at 1 Bl Com (5th edn) 268, A. Todd *Parliamentary Government in England* vol 2, pp. 726-44.
6   O. Hood Phillips *Constitutional and Administrative Law* (4th edn, 1967) p. 360.

or which judges should compose a particular appellate court, had it in his power to influence the result of that case. Further, as the appellate courts became prestigious after the Judicature Acts, it could be argued that a judge who sought promotion to an appellate court might seek to please accordingly. Equally, pressure might be brought upon an infirm judge to resign. That happened in the case of no less a figure than James Fitzjames Stephen for it appears that the Lord Chancellor urged him to resign on the grounds of ill health, despite a government statement made in 1891 to the effect that the Lord Chancellor exercised no such disciplinary powers in relation to the judges. Similarly, a judge might choose to retire if he appeared to be in breach of ethics. In 1934 Mr. Justice McCardie committed suicide once it appeared that certain allegations concerning him were about to be made public. However, during the whole of this period it was never necessary to use the formal machinery for the dismissal of a judge.

Granted, then, that for all practical purposes the judges were independent, were they impartial? Of course, it is easy enough to pick out particular instances of apparently intemperate or partial conduct: judges are fallible and it would be strange if, over a span of 200 years, there were no such examples of apparently partial conduct. A more valid critique is that as members of a small and privileged social elite, they were necessarily insensitive to many of the social nuances of the community within which they lived. A distinguished judge, Scrutton LJ, expressed his own fears upon that point as follows:

'This [impartiality] is rather difficult to obtain in any system. I am not speaking of conscious impartiality; but the habits you are trained in, the people with whom you mix, lead to your having a certain class of ideas of such a nature that, when you have to deal with other ideas, you do not give as sound and accurate judgments as you would wish. This is one of the great difficulties at present with labour.... It is very difficult sometimes to be sure that you have put yourself into a thoroughly impartial position between two disputants, one of your own class and one not of your own class. Even in matters outside trade-unionist cases (to some extent in workmen's compensation cases) it is sometimes difficult to be sure, hard as you have tried, that you have put yourself in a perfectly impartial position between the two litigants.'[7]

It is a point upon which no conclusive judgment can be reached however. The judges were true to the values and traditions of a legal system of which they were the most important interpreters and the chief protectors. At times the small circle of the Bar and of the judges was insensitive to changing commercial and social needs. In particular many judges, brought up in individualist philosophies, tended to be unsympathetic to the collectivist approach of a growing trade union movement at the beginning of the twentieth century. Such an example illustrates the fact that at times the judges were slow in reacting to new questions, but does not prove that the judges were not impartial in applying the law, as the law then stood.

7 Scrutton LJ (1923) 1 CLJ 6 at 8.

Chapter 4

The courts: an introduction

1 General introduction

Blackstone defined a court as a place wherein justice was judicially administered.[1] He explained that the existing 'prodigious variety' of courts was the
reflection of a national policy of bringing justice home to every man's door by
constituting as many courts of judicature as there were manors and townships in
the kingdom. Such little courts communicated with superior courts which 'were
respectively constituted to correct the errors of the inferior ones, and to determine such causes as by reason of their weight and difficulty demanded a more
solemn discussion'.[2] Certain qualities or values appeared to be implicit in such a
legal system. First, justice was to be dispensed in accordance with established
legal principles. Secondly, justice was to be accessible to every man. Thirdly, the
legal system amounted to a coherent whole.

Necessarily the principles by which the courts sought to do justice reflected
certain values. This is true of the substantive or actual rules of law. It is true also
of the rules of procedure, which set out the formal steps which must be followed
in court proceedings, of pleadings, which are the documents prepared alternatively by the parties to a civil case until the point at issue between them is clear,
and of the law of evidence, which sets out the matters which may or may not be
used to prove or disprove the matter in issue between the parties. In particular
such rules express lawyers' values as to how best justice may be achieved. They
are of the greatest importance. After all a legal right is of little value, if it cannot
be obtained in practice. Indeed, one of the most highly prized rules of all was
procedural. That was the use of a jury which effectively left the point in issue to
be decided by 12 ordinary citizens rather than by a judge who was appointed by
the government of the day. Important social consequences flowed from the
application of such rules. In particular it was desirable in the public interest that
the lawyer did not allow a search for truth to result in rules of procedure and

1 3 Bl Com (5th edn) 23.
2 3 Bl Com (5th edn) 24, 30.

evidence which were overelaborate and overexpensive. It might be preferable to give the public substantial justice rather than a more perfect, yet more expensive and less speedy, form of justice. Indeed, over the years there was manifested a strong public interest in ensuring that justice was neither unduly expensive nor unduly delayed.

In 1820, for example, the radical author of the *Black Book* had alleged that justice was not only most shamefully delayed but, from its dearness in many cases, wholly unattainable.[3] His may have been an exaggerated view — some delay is inherent in every case, more especially if the facts are complex. Nor is there any reason why lawyers should not be paid an appropriate rate for the exercise of their professional skills. Even so, the theme which runs throughout the whole of the nineteenth-century discussion of the courts is that of the search for a system in which there shall be less unreasonable delay, less unreasonable expense.[4] Even as late as 1913 a legal magazine reflected ruefully upon the 'hopeless state of congestion in the superior courts'.[5] The position seemed little better even in 1950. Were such unfortunate qualities inherent in the system? Was society asking too much of its legal system? Were the twentieth-century delays due in part simply to the fact that the legal system was becoming more accessible? It was now understood rather more clearly than it had been in Blackstone's day that, if a court were to perform its social function effectively, its rules of procedure and its mode of administration were of the utmost importance,[6] yet there was little real attempt to offer legal aid to those who were too poor themselves to pay a lawyer. To that extent the legal system failed to meet Magna Carta's longstanding promise that justice would be denied to no man.

Did the legal system amount to a coherent whole? To a large extent that was true of the superior courts, but less true of the local courts. However all attempts to organise the courts centrally e.g. through the medium of a Ministry of Justice, ended in failure.

2 The system of courts as a whole

The courts were classified as being either of a public and general jurisdiction throughout the whole realm or of a private and special jurisdiction in some particular parts of the realm.[7] Of the former sort there were the courts of common law and equity, the ecclesiastical courts and the courts military and maritime. Examples of courts of special jurisdiction were the commissioners of sewers whose jurisdiction included the cleansing of rivers and public streams; the palace court at Westminster, which might hear all personal actions such as an action for the recovery of a debt, personal chattel or damages which arose between parties within 12 miles of the royal palace at Whitehall; the courts of the counties

3 J. Wade (ed) *The Black Book* p. 219.
4 A.H. Manchester 'Legal Administration' in W.R. Cornish and others *Crime and Law*.
5 (1913) 134 LT 471, 571.
6 More recently a Royal Commission on Assizes and Quarter Sessions (Cmnd. 4153) para. 112, has stated that the modern expectation of the system is that of convenience, quality and economy, the overall requirement being 'to make high quality justice conveniently available at low cost'; G. Sawer *Law in Society* pp. 70-2; cf. W. Paley *Principles of Moral and Political Philosophy* pp. 497-503.
7 3 Bl Com (5th edn) chaps. 1-4.

palatine of Chester, Lancaster and Durham, and the stannary courts in Devonshire and Cornwall for the administration of justice among the tinners of those areas. Possibly the most important of such courts, however, were the courts of requests, or courts of conscience for the recovery of small debts whose jurisdiction was conferred by local Acts of Parliament and which were created quite often during the late eighteenth and early nineteenth centuries.

A further distinction needs to be made between courts of record and courts not of record. All courts were the king's courts by virtue of his crown and royal dignity so that no other court had the authority either to fine or to imprison. The creation of a new court with power to fine or to imprison made it instantly a court of record. A court not of record was the court of a private man such as the courts-baron which were incident to every manor. It is also necessary to distinguish between wrongs. Private wrongs, or civil injuries, were an infringement of the private or civil rights belonging to individuals. For example, the breach of an agreement between two individuals might result in a form of civil action for breach of contract. Public wrongs were regarded as a breach and violation of public rights and duties which affected the whole community: such wrongs were regarded as crimes so that their remedy involved the institution of criminal rather than civil proceedings. Finally, the distinction between the superior courts of public and general jurisdiction, essentially the courts at Westminster, and the inferior courts, whose jurisdiction was confined to particular localities and whose jurisdiction was limited should be noted.

In the chapters which follow the distinction between superior courts of public and general jurisdiction and inferior courts is followed together with that between courts which exercised a jurisdiction in civil matters and courts which exercised a jurisdiction in criminal matters. First, however, some further consideration is given to particular aspects of those qualities inherent in the legal system to which reference was made above. These are that jewel in the crown of the common law, the palladium of the Englishman's liberties in the view of many lawyers, the jury; the question of legal aid, and the administration of the courts.

3   The jury

a) *Introduction*

i) *Origins.* A jury was a body of neighbours summoned by a public officer to answer questions upon oath.[8] In its origins it was a royal administrative device whereby representative inhabitants of the locality were required to offer information to the Crown regarding the public life of their locality. Such information might include matters of an administrative, financial, judicial or police nature. That wide area of responsibility was reflected even as late as the nineteenth century in the many duties of the grand jury. For example, money might not be granted for the repair of any bridge until that bridge was 'presented or indicted for insufficiency, inconveniency, or want of reparation'.[9] However, it was in its judicial capacity as a convenient and more acceptable method for deciding the

---

8   F. Pollock and F.W. Maitland *History of English Law* vol 1, p. 117.
9   S. and B. Webb *The Parish and the County* p. 452.

issue between litigants than medieval methods such as trial by battle and trial by ordeal, that jury trial became not only accepted but even highly valued as a distinctive, even constitutional, mark of procedure at common law. Trial by jury was available in both civil and in criminal cases.[10] Typically such a trial was heard by a petit jury made up of 12 people. However, we shall see that other forms of jury known as the special jury and the grand jury also had important functions.

ii) *Public esteem.* Blackstone wrote:[11]

'Trial by jury ever has been, and I trust ever will be, looked upon as the glory of the English law...it is the most transcendent privilege which any subject can enjoy, or wish for, that he cannot be affected either in his property, his liberty, or his person, but by the unanimous consent of twelve of his neighbours and equals.'

Such sentiments remained strong. They remained strong, at least in the case of the criminal jury, even in the second half of the twentieth century.[12] Naturally Blackstone opposed the creation of all new tribunals, such as courts composed of justices of the peace or courts of conscience, in which jury trial was not available.[13] Thus in mid-nineteenth century provision was made for jury trial not only in Chancery but even in the county court which had been designed expressly for the more speedy recovery of small debts. Paradoxically, it is from that same period that there was an increasing recognition of the fact that jury trial was not appropriate in all cases, yet majority public sentiment continued to feel, with Blackstone, that summary proceedings might be convenient:

'(as doubtless all arbitrary powers, well executed, are the most convenient) yet let it be again remembered that delays, and little inconveniences in the forms of justice, are the price that all free nations must pay for their liberty in more substantial matters...'[14]

It was a laudable, and powerful, sentiment. When it was coupled with the mystery in which the deliberations of the jury was shrouded, it was clear that a rational appraisal of the jury process would be difficult.

iii) *Changing function.* The function of the jury had evolved gradually. In its origins it had been a representative body, necessarily independent, which communicated its own knowledge of the facts. It had become very much a judge of the facts in issue.[15] As such it appeared less reasonable that it should remain independent in the sense that there could be no review of, or appeal from, its decisions. Further, once the Act of Settlement and subsequent practice had

---

10 For the early history of the jury see W.S. Holdsworth *History of English Law* vol 1,
    pp. 298-350, T. Plucknett *A Concise History of the Common Law* p. 107, A.K.R. Kiralfy
    Historical Introduction to English Law (4th edn, 1958) p. 240, J.B. Thayer *A Preliminary
    Treatise on Evidence at the Common Law*, W. Forsyth *History of Trial by Jury.*
11 3 Bl Com (5th edn) 379.
12 Report of the Departmental Committee on Jury Service (Cmnd. 2627) para. 6. See *Ward v
    James* [1966] 1 QB 273 for a modern judicial appraisal of jury trial in civil cases; cf. *Ford v
    Blurton* (1922) 38 TLR 801.
13 4 Bl Com (5th edn) 344.
14 3 Bl Com (5th edn) 352.
15 It was only in 1856 that a trial could be moved to the Central Criminal Court if it was feared
    that a local jury would be partial: Plucknett *A Concise History of the Common Law* p. 128.

assured the independence of the judiciary, the value of the jury as a protector of the defendant against a judge was diminished. Blackstone continued to view the role of the grand jury in criminal cases as the first part of a twofold barrier i.e. the presentment by the grand jury and the trial by the petit jury, between the liber-´ ties of the people and the prerogative of the Crown,[16] and in 1824 a commentator in the *Westminster Review* maintained the traditional suspicion of the judges.[17] In 1879, however, the *Law Times* saw the role of the grand jury as being rather to act as a check 'upon the vagaries of the unpaid magistracy in respect of com- mittals'.[18]

Such shifts in the public perception of the jury necessarily affected its role, but the jury had rarely been as totally irresponsible as some critics, such as Bentham, had asserted.[19] In particular a number of technical devices, as described below, had limited its role.

b) *The role of the jury*

i) *Introduction.* Coke had set out the basic principle quite clearly. The judges did not pronounce upon a question of fact; the jurors did not pronounce upon a question of law.[20] In practice that principle was qualified quite considerably. The rules of evidence established the matters about which jurors might, and might not, be informed. It was not possible in all cases to distinguish clearly between questions of law and questions of fact. It was possible also to limit the role of the jury by means of a number of other technical devices. On the one hand, it could be argued that once jurors were no longer liable to punishment for bringing in a verdict which might be held to be perverse, they were in a sense irresponsible i.e. if they disregarded the instructions of the court, they them- selves were determining the law.[1] On the other hand judicial influence, the oft- blurred distinction between law and fact, and the limitations referred to above meant that in fact few juries exceeded the conventions of their day regarding the role which they were to play.

Public debate concerning the proper limits of that role had been at its height during the second half of the eighteenth century following a number of libel cases. In the Almon case[2] Lord Mansfield held that it was for the judge alone to determine whether a libel was criminal: the jury was to determine only the fact of publication and whether the libel meant what the indictment alleged that it meant. In effect Fox's Libel Act 1792 reversed that judicial position by declaring that on any trial or information of libel, the jury might give a general verdict of guilty or not guilty on the whole matter. The Act also contained the proviso that in trials for criminal libel the judge might give 'his opinions and directions to the

16   4 Bl Com (5th edn) 343.
17   (1824) 1 Westminster Review 146.
18   (1879) 67 LT 381.
19   J. Bentham *The Elements of the Act of Packing as applied to Special Juries particularly in cases of Libel Law.*
20   Co Litt 155b.
  1   A.W. Scott 'Trial by Jury and the Reform of Civil Procedure' (1918) 31 HLR 669, M.D. Howe 'Juries as Judges of Criminal Law' (1939) 52 HLR 582, cf. Anon. 'The Changing Role of the Jury in the Nineteenth Century' (1964) 74 YLJ 170.
  2   *R v Almon* (1770) 20 State Tr 803. See T.P. Taswell-Langmead *English Constitutional History* (11th edn, 1960) p. 666.

jury in the matter in issue...in like manner as in other criminal cases'. The Act indicates, however, that it was for the judge to determine questions of law.

That power meant that the judges were enabled to restrict the influence of the jury. It was used to some purpose in the interpretation of the law regarding trade union picketing. Similarly, although it was for the jury in cases of contract to determine whether the goods in question were necessaries in the circumstances of the particular defendant, it was for the judge first to determine whether in law they were capable of being necessaries. It was a decision which was arrived at in an era when many shopkeepers were likely to serve on juries and when, as Cornish has pointed out, the most unlikely articles were being found to be necessaries.[3] Again, at common law no test is more familiar than that of reasonableness. On occasion the judges sought to guide the jury in their determination of what was reasonable. For example, before 1946, the defendant who was charged with murder, but claimed that he had been provoked, was required in law to show only that a reasonable man would have used violence in the circumstances of that particular case. However, in 1946 the House of Lords resolved that in law words alone could not amount to such provocation as would reduce a charge of murder to one of manslaughter.[4]

ii) *New trial.* If a jury found the prisoner guilty, contrary to the evidence, their verdict could be set aside and a new trial granted by the Court of Queen's Bench.[5] Upon its institution in 1907 the Court of Criminal Appeal was enabled to exercise a similar power to quash a verdict of guilty which it considered unreasonable or which could not be supported by the evidence.

iii) *Special verdict.* If any difficult matter of law arose from the facts proved in the case, the jury might bring in a special verdict. They stated the facts as they found them to be proved, and then concluded conditionally that if upon the whole matter the court should be of opinion that the issue ought to be found for the plaintiff, the jury then found for the plaintiff and assessed the damages accordingly — otherwise they found for the defendant.[6] This was used frequently in civil actions for libel and also in criminal cases.[7] If either party were dissatisfied with the decision, he might appeal to the proper court of error in Exchequer Chamber.

A judge might, therefore, exercise some control over a jury by this means — the jury simply answered a number of questions put by the judge.

iv) *Special case.* If the law which governed the case were doubtful, counsel upon both sides might agree upon a statement of facts and state a special case for the opinion of the proper court of error in the Exchequer Chamber. The proceedings were very similar to those upon a special verdict, the chief difference being that a special case was not entered on the record:[8] therefore the question

---

3 W.R. Cornish *The Jury* p. 108.
4 *Cornish* p. 104, *Holmes v Director of Public Prosecutions* [1946] AC 588.
5 H.J. Stephen *New Commentaries on the Laws of England* vol 4 (4th edn, 1858), p. 499.
6 H.J. Stephen *New Commentaries on the Laws of England* vol 3 (4th edn, 1858), p. 625.
7 *R v Wheat and Stocks* [1921] 2 KB 119, cf. Cornish *The Jury* p. 111.
8 *Stephen* pp. 625-6.

could not proceed on a writ of error in a higher court.[9]

v) *Law and fact*. The object of special pleading was to develop the precise point in controversy between the parties and to present it in a shape fit for decision. If that question consisted of a matter of fact, the parties were enabled to prepare their proofs for the jury. If it turned out to be a matter of law, they had the means of obtaining immediately the decision of the cause, without the expense and trouble of a trial, by demurrer i.e. by referring the legal question so evolved to the determination of the judges.[10] Such use of special pleading conferred greater power upon the judges at the expense of jury trial. For many years, however, that process had been encouraged by the practice of 'giving colour', a process based upon a fiction whose sole object was to avoid jury trial.[11]

vi) *The influence of the judge*. On occasion a judge might influence the jury or at least give the appearance of trying to do so. There are professional anecdotes concerning the manner in which it is possible, for example, to sum up in a way which the transcript shows to have been completely objective, yet the inflection of the voice or facial expression may convey a far less neutral approach. Occasionally a judge might convey his views in an even more forthright manner. Cornish writes of Mr. Commissioner Kerr who was once reported to have disposed of a case at the Central Criminal Court with the words: 'Gentlemen of the jury, the man stole the ducks. Consider your verdict.'[12] Further, Larkin[13] suggested (in 1943) that, at all events in cases where the only outstanding questions were questions of law, the judge might direct the jury to return a verdict of guilty. Such a proposition is surely very much in line with Coke's traditional allocation of questions of law to the judge and questions of fact to the jury.

vii) *The independence of the jury*. In the final analysis, however, the jury might return whatever verdict it chose. On occasion juries reacted against laws or punishments of which they disapproved by failing to convict in such cases. In the time of the 'Bloody Code' many juries are said to have refused to convict defendants upon a capital charge, despite the overwhelming nature of the evidence against the defendant. Such cases were cited by Jerome Hall in support of his theory that a form of equity existed in the criminal sphere.[14] Others have used them to argue in favour of the jury system generally on the grounds that in such cases the humanity of the jury rightly mitigated the rigours of the Bloody Code. On occasion, however, it can be argued that the exercise of such a licence on the part of the jury has not been in the public interest. For example, juries have been extremely reluctant to convict motorists, who have caused death by their driving, of manslaughter, although they would convict them of dangerous driving. In 1938 a Home Office representative told a select committee that he believed that in such cases juries were deterred by 'the feeling that a charge of manslaughter

---

9   ·Common Law Procedure Act 1854, ss. 32 and 34.
10   Second Report...by the Commissioners appointed to inquire into the Practice and Proceedings of the Superior Courts of Common Law no. 123 (1830) p. 45.
11   J.B. Thayer *A Preliminary Treatise on Evidence at the Common Law* pp. 233-4.
12   Cornish *The Jury* p. 112.
13   [1943] 1 All ER 217, M.J. McConville 'Directions to Convict — A Reply' (1973) Criminal Law Review 164.
14   J. Hall *Theft, Law and Society*.

may in law result in a sentence of penal servitude for life, which they feel in most cases to be quite incommensurate with the facts of the case before them. They do not realise at the same time that manslaughter may vary enormously and may be perfectly well met by an almost nominal penalty in some cases.'[15] The committee accepted that view and concluded that in addition to the existing right of juries to find persons committed for manslaughter guilty of the lesser charge of dangerous driving, they should also be given the alternative of finding them guilty of driving without due care and attention.[16] It seems, therefore, that in such cases of manslaughter juries were again exercising a form of criminal equity, although they did so upon a false view of the law.

c) *The composition of the jury*

Juries at the assizes tended to be composed of the gentry, for the visit of the assize judge was a considerable social event — juries at quarter sessions tended to be far less socially exalted. By his Juries Act 1825 Peel consolidated existing practice. The chief qualification of the juror was that he must hold one of a number of interests in land. Cornish has pointed out that the property qualifications were liberal by the standards of 1825 in that they were less stringent than those for most parliamentary electors until the Reform Act 1832. Yet it remained true that the jury was not representative of the population as a whole, and even in 1913 a Home Office committee recommended only a small change in that qualification. In this respect the principle of trial by one's peers was not fully achieved in practice.[17]

During the fourteenth century the number of jurors was fixed at 12, a number which Coke invested with a mystic significance. Those particular jurors were called by successively drawing out of a box, into which they had been put previously, the names of the jurors on the panels annexed to the *nisi prius* record. The 12 persons whose names were first called and who appeared were sworn as the jury, unless some just cause of challenge or excuse were brought forward with regard to any of them. Such challenges could be made on the grounds, inter alia, of partiality on the part either of the sheriff who had drawn up the panel of jurors or on the part of an individual juror.[18] It was not possible, however, to ensure in this way that a jury was competent to hear a particular case, especially if that case were of a complex nature. The special jury could fill that role, in theory at least.

d) *The special jury*

Either plaintiff or defendant might choose to have the case heard not by a common jury but by a special jury. The special jury consisted of persons who, in addition to the ordinary qualifications, were of a certain station in society — esquires or persons of higher degree, bankers or merchants.[19] According to Blackstone, such juries had been introduced in trials at bar, when the causes were of too great nicety for the discussion of ordinary freeholders or where the sheriff was suspected of partiality.[20] Lord Mansfield made use of such juries when he was

---

15   Report of the Select Committee on the Prevention of Road Accidents HL 35, 192 (1938) p. 435.
16   HL 2.52 para. 55.
17   Cornish *The Jury* pp. 26-7, Committee on Juries 1913 (Cd. 6817).
18   Stephen *New Commentaries on the Laws of England* vol 3, pp. 595, 596, 600.
19   *Stephen* p. 591.
20   3 Bl Com (5th edn) 357, Thayer *A Preliminary Treatise on Evidence at the Common Law* n. 31, p. 95.

developing the principles of commercial law. Their use in the criminal sphere, in cases of sedition, towards the end of the eighteenth century was strongly opposed, however.[1] There was a gradual widening of the qualification, to the extent that in 1913 a Home Office committee became rather concerned,[2] but this was a longstanding criticism. As long ago as 1824 a critic had commented upon a general lack of intelligence, education and social standing among many special jurymen.[3]

Nor were allegations of packing a jury unknown. Such an allegation was made by John Horne in 1777 during proceedings before King's Bench upon an information by the Attorney-General for libel. Horne alleged that libel was always tried by special jury, although the special jury had been designed for use in more complex cases, because the Attorney-General believed that the majority of such special jurors would be sympathetic to the government's case. Horne also objected to the discretion which the Master of the Crown Office exercised in choosing some jurors and rejecting others.[4] Bentham and others were to emphasise such points over the years,[5] but there was little change.

By the early years of the twentieth century the use of the special jury in criminal cases had almost died out. They were still used in personal injury cases because, writes Cornish,[6] of the belief that people of higher status were likely to think in larger terms when it came to assessing damages. The special jury was abolished only in 1949.

e) *Consideration of verdict and the unanimity rule*

The jury was permitted to withdraw in order to consider its verdict. In order 'to avoid intemperance and causeless delay' the jurors were to be kept without meat, drink, fire or candle, unless by permission of the judge, until they were agreed unanimously. Should they not have arrived at such a decision before the judges were due to leave the town, then even in mid-nineteenth century the jurors were subject in theory to the old rule that they might be carried round the circuit from town to town in a cart. In practice, in such cases a juror often might be withdrawn by consent of the parties to the suit, so that no verdict could be given; or the whole jury might, with like consent, be discharged from finding any verdict; or the jurors might, even without such consent, be discharged by the judge, after having retired for a considerable time e.g. a night, for deliberation.[7]

The rule regarding unanimity appears to have become settled during the fourteenth century. In the event of a difference of opinion, it did have the advantage of compelling the whole jury to reconsider the question fully, for the jury could not be discharged until they had delivered their unanimous verdict. In the view of the common law commissioners it was absurd that the rights of a party, in questions of a doubtful and complicated nature, should depend upon his ability to satisfy 12 persons that one particular set of facts was the true one. As it

1   Cornish *The Jury* p. 32.
2   1913 (Cd. 6817) para. 241.
3   (1824) 1 Westminster Review 146.
4   20 State Tr 651 at 685 ff.
5   *Cornish* p. 19.
6   *Cornish* p. 33.
7   *Cornish* p. 623. Contrast (1848) 12 LT 55 which reports a verdict given contrary to the convictions of many members of the jury under compulsion of 'the gnawings of hunger'.

was notorious, they continued, that upon such questions a body of men so numerous were often found to differ irreconcilably in their views, it was obvious that the necessity of returning in every case a verdict, and a unanimous one, before they separated, must frequently lead to improper compromise among the jurors of their respective opinions. There was a danger also, they suggested, that such a practice might produce a corrupt verdict; all who were much conversant with the courts must frequently have heard the remark, in cases where the verdict had been very long in suspense, that one or other of the contending parties had a friend upon the jury.[8] The commissioners recommended that if, after a deliberation of 12 hours, 9 out of the 12 concurred, their verdict should be received. That recommendation was not accepted.

Having arrived unanimously at its finding, the jury also assessed damages in appropriate cases. Should there be difficulty in reaching agreement upon the amount of damages, the practice of 'squaring a jury' overcame the difficulties of the unanimity rule to some extent. In such cases the jurors might each write down the damages which he felt were appropriate, a total was arrived at and then divided by 12. That average was then awarded.[9]

f) *The criminal jury*

No person could be tried upon a charge of felony, unless upon an indictment i.e. the presentment or preparatory accusation of 12 or more of his fellow subjects of the grand jury. The mid-nineteenth century provisions whereby in certain cases larcenies might be disposed of summarily before justices without indictment were not regarded as an exception to that rule, since the consent of the person charged was required before such a course could be taken. The truth of every accusation, whether preferred in the form of an indictment by the grand jury or of an information by justices was then determined by the unanimous suffrage of 12 equals and neighbours, indifferently chosen, and above all suspicion i.e. the petit jury.[10]

i) *The grand jury.* The sheriff was required to return to every sessions and to every assizes, 24 good and lawful men of the county, some out of every hundred, 'to inquire, present, do, and execute all those things...which should be commanded them'. They were to be freeholders and, in Blackstone's view, they were 'usually·gentlemen of the best figure in the county'.[11] They were to number at least 12 and no more than 23. The judge upon the bench instructed them as to the articles of their inquiry: typically, his 'charge' to the grand jury would survey the state of crime in the area and offer his own thoughts upon it.

The grand jury then withdrew to sit and to receive indictments which were preferred to them in the name of the king but at the suit of any private prosecutor. Since the task of the grand jury was merely to determine whether there was sufficient cause to call upon the party charged to answer the accusation, it heard evidence only on behalf of the prosecution. The grand jury was abolished only in 1933.

---

8   Third Report...by the Commissioners appointed to inquire into the Practice and
    Proceedings of the Superior Courts of Common Law no. 92 (1831) pp. 69-70.
9   Cornish *The Jury* p. 624, (1868) 45 LT 157.
10 4 Bl Com (5th edn) 343.
11 4 Bl Com (5th edn) 299.

ii) *The petit jury*. The petit jury was governed by rules which were very similar to those which governed the jury in civil causes. In the case of misdemeanours the trial might even be by a special jury, as in civil actions, but this applied only to prosecutions in Queen's Bench and was not allowed before commissioners of oyer and terminer and gaol delivery or at the sessions of the peace. Yet some points are worthy of note. A member of the grand jury which had found the indictment could not sit upon the petit jury. Further, in addition to the right to challenge jurors for cause, the prisoner in cases of felony was allowed a number of peremptory challenges in which he was not required to show any cause at all. At common law 35 such peremptory challenges were allowed, although statute reduced this to 20. One commentator described this provision as 'full of that tenderness and humanity to prisoners, for which our English laws are justly famous'. It was based upon the views that the defendant should have a good opinion of his jury and because the defendant might wish still to reject a juror, although his challenge for cause had failed.[12]

The verdict of the jury might be either general, as guilty or not guilty, or special, in which the circumstances of the case were set out for the judgment of the court e.g. did these facts amount to murder or manslaughter? The old practice of fining, imprisoning or otherwise punishing jurors who found a verdict contrary to the direction of the judge had long been abandoned.

g) *The popularity of the jury*

Over the years there was a decline in the use of the jury as a method of trial.[13] Very probably that is one aspect of the legal system as it existed in 1950 which would have struck the eighteenth-century lawyer most forcibly. It was a decline which was far more marked in the case of civil actions, yet it is apparent even in criminal cases.

Blackstone had been concerned at the growth of summary trial, a process which denied the defendant trial by jury. It was a process which Peel's legislation of 1827 accelerated by conferring upon justices of the peace a jurisdiction in some of the less serious cases of larceny. Similarly, in 1855 statute provided that in cases of simple larceny not over five shillings, or attempted larceny from the person or attempted simple larceny, the defendant might be tried at petty sessions if the justices thought fit and if the defendant agreed. That provision amounted to a tolerable compromise between easing the pressures of jury trial upon the legal system and meeting what the public generally felt was the subject's constitutional right to jury trial in a criminal case. Its immediate effect was a sharp reduction in the number of jury trials upon indictment. There was also an increase in the number of indictable offences which were tried summarily i.e. there was a rise in the total number of indictable charges. Jackson's conclusion upon this point was that people would not prosecute many offences of small importance when such prosecutions involved trial by jury with its attendant trouble and expense, but that given a simple, quick and cheap procedure there was greater readiness to resort to the courts. The policy was believed to have been a success and its scope was extended by statute during the remaining years of the nineteenth century.

12   H.J. Stephen *New Commentaries on the Laws of England* (4th edn, 1858) vol 4, pp. 485-90.
13   See R.M. Jackson 'Incidence of Jury Trial During the Past Century' (1937-38) 1 MLR 132.

The decline in the use of the jury in civil actions was even more marked. Especially remarkable is the fact that juries were so little used in the new county court. In 1867 542560 causes were determined in the county courts. Only 856 of those causes were tried before a jury.[14] After 1935 it could be asserted that jury trials in county courts had practically ceased to exist. Yet Jackson points out that in the superior courts of common law during the period prior to the enactment of the Judicature Acts trial was by jury in well over 90 per cent of the cases tried.[15] Indeed, the possibility of jury trial had been extended to Chancery in 1858; the new Court for Divorce and Matrimonial Causes enjoyed similar powers. The judicature commissioners and a departmental committee which reported in 1913 favoured a more restricted right to trial by jury in civil causes. No such change was made until the Juries Act 1918 provided that all cases in the High Court should be before a judge without a jury unless the Court saw fit to order a jury, subject to a right to jury trial in certain cases. That legislation was repealed in 1925. Further restrictive legislation was introduced in 1933 — which applied only to the King's Bench Division but took away any absolute right to a jury.

The popularity of the jury in civil causes varied over the years. Jackson has shown that during the period 1922 — 33 there was an increase in the number of cases tried with a jury. Yet the decline in jury trial over the period in review did amount to a revolution in practice. Originally, the reverence in which jury trial was held had meant that the existing system was virtually sacrosanct until 1854 when issues of fact might be tried by a judge alone, albeit with the consent of the parties. Yet in the twentieth century substantial changes in the right to jury trial were made with little public protest. Perhaps the avoidance of the old bogeys of delay and expense were beginning to influence litigants, and their advisers, rather more than the traditional arguments in favour of the jury.

h) *Reform*
Public opinion valued the jury highly throughout this period. Accordingly, criticism of the jury tended to be reformist rather than abolitionist. There was more criticism of the use of the jury in civil cases than in criminal cases and in criminal cases there tended to be far more criticism of the grand jury than of the petit jury.

The common law commissioners had suggested as early as 1830 that trial by jury was unsuited to the minute and patient investigation which was necessary in matters of account. In 1853 their successors not only agreed upon that point but went on to suggest that trial by jury might be superseded if the parties themselves preferred that the case should be tried by a judge, a suggestion which was taken up by the Common Law Procedure Act 1854.[16] In 1869 the judicature commis-sioners took the process a step further when they suggested that more regard should be paid to the nature of the questions to be tried. Trial might be in any division of the court by (1) a judge, (2) a jury, or (3) a referee. In the view of the commissioners the plaintiff should be at liberty to give notice of trial by any one

14 (1868) 45 LT 441, cf. First Report of the Commissioners...into the State of the County Courts...no. 1914 (1855) p. 12.
15 R.M. Jackson (above) 1 MLR 132 at 144, 139.
16 Second Report on the Practice and Proceedings of the Superior Courts of Common Law no. 123 (1830) pp. 25-7, Second Report of...Commissioners for inquiring into the Process, Practice and System of Pleading no. 1626 (1853) pp. 5-6.

of those modes which he might prefer, subject to the right of the defendant to move the judge to appoint any other mode.[17] Nothing came of that particular proposal.

On the whole criticism tended rather to be reformist and went especially to the jury's composition, ability, and irresponsibility. In 1848 *The Times* voiced quite a common complaint to the effect that a 'stranger unacquainted with the wisdom of our modern jury laws, and judging only from the looks and acts of the "worthy and upright dozens" before him, would inevitably conclude that the sheriff was under an obligation to leave out of the box every man who had any external pretensions to education or intelligence'. This was because if he 'were to place gentlemen on the common jury lists who have pretensions to be on the special jury panels, he would give mortal offence to the aristocracy of his bailiwick'. The result was that special juries tried relatively trivial questions 'while utterly unimportant questions as to whether he should be hanged for treason, transported for felony, or imprisoned for misdemeanour, are left to the adjudication' of such common jurymen.[18] There can be little doubt but that *The Times* was accurate enough in its assessment of the social class of special and common jurymen respectively. In 1878 Lord Coleridge alleged that there had been a systematic evasion of the law by the undersheriffs in the construction of the panel in favour of the rich and against the poor. In future, announced Lord Coleridge, if any jury list did not contain a due proportion of both rich and poor, as required by the law of the land, he would treat it as a contempt of court.[19] It was a social distinction which also marked off the grand jury from the petty jury, so much is clear from the evidence given to the Select Committee on Municipal Corporations which reported in 1833. Grand juries in Kingston-on-Hull, a typical enough example, were 'always very respectable...it has always been considered a compliment to be put on the grand jury'.[20]

Granted that to have composed a jury of the defendant's equals in terms of social class would have been a difficult task, did such social differences really matter? In the great majority of cases in which there was a consensus as to the aims of the law, any difference in social class probably did not influence the jury. In any event the defendant was at liberty to challenge. However, in cases of sedition, a misdemeanour, it was possible to use a special jury. Arguably, the social bias of such a jury could have been inclined rather to find for the prosecution in such cases. So far as the ability of the jurors is concerned, it must be remembered that education did not become available to all children, even in an elementary form, until 1870. Therefore, it is fair to assume that even many of those who qualified as jurymen would barely have been literate. Such jurymen might well have found it difficult to assess the evidence in the more complex cases. The *Law Times* claimed in 1848 that every lawyer could recall at least 50 instances which revealed the jury's lack of understanding. Should the qualifications be raised, then, and the distinction between special and common juries abolished?[1] Or, as J.F. Stephen, believed, ought special juries to be available in all appropriate

17   First Report of the Judicature Commissioners no. 4130 (1869) p. 13.
18   (1848) 11 LT 425.
19   (1878) 22 Sol Jo 783.
20   Report from the Select Committee on Municipal Corporations no. 344 (1833) q. 7035 ff.
 1   (1848) 11 LT 425.

criminal cases e.g. cases of fraud? It does seem, however, that the special jury was not always all that it might have been in terms of expertise in dealing with the issue before it. In 1910 Scrutton KC, who later became a most distinguished judge, protested at the composition of a special jury summoned to try an important question relating to the custom of the Port of London in the Commercial Court on the grounds that the jury consisted of 'a butcher, a horsedealer, three artists and various small tradesmen'.[2]

Most proposals for reform sought to remedy such stated blemishes upon the system. That was the purpose of the resolutions which the Law Amendment Society passed in 1867. The Society suggested that no person should be excused from being in a common jury by reason merely of his being on the special jury list, unless he had actually served; the machinery for making out, completing and publishing jury lists should be assimilated to that for making out, publishing and completing lists of voters; reasonable allowances should be paid; the qualifications of grand jurymen, both at the assizes and quarter sessions should be specified by law. The Society also recommended that in all criminal cases it should be competent for a judge of the superior court to order the jury to be taken altogether or in part from the special jury list on such terms as might be reasonable.[3] Such questions were duly considered by various select committees and the Juries Act 1870 became law. Early in the twentieth century a Home Office committee recommended a reduction in the minimum rateable value of the property qualification.[4]

The grand jury was criticised very strongly over the years. In 1836 an MP had proposed its abolition.[5] Its secretive procedure was especially open to criticism. In 1879 the criminal code commissioners strongly criticised the virtually unhindered freedom of an individual complainant to go before a grand jury. The commissioners proposed that only proceedings before magistrates should be adopted in future.[6] Yet the grand jury was not abolished until 1933.

The 1853 commissioners put the case for the jury eloquently enough:

> 'Trial by jury, long the peculiar feature of the law of England, has in recent times been much canvassed, and its excellence as a judicial institution questioned. It has been urged that twelve men, taken at hazard from the body of society, unused to judicial duties or forensic discussions, cannot possess the same aptitude for judicial investigations as a judge, in whom a professional education, the habit of considering the effect of evidence, a long course of training and experience, have developed all the faculties which are required for the judicial office. To this it is added, that the sense of responsibility is weakened by being divided among a number of persons, and that such is peculiarly the case with a jury, who, filling the judicial office only for the moment, merge again, as soon as the trial is over, into

2   (1910) 128 LT 285.
3   (1867) 43 LT 210.
4   Report from the Select Committee...to inquire as to the Law relating to the Summoning, Attendance and Remuneration of Special and Common Juries...no. 425 (1867), Report from the Select Committee on the same subject in the following Session...no. 401 (1867-68). For further contemporary criticism of the jury see (1872) 41 Westminster Review 289.
5   (1835) 9 Legal Observer pp. 195-7, (1836) 11 Legal Observer 492.
6   Report of the Royal Commission appointed to consider the Law relating to Indictable Offences (1879) no. C-2345 p. 32.

the body of society....Further, it is urged that the want of permanency in the tribunal precludes the adjournments which sometimes, in the course of trials, become necessary to enable complete justice to be done. It is added, that in recent times trial by jury has been much dispensed with. The jurisdiction of courts of equity to try questions of fact without a jury, in certain cases where juries have been hitherto required, has been recently extended. Justices of the peace and commissioners of various kinds exercise jurisdiction in criminal and other matters without the assistance of a jury. And the experience of the county courts, in which the suitors may, if they think proper,. demand a jury, but in point of practice do not, is referred to, to show that cases may be left with perfect satisfaction to the suitor, to the decision of a judge, without the intervention of a jury.'[7]

Those, and similar criticisms were repeated frequently over the years. Of course defenders of trial by jury did not deny that there were faults in the system. When Baron Bramwell was asked in 1869 whether he had any cause to be dissatisfied with jury trial, he expressed himself satisfied but granted that there were 'cases in which juries go wrong: for instance, in an action against a railway company...in actions for discharging a servant...in actions as to malicious prosecution...and in cases of running down they always found for the plaintiff.'[8]

The common law commissioners summarised the defence of the jury as follows. A trial was a trial by a jury assisted by a judge. The jury members brought their own expertise to court. Being called upon to act on a temporary occasion only, the juryman came fresh to his task and was prepared to take a liberal rather than a literal view of his task. He also acted as a check upon the judge. With regard to cases before justices 'necessity or extreme convenience requires more speedy and summary proceedings than are consistent with the intervention of a jury'. Cases in the superior court were of a more difficult character than those in the county court where the practice of not usually asking for trial by jury had a 'considerable effect in preventing litigants from insisting upon trial by jury in the county court'. The commissioners' conclusion in 1853 was that while

> 'we feel that there are cases in which a jury may advantageously be dispensed with, yet, being of opinion that trial by jury on the whole works well and enjoys the confidence of the public, we do not think ourselves warranted, except in cases of mere account, to recommend that trial by jury should be superseded, unless the parties themselves prefer that the case should be tried by a judge'.[9]

Accordingly, the argument continued. Chalmers who had done much for reform by his codifying measures, was a staunch defender of trial by jury even in civil cases. He argued that disagreement among the jury was proper when the evidence was not good enough — if 'a race really ends in a dead heat, is it right that the umpire should be obliged mentally to spin a coin and to say that one horse or the other is the winner?' — he approved of the jury not giving reasons

7   Second Report...of Commissioners for inquiring into the Process, Practice and System of Pleading no. 1626 (1853) pp. 3-4. Cf. (1878) 65 LT 430. See also Report from the Select Committee on County Courts Jurisdiction (No. 2) Bill no. 267 (1878) minutes of evidence.
8   (1869) 47 LT 337.
9   Second Report no. 1626 (1853) p. 5.

for they should not be bound by precedents and he argued that, although juries were suspect in some types of case, individual inconvenience was counter-balanced by public policy.[10]

i) *Conclusion*

On occasion the jury had demonstrated its independence. Yet it would be hard to sustain a view of the jury as a bulwark of the citizen's liberty: its decisions are too inconsistent for that.[11] That is a picture which is locked in professional and public myth. Yet, aided by the necessary secrecy of the jury process, it is a picture which is none the less a very real factor even at the present day in any assessment of the jury's modern role. Historically, however, we can see a gradual public disenchantment, especially in civil cases, of trial by jury in the interests of a speedier and less expensive trial process.

4 Legal aid[12]

Little legal advice or legal representation was available in practice to those who could not pay for it. Such an omission was all the more surprising since statutory provisions for legal aid to needy litigants in civil cases in superior courts were of long standing and the 'dock brief' was an established institution amongst crim-inal lawyers. However, it was not until the twentieth century that any widespread and lasting protest at the lack of legal aid began to be expressed. Indeed, it was only in 1949 that a modern system, however inadequate it was in some respects, was established.

a) *Civil causes*

i) *Proceedings* in forma pauperis. Statute provided that paupers i.e. those who swore that they were not worth £5 in the world, except their wearing apparel and the matter in question in the cause, were exempt when plaintiffs from the pay-ment of court fees. In addition they were entitled to have counsel and attorney assigned to them by the court, without fee, and were excused from paying costs when they were unsuccessful. On the other hand, before Blackstone's day at all events, a judge in such a case might give a pauper who had been non-suited a choice either of being whipped or of paying costs. The spirit of that latter provi-sion lived on long after Blackstone's day.

Such provisions were not available to a pauper defendant, nor were they completely free. For example, about the year 1786 the minimum preliminary fees payable by a pauper to the Court of Common Pleas were 6s 6d. Nor were these provisions available in all courts but only in the courts of common law. Strangely enough, therefore, such provisions did not apply in the new county court after 1846, despite that court's avowed aim of bringing justice to persons of small means. Nor did proceedings *in forma pauperis* make any provision for the giving of preliminary legal advice.

---

10 (1891) 7 LQR 15.
11 R.M. Jackson *The Machinery of Justice in England* (6th edn, 1972) p. 390.
12 I am indebted to the following works: R. Egerton *Legal Aid*, B. Abel-Smith and R. Stevens *Lawyers and the Courts*, J.M. Maguire 'Poverty and Civil Litigation' (1923) 36 HLR 361.

ii) *The Rules of 1883*. The creation of the county court in 1846, and of the divorce jurisdiction in 1857, together with the possibilities of personal accident litigation, had created new and wider fields for litigation.

There was little change with regard to legal aid. Rules which were made in 1883 raised the limit of £5 to £25 and provided that relief might be granted to the defendant as well as to the plaintiff. On the other hand it was still necessary to obtain an opinion from counsel and an affidavit from a solicitor upon the merits of the case. As the new Rules did not indicate how the would-be litigant might do this, they appear to have been of little real help to the great majority of litigants.

iii) *The Rules of 1914*. The new Poor Persons Rules extended the financial limits by providing that certificates might be granted to applicants who were not worth £50, 'or such larger sum not exceeding £100 as a judge personally under special circumstances may direct'. Administration was in the hands of a Poor Persons' Department. Yet the Rules applied only to proceedings in the High Court and the Court of Appeal, nor did they make any provision for the giving of legal advice.

b) *Criminal causes*
Any defendant who was unable to pay the normal fees, might have the services as a 'dock brief' of any barrister who was in court and gowned. That system survived throughout the whole of this period, although the Poor Prisoners' Defence Act 1903 largely supplanted it.

There had long been criticism of the existing lack of provision. In 1851 a correspondent of the *Law Times* maintained that it was the duty of the state to allow or assign counsel to prisoners who really could not afford them — otherwise 'the Act for allowing counsel to make a speech in felony cases was a cruel aggravation of the distinction between the man who had a guinea or friends and the man who had not'.[13] By the beginning of the twentieth century such sentiments had become eminently respectable. In 1901 Dr. Goudy, who was Regius Professor of Civil Law at Oxford, in referring to the work of the Mansfield Settlement, said that the state had a duty to provide professional assistance for the poor: he had always thought it 'rather a scandal' that the criminal law should leave prisoners so much as it had done without professional men to defend them in the dock. The 1903 Act was a 'halting attempt', in the *Law Times'* phrase, to remedy that position.[14]

The Act provided that either the magistrates who were committing an accused person for trial, or the judge before the hearing of the trial, might certify for legal aid. Thereupon solicitor and counsel might be assigned at public expense. Yet there were serious draw-backs. In particular the Act limited legal aid to those prisoners who had disclosed their defences; nor did the Act provide for legal aid before committal.[15]

c) *Legal aid 1914-1950*
The 1914 Rules regarding the Poor Persons Procedure had not worked well.

13   (1851) 18 LT 134. Cf. (1851) 18 LT 161.
14   B. Abel-Smith and R. Stevens *Lawyers and the Courts* p. 151.
15   *Abel-Smith and Stevens* p. 151.

Relatively few lawyers were willing to undertake such work yet the growing amount of marital breakdown during the First World War had led to a greatly increased demand upon the existing system. A committee of inquiry, which was appointed in 1919, came up with little that was new. However, in 1920 the income limit was raised to £2 a week, with the proviso that in exceptional circumstances it might be raised to £4 a week.

A further committee reported in 1925. Once again the main concern was the lack of solicitors who were willing to undertake this work. It was decided that this problem might be overcome more readily if the administration were placed in the hands of the profession itself rather than of the Poor Persons Department. Accordingly, the Law Society undertook the administration of the scheme in 1926.

That resulted in a far greater number of solicitors throughout the country contributing to the scheme. Yet public demand for such services continued to grow with the result that public expectations were still not met. A further inquiry had little new to offer; the more liberal matrimonial legislation of 1937 made further demands upon the system, and an impasse appeared to have been reached. On the one hand the individual lawyer expected to be paid a reasonable fee for all the work which he undertook other than a limited number of 'charity' cases. On the other hand both the state and the legal profession rejected any proposals which tended towards nationalisation even of a part of legal services or to any encroachment upon the independence of the legal profession. The problem was acute.

The increased rate of marital breakdown during the Second World War made the problem even worse. The need was such that in 1942 a department of the Law Society began actually to conduct such divorce cases. The creation of numerous Citizens Advice Bureaux at much the same time also pointed to a widespread need for legal aid. Accordingly, in 1944 a committee was appointed to inquire into all aspects of legal aid and advice. The report of that committee, the Rushcliffe Committee, was to be influential.[16]

Nor had any substantial advance been made in respect of criminal legal aid. On the whole the Finlay Committee appeared even to believe that the existing system was working reasonably well. Popular dissatisfaction with that view led to the enactment of the Poor Prisoners' Defence Act 1930. This Act provided that it was no longer necessary for a poor person to disclose his defence. Any person charged with an indictable offence might be granted a defence certificate if his means were insufficient to enable him to obtain legal aid, if this were desirable in the interests of justice. In certain circumstances a certificate might be granted also in respect of proceedings before magistrates. However, there was considerable dissatisfaction with the manner in which the Act was administered.[17] The charitable origins of legal aid lingered on.

The Rushcliffe Committee found that the existing service had become 'totally inadequate and that this condition will become worse'. The report was published in 1945. Upon it was based the Legal Aid and Advice Act 1949 which the

16 Report of the Committee to enquire into the Poor Persons' Rules (Cmd. 430), Report of the Poor Persons' Rules Committee (Cmd. 2358), First Report of the Committee on Legal Aid for the Poor (the Finlay Committee) (Cmd. 2638), Report of the Committee on Legal Aid and Legal Advice in England and Wales (Cmd. 6641).
17 Abel-Smith and Stevens *Lawyers and the Courts* p. 163.

Attorney-General described as 'the charter of the little man to the British Courts of Justice'. Certainly, the new Act extended legal aid to county courts, to magistrates' courts, and even to tribunals in which audience was normally granted to barristers and solicitors. Further, the Act also considerably extended the range of those who were eligible to receive legal aid. An important feature of the new measure was that it was to be administered by the lawyers themselves through the Law Society, rather than by any governmental body. There had been widespread agreement that such an approach was necessary for two reasons. First, it would help to secure the necessary co-operation of the legal profession. Secondly, it was believed that it would help to underwrite the independence of the profession from government: such independence was thought to be desirable, since from time to time members of the profession might be involved in legal conflict with the government. So far as criminal proceedings were concerned, the Act provided that any doubts as to the desirability of having legal aid were to be resolved in favour of granting such legal aid. In addition the Act simplified in certain cases the machinery by which application could be made for it.

At last it appeared that all citizens were to have the legal process made accessible to them. Yet the history of this question was strewn with previous such good intentions. In practice much would depend upon the spirit in which the new legislation was administered.

5   Administration

a) *Staffing the court system*

Neither the court system as a whole nor individual courts were subjected to any uniform pattern of control or administration. Within the superior courts administrative posts were regarded usually as the property of a particular individual which he might manage or dispose of in much the same manner as he would any other freehold interest. If the legislature were to propose the abolition of such a freehold interest in property, it would be necessary to pay proper compensation to the holder of that interest; that was a process the very expense of which might delay changes. Further, as other courts, such as the new county court of 1846, were created no clear pattern of responsibility for overall administration of the court system emerged. Yet it had long been reasonably clear that an efficient administration was as necessary to the reduction of undue expense and delay as the reform of procedure.

In 1810 commissioners reported that there were no saleable offices in Chancery or Exchequer but that there were several in King's Bench. The Chief Justice held the right of appointment to several such offices, including that of the Chief Clerk. In his turn the Chief Clerk held the right of appointment to three further offices. In practice the offices were usually performed by a deputy who received only a relatively small proprtion of the fees paid by litigants to that office. For example, the Chief Clerk received upon average £6280 per annum; the Deputy, who actually performed the duties of the office was paid only £200 per annum. In the case of offices performed by deputy, total receipts were slightly more than £15000 while payments to deputies amounted only to £1356. Similarly, in 1810 there had been 242 such offices in the ecclesiastical courts with a total net income of £297000; however, in 1834 there were just 100 such offices whose total net emoluments amounted to rather less than £98000.[18] That reduction in the number of such offices reflected a growing public disapproval of saleable offices and sinecures. 'Anything in the nature of a sinecure office, with emoluments attached to it at the public charge', reported a parliamentary committee in 1834,[19] 'is alike indefensible in principle, pernicious as a means of influence, and grievous as an undue addition to the general burthens of the Nation...' Further, some offices were virtually sinecures. For example, in Chancery the Six Clerks drew salaries which ranged from £885 per annum to £2000 per annum for their two months work in the year. A new age demanded change: administrative efficiency was a new national watchword.

However, old customs must be respected. Commissioners had commented in 1810 that when the sale of offices in the several courts at Westminster should be prohibited, provision might be made towards the payment of salaries to the Chief Justice and the other judges of King's Bench. That goal was achieved within a very few years. Yet the payment of adequate compensation to the holders of all offices was a matter which governments found it more difficult to arrange on occasion, and critics who objected to what they felt was overgenerous compensation were also influential.

Clearly such a system could lead to undue expense, although this should not be exaggerated. It had been a system which had served medieval governments well in that essential public duties were performed at no cost to the Crown. A reduction in the number of such offices would not necessarily lead, however, to any marked increase in administrative efficiency. Possibly a more important matter was the payment of court officials by fee for this method was not conducive to efficiency. This was true especially of the Master's office in Chancery. Holdsworth has described the procedure before the Masters as being 'almost inconceivably dilatory. For every attendance at a Master's office a warrant must be taken out, and a fee paid...the Master and his clerks were paid by fees for each piece of work done. Every warrant, every copy, every report, carried its fee. This led to the abuse of compelling the suitor to take office copies.'[20]

By 1840 there was a widespread acceptance, even among lawyers, of the view that the arrears in Chancery were so great as to amount almost to a denial of justice. There was some hope that, upon the abolition of Exchequer's equity jurisdiction, a Chancery with an enhanced judicial strength would be able to cope. That turned out not to be the case. In a forthright memorandum the Incorporated Law Society commented in 1851 that:

> 'The Masters' offices call for the greatest attention, for to them, as at present constituted, is to be attributed a large proportion of the delay which has been charged, sometimes mistakenly, but often justly, upon equity procedure. One main defect in these subordinate tribunals is, that no

18 Report of Commissioners on Saleable Offices in Courts of Law no. 358 (1810), Report on the Court of King's Bench no. 292 (1818), Report of Commissioners on Duties, Salaries and Emoluments of the Officers of the Court of Chancery no. 428 (1816), Report on the Court of Common Pleas no. 3 (1819-20), Report on the Court of Exchequer and Exchequer Chamber no. 125 (1822).

19 Report from Select Committee on Papers and Returns respecting the Nature, Tenure and Emoluments of all Sinecure Offices within the United Kingdom no. 519 (1834) p. 3.

20 W.S. Holdsworth *A History of English Law* vol 1, pp. 423 ff. and *Charles Dickens as a Legal Historian*.

sufficient or continuous control is exercised over the proceedings....Besides this, the machinery itself in the Masters' offices is in many cases uselessly expensive, and is not calculated to insure expedition, even where all the parties do their utmost to provide it.

A further mischief attributable to the present system is the serious loss of time and money in the transmission of causes from the Court to the Master, and from the Master back again to the Court...Nor does the evil end here: for if exceptions be taken to the finding of the Master, they can only be heard by the Court in their turn as a cause, involving nearly as much expense as an original hearing; and where the exceptions prevail, they frequently render the Master's report, and all that has been done by him, useless.

Nearly the whole of this delay and expense would be avoided by commencing and keeping the cause before one tribunal...No alteration in the practice can be effective unless the business of the Master's office be placed upon a different footing.'[1]

Over the years a number of important changes were introduced. The judges were paid by salary. Saleable offices, sinecure offices and offices which were virtually sinecures were reduced in number or even abolished altogether. There was a tendency to put the judge fully in charge of proceedings in his own court. For example, the Court of Chancery Act 1852 abolished the old office of Master and provided that the judges themselves, sitting in chambers, were to carry out the major portion of the work which the Masters had done in the past — subordinate clerks were to perform the remaining duties. The Lord Chancellor, with the advice of two other Chancery judges, was also empowered to make general rules and orders for the conduct of 'chamber' business. All such changes were valuable in themselves, yet they were introduced slowly and on the basis of no comprehensive principle or plan. For example, judges of the new county court were paid by fee until 1850. Judicial patronage especially was to linger for some time. Indeed, it existed even within the new county courts whose judges were alleged often to believe that their own sons were especially well fitted for the office of registrar. Unfortunately, that was a charge which led to the disgrace even of a Lord Chancellor, Lord Westbury. On the other hand judicial patronage in such matters was by no means indefensible. A case could be made for a judge being responsible in every way for the staff of his court as a part of his responsibility for the efficient running of that court. It was possible also to fear that serious evils might result if patronage were to be centralised. The centralising and efficiency seeking pressure of the new bureaucracy was largely unsympathetic to such arguments. A committee on civil service expenditure not only considered the question of the legal offices but concluded that there was considerable scope for economy with regard to them. In its view, the legal establishments were 'unduly expensive and it is clear that the absence of any uniform principle in their regulation must produce mischievous results.' As the lawyers suggested that that committee had concerned itself with cost to the exclusion of considerations of efficiency and that — as Selborne LC pointed out — no witness before it had been familiar with the actual duties of the legal departments, a separate commission into the

1 Report and Correspondence received by Her Majesty's Commissioners from Incorporated Law Society no. 216 (1852) p. 5.

legal departments was established.[2] The result was that, after a comprehensive inquiry and the passage of several years, a central office for the Supreme Court was established in 1879.

Patronage continued and was vested effectively in the head of each division. That was a practice which continued to lead to quite justified charges of nepotism. Even as late as 1915 a royal commission found that the qualifications required for administrative officers in the Supreme Court were often less than adequate. In addition personal influence was said to count unduly in securing nomination to a post. Yet the commissioners' recommendation that the power of appointment should be vested almost entirely in the Lord Chancellor, acting on advice, appears to have been rejected largely on the grounds that the rights of the Lord Chief Justice and of the President of the Probate Division could not be interfered with.[3] Some minor changes were implemented in 1925. Yet it was only in 1946 that it was provided that the clerks of assize were to be appointed by the Lord Chief Justice rather than by the judge who was the last on that particular circuit.

The administration of the inferior courts presented an equally confusing picture. Within the county courts it was the county court judge who until 1934 appointed to the important office of county court registrar. However, the tendency did appear to be to vest more responsibility in the Lord Chancellor's department.

b) *The Lord Chancellor's department*

The Lord Chancellor's department was by no means the only government department which was concerned with legal administration in some form. In many ways it was to become the most significant such department. Of course, the Lord Chancellor had always been charged with a considerable number of administrative duties. In Lord Eldon's day the Lord Chancellor had been attended by a number of officials who served him in a personal capacity.[4] In 1873 the principal secretary to the Lord Chancellor outlined his more important administrative duties as follows:

'letters from departments of state, from members of both Houses of Parliament, and others relating to bills dealing with legal subjects, from legal associations and private individuals suggesting alterations in the law, from applicants for patronage in legal and other civil departments, and from judges and officers of the courts (as well as from the Treasury) on the subjects of duties, salaries, and pensions. To investigate (when necessary) any matter of complaint affecting the administration of justice made to the Lord Chancellor, and to place papers relating to suitors and their claims before the solicitor to the suitor's fund under his lordship's direction. To take the Lord Chancellor's directions upon matters affecting the bankruptcy and county courts administration, and to communicate under those directions with the officer of the Treasury appointed to assist his lordship in such matters. To communicate constantly with the following legal

---

2 First Report of the Select Committee on Civil Services Expenditure no. 131 (1873) p. 131. Legal Department's Commission no. C-1245 (1875).
3 Sixth Report of the Royal Commission on the Civil Service 1915 (Cd. 7832) para. 4, D.N. Chester and F.M.G. Willson *The Organization of British Central Government 1914-1964* (2nd edn, 1968) chap. III.
4 Sir C. Schuster 'Problems of Legal Administration' *Politica* (1937) pp. 239, 337.

offices: — The Patent Office, the Crown Office, the Registrar's Office, the Record and Writ Office, the Lunacy Office, the Paymaster-General's Office, and to daily transact business with the clerks in the principal secretary's office. To assist the Lord Chancellor, in any way required by him, in the preparation and revision of legislative measures under his charge in the House of Lords. To examine the evidences of pedigree for the purpose of issuing the writ to enable a peer to take his seat in the House of Lords, and to report upon the same to the Lord Chancellor...To receive all memorials...relating to the magistracy of the country...[5]

Those duties were performed by the principal secretary assisted by a staff of four. Even in 1914 the Lord Chancellor's office had a staff of only ten, although it is true that by that time other departments which were answerable to the Lord Chancellor did employ considerable staffs, for the Lord Chancellor's duties were not confined to those listed above. There was the appointment of judges to the superior courts. After the Judicature Acts he was responsible for the Supreme Court offices, which in 1914 employed a staff of 900, and there were other like duties. The extent to which the Lord Chancellor, a transient political figure who was charged with so many duties and who yet had so small a personal staff, might be responsible for the efficient performance of the more mundane, yet vitally important, duties such as the smooth running of those courts for which he was responsible remained an open question. Ever since the Judicature Acts, however, there had been a tendency to make the legal departments responsible to the Lord Chancellor's office and to the Treasury.

c) *Other departments*

In 1914 the Treasury was responsible for the county courts. The Home Office made rules in respect of the keeping of accounts by justices' clerks and the payment of allowances to JP's and to witnesses.[6]

d) *Proposals for a Ministry of Justice*

Some critics of the legal system believed that the responsibility for the administration of justice lay in too many hands with the result that there was too much expense, too much delay and too little reform. It was suggested that the establishment of a Ministry of Justice would remedy such matters. That appeared to be a reasonable solution which was in line with much of the best contemporary thinking from Queen Victoria's earliest days on the throne. Health, Education and Trade, for example, became great departments of state. Would not law also benefit from such administrative concern?

Bentham advocated the creation of a Ministry of Justice.[7] In 1850 *The Times* even predicted that Baron Parke was to be created a Peer with a view to becoming a Minister of Justice. Further, *The Times* was quite clear as to what the duties of such a Minister were to be:

---

5   Legal Department's Commission no. C-1245 (1875) p. 230, q. 2547. Cf. First Report...Legal Departments Commission C-1109 (1874).
6   D.N. Chester and F.M.G. Willson *The Organization of British Central Government 1914-1964* (2nd edn, 1968) pp. 129 and 132.
7   Draft Constitutional Code — Works ix, 597; B.N. Cardozo 'A Ministry of Justice' (1921) 35 HLR 113, 114.

'(1) this officer would have under his especial care the final supervision of the instruments to which the seal is affixed, such as charters, letters patent, titles of honour, &c.

(2) He would preside over the administration of justice, that is to say, he would take care that the whole machinery devoted to that purpose was constantly in the highest state of efficiency, and that excessive arrears, amounting to a denial of justice, should not occur.

(3) He would concur with the judges of the several courts in framing and sanctioning rules of practice.

(4) He would frame the annual reports on the state of civil and criminal justice.

(5) He would preside over, or cause to be conducted, those inquiries into the state of the law which have been assigned from time to time to various commissions, but hitherto with very inadequate results, because no Minister of the Crown is personally responsible for the successful termination of such inquiries.

(6) He would be especially charged with the legal business of the government in the Upper House; with the legal bills, and particularly with measures for the reform of the law, which are now thrown upon men wholly engrossed with other pursuits, or absorbed in the administration of the laws they are called upon to alter or reform.

(7) He would regulate the assizes, gaol deliveries, and occasionally special commissions.

(8) He would direct government prosecutions, informations in charitable suits, &c. to be instituted by the Attorney-General.

(9) He would exercise the legal patronage of the Crown, in conjunction with the Prime Minister, and would be responsible for legal appointments at home and in the colonies.

(10) He would receive recommendations to mercy and similar communications from the judges, or petitions for pardon, and advise the Crown in the exercise of the prerogative of mercy — a duty of the highest importance, which now devolves on a Minister filling the office of Secretary of State, but who may be unacquainted with the rules of legal evidence and the administration of criminal justice.

The *Law Times* welcomed the proposals as containing 'the germ of real, practical, useful, and safe law reform,...in itself it will be the greatest improvement that has yet been accomplished in our legal institutions.'[8] Some years later the challenge was taken up by Napier, who had been active also in the field of legal education. Napier told the Commons in 1857 that responsibility for the administration of justice was 'distributed amongst a variety of officers', suggested that the time had come when 'a vigorous remedy is required for incoherencies, the delays, and the other defects of our legal and judicial system' and concluded that:

'the remedy for the existing evil...is the establishment of a central office, charged with the general supervision of our whole legal and judicial business, who would be able to watch the working of the existing system, communicate with the judges as to defects and requisite reforms, and

8 (1850) 16 LT 293.

receive, and if thought proper, act upon the suggestions which might be received from various quarters. At present, if anyone had any suggestions to make with respect to legal reform, there was no member of the government who had the power to receive and act upon such suggestions.'[9]

At much the same time the Law Amendment Society favoured the establishment of a Board of Justice on the same footing as the Board of Trade. The Lord Chancellor was to be its president but the department should be directly responsible to the Commons. J.F. Stephen also favoured the creation of such a department. The *Daily News* and the *Pall Mall Gazette* were also in favour. The most influential support was that given by the Lord Chancellor in 1863.[10]

The reformers were not united in their detailed proposals. Their case was all the weaker as a result. Collier had supported Napier in 1857 but had then gone on to differ from him in some respects. Similarly, Brougham had supported the Lord Chancellor in 1863 — but had then gone on to maintain that 'it would be entirely out of the question' to allow a Department of Justice to have anything whatever to do with revising the decisions of courts of law and equity, as the Lord Chancellor had suggested. It was such conflicts of opinion amongst the reformers themselves which led Palmerston to note ruefully that, although people were generally agreed upon the defects, there was 'every sort of difference of opinion' with regard to remedies.[11] Others tended either to dismiss or to reject the reformers' proposals. The *Solicitors' Journal*, suspicious at the slow progress of law reform, despite constant talk of it, suggested that 'the house and the government are at their wit's ends on the subjects of law amendment' and believed that if, 'by a trifling change', the Lords Justices' Court was to take all the appellate work, the Lord Chancellor would then be able to give appropriate time to preparing and revising new bills.[12] The *Jurist* took a still stronger line. It objected to the creation of new officers and any consequent reimbursement to the holders of offices which were to be abolished; suggested that this country would be borrowing such an institution 'from a country which we do not think Englishmen will better themselves by imitating'; and went on to object on constitutional grounds to any such institution having the power to approve all bills or to revise the decisions of the courts 'without the presence of counsel, or the usual checks on judicial indolence or misconduct.... Have those who bring forward such a plan as this reflected on the degradation to which it would expose the Bench?'[13]

Discussion next arose following the report in 1873 of a parliamentary committee on civil service expenditure which not only considered the question of the legal offices but concluded that there was considerable scope for economy with regard to them.[14] Subsequently, the Legal Department's Commission heard a certain amount of evidence upon the subject of a Ministry of Justice. The

9   144 Official Report (3rd series) cols. 539, 542. Cf. *Transactions of the National Association for the Promotion of Social Science* (1862) p. 199.

10   (1857) 1 Sol Jo 424, cf. (1868) 13 Sol Jo 109, 110, *General View of the Criminal Law of England* p. 322, (1857) 1 Sol Jo 426, (1870) 48 LT 347, 171 Official Report (3rd series) cols. 791 ff.

11   144 Official Report (3rd series) cols. 545, 792, 573.

12   (1857) 1 Sol Jo 181, contrast (1857) 1 Sol Jo 426, 462.

13   (1859) 5 Jur (n.s.) 332, (1863) 9 Jur (n.s.) 299, 300-301.

14   First Report of the Select Committee on Civil Services Expenditure no. 131 (1873) p. 131.

evidence of Childers was especially persuasive. He maintained that any such new department 'must be a department which is in a position to take the initiative, to take a continuous view of the business of the establishment, and to deal with these establishments as the head of any other great public department deals with his own establishments'. Further:

> 'the control over such large establishments ought to be in a responsible minister. I say a responsible minister, as distinct either from the indirect control of the Treasury or the control of the judges of the superior courts....I believe it is incompatible with the position of the learned judges of the superior courts that they should be held by parliament responsible for the administration of these enormous civil establishments. The theory of our constitution as to a judge is, that he should not be, except in a very limited sense indeed, responsible to parliament. It may be his duty to pronounce judgments, and to take proceedings which the House of Commons itself may not approve of. I think it is, therefore, quite inconsistent with the position of independence on the seat of judgment that the learned judges should have the other function of controlling the organisation of what are practically huge civil establishments, provided for by votes of the House of Commons. If this state of things be maintained the judges have two relations to Parliament: with respect to one-half of their duties the relation of almost entire independence,...and with respect to the other a position of ordinary dependence like any other minister. It appears to me, therefore, that parliament ought to have a responsible minister of the Crown — a "Minister of Justice",...to look to in regard to these establishments.'

A further member of parliament in reply to Baron Bramwell, denied that the Lord Chancellor and the judges necessarily knew more than anybody else about such matters: further, a law department ought not to be created — on the analogy of the War Office and the Admiralty — because:

> 'it is not constructed as a department. The judicial bench is not a part of the government, and therefore it is not constructed with a view to the fulfilment of administrative functions.'[15]

There the matter rested for some years. The proposals which had been made over the years were themselves the victims of the very lack of a reforming agency to which they had drawn attention and, perhaps, to a lack of enthusiasm for such changes among the leaders of the profession.[16]

Once again the matter was to be raised in the context of a more general inquiry. On this occasion it was the inquiry into the machinery of government which was headed by Lord Haldane, a future Lord Chancellor, and which reported in 1918. In words which would have been familiar to their nineteenth-century predecessors, they commented that there was no functionary who could

---

15   Minutes of Evidence taken by the Commissioners appointed to inquire into the Administrative Departments of the Courts of Justice no. C-1245 (1875) q. 9242, q. 9232, q. 9355-6 and q. 9347. H.C.E. Childers (1827-1896) was a former financial secretary to the Treasury (1865), a member of the Judicature Commission, first Lord of the Admiralty (1868-1871), and chancellor of the duchy of Lancaster (1872).

16   Lord Selborne, in his evidence to a select committee (see n. 15, above) and Baron Bramwell in terms of questions asked by him as a member of the Legal Department's Commission (n. 15, above), appear to me to indicate such a lack of enthusiasm, unless the Lord Chancellor were to be at the head of such a new administrative department.

properly be called a minister responsible for the subject of justice. They continued:

> 'We are impressed by the representations made by men of great experience, such as the President of the Incorporated Law Society, as to the difficulty of getting the attention of the government to legal reform, and as to the want of contact between those who are responsible for the administration of the work of the commercial courts and the mercantile community, and by the evidence adduced that the latter are, in consequence and progressively, withdrawing their disputes from the jurisdiction of the courts.'[17]

The Haldane Committee went on to recommend the establishment of a Ministry of Justice. That minister was to assume the responsibilities for legal administration which were then exercised by the Lord Chancellor and the Home Secretary. In addition he would have 'experts charged with the duty of watching over the necessities of law reform, and of studying the developments of the subject at home and abroad'. The Law Society welcomed the proposals but the Bar Council was opposed strongly to any changes in the responsibilities which were then exercised by the Lord Chancellor's office.[18] Haldane's recommedations were not accepted. In practice the responsiblities of the Lord Chancellor tended to increase e.g. in the question of the appointment of judges, although there was some clarification of the respective responsibilities of the Lord Chancellor and the Home Secretary.[19] Accordingly, even in mid-twentieth century the administrative arrangements still bore the stamp of their piecemeal origin — complaints of undue expense and delay continued. As yet, however, lawyers generally showed little public awareness of the vital role which an efficient administration could play in reducing such undue expense and delay — and of the benefits which that might confer upon both the public and the profession.[20]

17   Report of the Machinery of Government Committee 1918 (Cd. 9230) pp. 63, 64, cited by Cardozo (1850) 16 LT 293.

18   B. Abel-Smith and R. Stevens *Lawyers and the Courts* pp. 131-2.

19   D.N. Chester and F.M.G. Willson *The Organization of British Government 1914-1964* (2nd edn, 1968) p. 139.

20   For a modern statement of opposition to a Ministry of Justice by a future Lord Chancellor see G. Gardiner 'The Machinery of Law Reform in England' (1953) 69 LQR 46.

Chapter 5

Inferior civil courts

1 Local justice and legal values

The demand for local and inexpensive justice has long been present in our society. Blackstone recognised it; William Hutton, a commissioner of Birmingham's court of requests, although not a lawyer, also recognised it. He wrote in 1787 that nothing was so necessary:

> 'in the whole system of English jurisprudence, as a concise method of recovering property, and terminating disputes. This is the great hinge upon which the welfare of a nation turns. The more a people increase their trade, the more they must venture their property; how necessary is it then to enact such laws as will best secure that property, and, when in danger, point out the easiest method to recover it.[1]

Blackstone's hope had been that the ancient county court, which was already a part of the existing legal system, would be revived; Hutton's panacea was a national extension of the courts of requests, much less formal bodies, whose judges were often laymen. How much law, how much legal certainty, then, was needed in local courts? The lawyers, who tended to dominate the nineteenth-century inquiries of a legal nature, favoured the traditional approach, despite its admitted inconveniences. The common law commissioners acknowledged in 1833 that if justice in cases of small claims was to be administered

> 'according to the ordinary rules of evidence in a court regulated by certain rules of practice, the proceeding ceases to be remedial in its effect. If, on the other hand, all such restraints be dispensed with, the tribunal becomes arbitrary, and its decisions too vague and uncertain to be satisfactory.'[2]

Similarly, in 1855 the county court commissioners agreed after the formation of the new county court in 1846 that 'considerable expense and delay necessarily result' from bringing the machinery of the superior courts into full activity: in the county courts proceedings were 'simple, cheap, speedy and final'. Even so, they

---

1 W. Hutton *Courts of Requests* p. 9. See p. 113, below for courts of requests.
2 Fifth Report of the Commissioners...into the Practice and Proceedings of the Superior Courts of Common Law no. 247 (1833) p. 11.

were of the opinion that the 'inconveniences incident to the administration of justice in the superior courts are counter balanced by the greater certainty in the application of the rules of law, than can be expected in a tribunal so constituted as the county court.'[3] That conviction of the lawyers was a major factor when reform in this field was considered.

2   Forms of local court

There were many local courts. In their prime they exercised a quite bewildering jurisdiction over matters other than those which we would regard as being questions for the courts at the present day. Arrangement might be reached regarding the management of the common pasture, or various officers such as the aleconner or the boroughreeve might be appointed, in addition to the courts' undoubted jurisdiction in the types of dispute which are more familiar to us at the present day. The more familiar of the local courts were the court of pie poudre, the court baron, the court of the hundred and the county court.

a) *The court of pie poudre*
The court of pie poudre was said to have been instituted to do justice for all injuries done in that very fair or market and to owe its name either to the dusty feet of the suitors or because justice was done there as speedily as dust could fall from the foot.[4]

The injury must have been done, complained of, heard and determined within the compass of one and the same day.

b) *The court baron*
The court baron was a court incident to every manor in the kingdom. The lawyers regarded the court baron as being of two types, although the distinction may not always have been observed in practice. On the one hand there was the customary court of the copyholders i.e. those who held land of the lord of the manor by customary tenure in which their estates were transferred and other matters relative to their tenures were transacted. On the other hand there was the court of the freeholders of the manor; its most important business was to determine by writ of right all controversies relating to the right of lands within the manor, although it might also determine any personal actions where the debt or damages did not amount to forty shillings.

c) *The court of the hundred*
The hundred court was essentially a larger court baron, being held for all the inhabitants of a particular hundred instead of a manor.

Even in Blackstone's day both the court baron and the hundred court had fallen into equal disuse with regard to the trial of actions, as causes were liable to removal from those courts. For example, proceedings on a writ of right could be

---

3   First Report of the Commissioners appointed to inquire into the State of the County Courts no. 1914 (1854-55) p. 24.
4   3 Bl Com (5th edn) 32, S. and B. Webb *Manor and Borough*.Yet Holdsworth writes that the court was in a state of 'total decay' in the sixteenth and seventeenth centuries: W.S. Holdsworth *History of English Law* vol 1, p. 540. Cf. Report from the Select Committee on Municipal Corporations no. 344 (1833) q. 2744-79 and q. 3657.

removed into the county court by a precept from the sheriff called a tolt, while proceedings in all other actions could be removed into the superior courts by the king's writ of pone, or *accedas ad curiam* according to the nature of the suit. In addition their proceedings could be reviewed by writ of false judgment. Yet in 1833 the common law commissioners treated them as existing institutions.[5]

d) *The county court*

The county court existed in every county. It was not a court of record but was incident to the jurisdiction of the sheriff. It held pleas of debt or damages under the value of forty shillings. It might also hold plea of many real actions and might entertain all personal actions to any amount by virtue of a special writ called a justicies which empowered the sheriff, for the sake of dispatch, to do the same justice in his county court as might otherwise be had at Westminster. However, the fact that the general jurisdiction had long been limited to 40 shillings only, now a relatively small sum in the light of the fall in the value of money, made the court less attractive to suitors. In addition, quite often the real actions and even the suits commenced by justicies might be removed from the county court by a defendant without giving security. Accordingly, the additional jurisdiction was little more than nominal. In Blackstone's day the county courts for the most part had fallen into disuse and no doubt merited the judgment of commissioners in 1833 to the effect that they had fallen into 'a state of comparative inutility'.[6]

e) *Inadequacy of local courts*

The local courts were quite inadequate for the transaction of the numerous civil disputes for which they ought to have provided a forum. That inadequacy was of long standing. It can be traced back to the interpretation of the Statute of Gloucester (1278). The statutory intention had been simply that the judges of the superior courts should not be required to deal with cases in which less than 40 shillings was in dispute. However, the judges interpreted the statute to mean that the county courts might not hear any personal actions in which the sum in dispute exceeded 40 shillings. Here and there some county courts may have served their areas well from time to time, yet the overall picture was one of decay and disuse.

f) *The court of requests*

A popular local court at this time was the court of requests. Accordingly, although Blackstone classified such courts as being of special jurisdiction, it will be appropriate to consider these courts for the recovery of small debts at this point. Modelled upon a court established in London during the reign of Henry VIII whereby two aldermen and twelve commoners were appointed to be commissioners to sit 'in the Court of Requests, commonly called the Court of Conscience, in the Guildhall' to hear and determine all matters of debt not amounting to the sum of 40 shillings, it should be distinguished from the better known and more powerful Court of Requests. Each court was instituted by a particular

---

5 Fifth Report of the Commissioners...into the Practice and Proceedings of the Superior Courts of Common Law no. 247 (1833) pp. 9 ff.

6 Fifth Report no. 247 (1833) p. 6, 3 Bl Com (5th edn) 33-5, H.J. Stephen *New Commentaries on the Laws of England* (4th edn, 1858) pp. 377 ff. On the forms of action see p. 132, below and chap. 12.

Act of Parliament. After 1747, however, such Acts were no longer entitled 'Acts for erecting courts of conscience' but were usually titled 'Acts for the more easy and speedy recovery of small debts'. Such Acts invariably preserved all older jurisdictions whether ecclesiastical, manorial, communal or municipal. In Blackstone's day it was usual in these courts to determine a case in accordance with 'equity and good conscience'.[7] In later years, however, it became more usual to declare that law should be followed. As local courts, the courts of requests could only exercise a strictly local jurisdiction. In Birmingham, for example, the jurisdiction of the court extended only over the manor of Birmingham while the town had expanded far beyond those limits. It was said to be an everyday practice for debtors to remove a few streets with a view to escaping the jurisdiction. The court might execute judgment against either the body or the goods: from 1786 it was provided that imprisonment should be for no longer than 20 days for up to 20 shillings and up to 40 days imprisonment for up to 40 shillings.

William Hutton, a commissioner of the Birmingham court of requests in the later eighteenth century, gives us a lively picture of a busy and popular court. Other portraits of the Birmingham court were less flattering.[8] What was clear was that as the wealth and numbers of the population increased and as the towns and cities grew in size, a demand for local and inexpensive justice had never been more merited. The common law commissioners summarised the national situation well enough in 1835:

> 'The rapid increase of population, wealth and commerce has given rise to extensive credit, and has thus naturally increased to a great extent the claims on public justice: new and complicated relations have given rise to a system of laws adapted to the exigencies of commerce, and have rendered necessary a considerable change in the practical administration of the law.'[9]

The circuit system had long since virtually destroyed any efficient system of local justice.[10] The assizes, with their pomp and ceremony, visited all parts of the country regularly. Inevitably, local courts were regarded as inferior to them. Yet the justice administered in the superior courts was far from being of the speedy and inexpensive character which was desirable in so many suits, at all events when the sum in issue was relatively small.

3   Possible reforms

Clearly all was far from well with the local courts in general. Lord Althorp promoted several bills during the period 1821-25 with a view to securing the speedier recovery of small debts in the county courts. In 1824 one such bill secured a third reading in the Commons: in the Lords, however, it was held up by the formidable Lord Ellenborough. Althorp then persuaded Sir Robert Peel, the Home Secretary, to introduce a later bill, as Althorp believed that a cabinet officer

7   3 Bl Com (5th edn) 81, W.H.D. Winder 'The Courts of Requests' (1936) 52 LQR 369.
8   J. Parkes *The State of the Courts of Requests and the Public Office in Birmingham* (pamphlet), R. Jenkinson *First Proceedings in... Watkins v Jenkinson...*(pamphlet).
9   Fifth Report...into the Practice and Proceedings of the Superior Courts of Common Law no. 247 (1833) p. 17.
10   On the circuit system see p. 164, below.

would have a better chance of getting the measure through.[11] This bill would have extended the jurisdiction of the existing county courts from £2 to £10. Further proceedings were held up in 1828 until a means of compensating the holders of certain sinecure offices was devised. It was left to Brougham, who addressed himself to the question in 1830, to give a fresh impetus to reform in this field. He told the Commons:

> 'If a man were told that there was a country, in which, in order to recover a debt of 61, or 71, it was necessary that the creditor should begin with the expenditure of 601, or 701 of his own money...I think the man who was so told would at once assert, that, whatever other advantages such a country might possess, it was unfortunate in its system of law....That it must be a poor country, he would think quite obvious — of no commercial power — of no extent of capital — of no density of population....Yet this was England.'[12]

Brougham's view was that the jurisdiction of the old county courts should be extended from £2 to £100 and that they should be presided over by judges of some learning and skill who should be paid accordingly. Little opposition was expressed in the Commons and the bill, duly amended, had a second reading in June 1830. There was no opposition to it on its first reading in the Lords in December 1830. However, an article in the *Legal Observer* of 1831 illustrated the opposition which the bill was soon to face. It claimed that Brougham's proposals would subvert the existing system of administration of justice, for proper local judges could not be obtained, or so it was said, for a mere £1500 per annum — there would be a disastrous effect upon the metropolitan bar; and there was, too, the question of the patronage which would accrue to the Lord Chancellor of the day in the appointment of such judges.[13] Accordingly, when Brougham, who was now Lord Chancellor, introduced his bill again in March 1833, after meeting the demands of the Reform Bill, it met with determined opposition.

Meanwhile, in April 1833, the Fifth Report of the Common Law Commissioners, which dealt with inferior courts, had been published. It is an authoritative document. Of the hundred courts and courts baron the commissioners commented that incompetent juries, 'an ill-regulated course of pleading, and the practice of allowing costs wholly disproportioned to the cause of action, and which frequently amounted to 71 or 81 on each side, though no greater sum than 40s can be recovered, render these courts inoperative for any useful purpose'. Of the county court the commissioners' view was that the

> 'limitation of jurisdiction in point of amount; the annual change of the officers who preside in these courts; the want of competent juries; the lengthened pleadings, heavy costs, unnecessary delay, and a vicious system of practice, attended with enormous abuse and oppression committed by bailiffs in the execution of process by improper agents, render these courts

11 N. Gash *Mr. Secretary Peel*, A.L. Cross 'Old English Local Courts and the Movement for their Reform' (1942) 30 Michigan Law Review 369, Minutes of Evidence taken before the Select Committee on the Bill for Preventing Delays and Expenses in the Proceedings of County Courts, and for the more easy and speedy Recovery of Small Debts in England and Wales no. 276 (1825).
12 24 Official Report (new series: 1830) cols. 244-245.
13 (1831) 1 Legal Observer 104, 105.

inefficient for the administration of justice, and the subject of general complaint'.

Nor did the courts of requests escape censure. Blackstone had criticised their wide discretionary powers and the absence of a jury. The commissioners were of like mind. 'So much is left to the discretion of those who decide the cause', reported the commissioners in 1834, 'that they ought to be persons of considerable ability and learning to perform their functions with propriety. But they consist, in general, of commissioners whose pursuits in life can give no assurance of their possessing these qualities.' They continued:

'There is a suspicion, too, (whether well or ill-founded it is difficult to determine) that their decisions are often wanting in impartiality.

We may observe, that the facility of obtaining execution against the goods and even the person of the debtor, in courts of request, has been represented to us as injurious, by encouraging the giving of credit, and the incurring of debts to a mischievous extent, and that whilst the labourer is obtaining credit for necessaries at an enhanced price, he is enabled to waste his ready money in procuring indulgences which he cannot obtain on credit...

We have also to observe, that the power given to these courts of imprisoning debtors for small sums is productive of very distressing and injurious consequences. Instances have occurred of the imprisonment of defendants for several weeks in respect of debts to the amount of 18d. or 2s.; and the certain effect of the practice of imprisonment in such cases is irreparable injury to the habits, feelings and morals of the lower classes of society.'

The commissioners' overall conclusions were clear enough, namely:

'the present inferior courts are more or less open to some or all of the following objections:-

That their jurisdiction is in general too limited in point of amount and local extent.

That frequently suits are removable into the higher courts without security.

The want of competent judges and juries.

The want of efficient inferior ministers to serve and execute process.

The want of sufficient and simple process to compel an appearance.

The use of complicated and expensive pleadings.

The distance of the place of trial from the residence of the parties and witnesses.

The want of sufficient means to compel the attendance of witnesses.

Delay.

The facility of evading execution.

The abuses occasioned by entrusting the execution of process to improper agents, for whose misconduct no superior is responsible.

The want of appeal.

The expense of the proceedings as compared with the amount of the demand.'

In the commissioners' view the defects of the inferior courts as then established were so numerous and complicated that it would be easier to devise new institutions than to introduce effectual improvements into the existing courts.

Accordingly, they recommended that the whole kingdom should be divided into districts for the purpose of establishing local courts upon an uniform system. The utmost distance of parties from the nearest place of trial should not exceed 20 to 25 miles. They suggested £20 as the limit to the jurisdiction of such courts, a sum which in their view was much less in real terms than the £2 which was the limit to the jurisdiction of the old county court. Such jurisdiction should also be exclusive rather than concurrent with that of other inferior courts. Further, it was most important that their judges should be persons of learning and experience and that their tenure of office should be permanent: they suggested that barristers of at least ten years standing should be selected for the office. They believed also that the advantages to be derived from the permanent residence of the judge within his district far outweighed the risk of any disadvantage to the suitors from the local prejudices or feelings of the judge: in particular such a judge would be able to regulate and to determine the interlocutory business which would be occurring continually.[14]

Were the commissioners, distinguished lawyers all, justified in their criticisms of the inferior courts and in particular of the courts of requests? Certainly, the popularity of such courts did not diminish in the years following the publication of the Report. Winder states that between the years 1835 and 1846, both exclusive, 49 Acts establishing such courts were passed. Several of those who gave evidence to the commissioners were reasonably well pleased with the existing courts of requests. John Turner of Birmingham believed that the Birmingham court of requests 'has of late years been much better conducted, by a more vigilant attention to its management' and that the hundred court was unnecessary in Birmingham by the sufficiency of the court of requests,[15] although other Birmingham men of that period and later spoke with horror of both courts. It can be agreed, too, that the proposals, radical though they were in some ways, of the distinguished lawyers who formed the commission, showed in their concern for the qualifications of the judge rather less of a concern for inexpensive, albeit substantial justice, and rather more concern for traditional legal values. Certainly the judge of such a court must be worthy of respect, yet need he also be of some legal standing? In the criminal courts, after all, lay magistrates exercised quite considerable powers. At all events Brougham's Bill was defeated on its third reading in July 1833. The grounds of opposition were varied. There was some opposition to placing extensive patronage in the form of fresh judicial appointments into the hands of the Lord Chancellor. The key objection appears to have been that the proposals would downgrade the metropolitan Bar. It was alleged that local bars would be inferior in quality. Yet, as judges of the superior courts were selected from the Bar, it was claimed that there was a strong public interest in maintaining the quality of the Bar.[16]

Despite the Report's trenchant criticisms of the existing local courts and the fact that the commissioners' views were close to those of Brougham, no more was done for over a decade. Legal business continued to go of necessity to the superior courts in London — and it appeared that the local courts were to

14 Fifth Report of the Commissioners...into the Practice and Proceedings of the Superior
     Courts of Common Law no. 247 (1833) pp. 9, 12, 5-6, 18, 20-21.
15 (1936) 52 LQR 369, 381, Fifth Report (above) Appendix (2nd series) p. 83A.
16 (1833) 6 Legal Observer 1, 2, 35.

remain unreformed. However, in 1842 it was decided to extend the bankruptcy jurisdiction throughout the country. Accordingly, there was a need for efficient local courts, if only to administer the bankruptcy jurisdiction. In fact the opportunity was taken to adopt the old proposals regarding local courts. So it was that in 1846 the new county court was established with little or no opposition offered to the principle of the measure, despite the fears of many lawyers for the future of the profession as a result of its enactment.

4   A modern county court

a) *The new court is established*
The title of the Act of 1846 'for the more easy recovery of small debts and demands in England' set the bounds of the role which the modern county court was to fulfil. The Act provided that each county might be divided into districts. In each of the districts so appointed, and at such towns and places therein as Order in Council might specify, the county court was to be held at least once every calendar month or at such other interval as should be directed by a principal secretary of state. Broadly speaking, the districts coincided approximately with the poor law unions — alterations were made subsequently by orders in council under successive County Court Acts. By 1855 there were 60 different divisions or circuits and to each a judge was appointed. At that time there were in all 495 districts distributed in numbers ranging from one to 13 among the divisions or circuits. A suit might be commenced in any district in which the defendant, or one of the defendants, should dwell or carry on business at the time or (by leave of the court) in any district in which he should have dwelt or carried on business within six calendar months before, or (by leave of the court) in any district in which the cause of action arose, without regard to the place of residence or business. The court was to have all the jurisdiction and powers of the old county court for the recovery of debts and demands. As modified in the early years of the court, the essence of that jurisdiction was as follows.

The court had jurisdiction over all personal actions where the debt, damage or demand claimed was not more than £50, with the exception of the action of ejectment for the recovery of land, and of actions in which the title to any corporeal or incorporeal hereditaments should be in question or in which the validity of any devise, bequest, or limitation, under any will or settlement might be disputed, or for any malicious prosecution, or for any libel or slander, or for criminal conversation, or for seduction, or breach of promise of marriage. By agreement in writing of both parties, the jurisdiction was also made capable of embracing all actions whatever which might be brought in any superior court of common law. In order to encourage litigation in the county courts with regard to small accounts it was provided that if in actions of covenant, debt, detinue or assumpsit (not being for breach of promise of marriage) the plaintiff should recover no more than £20; or if in actions for a wrong, independent of trespass, trover, or case (not being for malicious prosecution, libel, slander, or seduction) the plaintiff should recover no more than £5 — then the plaintiff should have judgment to recover such sum only, without costs, unless the court were of opinion that there was sufficient reason for bringing the action there. In addition the county court had a varied auxiliary jurisdiction over a number of miscellaneous matters. Features of the court were the extension of its jurisdiction over the years and that it exercised jurisdictions not only in law and equity but even in the quite complex field of bankruptcy: certain county courts also exercised a jurisdiction in admiralty matters. The judges were to be appointed by the Lord Chancellor who might also, if he thought fit, remove any such judge for inability or misbehaviour.

The procedure in the county court was far different from that which was known in the superior courts. A most notable feature was the absence of pleadings. Secondly, the parties to the action were competent witnesses i.e. might give evidence on their own behalf even in 1847 in the county courts, although it would be some years before this was possible in the superior courts. Thirdly, the courts were accessible not only because they were local but because the court office was open on most days and it was possible for litigants, or intending litigants, to go there for assistance. Finally, although the parties might appear in person, solicitors were entitled by statute to audience as advocates — a factor which tended to reduce the costs of the litigant who wished to be legally represented.[17]

There is some inconclusive academic dispute as to whether this was essentially a continuation of the old county court, a new county court, or a fusion of the two.[18] Undoubtedly, however, the modern county court was successful in recovering small debts reasonably expeditiously and at relatively little cost. Indeed, the courts' very success in that sphere masks the fact that its potential in other areas lay undeveloped.

The courts set about their work with such enthusiasm that by the end of 1847 there had been 429215 plaints, in claims totalling £1352035, the average amount claimed being three guineas. According to Smith,[19] this was a typical figure in the years which followed. Smith also states that plaintiffs appear to have succeeded in realising just 50 per cent of the amount they claimed during this period i.e. about £33m out of £66m and that the claims were, indeed, for the most part, small debts. Certainly the Commission on the County Courts which reported in 1855 seemed well satisfied with their work, commenting that:

> 'the experiment has been eminently successful, and benefits have been conferred on the community by means of these courts, which it is perhaps difficult to exaggerate. Honest claims have been enforced, and injuries have been redressed, which the expense, distance and delay incident to the proceedings of the superior courts, placed in effect beyond the power of the law. Facility to enforce rights has checked the commission of wrongs, and thus a more desirable state of credit and morality has been produced.'[20]

Yet, the commission was not inclined to recommend any marked extension of the courts' jurisdiction.

Ought that jurisdiction to have been extended? When George Bramwell QC

---

17 Judge Snagge 'Fifty Years of the English County Courts' (1897) 42 Nineteenth Century 560, S. Rosenbaum 'Studies in English Civil Procedure' (1915) 64 Univ of Pennsylvania Law Review 357, 472, 583.

18 W.S. Holdsworth *History of English Law* vol 1, p. 191, T.F.T. Plucknett *A Concise History of the Common Law* (5th edn, 1956) p. 208.

19 H. Smith 'The Resurgent County Court in Victorian Britain' (1969) 13 AJLH 128.

20 First Report of the Commissioners appointed to inquire into the State of the County Courts no. 1914 (1854-55) p. 25.

gave evidence to the commission and had not favoured extending the jurisdiction, it was put to him that '...in the year 1851 which was the year after the
jurisdiction had been extended from 20l to 50l, there were 13000 plaints
entered in the county courts for cases between 20l and 50l, that about 8000 of
those cases were tried; that there were 30 appeals, and that in only eight cases was
the judgment reversed'. Bramwell was unmoved. In his view the question was
rather that suitors should be encouraged to sue in the superior courts — on the
grounds that it was in the public interest that the law should be kept certain in
this way. That view may have been quite common among lawyers, especially
barristers, although a solicitor in extensive practice did tell the commission that
he favoured granting the county courts exclusive jurisdiction in tort cases up to
the amount of £50.[1] The result was that, although the jurisdiction was amended
frequently over the years, no substantial change was affected. Accordingly, the
discussion concerning the jurisdiction continued. In 1868 the *Westminster
Review* analysed 86 causes which had been entered for trial at the spring assizes
for Surrey. In some 60 cases, the *Review* stated, the cause was found not to be fit
for trial. Of the 26 cases for trial — almost all of them cases of debt or contract
under £100 or of tort under £50 — few were fit for trial in the superior courts for
they turned upon questions of disputed fact or the credibility to be given to
witnesses. In the opinion of the *Review*, such figures showed that actions were
brought needlessly in the superior courts, probably with a view to discouraging
the honest suitor concerned at the expense involved.[2]

In the light of the sporadic yet continuing discussion regarding the courts'
jurisdiction, it is surprising that some aspects of the existing jurisdiction were
neglected. Smith has pointed out that the tort litigation which one would expect
to have been heard in the county courts as a result of accidental injury and death
on the roads and railways and in factories and mines was not being heard there,
although in 1870 a distinguished lawyer stated that half the time of the nisi prius
courts was devoted to accident cases. Why was this? Smith suggests that it may be
that plaintiffs sought the more ample damages which could be awarded by the
superior courts. There was, too, the rule regarding venue, a railway company's
place of business being deemed to be its office so that a litigant might in any event
be faced with the costs of bringing an action either in the place of the accident or
of that office. There was also a general lack of awareness, apparently even
among the factory inspectorate, of the provisions of the County Courts Act and
the interest of many in the legal profession in preserving more or less intact the
existing jurisdiction of the superior courts.

b) *The Judicature Commission*

The judicature commissioners missed the opportunity both to establish the
respective roles of the superior courts and the county courts and to set fresh
bounds to the jurisdiction of the county courts. Six commissioners did not sign
the report on county courts at all; a further nine commissioners, although they
signed the report, expressed varying degrees of dissent. Of those who did not sign
at all, the opinion of a distinguished lawyer, Blackburn J, is especially
interesting. He maintained that change might destroy the efficiency of the

1   First Report (above) p. 151, q. 1316, p. 59, q. 15.
2   (1868) 34 Westminster Review 319.

county court as a court for the recovery of small debts. Further, he doubted the expediency of setting up such an intermediate class of court at all as he attached much importance:

> 'to the keeping up the great central bar of England. The only real practical check on the judges is the habitual respect which they pay to what is called "the opinion of the profession", and the same powerful body forms, as I think, a real and the principal check on the abuse of patronage by the government.'[3]

c) *1878-1950*

In the view of one critic the report of the Judicature Commission had dealt a death blow to reform for that generation. Yet discussion regarding the jurisdiction rumbled on. In 1878 most witnesses before a select committee favoured an extension of the common law jurisdiction, although the President of the Law Society not only opposed any such move but asserted that the court was unpopular and that there was a want of public confidence in it.[4] Other reasons advanced for not extending the jurisdiction were that as a general rule the county court judges were not competent to exercise an increased jurisdiction, that they were 'out of touch with the other judges and leaders of the legal profession', that there would be an increase in judicial salaries and it was felt that the interpolation of heavy cases in the county court would lead to the interests of small suitors being neglected. Indeed, the Lord Chancellor's committee reported in 1909 that the county courts were already 'heavily taxed' in terms of the burden of work which had been thrust upon them. This was true enough.[5] The statistics showed that the bulk of litigation was carried on in the county court. Judge Snagge pointed out in 1904 that while the volume of plaints etc. entered in the county court had for nearly half a century increased almost exactly in the same ratio as the population, and while the Chancery Division had pursued the even tenor of its way, the number of writs etc. which had been issued in the Queen's Bench Division, after increasing in proportion with the population until 1876, suddenly dropped from 127000 in that year to 83000 in 1858, had never since reached an average of 100000, and was then less than 68000. Judge Snagge commented:

> 'The remarkable drop in the number of writs in the Queen's Bench Division which occurred between 1867 and 1873 was due partly to the paralysis of commercial business...but chiefly to the effect of an Act of Parliament, passed in 1867, which provided that costs should not be recoverable in the superior courts where the cause of action, if in contract, should involve an amount of less than £20, or if in tort of less than £10.'

The judge also pointed out that the quinquennial average of cases tried in the Queen's Bench Division had gone down. In 1895 it had been 5098; in 1901 it was 3623. Two-thirds of the ordinary business of the King's Bench Division had

---

3 Judicature Commission: Second Report of the Commissioners no. C-631 (1872) p. 26, (1872) 16 Sol Jo 798.

4 County Courts Jurisdiction (No. 2) Bill: Reports from the Select Committee no. 267 (1878).

5 Report of the Lord Chancellor's Committee on County Court Procedure no. 71 (1909) p. 15, Second Interim Report of the Business of Courts Committee (Cmd. 4471) p. 47, (1889) 5 LQR 3. Cf. (1902) 18 LQR 237 and (1893) 9 LQR 321.

drifted to the county courts. Would those people really go back to a more expensive High Court?[6]

There were a number of piecemeal extensions of the jurisdiction. The Employers' Liability Act 1880 introduced a considerable new jurisdiction to the county court. Indeed, in 1887 it was said that the functions of the county courts were regulated by ten exclusively county courts' Acts and also by 42 other Acts which incidentally gave jurisdiction to, and imposed duties upon, the county court. The County Courts Act 1888 sought to remove inconsistencies. Yet the piecemeal process continued. In 1909 a committee pointed out just how varied and anomalous the jurisdiction was. There was the jurisdiction in admiralty cases, under the Workmen's Compensation Acts, and under the Bankruptcy Acts outside London where every kind of complication arose and the jurisdiction was unlimited. On the other hand, the jurisdiction on an ordinary contract such as a Bill of Exchange was limited to £100.[7]

Critics continued to press for an extension of that jurisdiction. In particular, there was constant pressure for a jurisdiction in divorce to be conferred upon the county court. The voices of those who were opposed to any liberalisation of the divorce laws were added in this respect to the customary objections to extending the jurisdiction. Yet, quite apart from divorce, there were ample grounds for extending the jurisdiction. In 1934 the *Solicitors' Journal* declared roundly that unless the jurisdiction of the county courts were extended further there would be no effective relief of congestion in the High Court or cheapening of the administration of justice.[8] Predictably, the Hanworth Committee had refused in 1933 to recommend any increase in the limit to the jurisdiction. Their reason was familiar enough: the primary function of the county courts was the collection of small debts and an extended jurisdiction would hamper that function. Nor was the committee prepared to recommend that money be spent on improving the court accommodation which would be necessary, if the jurisdiction were to be extended.[9] Accordingly, the jurisdiction remained substantially unchanged. Future inquiries tended to focus, sensibly enough, upon reducing the amount of time which litigants were compelled to wait at court.[10] As a result procedures were recommended which in many cases the best county courts had already adopted. Accordingly, even in 1950 the relationship of the county court to the superior courts was not based upon any clear pattern. The county courts had been instituted on a national basis. Yet for the most part their development, especially the extensions of the jurisdiction, had been no more than a piecemeal response to the particular demands of the day. The granting of jurisdiction under the Workmen's Compensation Acts had been rather more imaginative. Unfortunately, it had not been a success for reasons which lay largely outside the control of the county courts. Moreover, the county court had grown despite what

6   Judge Snagge 'Fifty Years of the English County Courts (1897) 42 Nineteenth Century 560, (1904) 48 Sol Jo 669, 696.
7   (1887) 3 LQR 1, Report of the Committee appointed by the Lord Chancellor to inquire into...County Court Procedure no. 71 (1909).
8   (1934) 78 Sol Jo 144. Cf. (1933) 175 LT 203, 222, 351, 366. On county court costs see also (1948) 206 LT 220, 236, 254, 281.
9   Second Interim Report of the Business of Courts Committee (Cmd. 4471) pp. 48-9.
10   Committee on County Court Procedure: First Interim Report (Cmd. 7468/48), (1948) 11 MLR 470.

was at best often no more than lukewarm approval on the part of senior members of the Bar. Yet the county court had grown; no serious criticism had been made of the quality of justice which was administered in it; it was a court which was clearly popular with litigants. It had been a success.

5 Magistrates' courts

In 1878 a certain amount of publicly expressed concern for the wife who suffered an aggravated assault at the hands of her husband persuaded parliament to confer a civil jurisdiction upon magistrates' courts. Henceforth, justices of the peace before whom a husband had been so convicted might, if satisfied that the future safety of the wife was in peril, order that the wife should be no longer bound to cohabit with her husband. Such order was to have the force and effect in all respects of a decree of judicial separation on the ground of cruelty. Further, the court might award a weekly sum to the wife by way of maintenance and might also give to the wife the legal custody of any children of the marriage under the age of ten years. This considerable provision was the result of no legislative forethought. What happened was simply that a straightforward matrimonial bill, which had nothing whatever to do with marital violence, was introduced into the House of Lords. Lord Penzance, a former President of the Court for Divorce and Matrimonial Causes, then obtained leave to introduce the clause which offered protection to the wife. Apparently Penzance had been influenced considerably by the powerful arguments of Frances Power Cobbe in her persuasive article upon 'Wife Torture'.

It is remarkable that so important a provision was undertaken by a private member during the course of a debate upon a substantially different matter. It was unfortunate that what amounted to a matrimonial remedy should attach to criminal proceedings, although it was clearly more convenient and cheaper for the wife to secure an order from the court which had convicted her husband rather than to petition the High Court for a judicial separation. Yet the measure was successful. In succeeding years the powers of magistrates to grant maintenance and separation orders were increased. In 1907, 6734 wives obtained separation orders. It is true that the Gorell Commission was unhappy that a court, whose main duties were of a criminal character, should entertain such applications. However, during the twentieth century this jurisdiction was to become firmly established.[11]

6 Quarter sessions

Quarter sessions exercised a considerable jurisdiction in both civil and criminal matters. Among the most important and typical heads of the civil jurisdiction were questions of administration such as the state of the roads and of the bridges as well as questions relating to carriers' rates and the wages of servants. However, in 1888 the county councils took over a great deal of the civil jurisdiction of quarter sessions. Perhaps the most important of the remaining duties of quarter

11 Reports to the Secretary of State for the Home Department on the State of the Law relating to Brutal Assaults no. C-11.38 (1875), (1878) 32 Contemporary Review 55, Report of the Royal Commission on Divorce and Matrimonial Causes 1912 (Cd. 6478). See also chap. 15.

sessions were those which went to liquor licensing and to the appointment of a prison visiting committee of justices. There was also a considerable appellate jurisdiction which included questions such as bastardy orders, rating appeals and settlement of poor persons.[12]

7   Borough and local courts of record

Many local courts of record had been established either by royal charter, or by local and personal Acts of Parliament or by prescription. Forty-two such courts had been abolished in 1883. During the twentieth century most such courts were in abeyance yet the corporation in question might still be compelled by mandamus to hold the court. In 1931, 17803 plaints were issued in such courts.[13]

8   Hundred and manorial courts

For the most part the civil jurisdiction of the hundred court was abolished in 1867 when statute provided that no action which could be brought in a county court should thereafter be brought in a hundred court not being a court of record.[14]

---

12   8 *Halsbury's Laws of England* (2nd edn) 621-2. For petty sessions see chap. 7.
13   Ibid. 669.
14   Ibid. 764.

Chapter 6

Superior courts of civil jurisdiction

1 Introduction

We will now consider the superior courts of public and general jurisdiction, whose function was to remedy civil wrongs. Perhaps the most outstanding feature to the modern eye of the eighteenth-century system is that such courts exercised quite separate jurisdictions which often both competed, and even clashed, with each other.

2 The separation of the jurisdictions

In Blackstone's view the division of labour between the courts worked well.[1] Yet all was not entirely well with the theoretically separate roles of the courts of common law, Chancery, and the ecclesiastical courts. Blackstone himself wrote that 'it seems the height of judicial absurdity, that in the same cause between the same parties, in the examination of the same facts, a discovery by the oath of the parties should be permitted on one side of Westminster Hall, and denied on the other'.[2] Moreover, the legal and equitable jurisdictions might conflict to the extent that by the use of the injunction a court of equity might deprive the plaintiff at law of the benefit of the judgment which he may have obtained at great cost.[3]

The Law Amendment Society summed the question up convincingly in a paper which it presented to the Home Office in 1851.[4] First, the Society argued, there was the uncertainty of the jurisdictions. They cited a case in which several shareholders of a company filed a bill against the directors, alleging their continuance in office to be illegal and praying for an injunction. The defendant

1 3 Bl Com (5th edn) 59-60.
2 3 Bl Com (5th) edn 382.
3 (1827) 45 Edinburgh Review 469.
4 First Report of the Special Committee (of the Law Amendment Society) on the Policy of the Distinction between Law and Equity Procedure no. 223 (1851). Contrast W.S Holdsworth *History of English Law* vol 12, pp. 583 ff.

demurred on the ground that the remedy was at law: after seven days argument, the Vice-Chancellor of England overruled the demurrer, thus establishing the right of the plaintiffs to sue in equity. After five days argument, the Chancellor reversed the judgment of the Vice-Chancellor, and allowed the demurrer, thus deciding that the plaintiff's remedy was at law. The result was that despite the enormous expense of these proceedings, nothing whatever had been determined as to the merits, and the plaintiffs were left to renew their suit anew in a court of law, with a possibility of being met there with an argument that their remedy, if any, was in equity. Secondly, there was the incompleteness of the remedy. In many cases equity would not give relief until the plaintiff had established his right at law e.g. in the instances of bills for the delivery up of title-deeds or for an injunction against a nuisance. Could any reason be given, asked the Society, 'why the court which decides the right should not establish it, or why the court which establishes it should not decide it?' Moreover, there was equity's practice of sending issues of fact to be tried by a jury in a court of law, for courts of equity did not make use of a jury. By way of example of how badly this system might work in practice, the Society cited a case involving a railway company in which after three arguments and judgments in equity, two verdicts of juries, and one argument at law, the suit remained still undecided. Thirdly, there was the antagonism of the jurisdictions. Some contracts e.g. bonds without consideration, contracts obtained by equitable fraud, and part-performed contracts within the Statute of Frauds were valid at law but invalid in equity. Accordingly, courts of law were bound to give effect to the legal, and courts of equity to the equitable, interest. It was perfectly possible, therefore, for a litigant to succeed in one court but to fail in another.

After due consideration of these and other disadvantages in the existing system, the Society recommended that 'justice, whether it relate to matters of legal or equitable cognisance, may advantageously be administered by the same tribunal', that 'where the principles of law conflict with those of equity, the latter shall prevail to the exclusion of the former' and that 'all litigation, whether it relate to matters of legal or of equitable cognisance, may advantageously be subjected to the same form of procedure'. It was a formula which smacked very much of that which the judicature commissioners were to recommend over 20 years afterwards. Nor was the formula completely new, at least in its essentials, even in mid-nineteenth century. Twenty years before that the common law commissioners had suggested that a court should itself be able to do complete justice.[5]

The overlapping of jurisdictions extended to the jurisdiction of the ecclesiastical courts. The Chancery commissioners acknowledged in 1852 that:

'if a testator by his will disposes of his real and personal estate, and the validity of the will is disputed, the same question between the same parties may become the subject of litigation in the ecclesiastical courts, in the common law courts, and in the Court of Chancery; and the parties entitled under the will may be under the necessity of resorting to these several jurisdictions before they can finally establish their rights, and be put in

5   Third Report...by the Commissioners...into the Practice and Proceedings of the Superior
     Courts of Common Law no. 92 (1831).

possession of the testator's property'.[6]

What was to be done? Certainly lawyers other than Blackstone had been aware for some years of the possible absurdities of the position. In 1742 the Lord Chancellor, Lord Hardwicke, had hoped that the legislature would find a remedy for the division of work between equity and the ecclesiastical courts. In the latter half of that century Lord Mansfield attempted, unsuccessfully as it turned out, some degree of fusion between the principles and rules applied by the courts of law and equity. Indeed, that attempt can be seen as but a further step in the process whereby since at least 1706 various statutes had introduced into the common law courts procedures and doctrines which originally were the province of equity.[7] Clearly such measures had failed to meet the need.

In 1852 the Chancery commissioners recognised that the mischiefs which arose 'from the system of several distinct courts proceeding on distinct and in some cases on antagonistic principles, are extensive and deep rooted'.[8] The common law commissioners had recently come to a similar conclusion.[9] Consequently, in mid-nineteenth century several statutory measures mitigated the worst features of the system in the following manner:

> 'By virtue of these Acts the Court of Chancery is now not only empowered, but bound to decide for itself all questions of common law without having recourse as formerly, to the aid of a common law court, whether such questions arise incidentally in the course of the suit, or constitute the foundation of a suit, in which a more effectual remedy is sought for the violation of a common law right, or a better protection against its violation than can be had at common law. The Court is further empowered to take evidence orally in open court, and in certain cases to award damages for breaches of contract or wrongs as at common law; and trial by jury, — the great distinctive feature of the common law, — has recently, for the first time, been introduced into the Court of Chancery.
>
> On the other hand, the courts of common law are now authorised to compel discovery in all cases, in which a court of equity would have enforced it in a suit instituted for that purpose. A limited power has been conferred on courts of common law to grant injunctions, and to allow equitable defences to be pleaded, and in certain cases to grant relief from forfeitures. These changes, however, fall far short of the recommendations of the common law commissioners, who in their Final Report had expressed the opinion, that power should be conferred on the common law courts "to give, in respect of rights there recognised, all the protection and redress which at present can be obtained in any jurisdiction".'[10]

Here, then, was a further step towards reform, however tentative. The judicature commissioners were clearly of the opinion that such measures had not

---

6 First Report of...Commissioners...into the Process, Practice and System of Pleading in the Court of Chancery no. 1437 (1852) pp. 3-4.
7 *Montgomery v Clarke* (1742) 2 Atk 378 at 379. C.H.S. Fifoot *Lord Mansfield* pp.183 ff., T.F.T. Plucknett *A Concise History of the Common Law* (5th edn, 1956) pp. 210-11.
8 First Report no. 1437 (1852) p. 1.
9 Second Report of...Commissioners for Inquiring into the Process, Practice and System of Pleading in the Superior Courts of Common Law no. 1626 (1853) p. 45.
10 Judicature Commission: First Report of the Commissioners no. 4130 (1869) p. 6. The Common Law Procedure Acts of 1852 and 1854, the Chancery Amendment Act 1858.

amounted to a sufficient remedy. Indeed, Holdsworth cites a contemporary commentator to the effect that the fusion of the several jurisdictions had gone little further than to add to that which was artificial in the Court of Chancery, the not less obscure technicalities which were peculiar to the courts of law.[11] Accordingly, a question long mooted by Blackstone and hinted at by Hardwicke, was to be left for the consideration of the judicature commissioners, who were appointed in 1867.

3   The superior courts of common law

There were three superior courts of common law, namely, the Court of Common Pleas, the Court of King's Bench and the Court of Exchequer. All three sat in Westminster Hall.

a) *Common Pleas*

The Court of Common Pleas had been dubbed by Coke as 'the lock and key of the common law' for it was only in that court that real actions i.e. actions which concerned the right of freehold or the realty, could be originally brought. Personal pleas i.e. actions for the recovery of a debt, personal chattel, or damages were also determined there, although King's Bench had a concurrent authority with regard to some of them. In Blackstone's day there were four judges in Common Pleas — the Chief Justice and three puisne judges. They sat every day in the four terms to hear and determine all matters of law arising in civil causes, whether real or personal, or mixed and compounded of both. Common Pleas had an original jurisdiction as well as upon removal from the inferior courts. However, a writ of error lay from Common Pleas to King's Bench[12] and at a later date into Exchequer Chamber. Common Pleas also laboured under two disadvantages. Until 1847, the serjeants at law had exclusive audience in it during term: this restrictive and costly practice endeared the court neither to lawyers generally nor to litigants. Secondly, attorneys also disliked the requirement that they must pay a proportion of the fees which were due much earlier than was customary in other courts.

b) *King's Bench*

The Court of King's Bench was described by Blackstone as the 'supreme court of common law in the kingdom'. King's Bench had jurisdiction to keep all inferior jurisdictions within the bounds of their authority, a function which it exercised by means of the prerogative writ of prohibition: it might also command magistrates and others to carry out their duties by means of the prerogative writ of mandamus. In addition it had jurisdiction over both criminal and civil causes. So far as civil causes were concerned it enjoyed a general jurisdiction over all actions between subject and subject with the exception of the real actions. Proceedings in error lay to King's Bench in Blackstone's day from Common Pleas

---

11   W.S. Holdsworth *History of English Law* vol 1, pp. 637-8.
12   3 BL Com (5th edn) 40. Cf. H.J. Stephen *Commentaries on the Laws of England* (4th edn, 1858) vol 3, p. 392. During the nineteenth century each common law court acquired an additional judge. See also I.H. Jacob 'Civil Procedure since 1800' in P. Allsop (ed) *Then and Now 1799-1974* p. 159.

and from all inferior courts of record — after 1830 proceedings in error were taken from King's Bench into Exchequer Chamber. The Court of King's Bench was composed of a Chief Justice and of three puisne justices who were, by their office, the sovereign conservators of the peace and supreme coroners of the land.[13]

c) *Exchequer*

The Court of Exchequer was both a court of law and, until 1841, a court of equity. In the exercise of its jurisdiction as a court of law, it administered redress between subject and subject in all actions, with the exception of the real actions. Further, in the exercise of its ancient revenue jurisdiction it ascertained and enforced the proprietary rights of the Crown against the subjects of the realm. On the equity side Exchequer had had a wide jurisdiction. In this respect it was the original and usual jurisdiction for tithes. Further, when the object of an equity suit was to obtain an injunction to stay a trial at law, it might in many cases be preferable to file a bill in the Exchequer rather than in Chancery because in the Exchequer an injunction would stay a trial, whereas in Chancery an injunction would not stay a trial but only execution, unless it was obtained before declaration. Another advantage which resulted from instituting an equity suit in Exchequer was that, if a question of law arose during the exercise of the equitable jurisdiction, the court would decide it without the delay and expense of referring it to another jurisdiction. The Court of Exchequer was composed of the Chief Baron and of three puisne barons. However, one statute had provided in 1817 that the Lord Chief Baron alone might hear and determine alone all causes, matters and things in the Court of Exchequer as a court of equity. Although the court had become unpopular for other reasons e.g. its fees were higher than those of Chancery, it was this statute which had the unexpected consequence of damaging the Exchequer severely on the equity side. The reason was simply that as a result of the statute there was in practice no longer any effective appeal in equity cases.[14]

d) *Competition for business*

Over the years the three courts had competed fiercely with each other for business. After all, both the judges and the officers of each of the courts were dependent for the greater part of their income upon the fees which were paid by litigants in their particular court; the judges were first paid by salary alone only in 1825.[15] In that struggle between the courts the legal fiction had played a considerable part by allowing one court to encroach upon the jurisdiction of another. By the early nineteenth century the result was twofold. First, the jurisdiction of the three superior courts of common law was virtually co-extensive. Brougham was able to tell the House of Commons in 1828:

> 'The jurisdiction of the Court of King's Bench, for example, was originally
> confined to pleas of the Crown, and then extended to actions where

---

13   3 Bl Com (5th edn) 41.
14   3 Bl Com (5th edn) 44, *Stephen* p. 391, E. Chitty *The Commercial and General Lawyer* (2nd edn, 1841) pp. 988-9. See also W.H. Bryson *The Equity Side of the Exchequer* pp.161-2.
15   B. Abel-Smith and R. Stevens *Lawyers and the Courts* p. 38.

violence was used — actions of trespass, by force; but now, all actions are admissible within its walls, through the medium of a legal fiction, which was adopted for the purpose of enlarging its authority, that every person sued is in the custody of the marshal of the court and may, therefore, be proceeded against for any personal cause of action. Thus, by degrees, this court has drawn over to itself actions which really belong to…the Court of Common Pleas. The Court of Common Pleas, however,…never was able to obtain cognizance of — the peculiar subject of King's Bench jurisdiction — Crown Pleas.…The Exchequer has adopted a similar course for, though it was originally confined to the trial of revenue cases, it has, by means of another fiction — the supposition that everybody sued is a debtor to the Crown, and further, that he cannot pay his debt, because the other party will not pay him, — opened its doors to every suitor, and so drawn to itself the right of trying cases, that were never intended to be placed within its jurisdiction.'[16]

Secondly, there was now less justification for maintaining nominally separate jurisdictions and procedures.

e) *Respective popularity of the common law courts*

In 1828, when Brougham gave that address to the Commons, King's Bench, profiting not only from its own merits but also from the disadvantages described above of the other courts, was the most popular of the common law courts with litigants. Of the actions brought in 1823, there were 43454 in King's Bench, 13009 in Common Pleas and 6778 in Exchequer. Over the five-year period 1823-27, 281109 actions were commenced in King's Bench, 80158 actions were commenced in Common Pleas, and 37197 actions were commenced in Exchequer.[17] Not surprisingly, the common law commissioners wrote in 1829 that King's Bench was 'immoderately over burthened', that the judges of Common Pleas were 'fully occupied in term, and much engaged in vacation also' but that the puisne barons of the Exchequer were 'comparatively little occupied either in term or vacation' to the extent that much of their time might be devoted to the relief of King's Bench.[18] Indeed, much of the business of the courts could be conducted only during the course of one of the legal terms. Yet a term lasted a mere three weeks and there were only four terms. As commerce expanded and as new forms of technology, such as the railway, were developed, it was likely not only that there would be enough business for all courts but that they would be placed under increasing pressure. In the admittedly exceptional year of 1846, 24000 writs more than in the preceding year were issued in connection with the railway speculations of the period.[19] It was therefore all the more necessary that the common law jurisdictions, especially King's Bench, should streamline their procedures to meet both the existing and the likely future pressures upon their time.

16   18 Official Report (2nd series) cols. 132-133.
17   First Report…by the Commissioners appointed to inquire into the Practice and Proceedings of the Superior Courts of Common Law no. 46 (1829) p. 11.
18   First Report (above) p. 17.
19   Report from the Common Law (Judicial Business) Commissioners no. 2268, Sess. 2 (1857) p. x.

f) *Procedure and pleading*

Brougham had urged strongly that an increase in the number of judges was necessary and that reforms in procedure and pleading also were needed. As a result of his speech the common law commissioners were appointed. All distinguished lawyers, they published their first report in 1829. Immediately, they expressed an awareness of the lawyers' constant dilemma:

> 'To render proceedings shorter, cheaper and more certain, is the great object to be proposed in recommending any alteration in the established course of practice. But we are well aware that certainty cannot be attained without precision; that precision is often inconsistent with brevity; and that whatever increases length increases cost.'[20]

However, their inquiries into the common law process soon revealed a number of areas which were ripe for reform.

i) *Mode of commencing suit.* First, there was the mode of commencing a suit. In theory it was possible to commence an action in numerous ways. Since the object of all these processes was either simply to enforce the defendant's appearance, or to enforce it in such a manner as to obtain security at the same time for ultimate execution on his person in satisfaction of the debt, the commissioners were able to recommend that the primary forms of process should be reduced to two — summons where the plaintiff intended merely to compel appearance, and *capias.* Accordingly, the Uniformity of Process Act 1832[1] abolished the fictitious processes and provided for a uniform writ of summons in most cases. In effect, therefore, that measure was an expression of existing practice.

ii) *Arrest.* The principal object of the process, or the mesne process, then, was the enforcement of appearance. A further object was the arrest of the defendant's person so that it might be available and subject to execution. Clearly it was hard to allow a defendant to be deprived of his liberty on the mere allegation of his adversary that a debt was due, even though the allegation were made on oath, especially when there appeared to be no danger of the defendant's endeavouring to abscond before judgment and execution could be obtained. Further, when the debt was small, the effect of a writ by way of arrest was not merely to prevent the escape of the debtor, but in a vast number of cases to enforce by the mere apprehension of imprisonment, immediate payment or compromise. At all events the common law commissioners concluded that the very large majority of those against whom process of arrest had been taken out were driven by it to immediate payment or terms of compromise, and either avoided any commitment to actual custody, or obtained a speedy discharge. Understandably, therefore, plaintiffs tended to argue that this power was essential to their security and to the maintenance of credit.[2]

Figures given to the common law commissioners showed that between 12 February 1830 and 12 February 1831, 28761 warrants were issued, that 3429 defendants had been taken to gaol and that on 12 February 1831, 829 people

---

20 First Report (above) p. 7.
1   2 & 3 Will 4, c. 39. First Report (above) p. 72ff.
2   First Report (above) p. 71.

were in custody.[3] The commissioners suggested that it only gratified a malicious disposition to resort to this process if the debtor, on being required, would have discharged the debt; and to arrest the debtor who did not have the means manifested only vexation and resentment. Accordingly, the commissioners concluded that in principle the power of arrest ought to be confined to cases of actual or meditated fraud. After suggesting some measures for the better protection of the creditor, they recommended, therefore, that nobody should be arrested for debt, unless the plaintiff or someone on his behalf, should make an oath that a debt to the amount of £20 was due, and that he believed that the defendant was about to abscond.[4] That provision was implemented substantially by the Judgments Act 1838[5] which abolished arrest on mesne process in all cases, except those in which it appeared that the defendant was about to leave the country in order to avoid meeting the claim against him.

The Judgments Act 1838 was the most determined attempt up to that time, although it was by no means the first attempt,[6] to purge the civil process of unduly punitive methods. That issue was a very real one. Between 1830 and 1834 as many as 12000 to 15000 debtors were committed to prison after judgment each year.[7] Even after 1838 it still remained possible to seize the debtor's body in satisfaction of a debt actually adjudged to be due. Only in 1869 was the civil process purged of the power to imprison, except in those cases in which the debtors were deemed to have been 'fraudulent' or to have been contemptuously resisting an order to pay which they could, if they chose, obey. On the whole the county court judges were very ready to find such fraud or contempt. The result, in the view of a select committee which reported in 1873, was that the real tricksters rarely went to prison: that fate was reserved for those who were incapable of managing their own affairs.[8] Yet that system survived until well after 1950. Its survival bore vivid witness to the strength of the apathy and drift with which so much of the administration of justice was clouded: there was no effective check on whether statutory objectives were being achieved.

iii) *Form of action: evidence.* The incorrect choice of the appropriate form of action, and on occasion that was all too possible a mistake in law, would be fatal to the plaintiff's cause. Nor could there be a joinder upon the same writ of two forms of action. The consequent expense and delay to the litigant, and not least to the business community, was tremendous. Nor could either plaintiff or defendant give evidence on their own behalf upon the ground that they had an interest in the case. It was for this reason that Mr. Pickwick was unable to go into the witness box to explain how Mrs. Bardell had come to believe that he had promised to marry her. That situation was remedied only in 1851 after a determined

3 Fourth Report...by the Commissioners appointed to inquire into the Practice and Proceedings of the Superior Courts of Common Law no. 239 (1832) p. 92. This report deals fully with the question of arrest and imprisonment for debt in civil suits.
4 Fourth Report (above) p. 33.
5 Cf. Debtor's Act 1869, s. 6.
6 E. Jenks *A Short History of English Law* (3rd edn, 1924) pp. 354-5.
7 Return of the Number of Persons Confined for Debt no. 199 (1830-34, 1835) cited by W.R. Cornish 'Criminal Justice and Punishment' in W.R. Cornish and others *Crime and Law in Nineteenth Century Britain* p. 49.
8 Report no. 348. See *Cornish* p. 49.

campaign which was able, inter alia, to point to the successful experience of the county court judges in such matters.[9]

iv) *Special pleading.* The considerable art of special pleading, as it was actually practised, was also a source of mutual incomprehension between lawyer and litigant. The avowed object of special pleading was worthy enough. That object was to develop the point in controversy between the parties so that, if it should turn out to be a question of law, it might be referred to the judges, or, if matter of fact, to trial by jury. The parties were then at issue.[10] Special pleaders were employed to this end which, in theory at least, might well have assisted usefully in the speedy despatch of business. In practice, in the view of many critics, the work of the special pleader usually had quite the contrary effect. One contemporary critic wrote of special pleading that its absurdities were 'enough to make a horse laugh; a drizzling mass of empirical inventions, circuitous procedure, and unintelligible fiction, calculated for no purpose but to fortify monopoly and wrap justice in deceit and mystery'. On the whole the lawyers tended to regard such criticism as uninformed and so unworthy of serious comment.[11] However, the Civil Procedure Act 1833,[12] although it accepted that laymen could not themselves reform so technical an area of the law, did require the common law judges to produce within five years for the approval of parliament a set of rules and orders which would govern pleadings. The object was to reduce delays, formalities and expense. So were born the Hilary Rules which were published in 1834. Unfortunately, they did little to reduce either complexity, delay or expense. Indeed, it was during the subsequent period that Baron Parke, who had been one of the original common law commissioners, dominated the common law bench. Lord Coleridge later recalled having heard Parke 'rejoice at non-suiting a plaintiff in an undefended cause, saying, with a sort of triumphant air, that those who drew loose declarations brought scandal on the law'.[13] Once again the traditional approach of the lawyers had undermined the statutory aim of greater simplicity.

v) *Trial.* The matter than came before the court either at Bar at Westminster or at nisi prius i.e. on assize. Witnesses might be examined and cross-examined, unlike Chancery. The verdict was usually delivered immediately.

vi) *Remedies.* Judgment might be given for the recovery of money, goods or land or, rarely, for an account and the costs of the action.[14]

g) *Reform*
Some changes were made during the 1830s, therefore. Yet when decisive action was taken, by incorporating the Welsh system into the English following

---

9   W.S. Holdsworth *Dickens as a Legal Historian* p. 117, Answers of the County Court Judges upon the Examination of Parties no. 21 (1851).
10 H.J. Stephen *Commentaries on the Laws of England* (4th edn, 1858) vol 3, p. 568.
11 For an account of the public opinion of the day see E.R. Sunderland 'The English Struggle for Procedural Reform' (1925-26) 39 HLR 725.
12 3 & 4 Will IV, c. 42.
13 C.H.S. Fifoot *Judge and Jurist in the Reign of Victoria* pp. 13-14.
14 Jacob 'Civil Procedure since 1800' in P. Allsop (ed) *Then and Now 1799-1974* p. 166.

recommendations made by the common law commissioners in 1829, the consequences for Welsh litigants were unhappy. Similar proposals for the Welsh Court
of Great Session had been made as early as 1780 and with the same motive which
inspired the commissioners in 1829 i.e. to have an additional number of judges.
Therefore, there is some truth in the allegation that the Welsh judicature fell a
victim not to its own defects but to the desire of English lawyers to have more
judges. Now Welsh people also were subjected to the torments of the unreformed
English system. The common law commissioners were unwilling, perhaps
because of their own legal background and because they were aware of what was
politically possible, to make radical proposals. They made no effective proposals
to remedy the pressure upon King's Bench. It was no surprise, therefore, when
arrears in Queen's Bench in 1837 were substantial — this may have been the
broad pattern in subsequent years.[15] One legal magazine, it is true, claimed in
1838 that the delay before a case could be heard in court was of incalculable
benefit since in that time 'passions have time to cool, the angry feeling that
prompts to litigation may subside, and if there are some obstinate spirits who are
disposed to fight to the last, their ability to carry on the warfare is put an end to
by the ruinous expense of the long-protracted context'.[16] Over the previous
decade, however, public patience with respect to such arguments on the part of
lawyers had diminished considerably. Now the *Law Times* sought to warn the
lawyers of the 'War Against the Lawyers'. With the enactment of the County
Courts Act in 1846 such lawyers were far more ready to preach the inevitability of
reform. The *Law Times* suggested, for example, that the institution of the
county court meant that

> 'it would be necessary for the superior courts to adopt without delay all
> those improvements which were found to facilitate the administration of
> justice in the county courts; such as, the admission of the parties as
> witnesses; more speedy execution, without permitting the lottery of delay
> by new trials, except with security given for judgment and costs; and allow-
> ing the parties, if they please, to dispense with a jury'.

In 1850 the *Law Times* adopted a less radical tone; the superior courts would
maintain their position, they assured their readers.[17] Nevertheless, by mid-nineteenth century it was clear that the country positively demanded legal reform
and at last the lawyers recognised that something had to be done about it. So
were born the Common Law Procedure Acts of 1852 and 1854.[18] A fresh Common Law Commission had published in 1851 a rather more critical look at the
common law system than had its predecessor.[19] For example, although it recognised that the writ of summons which had been introduced by the Uniformity of

---

15   Baron Bowen 'Progress in the Administration of Justice during the Victorian Period' in
     Select Essays in Anglo-American Legal History vol 1, pp. 519, 523, (1847) 8 LT 303, W.L.
     Williams 'The King's Court of Great Sessions in Wales' (1966) 26 Y Cymmrodor 1, W.R.
     Williams *The History of the Great Sessions in Wales*, D. Williams *A History of Modern
     Wales* pp. 29 ff., First Report of the Royal Commission on Practice and Proceedings of the
     Courts of Common Law no. 46 (1829) pp. 35-6, W.H. Winder 'Equity in the Courts of
     Great Sessions' (1939) 55 LQR 106.
16   (1838) 2 Jur 73.
17   (1850) 16 LT 78.
18   15 & 16 Vict, c. 76, 17 & 18 Vict, c. 125.
19   First Report of...Commissioners for inquiry into the Process, Practice and System of
     Pleading in the Superior Courts of Common Law no. 1389 (1851).

Process Act was 'a great improvement' on the former modes of commencing actions, it believed that the requirement in the existing writ of stating the nature or subject matter of the action was 'utterly useless' and led to 'much fruitless expense and delay'. Therefore, the commissioners recommended that there should be one general form of writ for every action and that it should not be necessary to mention any form or cause of action in the writ. Special attention was given to the 'difficult and anxious' question of pleading. In all the Report was a thorough piece of work which in turn gave birth to useful legislation. The Common Law Procedure Acts of 1852 and 1854 are lengthy statutes. It was provided that there should be one general form of writ of summons in personal actions. Pleadings were simplified. There was to be a considerable power of amendment during the course of the proceedings. Technicalities regarding the joinder of parties and of claims were abolished. Procedures to assist the conduct of arbitrations under the supervision of the court were laid down.

Understandably, such changes altered the balance of litigation within the courts. For example, the judge at chambers now heard the great bulk of those applications respecting matters of practice which were formerly brought before the full court. Certain practices had become obsolete or had been abolished. However, it did seem reasonable to suggest that new legislation e.g. concerning joint-stock companies and the railways, had introduced entirely new business which may have outweighed 'in difficulty and importance those that have ceased to exist'.[20] Yet the Common Law Procedure Acts amounted, as has been indicated already at the beginning of this chapter, to no more than a halfway house on the road to more radical reform. Indeed, some of the accomplished reforms were more apparent than real. For example, although the writ of summons was no longer to mention the cause of action — yet the appropriate form of action had to be declared in the pleadings. It is true that Baron Parke was said to have been so disturbed by the new measures that he resigned in 1855. Nevertheless the question which remained was whether the Judicature Commissioners, who were appointed in 1867, would feel able to put forward more thoroughgoing proposals.

4   The High Court of Chancery

a) *Origin and nature of the jurisdiction*
Chancery's jurisdiction was complementary to that of the courts of common law — it sought to do justice in cases for which there was no adequate remedy at common law. It had originated in the petition, not the writ, of the party who felt aggrieved to the Lord Chancellor as the 'keeper of the King's conscience'. In its origins, therefore, Chancery's flexible concern for justice complemented admirably the formalism of a medieval system of common law which had begun to adhere strictly, perhaps overstrictly on occasion, to prescribed forms.[1] By 1800,

---

20   Report from the Common Law (Judicial Business) Commissioners no. 2268, Sess. 2 (1857) pp. x-xi. For example, justifying bail had become obsolete and special demurrers had been abolished.
1   Report...by the Commissioners...into the Practice of the Court of Chancery no. 56 (1826) pp. 6-7.

however, Chancery's system was itself regarded as being both consistent and certain. Indeed, pride was taken in this changed approach. Lord Eldon, the Lord Chancellor who dominated Chancery during the first quarter of the nineteenth century, stated:

> 'the doctrines of this court ought to be as well settled and made as uniform as those of the common law, laying down fixed principles, but taking care that they are to be applied according to the circumstances of each case. I cannot agree that the doctrines of this court are to be changed with every succeeding judge. Nothing would inflict or give me greater pain in quitting this place than the recollection that I had done anything to justify the reproach that the equity of this court varies like the chancellor's foot.'[2]

Nevertheless, even in Lord Eldon's day, Chancery bore the marks of its origin. Relief was wholly discretionary in its nature; the court sought to achieve perfect justice in every case.

b) *The role of the Lord Chancellor*

The Lord Chancellor bore the brunt of the judicial work, a task which was rendered all the more difficult by the fact that until mid-nineteenth century the Lord Chancellor was also a considerable political figure with corresponding duties. The value of the judicial assistance which the Master of the Rolls gave was diminished by the fact that from his decision there might be an appeal to the Lord Chancellor. Accordingly, a Vice-Chancellor was appointed in 1813.

c) *Jurisdiction*

Chancery's jurisdiction was varied. Chancery even exercised a common law jurisdiction, although this occupied a 'very inconsiderable portion' of its time.[3] Here we consider only its extraordinary jurisdiction as a court of equity. In 1826 the Chancery commissioners explained how that jurisdiction had grown, as follows:

> 'One great source of the extension of the jurisdiction of courts of equity has been, the invention of new modes of disposing of property, particularly in the form of trusts, and the ingenuity of fraudulent contrivances; to which may be added, the power of disposition of all property by will; the vast increase of personal property, which may be disposed of by deed or will, or distributable according to law, upon intestacy; the difficulty of obtaining complete justice, under the forms of the common law, against persons accountable for property to others, as executors or administrators, or as trustees or agents; or as partners in trade, or joint owners of property; or in a vast variety of other ways in which parties may become so accountable; the demand of justice, for the specific execution of contracts, of various descriptions; and the complication of interests, arising from intricate transactions, for which the course of the common law, in the simplicity of its proceedings, can give no adequate remedy.'[4]

The cases of most frequent occurrence in Chancery could be classified under the following three heads: (1) All covins, frauds and deceits, for which there was no remedy in the ordinary courts of law. Fraud was the most fertile source of

2   *Gee v Pritchard* (1818) 2 Swan 402 at 414.
3   Report no. 56 (1826).
4   Report no. 56 (1826) p. 7.

litigation. It included purchases by trustees, attorneys, or others in a fiduciary situation, of the trust property; sales or agreements by expectant heirs; and gifts by a ward to his guardian. (2) Accidents, for example, in the case of a mistake in a deed, equity might not only rectify the mistake but also compel the execution of a proper deed. If a deed were lost, equity, in the exercise of a concurrent jurisdiction with common law, might afford relief. (3) Jurisdiction over trusts and trustees. This included not only express trusts created by deed or will, but also those which were implied from the circumstances of the party having accepted some office, as that of executor or administrator.

One head of equitable jurisdiction which was to be extended in the twentieth century was that of wardship. If an infant had property, Chancery might care both for that property and for the infant, even beyond the age of 21, until all the objects of the guardianship had been fulfilled. Finally, there was a statutory jurisdiction in cases of bankruptcy, charitable uses, the Arbitration Acts and the Friendly Societies Acts.[5]

d) *Allegations of undue delay and expense*

It was a formidable, and a growing, jurisdiction which might have taxed to the limits the efficiency of the best organised of courts. As Chancery was less than well organised, it was scarcely surprising that allegations of delay and expense were aimed at it with some bitterness during the first half of the nineteenth century. Such allegations became substantial during Lord Eldon's long tenure of the Woolsack. Although some of that criticism may have been inspired by opponents of Eldon primarily on political grounds, it must be conceded that Dickens' horrendous picture of Chancery in his *Bleak House*, and especially in the great trial of *Jarndyce v Jarndyce*, presented all too true a picture of Chancery during the first half of the nineteenth century. Holdsworth has even suggested that the physical fog, amidst which *Bleak House* opens, aptly typifies the moral fog which enveloped Chancery procedure.[6] M.A. Taylor, a well-known critic of the court during the early years of the century, complained constantly but to little effect in the House of Commons of delays in Chancery. Later critics such as Williams and Parkes were also able to cite instances of Chancery's tremendous delay and expense and of the ruin which they said it brought upon many litigants.[7] Lord Cottenham LC told the House of Lords in 1839 that it would be impossible to dispose of the causes then down for hearing before him in less than three years.[8] In 1840 an experienced Chancery practitioner advised a select committee of the House of Lords that once:

> 'you get to a certain point in the delays of a court, those delays alone operate as a choke, if I may so call it, upon the public, however urgent the demand for courts of justice may be. Parties will come into court if they can get their rights decided within some definite time — say two or three

5 E. Chitty *The Commercial and General Lawyer* (2nd edn, 1841) pp. 980-4. A covin was a secret assent determined in the hearts of two or more to the defrauding and prejudice of another.

6 W.S. Holdsworth *Dickens as a Legal Historian* p. 85.

7 W.S. Holdsworth 'The Movement for Reforms in the Law (1793-1832)' (1940) 56 LQR 208 at 221, 19 Official Report (1st series) cols. 263-264, 5 Official Report (new series: 1821) col. 1034.

8 J.B. Atlay *The Victorian Chancellors* vol 1, p. 407.

years: but tell a man that he must wait four or five, or eight or ten years, and he will give up his rights, or compromise them, rather than come into a court which imposes such oppressive terms as the price of its assistance.' It was for this reason, the practitioner believed, that the number of suitors in Chancery had not increased in proportion to the increase in the country's wealth but that the delays of the court practically operated as a prohibition.[9] The situation grew even worse. The result was that in 1850 a competent contemporary observer was moved to comment that the most popular measure which could be introduced into the House of Commons would be one for the abolition *sans phrase* of the Court of Chancery.[10]

e) *Early reforms*

Of course some reforms had been implemented during this period. An additional Chancery judge had been appointed to assist the Lord Chancellor in 1813 — yet it was possible for an appeal to be made from him to the Lord Chancellor. In 1831 the bankruptcy jurisdiction was transferred from Chancery to a chief judge in bankruptcy and in 1841 Exchequer's equitable jurisdiction was transferred to Chancery. Moreover, in 1833 statute simplified dealings in real property while other statutory measures, made for greater efficiency in administration.

It seems, too, that the judges worked hard. Eldon, it is true, was said to have been subject to a 'cunctative habit'. Undoubtedly Brougham worked hard, albeit with such an alleged lack of understanding of Chancery practice that he soon brought upon himself the enmity of the Chancery Bar, the result apparently being that on the termination of his Chancellorship the arrears were much the same as they had been upon the termination of Eldon's Chancellorship. Lord Cottenham told how, on leaving the House of Lords at four in the morning, he had called at Vice-Chancellor Shadwell's house and had found that that judge had just risen to begin his duties for the day. Small wonder, then, that should such a judge be ill — as Lord Cottenham was during his second Chancellorship — the arrears mounted even faster.[11] It was Lord Cottenham who, by the General Orders of April 1850, introduced a considerable change in Chancery procedure. By those orders

'in a great number of specified cases, without any formal pleading at all, by the filing of what is called a claim, heard summarily on affidavits, and, if necessary, on counter affidavits, the Court is enabled at once to pronounce a decree between the parties. Besides the specified cases, the Court is authorised, in every case in which it thinks fit to permit a claim to be filed.'

The Chancery commissioners, in their Report of 1852,[12] continued:

'The extent to which this new system has been used is shown by the number of claims filed. The Order came into operation on 22 May 1850, between which time and 12 January 1852, 1969 claims have been filed in almost

---

9   J. Wigram 'Minutes of Evidence taken before the Select Committee of the House of Lords...[on]..."An Act for Facilitating the Administration of Justice" ' no. 160.1 (1840) q. 86.

10   J.B. Atlay *The Victorian Chancellors* vol 1, p. 450.

11   *Atlay*. On court administration see p. 102, above.

12   First Report of...Commissioners...into the Process, Practice and System of Pleading in the Court of Chancery no. 1437 (1852) p. 13.

every variety of case.…In a small number of the cases heard the Court has felt itself unable to deal satisfactorily with the matter by way of claim, and has left the parties to proceed by Bill.'

At much the same time Lord Cottenham declined to hear original causes so that the Chancellor's Court became virtually a court of appeal from the Master of the Rolls and the Vice-Chancellor. Statutory sanction was soon given to this practice and two Lord Justices were authorised to exercise the same judicial powers as the Lord Chancellor, either jointly with him or in his absence.

f) *Report of the Chancery Commission 1826*

It was reasonably clear, however, that still more radical action was needed, if Chancery were to operate efficiently. Would the reformers be able to grasp the nettle of Chancery reform? An opportunity had been missed by the Chancery Commission which reported in 1826 and which showed a remarkable lack of awareness that any problem existed at all. Of the allegations of delay, the commissioners, whose chairman was Eldon, remarked that they were based upon 'ignorance, or partial acquaintance with the subject'. They pointed out that the administration of a trust might 'most beneficially endure' as long as the trust continued: in that sense 'a Chancery suit will usefully endure for more than half a century'.[13] Other cases which involved fraud and the investigation of accounts were complex. It was a comment which recognised, but did not examine critically, the fact that Chancery acted both judicially and administratively. More importantly still, Chancery employed the same procedure in both types of case, even though there may have been no dispute in issue between the persons involved. That was surely the type of point which, in the light of the tremendous amount of public criticism to which Chancery had been exposed, the commissioners should have examined critically. In fact their proposals lacked bite. As one critic put it, the proposals were not so much a remedy but a palliative.[14] However, a remedy demanded that the reformers should look critically both at Chancery procedure and (as was noted in chapter 4) at the administration of Chancery.

g) *Procedure*

Chancery procedure was lengthy and complex. Of those various proceedings, which the Chancery commissioners describe in their Report of 1852, a brief description of a few will be indicative of Chancery's approach. It should be remembered, however, that a cardinal feature of that procedure was that the parties did not give evidence orally in court: all was reduced to writing.

i) *Bill.* The party applying to the Court addressed a petition to the Lord Chancellor stating his case and praying for relief. This petition was called a bill: it was drawn and signed by counsel. Such an original bill consisted of nine parts and was of an impressive length. Of particular importance was the seventh or interrogating part which prayed that the parties complained of might answer all the matters contained in the bill, not only according to their positive knowledge

---

13   Report by the Commissioners into the Practice of the Court of Chancery no. 56 (1826) p. 9.
14   (1827) 45 Edinburgh Review 469.

of the facts stated, but also according to their remembrance, information, and belief.[15] It was of this part that Bowen, a distinguished judge of the later Victorian era, wrote that it 'converted the original allegations into a chain of subtly framed inquiries addressed to the defendant, minutely dovetailed and circuitously arranged so as to surround a slippery conscience and to stop up every earth....It was inevitably...elaborate and...long...and truth found no difficulty in disappearing during the operation.'[16] More bluntly John Wesley, when served with such a bill, described it as being:

> '42 pages in large folio to tell a story which needed not to have taken up 40 lines, and stuffed with such stupid senseless improbable lies, many of them, too, quite foreign to the question, as I believe would have cost the compiler his life in any heathen court of Greece or Rome, and this is equity in a Christian country'.[17]

More bluntly still, Bentham simply called it 'a volume of notorious lies'.[18] The elaboration at least was no doubt necessary in the light of Chancery's inability to hear oral evidence.

The Chancery commissioners of 1852 explained that in the interrogating part of the bill every statement and charge:

> 'is converted into a series of questions framed on the principle that the defendant may possibly be a dishonest defendant disposed to answer evasively and, therefore, suggesting modifications of the statement or charge. For example, if the statement be of a deed bearing a certain date, and made between and executed by certain parties, in certain words, or to a certain effect, the questions would be whether such a deed of that date or some other and what date, was not — made between and executed by such parties, or some, and which of them, or some other, and what parties — in such words, or to such effect, or in some other and what words, or to some other and what effect. In general, all the allegations of the bill are converted into interrogatories of a similar character. Originally, these interrogatories were used much more sparingly, and were confined to those matters supposed to be within the knowledge of the defendant, as to which it was considered necessary or desirable to extract admissions from him. But in course of time this practice was altered, and the easier process was adopted of transmuting all the statements into questions of the nature above described. The number of folios and the expense to all parties concerned were thereby greatly increased.[19]

The Chancery Report of 1826 had not felt that this question of the original bill called for any comment. In 1852, however, the Chancery commissioners wrote that, although it was difficult to guard against prolixity, especially when fees were based upon the number of folios which the office staff had prepared, the principal remedy for it must be found in a different mode of professional

---

15   E. Chitty *The Commercial and General Lawyer* p. 990.

16   Baron Bowen 'Progress in the Administration of Justice during the Victorian Period' *Select Essays in Anglo-American Legal History* vol 1, pp. 524-5.

17   A. Birrell 'Changes in Equity, Procedure, and Principles' in *A Century of English Law* pp. 177, 182.

18   *Birrell*.

19   First Report into the Process, Practice and System of Pleading in the Court of Chancery no. 1437 (1852) p. 5.

remuneration and in the determination of the judges and of taxing officers to repress it.[20]

After answer and any necessary amending bill had been made, the pleadings were complete and the cause was at issue. The papers were then laid before counsel to advise as to evidence and, if necessary, to prepare interrogations of witnesses.

ii) *Evidence: interrogatories for examination of witnesses.* It was an unsatisfactory process. William Vizard, a solicitor of some 24 years' experience who had a considerable experience of proceedings in Chancery, in 1824 told the Chancery Commission:

> 'those interrogatories are prepared not to meet the evidence supposed to come from one witness, but a variety of witnesses, all speaking partially to the same point, though not precisely to the same; the necessary consequence is, that a witness has to be instructed by the solicitor so as to enable him to understand the question, and in part to adjust the answer he has to give; the witness is then examined without the presence of the solicitor, or any one representing the parties, or any one acquainted with the circumstances of the case, to see that all the information wanted is drawn forth; the necessary consequence of that is, that the witness has either simply to answer the interrogatories as they are read to him or he must be instructed by the person examining him; in the one case, the risk is run of having an imperfect answer; in the other, it appears to me very improper that any person should be instructing a witness, particularly in the absence of the parties concerned.'[1]

Despite anxious consideration of points such as that, however, the Chancery commissioners of 1824, had nothing to suggest other than that the examiners should be persons of experience.[2] However, in 1851 the Council of the Incorporated Law Society commented that the method of taking evidence by written interrogatories before an officer of the court was 'extremely defective and unsatisfactory'.[3]

Now the issue was ready for trial. Even then there was further scope for delay.

iii) *Bill of revivor and supplement.* Bills of revivor and bills of supplement had to be filed upon the death or marriage of a party to the suit or upon the birth of a party into the suit. On

> 'the death of a plaintiff his legal personal representative or heir, as the case may be, files a fresh bill against all the parties to the original suit, who are all served and have all to enter appearances; each separate solicitor taking an office copy of the bill of revivor, for which he pays office fees. Similar proceedings take place on the marriage of a female plaintiff....The cases, moreover, in which a simple order of revivor will suffice are comparatively rare. If the transmission of an interest be anything other than simple

20 First Report no. 1437 (1852) pp. 5 and 24.
1   Report...by the Commissioners...into the Practice of the Court of Chancery no. 56 (1826) Appendix A, q. 153.
2   Report no. 56 (1826) pp. 13-14.
3   First Report of...Commissioners...into the Process, Practice and System of Pleading in the Court of Chancery no. 1437 (1852) p. 20.

transmission by marriage, heirship, executorship, or grant of administration, the bill must be what is called a bill of supplement....We are of opinion, that, without any inconvenience, bills of revivor, and in such simple cases as we have described supplemental bills may be dispensed with...'[4]

Not surprisingly, a wag had declared that 'a suit to which 50 defendants were necessary parties...could never hope to end at all, since the yearly average of deaths in England was one in 50, and a death, as a rule threw over the plaintiff's bill for at least a year'.[5] In an extreme case, that of the winding-up of a large joint-stock company, the large number of parties had made a suit in Chancery impracticable.

Accordingly, statute had provided a remedy in the form of a short petition etc.[6] If it could be done in that case, why could it not be done in other cases?

iv) *Rehearing and appeal.* Furthermore, any point could be raised by way of rehearing and appeal (1) before the Master of the Rolls, (2) before the same person by way of rehearing, (3) before the Lord Chancellor.

h) *Attitude of lawyers*

Clearly such a procedure made for unnecessary expense and delay. However appropriate it may have been in the more leisurely world of 1750, it was scarcely suited to the bustling commercial world of 1850. Yet even at a time when Chancery appears to have been inundated with work following the collapse of the railway boom, lawyers tended to view the whole problem as exclusively legal. For example, the Master of the Rolls, in seeking to exclude lay members from the Chancery Commission, commented upon the 'great number of technicalities which the members of the Commission were intimately acquainted with, and which it was not possible for any lay member to be acquainted with'.[7] In similar vein all the witnesses whom the commissioners heard in preparing their First Report were connected with the law: not one was associated directly with commerce.

i) *Reform*

However, in that Report the Chancery commissioners did recognise that all was not well with the court by any means. Legislation followed speedily which provided, inter alia, for the more speedy and efficient despatch of business and amended the practice and course of proceedings accordingly.[8] Undoubtedly, therefore, 1852 was an important year in the history of the Court of Chancery. Yet as soon as 1858 a legal magazine was moved to complain that delays in Chancery were again 'growing to be a very serious evil, and will again require the

---

4   Chancery Commission: First Report no. 1437 (1852) p. 20 and see also p. 9.
5   Baron Bowen 'Progress in the Administration of Justice during the Victorian Period' *Select Essays in Anglo-American Legal History* vol 1, p.526.
6   Joint Stock Companies Act 1848.
7   117 Official Report (3rd series) col. 1366.
8   Court of Chancery Act 1852, Chancery Amendment Act 1858.

interposition of parliament'.[9] The particular concern at that time was with the staffing of the court. Undue delay, seemed ever to be present in Chancery proceedings.

5 The ecclesiastical courts

a) *Structure*
Separate ecclesiastical courts had existed in England since the time of William the Conqueror, who provided that they should have care of 'pleas affecting episcopal jurisdiction' and 'any cause concerning the government of souls'. To some extent the courts differed according to whether they were in the province of Canterbury or that of York. The basic structure was ratified by a statute of Henry VIII.[10] The first appeal was from the sentence of the archdeacon, if the suit had begun in his court, to his diocesan, thence to the archbishop, and finally to the king, although local usage might blur that outline of authority. Within the province of Canterbury, the court of appeal from the courts of bishops or ordinaries within the province was known as the Court of Arches and was presided over by the Dean of the Arches. Whereas the majority of the ecclesiastical courts had ecclesiastics as judges the Court of Arches, the Prerogative or Testamentary Court and the Consistory Court of London enjoyed the services of the civilian lawyers of Doctors' Commons who also practised before, and presided in, the High Court of Admiralty. In the late 1820s there were some 372 ecclesiastical courts, which included some 36 provincial and diocesan courts.

b) *Jurisdiction*
It was clear to many people that the 'godly discipline' which the Conqueror had enjoined upon the courts had long extended to matters which many regarded as being more secular in nature. During the period 1827-30, of all ecclesiastical business in the provincial and diocesan courts of England and Wales, nearly one half was in testamentary matters. Questions such as church rate, church seats and tithes took rather less than a quarter of the courts' time. Matrimonial business, which referred to the courts' exclusive jurisdiction in such questions as the annulment of marriage, accounted for some 5.31 per cent of the courts' business. The exercise of such jurisdiction by church courts must be seen in the context of an increasing public awareness of anomalies and abuses within the Church of England, of the dissenters resentment at what they felt were the privileges of the Church, and of the increasing public demand for divorce.[11]

c) *Reform*
A fresh momentum was given to the debate during the 1830s by the appearance of three reports. The Report of the Commission on the Ecclesiastical Courts, the Fourth Real Property Report and the Report of the Select Committee on

9   (1858) 31 LT 221.
10   For the Restraint of Appeals 1532.
11   A.H. Manchester 'The Reform of the Ecclesiastical Courts' (1966) 10 AJLH 51, 57 n. 20.
     The figures are based upon statistics given in Reports of the Commissioners on the Practice and Jurisdiction of the Ecclesiastical Courts of England and Wales no. 199 (1831-32) at Appendix D, no. 11, and no. 567 at p. 12.

Admiralty Courts,[12] all agreed that the provincial courts should be abolished, although there was no agreement upon what role, if any, should be reserved for the civilian lawyers of Doctors' Commons. Certainly, the Admiralty which placed a high value upon the civilians' learning in the field of public international law, exercised some influence at one stage in preserving the existing jurisdiction on behalf of the civilians: indeed, it was suggested that the Admiralty committee had been appointed largely with a view to answering proposals which had been made in the Fourth Real Property Report.[13] Neither civilians nor leading churchmen stood in the way of moderate reform. Yet those Church people who opposed any reform — for example, on the ground that such reform would drive a further, and undesirable, wedge between Church and State — were united in effect in their opposition to reform with those who opposed ecclesiastical courts simply because they were ecclesiastical courts and so had no wish to see a reformed system. Eventually, the continuing struggle regarding reform became entangled with the increasing public demand for divorce. In 1857 when, after prolonged public debate, divorce was introduced by statute to England and Wales, this new jurisdiction was entrusted to a new Court for Divorce and Matrimonial Causes in addition to the existing matrimonial jurisdiction which had been exercised by the ecclesiastical courts.[14] At the same time the Court for Probate was also created.

Doctors' Commons, and its magnificent library, soon disappeared. Yet the new court was to follow the principles which had been established in the ecclesiastical courts, if modern authority were lacking. To that extent the work of the distinguished jurists of Doctors' Commons lives on.[15]

6   The Court of Admiralty

The Court of Admiralty had jurisdiction to determine all maritime injuries which arose upon the seas or in parts out of the reach of the common law. The Judge of the Admiralty also held a special commission from the Crown to adjudicate on prize of war and power also to decide on questions of booty of war. Appeals used to lie to the Court of Delegates until that jurisdiction was transferred to the Privy Council in 1833. The Court of Admiralty was not a court of record. However, a number of statutes improved its practice and extended its jurisdiction.[16]

7   From the Judicature Acts to 1950

a) *The appointment of the Judicature Commission*
The appointment of the Judicature Commission in 1867 was seen at the time as a

---

12   Fourth Report of the Commissioners of Inquiry into the Law of England respecting Real Property no. 226 (1833), Reports no. 199 (1831-32) etc. (n. 11, above), Report from the Select Committee on the Prerogative Court, Admiralty Court...no. 670 (1833). All but one of the Reports wished Doctors' Commons to continue.

13   (1834) 11 Law Magazine 447.

14   For the new court's jurisdiction etc. see chap. 15, 'The family and the law'.

15   A.H. Manchester 'The Principles and Rules of Ecclesiastical Law and Matrimonial Relief' (1968) 6 Sydney Law Review 25.

16   H.J. Stephen *Commentaries on the Laws of England* (4th edn, 1858) vol 3, pp. 429-31.

highly significant step. The *Law Times* foresaw 'the accomplishment of the greatest law reform as yet adventured'.[17] Sir Roundell Palmer — who was to be responsible as Lord Chancellor Selborne some years later for much of the resulting legislation — had suggested on 30 July 1867 that a royal commission with wide terms of reference should be appointed. The government agreed, with the result that a commission was issued on 18 September 1867. With the exception of Ayrton — and he had practised as a solicitor in Bombay until 1850 — and of Childers, the judicature commissioners were all lawyers. Indeed, they represented differing areas of expertise, and of self-interest, within the profession. Hollams and Lowndes, for example, were London solicitors: Bateson was a Liverpool solicitor. The *Solicitors' Journal* attributed the subsequent appointments of Phillimore and Bramwell to a wish to strengthen the civil and common law elements upon the Commission, in the belief that the Chancery element was too strong.[18] The judicature commissioners produced five reports. The first, and the most influential, report was dated 25 March 1869; the fifth, and final, report was dated 10 July 1874.

b) *The profession and reform*
At the time there seems to have been a fair degree of consensus within the profession as to the broad outline of reform. In 1868 a group of Liverpool solicitors — Selborne later acknowledged their assistance — suggested that all the existing courts should be merged into one supreme tribunal and that pleading and practice should be assimilated by the creation of a new and uniform system.[19] At much the same time Sergeant Pulling suggested to the commissioners that, inter alia, there should be a consolidation of the three superior courts of common law and the establishment by such means of one Supreme Court. Of course, there were some dissentient voices. Some lawyers sought to reject an amalgamation of the courts on the grounds that a judge could be expected to have only a limited expertise.[20] On the whole, however, there does appear to have been a broad consensus within the legal profession not only that reform was desirable but also as to the broad aims of such reform. Such consensus surely augured well for the work of the commissioners.

c) *The proposals of the Judicature Commissioners*
Their first report[1] covered the jurisdiction of law and equity, the constitution of a proposed Supreme Court, the general principles which were to govern questions of procedure, pleading and of evidence in that court, certain questions concerning sittings and assizes, juries, appeals, and a court of appeal.

With regard to the distinction between law and equity, the commissioners believed that, despite the efforts which had been made over the years to ameliorate its defects, such defects could not be remedied completely by any mere transfer or blending of jurisdiction between the courts as they were then constituted. The commissioners suggested that the first step towards meeting and surmounting the defects complained of would be the consolidation of all the

17 (1867) 43 LT 370.
18 (1869) 13 Sol Jo 489.
19 (1868) 12 Sol Jo 631.
20 (1868) 45 LT 134, cf. (1868) 12 Sol Jo 621 and (1869) 13 Sol Jo 91.
 1 Judicature Commission: First Report of the Commissioners no. 4130 (1869).

superior courts of law and equity, together with the Courts of Probate, Divorce, and Admiralty, into one court, to be called 'Her Majesty's Supreme Court', in which court should be vested all the jurisdiction which was then exercisable by each and all the courts so consolidated. Thereafter no suitor could be defeated because he had commenced his suit in the wrong court nor could the suitor be driven from law to equity and vice versa. The Supreme Court thus constituted would be divided, however, into as many chambers or divisions as the nature and extent or the convenient despatch of business might require. Yet all suits would be instituted in the Supreme Court and not in any particular chamber or division of it. However, the distinctive titles of the former courts were to be retained so as to ease the transition from the old system to the new. All judges of the existing superior courts would become judges of the Supreme Court: thus every judge, although he belonged to a particular division of the Supreme Court, would be competent to sit in any other division of the court.

The commissioners also recommended that as much uniformity should be introduced into the procedure of all the divisions of the Supreme Court as was consistent with the principle of making the procedure in each division appropriate to the nature of the cases, or classes of cases, which would be assigned to each. Accordingly, all suits should be commenced by a document to be called a writ of summons and such writs should be issued from one office. The commissioners further recommended, after criticising the existing forms of pleading, that the best system would be one which combined the comparative brevity of the simpler forms of common law pleading with the principle of stating intelligibly and not technically, the substance of the facts relied upon as constituting the plaintiff's or defendant's case, as distinguished from his evidence. They stated that it was upon this principle that most modern improvements of pleading had been founded, both in the United States, the colonies, the Indian possessions and in the practice recently settled for the courts of Probate and Divorce. Accordingly, they recommended that a short statement constructed on this principle of the facts constituting the plaintiff's cause of complaint, not on oath, to be called the declaration, should be delivered to the defendant. They also recommended that usually evidence at the trial should be by oral examination in open court. Further, power should be vested in the Supreme Court to regulate from time to time by general orders the procedure and practice in all its divisions.

d) *The reception of the proposals*

The changes recommended by the commissioners were seen as far reaching. One newspaper commented that they were well nigh revolutionary: the *Law Times* wrote that rumour 'has not exaggerated the extent and importance of the changes recommended by the commission'. There was also a note of approval. On the whole the *Solicitors' Journal*, for example, approved the recommendations. In December 1869 a deputation from the law societies of Liverpool, Manchester, Birmingham, Leeds, Newcastle and Bristol met the Lord Chancellor and urged that the government should introduce legislation in the ensuing session to implement the recommendations which had been made in the First Report.[2] In 1870 Lord Hatherley, the Lord Chancellor, introduced two

2   (1869) 13 Sol Jo 489. For assizes see chap. 7, for appeals see chap. 8.

bills which would have implemented in the main the recommendations of the commissioners. Yet they were not carried.

There had been some influential opposition. Cockburn, the Lord Chief Justice, wrote to the Lord Chancellor ópposing the reforming legislation and it may be that he reflected the views of the common law bench. The Lord Chief Justice wrote in a style similar to that in which he was later to write of Stephen's codification proposals i.e. he accepted the principle of the measure but had reservations, mainly of little consequence, regarding the suggested reforms. He regretted, for example, the abolition of the distinctive jurisdiction of Queen's Bench, the want of more specific legislation as to principles which should guide the framing of rules and orders, and an assumed loss of independence by the courts. Yet it was something that the Lord Chief Justice and his colleagues should support the reforms in principle.[3] In the view of an American magazine it was accepted that the proposed reforms would ultimately be carried through to such an extent that conservatism seemed to have lost heart in England. Vice-Chancellor Malins was said to be the only judge on either bench 'who gives out that he will resist à l'outrance in the good old-fashioned way'.[4] Accordingly, it may well be that the reason why Lord Hatherley's measures actually failed, despite the feeling in their favour, was simply because they did not amplify and explain sufficiently just how the general scheme proposed by the commissioners was to be put into operation — certainly that was to be Selborne's view.[5]

e) *The Judicature Bill*

Selborne, now Lord Chancellor, introduced a Judicature Bill which was founded upon the commissioners' first report. Taking care not to repeat Hatherley's mistakes, he wrote later:

> 'as soon as my Bill was prepared before the meeting of Parliament, I sent copies of it to Lord Cairns, Lord Hatherley, Lord Westbury and Lord Romilly, the two Chief Justices (Cockburn and Bovill), Chief Baron Kelly, the Lords Justices (James and Mellish), and the Attorney and Solicitor-General: giving them the opportunity of suggesting objections and amendments. The result was that when, on 14 February 1873, I explained my scheme to the House of Lords and presented the Bill, I had received general assurances of approval from the most influential of them, and expressions of opinion, encouraging on the whole, even from those (particularly Lord Westbury and Lord Romilly) who were more disposed to be critical. As soon as it was introduced, I sent copies to every judge, inviting from all free comment and friendly suggestion. The result was to strengthen me in many ways. From bench and bar of the common law courts, I obtained cordial and decided support; and if I could not say quite as much of those whose special experience was in equity, and who were distrustful of the effect of the proposed fusion of jurisdictions upon equitable jurisprudence, I succeeded in disarming, even from that quarter, active opposition; while from Lord Cairns and Lord Hatherley, whose authority

3   (1870) 14 Sol Jo 567.
4   (1870) 15 Sol Jo 67.
5   214 Official Report (3rd series) col. 334.

could not be gainsaid, I received powerful and consistent help.'[6]
The Chancery Bar's opposition was based in the fear that equitable principles
would be swamped. On the other hand some common law men protested at 'the
intentional subordination of our common law judicature to that of the Court of
Chancery'. There was also some reasonable doubt as to just what was meant by
the fusion of law and equity. On the other hand it was reported in May 1873 that
the Associated Northern and Midland Law Societies had discussed the Bill clause
by clause and, with some unimportant amendments had approved it: the Incorporated Law Society and the Associated Provincial Law Societies appear to have
taken similar positions at a later date.[7]

When the Lord Chancellor presented his measure to the House of Lords in
February 1873, he said that there were four points, namely: the artificial separation of the legal and equitable jurisdictions; the uniting of all the jurisdictions of
the separate superior courts of law and equity then in existence; provision for
cheapness, simplicity and uniformity of procedure; the improvement of the constitution of the courts of appeal.[8] The Lord Chancellor's measure was well nigh
upset by a conflict over the appellate system; and various amendments were
introduced before the Judicature Act 1873 and the Appellate Jurisdiction Act
1876 became law. Even so it will be convenient to follow the Lord Chancellor's
classification in the outline which follows of the chief provisions of the Judicature
Act 1873.

First, all the existing superior courts were merged into one Supreme Court of
Judicature. The Supreme Court of Judicature Act 1873[9] provided at sections 3 to
5 for the union of the existing courts into one Supreme Court, for the division of
the Supreme Court into a court of original and a court of appellate jurisdiction,
and for the constitution of a High Court of Justice. Section 16 provided that:

> 'the jurisdiction by this Act transferred to the High Court of Justice shall
> include (subject to the exceptions hereinafter contained) the jurisdiction
> which, at the commencement of this Act, was vested in, or capable of being
> exercised by, all or any one or more of the judges of the said courts...'

Section 24(5) emphasised the new unity by providing that no injunction or prohibition should issue from any tribunal of the Court to restrain any proceeding
pending in any other.

Certainly the names of the old courts remained as the names or titles of the
divisions of the new High Court of Justice.[10] However, the reality was to be that
such division of work was to be purely a matter of convenience — since all the
new divisions of the Court exercised concurrent jurisdiction. In this way a key
aim of the Act, as set out at section 24(7), was to be achieved, namely:

> 'all matters so in controversy between the said parties respectively may be
> completely and finally determined, and all multiplicity of legal pro-
> ceedings concerning any of such matters avoided'.

Secondly, it was provided that in the High Court the rules of law and of equity

6   R. Palmer *Memories Personal and Political* vol 1, pp. 300-301.
7   (1873) 55 LT 52, 21, 93.
8   214 Official Report (3rd series) cols. 336-337.
9   36 and 37 Vict., c. 66. By 38 and 39 Vict., c. 77, s. 9 the London court of bankruptcy was
    not to be merged in the Supreme Court: but it was again merged by 46 and 47 Vict., c. 52,
    s. 93; see W.S. Holdsworth *History of English Law* vol 1.
10 Holdsworth *History of English Law* vol 1, p. 638, n. 4.

should be administered concurrently, but that 'in all matters, not hereinbefore mentioned, in which there is any conflict or variance between the rules of equity, and the rules of the common law, with reference to the same matter, the rules of equity shall prevail'.[11] In this manner was the fusion of law and equity said to have been achieved. In practice it meant very little. Equity's days as a vital, innovating force were long past. For many years before the Judicature Acts law and equity had complemented each other harmoniously — in subsequent years they would continue to run paralleled with each other. The Judicature Acts had done no more than fuse the administration of law and equity.

Thirdly, a uniform code of procedure was created which was outlined in the Schedule to the Supreme Court of Judicature Act 1873.

The final issue, that of the appellate jurisdiction, is dealt with in a separate chapter on appellate courts (chapter 8). The Acts were in fact much amended,[12] and delayed versions of the judicature commissioners' proposals. Further amendments were to be made at regular intervals over the years. In 1881 the King's Bench, Common Pleas and Exchequer Divisions were merged in the King's Bench Division. The Lord Chief Justice of the King's Bench Division became the Lord Chief Justice of England. Nevertheless, legislation along the lines which Selborne had contemplated was enacted. It was a considerable achievement.

Certainly, contemporaries believed that the Judicature Acts amounted to a very real achievement. 'The Judicature Act crowns the edifice of legal improvement, which has been slowly built up since the beginning of the present century', wrote a contributor to the *Edinburgh Review* in 1875.[13] Nor was this commentator in any doubt as to its efficacy:

> 'Its application, though delayed by the suspensory Act of last session, cannot fail, in the course of a few months, to effect those improvements in the administration of law which have been the desire of law reformers for half a century.... These proposals once made facts, the tide of necessity will have passed by the ancient legal land marks, and will have borne the ark of the law to a point only dreamed of by Lord Brougham, Sir Samuel Romilly, and Sir James Mackintosh.'[14]

It is a popular view of the Judicature Acts. Unfortunately, the Acts in some respects led to disappointing results.

f) *The effects of the Judicature Acts*

Complaints, which were supported by lawyers, of delay and expense were made quite soon after their enactment. It was estimated that the costs of an ordinary common law action had increased by anything from 20 per cent to 50 per cent. The machinery of litigation was now said to be over-precise and elaborate e.g. discovery of documents and interrogatories were only of occasional use. In particular, a distinguished Victorian judge alleged, the new — supposedly simplified — rules of pleading were 'so confused and inartistic as to be in many instances only a source of embarrassment and expense'. Not surprisingly,

11 Section 25(11).
12 The proposals regarding juries and appellate courts especially had been changed.
13 (1875) 141 Edinburgh Review 179, 180.
14 141 Edinburgh Review 179.

commercial litigation was said to have 'almost entirely left the legal tribunals'. Above all, perhaps, there had been a great increase in the number of appeals: this in itself was a considerable cause of delay and of expense. In addition, as the distinguished judge, Lord Bowen pointed out, it tended 'to make the Court of Appeal the pivot of the new system, just as the Courts of Banc were the pivot of the old'. In itself that was not necessarily a misfortune, but it added to the delay in, and expenses of, cases which now went to appeal in some numbers. In 1890 the *Law Times* even suggested that a royal commission might be appointed so that 'the government may know the truth, and that before it is too late something may be done to restore public confidence in the courts'.[15]

No effective action was taken, although it is true that a number of minor changes was made. In particular, after one judge was believed to have been guilty of both considerable unnecessary delay and of a woeful lack of knowledge in a commercial case, judicial initiative led to the creation of the Commercial List within Queen's Bench with a view to ensuring that appropriate commercial cases were heard by a judge with some commercial knowledge. Yet arrears continued to mount, especially before King's Bench. In 1908 the *Law Times* referred to the 'chaos' in King's Bench; in 1913 it referred to the 'hopeless state of congestion in the courts'.[16]

The Judicature Acts had given their blessing to, or even introduced, useful changes. The administrative fusion of law and equity advanced existing practice usefully enough. The changed approach to procedure and to pleading which stressed the merits of the action was refreshing, even if initially the means of implementing that approach were found wanting. Nor was it surprising that it took some time before litigants, lawyers, and judges settled down to the new appellate process. Unfortunately, little had been done to banish the old enemies of delay and of expense. The judicature commissioners as a group lacked the will to implement any radical reform. The role of the judicature commissioners had been simply to set the seal upon consensus and to spell out the resulting details: it was a useful but limited role which did little to revitalise the courts by reducing unnecessary delay and expense.

Surprisingly little was done during the first half of the twentieth century to counter the constant complaints which were made of the superior courts, especially their delay. A Judicial Council rarely met. Two inquiries, which were headed by Hanworth and Peel respectively, were launched in the 1930s. They achieved little of note. In the late 1940s rather more was expected of the inquiry headed by Lord Evershed. Yet there was little apparent enthusiasm for change amongst either the profession or the public.[17] An age old legal machine lumbered on into the second half of the twentieth century.

8   Alternatives to the courts

a) *Introduction*
The role of the courts, as it was perceived during the eighteenth and nineteenth

---

15   Lord Bowen 'Law Courts under the Judicature Acts' (1886) 2 LQR 1, (1890) 89 LT 152, cf. (1891) 92 LT 90.
16   (1908) 126 LT 161, 251, 395, 419, 465, (1913) 134 LT 471, 493, 517. Scrutton LJ 'The Work of the Commercial Courts' (1923) 1 Camb LJ 6, 15, R.F.V. Heuston *Lives of the Lord Chancellors 1885-1940* p. 45, cf. (1944) 60 LQR 324.
17   B. Abel-Smith and R. Steven *Lawyers and the Courts* chap. 10.

centuries, had evolved only gradually by way of response to particular social, economic and political pressures. If the courts were to continue to play a significant role in society, it was essential that they should continue to respond positively to such pressures. Two particular challenges were offered to the system during this period. First, there was the rise of the administrative tribunal — and the rejection of the tribunal of commerce. Secondly, there was the growth of arbitration.

b) *The administrative tribunal*

i) *Judicial and administrative roles in medieval times.* During the nineteenth century new social factors, especially those which were consequent upon the growth of the cities, led to fresh approaches to problem-solving in the public sphere. Such a reallocation of judicial and administrative responsibilities was not new. Medieval government had never distinguished clearly between the manner in which it dealt with questions of law and questions of administration. Eventually, a rough division of responsibilities had been evolved. By and large the Exchequer dealt with financial questions, Parliament dealt with legislation, the courts adjudicated upon legal questions and the Council was concerned primarily with executive duties. That division of duties was not clear cut. Plucknett has pointed out that Parliament and Exchequer both had considerable judicial business, that the courts did a certain amount of administrative work, and that the Council had a large share in judicature as well as in legislation.[18] Not surprisingly, the legal system of the mid-eighteenth century bore the mark of these origins. For example, the duties of the justice of the peace were both judicial and administrative, as were those of the Lord Chancellor. The history of the Court of Chancery is one of an evolution from a wholly unfettered exercise of administrative discretion in medieval days to a situation in Eldon's days when equitable principles appeared to be as settled as those of the common law. Even then, some of Chancery's functions were wholly administrative. At the same time the minister in charge of the Home Department exercised a judicial function in deciding whether or not to recommend the pardon of a convicted criminal.

ii) *Early tribunals.* In addition there had long existed a number of specialised tribunals. The commission of sewers dates from the thirteenth century; Star Chamber and the Court of Requests were administrative tribunals. During the Tudor period in particular there was a marked increase in the numbers of such tribunals. After Parliament's victory they were regarded less favourably. They smacked of a more autocratic past. Henceforth, the courts of common law were to be supreme in adjudicating upon the law. The price of the supremacy of the courts in that sphere was their recognition in practice, no matter what lip service they paid at times to traditional doctrines of natural law or of the role of the common law, of the overall supremacy or sovereignty of Parliament. Accordingly, the courts were reluctant to pronounce upon what appeared to be questions of policy. In a sense, therefore, it was scarcely surprising that Dicey should have maintained that England and Wales had no system of administrative law. Yet,

18 T.F.T. Plucknett *A Concise History of the Common Law* (5th edn, 1956) p. 146.

even as he wrote, events had already overtaken him: he might have claimed with accuracy only that England and Wales had no coherent system of administrative law. Social necessity had already spawned a wide range of tribunals.[19]

iii) *Nineteenth-century-tribunals and twentieth-century origins of the modern system*. No more daunting problem faced the early Victorian administrators than that of public health. A great deal of public health legislation was enacted. Certainly the Public Health Act 1848[20] was a comprehensive measure. A General Board of Health was created: provision was made also for the creation of local boards of health which were charged with various duties. For example, a local board might require a person to carry out improvements to his property. In default thereof, the board might itself carry out the improvements and exact the cost from the owner. Statute then went on to provide that:

> 'Where any person deems himself aggrieved by the decision of the local authority in any case in which the local authority are empowered to recover in a summary manner any expenses incurred by them...he may, within 21 days after notice of such decision address a memorial to the Minister of Health stating the grounds of his complaint, and shall deliver a copy thereof to the local authority; the Minister of Health may make such order in the matter as to the said Minister may seem equitable, and the Order so made shall be binding and conclusive on all parties.[1]

Clearly such legislation encroached upon the existing role of the courts.

Other legislation sought to maintain a role for the courts. For example, statute provided in 1854[2] that all railway and canal companies were to 'afford all reasonable facilities for the receiving and forwarding and delivering of traffic' and that no company was to 'make or give any undue or unreasonable preferences or advantage' to any person or firm or class of traffic, or to manifest 'any undue or unreasonable prejudice or disadvantage' towards anyone. Complaints might be made to Common Pleas which might itself make inquiries and have the assistance of experts. Unfortunately, the system did not work well in practice. A select committee which reported in 1872 commented:[3]

> 'The decisions of the courts as between different classes of traders have...been satisfactory in principle, and there seems no reason to suppose that any tribunal specially constituted would come to sounder conclusions. But then it is urged that the expense of going before the Court of Common Pleas is so great as to give the wealthy companies great advantages over private traders...a court constituted of persons specially acquainted with the subject would settle questions of this kind without the expense and difficulty which is necessary in order to obtain decisions from a court of law. It is further urged that questions concerning the fairness of charges are matters of administrative policy rather than simple questions of law,

---

19   On tribunals generally see W.A. Robson *Justice and Administrative Law* (3rd edn, 1951). Cf. R.E. Wraith and P.G. Hutchesson *Administrative Tribunals* (1973), and W.S. Holdsworth *History of English Law* (1964) vol 14, p. 183.

20   See H.J Stephen *New Commentaries on the Laws of England* (4th edn, 1858) vol 3, p. 270.

1   Public Health Act 1875, s. 268.

2   Railway and Canal Traffic Act 1854.

3   Report from the Joint Select Committee...on Railway Companies Amalgamation no. 364 (1872) p. xviii.

and would be better dealt with by a special tribunal. There is considerable force in these arguments.'

The evidence certainly supported that final point. The commercial manager of an ironworks maintained that in the case of a small trader, it was almost impossible for him to bring a great railway company to book in a court of law. Taking the example of the Poor Law Board and the Committee of Council on Education, he said:

'some of the functions of the Poor Law Board are judicial,...but I should think a very large portion of their duties is that of deciding points for parties who appeal to them; they do not give a judicial decision, but they have got the cases all before them: they know what has arisen up on the subject before, and they give advice, and armed with that advice or with that decision the parties are then prepared, if necessary, to appeal to the law.'[4]

Accordingly, statute provided in 1873 for the transfer of Common Pleas powers to railway commissioners.[5] In 1888 further legislation provided that there were to be three commissioners.[6] One commissioner was to be experienced in railway matters — he would be appointed by the Crown upon the recommendation of the Home Secretary. A second commissioner was to be a judge of the High Court who would be appointed by the Lord Chancellor. Any person or representative body might take proceedings. The finding of the commissioners on any question of fact was final. Upon a question of law there could be an appeal to the Court of Appeal. In several respects this new tribunal was administrative in nature. Yet there was still a very strong bias towards the ordinary judicial system. The president of the Commission was a judge of the High Court, his opinion was to prevail on any question of law to the Court of Appeal. The traditional legal system appeared destined at least to influence strongly the characteristics of any future tribunals, no matter how varied the field which such tribunals might cover.

Indeed, it was upon the ordinary courts that the new jurisdiction in workmen's compensation was conferred in 1897.[7] Workmen were to be compensated for injuries 'arising out of and in the course of employment'. Despite the hopes which had been entertained of a speedy and inexpensive process based upon private agreement or arbitration, in practice many such cases went before county court judges. A considerable number of cases even went on appeal to the House of Lords. Accordingly, the process was often far from being either speedy or inexpensive. For that the courts and the lawyers incurred a considerable degree of blame. At much the same time there was also a considerable feeling that the courts had mishandled the trade union cases at the turn of the century. It was scarcely surprising, therefore, that when the Liberal Government introduced a new scheme of social insurance in 1911, provision was made for resort, not to the courts, but to a new form of tribunal. The origin of that tribunal may also have been due to the fact that the originators of the new scheme based themselves upon the German model which used such a system of tribunals.[8]

---

4 Royal Commission on Railways, Minutes of Evidence taken before the Commissioners no. 120252 (1867) q. 15467. One witness, distrusting the jury, wished to remove all questions which involved a railway before a special tribunal (q. 16844).
5 Regulation of Railways Act 1873.
6 Railway and Canal Traffic Act 1888.
7 60 and 61 Vict, c. 37.
8 Wraith and Hutchesson *Administrative Tribunals* p. 28.

In the first instance applications for unemployment benefit were to be made to an insurance officer who was appointed by the Board of Trade. In the event of a dispute the insurance office could be required to refer the matter to a 'court of referees'. Such courts were composed of a chairman who was appointed by the Board of Trade, one member who was drawn from an 'employers' panel' and one member who was drawn from a 'workmen's panel'. A further appeal might be made to an 'umpire' who was appointed by the Crown. It is in this form of tribunal that we find the true origins of the modern tribunals which multiplied so rapidly.[9]

iv) *Lawyers' attitudes.* The attitude of the lawyers to the creation of such a multitude of tribunals naturally varied just as the tribunals varied in their nature. On occasion the lawyers did not oppose, they even welcomed, the creation of tribunals which were to deal with matters which they felt lay outside their own traditional role. The lawyers did oppose vigorously the creation of tribunals which appeared to rival that traditional role. Such lawyers were to find an enthusiastic champion in the 1920s in the Lord Chief Justice, Lord Hewart. The rapid increase in the number of tribunals and the use of delegated legislation alarmed Lord Hewart to such an extent that in 1929 he made a highly critical and well publicised attack upon 'The New Despotism'.[10] As a result of Lord Hewart's criticism the Committee on Ministers' Powers (the Donoughmore Committee) was appointed.[11] So far as tribunals were concerned, the Committee rejected Lord Hewart's position. The Committee also went on to recommend that judicial, as contrasted with quasi-judicial, decisions should be left to the ordinary courts. It could be argued that such a distinction was both vague and legalistic, yet it appealed to many lawyers. Lord Greene MR commented in 1944 that 'on principle...questions of law ought to be decided by the courts and no other tribunal. Special tribunals may well be as good tribunals of fact as a judge or a jury.'[12] Accordingly, on questions of law there should be an appeal to the courts and legal representation should be allowed. It was an attitude which was given judicial expression in 1951 in *R v Northumberland Compensation Appeal Tribunal, ex parte Shaw* the Court of Appeal affirmed that certiorari lay not only to see that inferior tribunals kept within their jurisdiction but also to see that they observed the law.[13]

In practice the lawyers had tended to feel uneasy when they were asked to work without guidance outside what they regarded as their traditional role. For example, in 1854 Lord Campbell opposed the new Railway Act on the grounds that it sought to turn the judges of the common law into railway directors. He went on:

> 'no rule was laid down, which they were to enforce. The whole of this enacting law, as far as railways were concerned,...said...that railway

---

9   Wraith and Hutchesson p. 34. Cf. B. Abel-Smith and R. Stevens *Lawyers and the Courts* p. 116.
10   Lord Hewart *The New Despotism.*
11   Cmd. 4060.
12   Haldane Memorial Lecture, 1944 cited by Sir H. Slesser (himself a former Lord Justice of Appeal) with apparent approval in his book *The Administration of the Law* p. 121. Lord Greene made it clear that the tribunals did have a useful role to play.
13   Sir A. Denning *Freedom Under the Law.*

companies ought to act honestly; and common-law judges were to be called on to say whether railway companies had acted honestly or not. They had no statutable or common law authority to which they were referred; no decisions of their predecessors to guide them; but, to be able satisfactorily to discharge their new functions, they must go as apprentices to civil engineers and travel upon the railways, in order to acquire some knowledge of engineering, and of the manner in which the railways were conducted...

...The judges, then, had first to try upon affidavit whether the trains were sufficiently equipped, whether time had been properly kept, and the fares were just and reasonable, without favour to one or prejudice to another. Hitherto, the maxim had been, that the judges were to answer questions of law, and the jury questions of fact; but here they were called upon to answer questions of fact, upon which they must be wholly incompetent to form an opinion. It might be said that engineers might report to them; but the report of an engineer did not decide the case. The judge must hear the matter over again after this report was made.[14]

During the course of his reply the Lord Chancellor pointed out that the Bill enacted that companies must give reasonable facilities for traffic. 'Reasonable facilities' was the kind of phrase with which the common law was familiar. An innkeeper was bound to receive guests who presented themselves, and he might be indicted, or an action

'be brought against him, if he failed to give reasonable facilities in this way. The difficulty of saying what was reasonable, and what was unreasonable, had not stopped the wisdom of our ancestors in saying that this was a law which ought to be enforced. Then, again, a common carrier was bound to give reasonable facilities in taking all goods which were presented to him...he did not see that it was more difficult to say that a railway company had not given "reasonable facilities", than it was to say that a carrier or innkeeper had failed in complying with the requirements of the law affecting them.'[15]

To a large extent the Lord Chancellor was proved correct. The Select Committee of 1872 believed that the decisions of the courts under the Act were as acceptable as those which any tribunal was likely to give. What was unacceptable were the expense and delay which were inherent in the conventional court proceedings.

c) *Tribunals of commerce*

Lawyers were less amenable when it appeared that there might be any encroachment upon their traditional role, no matter what allegations were made regarding the delay and expense of the legal process. So much is apparent from the signal lack of success which met the pleas of commercial men for the creation of tribunals of commerce. The *Law Times* showed itself especially conscious of the force of such pleas. In 1851 it reported that there had been a meeting in the city to establish a tribunal of commerce: it wrote warningly of this 'dire symptom' of the growing impatience of the public with the existing system of law proceedings

14 133 Official Report (3rd series) cols. 596-597.
15 133 Official Report (3rd series) cols. 598-600.

and law charges — the lawyers must bestir themselves.[16] In 1857 it reported that a mercantile law conference had resolved that 'either tribunals of commerce should be established, or some means adopted to give speedier and more satisfactory justice in mercantile causes'.[17] To some lawyers it appeared that such tribunals were to be county courts with unlimited jurisdiction and with three judges instead of one, the judgment of the court to be the judgment of the majority. Such lawyers doubted whether a satisfactory administration of justice was compatible with such a condition of things: they feared, too, that such a change would mean the ruin of the Bar.[18] Lawyers tended to argue that what was wanted was not the creation of an amateur tribunal, as *The Times* had put it, but an end to 'costly, dilatory and vexatious procedures' within the existing courts.[19] Even so, in 1871 a select committee reported in favour of tribunals of commerce on the French model. Was it not becoming a serious question, asked the *Law Times*, whether the profession should not take the bull by the horns and so anticipate the action of such bodies as the Associated Chambers of Commerce? The alternative was that, as regards practice in the superior courts, the ruin of the Bar would be complete.[20]

The judicature commissioners refused to do so.[1] They collected great deal of evidence concerning the work of such tribunals overseas. However, in a report which was little more than two pages in length, they simply noted the diversity of opinion which existed as to the form which such tribunals should take and the diversity which existed in such tribunals overseas. They went on:

'Now, we think that it is of the utmost importance to the commercial community that the decisions of the courts of law should on all questions of principle be, as far as possible, uniform, thus affording precedents for the conduct of those engaged in the ordinary transactions of trade. With this view it is essential that the judges by whom commercial cases are determined, should be guided by the recognised rules of law and by the decisions of the superior courts in analogous cases; and only judges who have been trained in the principles and practice of law can be expected to be so guided. We fear that merchants would be too apt to decide questions that might come before them (as some of the witnesses we examined have suggested that they should do) according to their own views of what was just and proper in the particular case, a course which from the uncertainty attending their decisions would inevitably multiply litigation, and with the vast and intricate commercial business of this country would sooner or later lead to great confusion. Commercial questions, we think, ought not to be determined without law, or by men without special legal training. For these reasons we are of opinion that it is not expedient to establish in this country tribunals of commerce, in which commercial men are to be the judges.'

However, they did see a need for a court presided over by a legal judge who could

---

16   (1851) 16 LT 477.
17   (1857) 28 LT 303. Cf. (1865) 9 Sol Jo 1040, (1866) 10 Sol Jo 643, (1871) 15 Sol Jo 340, (1872) 17 Sol Jo 143.
18   (1871) 51 LT 390.
19   (1872) 17 Sol Jo 13.
20   (1871) 51 LT 390, 391.
 1   Judicature Commission: Third Report of the Commissioners no. C-597 (1874).

be assisted by two skilled assessors: they believed also that there should be sufficient judicial strength so as to avoid complaints of delay and of expense. There
were two notable dissentients — Lord Penzance, who in 1872 had refused to sign
the second report, in part because he upheld the traditional role of the superior
courts, now did not sign the third report because he was

> 'not satisfied that tribunals might not be established consisting of commer-
> cial men with adequate legal assistance, capable of settling commercial
> disputes in a satisfactory manner, at greater speed and at much less cost
> than at present. And I think the well-known fact that in the large majority
> of commercial disputes the parties avoid the courts of law and resort to
> private arbitration is strong to show the need of some such tribunals, and a
> cogent reason for making the experiment.'

The other dissentient maintained that not all mercantile legislation was hostile
in character.

Once again the influence of the Bar appears to have been successful in
resisting change. On this occasion, however, it seemed that a reasonable compromise was truly in hand for the general belief was that the Judicature Acts
would simplify procedure and pleading with a consequent reduction in the
delays and expense which had been inherent in litigation. Only time would show
that that had been a false hope. By that time commercial men appear to have
abandoned all hope of any radical change in the legal system and to be turning
even more to arbitration.

d) *Arbitration*

i) *Introduction.* Arbitration i.e. an agreement to refer the determination of a
dispute to a third party rather than go to law, has long been popular. In
Blackstone's day it was 'a considerable part of the business of the superior courts'
to set aside such arbitration awards when they were partially or illegally made, or
to enforce their execution.[2] It is fair to assume that an even greater number of
arbitrations was decided without recourse to the courts. We find that in 1953 the
Evershed Committee reported that it was troubled by a trend to arbitration.[3]
Clearly there has long been a public demand for arbitration. Clearly, also, the
lawyers and the courts have long been aware of that demand.

ii) *Law.* Parties might agree that their submission of the suit to arbitration or
umpirage should be made a rule of any of the king's courts of record. Any party
who disobeyed such an award was liable to be punished as for contempt of court,
unless such award were set aside for corruption or other misbehaviour in the
arbitrators or umpire. Later statutes provided that a court or judge might command the attendance of witnesses for giving evidence on oath and that the
appointment of an arbitrator might not be revocable by either party without
leave of the court. The Common Law Procedure Act 1854 also provided that
certain matters might be compulsorily remitted e.g. matters of mere account
which could not conveniently be tried in the ordinary way.[4]

---

2   3 Bl Com (5th edn) 17.
3   Final Report of the Committee on Supreme Court Practice and Procedure (Cmd. 8878)
    para. 895.
4   3 Bl Com (5th edn) 17, H.J. Stephen *New Commentaries on the Law of England* (4th edn,
    1858) vol 3, p. 357.

iii) *Merits and defects.* Blackstone believed that experience had demonstrated 'the great use of these peaceable and domestic tribunals, especially in settling matters of account, and other mercantile transactions, which are difficult and almost impossible to be adjusted on a trial at law'. Similarly, in 1791 a writer on arbitration suggested that arbitration allowed a decision to be reached without 'the unintelligible jargon of technical argumentation', but suggested that it was most appropriate only in complex cases. Even so, Brougham maintained that the provision of better facilities for arbitration, together with efficient county courts, would do a great deal to make justice less expensive.[5] Yet there were considerable faults in the system.

In 1867 the judicature commissioners pointed out that the powers given by the Common Law Procedure Act 1854 were limited to cases where the dispute related wholly or in part to matters of mere account, or where the parties had themselves before action agreed in writing to refer the matter in difference to arbitration. They continued:

> 'The system of arbitration which has thus been introduced, is attended with much inconvenience. The practice is to refer cases which cannot be conveniently tried in court either to a barrister or to an expert. A barrister can seldom give that continuous attention to the case which is essential to its being speedily and satisfactorily disposed of; and an expert, being unacquainted with the law of evidence, and with the rules which govern legal proceedings, allows questions to be introduced which have nothing to do with the matters at issue. In neither case has the referee that authority over the practitioners and the witnesses which is essential to the proper conduct of the proceedings. If the barrister or solicitor who is engaged in the suit, or even a witness, has some other engagement, an adjournment is almost of course. The arbitrator makes his own charges, generally depending on the number and length of the meetings, and the professional fees are regulated accordingly. The result is great and unnecessary delay, and a vast increase of expense to the suitors. The arbitrator thus appointed is the sole judge of law and fact, and there is no appeal from his judgment, however, erroneous his view of the law may be, unless perhaps when the error appears on the face of his award. Nor is there any remedy, whatever may be the miscarriage of the arbitrator, unless he fails to decide on all the matters referred to him, or exceeds his jurisdiction, or is guilty of some misconduct in the course of the case.'[6]

There were various forms of arbitration, not all of which required any decision as to the rights of the parties. For example, a contract might stipulate simply that price, quality etc. were to be determined by an arbitrator at a later date. However, public interest focussed upon two categories of arbitration in particular, industrial arbitration and commercial arbitration.

iv) *Industrial arbitration.* There had long been provision for industrial arbitration. Such provisions had met with little success. Even in the 1890s some still

---

5 W.S. Holdsworth *History of English Law* vol 3, p. 17, *History of English Law* vol 12, p. 393, *History of English Law* vol 13, p. 300.
6 Judicature Commission: First Report of the Commissioners no. 4130 (1869) pp. 12-13.

put their faith in such arbitration as a means of avoiding disputes. By then, however, workmen had long rejected such arbitration on the grounds that they could not accept the premise upon which the arbitrator might work. The employer felt that he must make at least a certain minimum profit; the employee wanted a living wage. Neither demand was necessarily unreasonable. Yet they could not always be reconciled. In the light of such a lack of consensus the task of the lawyer who was called upon to arbitrate was unenviable. Upon what principles should he proceed?[7] As compulsory arbitration began to appear in practice to mean the fixing of wages by a law over whose guiding principles they had little influence, workmen began to attach greater importance to conciliation.

v) *Commercial arbitration.* Commercial arbitration was outstandingly successful. Here there was a consensus as to the principles which should be applied. By and large lawyers and courts assisted in meeting the public expectation regarding the application of those principles. So in 1922 an English judge commented:

> 'That they [arbitrations] will continue their present popularity, I entertain no doubt, so long as the law itself retains sufficient hold over them to prevent any injustice on the part of the arbitrator, and to secure that the law that is administered by an arbitrator is in substance the law of the land, and not some home-made law of the particular arbitrator or the particular association.'[8]

That was not an uncommon attitude. Judges recognised that arbitrators were able to act speedily and that they were familiar with the relevant commercial technique and custom. On the other hand the judges believed that arbitrators were at a disadvantage in not being able to decide questions of law with the same precision as a court of law. Accordingly, the courts sought to determine points submitted to them in good faith with all due speed.[9] The consequence was that, in the view of an American author who wrote in 1934, the English arbitration system was 'working with precision and...[was]...used almost without exception by business'.[10] Recourse to such arbitration was not necessarily wholly voluntary. For example, standard insurance contracts included an arbitration clause as a matter of form. However, it was clear that arbitration attracted much popular support.

---

7 S. and B. Webb 'Arbitration in Labour Disputes' (1896) 40 Nineteenth Century 743, 747. The Webbs cite to similar effect the view of a county court judge who had acted as an arbitrator. See also chap. 14 and W.S. Holdsworth *History of English Law* vol 15, p. 32.
8 *Czarnikow v Roth, Schmidt & Co* [1922] 2 KB 478.
9 [1919] 2 KB 431 at 442-3.
10 P.G. Phillips 'Rules of Law or Laissez-Faire in Commercial Arbitration' (1934) 47 HLR 610.

Chapter 7

Courts of criminal jurisdiction

1 Introduction

a) *Courts of criminal jurisdiction*

There were numerous courts of criminal jurisdiction. By the beginning of the nineteenth century that jurisdiction was exercised for the most part by the Court of King's Bench and the assize courts, which heard the more serious, especially the capital, cases and by the county and borough courts of quarter sessions and the courts of summary jurisdiction which heard the less serious offences. The greater part of this chapter will be devoted to a discussion of those courts. It should be remembered, however, that the High Court of Parliament, the court of the Lord High Steward, the Court of Chivalry and the High Court of Admiralty were each invested with a criminal jurisdiction. At a lower level criminal jurisdiction might be exercised by the sheriff's tourn, the court leet, the court of the coroner and the court of the clerk of market. However, the criminal jurisdiction of these courts was little exercised during the nineteenth century.

b) *Allocation of case to a particular court*

Upon deciding to commit a prisoner for trial, the justice of the peace also decided whether the case was to be heard summarily, or upon indictment at quarter sessions or assizes.

2 Summary proceedings

Summary proceedings were such as were directed by Act of Parliament, there was no jury, and the person accused was acquitted or sentenced only by such person as statute had appointed for his judge. The common law was wholly a stranger to summary proceedings. Typical of the jurisdiction in Blackstone's day were all trials of offences and frauds contrary to the excise laws and other branches of the revenue. These were to be inquired into and determined by the commissioners of the respective departments, or by justices of the peace.

Another branch of the jurisdiction was that before justices of the peace for offences such as common swearing, drunkenness, vagrancy, idleness etc. which formerly had been punished by the verdict of a jury in the court leet. Generally speaking the summary jurisdiction was limited to such minor offences, of which minor nuisances and disturbances of good order afford other examples.[1] At this time, therefore, the justices had no jurisdiction with regard even to quite small larcenies.

During the nineteenth century the justices were given greater powers. It was a process which began in 1827 when they were given powers in relation to stealing deer etc. In 1847 justices 'in petty sessions assembled' were empowered to try offenders under 14 years of age on a charge of simple larceny.[2] The Criminal Justice Act 1855 conferred upon justices the power to try cases of theft and embezzlement of things of the value of less than five shillings, if the defendant consented. The Criminal Consolidation Acts of 1861 conferred wider powers still.

Motives for extending the summary jurisdiction varied. At a time when the criminal process did not distinguish between adults and juveniles, the criminal law commissioners had believed that juveniles might be spared the contaminating effects of prison while awaiting trial, if only the summary jurisdiction of the magistrates were increased. Such an increase in the summary powers would tend to diminish juvenile crime, they believed.[3] Secondly, there can be no doubt that the Criminal Justice Act 1855, by providing for local justice, met the needs of prosecutors, especially at a time when prosecutions were still largely private, when travel to a superior court may not have appealed to many potential prosecutors, and when many potential prosecutors may have believed that in the case, say, of a minor larceny, it was simply not worth the trouble of appearing before a superior court. The result of the Act was not simply to transfer the trial of a number of minor offences to the petty sessions but to increase considerably the number of such offences which were prosecuted at all.[4] The success of the 1855 Act marked a turning point in the history of the criminal process. Until the enactment of the Criminal Justice Act 1855 the distinguishing feature of the criminal process had been trial by jury: henceforth, there was to be a steadily increasing erosion of that 'palladium' of the liberties of the subject. The most notable extension of the jurisdiction occurred during the twentieth century when many motoring offences, together with a new and articulate social class of offender, were introduced to the summary jurisdiction. Inevitably, that meant that an ever sharper public scrutiny was aimed at the summary process.

The summary process was 'extremely speedy'. Before Blackstone's day any formal procedure was altogether lacking — justices had even disputed the necessity of a summons being issued to the person charged. Often during the eighteenth century, and even into the nineteenth century, the hearing might well be in the house of the justice. Brougham offered the notorious instance of the Duke of Buckingham hearing in his own home a charge brought by his own

---

1   4 Bl Com (5th edn) 277 ff., H. J. Stephen *New Commentaries on the Laws of England* (4th edn, 1858) vol 4, pp. 393ff.
2   An Act for consolidating and amending the Laws...relative to Larceny and other Offences..., An Act for the more speedy Trial and Punishment of Juvenile Offenders.
3   Third Report from the Commissioners on Criminal Law no. 79 (1837) p. 5.
4   D. Philips *Crime and Authority in Victorian England* p. 133.

gamekeeper against a neighbouring farmer. However, during the nineteenth century it became customary for regular divisional meetings, known as petty sessions, to be held. Even then the procedure to be followed before the magistrates' courts was vague and uncertain. How was the defendant to be caused to appear before the justice? What evidence might be introduced on his behalf? Might witnesses be compelled to attend? Such uncertainties led, through the medium of the writ of certiorari, to King's Bench quashing a considerable number of convictions before magistrates.[5] It is fair to assume, however, that throughout the country magistrates continued to exercise a considerable discretion which may have led to injustice in some cases and which certainly resulted in a lack of uniformity throughout the country as a whole.

In 1848 the measures which became known as Jervis' Acts sought to remedy these considerable defects in the criminal law. Their enactment both simplified the law and made all the more credible the further expansion of the summary jurisdiction. They established the procedure which was to be followed at the preliminary hearing before magistrates, they protected the justice from legal action in respect of any innocent breach of the law on his part, and they also dealt with the judicial work of the justices. The final Act, the Summary Jurisdiction Act 1848 consolidated and amended the previous provisions upon the subject. Upon either an information being laid or a complaint being made, the justice was to issue his summons to the party charged requiring him to appear and to answer. Witnesses also might be summonsed. The room in which the hearing took place was to be deemed to be an open and public court, to which all were to have access. These and other provisions did much to regularise the hearing before justices. There might be an appeal to quarter sessions. If a legal question were involved, the decision of quarter sessions might be reviewed by Queen's Bench. After 1848 the summary proceedings before justices adopted a modern form. Contemporary reformers had few criticisms to make of petty sessions beyond suggesting that they should not be held in a licensed house of any sort.[6]

During the twentieth century it was the advent of the motor car which revolutionised the work of such courts. Now it became increasingly common for a defendant not to appear personally in court upon the ground that it was unreasonable 'to require a defendant to come from a distance to appear in a comparatively unimportant case, since the cost of attending, including the loss of a day's work, might well exceed the penalty likely to be imposed by the justices'.[7] Much of the work was routine, therefore. Yet these ancient courts, staffed by a lay judiciary, continued to play a vital role in the legal system and also to command substantial public respect.

3 Quarter sessions

General quarter sessions were held in every county each quarter and enjoyed a wide jurisdiction. In practice, they seldom, if ever, tried any greater offence than

---

5 J. F. Stephen *History of the Criminal Law of England* vol 1, pp. 122ff.
6 Sir W. Jones 'Are any and what Improvements Necessary for the Administration of Justice in Petty and Quarter Sessions?' *Trans. of the Nat. Ass. for the Promotion of Social Science 1873* pp. 254, 258.
7 Report of the Departmental Committee on the Summary Trial of Minor Offences (Cmd. 9524) p. 6, para 6.

small felonies within the benefit of clergy for their commission provided that, if any case of difficulty arose, they should not proceed to judgment except in the presence of one of the justices of the Court of King's Bench or Common Pleas, or one of the judges of assize. Accordingly, murders and other capital felonies were usually remitted to the assizes; quarter sessions tried the smaller misdemeanours against the public. In most corporation towns borough quarter sessions were kept before justices of their own. Such courts usually had much the same authority as the general quarter sessions of the county.

Probably, it was not until the eighteenth century that the justices at quarter sessions began to distinguish, however informally, between the heavy administrative work, which was a most important part of the work of quarter sessions, and their judicial business. The extent of the business actually transacted and the adoption of a more efficient approach to it can be seen, however, in a newspaper advertisement of the latter half of the eighteenth century which was inserted by a clerk of the peace to the quarter sessions of the West Riding of Yorkshire:

'Notice is hereby given that the General Quarter Sessions of the Peace for the West Riding of the County of York will be opened at Pontefract on Monday...that the officers and Grand Jury will then be called over, the Chairman chosen and vagrants passed....On Tuesday morning...appeals will be heard. On Wednesday the Narrow Cloth Searchers will be sworn, and appeals to traverses tried. On Thursday morning the state of the bridges will be considered, the reports of the surveyors concerning them, and other reports relating to public works or business will be received, contracts for conveying vagrants treated upon, the Treasurer's, Clerk of the Peace's, and other accounts will be audited, and a Treasurer for the year ensuing elected. In the afternoon orders relating to the tolls of Castleford and Ferrybridge, to York Castle, the House of Correction, carriers' rates, wages of servants, artificers and labourers will be settled. On Friday morning the felons will be tried; at noon the Grand Jury discharged and all recognisances called. In the afternoon highways and persons indicted will be called over and process awarded against them. All the remaining business will be dispatched and the sessions closed that night if possible.'[8]

Evidence given to the Select Committee of 1833 on Municipal Corporations presents a similar picture. At Gloucester, for example, the mayor and aldermen presided. Six or twelve prisoners might be tried: all cases of life and limbs were sent to the assizes.[9]

As a court of justice quarter sessions was always open to the public and, therefore, to the press. Of course, they were local in their jurisdiction. Procedure, almost certainly, was lax. Often there was no chairman or, at all events, no regular chairman. In 1843 the *Law Times* suggested a form of petition which asserted the inadequacy of the existing courts of quarter sessions, suggested the establishment of local courts and also asked for 'the appointment of paid professional judges of experience and ability to preside at the courts of quarter sessions, and by assimilating the practice of the said courts to that of the superior

8 S. and B. Webb *The Parish and the County* p. 441.
9 Report from the Select Committee on Municipal Corporations no. 344 (1833) pp. 117-18, q. 2722-2734.

courts...all the objects of local courts as well as of a winter assize, may be accomplished at a trifling cost'.[10] Yet the proceedings were before a jury.

Few innovations of any real note were made over the years, although there were some extensions of the jurisdiction. However, lawyers who had practised in quarter sessions in 1840 would have experienced little difficulty in becoming accustomed to the quarter sessions of 1940. Certainly some of the criticisms of quarter sessions would have been familiar enough. For example, in 1933 a committee noted that in not less than 32 courts of quarter sessions out of a total of 65, chairmen trained in the law presided: the committee approved such a practice. Yet its report communicates no sense of urgency, although in 1938 a rather confused piece of legislation did seek to increase the number of legally qualified chairmen.[11] By and large, however, there was little public concern during this period with the structure of the courts of quarter sessions.

4 King's Bench and assizes

King's Bench was the country's principal court of criminal jurisdiction. On its Crown side that court had cognisance of all criminal causes from high treason down to the most trivial misdemeanour or breach of the peace. Into King's Bench also indictments from all inferior courts could be removed by writ of certiorari, and tried either at bar or at nisi prius i.e. at assizes, by a jury of the county out of which the indictment was brought. In practice it was this latter method which was by far the more usual method of proceeding in the nineteenth century.

The assizes exercised both a civil and a criminal jurisdiction. Therefore this section refers to the civil, as well as to the criminal work of the assizes. The circuit system of which they were a part originated before the time of Magna Charta. Judges, authorised by special commissions for the purpose, were directed to be sent into every county once a year. Blackstone wrote of the courts of assize and nisi prius as follows:

> 'These are composed of two or more commissioners who are twice in every year sent by the King's special commission all round the kingdom (except London and Middlesex where courts of nisi prius are holden in and after every term, before the chief or other judge of the several superior courts; and except the four northern counties where the assizes are holden only once a year) to try by a jury of the respective counties the truth of such matters of fact as are then under dispute in the courts of Westminster Hall.'[12]

The sheriff was ordered to have the jurors at Westminster by a certain day, unless before (nisi prius) that day the justices of assize came to his county. In practice it was arranged that the justices of assize would indeed come to his county before that day. The venue of the trial was local so that jurors might be selected who, in theory at least, would be representative of the locality. At the assizes the judges sat by virtue of five several authorities: the commission of assize and the attendant jurisdiction of nisi prius which were principally of a civil nature, the

---

10   (1843) 2 LT 58.

11   Second Interim Report of the Business of Courts Committee (Cmd. 4471) p. 43, para. 66, The Administration of Justice (Miscellaneous Provisions) Act 1938.

12   3 Bl Com (5th edn) 57.

commission of the peace, the commission of general gaol delivery whereby the judges, and others, were commanded to deliver gaol at a particular town of the prisoners therein and the commission of oyer and terminer whereby after enquiry by the grand jury, the justices were empowered to 'hear and determine' by the help of a petty jury.[13]

Much of the medieval pageantry which surrounded the assizes survived into the twentieth century. Trumpeters, javelinmen, the assize service offered all the hallmarks of a special local occasion. According to the taste of the observer, it all added up either to a useful and desirable reminder to the local community of the majesty of the law or to a tiresome and time-consuming repetition of outmoded ritual.

Above all it became increasingly obvious during the nineteenth century that the old county towns no longer necessarily afforded the most convenient centre for the transaction of business. The common law commissioners were aware of the problem in the 1830s when the Welsh courts were assimilated into the system.[14] In the large county of Yorkshire most of the population was in the West Riding rather than in the areas around the old county town of York. Similarly, in Warwickshire the population was greatest around the rapidly growing, industrial city of Birmingham rather than around the county town of Warwick. Necessarily a number of the less populous counties had relatively little business. Yet assize time was still allocated to them. In the view of the judicature commissioners this led to 'a great waste of judicial strength, and a great loss of time in going from one circuit town to another, and causes much unnecessary cost and inconvenience to those whose attendance is necessary or customary at the assizes'. Accordingly, the commissioners recommended that 'the venue for trial should be enlarged, and that several counties should be consolidated into districts of a convenient size — that such districts should for all purposes of trial at the assizes, both in civil and criminal cases, be treated as one venue or county, and that all counties or towns or cities, should for the purpose of such districts be included in an adjacent district or county...'[15]

Subsequent inquiries endorsed that approach — but to little effect. Yet all were at one in rejecting another possible solution — an increase in the number of judges. Invariably, such rejection was for a familiar reason. In 1913 the St. Aldwyn Commission expressed it as follows:

> 'No one will contend that more judges should be appointed than are really necessary. It must be remembered that the field of selection is limited, the more judges appointed the smaller it becomes, and therefore the less certainty of securing in those appointed the high level of ability, legal attainments, and mental and physical vigour, which are necessary to maintain the prestige of the English Bench. The smaller the number of judges the higher will be the standard of efficiency and the greater the prize for those selected.'[16]

13 4 Bl Com (5th edn) 262, J. F. Stephen *History of the Criminal Law of England* vol 1, pp. 95-6ff., E. Chitty *The Commercial and General Lawyer* (2nd edn, 1841) p. 1157.
14 First Report...by the Commissioners appointed to inquire into the Practice and Proceedings of the Superior Courts of Common Law no. 46 (1829) pp. 37ff.
15 Judicature Commission: First Report of the Commissioners no. 4130 (1869) p. 17.
16 1913 (Cd. 7177) p. 39, para. 63 — cited with approval in Second Interim Report of the Business of Courts Committee (Cmd. 4471) p. 33, para. 49.

Other solutions had been canvassed. The Assizes Relief Act 1889, which was passed in order to relieve the judges of assize from unnecessary work, provided that persons charged with offences triable at quarter sessions, should be tried at quarter sessions, unless the committing justices for special reasons directed otherwise. Yet that Act did not fulfil its author's intentions because committing magistrates treated the fact that assizes preceded the next practicable court of quarter sessions as providing a special reason for committing to the assizes.

In fact most civil work had been heard in London since a railway system which focussed upon London simply made London the most convenient centre for the transaction of much civil business. Yet because in practice, if not in theory, priority was given to going on circuit, the judges had less time for their London work with the result that, during the inter-war period, delays increased considerably. At the same time priority on assize was given to criminal cases with the result once again that the civil work suffered. Such problems were well known. Committees sat; various solutions were canvassed and resort was had to diverse expedients, of which Lord Denning's expedient of creating commissioners of assize, usually county court judges, for the purpose of tackling the greatly increased amount of divorce work after the Second World War was the most well known. However, to all intents and purposes the ancient system lumbered on, largely unchanged, even in mid-twentieth century.

5 The Central Criminal Court

Before the creation of the Central Criminal Court in 1834, London and Middlesex cases were tried at the Sessions House, Old Bailey, under a commission of oyer and terminer for the city of London, and a commission of gaol delivery for the gaol of Newgate. There were eight sessions at the Old Bailey in each year. The capital charges and other more serious offences were tried before two or more judges of the superior courts; other cases were tried before the recorder, the common sergeant, or one of the judges of the Sheriffs' Court, one alderman at least being always present. In 1834 statute placed the court upon its modern basis. Its national character was confirmed in 1856 when statute provided that, if it appeared that a local jury would not be impartial, the venue of the trial could be moved to the Central Criminal Court.[17]

6 Procedure

Procedure was seen as being essentially liberal. Blackstone maintained that both crimes and penalties were defined reasonably clearly, trials were public, torture was unknown, and every delinquent was judged by his equals.[18] These were highly relevant points to those reformers, both English and others, who had taken to heart Montesquieu's dictum that 'it is on the perfection of the criminal laws that the liberty of the individual depends',[19] who believed in the wisdom of Beccaria's insistence upon the importance to liberty of specific guarantees

17   T. F. T. Plucknett *A Concise History of the Common Law* (5th edn, 1956) p. 128.
18   4 Bl Com (5th edn) 3. Cf. L. Radzinowicz *History of the English Criminal Law* vol 1, pp. 714-19.
19   M. Ploscowe 'The Development of Present Day Criminal Procedures in Europe and America' (1935) 48 HLR 453.

rather than abstract declarations of principle, and for whom Voltaire's indictment of existing European procedures at criminal law as seeming 'to point only to the destruction of the accused' rang true. It may well be that this satisfaction with the English procedure was a factor which contributed to a relative lack of discussion of the topic in England during the nineteenth century. A further factor may have been the English reformers' preoccupation during the first part of the century with the campaign to reduce the incidence, perhaps even to abolish altogether, capital punishment which was then the penalty for numerous offences.

Characteristically, the criminal law commissioners in 1845 refrained from any discussion of general principle. They chose rather to concentrate upon particular matters. For example, the charge should be certain and the accused must be enabled to prepare for the trial by being provided with copies of indictments and depositions, lists of witnesses and jurors.[20] The Criminal Procedure Act 1865 established a model procedure. Yet old attitudes take a considerable time to dispel. There was the traditional need for what now seemed to be excessive care in drawing up the indictment. Until mid-nineteenth century any variance, however slight or immaterial, between indictment and proof was fatal to the prosecution. For example, the indictment might have charged the defendant with stealing a horse yet he was proved to have stolen a mare; or he might have been charged with stealing lambs and it turned out that he had stolen sheep. In both cases the prisoner would be entitled to an acquittal. Similarly it was necessary for an indictment for murder to be drawn up in considerable detail. It was necessary to specify the length and depth of the wound and the nature of the instrument used. If it turned out that the death was caused otherwise than as described in the indictment, the prosecution failed and the defendant was acquitted. In mid-nineteenth century Lord Campbell was responsible for an Act which mitigated some of the worst excesses of this obsessive technicality.[1] After all, in the light of the reduction in the number of capital offences, that technicality no longer served any humanitarian purpose. However, although the statute dispensed with excessive particularity in some cases, the old custom still prevailed in other cases. Accordingly, in 1879 the criminal code commissioners pointed out that it was then sufficient in an indictment for murder to charge that A wilfully, feloniously and of his malice aforethought did kill and murder B, instead of setting out the precise manner in which the murder was alleged to have been committed. On the other hand in a case of obtaining goods by false pretences, the particular false pretence used had to be stated and proved as laid, together with a proper averment that it was false to the knowledge of the person accused. The commissioners believed that the difference in practice between these two cases could be explained only by the fact that the inconvenience had been noticed in the one case but not in the other.[2]

In its essentials criminal procedure was very similar to civil procedure. In particular it was litigious and hardly at all inquisitional. Stephen has suggested that even the arrest of the prisoner and his detention before trial are analagous to

20   Eighth Report of...Commissioners on Criminal Law no. 656 (1845) p. 18.
1   An Act for further improving the Administration of Criminal Justice, (1876) 61 LT 338.
2   Report of the Royal Commission appointed to consider the Law relating to Indictable Offences no. C-2345 (1879) p. 36.

the law of arrest on mesne process at civil law,[3] subject to the exception that until 1898 he could not give evidence on his own behalf. In practice the speed and informality of summary criminal justice, especially before mid-nineteenth century, may well have amounted to a rough and paternalistic form of justice rather than justice according to law. That may well have been true also of justice in superior courts. Certainly one distinguished lawyer, looking back on trials at the Old Bailey in mid-nineteenth century, estimated that after dinner trials did not occupy on the average more than four minutes each.[4] It is true that in some respects the law may be seen as being biased in favour of the defendant. Indeed it has been argued that, during the late eighteenth century especially, factors such as the over-technicality of criminal procedure amounted to a form of criminal equity.[5] If that were the case, it was an uncertain equity which failed signally to meet the demands of the classical school for certainty in the criminal law.

7 Evidence

Some reforms of the law of evidence are worthy of attention. There was the question of the defence of prisoners by counsel. It was a settled rule at common law that, treason apart, no prisoner should be allowed a counsel upon his trial upon the general issue in any capital crime unless some point of law were to be debated; in theory the judge was counsel for the prisoner — the judge would see that the proceedings against the prisoner were legal and strictly regular. In Blackstone's view this rule seemed 'to be not all of a piece with the rest of the humane treatment of prisoners by the English Law. For upon what face of reason can that assistance be denied to save the life of a man, which yet is allowed him in prosecution for every petty trespass?' In Blackstone's view the judges of his day were 'so sensible of this defect...that they seldom scruple to allow a prisoner counsel to stand by him at the bar, and instruct him what questions to ask, or even to ask questions for him, with respect to matters of fact...'[6] However, it is clear from a report of 1836 by the criminal law commissioners that contemporary legal opinion was by no means unanimous on this question, although some respect was still accorded to the view of Hawkins, the author of a classic treatise upon the criminal law, that:

> 'This exclusion many have complained of as very unreasonable, yet if it be considered, that generally every one of common understanding may as properly speak to a matter of fact as if he were the best lawyer, and that it requires no manner of skill to make a plain and honest defence, which in cases of this kind is always the best; the simplicity, the innocence, the artless and the ingenuous behaviour of one whose conscience acquits him, having in it something more moving and convincing than the highest eloquence of persons speaking in a cause not their own: and if it be further considered, that it is the duty of the court to be indifferent between the king and prisoner, and see that the indictment be good in law, and the proceedings regular, and the evidence legal, and such as fully proves the point

3   J. F. Stephen *History of the Criminal Law of England* vol 1, pp. 506-7.
4   R. M. Jackson *The Machinery of Justice in England* (6th edn, 1972) citing the Memoirs of Sir Henry Hawkins (Lord Brampton), yet the example given is of a guilty plea.
5   J. Hall *Theft, Law and Society*; see chap. 9.
6   4 Bl Com (5th edn) 349-50.

in issue, there seems no great reason to fear but that, generally speaking, the innocent, for whose safety alone the law is concerned, have rather an advantage than a prejudice in having the court their only counsel. Whereas, on the other side, the very speech, gesture, countenance and manners of defence of those who are guilty, when they speak for themselves may often help to disclose the truth, which probably would not so well be discovered from the artificial defence of others speaking for them.'[7]

It was not a view which the commissioners shared. They had heard the opinion of an eminent lawyer that some people at least had been found guilty who might well have been acquitted, and rightly so, had they had counsel: they had heard evidence also regarding the differing approaches of the judges. Yet when a bill was introduced to allow the prisoner counsel, 12 of the 15 judges opposed it strongly; one judge even threatened to resign his office if the bill were to become law. Nevertheless, in 1836 a short Act enabled persons indicted of felony to make their defence by counsel or attorney, together with other useful measures such as allowing prisoners to have copies of depositions.[8]

It was not until 1898, however, that the defendant was allowed to give evidence on his own behalf — and that right may have been conferred rather with a view to securing convictions by encouraging the accused to give evidence and submit to cross examination than to guarding the interests of the accused.[9]

However it was for the prosecution to prove its case, just as the plaintiff in a civil case had to prove his case, with the additional element that the prosecutor must prove his case beyond all reasonable doubt rather than upon the civil balance of probabilities. Viscount Sankey LC summed up the law in 1935 in the leading case of *Woolmington v Director of Public Prosecutions* when he said:

'Throughout the web of the English criminal law one golden thread is always to be seen, that it is the duty of the prosecution to prove the prisoner's guilt subject to what I have already said as to the defence of insanity and subject also to any statutory exception. If, at the end of and on the whole of the case, there is a reasonable doubt, created by the evidence given by either the prosecution or the prisoner, as to whether the prisoner killed the deceased with a malicious intention, the prosecution has not made out the case and the prisoner is entitled to an acquittal. No matter what the charge or where the trial, the principle that the prosecution must prove the guilt of the prisoner is part of the common law of England and no attempt to whittle it down can be entertained.'[10]

It is in the context of this approach rather than in nineteenth-century practice, that we should place any presumption of the innocence of the defendant, a presumption which in its own right counted for little in the nineteenth century.[11] Certainly, the appearance of the accused person at the trial in the dock and reference to him as 'the prisoner' did little to foster any presumption of

7 Mr. Sjt. Hawkins *Pleas of the Crown* b. 2, c. 39, s. 2. Second Report from...Commissioners on Criminal Law no. 343 (1836) pp. 2ff.
8 An Act for enabling Persons indicted of Felony to make their Defence by Counsel or Attorney.
9 W. R. Cornish 'Criminal Justice and Punishment' in W. R. Cornish and others *Crime and Law in Nineteenth Century Britain* p. 58.
10 *Woolmington v Director of Public Prosecutions* [1935] AC 462 at 482.
11 J. B. Thayer *A Preliminary Treatise on Evidence at the Common Law* p. 551, G. Williams *The Proof of Guilt* p. 184.

innocence. However, by the standards of the day criminal trials appear on the whole to have been conducted fairly. Any substantial amendment and revision of criminal procedure still lay very much in the future even in 1950.

8 Conclusion

The nineteenth-century judiciary placed considerable emphasis upon the speed and certainty of criminal justice. Summary justice was especially speedy. Inevitably, there would often be some delay between a preliminary hearing and trial at quarter sessions or the assizes, simply because the defendant had to wait for the next sessions or the next assizes. However, the trial itself might then be conducted at one sitting, even well into the night.[12] In capital cases execution took place on the day next but one after that on which sentence was pronounced, unless that happened to be a Sunday; at a later date the sheriff, who was responsible for the execution, usually allowed two Sundays to intervene.[13]

During the first half of the twentieth century the introduction of legal aid and of changes in the appellate process both tended to increase the length of the trial process in many criminal cases. It was the beginning of a shift away from a process which emphasised primarily the community interest in speedy justice e.g. its deterrent value, even if that resulted in some individual injustices, to a process which placed an increasing emphasis upon the rights of the individual defendant in criminal cases.

12   H. J. Stephen *New Commentaries on the Laws of England* (4th edn, 1858) vol 4, p. 499.
13   E. Chitty *The Commercial and General Lawyer* (2nd edn, 1841) p. 1208.

Chapter 8

Review and appeal

1 Civil courts

a) *Introduction*

Proceedings in the nature of appeals, as Blackstone put it,[1] were available from the proceedings of the king's courts of law. Such proceedings were most certainly not appeals in the modern sense of a rehearing of the whole case. That approach, which evolved during the nineteenth century, was quite foreign to the common law system. The court at first instance was required to give detailed consideration to a case and might make considerable use of adjournments to allow it to do so: thereafter, there was a possibility of proceedings before the Court in Banc,[2] in other words, usually before the four judges of that particular court. At a time when each of the three great courts of common law was staffed by only four judges of some distinction, the old system may have worked well enough,[3] in so far as questions of law were concerned, for it was a common practice for the judge at nisi prius to reserve a difficult question for discussion with his colleagues at Westminster. Those discussions, which took place at Sergeants' Inn or in Exchequer Chamber, were purely informal. Yet clearly they were influential, especially if all the judges attended. In addition, a further hearing was possible in cases in which error was apparent on the record. However, the grounds upon which error might be granted began to appear to be unduly restrictive. By contrast it was possible in Chancery for there to be a review of the whole case. It is in such proceedings in Chancery that we find the genesis of the modern appellate system. Other appellate courts existed; in particular, the House of Lords exercised the final appellate jurisdiction.

1 3 Bl Com (5th edn) 402.
2 R. Sutton *Personal Actions at Common Law* p. 128, J. H. Baker *An Introduction to English Legal History* (1st edn, 1971) pp. 61-2;
3 Baron Bowen 'Progress in the Administration of Justice during the Victorian Period' *Select Essays in Anglo-American Legal History* vol 1, pp. 516 and 522.

b) *Common law*

i) *Suspension or arrest of judgment.* After the court of first instance had given judgment, the successful party could not have judgment entered until the term following the trial. In the interval the unsuccessful party might succeed in having that judgment suspended or finally arrested. He did this by applying to the Court in Banc for a rule to be served on the other side to show cause why an order should not be made by the court in his favour. If the court granted the rule, the point was argued before the court; if the court accepted the argument, the rule was made absolute; if the court rejected the argument, the rule was discharged. An arrest of judgment arose for some intrinsic cause which appeared upon the face of the record and which would render it erroneous and reversible. That would be the case if the declaration varied from the original writ e.g. if the writ were in debt or detinue and the plaintiff had declared in an action on the case for an assumpsit. Or the case laid in the declaration might not be sufficient in point of law to found an action. Alternatively, either party might apply for suspension of judgment by the grant of a new trial on the grounds, for example, of want of notice of trial, or that the judge had misdirected the jury so that they found an unjustifiable verdict, or if it appeared by the judge's report that the jury had brought in a verdict without or contrary to evidence or that they had given exorbitant damages.[4]

ii) *Error.* The writ of error was an original writ which issued out of Chancery. It lay for some error or defect in substance which appeared in the proceedings of a court of record. It lay to the same court in which the judgment was given, or to which the record was removed by writ of error, or to a superior court. However, the most usual species of the writ of error was that which was founded upon some supposed mistake of law, apparent on the face of the record, which might have formed a sufficient ground at the proper time for a motion in arrest of judgment, or a motion for a judgment *non obstante veredicto*; in such cases the writ of error was addressed not to the court in which judgment was given but to a superior tribunal. A number of statutes had sought to secure the suitor from the danger of being defeated by a matter of mere form. However, the common law commissioners pointed out in 1831 that such provisions did not embrace every case of formal objection. The commissioners were also of the view that the proceedings were attended with both 'unnecessary expense' and 'most unreasonable delay'.[5] The error was limited to a defect which appeared on the face of the record. The record contained only an entry of the declaration and pleadings, and the issue or issues joined thereon, with the award of the *venire facias* whereby the sheriff was to summon the jury, the judgment of the court and a number of formal matters. Inevitably, many questions could not ground a writ of error. For example, the writ of error was available neither to question the denial of a motion for a new trial or the admissibility of evidence or the judge's summing up.[6]

4   W. Tidd *The Practice of the Court of King's Bench in Personal Actions* (3rd edn, 1803) pp. 824-5.
5   H. J. Stephen *New Commentaries on the Laws of England* (1844) vol 3, Third Report...by the Commissioners appointed to inquire into the Practice and Proceedings of the Superior Courts of Common Law no. 92 (1831) pp. 31, 34. By a plea for entry of judgment *non obstante veredicto* an unsuccessful plaintiff claimed that the facts pleaded in answer to his claim were in law no answer to it.
6   *Tidd* (above) p. 711.

The court of Exchequer Chamber determined causes upon writs of error from the common law side of the Court of Exchequer. A further court of Exchequer Chamber exercised jurisdiction with regard to writs of error brought to reverse judgments in certain suits which had been begun originally in King's Bench. It was also into the Court of Exchequer Chamber, composed for this purpose of all the judges of the three superior courts of common law and, on occasion, of the Lord Chancellor, that there were sometimes adjourned from the other courts such causes as the judges upon argument found to be of great weight and difficulty, before any judgment was given upon them in the court below. From all the branches of this Court of Exchequer Chamber a writ of error lay to the House of Lords. This rather confusing situation was amended in 1830. Henceforth, the judgments of each of the superior courts of common law, in all suits whatever, were, upon proceedings in error in law being instituted for that purpose, subject to revision by the judges of the other two sitting collectively as a Court of Error for that purpose, in the Exchequer Chamber. Consequently, the composition of the court admitted of three different combinations, consisting of any two of the courts below i.e. those which were not parties to the judgment supposed to be erroneous. From each combination of this court proceedings in error could be taken to the House of Lords.[7] In the judgment of the judicature commissioners, this system led to 'very serious' inconveniences and also in many cases to 'great and unavoidable delays in the disposal of common law errors and appeals'. The difficulties were that the judges were able to devote only a very limited number of days after each term to the hearing of appeals and errors: each such period required to be broken up into three parts and the constitution of the court to be changed three times. Further, whenever there was a difference of opinion, it was possible that the majority of opinions taken together might be overruled by the minority.[8]

c) *Chancery*

Chancery had its own system of review. The party aggrieved by a decree might either petition the judge by whom it was pronounced for a rehearing of the cause by him or, if the decree had been made by the Master of the Rolls or by the Vice-Chancellor, he might apply, by way of appeal, to have the cause reheard by the Lord Chancellor. Further, a cause which had been reheard before the Vice-Chancellor or the Master of the Rolls, could be heard before the Lord Chancellor on appeal.

If the decree had been signed and enrolled, a reversal of it could be obtained only by a bill of review. This proceeding might be had upon apparent error in judgment on the face of the decree, or by special leave of the court, upon oath made of the discovery of new evidence which could not possibly be had or used at the time the decree was made. The appearance of a party to a bill of review could be enforced in the same manner as to an original bill.[9] Another mode of rectifying or setting aside a decree pronounced in Chancery was by appeal to the House of Lords. A party could not regularly appeal to the House of Lords from a decree made by the Master of the Rolls or by the Vice-Chancellor, until the same had

7 3 Bl Com (5th edn) 56, H. J. Stephen *New Commentaries on the Laws of England* (4th edn, 1858) vol 3, p. 412. Cf. W. S. Holdsworth *History of English Law* vol 1, p. 245.
8 Judicature Commission: First Report of the Commissioners no. 4130 (1869) pp. 24 and 21.
9 E. Chitty *The Commercial and General Lawyer* (2nd edn, 1841) pp. 1022-3.

been reheard before the Chancellor, unless the decree had been signed and enrolled; in that case the appeal was to be made directly to the House of Lords.

The Court of Appeal in Chancery was constituted in 1851. It consisted of two Lords Justices and the Lord Chancellor. Appeals from the Master of the Rolls and each of the Vice-Chancellors might be referred to this court, or they could be entertained by the Lord Chancellor sitting alone. From these appellate jurisdictions an appeal lay in turn to the House of Lords. In practice the Court of Appeal in Chancery usually sat in two courts. The Lord Chancellor presided alone in one court; the Lords Justices sat in the other court. However, the decisions under this system of a Lord Chancellor who lacked a Chancery background did not always enjoy the confidence of the profession. Yet if the Lords Justices differed in their opinion, the appeal failed, the judgment of the court below was affirmed, and a further appeal to the House of Lords often resulted. On occasion more than usually important cases were reserved for hearing, or were directed to be re-argued, before the full Court of Appeal. However, the engagements of the Lord Chancellor in the House of Lords confined within very narrow limits the time which could be allotted to sittings of the Full Court. The Court of Appeal in Chancery, both in what were technically called rehearings of decrees and decretal orders, and upon appeal petitions or motions, had all the powers possessed by the court of first instance. Therefore, it could allow amendments of the record and in some cases might receive new or further evidence, a practice which was contrary to that of the House of Lords.[10]

d) *Ecclesiastical and Admiralty courts: Courts of Probate and Divorce*
An appeal from the archdeacon's court went to the court of the diocesan, then to the archbishop. Within the province of Canterbury the court of appeal from the courts of bishops or ordinaries within the province was known as the Court of Arches and was presided over by the Dean of the Arches. If an appeal were then made to the king, such appeal was heard by the High Court of Delegates.

Brougham criticised the court in the following terms:

> 'the Delegates is one of the worst constituted courts which was ever appointed, and...the course of its proceedings forms one of the greatest mockeries of appeal ever conceived by man....The Court is thus formed: you take three judges from the common law courts, one from each; to these you add some half dozen civil lawyers, advocates from Doctors' Commons who the day before may have been practising in those courts, but who happened not to have been in the particular cause, in respect of which the appeal has been inserted. Now, only see what the consequence of this must be. The civilians, forming the majority of the Delegates, are, of necessity, men who have no practice, or the very youngest of the Doctors. So that you absolutely appeal from the three great judges of the Civil and Maritime Courts — from the sentences of Sir William Scott, Sir John Nicholl, Sir Christopher Robinson...to judges the majority of whom must, of necessity, be the advocates the least employed in the courts where those great authorities preside, the most recently admitted to those courts, and the most unqualified to pronounce soundly on their proceedings, if it were

10 H. J. Stephen *New Commentaries on the Laws of England* (4th edn, 1858) vol 3, p. 411, Judicature Commission: First Report of the Commissioners no. 4130 (1869) pp. 21-2.

decent that they should pronounce at all; for, out of so small a bar, the chances are, that the three or four eminent advocates have been employed in the case under appeal.'[11]

In 1832 the Delegates were abolished: henceforth ecclesiastical appeals and Admiralty appeals were to be heard by the Privy Council. The origins of the Privy Council's jurisdiction lay in the petitions to the Council from overseas possessions of the Crown which lay outside the jurisdiction of the courts at Westminster. Unfortunately, its composition was no more legally distinguished than was that of the Delegates. Accordingly, in 1833 an Act was passed 'for the better administration of justice in His Majesty's Privy Council'. In particular, there was to. be a Judicial Committee composed of those Privy Councillors who were, or had been, in high judicial office. Such legislation ensured that the Judicial Committee of the Privy Council began to assume the appearance of an ordinary court of justice, although traces of its origins remained in the fact that even in the twentieth century its decision took the form, not of a judgment, but of a report to the king.

The reconstituted Privy Council experienced problems. In 1844 Brougham told a committee that the main difficulty was the impossibility of finding a regular attendance of judges because of their other duties with the result that a case might have to be put off constantly.[12] Later in the nineteenth century it experienced difficulty in coping with the sheer mass of overseas appeals. During the twentieth century its role in hearing appeals from overseas began to be questioned as the Dominions became aware increasingly of their emergent nationhood. Yet the quality of its work remained unquestioned. And the Judicial Committee of the Privy Council retained its jurisdiction in ecclesiastical and admiralty matters.

Upon the creation in 1857 of the new Court of Probate and of the Court for Divorce and Matrimonial Causes appeals from the decrees and orders of the Judge Ordinary of the Divorce Court lay to the Full Court, consisting of the Judge Ordinary and two common law judges: in certain cases appeals also lay from the Full Court, or from the Judge Ordinary exercising the powers of the Full Court, to the House of Lords. From the Court of Probate appeal also lay to the House of Lords.

e) *House of Lords*

The house of peers was the supreme court of judicature in the kingdom. It might rectify any injustice or mistake of law committed by the courts below. In practice that power was limited severely by the procedural forms, especially that of the writ of error, to which reference has been made already. Yet it was a power which belonged to each member of the House and not simply to those who had had some judicial or legal training. The law reposed an entire confidence, wrote Blackstone,[13] in the honour and conscience of the noble persons who composed that important assembly, that they would make themselves masters of those questions upon which they undertook to decide since upon their decision all

11 18 Official Report (2nd series) col. 151.
12 Report from the Select Committee of the House of Lords appointed to consider...an Act for the better Administration of Justice in His Majesty's Privy Council no. 34 (1844) p. 81.
13 3 Bl Com (5th edn) 56-7.

property must finally depend. Usually most peers abstained from participating in the judicial business of the House, although a small number was required to sit with the judicial members.[14] That lack of participation in the judicial business may have been due originally rather to a distaste for judicial work than to any feeling of incompetence for the task.

Certainly there were occasions when peers abused their right to sit judicially by voting in such a matter in accordance with their purely personal or party preferences. One such notorious instance occurred in 1783 when the episcopal bench 'deliberately rejecting the counsel of the expert advisers of the House, was able to secure judgment in favour of the litigant who was one of their number'. Even as late as 1834 a case was decided without the benefit of any professional advice.[15] However, public opinion appears to have been opposed to the exercise of such a power. The publication in report form during the nineteenth century of cases heard in the Lords suggested that a growing professionalism existed both within the Lords and in the professional and public expectation of the manner in which this judicial power would be exercised. Finally, in 1844 upon the appeal from conviction of the Irish nationalist, O'Connell, the House determined that lords unlearned in the law should not vote upon judicial matters.[16] Unfortunately, the judicial quality of the House remained uncertain. In addition allegations of undue delay and expense were made from time to time.

A leading critic of the House was Bethell. On one occasion he even declared that the House of Lords 'was inferior to the lowest tribunal in what ought to be the accompaniments of a court of justice'.[17] However, when he gave evidence to a select committee in 1856, his criticisms were less startling. He stated that while the House was constituted 'of four most eminent learned Lords, diligently and constantly attending, upon whom we might count as always to be found there, the jurisdiction appeared...to be most satisfactorily exercised'. That was the case during Lord Lyndhurst's second Chancellorship which had ended in 1846. Subsequently some Chancellors sat alone. In Bethell's view the presiding by one, or even two, judges was unsatisfactory in the final administration of justice. More recently his dissatisfaction with the House had increased:

'principally from the circumstance that whenever the noble and learned Lords who constitute the tribunal differed in opinion, they did not reserve the matter for further consideration; they did not strive to attain to unanimity of judgment, but they made their differences of opinion public: frequently the appeals failed, and in many cases great injury was done by unsettling the law...'

Bethell believed that it would be more satisfactory if one written opinion were given in each case. Brougham's view was that it could amount to a deception upon the public if, when there was no unanimity in fact, the giving of one opinion suggested that there was unanimity.[18]

There had been constant allegations of delay and expense. A select committee reported in 1811 that it was 'indispensably necessary' that a greater proportion of

---

14   Report of the Select Committee on the Appellate Jurisdiction of the House of Lords no. 1823 (1823) p. 15.

15   52 LQR 203, 17 LQR 367.

16   W. S. Holdsworth *History of English Law* vol 1, p. 377.

17   139 Official Report (3rd series) col. 2120.

18   Report from the Select Committee of the House of Lords no. 264 (1856) pp. 1-7.

the time of the House of Lords should be employed in hearing appeals.[19] In 1824 a select committee wrote of the urgent necessity of disposing of the existing arrears. A chief cause of the arrears was said to be the great number of appeals from Scotland e.g. of 225 appeals which then remained unheard, 151 were Scottish appeals.[20] Earlier reforms such as the establishment of the Vice-Chancellor's court and increased sittings had been found ineffectual. Similar complaints were voiced in 1856 and, once again, in 1872. Clearly reform was overdue.

f) *Appeals from inferior civil courts*

From the court of pie-poudre a writ of error lay, in the nature of an appeal, to the courts at Westminster. From the court baron a writ of false judgment lay to the courts at Westminster to hear and review the cause. There could be no writ of error as the court baron was not a court of record. The hundred court also was not a court of record and it too was subject to a writ of false judgment. However, the above courts were soon to fall into disuse.

There was an appeal also from the new county court after 1846: it might go to a court of common law, to Chancery, or to Admiralty, according to the particular jurisdiction which was being exercised at that time. The result, in the words of the judicature commissioners, was that 'although we appear at first sight to have obtained that great *desideratum*, which the common law commissioners call "the consolidation of all the elements of a complete remedy in the same court", yet, as that remedy can only be had in three separate suits, the evil is equally great'.[1] The Judicature Acts solved that particular problem.

g) *Conclusion*

There could be little quarrel with the judgment of the judicature commissioners, made in 1869, that the systems of appeal which existed in the civil jurisdiction were both 'various and discordant'. The task of bringing order to that ancient, yet much amended, system, was rendered all the more difficult as the more modern concept of the appeal struggled to break free from age old forms and historic institutions. The judicature commissioners also pointed to the changing nature of the appeal by recommending that every appeal should be in the nature of a rehearing.[2]

h) *The new appellate system*

All appeals from petty or quarter sessions, from a county court, or from any other inferior court, which might previously have been brought to any court or judge whose jurisdiction was transferred to the new High Court, might now be heard and determined by a divisional court. The decision of the divisional court was to be final unless special leave were given to appeal to the Court of Appeal.

To the Court of Appeal, which was constituted a Superior Court of Record, was transferred all the appellate jurisdiction and powers of the Lord Chancellor

---

19 Report by the Select Committee...[on]...the more expeditious Hearing and Decision of causes brought into the House by Appeals and Writs of Error no. 70 (1811) p. 1.
20 Report of the Select Committee on the Appellate Jurisdiction of the House of Lords no. 1823 (1823) p. 4.
1   Judicature Commission: First Report of the Commissioners no. 4130 (1869) p. 8.
2   Judicature Commission: First Report no. 4130 (1869) p. 24.

and of the Court of Appeal in Chancery and of the Court of Exchequer Chamber. The Lord Chancellor was the president of the new court. And there was one ex officio judge, the Lord Chief Justice. In addition there were the ordinary judges of this court, the lords justices of appeal. It was provided that the Court of Appeal should have all the power, authority and jurisdiction of the High Court. To that end it was further provided that the Court of Appeal should have power to draw inferences of fact and to give any judgment and to make any order which ought to have been made, and to make such further or other order as the case might require.

The future role of the House of Lords was the occasion of rather more debate. In 1872 a select committee recommended that the Lord Chancellor should be joined upon a Judicial Committee of the House of Lords and Privy Council by four salaried members with appropriate judicial experience and by a number of members ex officio.[3] The judicature commissioners believed that the House of Lords should retain its appellate jurisdiction and Lord Hatherley so proposed in his Appellate Jurisdiction Bill of 1870. The Select Committee of 1872 also proposed the retention of that jurisdiction in the form of a Joint Judicial Committee of the House of Lords and of the Privy Council, although that proposal was carried only by a narrow majority. However, Selborne's Judicature Bill of 1873 made it clear that there were no longer to be appeals to the House of Lords. Appeals would go only as far as a new Court of Appeal, which would be staffed by nine permanent paid judges. There was little opposition to the measure which received the royal assent in August 1873 and was due to come into force in November 1874.

Disraeli and the Conservatives came into office in February 1874. Although Cairns, the new Lord Chancellor, was in general agreement with his predecessor's proposals, opposition had grown even within the new Cabinet so that in July 1874 Disraeli announced that the measure was to be dropped. Soon afterwards a bill postponing the coming into force of the 1873 Act from 1 November 1874 to 1 November 1875 passed through all its stages. Now the opponents of reform worked hard, with the result that when Cairns introduced his Appellate Jurisdiction Bill 1876, there was little serious opposition to it. Once again the House of Lords was to be the final appellate court. Yet law lords were to be created and the judicial sittings of the House were not to be tied to the House's legislative sittings. It was a compromise which kept the name of the House of Lords but made it in effect a court separate from the legislative body. The motive underlying the new proposals, as Stevens has shown, was to 'prop up the peers as a branch of the legislature' i.e. by giving it judicial duties to confirm it in its political role.[4]

The Appellate Jurisdiction Act 1876 provided that an appeal should lie to the Lords from any order or judgment either of the Court of Appeal in England or of any of the Scotch or Irish Courts, from which an error or appeal lay thereto at or immediately before the commencement of the Act (1 November 1876). Such an appeal was not to be heard and determined unless there were present not less than three 'Lords of Appeal' that is, three of the following persons: the Lord

3   Report from the Select Committee of the House of Lords on Appellate Jurisdiction no. 325 (1872) p. v,
4   R. B. Stevens 'Final Appeal: Reform of the House of Lords and Privy Council, 1867-1876' (1964) 80 LQR 343.

Chancellor, the lords of appeal in ordinary, and such peers as have held 'high judicial office', namely, the office of Lord Chancellor of Great Britain or Ireland or of paid judge of the Judicial Committee, or of judge of the High Court of Justice, or of the Court of Appeal, or of the superior courts of law and equity in England as they existed before the constitution of the High Court of Justice, or of one of the superior courts of law and equity at Dublin, or of the Court of Session in Scotland.

With regard to the lords of appeal in ordinary, it was provided that the Queen might appoint by patent qualified persons who would hold office during good behaviour and notwithstanding the demise of the Crown, but be removeable on the address of both Houses of Parliament.

The Court of Appeal was a completely new court. Over the years it was neces-sary, therefore, for it to solve a number of problems concerning its role. For example, it was only in 1944 that it decided upon the extent to which it was bound by its own previous decisions.[5] Certainly the Court of Appeal was kept busy. The Evershed Committee was told in mid-twentieth century that in the course of a normal year it dealt with about 600 appeals, of which 400 arose out of cases which had originated in the High Court — only about 5 per cent of the cases dealt with by the Court of Appeal formed the subject of appeals to the House of Lords.[6]

The House of Lords also took some years to establish itself. It was only in 1934 that statute qualified the traditional right of the subject to petition the king in parliament by providing that the judges should themselves grant leave to appeal.[7] The device of an Appellate Committee of the Lords was adopted only in 1948. However, although views differed as to the quality of the Lords' contribu-tion to the law, there could be no doubt but that this reformed and increasingly professional body was now widely respected amongst the legal profession.[8]

Clearly appeals have constituted an important factor in the cost of litigation at all times. Many lawyers regretted the failure of Selborne's attempt to eliminate the double appeal. In 1933 the Lord Chancellor asked the Hanworth Committee to consider whether the elimination or restriction of the rights of appeal to, within, or from the Supreme Court might reduce delay and expense. The Committee recognised the difficulty. For example, a county court case in which the sum at issue was no greater than £30 could be dealt with in turn by as many as four tribunals. Statute provided that after 1934 the Court of Appeal might hear appeals directly from the county court, thereby reducing the number of potential appellate tribunals.[9] However, for the most part the system established by the Judicature Acts remained unchanged even in 1950.

5 *Young v Bristol Aeroplane Co* [1944] KB 718.
6 Final Report of the Committee on Supreme Court Practice and Procedure (Cmd. 8878) p. 154, para. 478.
7 Administration of Justice (Appeals) Act 1934.
8 R. B. Stevens *Law and Politics: the House of Lords as a Judicial Body 1800-1976.* Cf. A. S. Turberville 'The House of Lords as a Court of Law, 1784-1837' (1936) 52 LQR 189.
9 Business of Courts Committee, Interim Report (Cmd. 4265), Second Interim Report of the Business of Courts Committee (Cmd. 4471). See also S. O. Clark 'English Appellate Procedure' (1929) 39 YLJ 76, Lord Cohen 'Jurisdiction, Practice and Procedure of the Court of Appeal' (1951) 11 CLJ 3, Lord Asquith 'Some Aspects of the Work of the Court of Appeal' (1950) 1 JSPTL (n.s.) 350. On appellate costs generally see (1900) 16 LQR 229, 236 and Final Report of the Committee on Supreme Court Practice and Procedure (Cmd. 8878) p. 153, para. 472.

2 Criminal courts

a) *Introduction*
Subsequent to the trial it was possible to bring proceedings in the nature of an appeal. There were proceedings in error; the judge might reserve a difficult question of law; there might be a motion for a new trial. Alternatively, there might be a reprieve or pardon. After 1848 a court which became known as the Court for Crown Cases Reserved might give further consideration to questions of law. It was only in 1907 that the appeal in criminal cases assumed its modern form with the creation of the Court of Criminal Appeal to which access was rather more liberal and which might hear appeals on both questions of law and questions of fact. The struggle for such a reform was a long one which throws considerable light upon nineteenth-century attitudes.

b) *Error*
A writ of error lay from all inferior criminal jurisdictions to King's Bench. It was granted only upon the fiat of the Attorney-General, its basis being that a notorious mistake appeared in the judgment or other part of the record. There might have been the want of a proper addition to the defendant's name; the sheriff or other officer of the court might not have been named properly. Other examples are an alleged irregularity in empanelling the jury, or in discharging a jury.[10] Such causes, commented Blackstone, were allowed out of tenderness to life and liberty but were 'not much to the credit or advancement of the national justice'. A distinction was made between cases of misdemeanour and cases of felony. In cases of misdemeanour the writ of error, although not allowed of course, was granted on sufficient and probable cause being shown to the Attorney-General; in such cases the writ was understood to be grantable of common right. In cases of felony they were only allowed ex gratia, and not without express warrant under the king's sign manual or at least by the consent of the attorney-general.[11]

The nature of the court record lay at the heart of all such proceedings. It was far from being a satisfactory document. It was so drawn up that many matters by which a prisoner might be prejudiced would not appear upon it. For example, neither the improper reception or rejection of evidence or a misdirection by the judge would appear upon the record. The writ of error applied, therefore, only to that small number of questions of law which concerned the regularity of the proceedings themselves. Accordingly, it was confined to 'a very small number of cases of rare occurrence'.[12]

c) *Reserving a question of law*
A judge might reserve a difficult question of law for the opinion of all the judges. As such proceedings were wholly informal, no judgment was given. If the judges thought that the defendant had been convicted improperly, he was pardoned. There was no mode for reserving cases which had arisen at the quarter sessions.

---

10   Report of the Royal Commission appointed to consider the Law relating to Indictable
 Offences no.C-2345 (1879) p. 37.
11   4 Bl Com (5th edn) 383, 385.
12   Report of the Royal Commission no.C-2345 (1879) p. 37.

d) *Motion for a new trial*

A motion for a new trial was confined to cases which had either originated in or had been removed into Queen's Bench and was confined to cases of misdemeanour. If a verdict of guilty had been given contrary to the evidence and not to the satisfaction of the judge, the court would, on the motion of the defendant, grant a new trial. Such a new trial would not be granted at the instance of the prosecutor unless the verdict appeared to have been obtained by some fraudulent or irregular proceeding on the part of the defendant.

e) *The reprieve and the pardon*

A reprieve was the taking back or withdrawing of a sentence for an interval of time whereby the execution of a criminal was suspended. In the eighteenth and early nineteenth centuries, when the Bloody Code was at its height, the judgment which was invariably in question, of course, was that of death. A reprieve could be granted either before or after judgment. The judge might not have been satisfied with the verdict, the evidence might be suspicious or the indictment insufficient, or there might have been such favourable circumstances in the criminal's character as to give room to apply to the Crown for either an absolute or a conditional pardon. Such arbitrary reprieves might be granted or taken off by the justices of gaol delivery, even although their session be finished and their commission expired. Further grounds of reprieve were pregnancy and insanity.[13]

The last available means of staying an execution was the Sovereign's pardon, the granting of which was a prerogative of the Crown. The effect of a pardon was to make the offender a new man, 'to acquit him of all corporal penalties and forfeitures annexed to the offence for which he obtains his pardon; and not so much to restore his former, as to give him new credit and capacity'. A pardon could be conditional — indeed, the validity of the pardon could depend upon such a condition. This was of frequent occurrence in the cases of felons who were pardoned on condition of transportation to some foreign country for life or for a term of years. If the king had been misinformed e.g. if there had been any suppression of truth, or suggestion of falsehood, the pardon would be void.[14]

It seems that at one time the king took a lively interest in the consideration of proper cases for pardon. Certainly that was the case with George III, and even in the late nineteenth century the real possibility of the sovereign's personal intervention was stressed.[15] However, this more active participation on the part of the sovereign appears to have lessened since the accession of Queen Victoria to the throne, in particular the personal presence of the sovereign when the fate of the capitally convicted was discussed. Stephen comments:

> 'This practice was discontinued at the beginning of the present [Queen Victoria's] reign, partly because the number of capital offences was so much reduced that there was no longer any occasion for it, partly because it would have been indecent and practically impossible to discuss with a woman the details of many crimes then capital.'[16]

13   4 Bl Com (5th edn) 383, 387. Cf. H. J. Stephen *New Commentaries on the Laws of England* (9th edn, 1883) pp. 467 ff.

14   4 Bl Com (5th edn) 389-95, H. J. Stephen *New Commentaries on the Laws of England* (9th edn, 1883) p. 481.

15   L. Radzinowicz *History of English Criminal Law* vol 1, pp. 121, 111, 113; (1904) 118 LT 207.

16   J. F. Stephen *History of the Criminal Law* p. 88.

Beccaria did not favour the exercise of such a prerogative on the grounds that it would, inter alia, weaken certainty of punishment. Blackstone, however, expressed the English position as follows:

> 'there is a magistrate, who has it in his power to extend mercy, wherever he thinks it is deserved: holding a court of equity in his own breast, to soften the rigour of the general law, in such criminal cases as merit an exemption from punishment. Pardons (according to some theorists) should be excluded in a perfect legislation, where punishments are mild but certain; for that the clemency of the prince seems a tacit disapprobation of the laws. But the exclusion of pardons must necessarily introduce a very dangerous power in the judge or jury, that of construing the criminal law by the spirit instead of the letter; or else it must be holden, what no man will seriously avow, that the situation and circumstances of the offender (though they alter not the offence of the crime) ought to make no distinction in the punishment.'[17]

Very little is known as to how the decision to pardon was actually exercised in practice. In mid-nineteenth century practice appeared to vary. In 1846, despite the strength of the evidence which was said to have been submitted regarding a man's innocence, the Secretary of State to the Home Office — as adviser to the Sovereign — declined to interfere on the ground that such evidence was not taken on oath, or subjected to cross-examination and, therefore, could not be received against the evidence formally taken at the trial. On the other hand, in a poisoning case in 1859 the Home Secretary was said to have conferred a pardon after referring the matter to a distinguished surgeon. The result, in Stephen's words, was that 'the private opinion of a single, eminent surgeon who might have been and was not called as a witness at the trial — who heard no witnesses, no counsel, no summing up — was allowed to overrule the verdict of a jury who had enjoyed all those advantages'.[18]

The old system creaked on. The practice was that a free pardon was given only in cases where innocence was proved; in such cases compensation was also given. However, if the prisoner was able merely to establish a reasonable doubt as to his guilt, sentence was simply remitted and the prisoner did not even receive reimbursement of the expenses which he had incurred in establishing the reasonable doubt. Inevitably, there tended to be more remissions than pardons. In 1905 one commentator stated that in the last 19 cases there had been only four free pardons as compared with 15 remissions. Inevitably, the Home Office had its critics — the 'minimum of trouble and responsibility appears to be the great object at which it aims', asserted one critic.[19] Equally inevitably, the Home Office had its defenders.[20] There was some misunderstanding of the role of the Home Office. That role was outlined in a Home Office memorandum submitted to the Beck Commission:

> 'In dealing with all cases, the principle is constantly kept in view that the Home Office, in advising on the exercise of the prerogative of mercy, is not a court of appeal or a court of revision. For this reason the Home Office will

17   4 Bl Com (5th edn) 390.
18   (1846) 8 LT 14, (1882) 73 LT 3.
19   (1904-5) 30 Law Mag and Rev 399, 420.
20   X.Y.Z. 'Criminal Appeals and the Prerogative of Mercy' (1899) 66 Fortnightly Review 510.

not, generally speaking, interfere on technical grounds; it will not interfere because evidence has been improperly admitted, or improperly rejected, or because the jury have been misdirected, unless it can be shown that a substantial injustice has been done. For the same reason it will not reopen a case merely because someone, sitting in the Home Office, who has not seen the prisoner and the witnesses nor heard the cross-examination, feels, on reading the printed evidence, some doubt as to whether he would have agreed with the jury. Further, it is constantly borne in mind that it is a matter of cardinal importance that the Home Office should act in co-operation with the judges; and a decided expression of opinion by an experienced judge on a case tried before him is hardly ever disregarded unless it clearly appears that there are strong grounds for believing him to be mistaken. As pointed out above, the judge who has seen the witnesses and heard the examination and followed the whole case in open court is in a much better position to form a right opinion than the Home Office; and if, notwithstanding the judge's opinion that the verdict is right, a doubt is still entertained, it has to be borne in mind that any ill-considered action in opposition to the judges might deprive the Home Office in future of the friendly assistance it now receives, and thereby greatly increase the difficulties of a task which is already one of great difficulty and delicacy.'[1]

Essentially the position remained much the same during the first half of the twentieth century. The Crown might grant a reprieve, which suspended temporarily the executing of the sentence or, within limits, might remit the whole or part of the penalty. The Sovereign, acting by the Home Secretary, might pardon offences of a public nature which were prosecuted by the Crown.[2]

f) *Attempts to extend the scope of review and appeal*
In 1836 E. A. Wilde, a solicitor and a former sheriff of London, told the criminal law commissioners that by his own personal exertions he had saved the lives of not less than six persons who had been improperly convicted within a period of only eight or nine months. Wilde was satisfied that many others had suffered punishment, although they would have been proven innocent had there been a court of appeal to which they might have stated their grounds of appeal. Accordingly, the *Legal Observer* wrote in 1836 of the necessity of establishing a Court of Appeal in criminal cases; in 1844 the *Law Times* asserted that it was a 'frightful anomaly' that there was no such court,[3] and in 1845 the criminal law commissioners said that the law was 'very defective as regards the means afforded for the correction of errors in criminal proceedings'. They went on to comment that:
'If, with a view to exclude the possibility of injustice, a man is to be allowed the benefit of a new trial where property to the amount of 20l is at stake, it is hard to deny him protection to the same extent where his life is in jeopardy. If the question whether a pauper be legally settled in parish A or parish B is not to be determined without power of appeal to the Court of Queen's Bench, it is harsh to condemn him to be transported for life to a

1 1905 (Cd. 2315), (1904) 118 LT 208.
2 O. Hood Phillips *Constitutional and Administrative Law* (4th edn, 1967) p. 256.
3 (1836) 12 Legal Observer 188, (1844) 2 LT 363.

penal settlement without power of appeal. The law in this respect is at variance with itself, and several evil consequences naturally result.'[4]

In February 1848 Ewart sought leave to introduce a bill which would give a right to appeal on both questions of law and questions of fact. He claimed that during the previous two months there had been ten cases which had shown the necessity of such an appeal.[5] Meanwhile Campbell introduced a measure in the Lords which proposed an appeal upon a question of law only. Upon Grey stating that a Lords' committee would probably be appointed before whom the judges could give evidence, Ewart did not proceed with his measure.[6] The evidence taken by that committee, and in particular the evidence of the judges, is of considerable interest.[7]

Some witnesses were for radical reform. Greaves, a distinguished criminal lawyer, favoured every prisoner having an absolute and unconditional right to appeal to one of the common law courts at Westminster upon questions of fact as well as questions of law. Similarly, Sir Fitzroy Kelly, a distinguished lawyer who later became a judge, maintained that perhaps one-sixth of all the cases of misdemeanour in which motions for a new trial had been made had resulted in the verdict being set aside as being against the evidence.[8] On the other hand none of the judges favoured an appeal upon a question of fact. The note was set by Baron Parke, a judge of 20 years standing and then the senior judge at Westminster Hall. Baron Parke favoured an improved mode of deciding doubtful questions of law which occurred at quarter sessions: he disapproved also of the practice whereby the judges did not give reasons in determining questions which had been reserved by them. However, he opposed a Court of Appeal in criminal cases upon questions of fact upon the ground that inconveniences would outweigh the supposed advantages. In his view the inconveniences were those of expense and of delay. If the benefits of an appeal were not to be confined in practice to the rich, then public assistance would have to be given to the poor, a great expense. Moreover, against any advantage which might be gained should be balanced 'one of the properties which is most advantageous to the due administration of criminal justice, and that is, a speedy determination of every charge of crime'. Yet if:

> 'this general power of appeal were given in all cases, the result would necessarily be a protraction of every criminal suit, and the advantage of a speedy conviction and punishment would be lost....I think that the complaints of the present mode of administering the criminal law have little foundation, for the cases in which the innocent are improperly convicted are extremely rare....I can say for myself that I can hardly call to my recollection any case with which I am personally acquainted in which I think that a person really innocent has been convicted by the jury.'

Moreover, additional judges must be appointed if there were to be such an appeal. He believed that the creation of such an appeal 'would add to the facilities of escape for guilt'. Nor did he accept that there was any inconsistency

4   Eighth Report of...Commissioners on Criminal Law no. 656 (1845) pp. 19-20.
5   96 Official Report (3rd series) col. 1299.
6   97 Official Report (3rd series) col. 1101.
7   Report from the Select Committee of the House of Lords...[on]...an Act for the Further Amendment of the Administration of the Criminal Law no. 523 (1848).
8   Report from the Select Committee no. 523 (1848) pp. 13, 27.

in allowing a right of appeal in civil but not in criminal cases. He maintained that disputes as to civil property were of a complicated nature as distinct from criminal cases where 'extremely few' such questions arose. In civil cases, he said, it was not as important to bring matters to a speedy termination as it was in criminal cases.[9]

g) *The Court for Crown Cases Reserved*
In 1848 a new court, which was later to become known as the Court for Crown Cases Reserved, was created to hear any question of law which the judge, or commissioner or justices of the peace before whom the case had been heard at first instance might in their discretion have reserved for it. The new court was composed of the judges of the three common law courts or any five of them, a Chief Justice or the Lord Chief Baron being one. It was designed to provide a better mode for determining difficult questions of law. As construed, the Act was held to mean that if a difference of opinion occurred between the five judges, the matter was to be referred to the whole body. That was found to be inconvenient. Further, a judge might not reserve a question unless he ruled it against the accused, although his opinion might be that, despite the point being doubtful, he ought to decide in favour of the accused. If, ultimately, it were determined that there had been an improper ruling against the accused, perhaps on some question of little weight, the court was required to avoid the conviction. The court had no power to grant a new trial.

Possibly to their surprise the judges of the new court were not inundated with appeals from quarter sessions. In 1849 the *Law Times* commented that three quarter sessions had resulted in a total of only 12 cases: it went on to suggest that an appeal upon the facts would produce a similar result. In fact this new court heard relatively few cases over the years — in 1907 it was said that on average it had heard only eight cases each year.[10]

h) *Further attempts at reform*
Even 18 years' experience of the work of the Court for Crown Cases Reserved did little to stimulate judicial enthusiasm in favour of allowing a more extended right of appeal in criminal cases. So much is apparent from evidence which was given to the Capital Punishment Commission in 1866. Of 11 witnesses who addressed themselves to the question only one favoured the establishment of a Court of Criminal Appeal. That witness, Sir Fitzroy Kelly, simply offered again his long-held opinion that if there were an efficient court of criminal appeal, 'the cases in which innocent men are convicted and punished would be greatly diminished'.[11] Kelly had little experience of criminal work. However, some lawyers did agree with him. For example, when Palmerston, as Home Secretary, asserted that there were no instances of wrongful convictions, the *Law Times* asked for a return of all pardons which had been granted over the previous ten years.[12] The same journal protested against inconvenience being set up as an answer to a demand for justice in any case, and suggested that the number of

9 Report from the Select Committee no. 523 (1848) pp. 3-9.
10 (1849) 12 LT 523, B. Abel-Smith and R. Stevens *Lawyers and the Courts* p. 99.
11 Report of the Capital Punishment Commission no. 3590 (1866) p. 137, q. 1101.
12 (1853) 21 LT 93.

judges be increased or, alternatively, that judges should be transferred from civil appellate work to appellate criminal work.[13] The leaders of the profession disagreed. Baron Bramwell commented, as Baron Parke had done previously, that you could not have a court of appeal 'without augmenting that uncertainty, which it is so desirable to diminish, and without giving more chances and more hopes; and you cannot have it without doing what it is also most desirable to avoid, namely, worrying prosecutors'.[14] By that latter point Bramwell was referring to the very real practical difficulty that prosecutions were still largely private. How many private prosecutors would be willing to run the additional financial risk of appellate proceedings? Bramwell conceded that one of the 'great objections' to the existing law was that, if new evidence were discovered, the only way of giving the prisoner the benefit of it was not to try him over again but to pardon him. Even so Bramwell contended that in practice no such mischief existed as would make it worthwhile to incur the mischiefs which the creation of a regular Court of Appeal would introduce. Further principled objections offered by S. H. Walpole were summarised as follows:

'(1)   Parties would be still as free to petition the Home Office to alter the punishment, and the objections which are now raised against the exercise of the prerogative by the Home Office, viz. that the Home Secretary is rehearing alone what has been determined by the judge and jury, would be ten times aggravated, because he would then be rehearing what had been determined by the Court of Appeal, and by the judge who had decided the case in the court below;

(2)   It would be an appeal for the rich and not for the poor;

(3)   If an appeal was admitted on the part of the criminal it must also be admitted on the part of the prosecutor; society could not be properly protected if appeals were granted as a matter of right.

(4)   Much matter is brought before the Secretary of State which could not be brought before a regular Court of Appeal.'[15]

These were principled and practical objections. Yet some of their point was removed as the police increasingly began to assume responsibility in practice for the conduct of prosecutions and with the origins in 1879 of the office of the Director of Public Prosecutions.

Now there was a considerable shift in professional opinion. In 1879 the criminal code commissioners argued persuasively in favour of an appellate court; reform seemed close in 1883; in 1892 even the judges recommended unanimously that some provision be made for the reconsideration of sentences on appeal.[16] That judicial concern stemmed not so much from a concern for the convict who had received an incorrect, perhaps even an excessive, sentence as from a belief that the existing practice of petitioning the Home Secretary was a means of by-passing the judiciary. In fact the Home Secretary received a very considerable number of petitions regarding sentence. It was alleged that there was a considerable lack of uniformity in sentencing practice. Others denied that

13   (1849) 12 LT 523.

14   Report of the Capital Punishment Commission no. 3590 (1866) p. 34, q. 229.

15   Report no. 3590 (1866).

16   Report of the Royal Commission appointed to consider the Law relating to Indictable Offences no. C-2345 (1879), (1883) 27 Sol Jo 327, cf. (1889) 87 LT 404 and (1895) 100 LT 29, (1906) 70 JP 171.

there was any real lack of uniformity in practice; trial judges had simply taken into account matters which only they could observe e.g. the demeanour of the witnesses.[17] Finally, there was an outcry over the case of the unfortunate Beck who was a victim of mistaken identity. The problem had long been recognised by some commentators. In 1846 the *Law Times* commented that all who had any experience of courts of justice would 'admit that there is nothing upon which men are at once so positive and so often mistaken as personal identity'.[18] However, the public outcry following the *Beck* case and the subsequent recommendations of the Beck Commission appeared to make reform inevitable. Not all lawyers agreed. In 1906 the Lord Chief Justice, Lord Alverstone, asserted that:

> 'the certainty, the expedition, the justice of our criminal procedure had been the admiration of jurists of all civilised nations; but the bedrock and foundation of all the system was the recognised duty of the prosecutor to make out his case, and upon the facts to satisfy a jury, and from the verdict of that jury there was no appeal'.[19]

It was an attitude which brought to mind Blackstone's old fear that the jury system would never be attacked openly but that it might be sapped and undermined by the introduction of 'new and arbitrary methods of trial'. It was an attitude which also ignored the view that in some cases the discovery of relevant new facts subsequent to the trial had made the verdict of that trial jury unsafe.

However, reform was imminent. Indeed, the Prevention of Corruption Act 1906 had already provided that any person aggrieved by a summary conviction under the Act might appeal to a court of quarter sessions. Soon there was a new Court of Criminal Appeal.

i) *The Court of Criminal Appeal 1907-1950*
The Criminal Appeal Act 1907 provided as follows at sections 3 and 4:

> '**3.** A person convicted on indictment may appeal under this Act to the Court of Criminal Appeal —
>
> (a) against his conviction on any ground of appeal which involves a question of law alone; and
>
> (b) with the leave of the Court of Criminal Appeal or upon the certificate of the judge who tried him that it is a fit case for appeal against his conviction on any ground of appeal which involves a question of fact alone, or a question of mixed law and fact, or any other ground which appears to the court to be a sufficient ground of appeal; and
>
> (c) with the leave of the Court of Criminal Appeal against the sentence passed on his conviction, unless the sentence is one passed by law.
>
> **4.**(1) The Court of Criminal Appeal on any such appeal against conviction shall allow the appeal if they think that the verdict of the jury should be set aside on the ground that it is unreasonable or cannot be supported having regard to the evidence, or that the judgment of the court before whom the appellant was convicted should be set aside on the ground of a wrong decision of any question of law or that on any ground there was a miscarriage of justice...

17 47 Official Report (4th series) col. 78, 57 Official Report (4th series) col. 1089, 1905 (Cd. 2315).
18 (1846) 8 LT 14.
19 (1906-7) 32 Law Mag and Rev (5th series) 314, 331.

Provided that the court may, notwithstanding that they are of the opinion that the point raised in the appeal might be decided in favour of the appellant, dismiss the appeal if they consider that no substantial miscarriage of justice has actually occurred...'

Section 10 provided for legal assistance to the appellant by providing that the court might assign solicitor and counsel to the appellant if 'it appears desirable in the interests of justice that the appellant should have legal aid, and that he has not sufficient means to enable him to obtain that aid'. The court was intended to be for the most part a final tribunal. Appeal to the House of Lords was to be allowed only in those cases where the Attorney-General certified that the decision of the Court of Criminal Appeal involved a point of law of exceptional public importance. In 1908 the composition of the court was amended so as to include all the judges of the King's Bench Division.

Many appeals were made each year: in 1951 there were some 1100. The most common grounds of appeal were three. The prisoner claimed that he was not guilty with the result that the notice of appeal amounted only to a repetition of the defence made at the trial. In numerous cases the prisoner alleged that he had been a victim of mistaken identity, albeit with little success as the court was unwilling to usurp the function of the jury, provided both that there had been evidence fit to go to it and that it had been directed properly. Thirdly, the prisoner alleged that his counsel had forced him to plead guilty or would not put up the defence which the prisoner wanted.

The court itself made a considerable contribution towards improvements in procedure, evidence and also in sentencing practice. It made little contribution, however, to an authoritative exposition of new or difficult points of substantive law, possibly due to pressure of other work, possibly because of the shifting composition of the court.[20]

j)   *The House of Lords*

Similarly, although the House of Lords made a number of well-known contributions to the criminal law during the twentieth century, its total contribution to criminal jurisprudence, even by 1950, was still relatively small.

---

20   Lord Goddard 'The Working of the Court of Criminal Appeal' (1952) 2 JSPTL (n.s.) 1, D. S. Davies 'The Court of Criminal Appeal: the First Forty Years' (1952) 1 JSPTL (n.s.) 425.

Chapter 9

The substantive criminal law

1 The province and prevalence of crime

The primary concern of the London magistrates, Fielding and Colquhoun, in the eighteenth century just as much as the Constabulary Commissioners in the middle years of the nineteenth century was a lack of security for person and property. It was in those areas that the criminals of Dickens' novels were especially active. It is a view of crime which the emphasis of the nineteenth-century statistics also tends to support. Indeed, it is a view of crime which is very much alive in the final quarter of the twentieth century not only in England and Wales but throughout the world.[1]

It was in this spirit that Blackstone divided all crimes into two groups. Those crimes which were *mala in se* were said to be forbidden by the superior laws and to gain no additional turpitude from being declared unlawful by the inferior legislature. In this category came offences such as murder, theft and perjury. All other crimes were *mala prohibita* i.e. 'those laws which enjoin only positive duties, and forbid any such things as are not *mala in se*...without any inter-mixture of moral guilt'. It would be a very wicked thing, wrote Blackstone, if every such law were a snare for the conscience of the subject. Interestingly enough, an example which he gave under this head was of an offence against the game laws, although, as we shall see, such offences aroused the unremitting ire of the country gentry.[2] Generally speaking common law offences, albeit supple-mented by statute, came into the first category; the latter category was held to be made up of statutory offences. An equally moralistic approach to the classifica-tion of crime was adopted by James Fitzjames Stephen, the greatest of the Victorian writers upon the criminal law, when in 1882 he commented upon the importance of the criminal law which 'stigmatises certain kinds of conduct as

---

1 H. Fielding *An Enquiry into the Causes of the Late Increase of Robbers*, P. Colquhoun *A Treatise on the Police of the Metropolis*, First Report of the Royal Commission on the Con-stabulary of England and Wales no. 169 (1839), L. Radzinowicz and J. King *The Growth of Crime* chap. 5, P. Collins *Dickens and Crime*.
2 1 Bl Com (5th edn) 54, 57-8.

189

crimes, the commission of which involves, if detected, indelible infamy and the loss, as the case may be, of life, property, or personal liberty'.[3] For Stephen most summary offences did not come within this category. He wrote that they 'do not form part of the criminal law properly so called, but are merely the sanctions by which other branches of the law are, in case of need, enforced'.[4] Stephen does not offer a satisfactory definition of crime. Nor is the distinction between *mala in se* and *mala prohibita* a classification which can be supported conceptually.[5] Yet it was cited with apparent approval in the Court of Criminal Appeal as late as 1934 and the relationship between morality and the criminal law remains a lively issue.[6] Blackstone's classification does illustrate the obvious fact that the community regards some offences in a much more serious light than others. Such societal standards may change in some respects over the years. Blackstone included witchcraft amongst the *mala in se* — offences against God and religion occupy a more prominent place in the nineteenth-century criminal texts than was to be accorded to them in the twentieth-century texts. Clearly, too, the prevailing social standard influences greatly contemporary attitudes towards the enforcement and punishment of particular offences. Large sectors of public opinion tended at times to look upon some quite serious offences as being scarcely criminal at all. In the eighteenth and early nineteenth centuries many looked in that light upon smuggling and offences against the game laws. Similar attitudes became more marked during the nineteenth century with the growth of numerous statutory offences of an administrative and regulatory nature. In the case of the truly minor offence this may be understandable up to a point. Yet it was an attitude to some new offences which rubbed off on persons whose conduct on occasion could have far more serious implications for the community. It was as difficult for the nineteenth-century manufacturer who had infringed the Factory Acts, however seriously, to regard himself as a criminal as the twentieth-century motorist who exceeds the speed limit. Such attitudes illustrate the lack in practice of any public consensus as to the proper bounds of the criminal law.

In fact the legislature gave little consistent attention to the criminal law as a whole. The criminal law's lack of unifying principle and its haphazard growth posed a threat to the efficient enforcement of all kinds of criminal offence. Blackstone had foreseen the danger clearly enough. In his view criminal legislation ought to be founded upon permanent, uniform and universal principles. However faults existed in the criminal legal system because of an overscrupulous adherence to some rules of the ancient common law, although they were redundant. These faults were the result of not repealing obsolete or absurd penal laws, and paying too little attention to the framing and passing of new laws. Had such attention been paid, Blackstone wrote, some offences would never have been made a capital crime. Strong words, indeed, from one who is often regarded as the arch apostle of complacency.[7]

Many capital criminal statutes were enacted during the second half of the

3   J.F. Stephen *A History of the Criminal Law of England* vol 1, p. ix.
4   J.F. Stephen *A History of the Criminal Law of England* vol 3, p. 266.
5   J.W.C. Turner 'The Mental Element in Crimes at Common Law' in L. Radzinowicz and J.W.C. Turner *The Modern Approach to Criminal Law* pp. 195, 221.
6   *R v Donovan* [1934] 2 KB 498 at 508, P. Devlin 'Morals and the Criminal Law' in *The Enforcement of Morals*, and the literature which that essay stimulated.
7   4 Bl Com (5th edn) 3-4.

eighteenth century. Radzinowicz has estimated that such capital statutes grew from about 50 to over 200 between 1688 and 1820.[8] Many of them dealt with offences against property. Of the criminal law during that period E.P. Thompson has written:

> 'The law was hated, but it was also despised. Only the most hardened criminal was held in as much popular odium as the informer who brought men to the gallows. And the resistance movement to the law of the propertied took not only the form of individualistic criminal acts, but also that of piecemeal and sporadic insurrectionary actions where numbers gave some immunity.'

Elsewhere Thompson has argued, at all events of the early eighteenth century, that 'property and the privileged status of the propertied were assuming, every year, a greater weight in the scales of justice, until justice itself was seen as no more than the outworks and defences of property and of its attendant status'. More recently still it has been claimed that:

> 'The ideology of the ruling oligarchy, which places a supreme value upon property, finds its visible and material embodiment above all in the ideology and practice of the law. Tyburn Tree, as William Blake well understood, stood at the heart of this ideology; and its ceremonies were at the heart of popular culture also.'[9]

It is a powerful indictment. What weight should be attached to it?

A great number of capital offences were created during the period 1688-1820. Many of the statutes relate to offences against property, but in order realistically to access the scope of legislation upon a particular topic, the substance of that legislation as a whole must be evaluated rather than simply counting the number of statutes which deal with that particular topic. The criminal offence of theft may be taken as an example. A legislature which was bent on protecting property at all costs might easily have enacted one statute, framed in the most general terms, which would have classified as theft the taking of any form of property. Such a statute would have been far more effective in protecting property generally than the numerous statutes which were enacted in a piecemeal manner over the years. In fact the common law of theft was quite restricted in scope. In addition the courts interpreted it fairly restrictively. The very abundance of criminal legislation during this period can be interpreted reasonably enough as a reflection of a restrictive, libertarian approach which sought to dub as criminal only that conduct which was categorised expressly as criminal. The emergence of the statutory offence of embezzlement, which is discussed later in this chapter, illustrates that point. The propertied classes showed a similar libertarian reluctance to establish regular police forces which might enforce such legislation effectively.

Nor is there any reason to suppose that the population did not support the criminal law as a whole. Thompson concedes that the population as a whole condemned many crimes e.g. wife or child murder. He then goes on to make much of offences such as coining, poaching, the evasion of taxes or excise or the

---

8 L. Radzinowicz *A History of English Criminal Law and its Administration* vol 1, p. 4.
9 E.P. Thompson *The Making of the English Working Class* (Pelican edn, 1968) pp. 64-6.
   D. Hay, P. Linebaugh, J.G. Rule, E.P. Thompson, C. Winslow *Albion's Fatal Tree* pp. 13, 18-26. Cf. E.P. Thompson *Whigs and Hunters* and J. Styles 'Criminal Records' (1977) 20 Historical Journal 977.

press-gang. Blackstone, too, had disliked such offences. The Whig, Brougham, was to express his dislike of the game laws in strong terms in 1828. Such offences are of considerable interest and importance — they are discussed in the next chapter. Yet popular dislike of them was by no means confined to the working class; nor were lay attitudes to them typical of attitudes to the criminal law as a whole.

The jury was a considerable guarantee of this. Also, in some areas at least of the country, working-class victims of crime were ready enough to prosecute. In the Black Country the unskilled and skilled working class made up a large proportion of the prosecutors during the period 1836-51.[10] Admittedly, this period is later than the period of which Thompson is writing and in addition there had by then been a considerable reduction in the number of capital offences. Yet there is little reason to suppose that working-class attitudes would have been different in the earlier period. Many offences were the product of the new commercialism. It has been said with some truth that virtually the whole of the modern law of theft was the creation of the second half of the eighteenth century.[11] That does not necessarily reflect any improper class interest. For example, the statutory offence of embezzlement was created at the very beginning of the nineteenth century at the instance of the bankers. Yet the shock with which the trade union world greeted the decision in *Hornby v Close* (1867),[12] which decided that a trade union could not prosecute one of its branch secretaries for embezzlement, suggests that, in 1867 at least, there was no rooted working-class objection to making use of the criminal law. Once again there is no reason to suppose that working-class attitudes to such conduct were different at any earlier period.

It is suggested, therefore, that throughout this period there was considerable public support, which spanned class barriers, for the greater part of the substantive criminal law. The game laws were an exception to that norm. There was popular pride also in criminal procedure, especially the jury, which was believed to be far ahead of continental practice. Criminal punishments, it is true, were severe. Yet the greater part of the mass of penal legislation was not enforced effectively. In addition relatively few were executed in practice by the beginning of the nineteenth century. Here again it does seem that, by and large, punishments at this time reflected the attitude to punishment of the whole community rather than any particular section of it.

There are no reliable figures regarding the incidence of crime in the eighteenth century: rather must we rely upon contemporary accounts. Henry Fielding and Patrick Colquhoun each give a disturbing picture of the London of their respective days. Fielding's grim account of the multitude of offences against the person and against property in 1751 was corroborated to a certain extent towards the end of the century by another London magistrate, Colquhoun, who referred to 'acts of violence' continually committed in and near London as well as to 'destroyers of lives'.[13] At all times he offered statistics of a remarkably specific,

10   D. Philips *Crime and Authority in Victorian England* pp. 125-6.
11   J. Hall *Theft, Law and Society* (2nd edn, 1952) p. 34.
12   [1867] L R 2 QB 153. L. Radzinowicz *A History of English Criminal Law and its Administration* vol 1, p. 9.
13   H. Fielding *An Enquiry into the Causes of the Late Increase of Robbers*, P. Colquhoun *A Treatise on the Police of the Metropolis* (7th edn, 1806) p. 93.

and quite alarming, nature. Although his statistical methods were open to question, Colquhoun was a competent and respected observer. We can well accept, therefore, that crime was prevalent in the London of his day, although it seems probable that violent crime was then of less frequent occurrence than it had been in the London of 1751: this may have been true of crime in general.[14]

Competent observers during the first half of the nineteenth century believed that violent crime was on the wane. That was the view of a select committee which reported in 1819. Similarly, in 1839 the Report of the Constabulary Commissioners — which is often known as Chadwick's Report, after its prime mover, Edwin Chadwick, who was an ardent advocate of a national police force and so not a man to play down the extent of crime — suggested that the age was less violent, despite the gloomy view which it took of the state of crime generally. The Report suggested that a decrease of violent and an increase of fraudulent crimes was the result of a gradual amelioration of the manners of the people. 'The fact of any act of violence having been inflicted in any burglary or depredation,' the Report stated, 'is in general deemed by the police presumptive evidence that the offence was not committed by an old or trained town thief.' The contemporary fears regarding unrestrained lawless behaviour of the railway navvies in the 1840s and the garotting scare in the London of the 1860s are equally consistent, as exceptions from the norm, with this belief.[15]

Statistics of a kind, which are admittedly unreliable, were available from 1805 and from the 1830s onwards individual statisticians sought to contribute towards an understanding of crime. Yet regular judicial statistics were not published until 1857. Many crimes would have gone unrecorded, especially before the foundation of regular police forces throughout the country in 1856; different police forces had different practices, while changes in law and practice make any attempt at a comparative study of the incidence of crime at different periods virtually an impossible task. Accordingly, it is difficult to assess the validity, in terms of the statistics, of contemporary beliefs regarding the rise or fall of crime.[16] However assumptions based upon the available statistics did influence contemporary policy. A select committee which reported in 1828 compared commitments for the periods 1811-17 and 1821-27. The committee found that there had been an increase in commitments of 86 per cent and in convictions of 105 per cent. After making every possible allowance for factors such as the increase in population and for a greater readiness to prosecute, it did appear that crime was on the increase. As the Commons would not yet sanction any radical reform in the police system, Peel, as Home Secretary, 'deliberately set himself against any further reduction in the severity of the penal code'. Towards the end of the nineteenth century it was possible to use the statistics both in support of the view that crime was increasing and also for the view that it was not,[17] but the belief, valid or not, of some observers that crime was increasing may well have

14 J.J. Tobias *Crime and Industrial Society in the Nineteenth Century* p. 44.
15 Report of the Select Committee on Criminal Laws no. 585 (1819). Cf. Report of the Select Committee on Criminal Commitments and Convictions no. 545 (1828), First Report of the Royal Commission on the Constabulary of England and Wales no. 169 (1839) p. 42, K. Chesney *The Victorian Underworld* p. 42.
16 V.A.C. Gatrell and T.B. Hadden 'Criminal Statistics and their Interpretation' in E.A. Wrigley (ed) *Nineteenth Century Society* p. 336. Cf. Tobias *Crime and Industrial Society in the Nineteenth Century* and Philips *Crime and Authority in Victorian England*.
17 N. Gash *Mr. Secretary Peel* pp. 341-2.

influenced contemporary attitudes towards legislation.[18]

However that may be, considerable improvements to the system of recording statistics were made in 1895;[19] which contributed to the increasingly popular science of criminology. Those statistics show that recorded indictable crimes during the twentieth century rose from an annual level of 100000 in the first decade, to 300000 in the late thirties and to 500000 in the mid-fifties. McClintock and Avison point out that the annual rate of growth of indictable crimes has remained remarkably constant over the years. Yet over the period 1900 to 1965 such offences increased by 1300 per cent while the population increased by only 47 per cent. Whether such figures mean that there has been a real increase in all kinds of crime or rather that the community is more ready to report and to record crime is a question which it is impossible to answer satisfactorily.[20]

2 The definition of crime

Crimes and misdemeanours were regarded in the eighteenth century as a breach and violation of the public rights and duties which were due to the whole community as distinguished from private wrongs or civil injuries which were regarded rather as an infringement of the civil rights which belonged to individuals. Accordingly, the criminal law was known very often as the pleas of the crown — 'so called, because the king, in whom centres the majesty of the whole community, is supposed by the law to be the person injured by every infraction of the public rights belonging to that community, and is therefore in all cases the proper prosecutor for every public offence'. Blackstone defined a crime or misdemeanour itself as an act omitted or committed, in violation of a public law, either forbidding or commanding it.[1] In that sense crimes and misdemeanours were synonymous. However, misdemeanours were confined to indictable offences which did not amount to felony and were generally punishable with fine and imprisonment. Felonies were such crimes as, independently of other punishment, occasioned at common law a total forfeiture of land or goods or both—generally a felony was a capital crime.[2]

3 Social control and preventive justice

Several factors contribute to the individual's decision to conform to society's minimum requirements. In addition to personal self-discipline, the persuasive influences of the family and of community values exercise a great influence.[3] Some contemporary observers believed that the increase in juvenile crime at the beginning of the nineteenth century could be attributed to a diminution of

18   For example, there was the enactment of the Criminal Evidence Act 1898.
19   H. Mannheim *Comparative Criminology* p. 99, T. Morris *The Criminal Area* p. 37 for the earlier period.
20   F.H. McClintock and N.H. Avison *Crime in England and Wales* chap. 2 especially at pp. 17, 18 and 23, N. Walker *Crimes, Courts and Figures.*
1   4 Bl Com (5th edn) 2, 5.
2   E. Chitty *The Commercial and General Lawyer* (2nd edn, 1841) p. 1049.
3   P. Laslett *The World We Have Lost.* On social control generally see R. Pound *Jurisprudence* vol 1, pp. 13, 291 and vol 2, pp. 188, 276, 349. Cf. A.P. Donaigrodzki (ed) *Social Control in Nineteenth Century Britain.*

parental influence, as parents were often required to work in the new factories while their children were unsupervised at home.[4] Similarly, a tendency to crime in particular families did not go unnoticed.[5] In like fashion the deeply felt assumptions and beliefs of the local community affected the attitudes of individual members of that community. This was especially the case in the small community where both the vicar and the squire continued to exercise considerable personal influence. Community disapproval might be expressed in a more tangible form. Many an unfortunate woman who was alleged, perhaps, to be a common scold, suffered the indignity of the ducking stool. The skimmity ride was aimed especially at fornicators and at those who had broken the marriage laws — the effigies of the offending couple would be tied to a horse and paraded while a crowd of villagers made a great noise outside their houses.[6] Many small communities virtually contained within themselves a self-regulating mechanism which required relatively little recourse to the more formal legal processes. Beatrice Webb's moving portrait of life in the small Lancashire town of Bacup in the 1880s gives us a glimpse of how such an atmosphere could be translated to a certain extent even to industrial communities.[7]

To such forms of social control, the concept of preventive justice constituted a powerful complement. Preventive justice consisted 'in obliging those persons whom there was probable ground to suspect of future misbehaviour, to stipulate with and to give full assurance to the public, that such offence as was apprehended should not happen by finding pledges or securities for keeping the peace, or for their good behaviour'. Such persons were required to enter into a recognizance, with one or more sureties, whereby the parties acknowledged that they were indebted to the Crown in the sum required. Such condition became void if the person concerned appeared in court on a named day and in the meantime had kept the peace. It was the justices of the peace, by virtue of their commission, who were empowered at their discretion to demand such securities.

The justice could bind over to keep the peace all those who in his presence made an affray

> 'or threaten to kill or beat another or contend together with hot and angry words, or go about with unusual words or attendance, to the terror of the people, and all such as he knows to be common barretors; and such as are brought before him by the constable for a breach of the peace in his presence, and all such persons as, having been before bound to the peace, have broken it and forfeited their recognizances...'

Moreover, the justices could bind over all those who were 'not of good fame', together with those who were guilty of scandal *contra bonos mores*, as well as *contra pacem*. So the justices might bind over 'all nightwalkers; eavesdroppers; such as keep suspicious company, or are reported to be pilferers or robbers; such as sleep in the day and wake on the night; common drunkards...whose misbehaviour may reasonably bring them within the general words of the statute'.[8]

---

4 Report of the Select Committee on Criminal Commitments and Convictions no. 545 (1828) p. 42 per William Payne, the Headborough of Birmingham.
5 For example, by Clay, the chaplain to Preston prison.
6 See Thomas Hardy's *Mayor of Casterbridge* chaps. 36 and 39, W. Andrews *Byegone Punishments*.
7 B. Webb *My Apprenticeship* (Penguin edn, 1971) pp. 166-85.
8 4 Bl Com (5th edn) 248-52.

Such powers were very wide indeed, if applied with any vigour. For example, they had a considerable part to play in the field of public order. Even as late as 1950 the authorities were not agreed as to all the offences for which the surety for good behaviour might be required.[9] Moreover, there was no right of appeal to quarter sessions against an order binding over a defendant.[10]

Over the years statute, in pursuance of the general aim of prevention, sought, inter alia, to control public houses frequented by thieves and to supervise discharged criminals, with mixed results.[11] Yet no effective moves to control drink, which was seen so often as a cause of crime, were introduced despite the licensing laws.[12] There was also a wide range of offences against 'the public police and oeconomy'. Such offences were 'a concern of the highest importance', wrote Blackstone. Offences against the public police and economy referred to:

> 'the due regulation and domestic order of the kingdom; whereby the individuals of the state, like members of a well governed family, are bound to conform their general behaviour to the rules of propriety, good neighbourhood and good manners; and to be decent, industrious and inoffensive in their respective stations. This head of offences must therefore be very miscellaneous...'[13]

Indeed it was. Of particular interest in this context were provisions which forbade 'idle soldiers and mariners, or persons pretending so to be', from wandering about the realm; gypsies were also subject to severe penal statutes. Common nuisances included, inter alia, all disorderly inns or ale houses, bawdy-houses, gaming houses, stage plays as well as eavesdroppers, lotteries and the common scold. It even included cottages 'if erected singly on the waste, being harbours for thieves and other idle and dissolute persons'.

In addition there were sumptuary laws and laws aimed at gaming. Finally, there was idleness which was, wrote Blackstone, 'in any person whatsoever...also a high offence against the public economy'. Thus:

> 'all idle persons or vagabonds, whom our ancient statutes describe to be "such as wake on the night, and sleep on the day, and haunt customable taverns and alehouses, and routs about, and no man wot from whence they come, ne wither they go" ',

were divided into three classes, idle and disorderly persons, rogues and vagabonds, and incorrigible rogues.[14]

The laws against vagrancy constituted a most potent form of social control. The first vagrancy statute had been enacted in 1349, just one year after the Black Death had killed about one half of the whole population. The statutes sought to ensure the labour supply by ensuring that, in Stephen's phrase, 'provisions as to vagrancy were practically punishments for desertion'. In Tudor times, however, the aim of the vagrancy statutes had altered. Now the aim was rather to prevent or to restrict criminal activities and punishments were much more severe. Yet the vagrancy laws were also the penal arm of the Poor Laws. Those laws amounted to a recognition on the part of the community that some of its members, through no

9   *Stone's Justices' Manual* (82nd edn, 1950) vol 1, p. 291, *Wilson v Skeock* (1949) 113 JP 294.
10   *R v County of London Quarter Sessions Appeals Committee, ex parte Metropolitan Police Comr* [1948] 1 KB 670, [1948] 1 All ER 72.
11   207 Official Report (3rd series) col. 1086.
12   B. Harrison *Drink and the Victorians*.
13   4 Bl Com (5th edn) 161-2.
14   4 Bl Com (5th edn) 164-70.

fault of their own, lived in great poverty—such people could not be allowed to starve. Accordingly, Elizabethan England adopted a dual system. On the one hand the state established a system of poor law relief whereby it undertook, through the medium of the parish, to contribute to the support and maintenance of the poor. That is, the impotent poor were to be relieved in and at the cost of the parish in which they were said to be settled. On the other hand the vagrancy laws were to ensure that the able-bodied vagrant did not abuse what was seen over the years as a generous system of poor law relief.[15]

The Poor Laws alone amounted to a powerful means of social control with regard to poor persons who were not settled in the parish. The vagrancy laws were still more powerful. An important Act of 1744 had classified offenders into three categories in ascending order of seriousness of offence: idle and disorderly persons, rogues and vagabonds, and incorrigible rogues.[16] The provisions were both specific e.g. in their prohibition of minstrels and betting at any unlawful games or plays, and general e.g. in forbidding persons who did not have the wherewithal to maintain themselves and were living idle without employment to refuse to work for the usual wages. Taken as a whole the provisions not only continued to aid the stability of the labour supply but also, if implemented, might well serve to prevent casual crime. Any persons might apprehend an offender; the constables were under a duty, subject to penalties, to do so and to 'convey or cause him to be conveyed to a justice of the peace'. Vagrants might be publicly whipped or sent to the house of correction or common gaol until the next sessions. After such punishment the justice might by a pass under hand cause the vagrant to be conveyed to the place of his last legal settlement. The recipient parish was required to employ the person conveyed until he should betake himself to some service or other employment.

Clearly such sweeping laws conferred upon justices very strong powers to restrain the activities of those within their jurisdiction who were regarded as undesirable. Even so they did not cover every type of behaviour which many regarded as undesirable. For example in 1770 Sir John Fielding told a Commons committee that great difficulty was found in dealing with common prostitutes 'they being...scarce, if at all, within the description of any statute now in being....This subjects watchmen, round-housekeepers, constables and even the magistrates themselves to prosecutions from low attorneys.'[17] Yet a remedy was at hand in the form of fresh legislation. Statutes of 1766 and 1788 were designed the better to preserve timber—offenders might be deemed to be vagrants. It was for 'hedge pulling' under these Acts that in 1800 six Gloucestershire women were stripped to the waist and flogged until, in the customary phrase, the blood ran down their backs.[18]

Further additions to the law were made during the course of the nineteenth century. The Act of 1824, which repealed all previous Acts, kept the old classifications. By virtue of that Act and other subsequent legislation Stephen could state as a general proposition that any person of bad character who prowled about, apparently for an unlawful purpose, was liable to be treated as

15 W.S. Holdsworth *History of English Law* vol 4, p. 392, J.F. Stephen *A History of the Criminal Law of England* vol 3, pp. 226-75.
16 R. Burn *Justice of the Peace and Parish Officer* (16th edn, 1788) vol 4, pp. 354 ff.
17 S. and B. Webb *English Poor Law History, Part I: The Old Poor Law* p. 353.
18 C.J. Ribton-Turner *A History of Vagrants and Vagrancy and Beggars and Begging* p. 205.

a rogue and vagabond. During the twentieth century vagrancy so defined continued to be a popular means of law enforcement, although the law was now aimed not only at the socially destitute who might be lodging in an outhouse but also at the potential thief who might have in his possession a picklock key etc. with intent feloniously to break into any building.[19]

4 The guilty mind: actus non facit reum nisi mens sit rea

It was commonly accepted in the case of all common law crimes, other than common nuisance, that a culpable mental element on the part of the defendant had to be proven. It was a principle which was summed up in the oft quoted maxim, *'Actus non facit reum nisi mens sit rea'*. That maxim stressed the moral responsibility of the individual before the law. The defendant was not to be found guilty unless he or she had the guilty mind, or mens rea, which the law prescribed for the criminal offence in question. In addition to proving that the defendant had this requisite mental intent, the prosecutor was then required also to prove that the defendant had committed the requisite unlawful act. We now consider the question of the guilty mind, or mens rea.

In its early days the common law had favoured a doctrine of absolute liability. Similarly, during the nineteenth century there was an awareness, quite apart from the more obvious traces of the older common law doctrine, that certain categories of unlawful conduct were to be punished as criminal even though the defendant in those cases lacked any clear intention to commit the unlawful act in question. Clearly there was little agreement at common law as to exactly what amounted to a guilty mind. As later theorists tended to stress the subjective approach to criminal responsibility, with a stress upon the defendant's foresight of the consequences of his action, approaches towards a consistent doctrine of mens rea became even more desirable.[20]

In an admirable search for general principle some nineteenth-century theorists suggested that the mental element could be defined by means of general rules which would apply to all crimes. Commissioners wrote in 1843 that mens rea:

> 'includes every case of intentional or voluntary wrong, where the mind is actively in fault; and comprehends also all cases where the mind is, as it were, negatively or passively to blame, and where hurt or damage results from want of exercising sufficient caution'.[1]

However, the moral culpability of the defendant in those two categories might differ considerably and in practice the cases took full account of this. Accordingly, the value of any general theory regarding the mental element was necessarily weakened considerably. What is the use, after all, of a general principle which is so highly qualified? Stephen expressed the reality of the existing legal situation much more accurately when he wrote in 1883 that the only means of arriving at a full comprehension of the expression mens rea was by a detailed examination of the definitions of particular crimes.[2]

---

19   Vagrancy Act 1824, s. 4; see also Larceny Act 1916, s. 28.
20   J.W.C. Turner 'The Mental Element in Crimes at Common Law' in L. Radzinowicz and J.W.C. Turner *The Modern Approach to Criminal Law* p. 195.
1   Seventh Report of the Commissioners on Criminal Law no. 448 (1843) p. 22.
2   J.F. Stephen *A History of the Criminal Law of England* vol 2, pp. 94-9.

The common law tended to describe rather than to define that mental element. When Foster wrote of the mens rea, or malice aforethought, of murder, he commented that in this instance malice meant that the fact of the killing:

> 'hath been attended with such circumstance as are the ordinary symptoms of a wicked, depraved, and malignant spirit....And I believe most, if not all the cases which in our books are ranged under the head of implied malice will, if carefully averted to, be found to turn upon this single point, that the fact hath been attended with such circumstances as carry in them the plain indications of a heart regardless of social duty and fatally bent upon mischief.'

In commenting upon theft, Hale was even less helpful. In a passage which Blackstone adopted, he wrote:

> 'In cases of larciny the variety of circumstances is so great, and the complications thereof so mingled, that it is impossible to prescribe all the circumstances evidencing a felonious intention, or the contrary: but the same must be left to the due and attentive consideration of the judge and jury, wherein the best rule is *in dubiis* to incline rather to acquit than convict.'[3]

Yet no matter how marked the lack in practice of general principle or how imprecise the mental element which was required for particular offences, the fact remained that at common law it was essential for the prosecution to prove that the defendant had a guilty mind.

The best proof of such a guilty mind was that the defendant had actually intended to commit the unlawful act e.g. to kill the victim. Yet by the doctrine of constructive or implied malice a person might be guilty of murder who had no intention to kill or to injure the deceased or any other person, but only to commit some other felony and the injury to the individual was a pure accident. Coke had actually written that if A, meaning to steal a deer in the park of B, shot at a deer, and by the glance of the arrow killed a boy who was hidden in a bush, that was murder, because the act was unlawful, even although A had not intended to hurt the boy or even knew of him. Foster modified Coke's doctrine to the extent that if the criminal intention were to commit a bare trespass, the offence would be no more than manslaughter. Stronger objections still to the doctrine were made during the nineteenth century. In 1839 commissioners sought to modify the law. They commented that whilst an accidental killing during the course of an unlawful act wholly unconnected with any danger or mischief to the person could not justly amount to murder, the same objections did not apply where the unlawful act was of a violent nature since in such cases the result was not a matter of pure accident wholly unconnected with the criminal intent. Yet their recommendation to that effect was not implemented. Other official bodies also considered this aspect of the law to be unsatisfactory. In 1883 Stephen wrote that even Foster's modified rule was 'cruel and indeed monstrous'.[4] In 1887 in *R v Serne and Goldfinch*[5] he showed his distaste for the rule by advising a jury that, rather

---

3 Foster's *Crown Law*, discourse on Homicide, 11, pp. 256-7, 4 Bl Com (5th edn) 232, Fourth Report of the Commissioners on Criminal Law no. 168 (1839), p. xxii, First Report of the Commissioners on Criminal Law no. 537 (1834) p. 3.

4 Fourth Report of the Commissioners on Criminal Law no. 168 (1839) p. xxix, Report of the Royal Commission appointed to consider the Law relating to Indictable Offences with an Appendix containing a Draft Code no. C-2345 (1879) p. 23, J.F. Stephen *A History of the Criminal Law of England* vol 3, p. 75.

5 (1887) 16 Cox, CC 311.

than apply the felony-murder rule, they might prefer to proceed upon the basis that the defendants had deliberately carried out an act which to their knowledge was obviously dangerous to life i.e. Stephen emphasised that the appropriate test was that of intention to kill rather than felony murder. It was a decision which may have had some influence. Yet in 1920 the House of Lords reaffirmed the felony-murder rule, at least to the modified extent which the criminal law commissioners had suggested in 1839, when in *Beard's case* Lord Birkenhead LC said:

> 'The evidence established that the prisoner killed the child by an act of violence done in the course or in the furtherance of the crime of rape, a felony involving violence. The Court (of Criminal Appeal) held that by the law of England such an act was murder. No attempt has been made in your Lordships' House to displace this view of the law and there can be no doubt as to its soundness...[6]

Such a finding may not have been necessary either to the decision in *Beard's case* or to cases which followed Beard. Yet it was to remain the law. Writing in 1945, Turner commented that the result of *Beard's case* was that:

> 'the highest tribunal in the land, by laying down as they did the law as to death caused in the course of commission of a felony of violence, nullified all the progress in improving the law of murder which had been achieved during the past century....The prisoner has only the thought of committing the felony: yet...he is to be sentenced to death although he never intended to kill anyone, or realised that he might kill anyone.'[7]

Despite such criticism the felony-murder rule was to remain an established part of the criminal law until 1957. Clearly there were sound policy reasons for a second category of that rule which established that it was murder where death was caused in the course of resisting lawful arrest by an officer of justice, if only an intention to resist arrest by force was proved.[8]

Ought killing by an unlawful act, although the defendant had not foreseen the consequences of that act, to be punishable as a criminal act at all, even as manslaughter? Such a policy surely both rendered the mens rea for such an offence an highly artificial concept and also made nonsense of a deterrent view of punishment, since in such cases the defendant's mind had not been directed at all to the criminal act in question. Some judges applied Foster's unlawful act doctrine without any qualms. For example, in *Fenton's case*,[9] D had committed a trespass, an unlawful act, by throwing stones down a mine as a result of which the victim had been killed. Tindal LCJ told the jury that as D's act was a trespass, the only question for them was whether D's act had caused the death of V. Other judges were reluctant to apply such a broad, constructive concept and a tendency did develop of limiting the doctrine to acts which were both unlawful

---

6 [1920] AC 479 at 493.
7 Turner 'The Mental Element in Crimes at Common Law' in Radzinowicz and Turner *The Modern Approach to Criminal Law* pp. 257-8, *R v Betts and Ridley* (1930) 144 LT 526, *R v Stone* [1937] 3 All ER 920, *R v Jarmain* [1946] KB 74. See S.G. Vesey-Fitzgerald 'The Reform of the Law of Murder' (1949) 2 Current Legal Problems 27, 35.
8 *Porter* (1873) 12 Cox, CC 444; cf. *Appleby* (1940) 28 Cr App Rep 1. The Report of the Royal Commission on Capital Punishment (Cmd. 8932), sets out the policy arguments for and against the felony-murder rule at paras. 72-90 and Appendix 7(b).
9 (1830) 1 Lew CC 179.

and dangerous, at all events if D had threatened V with some personal violence.[10]

At the same time a separate doctrine was emerging which made it clear that, although inadvertence on the part of the defendant would not found criminal liability for manslaughter, a high degree of negligence would do so. Yet whether it be in cases of the doctor's responsibility to his patients or of the motorist's responsibility to other road users,[11] the courts found it difficult satisfactorily to elucidate the extra degree of negligence which would distinguish liability for negligence at civil law from criminal liability for manslaughter. Attempts to distinguish satisfactorily between the unlawful act and criminal negligence doctrines of manslaughter also failed.[12] Similarly, during the first half of the nineteenth century there was considerable uncertainty as to the bounds of the requisite intent to steal. Some definitions of theft made *lucri causa*, or the intention of the defendant to derive a profit from his crime, an essential part of the offence of theft: other definitions regarded an intention to deprive the owner of his property to be sufficient evidence of the crime. The efforts of the courts to reconcile such differing definitions by annexing a vague and indefinite meaning to *lucrum* only increased the complexity of the law. In one case it was held that it was larceny in a servant clandestinely to take his master's corn to give to his master's horses. Some of the judges held that the additional quantity of corn would diminish the work of the men who had to look after the horses; so that the *lucri causa* i.e. to give themselves ease, was an ingredient in the case.[13] In time the courts solved many such problems. Much might depend also in practice upon contemporary professional understanding of the proper bounds of a particular crime. There was a gap, as it were, between the theoretically unsatisfactory state of the law on the one hand and the law as practised, perhaps quite satisfactorily, on the other hand. When Stephen spoke to a select committee in 1874 regarding the law of murder and of manslaughter, he commented:

> 'although there is an unspoken understanding about the law by virtue of which it is administered in a very satisfactory way, yet the theory of the law, if you look to books, is very bad indeed. I say, in addition, that this sort of unwritten understanding which I am speaking of is one which I defy anyone to learn out of books. You have to learn it by practice in the courts of justice, by getting acquainted with the view which the judges take of the subject, and in fact by translating for yourself the theory which you find in the great variety of writers...you will find, however, that you cannot learn it from them; you would have to learn the law as it really is from the practice of the courts.'[14]

Not surprisingly, the Draft Criminal Code of 1879, for which Stephen was largely responsible, sought to dispense altogether with the now highly technical concept

---

10   *R v Larkin* [1943] 1 All ER 217, *R v Jarmain* (1945) 31 Cr App Rep 39 at 43. Cf. *Kwaku Mensah v R* [1945] AC 83 at 90-91. See G. Williams 'Constructive Manslaughter' [1957] Crim LR 293. The question is also discussed in several Reports e.g. Fourth Report of the Commisioners on Criminal Law, Seventh Report of the Commissioners on Criminal Law no. 448 (1843) and the Draft Code no. C-2345 (1879).

11   *R v Bateman* [1925] All ER 45, *Andrews v Director of Public Prosecutions* [1937] AC 576.

12   *R v Larkin* [1943] 1 All ER 217 at 219.

13   *R v Morfit* (1816) Russ & Ry 307.

14   Special Report from the Select Committee on the Homicide Law Amendment Bill no. 315 (1874) pp. 2-3, q. 10.

of the malice aforethought or mens rea of murder and to substitute for it definitions of those intents which did constitute the requisite mental element in cases of murder.

On occasion the courts adopted a radical change. For example, in 1943 and 1944 they finally decided that a corporation could be found guilty of a criminal offence, even though mens rea was an essential element of the offence; previously it had been believed that a corporation aggregate could not be guilty of a criminal offence in ordinary cases, as it could not have a guilty mind. In effect, the new rule provided that, although a corporation could not be found guilty of a criminal offence simply because an employee of the corporation had committed a crime in the course of his corporate duties, the corporation could be found guilty of a criminal offence, if the mens rea of the employee were in effect that of the company. Impliedly, the rule was based upon the view that certain officials are the company and not merely agents of it.[15]

For the most part the courts continued to seek to solve difficult questions concerning the proper bounds of intent upon a case by case basis. Within the limits of their common law craft they fashioned a reasonably consistent approach. Yet attempts to formulate a tolerably consistent theoretical base, surely an essential feature of an avowedly democratic society, met considerable difficulties. The confused and shifting bounds of intention, recklessness and of negligence, together with the ever narrowing concept of the much older constructive intention, bore witness to the fact that the old maxim *actus non facit reum nisi mens sit rea* was itself subject very much to changing interpretations — themselves perhaps the results of a changing morality and attitude to crime — over the years.

5 No guilty mind: the doctrine of strict liability

From mid-nineteenth century mens rea was a requirement which the courts held had been omitted from an increasingly large number of statutory offences. In *R v Woodrow* (1846) Woodrow was charged with having in his possession 54 lbs of adulterated tobacco contrary to an Act of 1842. Quarter sessions found that Woodrow believed that the tobacco was genuine and had no knowledge or cause to suspect that it had been adulterated. Yet the Court of Exchequer found for the Crown. Baron Parke said:

> 'It is very true that in particular instances it may produce mischief, because an innocent man may suffer from his want of care in not examining the tobacco he has received, and not taking a warranty; but the public inconvenience would be much greater, if in every case the officers were obliged to prove knowledge. They would be very seldom able to do so. The legislature have made a stringent provision for the purpose of protecting the revenue, and have used very plain words.'[16]

---

15   *Director of Public Prosecutions v Kent and Sussex Contractors Ltd* [1944] KB 146, [1944] 1 All ER 119; *R v ICR Haulage Ltd* [1944] KB 551, [1944] 1 All ER 691; *Moore v Bresler Ltd* [1944] 2 All ER 515. Contrast 9 *Halsbury's Laws* (2nd edn) pp. 12-14. R.S. Welsh 'The Criminal Liability of Corporations' (1946) 62 LQR 345. Cf. Lee 'Corporate Criminal Liability' (1928) 28 Col LR 1181, L.C.B. Gower *The Principles of Modern Company Law* (2nd edn, 1957) pp. 136 ff., L.N. Leigh *The Criminal Liability of Corporations in English Law*, R.R. Pennington *Company Law* (3rd edn, 1973) p. 110.

16   *R v Woodrow* (1846) 15 M & W 404.

In *R v Prince* some years later the problem was rather more difficult for the charge in this case was no mere regulatory offence of the Woodrow type. Prince had taken an unmarried girl under the age of 16 out of the possession and against the will of her father. He had believed on reasonable grounds that she was over 16 but was charged with a breach of the statute which provided that:

'Whosoever shall unlawfully take or cause to be taken any unmarried girl, being under the age of sixteen years, out of the possession and against the will of her father…shall be guilty of a misdemeanour…'

In his dissenting judgment Brett J maintained that a mistake of fact on reasonable grounds to the extent that, if the facts were as believed, the acts of the prisoner would make him guilty of no criminal offence at all was an excuse, and that such excuse was implied in every criminal charge in every criminal enactment in England. The majority denied this. The words of the statute were plain and there was no need to add to them.[17]

The attitude of the courts to this difficult question continued to be ambivalent. In *Hobbs v Winchester Corporation* a butcher was held guilty of selling unsound meat even though he neither knew, nor could reasonably have known, that the meat was unsound. Kennedy LJ said:

'I think that the policy of the Act is this: that if a man chooses for profit to engage in a business which involves the offering for sale of that which may be deadly or injurious to health he must take that risk, and that it is not a sufficient defence for anyone who chooses to embark on such a business to say "I could not have discovered the disease unless I had an analyst on the premises".'[18]

Very often, therefore, the courts appear to have found no difficulty in applying a rule of interpretation which conflicted so sharply with the traditional position at common law. It may be true that in the divisional court some Lord Chief Justices showed greater enthusiasm than others for the doctrine. Lord Hewart tended to favour the doctrine: Lord Goddard tended to favour allowing a morally blameless defendant to escape conviction. However, the trend in favour of absolute liability had gone so far that in 1936 one commentator wrote of the eclipse of mens rea and suggested that in the case of modern statutory offences the maxim had no general application — the statutes were to be regarded as themselves prescribing the mental element which was prerequisite to a conviction. Later still, possibly influenced by Lord Goddard's approach, the courts began to reassert the requirement of mens rea.[19]

Of course, there could be no question but that statute bound the courts. Many judges may have believed that they were doing no more than abide by that fundamental legal principle. That could have been true both of Baron Parke in *Woodrow's case* and of Mr. Justice Blackburn in *Prince's case*. Yet clearly over the years there had been a shift in judicial policy in that the courts had gone beyond this in finding that some statutory provisions had created offences of strict liability. For the most party they were minor regulatory offences. The

17 (1875) 2 LR CCR 154, Offences Against the Person Act 1861, s. 55, R. Cross 'Centenary Reflections on Prince's Case' (1975) 91 LQR 540.
18 [1910] 2 KB 471 at 483.
19 W.T.S. Stallybrass 'The Eclipse of Mens Rea' (1936) 52 LQR 60. See generally: J.L.J. Edwards 'Malice and Wilfulness in Statutory Offences' (1951) 4 Current Legal Problems 247 and *Mens Rea in Statutory Offences*, C. Howard *Strict Responsibility*.

American writer, Sayre, has dubbed them public welfare offences. As such they might have been classified more satisfactorily as non-criminal, perhaps administrative, offences. Certainly their presence within the criminal code was offensive to those who believed that a primary function of the criminal law was to stress the moral responsibility of the individual: community standards outside that province could have been enforced by non criminal means.

6 The unlawful act

In addition to the 'vitious will' or mental element each crime was said to contain an unlawful act. In this book it is impossible to describe the unlawful act in crime generally. Yet no crime was more common than theft. Accordingly, a brief account of the history of theft offers us an insight into the changing bounds of unlawfulness at common law and into the factors which influenced such change.[20]

Medieval society developed distinctive civil remedies for the recovery of real property. It was necessary also to develop remedies for the recovery of certain forms of valuable moveable property such as cattle. In time a distinction arose between goods in possession, such as cattle, which in law could be stolen, and ferae naturae, or animals of a wild nature, and real property which in law could not be the subject matter of theft or larceny at criminal law. Eventually, such distinctions became recognised as limitations upon the subject matter of larceny. This in turn led to a list, as it were, of the subject-matter of larceny i.e. of the things which in law could be stolen. The converse of this position was that the medieval common law was equally clear with regard to what could not form the subject matter of larceny. Real property, ferae naturae, goods not possessed, choses in action and goods without pecuniary value, all lay outside the protection of the law of larceny. At common law, therefore, it was impossible to steal fixtures attached to houses, coal from the mines, or vegetables from the land for, as all these items were attached to the land, they were regarded in law as being immovables or real property. Further, the early common law understood larceny to be a forcible act against possession and it followed, therefore, that in cases where property had been obtained by deceit or fraud, such conduct, since it was not forcible in nature, did not amount to larceny. The history of larceny, or theft, is made up in large part of the attempts which were made to remedy such gaps in the law. Judges were to extend the law by reinterpreting the definition of larceny both as to its letter — by developing the concept of possession by means of legal fictions to include instances of what was called constructive possession, and as to its spirit — by a readiness to classify as criminal, conduct which formerly they had regarded as no more than sharp practice. It was inevitable also that legislation would play a significant role in re-equipping the medieval law of larceny to play an appropriate role in the new industrial Britain.

Larceny was defined as 'the felonious taking, and carrying away, of the personal goods of another'.[1] The requirement of taking implied that the consent of the owner was wanting; therefore no delivery of the goods from the owner to

---

20   First Report of the Commissioners on Criminal Law no. 537 (1834), Fourth Report of the Commissioners on Criminal Law no. 168 (1839), Draft Code no. C-2345 (1879), above.

1   4 Bl Com (5th edn) 230.

the defendant upon trust could amount to larceny. For essentially larceny was an offence against possession which always included a trespass or forcible taking. Yet what if the owner were to part voluntarily with the possession? After all, that was an every-day occurrence, even in medieval days, in cases of carriers of goods and hirers of horses or goods. Could not the carrier or the hirer be guilty of larceny of the goods entrusted to him? Indeed he could not. Yet by a process of reinterpretation a medieval court had extended the law as far as it possibly could in the case of a carrier to whom a bale had been entrusted and who had appropriated some of the contents of the bale. Possession of the bale had undoubtedly been passed voluntarily and lawfully to the defendant carrier — how, then, could he be held in law forcibly to have deprived the owner of the possession of a bale of which he the defendant carrier, was already in possession? The essence of the decision was that the carrier had been entrusted with the whole package but not with any particular part of it. Therefore, although he could not be found guilty of stealing the whole, he might be guilty of stealing a particular part of it. The Commissioners commented in 1834:

> 'Thus it has happened that the anxiety of the courts to subject by means of judicial constructions, bailees of various descriptions to the penalties of theft, where they embezzled property entrusted to them, has produced the singular anomaly, that if a carrier steal the whole package entrusted to him he is guilty of no offence; but if he break upon the package and steal part, he is guilty of felony.'[2]

Even in 1834 there was uncertainty as to the proper bounds of this particular gloss upon the medieval position at common law. The application in nineteenth-century England of the medieval rule regarding the realty meant that the criminal law was unable to protect some property adequately, as cases might turn upon small questions of fact. The taking of boxes which contained title deeds to real property might not amount in law to theft as such boxes were said to savour of the realty; in some cases all might depend upon whether the box was open or shut. The cases upon the meaning of 'taking and carrying away' also displayed a remarkable subtlety. For example, the lifting up of a bag from the bottom of the boot of a coach amounted in law to a taking and carrying away, though the thief was detected before he got it out of the boot. But the setting of a package on its end in the place where it lay for the purpose of cutting open the side, in order to steal the contents, was not a taking and carrying away.[3]

A further example of a gloss upon the traditional understanding of larceny was the judicial development of larceny by a trick. The facts of *Pear's case* were that Pear was indicted for stealing a horse, the property of Samuel Finch. Finch, a stable-keeper, had hired the horse to Pear so that Pear might go to Sutton in Surrey and back. Upon being asked, Pear had given what was later found to be a false address: he had also said that he would return at about eight o'clock on the evening of the same day. He did not return. Instead he sold the horse on the very day he had hired it. Ashurst J reserved the case for the opinion of the judges, the question before them being:

> 'Whether the delivery of the horse by the prosecutor to the prisoner, had so far changed the possession of the property, as to render the subsequent

2　First Report no. 537 (1834) pp. 7, 9.
3　Fourth Report no. C-2345 (1879) pp. liii, lvii.

conversion of it a mere breach of trust, or whether the conversion was felonious?'[4]

The judges were said to have differed considerably about this case. According to ordinary English usage, the defendant Pear had surely had the possession rather than the mere custody of the horse. Therefore, he could not be found guilty of larceny for, being already possessed of the horse, he could not have taken the horse out of the possession of another. He could be guilty of no more than a mere breach of trust. However, a majority decided that, as the jury had found that in hiring the horse the prisoner had been fraudulent, 'the parting with the property had not changed the nature of the possession, but that it remained unaltered in the prosecutor at the time of the conversion'. Pear was therefore guilty of felony on the ground that a previous felonious intent existed in the mind of the defendant to steal the property in question.

The courts developed the doctrine of constructive possession still further during the second half of the eighteenth century. If a servant were to appropriate property which a third party had passed directly to him in the expectation that the servant would pass that property on to his master, such conduct would not amount to larceny. The reason was clear enough in law. As the master had never been in possession of that property, the servant could not be found guilty of the legally essential requirement of taking the property out of his master's possession. As the number of banks grew dramatically during the second half of the eighteenth century and clerks or servants handled large sums of money, the courts sought to offer the protection of the criminal law to such masters. For example, if a servant placed money or goods received from a third person into any receptacle owned by the master, such money or goods were held to be in the possession of the master. In *R v Chipchase*[5] (1795) the defendant, who was confidential clerk to a merchant, had taken a bill from amongst other bills on his employer's desk where it had been placed by another clerk. Had the bill been in the possession of the employer, then? The court held that in such circumstances the bill had been in the constructive possession of the employer. Accordingly, the defendant was guilty. Yet surely there were limits beyond which the courts could not take a doctrine of constructive possession? The law faced up to this awkward reality in 1799 in the case of *R v Bazeley*.[6]

Bazeley was the principal teller at a London bank: his duty was to receive and to pay money, notes and bills at the counter. On one occasion he kept back a note for £100 which a customer of the bank had handed to him and put it into his own pocket. Was this larceny? On the one hand the Crown argued that Bazeley's employers had constructive possession of the bank note. Crown counsel claimed that in the case of personal chattels, possession in law followed the right of property. Moreover, counsel maintained that the person paying in the money had not deposited it with Bazeley as a matter of trust to him, for it was paid to Bazeley at the counter of the bank of which Bazeley was an employee. Accordingly, the payment to Bazeley was a payment to his employer, so that Bazeley's receipt of the money vested the property *eo instanter* in his employer's hands and gave them legal possession of it. On the other hand counsel for Bazeley denied

4   (1780) 1 Leach 212. First Report no. 537 (1834) p. 8.
5   (1795) 2 East, PC 567.
6   (1799) 2 Leach 835.

that the employers had ever had either the actual or the constructive possession of the note. Constructive possession did not arise. Blackstone had said that property in possession subsisted only where a man had both the right to, and also the occupation of, the property. 'The prosecutors in the present case', continued counsel, 'had only a right or title to possess the note, and not the absolute or even qualified possession of it. It was never in their custody or under their control.' After referring to what he said were analogous cases at common law, counsel maintained that such possession would arise 'by mere implication of law; and it is an established rule, that no man's life shall be endangered by any intendment or implication whatsoever'. The case was argued before nine of the judges in Exchequer Chamber on 27 April 1799. No public opinion was delivered. However, the report states that it was said that the judges were of opinion that the bank note never had been in the legal custody or possession of the prosecutors. Accordingly, the prisoner was pardoned.

Statute altered the law with some speed. Later in 1799 statute provided that clerks and servants who embezzled property received for their masters or principals were guilty of stealing the same.[7] Yet what of those who were not clerks or servants but who received monies from the public? What, for example, of the stockbroker for he was neither a clerk nor a servant? Clearly such a person was not within the statute. Once again parliament plugged that particular gap in the law by providing that in future such conduct by any stockbroker or certain other functionaries would amount in law to a misdemeanour. So it went on through the century.[8]

Finally, the judicial attitude towards offering the protection of the criminal law to the victim of cheating or deceit changed radically during the second half of the eighteenth century. Hawkins had expressed the traditional reluctance at common law to regard such cases as criminal in this way:

> 'It seemeth to be the better opinion, that the deceitful receiving of money from one man to another's use, upon a false pretence of having a message and order to that purpose, is not punishable by a criminal prosecution, because it is accompanied with no manner of artful contrivance, but wholly depends on a bare naked lie; and it is said to be needless to provide severe laws for such mischiefs, against which common prudence and caution may be a sufficient security.'[9]

However, in 1757 statute provided for an offence of knowingly and designedly by false pretence or pretences obtaining any money etc. with intent to cheat or defraud any person of the same.[10] Finally, in *Young's case* some years later the courts showed at last a willingness to apply the statute generally. The legislature had seen, said Ashurst J 'that all men were not equally prudent, and this statute was passed to protect the weaker part of mankind'.[11]

Judicial attempts through the medium of the common law to extend the old definition of larceny so as to bring more modern forms of wrongdoing within its scope had led to a high degree of technicality and obscurity in the law of theft.

---

7 An Act to protect masters against embezzlements by their clerks or servants.
8 J.F. Stephen *History of the Criminal Law of England* vol 3, p. 153.
9 1 Hawk PC chap. 71, s. 2.
10 An Act for the more effectual punishment of persons who shall attain...possession of goods or money, by false or untrue pretences...
11 (1789) 3 Term Rep 98 at 103.

Even if we except some of the cases such as *Chipchase* from this harsh judgment, surely no other assessment can fairly be made with regard to the technical character of some of the cases upon 'takes and carries away' or upon the nature of the victim's possession in cases of larceny by a trick, or upon the obscurity, even in the nineteenth century, which surrounded the limits of the medieval *Carriers' case*. Yet there was a point beyond which the judges were not prepared to go, as they showed in Bazeley, in so extending the law themselves. The legislature must act if the more extensive gaps in the law were to be filled, especially at a time when these were capital offences.

Such remedial legislation tended to abhor general principle. Often casual in its nature and slovenly in its execution, it aimed invariably rather to remedy a single particularly pressing evil of the day. In its turn such legislation created its own problems. Anomalies existed with regard to punishments in that there were inconsistencies in the punishments established for some offences. More seriously still, overlapping offences existed which aimed substantially at the same evil and whose separate existence could be explained only in terms of their technical legal definitions and justified up to a point only by understanding the limited legal options which had been available to the judges, and perhaps we may add to the legislators, who had created them. As late as 1966 a committee could report:[12]

> 'The fact that misappropriation of property is dealt with under the three separate heads of larceny, embezzlement and fraudulent conversion inevitably makes for difficulty and complication. Whether a misappropriation is larceny or embezzlement may depend on subtle questions such as whether the clerk or servant has placed the property in what the law regards as the employer's possession. Thus a cashier who misappropriates money before putting it into the till commits embezzlement; after it goes into the till the money is regarded as being in his employer's possession and misappropriation of it is larceny. If the offender is not a clerk or servant but stands in some other fiduciary relation to the person defrauded, his offence will be fraudulent conversion. It seems wrong that cases which differ little in essence should fall under one or other of these offences depending on matters of detail, which moreover may be difficult to ascertain before the trial. It is also wrong that the time of the courts should be occupied with deciding such technicalities and that a conviction or acquittal should depend on them.'

With regard to the distinction between false pretences and larceny the report commented:

> 'The essential difference between this offence and larceny is that in larceny the victim does not part with the ownership but in obtaining by false pretences he does. But since "obtaining the possession by any trick" amounts to a taking for the purpose of larceny, it is notoriously difficult to draw any logical distinction between larceny by a trick and obtaining by false pretences and to decide whether a particular case amounts to the one offence or the other. The matter is made worse by the fact that the two offences are construed as being mutually exclusive.'

Commissioners made severe criticisms of the law in 1834. In 1879 the commis-

---

12   Eighth Report of the Criminal Law Revision Committee on Theft and Related Offences (Cmnd. 2977) paras. 15 and 19.

sioners on the Draft Criminal Code stated that the law was 'most objectionable, not only on account of its extreme intricacy and technicality, but also because the numerous exceptions made to the common law rule are inconsistent with the principle on which it depends'. Accordingly, the Bill treated theft, criminal breach of trust, and obtaining property by false pretences as three ways of committing one offence — termed 'fraudulent misappropriation'. Yet many believed that in practice the law worked reasonably well[13] and reform did not occur until 1968.

7 The later growth of the criminal law

The common law of crime had shown itself capable of growth to a certain extent in its development of the law of theft. Further, the flexibility — or lack of precision, as the case may be — of the common law rules gave some scope for the development of existing offences. By 1879 it seemed that no attempt would be made in future by the judges to declare acts to be offences at common law, although no such declaration had been made before in respect of such conduct. For example, the commissioners noted the old principle of the inherent judicial power of the court of King's Bench to act as *custos morum* of all the king's subjects — but did not think that any attempt to exercise it would be made in their day.[14] How surprised they would have been when in 1962 in *Shaw v Director of Public Prosecutions* Viscount Simonds declared that there remained in the court a residual power, where statute had not intervened, to superintend those offences which were prejudicial to the public welfare, stating 'gaps remain and will always remain since no one can foresee every way on which the wickedness of men may disrupt the order of society'.[15] Similarly, as late as 1932 in *R v Manley* the Court of Criminal Appeal approved an early nineteenth-century dictum to the effect that: 'All offences of a public nature, that is, all such acts or attempts as tend to the prejudice of the community, are indictable.' Accordingly, the court gave birth to a doctrine of public mischief and opened up what one commentator described as 'a gloomy vista of indefinite criminal liability'.[16]

Even in Blackstone's day the encroachment of statute upon the common law of crime was becoming ever more marked. Nor was this a matter only of complementing the common law. Statute created new offences, many of them summary. It was a process which Blackstone regretted. By mid-nineteenth century a flood of such legislation had changed the character of much of crime. Factory Acts and Public Health Acts were typical of such legislation and of the society which they helped to regulate. Yet the general public continued, like Blackstone, to regard such offences, together with many of the motoring offences of the twentieth century, as carrying little moral censure. That was reserved for the offences which had been known to the law for so many years. By and large the twentieth century saw no substantial change in the substantive law regarding such offences.[17]

13 Draft Code no. C-2345, (1879) First Report no. 537 (1834). Cf. Eighth Report (Cmnd. 2977) para. 6.
14 Draft Code no. C-2345 (1879) p. 9.
15 [1962] AC 220 at 268.
16 [1933] 1 KB 529, W.T.S. Stallybrass 'Public Mischief' 49 LQR 183, J.C. Smith and B. Hogan *Criminal Law* (3rd edn, 1973) p. 591.
17 R. Burrows 'Criminal Law and Procedure' (1935) 51 LQR 36.

Chapter 10

The enforcement of the criminal law

1 Introduction

The primary responsibility for the enforcement of the criminal law lay with the private citizen and with the local community. That was inevitable at a time when travel and communications were both slow and arduous. A more mobile and sophisticated country demanded more sophisticated and efficient forms of law enforcement. Yet the old philosophy remained the basis of the law, subject to continual amendment. In such a patchwork system the spirit in which the law was enforced was often even more important than the letter of the law.

The efficient enforcement of the law regarding the key offences against the person and against property is a problem which is always with any society. In mid-nineteenth century the country was also seeking to come to grips with the new statutory offences under the Factory Acts and the Public Health Acts and to cope with problems such as the effect of drink as a factor contributing to crime. The development of a modern system of enforcing the criminal law was a unique Victorian contribution to the legal process. In the twentieth century the advent of the motorcar also posed particular problems in terms of law enforcement. In the late eighteenth and early nineteenth centuries, however, the country faced three quite exceptional law enforcement problems. Those problems were smuggling, the game laws and public order. The manner in which the country tackled those particular problems tells us something about contemporary attitudes to enforcement of the law and of the resources which were available to enforce the law.

2 Particular problems of enforcement

a) *Smuggling*
'Will Washington take America, or the smugglers England first?', wrote the tenth earl of Pembroke in 1781, 'The bett would be a fair, even one.' Nor was this an inflated estimate of either the effrontery or the power of the smugglers,

despite the best efforts of the governments of the day to enforce the law. The Hawkhurst gang maintained a reign of terror in Kent and Sussex. As many as 500 men could be raised in less than an hour and the smugglers did not hesitate to attack those who opposed them. Indeed, on one occasion in 1747, the local militia at Goudhurst was compelled to beat off a determined attack upon their village under the threat that the gang would murder all the inhabitants and burn down the village. In 1783 Commissioners of Excise wrote: 'Armies of smugglers are every day riding with impunity through the counties upon the sea coast, and sometimes enter the capital at noon day.' It was said that in some areas the smugglers were so resolute and so numerous that the excise men were not prepared to challenge them, even with the aid of a large military force. Above all, perhaps, in view of its political influence, the East India Company suffered heavy financial losses as a result of the activities of the smugglers. The deputy-accountant of the East India Company estimated that at least seven and a half million pounds of tea, the staple of smuggling, must have been smuggled into Great Britain and her dependencies each year during the period 1773-82; this figure compared with legal imports of under five and three quarter million pounds annually.[1]

Yet the law was clear, punishment was severe, and — by the standards of the day — enforcement was rigorous. Blackstone wrote that smuggling was:

'restrained by a great variety of statutes, which inflict pecuniary penalties and seizure of the goods for clandestine smuggling; and affix the guilt of felony, with transportation for seven years, upon more open, daring and avowed practices...19 Geo 11,c. 34...makes all forcible acts of smuggling, carried on in defiance of the laws, or even in disguise to evade them, felony without benefit of clergy; enacting that if three or more persons assemble, with firearms or other offensive persons, to assist in the illegal exportation or importation of goods, or in rescuing the same after seizure, or in rescuing offenders in custody for such offences; or shall pass with such goods in disguise; or shall wound, shoot at, or assault any officers of the revenue when in the execution of their duty; such persons shall be felons, without the benefit of clergy.'[2]

Statute sought to enforce these widely drawn laws by offering rewards. Further, by the standards of the day the cost of the preventive service was quite sizeable — by 1819 it amounted to £546402. It was all to little avail.[3]

The duties, especially that upon tea, were high so that the profit to the smuggler must have been considerable. Some smugglers, like the Hawkhurst gang, enforced their will by the most unscrupulous means. Yet such a lawless situation could surely not have been maintained had the smugglers not enjoyed the sympathy of a great deal of public opinion. Even Blackstone recognised that 'the laws themselves,...by imposing high duties on commodities increase the

1 G. D. Ramsay 'The Smugglers' Trade: A Neglected Aspect of English Commercial Development' *Transactions of the Royal Historical Society* (1952) 5th series 11, W. A. Cole 'Trends in Eighteenth Century Smuggling' The Economic History Review (1959) series 2, 10-11, p. 395, N. Williams *Contraband Cargoes*, Hoh-Cheung and L. A. Mui 'William Pitt and the Enforcement of the Commutation Act, 1784-1788' 76 English Historical Review 453.
2 4 Bl Com (5th edn) 155.
3 L. Radzinowicz *History of English Criminal Law* vol 2, pp. 64-5, N. Williams *Contraband and Cargoes* p. 148.

temptation to evade them';[4] and we may interpret the complaint made in 1781 of the excise men of Ipswich that several of the local militiamen had been, and still were, smugglers themselves as some evidence of wide public sympathy for the smugglers. At a more rarified level Adam Smith who, despite his innovating qualities, nevertheless had a due regard for the realities of the day, expressed the view that 'the existing high duties were not only impolitic, but so impolitic that "nature never meant" them to exist'; he regarded smugglers as persons who were in many cases 'incapable of violating the laws of natural justice'.[5] Indeed, in Adam Smith's view, to 'profess a scruple in buying wares on which the duty had not been paid would have been regarded as hypocrisy and would have suggested the suspicion that so much pretended honesty must of necessity have been a cloak for knavery greater than the average'.

What was to be done? In 1784 a parliamentary committee suggested that only a reduction in duty would diminish smuggling. This was done by means of the Commutation Act 1784[6] which reduced custom and excise duties on tea from 119 to 12½ per cent. The manner in which this was done was a highly skilled and technical operation whose success was not assured until 1788. However, its success did ruin the smugglers' trade in tea. Of course, smuggling did not thereby come to a complete end. There was a great revival in smuggling after the Napoleonic Wars. Yet smuggling was now no longer a threat to public law and order. But whose had been the victory?

b) *The game laws*[7]
In similar vein to the spirit of Pitt's Commutation Act Robert Peel was to assert that the fact that the game laws were 'practically evaded and violated every day' was itself a sufficient reason for their repeal.

The validity of Peel's assertion was unassailable. Public banquets, inns and private houses alike were served with an abundance of game. One wholesaler acknowledged an annual sale of 19000 head of game. Yet the law was clear and by the standards of the day it was enforced quite rigorously. The essence of the offence was that of destroying such beasts and fowls as were classified as game, which was royal property, unless the Crown had given permission to do so by the grant of either a free warren or a manor. It followed, therefore, that in law all persons who killed game outside their own territories, or even upon their own estates, without the king's licence expressed by the grant of a franchise, were guilty of encroaching upon the royal prerogative. Indeed, a man held a qualified and transient property, or legal interest, in such game only for so long as the game continued within his liberty. Those who were not qualified to kill game were guilty not only of that original offence but also of the aggravations created by numerous statutes for preserving game.[8] The qualifications for killing game

---

4   4 Bl Com (5th edn) 156.
5   Cited by L. O. Pike in *A History of Crime in England* vol 2, pp. 400-401.
6   Select Committees of the House of Commons published three reports during the period 24 December 1783 to 23 March 1784 — see J. Ehrman *The Younger Pitt* p. 242.
7   C. Kirby 'English Game Law Reform' in *Essays in Honour of W. Cortez Abbott* p. 345, C. Kirby 'The English Game Law System' (1932-1933) 38 Am Hist Rev 240, C. Kirby 'The Attack on the English Game Laws in the Forties' (1932) 4 Journal of Modern History 18, cf. P. B. Munsche 'The Game Laws in Wiltshire 1750-1800' in J. S Cockburn (ed) *Crime in England 1550 1800* p. 210 and D. Hay 'Poaching and the Game Laws on Cannock Chase', D. Hay and others in *Albion's Fatal Tree* p. 189.
8   4 Bl Com (5th edn) 174 ff.

or, more properly, the exemptions from the statutory penalties, were as follows:
'(1) The having a freehold estate of 100l per annum; there being 50 times the property required to enable a man to kill a partridge, as to vote for a knight of the shire. (2) A leasehold for 99 years of 150l per annum. (3) Being the son and heir apparent of an esquire (a very loose and vague description) or person of superior degree. (4) Being the owner, or keeper, of a forest, park, chase or warren. For unqualified persons transgressing these laws, by killing game, keeping engines for that purpose, or even having game in their custody, or for persons (however qualified) that kill game, or have it in their possession at unseasonable times of the year, there are various penalties assigned, corporal and pecuniary, by different statutes; on any of which but only on one at a time, the justices may convict in a summary way, or prosecutions may be carried on at the assizes. And, lastly, by statute 28 Geo 11, c.12 no person, however qualified to kill, may make merchandize of this valuable privilege, by selling or exposing to sale any game, on pain of like forfeiture as if he had no qualification.'[9]

It may not have escaped the notice of some poachers at least that in law such qualified property amounted to a distinct exception from the general principle that with regard to 'animals ferae naturae, all mankind had by the original grant of the creator a right to pursue and take any fowl or insect of the air, any fish or inhabitant of the waters, and any beast or reptile of the field'. And 'this natural right', continued Blackstone,[10] 'still continues in every individual, unless where it is restrained by the civil laws of the country'. Blackstone even regarded the general offence against the game laws as being of a 'questionable' nature and suggested that:

'the only rational footing, upon which we can consider it as a crime, is, that, in low and indigent persons it promotes idleness, and takes them away from their proper employments and callings; which is an offence against the public police and economy of the commonwealth'.[11]

At much the same time Willes J, in a dissenting opinion, expressed the view that 'the game laws are already sufficiently oppressive and therefore ought not to be extended by implication'.[12] Yet these were minority views in the context of the dominant public opinion of the day. For attempts were made to enforce the law.

Whole armies of gamekeepers, who enjoyed special legal powers, were employed for this purpose. Occasionally landowners pooled their forces. For example, the Society of Noblemen and Gentlemen for the Preservation of the Game was active during the latter half of the eighteenth century. According to Kirby, the Society encouraged 'informers, drew up a scale of rewards, set up a special watch in London and Westminster with a view to getting at the nub of the difficulty in the sale of game and requested qualified persons to label all legitimate parcels of game with care to make deception more difficult'. Man traps and spring guns were laid; still more repressive measures were enacted. Nor should it be forgotten that many country gentlemen were themselves justices of the peace and so were especially well placed to enforce the game laws. Indeed, in

9   2 Bl Com (5th edn) 417.
10 2 Bl Com (5th edn) 403.
11 4 Bl Com (5th edn) 174.
12 *Jones v Smart* (1785) 1 Term Rep 44 at 49.

certain cases one justice alone might punish the poacher. It was an opportunity which many justices used to the full. 'There is not a worse constituted tribunal on the face of the earth', asserted Brougham in 1828,[13] 'than that at which summary convictions on the game laws take place....I mean...a brace of sporting magistrates.' Not surprisingly, perhaps, commitments for offences against the game laws continued at a high level.

Occasionally voices were raised against the game laws. In 1782 Charles Turner told the House of Commons that the game laws were 'cruel and oppressive on the poor'. Yet that and later attempts at reform were to achieve nothing. However, in 1827 spring guns were prohibited as a means of preserving game. In 1828 the Lords appeared to favour reform and a Select Committee of the House of Commons, although it saw little that needed amendment in the game laws themselves, called for a change in the laws respecting qualification and the sale of game. It did seem that change of a kind was on the way.

The Game Act 1831,[14] whose most striking feature was that it removed the legal qualifications for killing game, was enacted by the incoming Whig government. Licensed dealers might now sell game. Here, then, was some reform: after all, this Whig Act ensured that exclusive sporting privileges disappeared almost without trace. Yet the Act was no thoroughgoing measure of reform. It was enacted primarily to please the new middle classes who were outside the existing qualifications — how socially galling that must have been — and yet who wished to have game on their tables — how socially necessary that was! Accordingly, the Act did nothing to alleviate the distress of the agricultural labourer by restoring the common law principle that all mankind had a natural right to take animals ferae naturae. Nor did it help the farmer by protecting him from the landlord's insistence that the lease should reserve the game to the landlord — although the game would continue to damage the farmers' crops.

It is possible that this failure to alleviate the misery of the agricultural labourer may have contributed to the incendiarism which became a characteristic form of rural protest after 1830. However, the question of game law reform did not come to the fore again until 1844 and it did so then largely because the Anti Corn Law League, and John Bright in particular, had chosen to link the question of game law reform with its own campaign. With the repeal of the Corn Laws much of the sting went out of the campaign. A select committee, which reported in 1846, presented a bland report and little was done. Over the remaining years of the century the questions of the game offences themselves — originating to some extent in the poverty of the people — and of the accompanying allegations of unequal and excessive punishments faded from the forefront of the public consciousness, a process to which increasing prosperity contributed from 1850 onwards.

c) *Public order*[15]

On the one hand it can be argued that a country which surrenders its capital to

13   18 Official Report (new series: 1828) col. 166.
14   An Act to amend the Laws in England relative to Game.
15   E. J. Hobsbawm and G. Rudé *Captain Swing*, J. Stevenson and R. Quinault *Popular Protest and Public Order*, L. Radzinowicz *History of English Criminal Law* vol 4, E. P. Thompson *The Making of the English Working Class* p. 533, D. Williams *Keeping the Peace*, F. C. Mather *Public Order in the Age of the Chartists*, T. A. Critchley *The Conquest of Violence*, G. Dangerfield *The Strange Death of Liberal England*.

rioters for several days and whose Lord Chief Justice escapes rioters at his front door only by climbing over his rear garden wall in some haste, as happened to Lord Mansfield in London during the Gordon riots of 1780; which deployed rather more troops to counter the Luddite threat than it had employed in the Peninsular War to help to counter the forces of Napoleon; which tried 1976 prisoners in 34 counties in the aftermath of the Swing riots and which believed itself to be on the verge of insurrection in the 1840s, especially in 1842, was a country in which, to say the least, the maintenance of public order was a most difficult task. On the other hand out and out violence was relatively infrequent over the country as a whole and the conduct of the participants in public disorders was often highly restrained or even ritual in its nature.

It was the local magistrate who was the key decision-maker. When the riot was not wholly local — and the concept of the riot covered a great many possibilities — the individual magistrate alone could not cope, as the Luddite disturbances and the Swing riots both illustrate.

The Luddite disturbances, whose characteristic was machine breaking, produced rioting of an extremely serious nature during the period 1811-12. Indeed, on occasion mills were attacked, and even sacked and fired, by groups of several hundred men. One mill-owner, who was especially disliked, was assassinated. The disturbances were spread over a wide area in the North of England and in the Midlands. How did the authorities cope with this unusual situation? All available forces were called out — special constables, voluntary associations, yeomanry and militia. In 1812 there were actually 12000 troops in the disturbed areas. Yet the Luddite's security system, aided by the sympathy — or at least the passive acquiescence — of many of the people remained largely intact. The authorities found it especially difficult to persuade anybody to give evidence against a neighbour. To act the part of informer, writes Thompson, 'was a breach of the moral economy, entailing a sentence of outlawry from the community. Even the local magistrates could not view Benjamin Walker, the accomplice who turned king's evidence against Mellor, in any other light than as a Judas.' Even after a number of Luddites had been convicted, even after the end of the war, some unrest continued. It was clear that the army still had a role to play in the keeping of the peace.

It was the Swing riots which again stretched to the limit all of the national resources which were devoted to the keeping of the peace.[16] The first rural outbreaks occurred in the summer and autumn of 1830 in Kent and Surrey. As the riots spread the Tory government dispatched such troops as were available to the affected areas but they were dispatched to protect the towns alone. It was the duty of the magistrates to protect individual properties. Accordingly, Peel had urged the Horsham magistrates 'to enrol specials', form voluntary associations and even, if they wished, revive the old corps of yeomanry cavalry. Therefore, outside a few strategic centres, the justices were left largely to fend for themselves. Yet invitations to join the yeomanry, sometimes at least, fell on deaf ears: there was often a similar reluctance to enrol as 'specials'. However, various kinds of association for the protection of private property were formed; some

---

16   This account is based wholly upon that given by Hobsbawm and Rudé in *Captain Swing*. *Beatty v Gilbanks* (1882) 9 QBD 308, *Wise v Dunning* [1902] 1 KB 167, *Lansbury v Riley* [1914] 3 KB 229.

magistrates set up a nightly watch on farming property, noblemen organised forces composed of their labourers and tenants. Meanwhile Melbourne had succeeded Peel at the Home Office. After taking office he issued a proclamation offering rewards of £500 for bringing rioters and incendiaries to justice. This, and other measures, met with some success, although, to the annoyance of Melbourne, not all magistrates were unsympathetic to the disaffected. Yet it was not force alone, in the view of Hobsbawm and Rudé, but a combination of 'energetic' and conciliatory measures which brought the riots to an end. Even so, repression certainly had its place: over 1900 rioters awaited trial in more than 20 counties.

The riots themselves, which began in 1830, had been a manifestation of agricultural discontent. Ricks and barns were burned down, threshing machines were broken as various demands and threats, signed Captain Swing, were made upon the local gentry and clergy. Retribution was heavy. 'From no other protest movement of the kind — from neither Luddites nor Chartists, nor trade unionists — was such a bitter price exacted', write Hobsbawm and Rudé, 'In the south of England there were whole communities that, for a generation, were stricken by the blow.'

There were to be other serious disturbances. Indeed, Mather has written that the disturbances of 1842 were the most intense of any kind that occurred in Britain from the time of the French Revolution to 1848. It led to correspondingly determined action by central government to put them down. One new policy feature, which is noted by Mather, was that the Home Secretary encouraged magistrates to suppress all large meetings in the disturbed areas on the ground that in present circumstances they had 'a manifest tendency to create terror and to endanger the public peace'. Thereby, comments Mather, 'he removed one of the principal means by which advice to strike until the People's Charter became law was disseminated'. Throughout this period the influence of the Home Secretary is pervasive. Lord Sidmouth's employment of informers, the giving of advice to magistrates — often at their request — the capacity to dispatch contingents of Metropolitan police or of troops to assist in the suppression of local disorders, all added up to an influential role. Peel in particular played a notably even-handed role. Yet all Home Secretaries, whether from necessity, in days of poor communications before the advent of the railway, or from choice, as the idea of improved regular police forces became more current in the 1840s, insisted that the prime responsibility for the maintenance of public order continued to remain with the neighbourhood. It was an attitude which was to culminate in the creation of regular police forces throughout England and Wales in 1856, a year which marks a watershed in the maintenance of public order.

There was less violence after 1850, although there were particularly disturbed periods during the 1880s and in 1910-14. Winston Churchill's arrival at the Home Office in February 1910 heralded the greatest use of soldiers for the maintenance of order since Chartist days, while 1911 was probably the country's most violent year since 1842. On the whole, however, during this period a new 'respectable' working class posed no threat to the maintenance of law and order.

Perhaps the highwater mark was reached when the great Chartist demonstration of 10 April 1848 on Kennington Common, a demonstration which could have sparked off a massive confrontation, passed off peaceably. This was, wrote

Palmerston, 'a glorious day, the Waterloo of peace and order', not least, perhaps, because the troops had remained in the background. On other occasions, too, the police had shown their worth e.g. in 1833, 30 police had dispersed 3000 miners. There can be little doubt, despite disturbances in Hyde Park and Trafalgar Square, that during the second half of the nineteenth century a changed national mood, together with widespread public support for the new police, had created a new public order situation. It is true that troops were called out at Featherstone in 1893 — troops had been called out nationally on 24 occasions, on two of which they had opened fire, during the period 1869-1910 — and opened fire. Two people were killed. Yet one interesting feature concerning the Featherstone incident is that police were not available as they had been called away to other duties.

The preventive powers of the magistrates were used as a number of cases show — *Beatty v Gilbanks, Wise v Dunning* and, during the suffragette period, *Lansbury v Riley,* and the regulations which governed the use of Hyde Park and Trafalgar Square demonstrated that administrative powers might be used to govern those who wished to hold public demonstrations.

However, the years 1910-14 were, it seemed, the beginning of a truly testing period. The question of Home Rule for Ireland, the activities of the militant suffragette movement, and a period of marked industrial unrest were truly questions of public concern as they appeared to mark a weakening acceptance of the constitutional and legal system. So much is apparent from the doubts which arose over the army's attitude to the Home Rule question, over the suffragettes' new forms of demonstration, including arson and other damage to property, as well as the calculated disrespect which some suffragettes showed for the court upon being tried upon various charges, and from the possibility that the country was heading towards a general strike. Such points may be exaggerated. Certainly, the machinery for the maintenance of law and order, and the law itself, were adequate if there were a national will to use them. Before that question arose, however, the country went to war.

During the period 1919-50 there was no comparable challenge to public order. A certain amount of unrest after the First World War and a considerable number of arrests made during the General Strike of 1926 gave some passing cause for alarm. However, there was to be no determined challenge to the enforcement of the law itself. How different it all seemed from the position in the late eighteenth and early nineteenth centuries.

Of course, even in 1750 there had been widespread public support for much of the criminal law. In a country which relied so heavily upon private prosecution of offences, rather than prosecution by the state, it could not be otherwise. Further, it must remembered both that smuggling was confined to particular areas and that public order offences, although serious on occasion, were sporadic. Even so, the problems posed by the prevalence of smuggling and by offences against the game laws and public order were serious enough for any country. Clearly there was a limit, however blurred in practice, beyond which many people were not prepared to support the criminal law. Clearly, also, there were limits beyond which the state, reliant upon a motley collection of inefficient police agencies, found it impracticable, or even impossible to enforce the law. They were limits which pragmatic and sensitive politicians such as Pitt and Peel sought to observe in practice. All criminal prohibitions must command substantial public assent. Yet until Peel established a regular police force in London in 1829 there was little public wish to strengthen the forces of law and order — that public attitude remained prevalent until mid-nineteenth century. In a free country it was preferable that a certain amount of crime should go unchallenged rather than that paid, organised government agents should be available to repress the liberties of the people.

It is to the story of the establishment of such regular forces for the preservation of law and order that we now turn. Certainly, there can be no doubt but that in 1750 they were inadequate for regular policing.

3   The personnel of enforcement

a) *Community and individual responsibility*
The Statute of Winchester (1285) emphasised that the responsibility for policing a district was local. The statute specified three measures which were designed to assist in keeping the peace. There was a system of watch and ward, hue and cry, and the assise of arms. In addition certain duties were laid upon two constables in every hundred and franchise:[17] they executed the community responsibility. Each subject was under a duty and a right to keep the peace, a point which Lord Mansfield affirmed extrajudicially during the course of a debate upon the Gordon riots. It followed that the voluntary military associations, as associations of citizens pledged to unphold the law, were lawful in their nature;[18] it was their cavalry which became known as the yeomanry. Citizens were under an obligation to join the posse comitatus to keep the peace and to pursue felons, upon the sheriff of the county requiring them to do so.[19] Citizens might be engaged also in the militia. Statute required each county to raise a stated number of men and the members were obtained by ballot.[20]

b) *The constable*
In practice this individual and communal responsibility was usually exercised in the person of the constable. Constables were of two sorts, high constables and petty constables. They were appointed at the court leet of the franchise or hundred over which they presided, or, in default of that, by the justices at quarter sessions and were removable by the same authority. Petty constables were inferior officers in every town and parish who were subordinate to the high constable of the hundred. They were chosen by the jury at the court leet or, if no court leet were held, they were appointed by two justices of the peace.[1] For example, each year at Birmingham the court leet of the manor of Birmingham appointed two constables, together with an headborough as assistant to the constables. Their duties in 1779 were as follows:

> 'The office of constable:
> these officers are annually elected by the jury; and their duty is to suppress all riots and affrays within the manor, to arrest all felons, nightwalkers and

17   4 Bl Com (5th edn) 289-92.
18   Radzinowicz *History of English Criminal Law* vol 4, p. 108.
19   1 Bl Com (5th edn) 122, 343-4.
20   F. W. Maitland *The Constitutional History of England* pp. 456-7.
1   1 Bl Com (5th edn) 355-6.

suspicious persons, which they may do of their own authority; and they may charge and command any person, to assist them in the execution of their office, if need require, and they are to be attendant on the justices of the peace, and to execute their warrants; and they have a power, by virtue of their office, of billeting the officers and soldiers, which they are to do fairly and impartially.

The office of headborough:

this officer is annually elected by the jury, and is a secondary constable, and in the absence or on the death of a constable, it is his business, to do and execute the duties of the constable, and when required, he is personally to assist the constable in preserving the public peace.'[2]

It seems that in addition the headborough at Birmingham was the prison keeper and was in charge of the public office. He was assisted by six officers who were sometimes called 'thief takers' and who dealt with felons. It was the headborough who was regarded as the chief officer of the local police.[3] Special constables were appointed to meet particular needs e.g. if it appeared to any two JP's that any tumult, riot or felony had taken place or might reasonably be apprehended and if they were of opinion that the ordinary officers were insufficient, they might appoint special constables for a limited time for some particular parish, township or place.[4]

The constable worked closely with the justice of the peace by executing his warrants[5] and, in practice, by acting as his executive agent.

c) The justice of the peace

The justice's commission, upon which his powers and duties depended, empowered him simply to conserve the peace. It also gave him all the powers of the old conservators at common law in suppressing riots and affrays, in taking securities for the peace, and in apprehending and committing felons and other inferior criminals. Like any other conservator of the peace he might enlist the help of others; he might also be indicted and fined, again like them, if he were negligent in seeing the peace kept.[6]

d) The military

The numbers and calibre of the persons available in an emergency to deal with a mob were often inadequate as Kennett in London, Pinney in Bristol and many other magistrates found. Until regular police forces were established throughout the country in 1857, therefore, it was not uncommon for the military to be called upon to deal with such disturbances. The military enjoyed no special powers; they were responsible at law for their actions. Commissioners, who included the eminent judge, Lord Bowen, restated the legal position as late as 1893. The two chief principles of law were that every citizen was bound to assist the civil

---

2 'The Duty of the respective Officers appointed by the Court Leet in the Manor of Birmingham, 1779' (pamphlet 72245 in the City of Birmingham Reference Library Collection).
3 C.C.H. Moriarty *The Formation of the Birmingham Police Force and its Present Organisation* (pamphlet: 1939).
4 H. J. Stephen *New Commentaries on the Laws of England* (4th edn, 1848) vol 2, cf. *Stone's Justices' Manual* (82nd edn, 1950) vol 2, p. 2788.
5 J. Burn *The Justice of the Peace and Parish Officer* (16th edn, 1788) vol 1, p. 385.
6 1 Bl Com (5th edn) 353-4.

authority in repressing disorder when called upon to do so, an obligation which admitted of no distinction between civil and military status, and that for such purposes of repression no more force than was necessary could lawfully be used. Other points were that:

1)   The presence of a magistrate was highly desirable, but if none could be found the soldiers would still be under a duty to act. In any event the final responsibility for firing lay with the officer in charge.
2)   The soldier was in no special position but was only a citizen armed in a particular manner.
3)   The order to fire should be given only when it was absolutely necessary to prevent crime or damage to property. When so ordered the soldiers should 'fire with all reasonable caution, so as to produce no further injury than what is wanted for the purpose of protecting person and property'.
4)   The Riot Act did not alter the provisions of the common law. Accordingly, the military could act before the termination of the statutory one hour.
5)   Soldiers were under no duty to differentiate between rioters and spectators, it being unreasonable to expect this.[7]

In addition to the obedience which he owed to the civil law, the soldier was required also to obey the lawful command of a military superior. The dilemma which the soldier could face was expressed graphically in the 1830s by General Napier:

> '[the soldier's] thoughts dwell upon the most interesting question, "shall I be shot for my forbearance by a court martial, or hanged for over zeal by a jury...when a riot has taken place and all is over...then come forth the wise, the heroic, the patriotic". "How undecided the officer was" exclaims the first, "he ought to have charged at once." "That redcoated butcher must be hanged", says another.'

Unfortunately, neither that law — nor military regulations — clarified the meaning of 'lawful command'.[8]

e)   *The foundation of regular police forces*[9]

Even as early as the second half of the eighteenth century, isolated measures were taken to strengthen the existing police forces. A customs force was already active; the Fielding Brothers had founded the Bow Street Runners; in 1785 Pitt's government proposed, without success, to establish a police force. The Middlesex Justices Act 1792 provided for the creation of seven magistrates' offices: at each office there were to be three stipendiary magistrates. One such magistrate, Patrick Colquhoun, pleaded eloquently in his influential Treatise on the Police of the Metropolis for the creation of improved police forces. Such a

---

7   Report of the Departmental Committee on the Featherstone Riot no. 381 (1893-4) p. xvii. Cf. the evidence of the Secretary of State for War, R. B. Haldane, in Report of the Select Committee on Employment of Military in Cases of Disturbances (1908), *Burdett v Abbott* (1812) 4 Taunt 401 at 449, *R v Pinney* (1832) 5 C & P 254, (1832) 16 Westminster Review 422.
8   *Johnstone v Sutton* (1785) I Term Rep 510 at 546, *Keighly v Bell* (1866) 4 F & F 763 at 790. For an example of the traditional suspicion of a standing army see 1 Bl Com (5th edn) 413-14.
9   P. Colquhoun *A Treatise on the Police of the Metropolis*, T. A. Critchley *A History of Police in England and Wales 900-1966*, N. Gash *Mr. Secretary Peel*, E. Midwinter *Social Administration in Lancashire*, L. Radzinowicz *A History of the Criminal Law of England* vol 4, J. M. Hart *The British Police*, F. W. Maitland *Justice and Police*.

police would prevent and detect crime, he wrote, and would secure 'the blessings of true liberty, and the undisturbed enjoyment of property'. Jeremy Bentham, too, favoured a centralised police force. However, traditional libertarian instincts were hostile to such proposals. In 1820 a committee which had considered a preventive police system was firmly of the view that such a system would be 'odious and repulsive' and incapable of execution. Even a committee chaired by Peel and composed of those who appeared to have a special understanding of the problem came to a familiar conclusion in 1822:

> 'It is difficult to reconcile an effective system of police, with that perfect freedom of action and exemption from interference, which are the great privileges and blessings of society in this country; and your committee think that the forfeiture or curtailment of such advantages would be too great a sacrifice for improvements in police, or facilities in detection of crime, however desirable in themselves if abstractedly considered.'[10]

Peel believed that the questions of crime, police and penal reform were interdependent. By 1827 the apparent rise in the statistics of secondary crime may have persuaded him that it was appropriate to spend rather less time on penal reform and to attempt once more to create a preventive police force. After all in 1822 London, with over one million inhabitants, had less than 400 men to police it and many of those men were suspect in both quality and discipline. Peel obtained statistics of crime and population from abroad and in 1828 he duly proposed another inquiry. That inquiry found that there had been a considerable increase in crime: it recommended police reform. Accordingly, on 15 April 1829, Peel introduced his Metropolitan Police Improvement Bill, whose main objects were to unite all the regular police under one authority and to meet local expenses from local taxation. Little interest was shown in the Bill — parliamentary attention was devoted largely to the question of Catholic emancipation. The Metropolitan Police Act became law on 19 June 1829.[11]

The heads of the new force were Colonel Rowan, who had seen distinguished military service in the Peninsular campaign, and Richard Mayne, an Irish barrister. The two men were styled commissioners, yet in practice they were not so much justices of the peace as executive heads of the new force. Deliberately they decided that ranks up to that of superintendent were to be drawn, typically, from ex-warrant officers and NCO's — there was to be no caste system in this new working force. The members of the new force enjoyed only the powers of the familiar constable of old. However, the general instructions which were issued to the new force made it clear that much was expected of its members. After stating that the principal object of the force was the prevention of crime, they required that the constable was to be 'civil and obliging to people of every rank and class' and 'must be particularly cautious not to interfere idly or unnecessarily in order to make a display of his authority'. Moreover, discipline was strict. Yet despite a high turnover of police officers, partly due to a large number of dismissals from the force, the force quickly became accepted. Indeed, a select committee was soon to report that complaints against the police 'have not been well founded'. It commented also that 'the Metropolitan force has imposed no restraint either

---

10   Report of the Select Committee on the Police of the Metropolis (1822) cited by N. Gash *Mr. Secretary Peel* p. 313.
11   N. Gash *Mr. Secretary Peel* p. 497.

upon public bodies or individuals which is not entirely consistent with the fullest practical exercise of every civil privilege and with the most unrestrained intercourse of private society'. Clearly the force was here to stay.

Policing outside London tended to be of the traditional kind. For example, in the growing industrial city of Birmingham the responsibility for policing was divided between three bodies — the improvement commissioners, the courts leet, and the justices of the peace.[12] Birmingham had obtained a local Act for the incorporation of a body of 'lamp', 'street', or 'improvement' commissioners in 1769. For the first seven years or so of their existence the Birmingham commissioners held few meetings and employed no regular staff. However, they did divide the town into 12 districts, appointing a committee for each. The first tasks which they undertook were concerned with questions such as the bow windows which obstructed narrow streets, yawning cellars and the removal of rubbish. As yet they appointed no police of any kind, although from 1789-1801 a nightly watch was provided by private subscription. In 1801, however, a new local Act was obtained which conferred wider rateable powers. Accordingly, the commissioners then undertook the task of providing a nightly watch. Henceforth, during the winter months only, a force of 60 men was engaged at the public expense. Even as late as 1829 the watchmen were employed only during the seven dark months of the year. In 1839 the commissioners provided about 30 day police and 180 night watchmen. A second responsible body was the court leet of the manor of Birmingham. Each year the court leet appointed two constables together with a headborough as assistant to the constables. Finally, there were the justices of the peace. They carried out their duties at the public office. It was scarcely a large force in a city which was growing so rapidly. Yet there is little sense of contemporary public concern on this account. For example in 1828 Birmingham's high constable told a select committee that he did not think that an increase in the police establishment would lead to a decrease of crime. At Bristol, it is true, in 1830, the mayor and aldermen had sought the establishment of 'a more efficient system of police founded upon that adopted in the Metropolis'.[13] That and other similar proposals may well have failed because of popular dissatisfaction with the existing state of the municipal corporations.

The Municipal Corporations Act 1835[14] required the 178 boroughs of England and Wales to appoint a watch committee and to set up a police force. It is important to remember, however, that this Act was far from being concerned primarily with the reform of the police. Primarily, it was concerned with municipal reform. It is not surprising, therefore, that as a measure of police reform the Act had considerable defects. In particular Mrs. Hart has criticised the quality of the new borough forces.[15] In her view reform really meant the extent to which London reforms were introduced e.g. putting all the police of the

---

12   S. and B. Webb *Statutory Authorities for Special Purposes* (1963 edn) p. 239, C.C. H. Moriarty 'The Formation of the Birmingham Police Force and its Present Organisation' (pamphlet: 1939).

13   For a brief survey of the Bristol Riots see L. Radzinowicz *A History of English Criminal Law* vol 4.

14   See also Report from the Select Committee on Municipal Corporations no. 344 (1833).

15   J.M. Hart 'Reform of the Borough Police 1835-1856' (1955) 70 English Historical Review 411, J. M. Hart 'The County and Borough Police Act 1856' (1956) Public Administration 405. Cf. J. M. Hart 'Police' in W. R. Cornish and others *Crime and Law in Nineteenth Century Britain* p. 179.

town — except the City of London — under one authority, the provision of sufficient but not too many policemen, making the police a full-time occupation, paying the men fixed weekly wages and not according to the work they did, and generally improving their efficiency by the careful selection and instruction of recruits and by a strict enforcement of discipline. Mrs. Hart's conclusion was that the standard of policing remained low in the boroughs even after 1856, this being inevitable in a system which allowed nearly 250 separate forces in England and Wales.

How was it that the 1835 Act achieved so little for police reform? Quite simply, its sponsors had never intended that it should do very much for police reform. For his part Peel, a powerful minister, had worked hard to achieve police reform in London where the problems of crime and of the maintenance of public order were at their greatest. The Whigs had little enthusiasm for the establishment of regular police. For their part, therefore, they were prepared to tolerate a measure of police reform in the 1835 Act only as a necessary and minor incident to sweeping away the old closed corporations which were anathema to them. It was not surprising, therefore, that their proposals regarding the new borough forces were inadequate and defective. Yet the new borough forces, these incidental by products of the Whig philosophy would — as a new vested interest — surely stand in the way of any future attempts to establish a more unified police force.

A plea for such a force was made in the First Report of the Constabulary Commissioners.[16] The commissioners were appointed on 20 October 1836; the Report was signed on 27 March 1839. Their terms of inquiry had been:

'to inquire as to the best means of establishing an efficient constabulary force in the counties of England and Wales, for the prevention of offences, the detection and punishment of criminals, the due protection of property, and the more regular observance of the laws of the realm...'

The commissioners noted that there had been a decrease in violent crime, albeit with an increase in fraudulent crimes. Yet the overall picture was one of a huge social problem — 'the wide extent of moral corruption in operation throughout the country becomes fearfully manifest'. Moreover, 'the condition of the habitual depredator is, during his career, much higher than that of the honest labourer, living on wages which afford a share of the comforts of life'. The commissioners believed that, with the exception of the metropolitan police, the existing institutions had failed to combat the problem. What, then, was to be done? The commissioners proposed that an unified national police force should be created for the rural areas along the lines of the metropolitan force. In their view such a centrally directed, professional police force need not represent a danger to liberty. They wrote:

'The safe course for maintaining the freedom of the subject appears to us to be, not to render the authorities impotent, but to make them strictly responsible for the use of the power with which they may be invested for the public service....The great mass of evil indicated in our Report is ascribable not to the abuse, but to the neglect and disuse of beneficial powers. The chief and proper objection, as we conceive, to the police forces abroad

16 First Report of Commissioners appointed to inquire into the best Means of establishing an efficient Constabulary Force in the Counties of England and Wales no. 169 (1839).

are, that they act on powers which are arbitrary: the force which we propose could only act on powers which are powers which are legal, and for which they would be responsible to the courts of law, and ultimately to the Parliament.'[17]

The Report's prime mover is generally recognised to have been the Benthamite, Chadwick, who had had a long-standing interest in police matters. Indeed, he had contributed the section on 'Police' to Bentham's Constitutional Code. The influence of this interesting Report is more difficult to assess. Certainly Russell did not accept its major recommendations. Even as the commissioners had been completing their Report, Russell had been consulting magistrates throughout the country as to how a rural police force might best be organised. For in 1839 serious disorder appeared to be imminent as a result of Chartist activities. In a deteriorating situation Russell placed his first rural police bill before Parliament on 24 July 1839. In view of its origins it is not surprising that his County Constabulary Bill of 1839 permitted the magistrates in quarter sessions to establish — with the consent of the Home Secretary — a police force either for the whole county or for any particular division of it. The magistrates were to make all appointments and the costs were to be met out of the county rate. However, the Home Secretary was given some supervisory powers. Moreover, once such a force had been established, improvement commissioners were no longer to employ watchmen and constables. Even this quite modest Bill met strong Tory opposition — an opposition which suggests that politically the government may have been in no position to tamper further with the traditional powers of those traditional Tories, the county magistrates. At all events the Act was not implemented either speedily or fully. Even by 1848 the Act had not been implemented at all in fewer than half of the counties.

Accordingly, the government sought rather to strengthen the existing, time-honoured machinery of enforcement. The Parish Constables Act of 1842 — which has been described both as 'a gallant effort to put new life into the old constabulary' and as 'an Act for all seasons', provided that:

'every able bodied man resident in any parish, between the ages of 25 and 55, rated to the poor rate at £4 or more is liable to serve as a constable.'[18]

There were many exemptions from such services. The Act was a failure.

Meanwhile influential sections of public opinion continued to attempt to reject the reforms which had been introduced in 1839.

In Lancashire motions for the abolition of the force were carried, but the necessary majority of three-quarters was never obtained. Dissatisfaction was evident also in Essex, despite the fact that Captain M'Hardy was a most admirable chief constable. It was the arrival of Palmerston at the Home Office in December 1852 which marked a fresh and decisive approach towards police reform. In 1853 a select committee appeared to favour government aid 'towards defraying the cost of an approved and extended system of police without essentially interfering with the local management of that force'. Yet Palmerston's attempts to introduce radical legislation failed, largely in the face of opposition from the boroughs. It was left to a new but experienced Home Secretary, Sir George Grey, to carry such

17 Cited by T. A. Critchley in *A History of Police in England and Wales 900-1966* p. 75.
18 Section 5.

proposals in 1856. At last all counties were required to establish police forces for the whole of their counties. Despite some amendments which Grey was obliged to make, the new Act remained a substantial step forward.[19]

The impact of the Benthamites, the emigration theory, constant theft and the fear of theft, and fear of the Chartists may each have had some influence in establishing the new regular police forces. Certainly Edwin Chadwick was an avowed Benthamite and a keen advocate of police reform. Clearly the Benthamite arguments in favour of rational administration and the avoidance of waste were relevant to police reform. Quite possibly, too, the cause of police reform was affected by the Benthamite creation of the New Poor Law. Chadwick himself wished to use the police in support of the Poor Law and there was a wide-spread recognition of the links between crime on the one hand and the Poor Law and the vagrancy laws on the other hand. Yet whereas the Benthamites may well have been inspired by their Poor Law success to make greater efforts in the field of police reform, it is probably equally true that others were just as repelled by that Benthamite creation — notably the Tories who resented the new bureau-cracy which limited their own former privileges, and the working classes who had felt the harshness of the New Poor Law.

There seems to be no evidence in support of the emigration theory. This theory has it that on the formation of the metropolitan force criminals were driven from London to the boroughs: from the boroughs they were driven in turn to the rural areas. Accordingly, the rural areas were in need of a police force. Hart points out that any discussion is bound to be inconclusive in view of the lack of sound statistics. However, the case for reforming the borough police was argued on other grounds — the police in most towns were defective and shown to be so. Accordingly, the opportunity was taken to reform them when municipal reform generally was being undertaken. The Municipal Corporation Commis-sioners did not refer to any exodus from London; nor was it referred to in the debates on the Corporation Bill. Hart's conclusion is similar with regard to the rural police. Indeed, 'far from the reform of the town police causing the reform of the rural police, the deficiencies of the police in many towns (although admittedly mainly the unincorporated ones) were an added reason for taking action about the rural police'. Midwinter argues that constant theft and fear of theft was an important factor in police reform. He suggests that historians 'have perhaps been a little over-anxious to lay all police reform at the Chartist door'. He argues that the case as presented by the Constabulary Report, and in part accepted, for a reformed police was not Chartist centred. Secondly he points out that the rather innocuous permissive County Police Act of 1839 was 'hardly the thorough-going act of a state terrorised by Chartism and, although Chartist threats continued through most of the next decade only 22 counties had adopted the Act in full by 1853'.

It is impossible, therefore, to attribute convincingly the long drawn out course of police reform to any single factor. Yet the initial and continuing opposition to the creation of regular police forces did ensure that police powers would be limited simply to the powers which the constable had long enjoyed at common law and which scarcely exceeded those enjoyed by each subject.

19   County and Borough Police Act 1856.

4   The prosecution process

a) *Introduction*

The primary responsibility for the prosecution of crime lay with the private citizen. By mid-nineteenth century it had become clear that, in the case of minor offences at least, many citizens were reluctant to take up this public duty because of the expense and inconvenience which were involved. Accordingly, the newly established regular police forces in practice began to assume a considerable responsibility for many prosecutions. At much the same time public administrators began to exercise a discretion whether or not to prosecute under one of the numerous statutory offences e.g. the Factory Acts and the Public Health Acts, which had been created during this period. Yet the basis of the law remained unchanged. Only exceptionally were public officers granted legal powers which exceeded the powers of the citizen and the constable at common law. Nor was there any public prosecutor: the office of the Director of Public Prosecutions, the closest approximation to a public prosecutor, was created only in 1879.

b) *Rewards, immunities and pardons*

The state sought to encourage prosecutions through the considerable use which was made until well into the nineteenth century of rewards and of immunities. Numerous Acts of Parliament had conferred rewards and immunities upon those who brought felons to justice.[20] In London it was common practice to publish an advertisement offering a reward on the recovery of the articles stolen and the conviction of the offenders. Large rewards were offered for information leading to the conviction of Luddites. At a slightly later date the radical press was prepared to cite cases 'in which blood-money informers "planted" forged bank notes on innocent victims, and then secured the reward for their conviction'.[1] In the light of increasing public concern upon this point, the question of rewards was discussed in the House of Commons. A critic of the existing system told the House that some were reluctant to prosecute because of the question of blood money; others had been convicted falsely because of it. About 20 persons were said to have been the victims of such machinations in 1772. The first question which was said to be put frequently at trials to police officers and to witnesses was, what would they gain by the conviction? Rewards were abolished in 1818.[2] Immunities had also been granted. Statute provided, for example, that any persons apprehending and prosecuting to conviction a felon guilty of burglary or of private larceny to the value of five shillings, from any shop, warehouse, coach-house or stable, should be excused from all parish offices. The grant of such immunity was known as the award of a 'Tyburn-ticket', as the offences in question carried the death penalty so that a person convicted was likely to be sent to Tyburn for execution.[3] In addition free pardons might be conferred, indeed,

---

20 4 Bl Com (5th edn) 291-2.
1   P. Colquhoun *Treatise on the Police of the Metropolis* pp..383-4, E. P. Thompson *The Making of the English Working Class* (1968 edn) p. 533, L. Radzinowicz *A History of the Criminal Law of England* vol 2, pp. 147-55.
2   37 Official Report (1st series: 1818) cols. 691-693, cf. 38 Official Report (1st series: 1818) cols. 507-510. See also L. Radzinowicz *A History of the Criminal Law of England* vol 4, p. 223.
3   4 Bl Com (5th edn) 292, L. Radzinowicz *A History of the Criminal Law of England* vol 2, pp. 155-6.

they were often advertised.[4]

c) *The decision to prosecute*

Whether or not to prosecute was the decision of a private individual, usually the victim. The achievement of the aims of much social legislation during the nineteenth century did mean, however, that the decision whether or not to prosecute was now more complex. For example, the Home Secretary told the first factory inspectors that:

> 'Your best chance of success will be a courteous and conciliatory demeanour towards the millowners; and by impressing on their minds that the object of your visits is rather to assist them in conforming to the Act and Regulations thereon founded; and to explain what they may find it difficult to understand, rather than to fish out grounds for complaint. It should be kept in mind that the Act itself is a novelty...and that a gradual and quiet introduction of its observance by the body of manufacturers is the most likely method to perpetuate its benefits.'[5]

At a later stage the factory inspectors were to consult together with a view to introducing a certain amount of conformity of practice amongst themselves. The Medical Officer of Health might act in a similar manner in seeking to enforce the Public Health Acts.[6]

More usually it was the private individual who, with or without the aid of the constable, arrested the defendant. It was the private individual who was responsible for the prosecution of the case. Accordingly, if the magistrate did not deal with the case summarily, the magistrate would require the prosecution and the witnesses to enter into recognizances to prosecute the case. One can understand that at a time when travel was relatively difficult many private citizens might well be reluctant to undertake a time-consuming and expensive task, in the case, at all events, of relatively minor offences. The criminal law commissioners commented in 1845 that:

> 'The existing law...is by no means so effectual as it ought to be: the duty of prosecution is usually irksome, inconvenient, and burthensome; the injured party would often rather forego the prosecution than incur expense of time, labour, and money. When, therefore, the party injured is compelled by the magistrate to act as prosecutor, the duty is frequently performed unwillingly; and carelessly. It cannot be well performed in any case without the aid of an attorney nor without greater cost and expense than is usually allowed to the pary who prosecutes. Hence it happens but too often, that prosecutions are conducted in a loose and an unsatisfactory manner, from want of the means and labour esential to a just and satisfactory inquiry.
>
> The intrusting the conduct of the prosecution to a private individual opens a wide door to bribery, collusion, and illegal compromises. Independently of these obvious objections attending such a course, it frequently

---

4 L. Radzinowicz *A History of the Criminal Law of England* vol 2, pp. 41-2.
5 M. W. Thomas 'The Origins of Administrative Centralisation' (1950) 3 Current Legal Problems 214, 222, citing Parliamentary Papers no. 40 (1835) p. 698.
6 See generally W. Frazer *The History of English Public Health, 1834-1939* and R. A. Lewis *Edwin Chadwick and the Public Health Movement 1832-1854.*

happens that there is no person who can legally be called upon to prosecute; as in cases of homicide.'[7]

The creation of a public prosecutor became a recurrent theme amongst law reformers during the following years. Very often groups of individuals had sought to overcome this defect by forming themselves into a group or society whose object was to prosecute injuries alleged to have been done to members, usually to the property of members. Some such groups had quite specific aims, such as the protection of game or the suppression of vice or vagrancy. Of course the larger commercial enterprises were less reluctant to prosecute than individual tradesmen may have been.[8] Even so it was clear that the lack of a public prosecutor amounted to a considerable omission in the legal system. The judicature commissioners believed in 1874 that the appointment of public prosecutors 'would materially add to the efficiency of the administration of criminal justice',[9] but their Report lacked bite and it was not until 1879 that the office of the Director of Public Prosecutions was created. Initially his function was advisory: he passed cases on to the Treasury Solicitor. The issue was considered again in 1884. Yet it was not until 1908 that the office of the Director of Public Prosecutions began to assume its modern form and function. Even then, the Director of Public Prosecutions quite definitely did not regard himself as the Public Prosecutor, although in a growing number of serious offences statute gave him the sole duty to prosecute. Responsibility for prosecution still lay more frequently in the alternative between the private citizen, the chief constable, and the Director of Public Prosecutions.[10]

d) *Arrest*

An arrest was the 'apprehending or restraining of one's person in order to be forthcoming to answer an alleged or suspected crime'.[11] All persons were liable to arrest but no one was to be arrested unless he were charged with such a crime that would justify holding him to bail when he was taken. An arrest could be either: (1) by warrant or (2) by an officer without warrant or (3) by a private person also without warrant or (4) by hue or cry.

Once the justice of the peace had granted a warrant, the warrant was directed to the constable or other peace officer. The officer was bound to execute a warrant which he received and he would be indemnified in executing ministerially within the bounds of the jurisdiction of the executing magistrate a duly penned warrant, even if the magistrate had exceeded his jurisdiction. The warrant of a justice of the peace in one county had to be 'backed' i.e. signed, by a justice of the peace in another county before it could be executed in that other county.

Without warrant, an officer might:

---

7   Eighth Report from Her Majesty's Commissioners on Criminal Law no. 656 (1845) pp. 24-5. Cf. Royal Commission on County Rates no. 58 (1836) pp. 44, 61, 177, Second Report from the Select Committee appointed to consider the Expediency of adopting a more Uniform System of Police in England and Wales and Scotland no. 715 (1852–53) p. 270.

8   D. Philips *Crime and Authority in Victorian England* pp. 101, 120.

9   Judicature Commission: Fifth and Final Report no. C-1090 (1874) p. ix.

10   R. M. Jackson *The Machinery of Justice in England* (6th edn, 1972) p. 162, Sir E. T. Atkinson 'The Department of the Director of Public Prosecutions' (1944) 22 Can Bar Rev 413.

11   4 Bl Com (5th edn) 286.

'Arrest any one for a breach of the peace, and carry him before a justice of the peace. And, in case of felony actually committed, or a dangerous wounding whereby felony is likely to ensue, he may upon probable suspicion arrest the felon; and for that purpose is authorised (as upon a justice's warrant) to break open doors, and even to kill the felon if he cannot otherwise be taken; and, if he or his assistants be killed in attempting such arrest, it is murder in all concerned.'[12]

Mayne drafted regulations for the metropolitan police which sought to set out such law clearly. It seems that the police made every effort to abide by the law despite its omissions. For example, the power of the constable to arrest without warrant for misdemeanour was limited to cases of breach of the peace which took place within his own view; in all other cases the constable was required to obtain a warrant. The police soon pointed out that persons suspected of offences e.g. common assault were thereby enabled to escape.[13] Nor was such caution on the part of the police misplaced in cases of misdemeanour since it was unlawful to arrest an individual without a justice's warrant, if the improper conduct were at an end before the arrest took place.[14] Not surprisingly one critic suggested that the distinction between felony and misdemeanour should be abolished as it led to much litigation and prevented many offenders being brought to justice. Moreover, there was little logic in the distinction. 'If a man steals sixpence', wrote Greaves,[15] 'he may be apprehended at any time and any place; if he obtains 100l by false pretences, he cannot be apprehended at all, except in the very act.' Greaves went on also to suggest in 1844 that the jurisdiction of parish constables should not be limited to their parishes but should extend over a considerable area around, although constables appointed under the Municipal Corporation Act had jurisdiction over 15 miles round their borough. The existing law made it all too easy for the wrongdoer to continue a wrongful act e.g. a prize fight, in an adjacent parish.[16]

In fact little interest was shown and few changes were made in this area of law despite occasional recognition of its public importance. Even the provisions of the Draft Code of 1879[17] followed the existing law — apart from changes consequent upon the proposed abolition of the distinction between felony and misdemeanour — which showed little advance upon the position outlined above. What had happened was that individual statutes had increased the powers of constables in a piecemeal manner and so had glossed over the basic common law position that the constable differed but little from the private citizen in his powers of arrest. The metropolitan commissioners had shown what was to happen in this respect when they proposed to a select committee of 1834 that police should have power to clear public houses and to keep pathways clear.[18] Over the years the statutes which imposed such duties upon constables gave them corresponding powers. Often, too, local by-laws conferred special powers with

12 4 Bl Com (5th edn) 289.
13 Eighth Report from…Commissioners on Criminal Law no. 656 (1845) p. 32.
14 *Timothy v Simpson* (1835) 1 Cr M & R 757. Contrast *Baynes v Brewster* 5 JP 799, [1842] 2 LJR 24.
15 Eighth Report from…Commissioners on Criminal Law no. 656 (1845) p. 246. Greaves cited *Fox v Gaunt* (1832) 3 B & Ad 798.
16 Eighth Report no. 656 (1845) p. 246.
17 Report of the Royal Commission appointed to consider the Law relating to Indictable Offences no. C-2345 (1879).
18 Report of the Select Committee on the Police of the Metropolis no. 600 (1834) pp. 391, 187.

regard to specified matters upon the constables of that locality. As a result the powers of the police became correspondingly unclear.

Any private person who was present when a felony was committed was bound to arrest the felon. In following such a felon they might break open doors and if they killed him, provided he could not be taken otherwise, it was justifiable. A private person might also arrest a felon upon probable suspicion but could not justify breaking open doors to do it.

Fourthly, there might be an arrest following a hue and cry. Such a course, which provided for raising a posse of horse and foot for pursuing a malefactor from vill to vill, and from county to county, to the coast of the sea, was infrequently resorted to and was seen as of little use in the nineteenth century, although a statute of 1735 had sought to strengthen it.

e) *The preliminary inquiry, commitment and bail*

Upon the arrest of the defendant, he was carried before a justice of the peace who was bound immediately to examine the circumstances of the crime alleged. If the justice or justices were of opinion that the evidence was not sufficient to put the prisoner upon his trial, they ordered him to be discharged. If they were of the opposite opinion, or if the evidence raised a strong or probable presumption of his guilt, they either committed him to prison or admitted him to bail.[19] Over the years the role of the magistrate had changed. Initially, his role had been of an inquisitorial nature: after Jervis' Act of 1848 he was established rather in the role of a preliminary judge.[20]

In determining whether to commit the accused person to prison or to admit him to bail, the justices were aware of the importance of ensuring that the suspect would be available for trial. Even so, it had been determined in *R v Scaife and Wife* that the propriety of admitting a prisoner charged with felony to bail ought to be determined with reference to the possibility of his appearing to take his trial and not with reference to the probability of the guilt or innocence of the party.[1] Excessive bail was not to be required, yet if the magistrate took insufficient bail, he was liable to be fined if the person bailed failed to appear for trial.[2]

Subsequently, the matter came before the grand jury. If the grand jury found that there was a case to answer, the matter then came to court for trial.

5 Administration

a) *Introduction*

Until mid-nineteenth century at least, the administration of the criminal process amounted very often to a lottery. There was a discretion as to whether or not to prosecute at all; prosecutors, judges and juries might choose, or not, to temper the rigours of the Bloody Code; the deliberate maladministration of a law might even subvert its avowed intent; there was often a lack of consistency in sentencing

---

19   H. J. Stephen *New Commentaries on the Laws of England* (4th edn, 1858) vol 4, pp. 416-17.
20   J. F. Stephen *A History of the Criminal Law of England* vol 1, p. 221.
 1   Eighth Report from...Commissioners on Criminal Law no. 656 (1845) p. 6.
 2   *Stephen* p. 418.

which is exemplified by Romilly's story of the two criminals who pleaded guilty at separate trials to their joint guilt on a charge of stealing chickens — the first was imprisoned for six months, the second was transported. Clearly much depended upon the spirit in which the criminal law was administered. That spirit must have been as essential to the fair conduct of a criminal process in which so much depended upon the largely unsupervised discretion of its administrators as was the professional understanding of the substantive criminal law to an accurate interpretation of that law in court.

b) *The administration of the vagrancy laws*
Some reference has been made already to the prosecution process. For a striking example of the manner in which the clear aim of a law was avoided, we may turn to the administration of the vagrancy laws during the first quarter of the nineteenth century. All the evidence points to a legislature and a central government which was determined to curb vagrancy. In 1821 a Select Committee Report in commenting upon a failure to accomplish the statutory objects remarked: 'The abuses tolerated and the frauds practised under these laws have been unquestionably proved by the evidence.' Similarly, a member of parliament had claimed that the country was overrun with paupers. He said that he did not complain of the truly destitute but of the idle vagrants who made a large subsistence by their vagrancy.[3]

One important factor was that under the vagrancy laws the moving parish was put to no expense, as it was under the Poor Law, if it wished to move an unsettled person. Under the Vagrancy Acts the county treasurer repaid all expenses and actually paid a reward, while the constable was required to journey no further than the next parish. Moreover, the parish of destination had no right of appeal. Accordingly, many were classified as vagrants who were not vagrants. The Report tells us:

> 'The county reward of 10s, at present payable, has in some instances converted the apprehension of vagrants into a regular trade, so disgraceful in all its branches as even to prevent the more respectable constables from interfering with vagrants, from a dread of sharing the obloquy attached to their apprehension. It is in evidence that it has led to a system of collusion between the apprehender and the vagrant, and that the latter has voluntarily entered, or been invited into the district of the former, and even been bribed to commit an act of vagrancy with the view of procuring the reward of 10s, which in some cases has actually been divided between the parties.'[4]

At the other end of the scale the more frugal JP's discouraged reward-seeking constables. The Committee despaired also of the system of passing vagrants. The system of the justices' 'free pass', which Burn had described as a 'pernicious practice' as long ago as 1764, amounted to an extra-legal written passport or certificate of character for the use of any person setting out on a long journey. Such findings led the Committee to conclude that an abolition of the system of passing English vagrants should be accompanied by more extended forms of

---

3 Report of the Select Committee appointed to take into consideration the existing Laws relating to Vagrants...no. 543 (1821).
4 Report no. 543 (1821) p. 3.

imprisonment. The reward system should also be discontinued and a central office in London should be established to put into force the laws against habitual vagrants. Some minor reforms were introduced e.g. with regard to passes. Yet the whole system was soon to be caught up with the radical Benthamite revision of the Poor Laws, of which the vagrancy laws in a sense were but the penal arm, in 1834.

The question of the administration and enforcement of the vagrancy laws, quite apart from the trial process, cannot be seen in isolation from the considerable and vexed problem of the administration of the Poor Laws. Woodward has pointed out[5] that the cost of Poor Law administration rose from £619000 in 1750 to almost £8m in 1818, or 13*s* 3*d* per head of the population in England and Wales. Woodward states also that the law of settlement enabled manufacturers in towns to escape the burden of maintaining unemployed workmen in times of depression; they could take men from their villages in good times and send them back again when there was no work for them. It can been seen, therefore, that the administrative abuse of the vagrancy laws was but part of a wider system of abuse which was supported by powerful economic interests. The abuse of the vagrancy laws was also in the economic interests of the parishes, which were thereby able to shift on to the county a burden which they would otherwise have been compelled to shoulder themselves, of corrupt constables, of carriers who made a profitable business out of the carriage of vagrants, and of many vagrants themselves who undoubtedly manipulated the vagrancy laws for their own benefit by sharing in the rewards which were offered for their apprehension and by using the conveyance system to their own ends. Yet we should not forget the growing humanitarianism of many justices who shrank from whipping a fellow human being whose only fault appeared to be that he was without means. No doubt many such justices welcomed the opportunity of moving on such people without cost to their own neighbours, whatever the legal niceties may have been.

c) *A criminal equity?*

In the area of vagrancy we have an instance, therefore, of the manner in which administrative practices may produce in practice a result far different from that which the substantive law appears to indicate. Such a phenomenon was especially obvious in the administration of the Bloody Code when a whole range of technical devices mitigated the literal rigour of the law. Jerome Hall has shown[6] how the administrative practices of this period, influenced by a number of extra legal factors, transformed a formally barbaric criminal code into relatively moderate, actual law. In the first quarter of the nineteenth century only a small, and steadily declining, proportion of those condemned were actually executed. Victims might choose not to prosecute, prosecuting counsel might choose not to press a capital charge, judges tended to construe capital statutes very narrowly indeed, juries might refuse to convict an accused person of a capital offence despite that person clearly being guilty as charged. Such factors led Hall to conclude that:

> 'there is represented in the history of the criminal law from the seventeenth century to the present day a process roughly analogous to that described by

5   Sir L. Woodward *The Age of Reform 1815-1870* (2nd edn, 1962) pp. 449-50.
6   *Theft, Law and Society.*

Maine in his *Ancient Law*. There is first the formal body of rules which, with changes in conditions and passage of time, lag behind the needs of the community. There results in the civil law the growth of equity, a superior body of rules. In the criminal law the absence of a dual system of courts confines change in the case law to the narrow limits of judicial redefinition of this law. Accordingly, practices analogous to equity in civil proceedings develop in the trial of criminal cases which, in effect, supersede and are superior to the rules of law. Finally, the legislature takes cognisance of what is being done and what has in fact been established, and enacts legislation which directs these practices into expressly legal avenues. Whereupon a new cycle sets in.'[7]

Certainly there is some authority for the view that a reluctance to enforce the capital statutes was due to an increasing humanitarianism. Witnesses before the 1819 Committee[8] had testified to an unwillingness in many instances to prosecute for a capital offence; the available statistics do show that an increasing proportion of those sentenced to death was spared; statute forbade the whipping of women for vagrancy; at a later date women were not to be whipped at all; the Webbs report that on occasion passers-by could be very hostile indeed to the constable who was whipping a person according to law. Did such factors lead to a form of criminal equity?

The extension of benefit of clergy to all persons does support such a theory, but many offences were to be exempted quite expressly from benefit of clergy. Certainly administrative practices during the trial of cases often softened the apparent rigour of the law: we may suspect that in many other cases the rigour of the law was undiminished — that is a belief which Romilly's anecdote concerning the two criminals who pleaded guilty at separate trials to their joint guilt but who received disparate sentences supports. Yet, if some parishes did not whip vagrants, others did. Above all the policy of discretionary selection did not make it clear which capitally convicted persons would be spared execution.

During the late years of the eighteenth and early nineteenth centuries, therefore, administrative practices to a large extent transformed the letter of the substantive criminal law during the trial process in particular. In view, however, of the generality of this shifting body of practice and its uncertainty in particular cases, it should probably not be regarded as more than superficially analogous to equity in the civil sphere.

d) *Administrative inconsistency and the spirit of enforcement*
The discretion whether or not to prosecute remained flexible and remarkably ill-defined, despite the greater consistency which the Director of Public Prosecutions introduced after 1879. Inconsistencies became especially marked during the twentieth century in the enforcement of the road traffic law by different police authorities. A great deal depended, therefore, upon the wholly informal practices followed by the Director of Public Prosecutions and by individual chief constables. That modern system was rooted in the traditional legal insistence upon individual responsibility for the enforcement of the law: in a more mobile

---

7 J. Hall *Theft, Law and Society*.
8 Report from the Select Committee on Criminal Laws no. 585 (1819).

and complex modern society, however, the old rule tended rather to mean that important decisions, which now were made in practice by public officers, were not governed by law. Juries and courts also tended to be unduly inconsistent in the enforcement of road traffic offences. In that area of the law especially the spirit in which it was administered was particularly important.[9] Some degree of inconsistency was of course inevitable. Conferences of magistrates, a certain amount of judicial and Home Office guidance, and the work of the Lord Chancellor's office helped to achieve a greater measure of consistency. Yet the country still resisted the creation of a Ministry of Justice which might have instituted a greater measure still of consistency.

9   Select Committee on the Prevention of Road Accidents no. 192, HL (1938) q. 437 and
     q. 2477.

Chapter 11

The criminal and punishment

1 The growth of a science of criminology

At this stage it is appropriate that we should consider briefly the origins of the science of criminology.

Our society has rarely lacked commentators who were prepared to speculate upon the causes of crime. When the King addressed Parliament in 1751 he maintained that factors such as irreligion, idleness, gaming and extravagance had contributed to crime.[1] Colquhoun, like Henry Fielding before him, maintained that the public houses were a prime cause of virtually all the moral evils with which society was afflicted.[2] A select committee of 1828, although it noted an increase in the sale of spirits, attributed the chief cause of crime in the agricultural districts to the 'want of employment which was often produced artificially by the Poor Laws'.[3] There were many other similar reports. Such observations are of considerable interest. In so far as occasionally they even suggest, however obliquely, that some responsibility for criminal behaviour lay with society itself, they were potentially radical in their nature. It was the birth of an interest in statistics which first put such inquiries upon a more scientific basis.

Bentham had suggested such a course. He wanted 'bills of delinquency' to be prepared which would be comparable to the 'bills of mortality published annually in London; indicating the moral health of the country...as these latter do the physical'.[4] However, it was the French who, in 1827, introduced criminal statistics in a modern form. Quetelet and Guerry were the most renowned interpreters of those statistics.[5] Their method was to explore the incidence of crime in relation to age, sex, profession and education, economic conditions, climate,

---

1 L. Radzinowicz *A History of English Criminal Law* vol 1, p. 415.
2 P. Colquhoun *A Treatise on the Police of the Metropolis*, H. Fielding *An Enquiry into the Causes of the Late Increase of Robbers*.
3 Report of the Select Committee on Criminal Commitments and Convictions no. 245 (1828).
4 J. Bentham 'A View of the Hard-Labour Bill' in *Works* (ed Bowring 1838-43) vol 4, p. 29.
5 L. Radzinowicz *Ideology and Crime* pp. 33-5. Cf. L. Lindesmith and Y. Levin 'English Ecology and Criminology of the Past Century', (1937) 27 Journal of Criminal Law, Criminology and Police Science 801 and T. Morris *The Criminal Area* chap. 3.

seasons and race. Radzinowicz has pointed out that two things were apparent from the figures as they were published year after year. First, the annual totals of recorded crimes, and of the main classes of crime, remained much the same. Secondly, a similar regularity was shown in the contribution to those totals made by the various sections of the population, living under various social conditions — young or old, urban or rural, poor or rich, male or female. 'It was the discovery of these regularities', comments Radzinowicz, 'that made a scientific approach possible. To bring them to light was the major achievement of Quetelet. Without it there could have been no understanding of crime as a social phenomenon.'

The work of Quetelet and Guerry was well known in England and reference was made to the French statistics in general.[6] In England, too, work of a similar nature was soon in progress. In particular, the Statistical Society concerned itself with such questions. Papers such as those presented by the Reverend John Clay, Rawson W. Rawson, and Joseph Fletcher are especially interesting. Clay's concern, as Chaplain to the Preston House of Correction, was with crime in Preston. He offered[7] a classification of the offences for which indictments had been preferred and, by giving the relevant figures for the previous year, was able to demonstrate in what areas 'criminality' had increased or diminished. With regard to committals for felony he was concerned both with the ages of the persons concerned — 33.32 per cent were aged 21 to 30, 30.75 per cent were aged 15 to 20 and 14.84 per cent were aged 31 to 40 — and with the causes of the offence. In this respect the major overall cause was attributed to 'various and uncertain', presumably miscellaneous, factors. Chief among the other factors stated was drinking, followed by idleness and bad company, want and distress, weak intellects, temptation and bad habits. Clay also gave a list of the trades and occupations of the various offenders, distinguishing the number of offenders who were under 21 years of age. He posed the question whether a recent strike had contributed to crime and recognised 'that more than one-third of the whole amount of criminality in the male population of Preston has been furnished by boys previously employed in the factories'. Yet few offences had been committed while the strike was actually in existence 'and a further proof of this may be found upon referring to the very few cases of weavers in the above list — a class which it is well known, has been labouring for the last two or three years under the severest privation'. Clay went on to comment that independently of general causes, there appeared to be a tendency to crime in particular families.

Joseph Fletcher's work was even more ambitious in its concept. His concern was with the 'moral and educational statistics of England and Wales'.[8] He analysed the criminal commitments in terms of class, locality, sex and whether times were good or bad. One most interesting feature of his work, however, was the use of shaded maps to illustrate the most important branches of the investigation. Maps showed:

1)   dispersion of population in England and Wales 1841;
2)   real property in proportion to the population in England and Wales in

6   (1833) 18 Westminster Review 356.
7   Clay contributed a number of statistical papers.
8   J. Fletcher 'Moral and Educational Statistics for England and Wales' (1848) 11 Journ Stat Soc 344 and also in (1849) 12 at 151.

1842-43 assessed to the property and income tax;
3) ignorance in England and Wales as indicated by the men's signatures by marks in the marriage registers 1844.

A further paper contained the following maps:

1) Crime in England and Wales as indicated by the criminal commitments of males to assizes and quarter sessions 1842-47.
2) Commitments in England and Wales for the more serious offences against the person and malicious offences against property 1842-47.
3) Commitments in England and Wales for all offences against property excepting only the malicious 1845-47.
4) Improvident marriages in England and Wales (those of males under 21 being so designated) 1844.
5) Pauperism in England and Wales 1844.

There then followed a number of detailed tables which analysed comprehensively the available statistics. In May 1849 Fletcher's conclusion was clear enough:

'In the case of the whole kingdom, however,...it would appear that a rapid progress in material civilisation, without a proportionate moral advancement, has thrown new and more frequent incentives to disorder among the people at large, which produce their worst effects on the recoil of each wave of industrial prosperity, amidst those classes whose moral ties to the existing framework of society are feeblest and least felt or understood, and to many of whom socialism or any other destructive theory would appear as consistent with their well-being, as the most cherished axioms of political science, or even the words of Christian truth itself. It is to such populations that we must especially turn our regards....It is not a question of letting "well" alone in their case, for it is "evil" that is marching upon us from among them with gigantic strides. Improved or invigorated institutions of education, police, providence, and sanatory administration, are essential to incorporate them into a healthy social fabric; and these, it is true, require for their erection and useful maintenance, the local exertions of Christian men...'

Fletcher's approach, then, conscious of the French model, was both comprehensive and careful. Essentially, he reflected the concerned middle-class, Christian, reformist approach to the question of the causation of crime which yet stopped short of asking awkward questions of society itself.

Henry Mayhew's work is far better known, although it has received inadequate recognition from twentieth-century criminologists.[9] His work was just as comprehensive and made equally extensive use of the available government statistics as Fletcher and the other statisticians. Indeed, in his classification of crimes, for example, he made a more intelligent use of such statistics. Perhaps his particular contribution — in the line of Gibbon Wakefield, of the constabulary commissioners and of others who had sought to persuade convicted criminals to tell their life stories — was his belief, which he based on his

---

9 See E.P. Thompson 'Mayhew and The Morning Chronicle' and E. Yeo 'Mayhew as a Social Investigator'. Both essays are in *The Unknown Mayhew* (ed Thompson and Yeo).

knowledge of, inter alia, criminals themselves, that the key to the causation of crime lay initially in a knowledge of the criminal himself: yet society, too, had a responsibility. He wrote:

'Crime is as much a business among us, as manufacturing or trading in any article of wealth...

That the juvenile offenders are the principal class from whom the old habitual ones are derived becomes positively indisputable, when the facts are brought clearly before the mind...

Notwithstanding these plain facts, however, learned professors will occasionally read papers before meetings of scientific gentlemen, in order to prove that fluctuations in the number of our criminals are due to the greater or less prosperity of the nation and that years of distress are years in which malefactors abound, and years of plenty those in which our murderers, and burglars, and pickpockets cease to indulge in their natural propensities...

...these sages...are unacquainted with the characters of the people concerning whom they are speculating...'[10]

He wrote that crime was made up of many elements and of the necessity of not confounding habitual criminals with casual criminals — casual criminals, he granted, might vary in numbers according to the prosperity of the nation.

Mayhew then went on by means of several tables to show the ratios of the accused to every 10 millions of population throughout England and Wales, and also the increase or decrease for each crime, arranged in classes and orders, during the several quinquennial and decennial periods from 1834 to 1853. In his view the existence of so large an amount of inequity in the land could not be accounted for except by the fact that offenders had 'been regularly born and bred to the business'. His conclusion was depressing:

'we have little faith in prison teaching, or even national reformatories, as a means of decreasing the offenders of the country. Crime, in its habitual form, seems to us as radically incurable as lock-jaw or confirmed consumption...

The only hope is to prevent juvenile delinquency...crime [is] but a moral pestilence, ordained by God to rouse us to our duty to those wretched actual or virtual orphans, whom, for some inscrutable reason, he has willed to begin life as outcasts among us.'[11]

Those that Will not Work is also of considerable interest for its discussion of London crime and criminal areas. Here again Mayhew stresses the evolution from juvenile crime to professional crime. In addition he has a number of maps and tables which illustrate, inter alia:

1) density of population in England and Wales;
2) intensity of criminality;
3) number committed for rape;
4) number committed for intent to ravish and carnally abuse;
5) a table comparing crime and ignorance in various countries by occupation, by education.

---

10 H. Mayhew *Criminal Prisons* pp. 439-40.
11 *Mayhew* p. 452.

Beyond the earnest contributions which were made to the annual proceedings of the National Association for the Promotion of Social Science, England and Wales made no further notable contributions to criminological studies until well into the twentieth century. Meanwhile, there had been an outstanding new departure with the publication in 1876 of the work of the Italian criminal anthropologist, Cesare Lombroso. In his *L'Uomo Delinquente*, which was based upon a study of the characteristics of convicts in the Italian penitentiaries, he explained his theory that crime was caused almost entirely by the anthropological characteristics of the criminal. Physical examination of many criminals and of their psychology convinced him — the characteristics of primitive men and of inferior animals were being reproduced.[12] Much of his work was criticised quite strongly even during his own lifetime — he died in 1913. Nevertheless, Lombroso was to have an influence which more than equalled that of his fellow Italian, Beccaria. Thus, comments Radzinowicz, whereas the 'classical school exhorts men to study justice: the positivist school exhorts justice to study men'. It was Lombroso's achievement, therefore, that he brought the criminal's individuality to the forefront 'as an element of the first importance in the study of crime'.[13]

The publication of Charles Goring's *The English Convict* in 1919 and of Cyril Burt's *The Young Delinquent* were excellent contributions to the international debate: there were a number of other worthy contributions. By and large, however, England and Wales made only a relatively small contribution, especially when contrasted with the work which was being done in Western Europe and, more especially, in the USA. However, the Association for the Scientific Treatment of Criminals, which later became the Institute for the Study and Treatment of Delinquency, was set up in 1931. In addition the Howard League continued its valuable work, even asking the Home Office in 1936 for further research. And, as always, the reports of royal commissions etc. contained the stuff of criminology.[14] Overall, however, it all amounted to very little.

It was the advent in the 1930s of Mannheim, Grunhut and Radzinowicz which was to confer both a certain academic respectability and some public recognition in the 1940s upon the study of criminology in England and Wales. The Criminal Justice Act 1948 enabled the Home Secretary and the prison commissioners to spend money on 'research into the causes of delinquency and the treatment of offenders and matters connected therewith'.[15] It was an important first step. Even so, and despite the alarm of the Home Office at the increase in juvenile delinquency during the 1940s, the government was prepared to allocate in its estimates for 1951-52 only £1500 for government research: between 1948 and 1957 just £12000 was allocated.[16] It was a small beginning, yet it was also a time of hope for criminological studies generally.

---

12 C. Lombroso *Crime: Its Causes and Remedies* (1911 edn, with introduction by M. Parmelee) p. xviii.
13 L. Radzinowicz *Ideology and Crime* pp. 56-8.
14 T.S. Lodge 'The Founding of the Home Office and Research Unit' in R. Hood (ed) *Crime, Criminology and Public Policy* pp. 11-13.
15 Criminal Justice Act 1948, s.77 (1) (b).
16 Lord Butler 'The Foundation of the Institute of Criminology in Cambridge' in Hood *Crime, Criminology and Public Policy* pp. 1-2.

2 Punishment

a) *Introduction*

In Blackstone's day capital punishment and transportation were common punishments.[17] At that time whipping and imprisonment were regarded as relatively mild punishments. By mid-nineteenth century, however, a remarkable change had taken place. For some 20 years or more there had been few executions and transportation was coming to an end. In Victorian England imprisonment, administered uniformly by a central authority, was to be the typical criminal sanction. By contrast, during the first half of the twentieth century a policy developed of seeking to avoid imprisoning many categories of criminal so far as possible but rather to adopt one of a number of alternative sanctions. During the whole period, however, a number of basic themes is evident. Above all, the public must be protected and the criminal deterred. There was talk also, even as early as the late eighteenth century, of the reformation of the offender. From that same period also there was a gradually increasing concern with juvenile delinquency. However, the distinctive feature of the country's system of punishments during the second half of the eighteenth century, which caused it to be dubbed the 'Bloody Code', was the incidence of capital punishment.

In 1810 Sir Samuel Romilly told the House of Commons that 'there was no country on the face of the earth in which there had been so many different offences according to law to be punished with death as in England'. In 1776 Colquhoun had estimated that there were 166 capital offences: in 1819 Fowell Buxton believed that there were 229 capital offences.[18] However, in the opening two decades of the nineteenth century there was an increasing tendency to execute fewer of those who had been convicted of a capital offence. In 1805 one out of every five persons who had been convicted of a capital offence was executed. In 1811 the proportion was one to nine. In 1818 just one out of twelve of those convicted of a capital offence was executed.[19] Penal theorists both overseas and at home had contributed to that position. Not surprisingly at that time, much of their work was directed to the question of capital punishment.

b) *Early penal theory*

The severity of contemporary punishments began to be questioned from about mid-eighteenth century. In his influential *L'Esprit de Lois*, which was published in 1748, and which soon reached a wide audience, Montesquieu pleaded that penalties should be moderate. Increasingly, the French philosophers began to spurn tradition and to seek to establish a state which would be based upon justice, reason, and equality. Did the contemporary, bloody criminal punishments really have a place in such a state? Inspired by such writings, the young Italian, Beccaria, published in 1764 his brief but highly influential work upon crimes and punishments. British writers soon contributed to the discussion. Some, like Eden and Bentham, followed in the tradition of Beccaria. Others, like Madan and Paley, tended to support the existing system. Even Blackstone

---

17 See generally 4 Bl Com (5th edn) 11-12.
18 See L. Radzinowicz *A History of English Criminal Law* vol 1, chap. 1.
19 Report from the Select Committee on Criminal Laws no. 585 (1819) Appendix no. 1, p. 134.

offered some guarded criticism of the existing system of punishments. For all these writers, however, it was the incidence of the death penalty which was of particular concern.[20]

Beccaria wrote that punishments must be prompt, certain and moderate. He suggested that the certainty of punishment was a more effective deterrent than rigour and cruelty; the criminal might believe that a severe punishment would not be inflicted in practice because the prosecutor, judge or jury might choose to exercise clemency. As punishments became more mild, clemency and pardon would become less necessary. Further, punishment should be proportioned to the offence. It was important to bear in mind that the true measure of crime was the injury done to society rather than the intention of the delinquent. True proportion was obtained when the evil of the punishment just exceeded the advantage of the crime — to ensure such excess the certainty of the punishment and the loss of the possible advantage from the crime must be taken into consideration. Laws marked by cruelty and ferocity violated the 'greatest happiness' principle and were contrary to the very object of preventing the commission of crimes. Not only did such punishments lead to impunity for many criminals through the exercise of clemency, it meant also that there was no incentive for the criminal to restrain himself to the extent of committing a lesser rather than a greater crime.

Beccaria was only 26 years old when he published his *Dei Delitti et delle Pene* (Of Crimes and Punishments). He had had little juridical training; nor had he any experience at all in the criminal field. Yet he wrote well, produced the book — which he wrote within a few months — at the right time and soon enjoyed international fame. Blackstone, Eden, Bentham and Romilly each acknowledged their debt to him.

In particular Blackstone noted Beccaria's view that crimes were prevented more effectually by the certainty than by the severity of punishment. Blackstone noted also that Beccaria had 'ingeniously proposed' that punishment should be proportionate to the crime. That might be too romantic an idea, suggested Blackstone, 'yet at least a wise legislator will mark the principal divisions, and not assign penalties of the first degree to offences of an inferior rank'. Blackstone even cast doubt upon the right of the state to inflict the death penalty for relatively trivial offences:

> 'It is therefore the enormity, or dangerous tendency, of the crime, that alone can warrant any earthly legislature in putting him to death that commits it. It is not its frequency only, or the difficulty of otherwise preventing it, that will excuse our attempting to prevent it by a wanton effusion of human blood. For, though the end of punishment is to deter men from offending, it never can follow from thence, that it is lawful to deter them at any rate and by any means; since there may be unlawful methods of enforcing obedience to the justest laws.'[1]

The fact that this distinguished legal commentator and judge could offer such measured and reasoned criticism of a wide-spread application of the death

20 L. Radzinowicz *A History of English Criminal Law* vol 1, p. 269, L. Radzinowicz *Ideology and Crime*, C. Phillipson *Three Criminal Law Reformers* p. 39, E.J. Heath *Eighteenth Century Penal Theory*.
1 4 Bl Com (5th edn) 2-11.

penalty must surely have influenced the course of reform over the years.

The status quo also had its supporters, of whom Madan and Paley were the most notable. Madan, whose *Thoughts on Executive Justice* was published in 1785, maintained that the value of a penalty depended solely on the degree of fear which that penalty was likely to generate. Moreover, punishment ought to be inflicted with a view to preventing future crimes. In Madan's view capital penalties were not being inflicted in as many cases as would be proper. It was only when mercy was granted in relatively few cases that the necessary degree of fear would be maintained which would prevent offences of a similar nature being committed in the future. William Paley's *Principles of Moral and Political Philosophy* was also published in 1785. It was an highly influential book. In Paley's view the factors to be taken into account in determining the degree of the severity of punishment to be inflicted were the facility with which the crime could be committed, the difficulty of its detection and the danger which it presented to the community. He concluded that capital punishment was the most effective means of preventing crime, albeit mitigated by a policy of discretionary selection. The commissioners on the criminal law in 1836 paid Paley the compliment of summarising his arguments as follows:

'(1) The practice is consonant to the ancient and approved maxim "*Poena ad paucos, metus ad omnes*". It accomplishes the purposes of capital punishment by a small sacrifice of human life; the penalty actually falling on a few offenders, whilst the fear of it falls upon all who are tempted to offend. This argument is supported by the subsidiary one, that the selection may be entrusted without danger to the executive magistrate.

(2) The selection of proper objects for capital punishment principally depends upon circumstances which cannot be defined beforehand, although in particular cases they are easily perceived after the commission of the offence.

(3) If death were only inflicted according to previous definitions there are many offences which would not be embraced by any of them; and the offenders would escape with impunity, or would avoid their merited punishment.'[2]

Paley differed from Madan, then, most markedly, in that Paley did not advocate a rigorous enforcement of the capital laws. Indeed, a prime factor in Paley's popularity and influence was his capacity — in this area at least — to rationalise and to justify existing practice.

It was not an approach which had ever appealed to Jeremy Bentham. Bentham's penal doctrine is expounded in his *An Introduction to the Principles of Morals and Legislation* and in his *Rationale of Punishment*. The former work was printed in 1780 but was not published until 1789; the latter work was published, in collaboration with Dumont, in French in 1811 under the title, *Théorie des Peines et des Récompenses*.

To Bentham punishment was an evil. He wrote:

'But all punishment is mischief; all punishment in itself is evil. Upon the principle of utility, if it ought at all to be admitted, it ought only to be admitted in as far as it promises to exclude some greater evil.'

Accordingly, it followed that punishment ought not to be inflicted where it was

2 Second Report from the Commissioners on Criminal Law no. 343 (1836) p. 29.

groundless i.e. 'where there is no mischief for it to prevent; the act not being mischievous upon the whole'; where it must be inefficacious i.e. 'where it cannot act so as to prevent the mischief'; where it is 'unprofitable', or too expensive; where the mischief it would produce would be greater than what it prevented; and where 'it is needless'; where 'the mischief may be prevented, or cease of itself without it: that is, at a cheaper rate'.[3]

When punishment was worthwhile, the legislator whose views were governed by the principle of utility, would have four subordinate designs or objects in mind. These were:

'(1) [to prevent] in as far as it is possible, and worthwhile, all sorts of offences whatsoever: in other words, so to manage, that no offence whatsoever may be committed.

(2) But if a man must needs commit an offence of some kind or other, the next object is to induce him to commit an offence less mischievous.

(3) When a man has resolved upon a particular offence, the next object is to dispose him to do no more mischief than is necessary to his purpose...

(4) The last object is, whatever the mischief be, which it is proposed to prevent, to prevent it at as cheap a rate as possible.'

Subservient to these four objects or purposes, Bentham laid down 13 rules or canons by which the proportion of punishments to offences was to be governed.[4] So, for example, the first rule provided that the 'value of the punishment must not be less in any case than what is sufficient to outweigh that of the profit of the offence'. He also suggested that, 'The greater the mischief of the offence, the greater is the expence, which it may be worthwhile to be at, in the way of punishment.' It is worth noting also that he provided that:

1) 'To enable the value of the punishment to outweigh that of the profit of the offence, it must be increased, in point of magnitude, in proportion as it falls short in point of certainty,' and

2) 'Punishment must be further increased in point of magnitude, in proportion as it falls short in point of proximity.'[5]

Bentham then turns to 11 properties to be given to punishment.

What, then did Bentham think of the death penalty? On the one hand it clearly met the properties of disablement, of being analogous to the offence and, at least in the case of the more serious offences, of popularity. On the other hand it was clear that the death penalty was neither remissible nor subservient to reformation — probably also it was neither frugal, nor equable nor variable. Ought the death penalty to be retained, then? Bentham's conclusion was that 'if in spite of all its defects capital punishment is to be retained in consideration of the effects it produces in terrorem, it ought to be confined to offences which in the highest degree shock the public feeling — for murders, accompanied with circumstances of aggravation, and particularly when their effect may be the destruction of numbers'. This was a highly radical position among the reformers of the day.

---

3   *An Introduction to the Principles of Morals and Legislation* chap. 13, pp. 158-9.
4   Op. cit.
5   Op. cit. pp. 165 ff. See generally L. Radzinowicz *A History of English Criminal Law* vol 1, p. 390, W.S. Holdsworth *A History of English Law* vol 13, pp. 40 ff.

These, then, were the theorists who contributed most to the debate. Now the struggle for reform was essentially political in its nature.

c) *The mitigation of capital punishments*

The political battle for a reduction in the number of offences for which capital punishment was the penalty — and at times even for the complete abolition of the death penalty — was waged over a number of years. Perhaps the first real skirmish in that battle was a speech which Sir Samuel Romilly made to the House of Commons on 18 May 1808. As Home Secretary during the 1820s Peel presided over the opening of a second stage. The third stage began in the 1840s with moves for the complete abolition of the death penalty: it ended in 1868 with the decision that executions — by then restricted effectively to cases of murder — would no longer take place in public. The final stage did not begin effectively until well into the twentieth century — capital punishment remained part of the law of the land even in 1950.

In 1808 Romilly succeeded in securing the repeal of a statute of Queen Elizabeth which made it a capital offence to steal privately from the person of another.[6] Even Paley had believed that this statute should be repealed. According to Romilly, only one offender had been executed by virtue of the provisions of this Act — that had been a pickpocket who was detected while exercising his trade in court, even as the judge was sitting. In 1810 he introduced three bills for the repeal of statutes which imposed capital punishment for stealing privately in a shop to the value of five shillings, for stealing property to the value of forty shillings in a dwelling house, and for stealing property to the value of forty shillings on board ship in navigable rivers. Romilly criticised a system whereby laws were passed but rarely administered and he refuted Paley's argument that it had been the legislature's intention that this should be so as the figures showed that from the second half of the eighteenth century to the beginning of the nineteenth century, there had been a considerable and fairly steady decrease in the number of executions. The laws in Romilly's day were the same as the laws then, so the statistics could have altered only as the result of another factor i.e. the fact that the ordinary citizen was unwilling to prosecute, the juror to convict and the judge to sentence to death. Moreover, such a system as this, he said, meant that there could be a considerable disparity between the punishments of criminals convicted of similar offences. The example which he gave was of two men who had stolen poultry. One received a sentence of six months imprisonment. Upon hearing of this, the other gave himself up. He was sentenced to transportation. Romilly also stressed the importance of certainty of punishment and argued that, if punishment were really certain, then punishment could be very light indeed. Finally, he believed that statute should guide the exercise of the judicial discretion.

He was unsuccessful both on this and on future occasions although he received some support. In 1809 a Quaker, William Allen, and a Benthamite friend of Romilly's, Basil Montagu, had founded 'The society for diffusion of knowledge upon the punishment of death, and improvement of prison discipline'. Romilly's wide reading of the continental authors, his acquaintance at an early stage with a number of leading French reformers, his respect for Bentham, his own humane

6   P. Medd *Romilly*, L. Radzinowicz *A History of English Criminal Law* vol 1, pp. 498 ff.

and liberal principles had promised much. Yet the efforts of this successful Chancery barrister were thwarted by the contemporary national dread of innovation, especially amongst the judiciary. By the time of his suicide, following the death of his wife, in 1818 Romilly had achieved very little indeed, therefore, in legislative terms. The measure of Romilly's achievement was that he had aroused the conscience of the nation upon the question of the incidence of capital punishment. Henceforth this was a question which was worthy of serious public debate.

Others, notably James Mackintosh and Fowell Buxton, continued the parliamentary struggle.[7] On 2 March 1819 Mackintosh moved for a committee to consider so much of the criminal law as related to capital punishment for felony. The government opposed the motion, despite the fact that numbers of petitions upon this question were now being presented to parliament, but was defeated by a majority of 19. The report is a document of considerable interest. The committee had sought information from potential prosecutors, traders, jurors, clerks at the offices of magistrates and the officers of criminal courts rather than from the judiciary who, said the committee, could know nothing of the cases which never came before a court of justice nor of the motives which influenced the testimony of witnesses nor really of the influence of punishment upon malefactors. After reviewing the evidence, the committee's conclusion was that in the case of forgery the punishment should be reduced in most instances, if the law were to be put into effect. Certainly striking evidence to that effect had been given. One banker told the committee that he himself was reluctant to prosecute in cases of forgery because of the severity of the law and that he had observed a similar reluctance among many bankers and traders.[8] The committee suggested also that other penal statutes such as that which made it a capital offence to break down the head or mound of a fish pond might safely be made punishable as a misdemeanour at common law.[9]

The report enjoyed no immediate legislative success. Indeed, the *Tory Quarterly Review* felt able to compliment the House of Lords 'which on this occasion again acted as a floodgate against the tide of legislation which is now rolling so impetuously through the House of Commons'.[10] Mackintosh introduced a Forgery Punishment Mitigation Bill in 1821. It was presented by Sir Thomas Fowell Buxton whose speech was regarded generally as a classic. He maintained that 'imprisonment, with hard labour and occasional solitary confinement, and constant inspection, and rigid discipline, is, in fact the punishment you require'. If the secondary punishment available was inadequate due to the neglect of the state, surely the felons should not be made to suffer. Yet it was all to no avail. The Bill, by then much amended, was rejected by a narrow majority. Even so the number of criminals who were actually executed diminished very considerably as the years went by.[11] Peel as Home Secretary presided in 1823 over the passing of five Acts which reduced the number of offences subject to capital punishment. Some had long been advocated, others were Peel's own idea. As Peel's

---

7 L. Radzinowicz *A History of English Criminal Law* vol 1, W.S. Holdsworth 'The Movement for Reforms in the Law 1793-1832' (1940) 56 LQR 33, 208, 340.
8 Report from the Select Committee on Criminal Laws no. 585 (1819) p. 15.
9 Report no. 585 (1819) pp. 6-7.
10 (1820 – 21) 24 Quarterly Review 232-3.
11 L. Radzinowicz *A History of English Criminal Law* vol 1, p. 558.

biographer remarks, with 'a reforming Home Secretary the citadel of legislative inertia had been finally outflanked'. Further legislation in 1827 aided the process.[12] Upon Russell becoming Home Secretary, he asked the criminal law commissioners to present at an early period, inter alia, the result of their inquiries regarding the infliction of capital punishments. They so reported on 9 June 1836. Their lucid and reasoned report is worthy of extended consideration.[13]

The principal consideration before the commissioners was whether it would be more beneficial to restrict capital punishment to cases in which ordinarily it would be implemented. They pointed out that sweeping definitions of criminal offences frequently classed crimes together without any consideration as to the penal consequences. For example, within the definition of burglary could be included both the hungry pauper 'who after it is dark breaks a pane of glass, and thrusts a hand through the broken window to seize a loaf of bread [and so] is just as liable to suffer death, as one of a gang of ruffians who break into a dwelling-house to pillage the inhabitants, and who execute their purpose with circumstances of the utmost violence and cruelty'. They concluded that the policy of discretionary selection tended to increase the number of offenders. In support of that view they pointed out that men were daily persuaded to engage in the most hazardous occupations. For example, on an average of 25 years, not fewer than 82 violent deaths had occurred amongst miners; by contrast the number of executions in England and Wales in 1834 and 1835 was 34 only in each year. These and other persuasive arguments, including a powerful rejection of Paley's stance, led the commissioners to conclude that the number of capital offences should be limited to crimes of peculiar atrocity.

However, capital punishment might 'have a very material and salutary effect in restraining offenders from acts of particular outrage and cruelty, when it is known that such aggravations will, on conviction, almost certainly be punished with death. It is important also to remark that the punishment of death may be inflicted in such cases without shocking the feelings of society'. The commissioners went on to insist that it was:

> 'Of the very essence of a law that its penalties should be definite and known; how else are they to operate on the fears of offenders, or to afford a practical guide of conduct?...The individual discretion which is now substituted for such general rules, is pregnant with uncertainty. For the discretion exercised in the selection of the persons who are to suffer death out of a number capitally convicted, must necessarily be subject to variations, depending on the peculiar notions of policy entertained by different individuals, or their firmness and resolution of mind.'

So offenders come to believe

> ·'that severity of punishment depends on accidental and casual circumstances, and is therefore precarious and uncertain....A malefactor sometimes, we believe, owes his life to the circumstance that it happens that others are convicted at the same assizes, whose guilt is greater than his own...'

Russell told the commissioners that he had 'attentively considered' their report,

12   N. Gash *Mr. Secretary Peel* pp. 329, 340.
13   Second Report from the Commissioners on Criminal Law no. 343 (1836) pp. 19 ff.

yet there appeared to be difficulties. Alterations in the criminal law should not be mingled with the question of a general digest. Indeed, it would be impossible, he wrote, to lay down any rule to be invariably observed. So he commented that 'in the seven years ending 1834, of fourteen persons found guilty of murder in London and Middlesex, only nine were executed: yet if any crime would admit of an invariable rule it would be murder'.[14] In fact numerous measures were introduced into Parliament in 1837 with the result that the number of offences for which capital punishment was the penalty was indeed reduced considerably.[15]

On 5 March 1840 Ewart moved for the entire abolition of the punishment of death. In putting this motion to the Commons he stated that he:

> 'Could not conceive a duty more important in a legislature, than to impress upon the people the sacred inviolability of human life; nor a duty more imperative upon it, than to set an example of regard for that inviolability of human life; nor a duty more imperative upon it, than to set an example of regard for that inviolability in its acts of legislation....Let us humanise our punishments and we should humanise our people.'

For abolition there were 90 members: against abolition there were 161 members, a majority of 71. Ewart maintained that society had a right to inflict such an amount of punishment as was necessary to its safety and preservation but no more, although the necessary amount of punishment changed at different periods of society. Statistics showed that the reduction in the number of capital offences had not increased crime. Nor did capital punishment act as a deterrent. Ewart maintained that even the witnessing of an execution had not deterred persons from committing crimes. For example, a clergyman who had attended 167 persons condemned to death had stated that 164 of them had been present repeatedly at public executions. Indeed, officials at Newgate prison had informed him that it was very rarely that anyone suffered the penalty of death there who had not seen the same punishment inflicted repeatedly. He objected also to the irrevocability of capital punishment and maintained that juries would not hesitate to convict if the punishment were not death. Finally, he claimed that the maintenance of capital punishment was the maintenance of the old principle of revenge for which the country was substituting a system of repentance and reform. Could they continue a system involving a principle contradicted by their own recent practice?

Russell, the former Home Secretary, who had long been sympathetic to the cause of penal reform, opposed Ewart's motion. Russell maintained that murder was a crime which excited the greatest horror, a crime apart, and so quite different from those offences from which the death penalty had been removed during the early 1830s. He believed that a greater number of persons was deterred from murder by fear of capital punishment than would be deterred by fear of punishment of a minor character. He agreed that this was a matter which was incapable of proof, but those who committed the crime well knew that they could have no expectation that these cases would excite the sympathy of the public, or that they could escape by the sympathy of the jury. It was the paramount duty of the government, Russell concluded, to protect the innocent and

14 Correspondence between the Secretary of State for the Home Department and Commissioners no. 88 (1837) pp. 5-6.
15 L. Radzinowicz *A History of English Criminal Law* vol 4, p. 317.

unoffending portion of the community. Even so, he pointed to the immense change which had taken place in the mitigation of the criminal law and was far from saying that he did not indulge hopes that the condition of society would become yet so far improved, that the aversion to the shedding of blood would gain such strength that without danger to the innocent and unoffending, the abolition of death as a punishment might be effected.

Ewart's motion was lost. Yet the abolitionist movement flourished for some years. Literary circles especially favoured abolition at this time. It was Thackeray who, after being among a crowd of 40000 which witnessed a public execution wrote: 'I pray to Almighty God to cause this disgraceful sin to pass from among us, and to clean our land of blood.' Of course, public executions gave rise to disgusting exhibitions on the part of the great multitudes which attended them, despite their supposed deterrent value. A Select Committee of the House of Lords was told in 1856 that many people went to a public execution 'as they would to a theatre, or the exhibition of a bull fight'. In the town where the execution was to take place 'the whole town for the day was a scene of drunkenness and riot and debauching of every kind'. So far as the criminal section of the population was concerned, it was believed 'that the present mode tended to glorify the criminal, and so invest crime with something like the honours of martyrdom, that criminals were commonly found to have been frequent attendants at executions, that the terrors of death were lightened by the spectacle and 'a hardening effect produced on those who were already tainted with crime'. Accordingly, the Committee proposed that executions should in figure be carried into effect within the precincts of the prison, or in some place securing similar comparative privacy.[16]

Such a proposal was scarcely pleasing to the abolitionists who might well have felt that for such spectacles to be out of sight of the public was to ensure that the question of capital punishment would be out of the mind of the public. Accordingly, they opposed the proposal and for some years nothing was done. However, much of the former enthusiasm for the abolitionist cause had waned. The arguments on either side were overfamiliar. Statistics, it was said, could be made to serve either side. Comparatively few people were executed anyway. Above all, perhaps, there was the feeling that murder was an especially repugnant offence for which society should exercise due retribution. Nevertheless, after further public discussion a Commission on Capital Punishment reported in 1866.[17] Executions were now to be in private, yet executions there were still to be, although a minority of five members of the Commission had advocated the total abolition of capital punishment.

The fears of the abolitionists were proved correct. With the exception of some discussion in the 1870s and 1880s there was to be no further effective action until well into the twentieth century. That action began in the early 1920s.[18] The creation in 1921 of the Howard League for Penal Reform, upon the amalgamation of the Howard Association and the Penal Reform League, and in 1925 of the

16 Report from the Select Committee of the House of Lords appointed to take into consideration the present mode of carrying into effect Capital Punishment no. 366 (1856).
17 Report of the Capital Punishment Commission no. 10438 (1866).
18 The account in the text of the twentieth-century campaign is based primarily upon E.O. Tuttle's *The Crusade against Capital Punishment in Great Britain*. Cf. G. Rose *The Struggle for Penal Reform*. See also J.B. Christoph *Capital Punishment and British Politics*.

National Council for the Abolition of the Death Penalty, under the direction of Roy Calvert, a Quaker, gave a strong impetus to reform. The high hopes which abolitionists held of government legislation when Ramsay MacDonald again formed a Labour Government in May 1929, with Liberal support, were to be disappointed. However, a select committee was appointed in December 1929. The report was a thorough piece of work which considered not only evidence from the United Kingdom but also a great deal of evidence from overseas witnesses. The committee's conclusion was that 'Capital punishment may be abolished in this country without endangering life or property, or impairing the security of society'.[19] The Report was tabled in the House of Commons in December 1930. Yet the government, led in this respect by J.R. Clynes, the Home Secretary, was unwilling even to discuss it. In fact the Conservative minority on the select committee had refused to accept the report. However, had Clynes showed any enthusiasm for it, there is little doubt but that the government would have been able to act. Nothing further was accomplished during the 1930s although a full scale debate upon capital punishment took place in the House of Commons in 1938.

Little attention was paid to such matters during the Second World War. Upon the return in 1945 of a Labour Government, which on this occasion enjoyed a massive parliamentary majority and so governed in its own right, abolitionist hopes were once again high. They were soon to be dashed. The controversy came to a head during the debates upon the Criminal Justice Bill. The House of Lords, and the Lord Chief Justice, Lord Goddard, stood in the way of change. In Autumn 1948 the Home Secretary, Chuter Ede, offered a crumb of comfort to the abolitionists. There was to be a royal commission to discover the best way of mitigating capital punishment. Yet its terms of reference excluded abolition. The membership of this new royal commission was announced in April 1949; it reported in September 1953. By then a Conservative Government was in power once again: abolition still lay some years in the future.

d) *Benefit of clergy*

After trial and conviction the judgment of the court followed, unless it were suspended or arrested by some intervening circumstance, of which the principal was benefit of clergy.[20] That benefit or privilege had originated in the right of the clergy to be tried only before the ecclesiastical courts. In the course of time it was extended to people, even women, who were not clergy, but who were able to prove their clergy by reading the 'hanging verse'. At the same time the privilege was withdrawn from the more serious felonies. Particularly during the eighteenth century the severity of the criminal law was increased greatly by the creation of new felonies without benefit of clergy.[1] Benefit of clergy was abolished altogether in 1827.[2]

Benefit of clergy was an administrative device of tremendous significance so far as the actual operation of punishment at criminal law was concerned. Through its operation a 'Bloody Code' which in theory was quite incredibly

---

19 Report from the Select Committee on Capital Punishment (1931) p. xcvi.
20 4 Bl Com (5th edn) 358.
1 J.F. Stephen *History of the Criminal Law of England* vol 1, p. 470.
2 An Act for further improving the Administration in Criminal Cases in England 1827, ss. 6 and 7.

punitive, in practice became far less so. After praying his clergy successfully, a convicted person might be liable to imprisonment for a year, to whipping, or, in some cases, to seven years transportation.[3]

e) *Transportation*

Transportation was quite common from the period after the Restoration. The prisoner was reprieved on condition that he agreed to be transported to the plantations, usually in the Americas. The prisoner was assigned to a settler — later, in Australia, he was assigned to the governor — his master had a 'property and interest' in his services for the term of his sentence, and had to be compensated, if he were pardoned early. Accordingly, it was possible to regard convict labour as only a particular type of indentured labour.[4] Offenders who had been transported but who were found at large, without lawful excuse, before the expiration of the term, were guilty of felony. Originally that offence was punishable by death; however, during the reign of William IV it was made subject instead to transportation for life.[5] Yet transportation was unknown at common law, although at common law it was possible for a criminal to be exiled when he had taken sanctuary and confessed his crime. However, during the eighteenth and early nineteenth centuries an 'immense number' of statutes authorised transportation.[6]

After the loss of the American colonies, the solution adopted was the incarceration of prisoners in the ships which may formerly have carried prisoners across the ocean. These ships were moored in river estuaries and became known as 'hulks'. A more lasting solution, after Cook's discovery of Australia, was adopted in 1786. Now convicts were to be transported to Australia. Convicts were so dispatched in great numbers. In all more than 150000 persons were transported during the period 1788-1867. Indeed, the halt in the upward trend in crime for a time during that period was probably due in part to the fact that so many criminals were transported.[7]

Many maintained that transportation was not a particularly severe punishment. For Paley it was 'a slight punishment' which placed the delinquent in a position not worse than that in which he was at the time when he committed the crime; further, it was unseen by others and so could not adequately perform its preventive function. Bentham, too, thought little of transportation as it meant that the effect of the criminal's punishment was lost upon the home community. Many others felt simply that transportation amounted to no punishment at all.[8] Of course, transportation did have its champions;[9] above all, the government made ample use of it.

Once awaiting transportaton the practice was said to be that usually the worst characters were sent first i.e. those who had been convicted before and bad

---

3   *Stephen* (above) p. 472, J. Hall *Theft, Law and Society* (2nd edn, 1935) pp. 110 ff.
4   A.G.L. Shaw *Convicts and the Colonies* pp. 28-30.
5   An Act for abolishing Capital Punishment in case of returning from Transportation.
6   *Stephen* (above) p. 480.
7   L. Radzinowicz *Ideology of Crime* pp. 60-61. In 1776 the hulks had been authorised for two years; they lasted for 82 years — Shaw *Convicts and the Colonies* p. 43.
8   L. Radzinowicz *A History of English Criminal Law* vol 1, p. 253, n. 75, J. Bentham *Theory of Legislation* chap. 9.
9   (1837) 5 British and For Rev 121.

characters from the gaol.[10] Conditions on the voyage were frequently atrocious, even in an age when sea travel generally was arduous. Many prisoners did not survive the journey. In part this may have been due to the fact that at first the contractors were paid by the numbers of convicts whom they took on board in England rather than by the number whom they delivered safely to Australia. Treatment in Australia also was often extremely harsh and even cruel. Stories abound of the most severe floggings and other such treatment which was meted out to convicts. Occasionally, convicts were fortunate to be subjected to humane and reasonable discipline such as that inaugurated all too briefly by Maconochie on Norfolk Island. His was an exceptional case. Of course, treatment in prisons at home was often brutal, and no doubt those who wished to see an end to transportation generally, may have overstressed the evils of the system on occasion, as was probably the case with some of the evidence which was given to the Molesworth Committee in 1837.[11] At all events the system came to an end in 1867. Pressure from Australian colonists had shown an increasing hostility to continued transportation. Transportation to New South Wales ceased in 1840: after 1846 nearly all convicts were sent to Van Diemen's land, where it was not necessary for a colonial government to consent to receive them. Finally, the last convict ship sailed — for Western Australia — on 12 October 1867.

Transportation had served both the home country and Australia reasonably well, a fact to which the cruelties practised under the system should not blind us. Shaw writes that economically it had greatly helped Australian development by providing a labour force and by making private investment more profitable; socially, it did no great harm. Its greatest evil, Shaw suggests, 'was to encourage brutality which an allegedly civilised community should deplore; but the early nineteenth century was a brutal age, in which pain and suffering were regarded as normal and inevitable if distressing in all walks of life'. As a severe deterrent transportation failed:

> 'partly because it was misunderstood at home, partly because it is hopeless to rely solely on deterrence to get rid of crime. Because of this failure, government opinion slowly turned against it....In fact transportation and assignment was the most effective reformatory punishment that was widely adopted before 1850; but at that time few accepted the principle that the aim of punishment and prison discipline should be reformation rather than the infliction of suffering, and most men would have agreed with Sir James F. Stephen that the "criminal law is mainly a system of licensed revenge".'[12]

f) *Whipping — corporal punishment*

In the early nineteenth century whipping was a common punishment which was inflicted upon both males and females, young and old. For example, at Nottingham in 1769 a young woman of 19 was found guilty at the quarter sessions of obtaining goods under false pretences, a statutory misdemeanour. The sentence

10 Appendix to Minutes of Evidence taken before the Select Committee of the House of Lords appointed to inquire into the present state of the several Gaols and Houses of Correction no. 42 (1835) Appendix; no. 440, pp. 254-5.
11 Report from the Select Committee on Transportation no. 518 (1837).
12 Shaw *Convicts and the Colonies* pp. 358-9.

was that she be stripped to the waist and publicly whipped on market day in the market place.[13] Most commonly it was a punishment which was visited upon vagrants, even whole families of vagrants — the usual form of sentence being that they be whipped until their backs be bloodied. As the movement for the mitigation of capital punishments gained some degree of momentum, public opinion appears also to have rejected what appeared to be the most objectionable or harsh cases of such punishment. In 1817 it was provided that women were no longer to be whipped in public, in 1820 it was provided that women were no longer to be whipped at all.[14] We may suspect also that a certain humanitarianism had long persuaded many justices not to whip vagrants whose fault appeared to be only that they were poor. In assessing the severity of whipping in contemporary eyes, we should bear in mind that such punishments were by no means unknown in home life. For example, in the eighteenth century it was quite common for the master or mistress to beat their servants. One wealthy lady who confided such an incident to her diary expressed astonishment that the young servant's mother had never beaten her daughter — the lady makes it quite clear that for her part she had done her duty by whipping her own daughters.[15] Similarly, a headmaster of Eton established a claim to fame at the beginning of the nineteenth century by the frequency with which he flogged his students.

In 1861 statute provided that, subject to some exceptions, males over 16 were no longer to be subject to corporal punishment. Those under that age would continue to be subject to such punishment.[16] Subsequently, flogging was introduced, however, for further offences beginning with the Garrotters Act 1863.[17] It is clear also that during these years many members of the judiciary continued to believe in the deterrent value of flogging in the case of some criminal offences at least. For example, in 1875 many judges were virtually unanimous in agreeing that flogging be introduced in an attempt to curb brutal assaults upon wives by husbands, a subject about which there was considerable public concern at that time.[18] It was the Criminal Justice Act 1948[19] which finally abolished the judicial corporal punishment of adults.

In fact there had been a steady reduction in its use during the twentieth century. At the beginning of the twentieth century it was used in 7 per cent of cases; in 1946 a writer was able to assert that it was 'practically disused'.[20] The statistics show that in 1900, 3260 persons were whipped; in 1938, 60 persons were whipped — 17 adults who were flogged for robbery with violence and 43 juveniles who were whipped for various offences.[1]

In the case of a juvenile in 1946 the position was that:

13   W. Andrew *By Gone Punishments* pp. 219-20, 224-5.
14   An Act to repeal an Act ... intituled An Act to abolish the punishment of public Whipping on Female Offenders ...
15   W. Andrew *By Gone Punishments*.
16   In 1914 the Criminal Justice Administration Act provided that no one should be whipped unless the offence specifically carried whipping as the penalty.
17   An outstanding instance of panic legislation.
18   Reports to the Secretary of State for the Home Department on the State of the Law relating to Indictable Assaults no. C-1138 (1875).
19   See generally L. Radzinowicz and J.W.C. Turner (ed) *Penal Reform in England*.
20   S.K. Ruck 'Developments in Crime and Punishment' in L. Radzinowicz and J.W.C.Turner (ed) *Penal Reform in England* pp. 1, 10.
 1   Op. cit. p. 12.

'Upon being found guilty of an indictable offence a boy who is under fourteen years of age may be ordered to receive not more than six strokes with a birch rod. In the London juvenile courts there have been no birchings for many years, and although in some parts of England this form of punishment is still used, it appears that the majority of courts can have little faith in this, judging by the small number of birchings now ordered.'[2] There had long been a quite substantial opposition to the flogging of adults. During the final quarter of the nineteenth century the most effective case for reform was put by the Humanitarian League. There was less opposition to the use of the birch upon juveniles. After all, corporal punishment was common in the schools. Further, it could be argued that, before juvenile imprisonment was abolished in 1908, the birching of a juvenile was a lesser evil than his imprisonment under the conditions which then prevailed.[3] An unsuccessful attempt was made by the government to abolish birching in the Children and Young Person's Bill 1932.

As a result of further pressure a Departmental Committee on Corporal Punishment was appointed in 1937.[4] So far as the birching of juveniles was concerned, the statistics tended to show that birchings had not acted as a deterrent to future offences. Further, a majority of magistrates and of probation officers wished to dispense with it.[5] Rose writes that in relation to flogging the evidence was even more impressive. Analysis showed that '55 per cent of those flogged were subsequently convicted of serious crime, as against 43.9 per cent of those not flogged'. The Committee also rejected claims which had been made of the effectiveness of floggings in putting down certain outbursts of crime e.g. the London garrottings, in the past. The judiciary and police tended to favour its retention; the Committee was unanimous in recommending that the courts should no longer have the power to order the corporal punishment of an offender.[6] That position was adopted finally by statute in 1948.[7]

g) *Imprisonment*

The history of imprisonment in England and Wales is a long one, yet the history of imprisonment as the usual, rather than as a purely secondary, form of punishment dates only from mid-nineteenth century. It was during that period that a great many of the present day prisons were built. Even now, therefore, our prison system itself lives largely within the confines of early Victorian buildings which were built within a remarkably short time to meet the pressing needs of the mid-nineteenth century and which expressed a mid-nineteenth century approach to punishment.

In the eighteenth century gaols were regarded primarily not so much as places of punishment as places of detention whose object was simply to ensure that the prisoner would be available for trial. Accordingly, the population of the gaol was extraordinarily varied: civil debtors and prisoners on criminal charges, both before and after trial, were mixed together indiscriminately, both male and

---

2   A.C.L. Morrison 'The Jurisdiction of Juvenile Courts' in *Penal Reform in England* p. 98.
3   G. Rose *The Struggle for Penal Reform* p. 208.
4   Report of the Departmental Committee on Corporal Punishment (Cmd. 5684).
5   *Rose* p. 210.
6   *Rose* p. 211.
7   Criminal Justice Act 1948.

female, young and old. Conditions within the prisons, which had not necessarily been built as prisons, were often poor and treatment harsh. Gaol fever was common. Indeed, in 1750 two judges were victims of it. Such poor conditions and bad treatment were not so much the result of state policy as of administrative chaos, of faults inherent in the system, and of a general indifference to the fate of the prisoner.[8]

There were county gaols for which the sheriff was responsible. Private persons were responsible, by franchise, for about half of the gaols. For example the Duke of Leeds owned Halifax prison and the Bishop of Durham owned the county gaol at Durham. Gaolers expected to make a living out of their occupation by the fees which they were enabled to charge prisoners. There were fees for food, fees for improved accommodation, fees for 'easement of irons', and so on. Woe betide the prisoner who could not pay his way. Increasingly, it became recognised that such institutions corrupted the inmates, especially the young, in their attitude to crime and to every kind of vice.

Gradually the justices were granted greater powers in respect of the prisons. It was an obligation for which they invariably showed little enthusiasm. It was rather the work of John Howard and of Elizabeth Fry which first began to raise the country's level of consciousness and feelings of responsibility in this area. Yet the legislature had shown quite a lively awareness of what was needed by an Act of 1779, in the enactment of which Blackstone had played a considerable part. It provided for the establishment of penitentiaries and for the work which prisoners were to do within them. Later Acts provided for the classification of prisoners and for justices to visit the gaols. Unfortunately, the justices neglected these duties.[9]

The working house or house of correction, known popularly as the bridewell, was the creation of the Tudors. It was supervised efficiently by the justices. Their aim was to provide work for those, especially vagrants, who might be reluctant to find work for themselves. As time went by, however, minor offenders were committed to them, sight was lost of the original aim of reformation, and the bridewell was seen very much as a penal institution. By the eighteenth century it was very often in practice a part of the common gaol, although it was only in 1865 that the distinction, long disused in practice, was finally abolished.[10] Bentham grappled with the prison question. Unfortunately, perhaps, he devoted the greater part of his attention to his cherished plan for a Panopticon although nothing came of that plan, despite an initial interest on the part of the government. It was Peel's arrival at the Home Office which marked the beginning of real change.

Peel realised that, if there was to be a reduction in the number of capital punishments, it would be necessary to improve secondary punishments. He was fortunate in taking over a bill which had already been prepared and which had already won the assent of the government. Peel's skill was essential, however, in securing the passage of the measure, especially in overcoming Eldon's lack of enthusiasm for it. Peel's Gaols Act consolidated 23 previous measures. By way of

8   I am indebted to L.W. Fox *The English Prison and Borstal Systems.*
9   W.S. Holdsworth *History of English Law* vol 10, pp. 180-3. Cf. S. and B. Webb *English Prisons under Local Government* and R.E.S. Hinde *The British Penal System 1773-1950.*
10   L.W. Fox *The English Prison and Borstal Systems* p. 25.

reform it provided for justices to execute the Act, to classify prisoners in accordance with the provisions of the Act, established rules regarding gaol hygiene and provided that further rules could be made by quarter sessions, subject to the approval of the judges. Visiting justices were to report to quarter sessions, quarter sessions was then to report to the Secretary of State.[11] In all it was a substantial legislative advance. Indeed, Peel's biographer has described it as 'a great reforming statute, introducing most of the principles of enlightened prison administration advocated by a generation of penal reformers'. Uniform principles had been laid down, there was to be a rudimentary form of central supervision. Yet the country was not ready for effective enforcement in this sphere any more than it was in other spheres of the national life. To achieve such enforcement was the key to true reform. Even so, although the Act was enforced only partially or not at all in many areas 'it did act as a tremendous stimulus to the more progressive, and a considerable number of the more important prisons were rebuilt under its influence'.[12] In 1835 statute provided that the Home Secretary might appoint inspectors of prisons who would report to him.[13]

On the whole the inspectors appointed appear to have been men of some calibre. One, William Crawford, had visited the USA in 1836 and had observed at first hand both the separate system which had been adopted in Pennsylvania and the silent system which had been adopted in New York State. Impressed, he informed Lord John Russell, the Home Secretary, of what he had seen. Crawford advocated the speedy adoption of the separate system. It seems that by 1856 the separate system was implemented fully in one-third of the prisons and carried out partially in a further one-third.[14] Yet, although Peel's Act had envisaged a reformatory regime and despite the improved arrangements for supervision, prison conditions were often harsh, even cruel. Allegations of cruel treatment were substantiated by an inquiry, begun after the death of a young prisoner, into conditions in mid-nineteenth century at Birmingham borough gaol.[15] Moreover, it had proved virtually impossible to provide constructive work, which might assist reform, without appearing to take much needed work away from honest men and women outside prison. The answer which the treadwheel and the crank provided must have appeared soul-destroying to many prisoners.

Sheer force of circumstance obliged the government to take further action, especially as the Australian colonies became increasingly reluctant to accept transported convicts. Pentonville was built in 1842 and a further 54 prisons had been built by 1848. It was a remarkable achievement which was to fashion prison history for well over the ensuing 100 years. An Act of 1850 provided for the appointment of directors of convict prisons:[16] their first chairman was Colonel Jebb. Treatment of prisoners amounted to an amalgam of existing methods. Imprisonment yielded separate confinement and hard labour; transportation

11 N. Gash *Mr. Secretary Peel* pp. 315-16, W.S. Holdsworth *History of English Law* vol 13, pp. 318-19, *Fox* pp. 34-5.

12 *Fox* p. 35.

13 An Act for effecting greater Uniformity of Practice in the Government of the several Prisons in England and Wales; and for appointing Inspectors of Prisons in Great Britain.

14 *Fox* p. 39.

15 Report of the Commissioners appointed to inquire into the Condition and Treatment of the Prisoners confined in Birmingham Borough Prison no. 1809 (1854).

16 An Act for the better Government of Convict Prisons.

yielded the practice of releasing the well-behaved prisoner upon ticket of leave before the expiration of his sentence, the use of prison labour upon public works, and a system of 'progressive stages' by means of which prisoners might gain ticket of leave more quickly. Indeed, Jebb and his senior colleagues appear even to have aimed at a system which would reclaim or reform the prisoner.

Local prisons were another matter. Both they and the convict prisons came under the scrutiny in 1863 of a Select Committee of the House of Lords. The Committee met at a time when public opinion was disturbed by an apparent increase in crime and especially by a number of cases of garrotting. The Committee was quite clear upon the object of imprisonment. The object of imprisonment was deterrence. There was to be 'hard labour, hard fare, and a hard bed'.[17] In that system separate confinement and the crank were each to play a major role. The Committee's recommendations, in which the judiciary had played a role, were adopted. In addition the Prison Act 1865 established mandatory provisions in some detail for the conduct of local prisons. The result, writes Fox,[18] was that the foundations of a coherent and uniform system of imprisonment had now been laid. By the Prison Act 1877[19] a further step along the path to uniformity was taken with the vesting in the Secretary of State of the ownership and control of all local prisons, which now were to be maintained out of public funds.

The application in practice of the public aims of deterrence, uniformity and economy was the life's work of Sir Edmund F. du Cane who was Chairman of the Prison Commissioners from 1877 until 1895. It was a considerable achievement by an outstanding public servant. Yet in the closing years of the 'du Cane regime', du Cane himself came under considerable attack for the alleged rigidity of his methods. Fox even writes that for 'death itself the system had substituted a living death'.[20] A press campaign initiated by a former prison chaplain, Dr. Morrison, culminated in the appointment in 1894 of a departmental committee under the chairmanship of the Under Secretary of State at the Home Office, H.J. Gladstone. The Gladstone Report was published in 1895.[1] It was to be an influential document. Fox commented in 1952: 'For fifty years it has held its place, comparable with that of the Cincinatti Principles in America, as the scriptural sanction of the English prison system.' Its 'unique achievement' was that it rejected the philosophy of uniformity and of severity which had been characteristic of the du Cane regime.[2]

The Gladstone committee believed in the reformation of the prisoner — prison treatment should have as its primary and concurrent objects deterrence and reformation. Accordingly, non-productive labour such as the crank and the treadmill was condemned, useful work was recommended. Greater attention should be paid to the needs of individual prisoners, a proposition which led them not only to view with disfavour both the separate and the silent systems but led to

17   Report from the Select Committee of the House of Lords appointed to consider the present state of discipline in gaols and houses of correction no. 499 (1863).
18   L.W. Fox *The English Prison and Borstal Systems* p. 47.
19   An Act to amend the law relating to Prisons in England (1877).
20   *Fox* p. 51. See also R. Cross *Punishment, Prison and the Public*, cf. L. Radzinowicz 'The Evolution of the Modern English Prison System' (1939) 3 MLR 121.
1   Report of the Departmental Committee on Prisons 1895 (C. 2nd series 7703).
2   *Fox* p. 56, N. McLachlan 'Penal Reform and Penal History: Some Reflections' in L. Blom-Cooper (ed) *Progress in Penal Reform* p. 7. See generally M. Grunhut *Penal Reform*.

the provision of workshops for labour in association and to the provision of educational facilities such as libraries.

The Prison Act 1898[3] reduced the number of offences punishable by flogging, established three divisions for the classification of offenders, and a regular system which allowed a prisoner by his conduct to earn remission of his sentence.

Finally, the Act left it to the Secretary of State to make rules for the detailed regulation of the prisons. Fox describes this as a 'more elastic procedure, which made it possible for changes to be effected without fresh legislation on each occasion' with the result that under it 'the natural development of fifty years was able to proceed without further intervention by parliament'. Fox points out also that the creation of a departmental committee, appointed by the Home Secretary, tended to replace the nineteenth-century style parliamentary committee.[4]

The return of the Liberal Government in 1906, with none other than Gladstone as Home Secretary, appeared likely to mark a new dawn for penal reform. Some important legislation did follow. The Probation of Offenders Act 1907[5] gave statutory recognition to a practice which had been growing for some 25 years within the context of the magistrates' traditional legal power to bind over the offender and give advice through a social worker. Craven describes the 1907 Act as 'the first of the twentieth-century parliaments' many confessions of faith in anything but prison'.[6] Yet Craven also reported that, although the number of cases dealt with by probation increased steadily, the enforcement of the Act's provisions varied throughout the country. For example, in 1922 over one-fifth of courts had not appointed a probation officer: in 1936 the percentage of persons found guilty of indictable offences and placed on probation varied from 43.8 per cent to 5 per cent in different courts.[7] The Children Act 1908[8] established juvenile courts. The Prevention of Crime Act 1908[9] created the borstal system as an alternative to prison for delinquents between the ages of 16 and 21. The same Act also inaugurated the sentence of preventive detention for the habitual criminal, although Craven states that it was little used and that in the form given it in 1908 it was destined to be abolished by the Criminal Justice Bill of 1938.

Nevertheless conditions in prison remained forbidding, to the extent that when the longserving chairman of the Prison Commission, Ruggles-Brise, retired in 1921 he was subjected to much the same kind of criticism as du Cane upon his retirement. That criticism stemmed largely from the experience of a number of imprisoned conscientious objectors during the First World War. In particular they alleged that the administration was unduly rigid and that in practice reform had little place. It may be that Ruggles-Brise himself did not give a high priority to reform. In that respect he reflected a substantial section of public opinion. Upon a more sophisticated level some officials had long doubted whether it was possible both to deter and to reform.

3   An Act to amend the Prisons Acts (1898).
4   *Fox* p. 58.
5   7 Edw 7, c. 17.
6   C.M. Craven 'The Trend of Criminal Legislation' in L. Radzinowicz and J.W.C. Turner (ed) *Penal Reform in England* pp. 18, 22.
7   Op. cit. p. 23.
8   8 Edw 7, c. 67.
9   8 Edw 7, c. 59, Criminal Justice Act 1925 regarding probation.

Perhaps the abiding characteristic of twentieth-century legislation was the wish to keep people out of prison. The Probation of Offenders Act 1907, the Children Act 1908, and the Prevention of Crime Act 1908 all had that aim. Similarly, the Criminal Justice Administration Act 1914[10] required magistrates to allow time for the payment of fines unless there were good reasons for not doing so, and Fox describes the Criminal Justice Act 1948, except in its provisions for the treatment of persistent offenders, as 'above all an Act for keeping people out of prison'.[11]

At the same time the influence of Alexander Paterson, a prison commissioner, led to some relaxation in conditions within prisons and to the establishment of open institutions. In theory at least the system was designed to 'turn out better men and women'.[12] Practice, due to lack of finance for new buildings and more trained staff, may have been another matter. In truth penal reform had advanced only at a snail's pace.

Yet Grunhut commented:

> 'Even in the face of such modest progress prison history shows one remarkable result. In little more than one century mankind made the extraordinary step from considering imprisonment as a mere substitute for the death penalty and a mortification closely allied to other form of bodily punishment to considering it as something which, by its underlying principles, is an appeal to the moral personality of the prisoner.'[13]

It is possible to take a different view. McLachlan comments that 'we are still suffering from disastrous policy decisions made more than a century ago' e.g. Jebb's programme of cellular prison building. That dead hand of the architectural past still seriously obstructs, he comments, 'if it does not in fact destroy, recent emphases on training and preparation for return to the outside world'. Even the 'prevention of deterioration' which R. Cross proposes as the main aim of prison reform must be hard to achieve in such an environment.[14] McLachlan's belief is, that if one takes a long view, the penal system has changed little.

As we survey the history of imprisonment, over a span of 200 years, it is easy enough to point to a number of administrative phases. Before 1865 there was the slow growth of a degree of uniformity and of central control. Then we had the successive regimes of du Cane, Ruggles-Brise and Paterson, with the avowed aim of reformation — and even of the avoidance of imprisonment altogether — coming in theory at least, increasingly to the fore. The reality was that theory lagged considerably behind practice, if only because society was unwilling, after that early Victorian bout of energetic prison building, to allocate adequate resources to modernise prisons and prison treatment. A more liberal society simply congratulated itself upon its modern penal theory and failed to implement that theory at more than a snail's pace. The result was that in 1950 society appeared far less aware, even than in 1850, of the objectives of imprisonment.

h) *Fines and other punishments*

Courts had always been able at common law and by various statutes to impose

10   4 & 5 Geo 5, c. 58.
11   L.W. Fox *The English Prison and Borstal Systems* p. 66.
12   *Fox* p. 77.
13   M. Grunhut *Penal Reform* pp. 131, 133, 62, 132.
14   R. Cross *Punishment, Prison and the Public* p. 85.

fines. As secondary punishments became more significant during the nineteenth century and as numerous statutory offences were also created, so also did the importance of the fine increase as a form of punishment. However, by the beginning of the twentieth century the fine had reached a peak in terms of the frequency of its imposition; its use simply remained constant during the first half of the twentieth century. The payment of fines was facilitated in 1914 when statute provided[15] that the courts must allow time for the payment of fines unless there were compelling reasons to the contrary. That provision alone reduced the number of defaulters who were imprisoned from 83187 a year between 1909 and 1913 to 11613 in 1933.[16] A further statute, enacted in 1935, reduced the number imprisoned in 1938 to 7936.[17]

The striking characteristic of the imposition, or at all events the administration, of punishments during the first half of the twentieth century was the great increase in the number of conditional releases.[18] Without doubt both the avoidance of imprisonment and the early release of prisoners characterised the penal system during this period. How successful such a policy was, whether in terms of deterrence or of the rehabilitation of the prisoner, is not clear. Few extra resources appear to have been allocated in support of such prisoners and for their part the police believed that an increase in crime could be attributed to this policy. Yet the facts were clear: Ruck wrote that at any given moment less than half the number of grown criminals were under detention in 1946 than had been in 1900.[19]

There were other punishments. For example, the eighteenth century knew branding and the pillory: the first half of the twentieth century saw the birth of an interesting number of experiments in penology. This book must confine itself to a discussion of the leading punishments.

i) *In conclusion*
Little thought was ever given to the scale of punishments within an overall scheme of criminal law. Anomalies abounded. Discretion continued to play a large part. At a time when capital punishment figured so largely in criminal punishments, this was understandable. Yet the attempts of the criminal law commissioners in the 1830s to introduce a certain measure of uniformity in criminal punishments generally met with little success.

Even by 1950 no general reconstruction of penalty structures had been accomplished. The maximum terms of imprisonment which were then possible amounted to an 'extraordinary collection' which exhibited 'a strange, biblical faith in multiples of 7'.[20] Other punishments did not so much add up to one coherent system as form part of a bewildering mosaic. Professor Milsom has written of crime's 'miserable history' before the age of reform, that it is one of

---

15   The Criminal Justice Administration Act 1914.
16   C.M. Craven 'The Trend of Criminal Legislation' in Radzinowicz and Turner (ed) *Penal Reform in England* p. 27.
17   Money Payments (Justices Procedure) Act 1935.
18   L. Radzinowicz 'The Present Trend of English Penal Policy' (1939) 55 LQR 273.
19   S.K. Ruck 'Developments in Crime and Punishment' in Radzinowicz and Turner (ed) *Penal Reform in England* p. 11.
20   D.A. Thomas *The Penal Equation* p. 50 (pamphlet: Univ. of Cambridge, Inst. of Crim., 1978).

'institutional expedients all sensible in their day, all in the long run tending to make the subject nobody's business'.[1] It is a harsh, yet a just, judgment which applies equally during the so-called age of reform during the nineteenth century and after not only to the substantive criminal law and its administration but also to criminal punishments.

1   S.F.C. Milsom *Historical Foundations of the Common Law* p. 353.

Chapter 12

Civil liability

1 The forms of action

a) *The various forms of action*

We have noted already that it was essential for the plaintiff to choose the technically correct form of action. At this point it is appropriate to say a little more
about the forms of action in general before we consider the question of civil
liability.

An action was said to be the means afforded by law of obtaining the remedy
for an injury. Actions were divided into criminal, or such as concerned pleas of
the crown, and civil, or such as concerned common pleas. Civil actions were
themselves distinguished according to their subject matter into either personal
actions, real actions or mixed actions. Personal actions were for the specific
recovery of goods and chattels, or for damages or other redress for breach of
contract or other injuries of whatever description, the specific recovery of real
property only excepted. Real actions were for the specific recovery of real
property e.g. land, only. Mixed actions partook of the nature of the other two,
being brought for the recovery of real property and also for damages for an
injury thereto.[1]

b) *Personal actions*

In this chapter we shall consider personal actions. Personal actions were in form
ex contractu or *ex delicto*. Those which were classified as being contractual in
their nature were principally assumpsit, debt and covenant.[2] Into the latter
category of delict or tort there fell trespass vi et armis, case, trover and replevin.
Detinue might be classified in either category. The plaintiff in a personal action
was required to allocate his complaint to one such prescribed form of action.

---

1 3 Bl Com (5th edn) 117 ff., E. Chitty *The Commercial and General Lawyer* (2nd edn, 1841)
   p. 945.
2 There were also actions of account, annuity and *scire facias*.

c) *Particular rules*

i) *Joinder of parties.* Rules regarding the joinder of parties made it especially important to distinguish accurately between contract and tort. Where there were several parties on either side of a contract, the action was required to be brought by or against all of them; if they were dead, the action should be brought by or against the survivors. The omission of a party as plaintiff who ought to have been joined, or the joinder of a party who ought not to have been joined, might be fatal to the action. The omission of a party as defendant who ought to have been joined could only be taken advantage of by a plea in abatement. It was a similar story in actions of tort. The joinder of a party who ought not to be plaintiff was fatal. Yet one very important distinction between contract and tort, namely, that torts were of a joint and several nature, meant that in cases of tort the plaintiff might proceed against all or any of the parties who was alleged to have committed the tort. Clearly the possibility of choosing whom to sue in such circumstances meant that a plaintiff might prefer to sue in tort rather than in contract. Irrespective of the justice of the matter, such a plaintiff might succeed in his case only if he could persuade the court upon the initial point that it was indeed proper for him to bring his case in tort rather than in contract.

Such rules were highly technical in their nature. Yet it was only in 1851 that commissioners recognised the validity of the criticism that they often tended to defeat justice.[3]

ii) *Survival of actions.* Upon contracts the action was to be brought by the party with whom the contract was made or, if he were dead, by his executors or administrators. Yet in tort the rule was far different, if either of the parties were dead. In such cases there could be no action for the rule was *actio personalis moritur cum persona*[4]. It was a rule which was amended by the Fatal Accidents Act 1846 — a measure which became known more usually as Lord Campbell's Act. Now statute provided that the death of the party injured through the act or default of another should not exonerate that other from any liability which would have rested on him for such act or default had the victim lived. Damages were not to form part of the deceased's estate, which would have made them subject to his debts, but were to be divided amongst his nearest relatives.

iii) *Joinder of actions.* No two of those forms of action could be joined in one action. That rule was inconvenient upon two grounds. In the first place it could lead to a litigant suffering undue inconvenience and expense. In 1851 commissioners gave the following example:

> 'If a man has a claim against his tenant for breach of a covenant to repair contained in a lease under seal, and a further claim against the same tenant for nonrepair of another house let by lease or agreement not under seal, he must bring two actions, one of covenant and the other of assumpsit, to enforce those claims. If he has a further claim for a trespass to

---

3 W. Tidd *The Practice of the Court of King's Bench in Personal Actions* (3rd edn, 1803) pp. 8-9, First Report of the Royal Commission on Pleading in Courts of Common Law no. 1389 (1851) p. 31.
4 *Tidd*, p. 8, W.S. Malone 'The Genesis of Wrongful Death' (1965) 17 Stanford Law Review 1043.

a third house which the same person has occupied under the pretence of its being let to him, a third action must be brought; and a fourth action would have to be brought if the defendant had done a permanent injury to premises let by the plaintiff to a third person.'[5]

Secondly, he might well suffer such undue inconvenience and expense simply because in some instances it was impossible to determine convincingly whether the claim should be in contract or tort. No satisfactory explanation of the distinction between contract and tort was made even by mid-twentieth century. Throughout these years the shadowy distinction between contract and tort haunted the courts. It was a problem which arose especially in the field of the common carrier and, of course, of the railway.

In *Govett v Radnidge* (1802)[6] the defendants had contracted with the plaintiff to load a certain hogshead. The hogshead was damaged as a result of negligence on the part of some of the defendants. Ought the plaintiff to have framed the action, which was not said to be against a common carrier, in contract or in tort? There was considerable authority which suggested that it should be in contract. If so, the defendants would not have been liable as a verdict had been found only against some, but not all, of them. Lord Ellenborough chose a bolder course, saying:

'What inconvenience is there in suffering the party to allege his gravamen, if he please, as consisting in a breach of duty arising out of an employment for hire and to consider that breach of duty as tortious negligence, instead of considering the same circumstances as forming a breach of promise implied from the same consideration of hire?'

As we look back with the benefit of hindsight we can see that, within the accepted limits of the forms of action as they were then understood, the courts were beginning to grope towards a broader concept of what today we call the duty of care in negligence. For Lord Ellenborough to recognise, however obliquely, that facts such as those in *Govett v Radnidge* might form the basis of an action in tort rather than in contract was to point to the manner in which the law was to develop. It was only in the early 1820s that it became accepted that the common carrier, when sued upon the custom of the realm, was liable in tort. It was a battle which soon was to be fought over again as the railways spread rapidly across the country. Generally speaking the courts became prepared increasingly to recognise a duty in many situations which would found an action in tort quite independently of any contract. Generally speaking the courts learned to cope adequately enough with the typical case of the negligently caused accident in the factory or on the roads or railways although they proved less adept at recognising 'organisational negligence' in accident cases i.e. that certain types of work were inherently dangerous. A new body of law emerged. Yet the old thinking was slow to disappear. It was only in *Donoghue v Stevenson*[7] (1932) that the concept of the duty of care received its classic formulation and negligence itself was recognised finally as an independent tort in its own right. In 1935 an outstanding authority upon the law of tort commented that the principle which was recognised in

---

5   *Tidd* pp. 9-10, First Report no. 1389 (1851). Yet debt might be joined with detinue and case with trover.

6   (1802) 3 East 62.

7   [1932] AC 562, [1932] All ER 1.

Donoghue would probably have been established earlier but for a tendency in some quarters to argue that because there was no contractual duty between manufacturer and consumer, therefore there could be no duty in tort.[8] Even then it was still possible to distinguish between tort and contract in terms of the different rules which governed survival of actions, joinder of actions, joint liability, and limitation of actions.

iv) *The end of the forms of action*. The Uniformity of Process Act 1832 and two statutes which were enacted in 1833,[9] simplified the forms of action considerably. Yet the forms of action which stayed remained distinctive. The Common Law Procedure Act 1852 introduced a further change. Henceforth, the form of action was not to be mentioned in the writ — yet it was still necessary for the correct choice of the form of action to appear in the declaration. The Judicature Acts 1873-1875 abolished finally the old forms of action. Yet they had shaped the law. Accordingly, in a famous sentence Maitland concluded: 'The forms of action we have buried but they still rule us from their graves.'[10]

2 Contract

a) *Introduction*

The modern history of contract falls into three periods. The origins of the modern doctrine are buried in the venerable forms of eighteenth-century law. Secondly, during the first half of the nineteenth century the judges began to develop the general, and classic, theory of contract which moulded the modern lawyers' understanding of the new doctrine. That period culminated in the publication of the influential academic treatises of Pollock and of Anson.[11] Finally, even during the second half of the nineteenth century but more especially during the first half of the twentieth century, there was a steady and increasing erosion of the classic theory. Each of those three periods reflected the changing and shifting economic beliefs and facts of their day.

b) *The early law of contracts*

i) *Contractual forms of action*. Blackstone wrote that there were three classes of express contracts — debts, covenants, and promises or assumpsit.[12]

1) Debt. Debt lay for a sum due by certain and express agreement upon simple contracts, specialties e.g. debts due under a deed, or records e.g. judgment debts. If I had agreed verbally to pay a man a certain price for a certain parcel of

---

8   P. Winfield 'The Law of Tort' (1935) 51 LQR 249, 254.
9   3 & 4 Will IV, c.27, s.36 and c.42, s.13.
10 See generally F.W. Maitland *The Forms of Action at Common Law*.
11 F. Pollock *Principles of Contract* (1875), W.R. Anson *Principles of the English Law of Contract* (1879). The Indian Contract Act 1872, although much criticised on some counts, sets out a classic approach to contract.
12 3 Bl Com (5th edn) 153-7, W. Tidd *The Practice of the Court of King's Bench in Personal Actions* (3rd edn, 1803) p. 4. Traditionally, *Slade's case* (1602) 4 Co Rep 91a has been stressed as the herald of modern contract. For an authoritative modern exposition see A.W.B. Simpson *A History of the Common Law of Contract*.

goods and I failed to do so, an action of debt would lie against me. Usually debt was brought on a special contract under seal which set out the sum due clearly. Yet a defendant might wage his law, a possibility which was surely a nonsense by 1750. Further, at one time the plaintiff was required to recover the whole amount which he claimed or nothing at all: however, before mid-nineteenth century it was settled that the plaintiff might prove and recover less than the sum stated. Debt could not be used to recover damages for breach of contract for, in legal consideration, it was confined to the recovery of a debt and not for compensation in damages. In fact debt, which as an action was not necessarily based upon contract at all, was not so much contractual in nature as a consequence of contract.

2) Covenant. Covenant to do a direct act or to omit one, which also was contained in a deed, was another type of express contract. The writ of covenant directed the sheriff to command the defendant generally to keep his covenant with the plaintiff or to show good cause to the contrary. If he continued in breach, or if the covenant were already so broken that it could no longer be performed specifically, the plaintiff might recover damages in proportion to the injury which he had sustained as a result of such breach. Covenant was used most often in respect of leases, mortgages, articles of agreement, charterparties of affreightment, indentures of apprenticeship, etc.

3) Promise or assumpsit. A promise was in the nature of a verbal covenant which wanted nothing but the solemnity of writing and sealing to make it absolutely the same. The remedy was an action on the case for the assumpsit or undertaking of the defendant. Some express agreements were deemed to be so important that, by virtue of the Statute of Frauds (1677), a note or memorandum in writing signed by the party to be charged therewith was required. Especially useful in view of the limitations of debt, which lay originally only for a fixed and determinate sum, was the action upon an implied promise for indebitatus assumpsit. Such an action was brought not to compel a specific performance of the contract but to recover damages for its non performance. I might declare that the defendant, being indebted to me for £30, undertook or promised to pay it but failed to do so. I might then assess my damages at such sum as I pleased and the jury might allow me either the whole or a lesser sum in damages.

ii) *A law of contracts.* For Blackstone the most usual contracts 'whereby the right of chattels personal may be acquired' were (1) sale or exchange (2) bailment (3) hiring and borrowing, and (4) debt. That classification may have been 'inelegantly selected and incongruously assembled', in Fifoot's words, yet it reflected the view of contemporary lawyers who, in pursuance of the traditional learning, as yet were not thinking in terms of a general theory of contract. However, in that Blackstone defined contract as 'an agreement, upon sufficient consideration, to do or not to do a particular thing', he offered later lawyers, who were to work towards a general theory of contract, a conceptual base upon which they might build. Within the flexible framework of assumpsit, that was a challenge to which they were soon to respond with some enthusiasm.

iii) *Fair dealing*. The England and Wales of the mid-eighteenth century was a relatively static and primarily agricultural society. Transactions were for the most part proprietary in their nature. Blackstone devotes the whole of one of his four volumes to a discussion of the law of property and even his relatively brief discussion of contract tends to be proprietary in its nature. At the same time the law played a considerable role in determining what amounted to justice or fair dealing in particular cases. A seventeenth-century Lord Chancellor had maintained that, 'The Chancery mends no man's bargain.'[13] Yet equity might act in various ways. The medieval Chancery had sought to support good faith and honest dealing with the result that Chancery might well regard a failure to carry out a promise as equivalent to bad faith. There was the question also of the extent to which Chancery might intervene to deny the enforcement of an unconscionable bargain with the result that a trader, who had not made use of a bond, might be unable to obtain the benefit of a bargain which he had struck. In like manner it was believed generally that a sound price given for a horse was tantamount to a warranty of soundness.[14] Similarly, a community view of a fair wage might be arrived at in that the servant was governed in that respect by the locally enforced concept of a fair wage rather than by the terms of a bargain freely arrived at between his employer and himself. His position rested upon status rather than upon contract.[15]

iv) *The rise of* caveat emptor. During the second half of the eighteenth century the equitable concept of substantial justice, which was prepared to examine the fairness of a particular bargain, was first questioned and then rejected. Now parties would obtain that for which they had bargained: the law would not annul a contract because everything had not been conducted within the bounds of a perfect sincerity. Lord Mansfield, who had been the apostle of a new commercial approach to legal problems, suggested that there must either be an express warranty of soundness, or fraud in the seller, in order to maintain an action.[16] The old approach of substantial justice was soon to be rejected outright. It was found to be, as a court put it at the turn of the century, a loose and unsatisfactory ground of decision.[17] Quite soon thereafter Baron Parke was emphatic upon the point that a purchaser could not recover unless he proved fraud on the part of the seller. In 1849 this outstanding common law judge even maintained that there was no implied undertaking on the part of a vendor that he was passing good title.[18]

Despite the existence of some common law authority of respectable antiquity which suggested that the promise, undertaking or agreement, which formed the basis of assumpsit, founded a like absolute liability, this was a substantially new approach. It was an approach which Adam Smith made both widely popular and intellectually respectable. It was an approach which was well suited to a commercial and individualistic age which was intent on dispensing with old restraints.

13 Lord Nottingham in *Maynard v Moseley* (1676) 3 Swan 651 at 655.
14 *Parkinson v Lee* (1802) 2 East 314.
15 See chap. 14 for an outline of the law regarding customary wages.
16 *Stuart v Wilkins* (1778) 1 Doug 18, contrast *Parkinson v Lee* (1802) 2 East 314.
17 *Parkinson v Lee* (1802) 2 East 314.
18 *Early v Garrett* (1829) 9 B & C 928, *Morley v Attenborough* (1849) 3 Exch 500.

c) *A classic theory of contract*

i) *Introduction.* Contemporary political and economic theory, continental theories of contract, a spirit of abstraction, and the appearance during the nineteenth century of persuasive academic texts on contract reshaped, and added to, old doctrine. The result was the rise and eventual dominance of a general theory of contract.

ii) *The new philosophy and freedom of contract.* Political and economic theory demanded an end to artifical restraints upon the individual. The role of the state was to be minimal: each individual was to be the best judge of his own interests. The philosophies of Adam Smith and of Jeremy Bentham had become highly influential. Their philosophy was captured in a general manner in the Report of a Select Committee on Gaming Laws which commented in 1844 upon some of the older laws which sought to protect people against the consequences of their own improvidence, to prescribe what clothes people should wear and what games they should play. The Committee concluded:

> 'Such regulations are out of date; and nobody now disputes the opinion of Adam Smith, that governments ought not to pretend to watch over the economy of private people, and to restrain their expense by sumptuary laws; but if that if they look well after their own expenses, they may safely trust private people with theirs.'[19]

Individual liberty was the watchword: contract was its legal spearhead. The aim, as Dicey has told us, was to secure to every person as much liberty as was consistent with giving the same amount of liberty to every other citizen; it was an aim which included the striking off of every unnecessary fetter which law or custom imposed upon the free action of an individual citizen. Statute repealed protectionist measures such as the crimes of forestalling and regrating and of usury. Other statutes such as the Marriage Act 1835 and the Combination Acts 1824-25 expressed an affirmative view of the new concept of freedom of contract.[20] Naturally the courts played their part. Usually third parties were not to inquire into the merits of an agreement. Agreements were presumed to have been concluded between equals — the role of the courts was simply to interpret that agreement, as an expression of the intention of the parties, and to enforce it. In a classic passage a Victorian judge affirmed such an approach, when he said:

> 'if there is one thing more than another which public policy requires, it is that men of full age and competent understanding shall have the utmost liberty of contracting and that their contracts, when entered into freely and voluntarily, shall be held sacred and shall be enforced by courts of justice'.[1]

For lawyers the concept of freedom of contract was simply indicative of the general approach which they should follow. At a time when the whole law of civil liability was being re-shaped, even such a general philosophy could be influential with regard to particular matters. For example, the reason why the master was

---

19   Report from the Select Committee on Gaming no. 297 (1844) p. iv.
20   A.V. Dicey *Law and Public Opinion in England during the Nineteenth Century* (2nd edn, 1962) p. 190.
1   Jessel MR in *Printing and Numerical Registering Co v Sampson* (1875) 19 LR Eq 462. See Sir D. Hughes Parry *The Sanctity of Contracts in English Law.*

said not to be liable at common law for an injury done to a servant because of the negligence of a fellow servant — the rule in *Priestley v Fowler*[2] — was rooted in contract. The injured workman was presumed to have entered into his contract of employment with a full knowledge of the risks involved. Similarly, in the running down cases it could be difficult for a plaintiff to recover in the absence of a contract. For such plaintiffs relief came only through the medium of remedial statutes and an expanded doctrine of tort.

iii) *The influence of continental treatises*. During the first half of the nineteenth century the lawyers, like everybody else, were exposed to the new political and economic doctrine. They were exposed also to a new kind of legal treatise, often continental, which stressed general principles rather than the more mechanical listing of precedents which was characteristic of legal texts in this country. The debt of our law to such treatises, although it is rarely acknowledged, is substantial. The work of Pothier was especially influential. Just how great a debt our law owed to the work of Pothier and other continental authors may be assessed easily enough by glancing at a traditional, yet able, practitioners' text such as that by Addison, which was published in 1849. Continental sources are acknowledged there in some abundance. Nor was this merely introduced in order to justify a decision already arrived at, after the manner of Lord Mansfield or Lord Stowell. The continental writers contributed substantially to the introduction of new doctrines into the developing modern law of contract.[3]

iv) *Offer and acceptance*. To that source we may attribute the importance which was to be attached in the formation of contract to an offer having been made by one party and accepted by the other party to a contract. The importance of such an acceptance was suggested, albeit tentatively, only as late as 1818 in *Adams v Lindsell*. The facts were that as they had put the wrong address on their written offer to the plaintiffs, the defendants did not receive the plaintiffs' response until a few days after they had anticipated receiving it. The defendants denied that there could be any binding contract between the parties until the plaintiffs' answer had actually been received. The court denied this, saying:

> 'if that were so, no contract could ever be completed by the post. For if the defendants were not bound by their offer when accepted by the plaintiffs till the answer was received, then the plaintiffs ought not to be bound till after they had received the notification that the defendants had received their answer and assented to it. And so it might go on ad infinitum. The defendants must be considered in law as making, during every instant of the time their letter was travelling, the same identical offer to the plaintiffs; and then the contract is completed by the acceptance of it by the latter. Then as to the delay in notifying the acceptance, that arises entirely from the mistake of the defendants, and it therefore must be taken as against them, that the plaintiffs' answer was received in course of post.'[4]

Here, then, was a decision on the particular facts of a contract by

2   (1837) 3 M & W 1.
3   C.G. Addison *Treatise on the Law of Contracts* (2nd edn, 1849), A.W.B. Simpson 'Innovation in Nineteenth Century Contract Law' (1975) 91 LQR 247 at 250.
4   (1818) 1 B & Ald 681.

correspondence, which was rooted in a particular view of commercial convenience rather than in theory or ideology, although its origins are to be found in Pothier's treatise. Yet in retrospect at least *Adams v Lindsell* was to be seen as an illustration of a general rule that, at least in the case of bilateral contracts, there must be an offer by one party and an acceptance by the other party. To Anson especially, later in the nineteenth century, this became an obvious general principle. It reflected a consensus theory of contract. It was a suitable means, in addition to the requirement of consideration, of analysing the idea of bargain which was central to thinking on contract. New cases blessed that approach. Old precedents were sought which appeared to justify it. In fact it amounted to new law.

Under the old law an action had lain for the breach of a promise. In the nineteenth century we moved, as Simpson has reminded us,[5] from that essentially one-sided conception of a promise broken to an essentially two-sided notion of a contract broken. It was an approach which went well with the new rhetoric of contract which attached so much importance to determining the intention of the parties to such a contract.

v) *The intention of the parties.* The more austere legal advocates of the new philosophy during the nineteenth century even advocated a subjective approach to contract. The courts were to implement the actual intention of the parties. The lawyers wish to establish some degree of certainty made it unlikely that so extreme a doctrine would be adopted. The parol evidence rule which provided that, where there was no ambiguity in a written contract, verbal evidence was inadmissible to annul or substantially vary it was well established in 1841.[6] Further, as the nineteenth century progressed, the judges became increasingly ready, often with the laudable view of giving business efficacy to agreements, to attribute to parties to a contract an intention, i.e. an implied term, which in reality had surely never occurred to them. In many such cases it was surely misleading to regard the court as implementing the intention of the parties in other than a technical sense. Although it had long been necessary for the courts to determine what the parties had intended, initially there was no trace in law of any necessity to show an intention to create legal relations, a quite different point, as an independent element in the formation of contract. Once again it was the authors who first enunciated such a doctrine; once again they based themselves upon continental influences; once again the courts followed. The acceptance of the doctrine in the second half of the nineteenth century was a manifestation in legal terms of contemporary ideology which stressed the importance of the individual will, although its role in contract was less than clear. However, the new doctrine did help to make clear those agreements which were to have no effect in law. This was quite helpful in respect of social engagements which few wished to see made enforceable in law.[7] Many critics believed that the doctrine was less helpful in the case of the powerful corporation, which may have been contracting with an individual consumer, and which used the doctrine to

5 Sir D. Hughes Parry *The Sanctity of Contracts in English Law.*
6 E. Chitty *The Commercial and General Lawyer* (2nd edn, 1841) p. 642.
7 *Balfour v Balfour* [1919] 2 KB 571. Cf. *Carlill v Carbolic Smoke Ball Co.* On the reception of the doctrine see *Carlill v Carbolic Smoke Ball Co* [1893] 1 QB 256.

evade responsibility before the courts by denying any contractual intention on its part to allow such recourse to the courts. Such an approach reflected well enough the nineteenth-century's approach to freedom of contract: it did not reflect the twentieth-century reality of the individual's inability to vary the standard form contracts of large corporations which often enjoyed a near monopoly of power.

vi) *Damages.* A similar tension between the rhetoric of the law and professional tradition, which sought to ensure a measure of certainty in the law, was evident in the law regarding damages. Here, too, homage was paid to the intention of the parties. Yet here, too, the law also tended to impose its own objective values.

When the contract was silent as to damages, it was the duty of the jury to reduce damages to a pecuniary value. Initially, the law offered little assistance to the jury. It was only in *Hadley v Baxendale* (1854)[8] that the courts established a general principle for the assessment of damages. Due reference was then paid to what the parties had contemplated. Yet the standard adopted was largely objective.

Baron Parke outlined the general principle in 1848 when he said:

> 'The rule of the common law is, that where a party sustains a loss by reason of a breach of contract, he is, so far as money can do it, to be placed in the same situation, with respect to damages, as if the contract had been performed.'[9]

That dictum failed to cast any light upon the limits, if any, which were to be placed upon a plaintiff obtaining the full benefit of his bargain. The law was feeling its way towards a solution to that problem by distinguishing between general damages, nominal damages, and special damages. Special damages might be awarded in respect of consequences which were not the 'immediate, necessary, and invariable result of the breach of contract, but may or may not exist, and be recoverable according to the particular circumstances of each case'. Recovery was to be allowed for all damages which were 'the fair and natural result', or 'the necessary and natural consequences', of the defendant's breach of contract. In 1849 the writer of a leading text offered the following example:

> 'If a cable is sold with a warranty, and the cable on trial does not answer the warranty, and is broken and lost, the general damage is the price paid for the cable. If the purchaser, relying on the warranty, has attached an anchor to the cable, and has consequently lost both his anchor and cable, special damage is sustained to the extent of the value of the anchor, which may be recovered in addition to the price paid for the cable.'[10]

Yet what was a 'necessary and natural consequence', or a 'fair and natural result', of the defendant's breach of contract? In the example given above would the plaintiff have been able to recover special damages if the broken cable had led to the plaintiff's ship damaging other ships? It was in just such terms, which went to the question of the remoteness of damage, that in 1854 the Court of Exchequer dealt with what became the leading case of *Hadley v Baxendale*.

8 (1854) 9 Exch 341, 23 LJ Exch 179. G. Washington 'Damages in Contract at Common Law' (1932) 48 LQR 90.
9 *Robinson v Harman* (1848) 1 Exch 850.
10 C.G. Addison *Wrongs and their Remedies: being A Treatise on the Law of Torts* (5th edn, 1879) p. 1058. Cf. W. Tidd *The Practice of the Court of King's Bench in Personal Actions* (3rd edn, 1803) pp. 798, 842.

Hadley v Baxendale established that the damges to which a plaintiff was entitled were such as the parties might have supposed to be the natural result of a breach of the contract; they were to be such as might have been in the contemplation of the parties at the time when the contract was made. The recovery of any special loss which might accrue to the plaintiff, but which did not flow naturally and obviously from the breach of contract, was to be dependent upon express terms in the contract itself.[11] To that extent the case was at one with contemporary theory regarding the enforcement of the intention of the parties. The case did make it clear, however, that the intention of the parties was to be determined by an objective standard. It is in this factor that much of the importance of *Hadley* lies. That principle was established after due consideration by a strong court.

What are we to make of it? It is clear that for some years the judges had been attempting to establish a principle regarding remoteness of damage. It was surprising that an acccptable general principle was not formulated before 1854. Once it did arrive, overseas influence was clear enough — Pothier's influence is evident. We know also that Baron Parke, who played a part in the decision in *Hadley*, was familiar with American writing upon damages. American courts had gone to some lengths to limit business risks and so standardise costs for the emergent industries by adopting an objective standard. It is not surprising that a similar principle took root in the England and Wales of mid-nineteenth century.

vii) *Consideration.* Amidst such concessions to contemporary political and economic thought and to the grafting of concepts of civil law, on to the body of the common law, one at least of the elements of contract at common law remained unchanged. Indeed, lawyers were to attach a fresh importance to consideration.

The term 'consideration' has a long history. Yet the nineteenth century was well advanced before the lawyers began to explore its meaning with any degree of precision: even as late as 1936 a distinguished law lord acknowledged that there was 'considerable uncertainty' as to what was meant by it.[12] We find, therefore, that especially during the period 1750 to 1840 there was some uncertainty as to what role, if any consideration was to play in an emergent general theory of contract. Lord Mansfield made the point clearly enough in 1765 when he said:

> 'I take it, that the ancient notion about the want of consideration was for the sake of evidence only: for when it is reduced into writing, as in covenants, specialties, bonds etc. there was no objection to the want of consideration. And the Statute of Frauds proceeded upon the same principle. In commercial cases amongst merchants, the want of consideration is not an objection.'[13]

In that case of *Pillans v Van Mierop* the facts were that the plaintiffs, who were merchants in Holland, agreed with White, a merchant in Ireland, that they, the plaintiffs, would accept White's bill for £800, provided that White gave them a confirmed credit upon a house of rank in London. White named the defendants:

11 *Flureau v Thornhill* (1775) 2 Wm Black 108. M.J. Horwitz *The Transformation of American Law 1780-1860.*
12 Lord Wright 'Ought the Doctrine of Consideration to be Abolished from the Common Law?' (1936) 49 HLR 1225 at 1226.
13 *Pillans and Rose v Van Mierop and Hopkins* (1765) 3 Burr 1664.

the plaintiffs paid the money. The plaintiffs subsequently wrote to the defendants, Van Mierop in London, who agreed to allow the plaintiffs to withdraw £800 upon the credit of White. Meanwhile White became bankrupt and the defendants then forbade the plaintiffs to draw upon them. Upon the defendants doing so, the plaintiffs refused to pay their bills. Upon trial a verdict was found for the defendants. Upon cause being shewn counsel for the defendants argued that the plaintiffs had given credit to White more than a month before the defendants had agreed to accept their draft. Therefore, the consideration was past and done before their promise was made. Accordingly, they argued that for one man to undertake 'to pay another man's debt' was a void undertaking unless there was some consideration for such undertaking: a mere general promise without benefit to the promisor or loss to the promisee was a *nudum pactum*. However, King's Bench found for the plaintiff.

Lord Mansfield acknowledged that this was 'a matter of great consequence to trade and commerce, in every light'. He pointed out that there had been no fraud. Further, both the plaintiffs and White had written to Van Mierop who had answered that they would honour the plaintiffs' draughts. This was, then, a question of law: a *nudum pactum* did not exist in the usage and law of merchants. Lord Mansfield then asserted that consideration went to evidence only and affirmed that if a man agreed that he would do the formal part, the law looked upon it, in the case of an acceptance of a bill, as if actually done. He concluded:

> 'This is an engagement "to accept the bill, if there was a necessity to accept it; and to pay it, when due": and they could not afterwards retract. It would be very destructive to trade, and to trust in commercial dealing, if they could. There was nothing of *nudum pactum* mentioned to the jury; nor was it, I dare say, at all in their idea or contemplation.'[14]

The report of Lord Mansfield's judgment does not cite a single case nor does it record that he answered directly defendant counsel's point regarding past consideration. A distinction between written and oral contracts was suggested and the importance of trust in commercial cases was stressed. However, other judgments were also delivered so that it is virtually impossible to extract any clear *ratio decidendi* from *Pillans v Van Mierop*. Even so, in subsequent cases Lord Mansfield sought to apply and even to extend his view of the importance that was to be attached to the intention of the parties and to moral obligation.[15]

Some of the judges opposed Lord Mansfield's view. In *Rann v Hughes* Lord Chief Baron Skynner observed:

> 'It is undoubtedly true that every man is by the law of nature bound to fulfil his engagements. It is equally true that the law of this country supplies no means, nor affords any remedy, to compel the performance of an agreement made without sufficient consideration.'[16]

In fact *Rann v Hughes* was not fully reported. The report did not in any event appear for some years, and it did leave open the question of just what would amount to 'sufficient consideration'. Even more influential was the reporters' note to *Wennal v Adney*,[17] often cited over the years, which argued that the

---

14   Ibid. at p. 1669.
15   *Trueman v Fenton* (1777) 2 Cowp 544, *Atkins v Hill* (1775) 1 Cowp 284.
16   4 Bro Parl Cas 27, (1778) 7 TR 350.
17   (1802) 3 Bos & P 247.

Mansfield approach should be confined to a number of exceptional stated cases: any wider application was denied on the ground that in each of the cases cited in support of such a wider application the party bound by the promise had received a benefit previous to the promise.

The matter does not appear to have been settled until as late as 1840 in *Eastwood v Kenyon*. Lord Denman CJ denied that the Mansfield approach was good law and went on to offer a policy statement in support of the rejection, saying:

> 'The enforcement of such promises by law, however plausibly reconciled by the desire to effect all conscientious engagements, might be attended with mischievous consequences to society; one of which would be the frequent preference of voluntary undertakings to claims for just debts. Suits would thereby be multiplied, and voluntary undertakings would also be multiplied, to the prejudice of real creditors. The temptations of executors would be much increased by the prevalence of such a doctrine, and the faithful discharge of their duty rendered more difficult.'[18]

Oddly enough, therefore, at a time when we might have supposed the influence of a laissez-faire type of market economy to have begun really to influence the law in seeking to implement the intention of the parties to the contract, subject only to the most decisive public policy factors, we find instead that the courts rather insist upon the presence of a real even though not an adequate consideration. This was so even though an absence of consideration might on occasion even defeat the intention of the parties. Why, then, did the courts re-affirm the technical view of consideration in *Eastwood v Kenyon*? Lord Denman CJ justified his decision in terms of broad public policy. It was not a convincing approach. The law already granted the validity of gratuitous promises, if those promises were contained in a deed. In principle, therefore, the law was not opposed to enforcing gratuitous promises. Further, it was surely not beyond the courts to determine, in the light of the parties' intentions, as did the continental courts, which agreements had been entered into with a view to their being legally enforceable.

The decision of the court in 1840 may have been influenced by the implementation of the Hilary Rules of 1834. Those rules had made special pleading even more important in practice. Now it was essential to distinguish far more clearly between the forms of action. The result was that, as Lord Denman's judgment in *Eastwood v Kenyon* illustrated, there was now an increased respect for the old learning of the common law, despite the fact that in Eastwood the plea was the general issue.[19] Yet at least it was clear now that consideration must be real, although not necessarily adequate.

In 1936 Lord Wright concluded that consideration ought to find no place in contract law. The true public policy was to ensure that 'people should keep their plighted word'.[20] In 1937 Lord Wright was chairman of a law revision committee which reported on consideration. Despite the strength of Lord Wright's views,

---

18 (1840) 11 Ad & El 438.
19 W.S. Holdsworth 'The New Rules of Pleading of Hilary Term 1834' (1923) 1 Camb LJ 261, W.S. Holdsworth *History of English Law* vol 8, p. 38.
20 Lord Wright 'Ought the Doctrine of Consideration to be Abolished from the Common Law?' (1936) 49 HLR 1225, 1253.

the committee did not so much recommend the abolition of the doctrine of consideration as its amendment. Even so its proposals aroused considerable opposition. It was conceded that some of the rules or accretions of consideration e.g. the rule in *Foakes v Beer* were unfortunate.[1] Certainly it was true that it would be impossible simply to abolish consideration without making further consequential amendments to other aspects of contract. However, there was to be no reform after the Wright report. Advocates of consideration would continue to deplore the 'accretions and the somewhat unfortunate air of learning with which it [consideration] has been invested' but would applaud it as 'nothing more or less than the sign and symbol of bargain'. Such advocacy tended to ignore whether such a concept was necessary to a modern law of contract.

The result was that the vaguely defined and flexible procedural concept of consideration, as it had been in 1750, became the focal point of a freshly-formulated general theory of contract during the nineteenth century. That this legalistic, albeit fluid, concept of bargain, rather than intention, was to be the touchstone of a new doctrine was a tribute both to the lawyers' influence and conservatism as well, perhaps, as to a certain insensitivity to the overriding public interest in ensuring rather that parties kept their plighted word than that they simply observed technical formalities — and on occasion used those technicalities to avoid keeping their word. It was all the more appropriate, therefore, that in the late 1940s equitable principles — the traditional means of softening the technical rigours of the common law — should be used to mitigate one particular injustice which had been caused in the name of consideration. This was the rule in *Foakes v Beer* (1884) which held that the payment of a smaller sum was no consideration for the discharge of a larger sum. In the *High Trees case* (1947)[2] the plaintiff landlord of a block of flats had promised to forego part of the rent while the flats were empty during the Second World War. Denning J held, obiter, that the plaintiff was bound by his promise. First, he relied upon an old equitable principle which held that in circumstances in which a plaintiff had led the other party to suppose that the plaintiff would not rely on his strict legal rights, then a court will not allow the plaintiff to enforce those rights, if that would be inequitable, having regard to the dealings which had taken place between the parties. Secondly, the *High Trees* principle might be used only as a defence: it could not found a cause of action. As the learned judge said some years later, the doctrine of consideration was too firmly fixed to be overthrown by a side wind.[3] Yet this bold and ingenious judicial use of old, equitable principles had shown that on occasion at least the courts might themselves tidy up at least the rough edges of the common law rather than wait, possibly in vain, for the legislature to act. It was a suitably exciting and promising note upon which to finish the first half of the twentieth century — and to begin the second half.

d) *The erosion of the classic theory of contracts*

i) *Introduction.* The freedom and the sanctity of contract were persuasive and

---

1   *Foakes v Beer* (1884) 9 App Cas 605 affirmed that a promise to pay less than the amount due could not in law be consideration.
2   *Central London Property Trust Ltd v High Trees House Ltd* [1947] KB 130. Cf. *Hughes v Metropolitan Railway Co* (1877) 2 App Cas 439.
3   *Combe v Combe* [1951] 2 KB 215, [1951] 1 All ER 767.

powerful general principles but they could never be absolute. It was impossible for the courts ever to enforce a contract which appeared to be contrary to public policy, however ill-defined that concept was. Yet if the courts were prepared, on the ground of public policy, to refuse to allow a contracting party to benefit by his fraud, to what extent should the courts frown also upon misrepresentation? To what extent should they be prepared to imply terms such as merchantable quality into a contract or to nullify a contract on the grounds of frustration or of mistake? During the second half of the nineteenth century the courts began increasingly to erode the classical theory of contract, as they sought to do justice to the parties in such cases.

ii) *Illegality.* It was inevitable that, even at a time when the virtues of freedom of contract were stressed, many agreements were deemed in law to be either illegal or unenforceable. That might be the case if such agreements were contrary to law, justice, morality, or public policy. Lord Mansfield stated in 1775 that the principle of public policy was that no court would lend its aid to a man who founded his cause of action upon an immoral or illegal act.[4] Numerous such agreements were illegal at common law. Examples were contracts for the sale of libellous prints, for printing an immoral publication, or for the rent of a house knowingly let for the purposes of prostitution. Into the same category came agreements which were contrary to public policy such as a stipulation in general restraint of trade; as an engagement not to carry on a particular business in any part of England; or in restraint of marriage generally; or a contract to pay a commission for recommending a customer; or a contract which had a tendency to prevent the due course of justice by dropping a criminal prosecution. Even more interesting is the fact that the lawyer of mid-nineteenth century also classi- fied under the general head of illegality cases where a person had been induced to enter into a contract by fraud or gross misrepresentation on the part of the person with whom he contracted. Statute also rendered a large number of agree- ments illegal. Usurious contracts and gaming contracts are notable examples.[5]

Lawyers were well aware of the anomalies and difficulties, which were inherent in the legal position. It was distasteful that a wrongdoer might benefit from his or her own wrongdoing, as might a prostitute in the example given above, who refused to pay rent. Shifts in public opinion also made this an area in which judges might well tread warily. The uncertainty and the breadth of this necessary qualification of the general principles of contract meant that it amounted to a qualification of the general principles themselves. Yet by and large the nineteenth-century judges showed remarkable loyalty to the classic theory.

iii) *Fraud, misrepresentation, mistake.* It was of the essence of the classic theory that no third party should pronounce upon the merits of a bargain. Accordingly, the judges showed a marked reluctance to extend the bounds of fraud, misrepre- sentation or mistake. It is true that contracts of insurance had long been *uberrimae fidei* (of the utmost good faith). It is true also that Lord Eldon suggested that if a single word were dropped which tended to mislead a party,

---

4 *Holman v Johnson* (1775) 1 Cowp 341, C.H.S. Fifoot *Lord Mansfield* p. 122.
5 E. Chitty *The Commercial and General Lawyer* (2nd edn, 1841) p. 661.

the principle of caveat emptor would not apply. More usually the position was
that:

> 'A collateral statement, made at the time of entering into a contract, but
> not embodied in it, must, in order to invalidate the contract on the ground
> of its being a fraudulent statement, be shown not only to have been false,
> but to have been known to be so by the party making it, and that the other
> party was thereby induced to enter into the contract.'[6]

Neither mere non-communication nor innocent misrepresentation was enough
to avoid the contract. Yet clearly the bounds of this doctrine were potentially
flexible in that by a process of construction the judges might well take so
generous a view of the bounds of fraud, misrepresentation or mistake as
effectively to change the law towards a view of substantial justice in practice if
not in theory. The judges proved rather reluctant to do so, despite the popularity
of the consensus or will theory of contract which, in logic should have led to a
fully fledged doctrine of mistake. However, in *Smith v Hughes* (1871)[7] the court
held that there was no legal obligation on the vendor to inform the purchaser
that he was under a mistake, not induced by the act of the vendor. As late as 1889
in *Derry v Peek* the House of Lords even took a decidedly restrictive view of
fraud. Lord Herschell went so far as to say that fraud meant a false statement
'made knowingly, or without belief in its truth, or recklessly, careless whether it
be true or false'.[8] Negligence was not enough, although prior to *Derry v Peek*
there had been some authority at least which suggested that in some circumstances an action for negligent misrepresentation could be maintained. Many
regarded the decision as having 'mischievous consequences' and some years later
legislation was introduced which countered the effect of *Derry v Peek* in respect
of the class of company cases in which it had a risen.[9] Of course *Derry v Peek*
continued to represent the position at common law. The twentieth century
judges showed a similar reluctance to extend the bounds of mistake,[10] although it
is true that in some circumstances equity was prepared to grant relief by way of
rescission of the contract and in such circumstances equity was prepared to adopt
a rather more liberal interpretation of fraud. Even so the judicial reluctance to
extend the bounds of misrepresentation had been quite marked — an affirmation of nineteenth century market place values in a mass-producing twentieth
century world.

iv) *The implied term*. The most marked erosion of the classic theory coincided
with a slow but steadily increasing use of the implied term. For some years it is
true that it had been possible to ground liability in indebitatus asssumpsit upon
an implied promise. In addition trade usage or local custom might qualify the
express terms which had been used in a contract.[11] For example, a tenant who
quit his farm at Candlemas or Christmas was entitled to reap corn which had

---

6   *Turner v Harvey* (1821) Jac 169, *Moens v Heyworth* (1842) 10 M & W 147. Cf. *Bannerman v
    White* (1861) 10 CB (n.s.) 8444.
7   (1871) 6 LRQB 597.
8   (1889) 14 App Cas 337 at 374. Contrast *Lindsay v Cundy* (1877) 2 QBD 96.
9   W.W. Kerr *On Fraud and Mistake* (6th edn, 1928).
10 *Bell v Lever Bros* [1932] AC 161.
11 E. Chitty *The Commercial and General Lawyer* (2nd edn, 1841) p. 642.

been sown the preceding autumn.[12] In all such cases the presumption was said to be that the parties had intended to contract with reference to such promise or to such known usages.[13] It followed that, since the courts held that they were simply giving effect to the intention of the parties, they would not imply any term which was at variance, or even inconsistent, with the terms of the contract.[14] Despite such practices it is clear that the judicial approach to the use of the implied term was cautious. The principle of caveat emptor dominated the law of contract during the first half of the nineteenth century, although increasingly that principle was subjected to exceptions as the judges sought to do justice in particular cases. Even so, it was as late as 1864 before a court held that, at all events in the case of goods sold in an open shop or warehouse, there was an implied warranty on the part of the vendor that he was the owner of the goods.[15]

At much the same time the courts became rather bolder in their use of the implied term in other types of case. The establishment of an independent doctrine of frustration of contract illustrates admirably such a shift in judicial attitudes.

If it were no longer possible to perform a contract the courts classified originally such impossibility of performance on the basis of an implied term. For example, in *Taylor v Caldwell* the court faced up to a situation in which a music hall, which had been previously hired for a number of concerts, was destroyed by fire. Blackburn J said:

> 'There seems to be no doubt that where there is a positive contract to do a thing, not in itself unlawful, the contractor must perfom it or pay damages for not doing it, although in consequence of unforeseen accidents, the performance of his contract has become unexpectedly burthensome or even impossible.... But this rule is only applicable when the contract is positive and absolute, and not subject to any condition either express or implied; ... In the present case, looking at the whole contract, we find that the parties contracted on the basis of the continued existence of the music hall at the time when the concerts were given; that being essential to their performance. We think therefore, that the music hall having ceased to exist, without fault of either party, both parties are excused.'[16]

In these circumstances, therefore, Blackburn J was prepared to hold that the contractor was not liable by implying a term into the contract. As the courts, seeking to do justice in the particular case, became more assured in their use of the new doctrine of frustration, it became clear that they were going beyond the intention of the parties. Accordingly, in 1941 the House of Lords recognised that the doctrine, now called the doctrine of frustration of contract, had been extended beyond the bounds of the implied term. Lord Wright said:

> 'in ascertaining the meaning of the contract and its applicaton to the actual occurrences the court has to decide, not what the parties actually

---

12 *Wiggleworth v Dallison* (1799) 1 Smith LC 598, cited in W.R. Anson *Principles of the English Law of Contract* (3rd edn, 1884) p. 241.

13 *Hutton v Warren* (1836) 1 M & W 466 at 475, per Parke B. Cf. *Mollet v Robinson* (1872) LR 7 CP 84, per Blackburn J.

14 See generally Sir D. Hughes Parry *The Sanctity of Contracts in English Law* pp. 39 ff.

15 *Eicholz v Bannister* (1864) 12 CBNS 708. Contrast *Laing v Fidgeon* (1815) 6 Taunt 108 and *Jones v Bright* (1820) 5 Bing 533.

16 (1863) 3 B & S 826.

intended, but what as reasonable men they should have intended. The court personifies for this purpose the reasonable man.'[17]

However, it was only rarely that the courts sought such an objective rationale for the use of the implied term itself. In *The Moorcock* (1889) Bowen LJ referred to the wish of the courts to give business efficacy to agreements and said:

> 'The question is what inference is to be drawn where the parties are dealing with each other on the assumption that the negotiations are to have some fruit, and where they say nothing about the burden of this unseen peril, leaving the law to raise such inferences as are reasonable from the very nature of the transaction.'[18]

A liberal interpretation of that dictum would indeed have conferred upon courts a power to make contracts for parties. On occasion the courts were invited to do just that: the Sale of Goods Act 1893 illustrates how extensive a use of the implied term had become accepted at that time. However, on the whole during the twentieth century the courts resisted that temptation. The dominant view, as expressed in 1939, was that which suggested that a court might imply a term only in circumstances in which, 'if while the parties were making their bargain an officious bystander were to suggest some express provision for it in their agreement, they would testily suppress him with a common "Oh, of course." '[19] Nevertheless, it is clear that during the twentieth century an increased use of the implied term had brought about a situation in which very often the courts chose to offer their own interpretation of what the parties had actually intended. Often the test of what was reasonable was as important in contract as it was in tort. It was all a far cry from that principled approach to the classic theory of contract which sought to implement the actual intention of the parties.

v) *The adhesion contract*. During the twentieth century a particular form of contract, the contrat d'adhésion, came into prominence. It was seen as a phenomenon which was characteristic of the mass-producing world. One party fixed the conditions of the contract in advance: the contract might then be accepted by anybody who was prepared to accept it in toto. Typically the party which fixed the conditions was a large company which, like a railway company, might be in a strong position to impose its will upon a reluctant customer. Increasingly, it began to seem unfair that such companies should be able to impose unreasonable conditions, especially wide exemptions from liability, upon captive customers. What, then, was the role in this area of law of any theory of freedom of contract?

In fact no theory of freedom of contract had any direct influence upon adhesion contracts. The origin of adhesion contracts lies in commercial necessities and convenience, as adjusted from time to time by the force of public opinion through the courts in terms of what was fair business practice. The issue arose in a modern form when common carriers began to use notices to limit the strict liability to which they were then subject. It was uncertain whether that

---

17 *Joseph Constantine Steamship Line Ltd v Imperial Smelting Corporation Ltd* [1942] AC 154 at 185.
18 (1889) 14 PD 64 at 68, 70.
19 *Shirlaw v Southern Foundries (1926) Ltd* [1939] 2 KB 206 at 227, [1939] 2 All ER 113 at 124.

liability was contractual in nature or tortious.[20] However, as the question of the validity of carriers notices came before the courts during the period 1800-30, they were regarded as contractual. In 1816 Lord Ellenborough was quite clear upon the point that notices might be used to exclude all responsibility whatsoever on the part of the carrier: 'If the parties in the present case have so contracted, the plaintiff must abide by the agreement and he must be taken to have so contracted if he chooses to send his goods to be carried after notice of the conditions.' Lord Ellenborough then added that 'if this action had been brought 20 years ago, the defendant would have been liable'.[1] However, the courts sought to insist that the effect of the notice should have been 'brought home' to the plaintiff and that clear language should have been used. Even so, the law became uncertain. The Carriers Act 1830 was an attempt to clarify the situation. The carrier was afforded a certain protection in respect of goods which were above £10 in value. On the other hand he was no longer allowed to limit his liability by public notice in respect of other goods.

Of course, the Act had been passed at the beginning of the age of the railway. Many of the cargoes which they carried did not come within the protection afforded the carrier by the Carriers Act 1830. In addition the railways carried passengers, a risky business. Inevitably, the railways sought to impose their own terms. Like the carriers before them they sought to enforce exemption clauses which excluded even a duty to take reasonable care. Public disquiet at this practice led to the enactment of the Railway and Canal Traffic Act 1854. Contracting out was allowed by special contract. However, the terms had to be reasonable and the consignor had to sign the contract. The latter requirement indicated the importance which was attached to the giving of notice, a point which was affirmed in *Parker v SER* (1877).[2] However, now it was no longer necessary to do more than what was reasonably necessary to bring the notice home to the plaintiff, a reversion to the early nineteenth-century position. Very often in the twentieth century a vendor might escape all liability by an appropriate use of language in a manner which would have shocked Lord Ellenborough. In *L' Estrange v Graucob* (1934)[3] an automatic machine failed to work properly. Yet the defendant escaped liability because the written agreement included a clause which stated that 'any express or implied condition, statement or warranty, statutory or otherwise, is hereby excluded'. The courts did attempt on occasion to protect a consumer through strict interpretation. In mid-twentieth century the courts were prepared to hold that an exemption clause did not allow a party to escape the basic duty which he had imposed upon himself when he entered into the contract.[4] By and large, however, during the first half of the twentieth century the courts had refused to police the reasonably satisfactory rules for the incorporation of standard terms which had been worked out during the nineteenth century. 'Freedom of contract, in the context of standard

---

20 In this section I am indebted to two articles by J.N. Adams, namely: 'The Standardisation of Commercial Contracts, or the Contractualisation of Standard Forms' (1978) 7 Anglo-American Law Review 136 and 'The Common Carrier in Legal History' (paper presented to the Fourth British Legal History Conference (1979)).
1 *Leeson v Holt* (1816) 1 Stark 186.
2 (1877) 2 CPD 416.
3 [1934] 2 KB 394, [1934] All ER Rep 16.
4 *Karsales (Harrow) Ltd v Wallis* [1956] 2 All ER 866.

form contracts', writes Adams, 'is not so much a nineteenth century aberration but a twentieth.'

e) *Conclusion*

At the beginning of this section on contract it was asserted that the modern history of contract fell into three periods. That is substantially true, yet clearly there was a considerable amount of overlap between those periods. They were not distinctive in the sense, for example, that at any time the classic theory ruled unchallenged. At the very time when to the lawyers of the day it may have seemed, with the publication of the classic treatises upon contract, that the classic principles were dominant, we can now see with hindsight that considerable exceptions to those classic principles already existed.

Professional traditions have contributed to that development. We should never underestimate the impact of professional tradition: the survival of the doctrine of consideration is some illustration of that point. There is, too, the very proper concern of the practitioner with regard to the manner in which the elements of a contract may be proved. That concern alone made it inevitable that an objective, rather than a subjective, standard should be adopted overall in contract. The concept of freedom of contract operated in a rather more general manner — it set the tone of the debate upon contract rather than settled its specifics. Indeed, one of the most notable features of nineteenth-century contract law i.e. the attempt to adopt a uniform and comprehensive set of general principles, may be attributed rather to the influence of continental treatises. Inevitably, the pragmatic approach of the English lawyer, the wish to do justice in particular cases, the wish to do what was reasonable, led quite obviously to a situation in which classic theory no longer described with any accuracy what the courts did. Further, during the twentieth century an expanded concept of social duty and of equality meant that the classic concept became wholly outmoded. Similarly, the simple fact that there was an extensive standardisation of commercial contracts, including the use of particular forms of contracts in particular industries, made it less realistic to think in terms of one general theory of contract. Increasingly, the general theory of contract appeared to be no more than residual in nature, as — for example — employment contracts and building contracts assumed features which were peculiar to themselves. In mid-twentieth century it was far too early to suggest that contract was dead in England and Wales.[5] Yet clearly the law was then entering upon a period of change as dramatic as that which had faced Lord Mansfield two hundred years earlier.

3 Tort

a) *Introduction*

In medieval days the law was concerned primarily to protect interests in land, in chattels, in domestic relationships. Physical security was protected only in so far as a direct and forcible assault was made upon it. Legal protection was offered through the medium of one of the writs of trespass which, by and large, imposed

---

5   G. Gilmore *The Death of Contract*.

liability upon a defendant irrespective of whether the defendant was at fault or blameworthy in any moral sense. This approach was suited well enough to the needs of a slow moving, predominantly agricultural society. New problems were presented by the growth of roads, railways and factories in terms especially of the personal injuries to which so many were now subjected. The law then sought to achieve a balance between doing justice to the injured and seeking to ensure in the public interest, although this was rarely articulated, that the new business interests upon which the prosperity of the whole country was seen to depend, were not unduly impeded. In an age of religion and of individualism it was fitting that the new standard chosen was to be that of fault. Fault or blameworthiness was to be the criterion of a defendant's liability. Negligence was to emerge eventually as an independent tort. Yet those rules of negligence were not applied uniformly in all cases of personal injury. To many it appeared that as a result workmen especially suffered. Finally, legislation was enacted which tended to impose upon employers an absolute liability, which made no reference to negligence, in respect of personal injuries to their employees in the course of their employment. The courts, too, had already established an important principle regarding the circumstances in which they would apply a general doctrine of absolute liability. With that decision in *Rylands v Fletcher* (1868)[6] it may have appeared that the law had turned an about face with a move from trespass, to negligence, to absolute liability. That turned out not to be the case, although it provides a suitable theme for the following pages.[7] By mid-twentieth century an independent and expanded tort of negligence dominated the law of tort. At the same time the community was becoming aware of the role which insurance played in so many cases of personal injury. It was then possible to argue that fault did not necessarily form the sole appropriate basis of compensation to the injured in a modern society.

b) *The emergence of a tort of negligence*

i) *Particular origins.* The origins of the tort of negligence lie in two sets of circumstances. First, there were the running down cases. Secondly, there were those cases in which it was alleged that there had been negligence in the performance of an undertaking or calling. Yet all conduct was subject to the procedural constraints of the appropriate available forms of action. In the first instance, therefore, we turn to the actions of trespass and of case.

ii) *Trespass and case.* Trespass vi et armis lay to recover damages for immediate wrongs which had been accompanied with force. It might take three forms, namely: trespass to the person, trespass to personal property and trespass to houses, lands, fisheries, or watercourses.[8] An essential feature of trespass was that the wrong complained of had been inflicted both forcibly and immediately.

Of course, not all injuries are inflicted in such a forcible and immediate

---

6 (1868) 3 LRHL 330, 37 LJ Ex 161, 19 LT 220, 33 JP 70.

7 W.A. Seavey '*Candler v Crane, Christmas & Co*' (1951) 67 LQR 466, 469, W. Friedmann *Law in a Changing Society* (2nd edn, 1972) chap. 5, C.O. Gregory 'Trespass to Negligence to Absolute Liability' (1951) 37 Virginia Law Review 359.

8 W. Tidd *The Practice of the Court of King's Bench in Personal Actions* (3rd edn, 1803) p. 7.

manner. To cater for such instances the law long ago developed the action of trespass on the case which was a 'universal remedy given for all personal wrongs and injuries without force'. That deviation from the general methods and forms of action was allowed 'where any special consequential damage arises which could not be foreseen and provided for in the ordinary course of justice'.[9] Case was said to be the remedy for all actionable matters of complaint to which the other forms of action did not apply.[10] Certainly it covered wide varieties of conduct. An action on the case might lie inter alia for some consequential hurt or damage which arose from public nuisances, or for criminal conversation, or for seducing or debauching wives, or in the respect of negligence in riding horses, driving carriages, navigating vessels, or performing works.[11]

Despite the scope of the action on the case, it was very important to be able to distinguish between trespass and case. Blackstone distinguished between them in the following manner:

> 'And it is a settled distinction, that where an act is done, which is in itself an immediate injury to another's person or property, there the remedy is usually by an action of trespass vi et armis; but where there is no act done, but only a culpable omission; or where the act is not immediately injurious, but only by consequence and collaterally; there no action of trespass vi et armis will lie, but an action on the special case, for the damages consequent on such omission or act.'[12]

A familiar illustration of the difference between trespass and case was as follows:

> 'Suppose a person throws a log of wood on a highway, and, by the act of throwing, another person is injured, the remedy in such case is trespass. But if the log reaches the ground, and remains there, and a person falls over it, and is injured, the remedy is case, as the injury is not immediately consequent on the act. So, if the defendant drive his carriage against that of another, the remedy may be trespass; but if the defendant's servant be driving, the remedy is case.'[13]

Now it was of the utmost importance for the plaintiff to decide whether an action in trespass or an action in case best fitted the circumstances of which he was complaining. It was vital that he make what turned out in law to be the correct choice for at common law it was impossible to join trespass and case. Therefore, if the plaintiff sued in trespass but the court decided that he should have sued in case, the plaintiff lost his action. Yet often it was difficult to determine before the trial whether the injury done to the plaintiff fell into the category of immediate or consequential injury.

In two valuable articles Prichard has rightly made a great deal of such important procedural points.[14] He has pointed out that the evidence might show either that the defendant had set in motion a force which thereafter he was

---

9   3 Bl Com (5th edn) 122.
10 First Report of...Commissioners for inquiring into the Process, Practice and System of Pleading in the Superior Courts of Common Law no. 1389 (1851), p. 31.
11 *Tidd*, pp. 6-7.
12 3 Bl Com (5th edn) 123.
13 See *Reynolds v Clarke* (1725) 2 Ld Raym 1399.
14 M.J. Prichard 'Trespass, Case and the Rule in *Williams v Holland*' (1964) CLJ 234, '*Scott v Shepherd* (1773) and the Emergence of the Tort of Negligence' (Selden Society Lecture 1976).

unable to control or that the wrong had been done by D's servant. In such circumstances it was preferable to bring case rather than trespass. If the plaintiff were allowed to bring case, he might join a count against D personally with one against him as master or with one alleging loss of control. In other similar cases, therefore, it was very much in the interests of the plaintiff that, if trespass and case could not be joined, then at least their boundaries should be blurred. In an age of mass transportation the problem became even more acute.

iii) *The running down cases.* Improvements in road building during the second half of the eighteenth century led to more people travelling more quickly. Inevitably, more people were injured and killed in running down cases. The advent of the railway accelerated the process dramatically. In a famous sentence Winfield reminded us that the victims of the railway included anything from a wandering cow to a minister of state.[15] The carnage increased dramatically as the nineteenth century progressed. During the four year period 1872-75 no fewer than 5231 people were killed and 16944 were injured in railway accidents: those figures yield an annual average of 1307 killed and 4236 injured. In such circumstances it was scarcely surprising that the law advanced dramatically to cope with this startling situation. In particular, a new body of law on negligence was developed. The bounds of negligence as a concept which had a part to play in other torts have always been shifting and uncertain. That is true also of negligence as a tort. However, even in 1865 a royal commission felt able to state that the law of negligence was the greatest safeguard of the public against railway accidents.[16]

In the late eighteenth century Lord Kenyon made it clear that, in determining whether the plaintiff should have brought his action in trespass or in case, his court would apply rigorously the immediate-consequential test which is outlined above. Lord Kenyon went on to extend the principle to cases of vicarious liability.[17] Not all courts favoured such an approach in view of the procedural difficulties in which it often placed a plaintiff who appeared to have a just claim. For some years, therefore, the courts were in a state of considerable uncertainty upon this point. It was a difficulty which was reflected in 1823 in *Lloyd v Needham*. The facts were that the plaintiff had been injured as a result of the defendant's negligent driving of a gig: the evidence proved that the act was violent and that the injury which resulted was immediate. Yet the plaintiff had brought an action of case. In his dissenting opinion Baron Graham said that this was clearly a case of direct and immediate injury. He continued:

> 'It is admitted that trespass would lie in this case, and if the mode of redress, and the form of action be matter of option, it appears to me that there is an end of all distinction in such cases, and that to insist on it would be futile and nugatory. It has been said that these nice distinctions of the old cases ought not to be preserved: yet the earlier books are full of them, — and I, for one cannot consent to give them up because I am fully convinced of their utility. It is also said that trespass may be waved (sic);

15 P. Winfield 'The History of Negligence in the Law of Torts' (1926) 42 LQR 184.
16 Report from the Commissioners on Railway Accidents no. C-1637 (1877) pp. 25-7. Cf. (1867) 125 Edinburgh Review 549. Of course, in contemporary Britain the carnage on the roads is far greater still.
17 *Day v Edwards* (1794) 5 Term Rep 648, *Savignac v Roome* (1794) 6 Term Rep 125.

but if you wave (sic) the trespass in such cases, in my opinion you wave (sic) everything which entitles you to seek redress in a court of law, and there is no longer any foundation for your action.'[18]

The majority of his colleagues in Exchequer disagreed. In effect, therefore, they had ignored the traditional distinction between trespass and case and had shown themselves to be prepared really to offer the plaintiff the option of bringing an action either in trespass or in case.

It was the Court of Common Pleas which ultimately formulated a definitive approach. In 1833 it held in *Williams v Holland* that where, through negligent and careless driving, one vehicle was caused forcibly to strike against another, an action on the case was maintainable for the injury done, although it had been immediate upon the violence, unless the act producing it were a wilful act.[19] It was a formula which proved successful in that it both combined a certain respect for the old precedents while ensuring that they did not bar the way to a satisfactory legal solution of a pressing social problem. Case, with its stress upon negligence, was to be available in virtually all of the numerous running down cases.

iv) *Negligence in the performance of an undertaking or calling*. By the early 1820s it had become clear that, in instances of negligence in the performance of certain undertakings or callings, the plaintiff could found his action in tort alone. This was true, for example, of cases which involved carriers or surgeons. Prichard tells us that such an action did not differ in any of its essentials from the non relationship action for highway accidents etc. All that was needed, he comments, was to fuse them: this was achieved by the adoption of a common standard of conduct — the reasonable man — and a common technique of pleading — the duty of care.

v) *Reasonable foresight: the duty of care*. The law had long been familiar with the concept of duty in certain circumstances. A duty might arise from a public calling, from bailment, from custom, or from the control of dangerous things. Winfield suggested that the duty of care originated in a judicial belief that a plaintiff could sue only if he could show that the defendant owed him a duty in contract. More recently Prichard has asserted that the duty of care has its origins in prior relationship negligence and sprang from a desire to develop a form of declaration which could be held to be exclusively tortious and not to suffer from any of the contractual rules about joinder. Such a duty was asserted, writes Prichard, where the plaintiff was least sure that it existed: it was the plaintiff, not the court or the defendant, who first mentioned duty.[20]

Lord Ellenborough had been prepared in 1802 to speak of considering a breach of contractual duty as tortious negligence. In 1837 Tindal CJ commented that, even if no contract governed the case, yet 'there is a rule of law which says you must so enjoy your own property as not to injure that of another'.[1] Here, then, is an implicit recognition that in some circumstances, irrespective of

---

18   (1823) 11 Price 608 at 613.
19   (1833) 10 Bing 112, 2 LJCP 190.
20   P.H. Winfield 'Duty in Tortious Negligence' (1934) 34 Col LR 41.
 1   *Govett v Radnidge* (1802) 3 East 62, *Vaugham v Menlove* (1837) 3 Bing NC 468 at 474.

contract, the law may impose a social duty. But how far should that duty extend? The courts were wary of imposing, under the head of duty, a liability which might virtually be unlimited. In rejecting such an approach in 1837 Baron Parke said:

> 'we should pause before we made a precedent by our decision which would be an authority for our action against the vendors, even of such instruments and articles as are dangerous in themselves, at the suit of any person whomsoever into whose hands they might happen to pass, and who should be injured thereby'.[2]

On occasion judges who were afflicted by such doubts did seek refuge in contract. *Winterbottom v Wright* (1842) is such a case. The facts were that A had contracted with the Postmaster General to provide a mail coach to convey mail bags along a certain line of road. B and others contracted to horse the coach along the same line of road. B and his co-contractors hired C to drive the coach. The court held that C could not maintain an action against A for an injury sustained by him while driving the coach, by its breaking down from latent defects in its construction. The defendant stressed that, if the action were to succeed, there would be no limit to such actions. Everyone 'of the sufferers by such an accident as that which recently happened on the Versailles railway, might have his action against the manufacturer of the defective axle'. On the other hand the plaintiff contended that the defendant should be responsible for damage which was the natural and immediate consequence of the negligence. The judges rejected that approach. Lord Abinger said:

> 'There is no privity of contract between these parties; and if the plaintiff can sue, every passenger, or even any person passing along the road, who was injured by the upsetting of the coach, might bring a similar action. Unless we confine the operation of such contracts as this to the parties who entered into them, the most absurd and outrageous consequences, to which I can see no limit, would ensue.'[3]

In time the courts became willing to grasp that particular nettle.

The courts established a list of duties of care which existed in particular circumstances. At much the same time the concept of the reasonable man, as the embodiment of the standard which was to be adopted in cases of negligence, probably began during the 1830s in cases of non relationship negligence. Despite the increasing importance of negligence as the nineteenth century progressed, the law continued to stress a catalogue of duties rather than the development of a general principle which might embrace all such duties. Brett LJ attempted such a generalisation in *Heaven v Pender* (1883).[4] He was ahead of his time. It was only in 1932 that Lord Atkin offered us what became a classic formulation in the leading case of *Donoghue v Stevenson*. The question before the court in that case was whether the manufacturer of an article of drink sold by him to a distributor, in circumstances which prevented the distributor or the ultimate purchaser or consumer from discovering by inspection any defect, was under a legal duty to the ultimate purchaser or consumer to take reasonable care that the article was free from defect likely to cause injury to health. In this case an unfortunate

2 *Langridge v Levy* (1837) 2 M & W 519 at 530.
3 (1842) 10 M & W 109.
4 (1883) 11 QBD 503.

consumer drank part of the contents of a bottle of ginger beer. Shortly afterwards there floated out from the bottle the decomposed remains of a snail. As a
result the consumer suffered shock and severe gastro-enteritis. Lord Atkin said:

> 'You must take reasonable care to avoid acts or omissions which you can
> reasonably foresee would be likely to injure your neighbour. Who, then, in
> law is my neighbour? The answer seems to be — persons who are so closely
> and directly affected by my act that I ought reasonably to have them in
> contemplation as being so affected when I am directing my mind to the
> acts or omissions which are called in question.'[5]

So broad a formulation — Lord Atkin had himself referred to Brett MR's
formulation in *Heaven v Pender* as 'demonstrably too wide' — gave rise to
considerable comment before it became established. It did have the capacity for
growth. As Lord Macmillan said in his speech, 'The categories of negligence are
never closed.' Now negligence was established as an independent tort. The age of
the consumer was dawning.

Yet it is useful to bear in mind that Lord Atkin had only found himself in a
bare majority. It was some years since American courts had held that, irrespective of contract, the manufacturer was under a duty towards the ultimate
consumer to take reasonable care that the manufactured article was free from
injurious defects. Resistance to such a move in England and Wales was due
largely to the argument that, because there was no contractual duty between
manufacturer and consumer, therefore, there could be no duty in tort. In his
dissenting speech in *Donoghue*, Lord Buckmaster had expressed such opposition
forcibly. He maintained that to the principle that 'the breach of the defendant's
contract with A to use care and skill in and about the manufacture or repair of an
article does not of itself give any cause of action to B when he is injured by reason
of the article proving to be defective', there were only two exceptions. Those
exceptions were where the article was dangerous in itself or had a defect known to
the manufacturer. In his view the majority decision was simply to misapply to
tort a doctrine which was applicable to sale and purchase. Not surprisingly, he
recommended that the 'dicta in *Heaven v Pender* should be buried so securely
that their perturbed spirits shall no longer vex the law'.

Initially, therefore, the courts in England and Wales sought to limit
drastically Lord Atkin's formula. Many believed that it was to be confined to the
manufacturers of products. Certainly it was to be confined to negligent acts
rather than extended to negligent statements.[6] Yet the doctrine clearly met the
needs of the community. Its limits would necessarily be uncertain as the courts
set about establishing its boundaries and as social conditions changed. By mid-
twentieth century the early doubts had been settled: the new doctrine was here to
stay.

c) *The ugly sisters of the common law*

i) *Introduction.* The possibility that a plaintiff might recover in negligence was
limited by three common law defences. The fellow servant rule, together with
the doctrines of contributory negligence and of assumption of risk were creations

---

5   [1932] AC 562 at 580.
6   See *Candler v Crane, Christmas & Co* [1951] 2 KB 164, [1951] 1 All ER 426.

of the nineteenth century. In an industrial society they began to be seen increasingly as a barrier to the just claims of the injured workman against his employer, although they were not confined to the master-servant relationship but were defences of general application. Inevitably, they became cast as the ugly sisters of the common law.

ii) *The liability of the employer.* Blackstone wrote:
> 'As for those things which a servant may do on behalf of his master, they seem all to proceed upon this principle, that the master is answerable for the act of his servant, if done by his command, either expressly given or implied.'

Blackstone offers a number of rather confused illustrations of this point. He then adds:
> 'whatever a servant is permitted to do in the usual course of his business, is equivalent to a general command'.[7]

The general principle upon which a master was liable to answer for accidents which resulted from the negligence or unskilfulness of his servants was that the act of his servant was in truth his own act for the master had set the whole thing in motion. In such circumstances the master was clearly liable if, either expressly or impliedly, he had commanded his servant to do an act which, through the negligence of the servant, resulted in damage to another. However, there had long been some authority which went beyond this by suggesting that 'if my servant doth anything prejudicial to another, it shall bind me, when it may be presumed that he acts by my authority, being about my business'.[8]

The doctrine of the liability of the employer, or *respondeat superior*, raised several difficult issues. For example, who was a servant? Far more contentious, however, was the exception made by the law when a servant was injured by the negligence of a fellow servant. In such circumstances the injured servant could usually not recover against his employer.

iii) *Common employment: the fellow servant rule.* The fellow servant rule established that, when a servant engaged to serve a master, he undertook, as between himself and the master, to run all the ordinary risks of the service. This included the risk of negligence on the part of the fellow servant whenever he was acting in the discharge of his duty, as the servant of the master who was the common master of both. This principle was suggested for the first time, and then only in very loose terms, in 1837; in 1850 it became established law.

In *Priestley v Fowler*,[9] the first of those cases, the facts were that the plaintiff was a servant of the defendant in his trade of butcher. The plaintiff had been required to take certain goods of the defendant in a van which belonged to the defendant and which was conducted by another of the defendant's servants. The van was overloaded and broke down, throwing the plaintiff upon the ground with such force that his thigh was fractured. The plaintiff brought an action in case. At assizes he obtained a verdict for £100. However, upon a motion in arrest

---

7   1 Bl Com (5th edn) 429-30.
8   W.S. Holdsworth *History of English Law* vol 8, p. 474, *Duncan v Finlater* (1839) 6 Cl & Fin 910, J.H. Wigmore 'Responsibility for Tortious Acts: Its History' in *Select Essays in Anglo-American Legal History* vol 3, pp. 520 ff.
9   (1837) 3 M & W 1.

of judgment, the plaintiff lost his action. Lord Abinger pointed to the novelty of the action. Accordingly, Lord Abinger was unable to cite a single case by way of authority but arrived at his decision by first assessing what the consequences of a decision to the contrary would mean:

'If the master be liable to the servant in this action, the principle of that liability will be found to carry us to an alarming extent. He who is responsible by his general duty, or by the terms of his contract, for all the consequences of negligence in a matter in which he is the principle is responsible for the negligence of all his inferior agents. If the owner of the carriage is therefore responsible for the sufficiency of his carriage to his servant, he is responsible for the negligence of his coach-maker, or his harness-maker, or his coachman. The footman, therefore, who rides behind the carriage, may have an action against his master for a defect in the carriage owing to negligence of the coach-maker, or for a defect in the harness arising from the negligence of the harness-maker, or for drunkenness, neglect, or want of skill in the coachman; nor is there any reason why the principle should not, if applicable in this class of cases, extend to many others. The master, for example, would be liable to the servant for the negligence of the chambermaid, for putting him into a damp bed; for that of the upholsterer, for sending in a crazy bedstead, whereby he was made to fall down while asleep and injure himself; for the negligence of the cook, in not properly cleaning the copper vessel used in the kitchen: of the butcher, in supplying the family with meat of a quality injurious to the health; of the builder, for a defect in the foundation of the house, whereby it fell, and injured both the master and the servant by the ruins.'

Lord Abinger's conclusion was clear:

'The inconvenience, not to say the absurdities of these consequences, afford a sufficient argument against the application of this principle to the present case.'

Yet the master was under some obligations:

'He is, no doubt, bound to provide for the safety of his servant in the course of his employment, to the best of the judgment, information and belief .... In that sort of employment, especially, which is described in the declaration in this case, the plaintiff must have known as well as his master, and probably better, whether the van was sufficient, whether it was overloaded, and whether it was likely to carry him safely. In fact to allow this sort of action to prevail would be an encouragement to the servant to omit that diligence and caution which he is in duty bound to exercise on behalf of his master, to protect him against the misconduct or negligence of others who serve him and which diligence and caution, while they protect the master, are a much better security against any injury the servant may sustain by the negligence of others engaged under the same master, than any recourse against his master for damages could possibly afford.'

The case which really established the rule was *Hutchinson v The York, Newcastle Railway* (1850).[10] The facts were that a railway servant who was travelling on a train was injured as the result of a collision between his own and

10 (1850) 5 Exch 351.

another train. The collision was due to the negligence of an engineer. Baron Alderson said:

> 'This [the neglect of the other servant] was a risk which Hutchinson must be taken to have agreed to run when he entered into the defendants' service, and for the consequences of which therefore they are not responsible.'

The same principle was affirmed by Chief Baron Pollock in a judgment delivered on the very same day in *Wigmore v Jay*.[11]

The courts then went on liberally to define the risks which were incident to the service and the meaning of the phrase common employment! In *Skip v Eastern Counties Railway Co* (1851),[12] a case of a railway accident, it was held that a risk arising from the circumstance that the company was in the habit of employing an insufficient number of hands to the knowledge of the person undertaking the service, was a risk incident to his contract of service. Baron Alderson said: 'The jury are not to be the judges of the sufficiency of the number of servants a man keeps. The plaintiff stayed in this situation three months, without having an under guard to assist him, and without making any objection.' Similarly, Baron Parke said, 'He goes into the service and willingly incurs the danger.'

In other cases a wide understanding was given to the phrase 'common employment'. It was held to include a labourer employed in loading bricks and a deputy foreman of platelayers. In another case it was held to include on the one hand a miner and an underlooker, whose duty it was to superintend the mining operations and on the other hand a workman employed by an engine-maker. The leading case of *Wilson v Merry* (1868) established:

1) a rejection of the view that the foreman might be considered the delegate of his employer, or that the question might be left to the jury;
2) the wide meaning which the English judges had given to the term 'common employment'.[13]

Wilson v Merry showed that the true criterion of the doctrine of common employment was not whether the person who caused, and the person who suffered from, the accident were fellow workmen in any strict sense of the word but whether the damage was within the risk incident to the service undertaken for reward. The rule was based not on the phrase 'common employment' but on the meaning of the contract. Once the master had selected proper and competent persons to do the job in question, and furnished them with adequate materials and resources for the work, he had done all that he was bound to do. Therefore, provided that the master employed competent servants, he was not required to warrant them beyond that. It was a position which created considerable controversy. In 1877 William Crawford, the secretary to the Durham miners, told a select committee that in his view the law of compensation was not extensive enough. He continued:

> 'The distance between the owner and the workmen is so great that the present law but very seldom reaches the former .... The moment an underground workman enters the cage to descend the mine his life is in the

11 (1850) 5 Exch 354.
12 (1851) 9 Exch 223.
13 (1868) LR 1 Sc & Div 326.

hands of a person, between whom and him there is not the least common employment. They are entirely different classes of workmen, engaged and overlooked by different managers, and between whom there is not the least oneness of employment. Nevertheless, by the negligence and oversight of these men, numbers of men and boys in our mines have lost their lives .... In common fairnesss and equity, I think that if the individual employer is responsible for his own act, so the owner who delegates his authority for the carrying on of the work to the one or many, ought to be responsible for the acts of all those that do what he himself would do, if he did not so delegate his power. Yet if the negligence or incompetency of any one of these men, or of all combined, cause the death of either one man or any number of men, the owners are at present beyond the reach of the laws. Instance upon instance might be given of what I am now saying ... the workman has a right to expect, and does expect, that in following his hazardous occupation his risks will be reduced to a minimum .... We only seek to render an owner responsible when in evidence it is shown that such accident might have been prevented by an exercise of necessary caution and ability by those in charge, and to whom for the time the owner had delegated alike his power and responsibility.'[14]

By way of contrast Mr. Cole, who appeared on behalf of the North of England United Coal Trade Association, argued:

'For the result of injury consequent upon the negligence of a fellow servant the owner is not responsible, nor would it be equitable that he should be; the workman having entered upon his employment with a full knowledge of this, the negligence not being within his power to control, and the negligence in most instances leading to loss and injury to the owner. When an injury is sustained by reason of the owner not having provided what was requisite, or works of an insufficient character, or furnished materials of an unsound or defective description; or selected grossly incompetent servants, then the owner is, and ought to be, liable, the act causing the injury proceeding from himself. In the case of coal mines the majority of accidents which occur, whose cause can be traced to any human agency, are the result of the negligence of some common workmen. The negligence in such cases, although committed during the period of their employment, arises from acts which are totally unconnected with the performance of the employment; that is to say, it arises from acts which it was in no way necessary or even expedient should be adopted by the workman for the purpose of executing the purpose of his employment. If, as an instance, the shaft of a coal pit fell in owing to its being insufficiently walled and timbered, in such a case the employer would be liable for injuries sustained by a workman, as the insufficiency of the walling or timbering was the result of not using due care in providing proper materials. The law reaches every possible case in which injury sustained by a workman in a colliery is attributable to the negligence of the master. It is impossible for a master to control the carelessness of a miner, in an act which is not done in the exercise of his ordinary employment, but which forbids it, and which is done in

14 Report from the Select Committee on Employers Liability for Injuries to their Servants
   no. 285 (1877) pp. 1-2.

direct opposition to his duty, and for which it would be hard that a master, who had by the rules laid down for his workmen forbidden this, and which rules had been violated against his will, should be held responsible. For instance, a workman might negligently strike a light in a dangerous place where safety lamps were used, or expose a candle, or negligently run over a fellow workman while driving waggons, or leave a door open when it should be shut; and there can be no reason why the owner should be held liable in such cases. The miners are quite cognisant of the risks that attend their employment. Then again as most accidents occur from some unavoidable cause, which neither the servant nor the master can possibly foresee ...'[15]

The select committee came out very much in favour of the status quo: in doing so it offered a rationale of the existing doctrine.

'There can be no doubt that the effect of abolishing the defence of "common employment", (as has been actually proposed in a bill submitted to the House) would effect a serious disturbance in the industrial arrangements of the country. Sooner or later the position of master and workman would find its level by a readjustment of the rate of wages, but in the meantime great alarm would be occasioned, and the investment of capital in industrial undertakings would be discouraged. Your committee cannot express their opinion on the question of the public policy involved in the existing law better than by adopting the language of the distinguished American judge who decided the case of *Farwell v Boston and Worcester Railway Corporation*. "When several persons are employed in the conduct of one common enterprise or undertaking, and the safety of each depends much upon the care and skill with which each other shall perform his appropriate duty, each is an observer of the conduct of the other, can give notice of any misconduct, incapacity, or neglect of duty, and leave the service if the common employer will not take such precautions and employ such agents as the safety of the whole party may require. By these means the safety of each will be much more effectually secured than could be done by a resort to the common employer for an indemnity in the case of loss of life by the negligence of each other." '[16]

In 1878 Lowe told the House of Commons that, if the law remained as it was, then 'what were believed to be the rights of the working classes have been gradually withdrawn from without their knowledge, and without the power of protesting, or of taking steps to protect themselves by an appeal to the legislature'. The *Law Times* agreed with him.[17] It was common knowledge that there was no trace of the rule in the law of France, Italy or Germany — only in the USA did the same rule exist. Finally, the rule appeared to favour a limitation upon the risk to invest capital in the new industries. Such a rationale appears to have been accepted in the USA. Similarly, in 1877 a select committee had suggested that, if the defence of 'common employment' were abolished, the investment of capital in industrial undertakings would be discouraged. Did not

15 Report no. 285 (1877) pp. 31 ff.
16 Report no. 285 (1871) p. iv.
17 (1878) 65 LT 22. Cf. F.M. Burdick 'Is Law the Expression of Class Selfishness?' (1911-12) 25 HLR 349.

that rule discriminate unfairly against workmen, then, in that it did not protect them to the same extent that it protected the public in general? And was this not done in order to protect capital rather than labour?

The facts of *Priestley v Fowler* were far removed from the new industrial scene of the railway and of the factory. Not surprisingly, therefore, the examples with which Lord Abinger illustrates his judgment are themselves far removed from the industrial scene. Whatever the uses to which *Priestley v Fowler* was to be put at a later date, the judgments in that case offer no indication that a judicial solicitude for capital inspired the decision. Indeed, there was no reason why those examples should be applied exclusively to the relation between master and servant: they are equally applicable to the relation between carrier and passenger. Several of the examples which Lord Abinger gives do not relate to the master-servant relationship at all. In fact *Priestley v Fowler* scarcely amounts to an authority for the rule for which it was later to be cited as the founding authority. We should remember also that Lord Abinger offered a rationale in terms of safety at work which should not be ignored. A similar rationale was offered in the American case of *Farwell* which soon became well known in England and Wales. At a time when effective safety legislation was largely unknown, this was an important factor. It was especially appropriate in the type of small business which gave rise to *Priestley v Fowler*. It was far less appropriate in the case of larger business undertakings in which it was wholly unrealistic to expect a workman to insist upon his fellow workmen observing the appropriate procedures. Yet it was in the case of just such an undertaking, a railway company, that the rule was first placed upon an authoritative footing.

What was new about *Priestley v Fowler* was that the plaintiff servant sought to recover in his capacity as a passenger. Should he have been treated no less favourably than a member of the public? The defendant did not stand in the relationship of a common carrier to the plaintiff servant, and *Winterbottom v Wright* was soon to show that the courts were reluctant to extend the emergent concept of duty. Nor did the plaintiff argue his case on the basis of any implied term in the contract of service. It can be argued, therefore, that upon its own facts *Priestley v Fowler* was not an unreasonable decision. In all it would be rather more interesting to know why *Hutchinson v The York Newcastle* adopted the fellow servant rule.

Change was on the way. The Select Committee of 1877 was well aware that, if the master were to be held liable in such circumstances, he might insure against liability. In 1877 a Royal Commission on Railway Accidents[18] recommended that in any action against a railway company for compensation for the death or injury of a servant through the defendant's negligence, the officials whom the company entrusted with executive authority should no longer be deemed to be merely the fellow-servants of their subordinates: the company should in every case be liable to its servants for the negligence of those to whom it delegated its authority as master.

Accordingly, with the Employers' Liability Act 1880, Gladstone's government introduced a new principle. In a limited number of cases in which an employer was to be made liable for the result of personal injury caused to his workmen, such employer was to be liable to the same extent that he would have been liable

18   Report from the Commissioners on Railway Accidents no. C-1637 (1877) p. 27.

'if the workman had not been a workman of, nor in the service of the employer, nor engaged in his work'. Of course, the common law principles applied in cases which fell outside the statutory exemptions. In addition there were other legal difficulties which beset the workman.[19] Before long, therefore, further changes were being discussed. It was scarcely surprising that the Workmen's Compensation Acts of 1897, 1900 and 1906 were more radical measures still. That legislation provided that:

> 'if in any employment personal injury by accident arising out of and in the course of the employment is caused to a workman, his employer shall ... be liable to pay compensation'.

Now compensation might be recovered irrespective of negligence on the part of either employer or fellow workman. The legislation had established a new legal principle in this area — the employer, who would usually be protected by insurance, is to be strictly responsible for the safety of his employees. Indirectly, through the medium of higher insurance premiums and the higher costs of goods and services, society had begun to acknowledge a community or social responsibility to workmen in such circumstances, although the doctrine of common employment was not abolished finally until 1948.[20]

iv) *Contributory negligence.* In 1884 Lord Blackburn declared:

> 'The rule of law is that if there is blame causing the accident on both sides, however small that blame may be on one side, the loss lies where it falls.'[1]

Although this rule of contributory negligence was a rule of general application, it was clearly of particular interest to workmen who had been injured at their place of employment. Its application was to be a source of controversy and of concern for lawyers throughout this period.

Butterfield v Forrester,[2] which was decided in King's Bench in 1809, is generally held to have established the modern rule of contributory negligence. The brief judgments give no indication that the judges believed that they were establishing what was to be an important principle. That importance was to become clear only some years later during the new railway age. The facts were that the defendant, in the course of doing house repairs, had put up a pole across part of the road. The plaintiff left a nearby public house at dusk but while there was still light enough to see the obstruction at a distance of 100 yards. However, the plaintiff, who was riding his horse violently, did not observe the obstruction but rode into it. As a result he was badly injured. Subsequently, he brought an action on the case. The court rejected his claim. Bayley J said that the accident appeared to have happened entirely from his own fault. However, in what was to be a seminal passage, Lord Ellenborough expressed himself as follows:

> 'A party is not to cast himself upon an obstruction which has been made by the fault of another, and avail himself of it, if he do not himself use common and ordinary caution to be in the right .... One person being in fault will not dispense with another's using ordinary care for himself. Two

19 H.D. Bateson 'Employers' Liability' (1889) 5 LQR 179. Cf. *Transactions of the National Association for the Promotion of Social Science* (1883) p. 162.
20 Law Reform (Personal Injuries) Act 1948. See also F.H. Bohlem 'Workmen's Compensation Acts: Their Theory and their Constitutionality' (1911-12) 25 HLR 328, 401, 517.
1 *Cayzev, Irvine & Co v Carron Co* (1884) 9 App Cas 873 at 881.
2 (1809) 11 East 60.

things must concur to support this action, an obstruction in the road by the fault of the defendant, and no want of ordinary care to avoid it on the part of the plaintiff.'

In *Bridge v The Grand Junction Railway Company* (1838) counsel contended that if there were negligence as well on the part of the plaintiff as of the defendant, then the defendant was not liable. Baron Parke was not prepared to go quite as far as that. He said:

'although there may have been negligence on the part of the plaintiff, yet, unless he might, by the exercise of ordinary care, have avoided the consequences of the defendant's negligence, he is entitled to recover: if by ordinary care he might have avoided them, he is the author of his own wrong'.[3]

Baron Parke's approach was at one with the principle which suggested that the plaintiff might recover, provided that the defendant had had the last clear chance of avoiding the incident. In practice, however, the courts, tended to apply the doctrine of contributory negligence with some enthusiasm, as Lord Blackburn's dictum above indicates.

Certainly, in some cases the law went far. In *Waite v North Eastern Railway Company* (1858)[4] an action was brought in respect of an injured child. There would not have been any injury to the child had there not been negligence on the part of an adult in whose care the child was at the time of the accident. As a result the child was unable to recover. That same principle of identifying the injured party; with another person had been carried even further in *Thorogood v Bryant* (1849).[5] In that case it was held that a passenger in a public conveyance, who was injured in a collision with another conveyance, was so far identified with the management of the driver to whom he had committed himself that he would have no right of action against the proprietors of the other carriage with which the collision took place, if it appeared that the accident was the result of a want of ordinary care on the part of both drivers. This was a much criticised decision. It was argued that in such a case both the wrongdoers or their employers should be liable to the passengers who had suffered from their combined negligence, and that it was highly unreasonable to restrict the passengers in each vehicle to an action against their own driver.[6]

Possibly, the law could have been extended even further, especially in the case of workmen, as the following exchange before the Select Committee in 1876 illustrates:

'whenever in any way a workman was in any sense a party to the negligence, or a party to the breach of the statutory regulations, you would not allow him to have any claim for damages? The general principle of law I think would be quite enough to prevent his claiming damage in such cases.

794. For instance, if there was neglect on board ship to put up the lights, you would not consider if a collision occurred that anybody on board would have claim for damages? — That would be carrying the doctrine of contributory negligence rather far to affect all the innocent people on board.

3 (1838) 3 M & W 244 at 248.
4 (1858) EB & E 719.
5 (1849) 8 CB 115.
6 (1868) 45 LT 62.

795. But they are all aware of the regulations; they are all aware of the fact that lights are not put up; it is patent to everybody; and if they never protest against it in any way in a certain sense, would they not all be parties to the negligence? — Certainly that would be a new principle in law ...

799. You would still require the workman to exercise some care as to the regulations, and whatever regulations they were they should be carried out? — If you have the power; but, practically, you could hardly put it into a law; you must leave that to juries. You could hardly say that it is the duty of every man employed in a mine to inform the manager about every violation of duty.'[7]

The doctrine does appear to have been in tune with society's attitudes at the time. Evidence to a select committee in 1876 showed that trade union leaders were by no means united in their opposition to a doctrine of contributory negligence. On the one hand it is true that Henry Broadhurst, who was Secretary of the Trade Union Congress Parliamentary Committee, was in favour of holding the master responsible in damages for an accident which might have been prevented by the men themselves, if they had been ordered to go on with the work and do it in a way which led to the accident. It was a point of view which shaded into that of George Howell, who was a kind of parliamentary agent in trade union matters and who had had considerable experience with the building unions. Howell maintained that the master ought always to be liable unless the workman had 'materially contributed' to his injury. On the other hand John Burnett, who was Secretary of the Amalgamated Society of Engineers, said that he had no quarrel with the existing law of contributory negligence and thought it reasonable. Similarly, F.W. Evans, who was General Secretary to the Amalgamated Society of Railway Servants, said that he would not make the company responsible at all for cases in which servants had undertaken unnecessary risks. Industry tended to support the existing law on the ground that any change in the law would result in increased costs to industry.[8]

To what do we owe the developed doctrine of contributory negligence during the second half of the nineteenth century? Was it developed as a rule to discriminate against the workman? On the one hand industrialists clearly favoured it. The courts must have been aware of that factor. Although Lord Ellenborough gave judgment in *Butterfield v Forrester* (1809) before there was likely to have been such an awareness among industrialists generally, it is possible to see that brief passage in which he set out the doctrine as not so much a precedent which bound future courts as an excuse which justified their acting in a manner which would reduce costs to industry, especially the railways. On the other hand more mundane legalistic reasons were probably far more influential. Older authority hinted that if the plaintiff's act were the proximate cause of the injury, he could not recover. Pleading practice might also prevent the plaintiff recovering for in response to the plaintiff's declaring in such circumstances upon the defendant's negligence, it would be open to the defendant simply to deny this simply by

---

7 Report from the Select Committee on Employers' Liability for Injuries to Their Servants no. 372 (1876) pp. 58-9. The questioner was Mr. Eustace Smith. The respondent was R.S. Wright, a distinguished lawyer.

8 Report no. 372 (1876). For industry I refer to the evidence of Mr. J. Knowles, a managing director of a colliery: Report from the Select Committee on Employers' Liability for Injuries to their Servants no. 285 (1877) p. 48.

pleading 'not guilty'. The defendant might demonstrate this easily enough merely by pointing to the plaintiff's own negligence.[9] The importance of such a procedural point cannot be overestimated. It does seem reasonably clear, therefore, that the doctrine had originated in suits outside the master-servant relationship. Legal texts of the 1870s placed no emphasis upon that relationship and by and large trade union leaders did not feel that the rule discriminated unfairly against their members. However, such attitudes can change, especially when workmen became critical of other aspects of the law.

From the later nineteenth century on the doctrine was subject to increasing criticism. In 1887 Fry LJ wondered why, in cases of contributory negligence, the courts might not apportion the loss. That was a position which was provided for by statute only in 1945.[10] Henceforth, damages were to be reduced to such extent as the court thought just and equitable having regard to the claimant's share in the responsibility for the damage. The Act also abrogated the doctrine of the last opportunity. Yet the doctrine of contributory negligence itself survived and even remained a defence to a master sued by his servant for breach of statutory duty.[11]

v) *Consent*. The linked principle that no injury was done to one who consented was also a rule of general application which had originated well before mid-nineteenth century. In an age which tended to emphasise both the freedom and the sanctity of contract, it was a principle which many believed often worked unfairly against the workman who was employed in a large, industrial undertaking. Had he really contracted to run many risks as part of his contract of employment? Baron Bramwell was a forthright, even an extreme, exponent of the classic, contractual approach. Speaking extra-judicially in 1877, he said:

> 'Why does he not leave the employment if he knows that it is dangerous? To my mind, it is a sad thing to hear men come into court, as I have heard them, and excuse themselves for not having done that on the ground that their bread depended upon it, or something of that sort. I should like to see a more independent feeling on the part of workmen, so that they would say, "I will have nothing to do, with a man who employs dangerous things or dangerous persons." '[12]

Such an approach expressed perfectly the classic ideology of contract, a bargain freely arrived at between equals. It did not represent the reality which faced the workman in the great industrial cities during the second half of the nineteenth century. Towards the end of the century the courts recognised this when they decided that a workman's knowledge of a dangerous situation amounted to no more than evidence upon which a jury might, or might not, find that the workman had agreed as part of his contract of employment to assume such a risk himself.[13]

d) *Easing the burden of proof*: res ipsa loquitur
Of course, it was for the plaintiff to prove that the defendant had been negligent.

9   Lord Wright 'Contributory Negligence' (1950) 13 MLR 2, 5.
10   Law Reform (Contributory Negligence) Act 1945, s.1.
11   F.R. Batt *The Law of Master and Servant* (5th edn, 1967) pp. 458 ff.
12   Report from the Select Committee on Employers' Liability for Injuries to their Servants no. 285 (1877) p. 63, q. 1157. Bramwell also stated that workmen were often insured against accidents.
13   *Smith v Charles Baker & Sons* [1891] AC 325.

However, in some cases the courts were prepared to accept that *res ipsa loquitur*, the thing speaks for itself. In *Skinner LB and SC Rly* (1850)[14] two trains which belonged to the same company collided. As a result the plaintiff had been injured. Alderson B said that as both trains belonged to the same company, it was unnecessary for the plaintiff to specify the negligence. It was an approach which was recognised in *Byrne v Boadle* (1863).[15] It was an approach which was of some help to plaintiffs, and not least in the railway cases, despite its limitations. The rule was said to be:

> 'There must be reasonable evidence of negligence; but where the thing is shown to be under the management of the defendant or his servants, and the accident is such as in the ordinary course of things does not happen, if those who have the management use proper care, it affords reasonable evidence, in the absence of explanation by the defendants, that the accident arose from want of care.'[16]

e) *Strict liability*

i) *Introduction.* In 1868 the House of Lords affirmed a tortious rule of strict liability. Now a man was responsible in certain circumstances irrespective of fault or negligence on his part. On several counts that decision in *Rylands v Fletcher*[17] was quite remarkable. This reversion to an earlier age's view of strict liability occurred at a time when a more modern concept of fault-based negligence was gaining ground. Secondly, it quite clearly runs counter to the allegation that the courts and the law were doing everything possible to limit risk to investment capital. Moreover, at all events in its early years, the decision was much canvassed to the extent that in 1879 the *Solicitors' Journal* referred to a classic passage in the case as 'household words' in the law courts.[18]

In November 1861 Fletcher, the plaintiff, brought an action against Rylands, the defendant. Put down for trial at Liverpool summer assizes in 1862, the case was referred to an arbitrator. The arbitrator stated a special case. That case was considered by the Court of Exchequer in Trinity Term 1865. Exchequer dismissed the action. The plaintiff, Fletcher, then appealed to Exchequer Chamber where he won his case. Now the defendant in his turn appealed to the House of Lords in 1868. The House of Lords upheld Exchequer Chamber's decision in favour of the plaintiff Fletcher. In brief the facts of this famous case, which were to become well known to generations of law students, were as follows. The defendant owners of a mill wished to improve the water supply to it. The landowner, Lord Wilton, gave permission for a reservoir to be built on his land and the defendants employed competent persons to carry out this work. Now it so happened that the plaintiffs held a mineral lease of the same Lord Wilton. They had opened an underground communication between their own colliery and old workings under the reservoir, although the land of third parties separated them from the defendant's land. In the course of building the reservoir the engineers

14 (1850) 5 Exch 787.
15 (1863) 2 H & C 722, 33 LJ Ex 13.
16 Per Erle CJ, *Scott v The London and St. Katherine Docks Co* (1865) 3 H & C 596 at 601.
   T.E. Lewis 'A Ramble with *Res Ipsa Loquitur*' (1951) 11 CLJ 74.
17 (1868) 3 LRHL 330. C.H.S. Fifoot *Judge and Jurist in the Reign of Victoria* pp. 41 ff.
18 (1879) 23 Sol Jo 599.

came across five old shafts. They failed to seal them properly. The result was that, once the reservoir was filled, water broke through these shafts and flowed along the underground communication into the mine of the plaintiffs. Damage was agreed at £937.

The plaintiff pointed to the recent case of *Williams v Groucott* (1863)[19] in which Blackburn J had said: 'When a party alters things from their normal condition so as to render them dangerous to already acquired rights, the law casts on him the obligation of fencing the danger so that it shall not be injurious to those rights.' His counsel then contended:

> 'The principle of law which governs the case is, that he who does upon his own land acts which, though lawful in themselves, may become sources of mischief to his neighbours, is bound to prevent the mischief from occurring or in the alternative to make compensation to the person injured. This will be peculiarly the case when the act done consists in the construction and use of artificial works, for the purpose of collecting and impounding in vast quantities an element which will certainly cause mischief if it escapes.'

For the defendants it was possible to distinguish *Williams v Groucott* upon its facts. Further, it was argued that the only obligation upon the defendants was to take reasonable care not to injure the property of others. The examples of absolute liability at common law, which admittedly did exist, were all said to be examples of actions on the custom of the realm. Counsel then argued that 'where the custom of the realm did not extend, the rule of the common law was that negligence must be shown'. These arguments were rejected. Although Exchequer had found for the defendants, both Exchequer Chamber and the House of Lords found for the plaintiffs.

ii) *The rule in* Rylands v Fletcher. In a classic passage in his judgment in Exchequer Chamber in 1866 Blackburn J expressed the 'rule' in *Rylands v Fletcher* as follows:

> 'We think that the true rule of law is that the person who for his own purposes brings on his lands and collects and keeps there anything likely to do mischief if it escapes, must keep it in at his peril, and if he does not do so, is prima facie answerable for all the damage which is the natural consequence of its escape ... it seems both reasonable and just that the neighbour, who has brought something on his own property which was not naturally there, harmless to others so long as it is confined to his own property, but which he knows to be mischievous if it gets on to his neighbours, should be obliged to make good the damage which ensues if he does not succeed in confining it to his own property. But for his act in bringing it there no mischief could have accrued, and it seems but just that he should at his peril keep it there so that no mischief may accrue, or answer for the natural and anticipated consequences.'

In his speech in the House of Lords Lord Cairns distinguished between what he called the natural user of land and the non natural use of land. The plaintiff

---

19 4 B & S 149, (1863) 32 LJQB 237.

could not have complained of the consequences of natural user. He might complain of the defendant's non natural user as:

> 'But for his act in bringing it there no mischief could have accrued, and it seems but just that he should at his peril keep it there, so that no mischief may accrue, or answer for the natural and anticipated consequence.'

iii) *Did* Rylands v Fletcher *establish a new rule?* The facts of the case had not fallen within the boundaries of any of the old forms of action. It was hardly trespass, although Baron Bramwell appeared to think differently, since the flooding was neither direct nor immediate. Nuisance was a more plausible possibility. For example, a man who constructed a projection which caused, or had a tendency to cause, an unnatural quantity of rainwater to descend on his neighbour's house and land was responsible in nuisance. Similarly, every occupier of land was entitled to the reasonable enjoyment thereof as a natural right of property, and might maintain an action against anyone who allowed filth or other noxious thing produced by him on his own land to interfere with this enjoyment, or who, by artificial means, caused things in themselves offensive to pass into his neighbour's property to the prejudice of his enjoyment thereof.[20] There was some discussion of nuisance in Exchequer Chamber. Yet the facts of *Rylands v Fletcher* failed to show that any nuisance in that case was both continuous and recurring, a fatal flaw. Was negligence appropriate, then? In the Court of Exchequer the majority held that, as the defendants had not been guilty of negligence, they were not liable for the harm done by the bursting of the reservoir. It is rather surprising that in Exchequer Chamber Blackburn J did not follow up the possibility of negligence as he was of the view that there were some injuries to land or property which were only actionable if produced through wilful or negligent behaviour.[1] Certainly much legal opinion since *Rylands v Fletcher* has been of the opinion that the facts could have been held to found liability in negligence. However, the two typical categories of conduct which spawned negligence in its modern form during the nineteenth century were those which were based upon injury to the person. *Rylands v Fletcher* was a case of injury to proprietary interests in land. In such cases the old authority to the effect that strict liability might be imposed for damage caused by animals or by fire was persuasive. Blackburn J did no more than to frame the older strands of authority into the form of a general principle.

iv) *The importance of* Rylands v Fletcher. The establishment of what appeared to be a new legal principle was clearly of considerable importance. The fact that it ran counter to much contemporary legal and economic thinking makes it all the more interesting. The implications of *Rylands v Fletcher* were clear enough to lawyers of the day. In 1879 a legal commentator wrote that in such circumstances:

> 'the beneficial use of property and the development of its value by enterprise and industry would be unduly restricted. If a landowner could not

---

20 *Fay v Prentice* (1846) ICB 828, *Hurdman v North-Eastern Rail Co* (1878) 3 LRCP 168, (1878) 47 LJCP 368.

1 G.H. Fridman 'The Rise and Fall of *Rylands v Fletcher*' (1956) 34 Can BR 810, E. Blackburn 'The Rule in *Rylands v Fletcher*' (1961) 4 Can BJ 39. See also J.H. Wigmore 'Responsibility for Tortious Acts: Its History' *Select Essays in Anglo-American Legal History* vol 3, pp. 474, 518, W.S. Holdsworth *History of English Law* vol 8, p. 465.

alter the natural state of things and construct anything without incurring the risk of liability for any damages occasioned by the unlawful act of a third person, or the unusual operation of the forces of nature in connection with such altered state of things, there are few alterations of an extensive nature that a landlord could safely make.'[2]

Was Blackburn J oblivious to such implications of his decision? Bohlen, an American writer, thought not. Writing in 1911 he suggested that the judiciary saw land as 'primarily a private domain, an estate from which the owner derives his power and dignity, within which he must be supreme and undisturbed by intrusions'. Reflecting the opinions of the aristocracy, either because they were recruited from the landed gentry or because they wished to become members of it, the judges would not look with favour upon a commercial development which was based upon manufacturing and the extractive industries.[3] It was an attractive and popular theory. Unfortunately, it did not fit the facts. An examination of the lives of the judges who had been involved in *Rylands v Fletcher* revealed no such aspirations. Moreover, although the landed classes may be accused of a number of sins, a reluctance to exploit their land for commercial gain certainly cannot be counted amongst them. A whole host of Enclosure Acts point to the existence of such a commercial spirit amongst an earlier generation of landowners. The Settled Land Act 1882, in whose enactment Lord Cairns played a considerable part, offers similar testimony to the existence of a similar spirit in the Rylands generation.[4] Indeed, it should not be forgotten that both the plaintiff and the defendant in *Rylands v Fletcher* were lessees of Lord Wilton.

How, then, did Blackburn J arrive at his decision in *Rylands v Fletcher*? In his judgment there is no evident awareness that he was establishing new law. Upon counsel in a case in 1872 claiming that the case before them raised a new point 'like the question in *Rylands v Fletcher* which had never before been decided until the adjudication of that case', he replied that he must have wasted his time in that case if he had not succeeded in showing that there was no law in that case which had not been law for the previous 300 years.[5] There is no reason to doubt him. So far from being based consciously upon social or economic motives, it appears far more likely that Blackburn J arrived at his decision rather through his awareness of the old precedents, coupled with his lawyer-like concern, and ability, to apply them. The radical nature of his decision lay principally in his gift for generalisation of the underlying principle, which lay latent in the old cases.

v) *The application of* Rylands v Fletcher. It was not a radicalism which was welcome to every lawyer. Quite soon a judge remarked that it was:

> 'not to be extended beyond the legitimate principle on which the House of Lords decided it. If it were extended as far as strict logic might require, it would be a very oppressive decision.'[6]

---

2   (1879) 23 Sol Jo 600.
3   F.H. Bohlem 'The Rule in *Rylands v Fletcher*' (1911) 59 Univ of Penn LR 298, 373, 423, R.T. Molloy '*Fletcher v Rylands* — A Re-examination of Juristic Origins' 9 Univ of Chic LR 266.
4   See chap. 13.
5   *Ross v Fedden* (1872) LR 7 QB 661.
6   *Green v Chelsea Water Works Co* (1894) 70 LT 547.

As negligence continued to develop, it was inevitable that any dividing line between strict liability and negligence would be queried. In 1886 Pollock recognised that the law might have been content with applying the general standard of reasonable care rather than by establishing an absolute duty. He was able to note that even by that early date the tendency of the decisions had been rather to encourage the discovery of exceptions to *Rylands v Fletcher* than otherwise.[7]

In fact the dicta of Blackburn J and of Lord Cairns express differing approaches. In the House of Lords Lord Cairns had concurred with Blackburn J. Of course, in future years the courts sought to harmonise the veiws of Blackburn J and of Lord Cairns. Yet Lord Cairns' view was quite distinctive. Whereas Blackburn J was looking back to an older concept of liability, Lord Cairns' approach was much more in tune with the contemporary approach which stressed blameworthiness. In fact Cairns' view was subversive of that of Blackburn J in that his use of the phrase 'non-natural use' allowed courts on occasion to avoid applying the rule. It was also successful to the extent that in mid-twentieth century a commentator was able to write that the development of the rule in *Rylands v Fletcher* proceeded on the footing that liability under it should be assimilated so far as possible to liability for negligence. Such an approach made it seem less worth while to treat the rule in *Rylands v Fletcher* as an independent rule than as simply one more category of liability in negligence.

It was a tendency which was emphasised during the 1940s when the courts made it clear that the rule in *Rylands v Fletcher* was not to be extended. Its fall was most apparent in the House of Lords decision in *Read v Lyons*.[8] The facts were that the plaintiff munitions inspector had been injured in the defendant's munitions factory where a shell, which was in the process of being manufactured, exploded. The plaintiff had not sought to prove negligence. Lord Simon stressed that the rule in *Rylands v Fletcher* went to the rights of adjoining land owners, although the case as a whole does not go so far as to deny that *Rylands v Fletcher* might still be relevant in cases of personal injuries. However, it was held that the plaintiff in this case could not succeed under the rule in *Rylands v Fletcher* as there had been no escape from the defendant's land. In the following year Lord Goddard made it clear that in his view also the rule in *Rylands v Fletcher* was not to be extended.[9]

4 Conclusion

Of course there were other torts, which have not been discussed in this chapter, which were of considerable importance. Yet the rapid growth of negligence overshadowed all else. That growth mirrored society's own concept of the expanding boundaries of social duty. In the light of contract's traditionally narrow concept of social duty and its increasing reliance upon objective standards, it began to appear increasingly that the yardstick overall of civil liability was becoming primarily tortious in nature. By 1950 tort and contract had moved quite close to each other in conceptual terms.

---

7   F. Pollock 'Duties of Insuring Safety: the Rule in *Rylands v Fletcher*' (1886) 2 LQR 52.
8   [1947] AC 156.
9   E. Blackburn 'The Rule in *Rylands v Fletcher*' (1961) 4 Can BJ 40.

Chapter 13
Property

1 Introduction

a) *Real property and personal property*

The law distinguished between real property and personal property. Things real, or realty, were said to consist of things substantial and immoveable, and of the rights and profits annexed to, or issuing out of, these. Realty consisted of lands, of tenements (which usually referred only to houses and buildings), or of hereditaments (whatever might be inherited, including lands and tenements). In this chapter we shall be referring to land law. Things personal, or personalty, were said to consist of goods, money, and all other moveables, and of such rights and profits as related to moveables.[1] Personal property rose to some prominence in law only during this period. It is a fascinating yet complex story to which we shall be unable to make any reference.

b) *Early reforms*

Between the Restoration and the Reform Act 1832 there were few changes of any note in the law of real property. The one notable change, the evolution of the modern strict settlement, which is discussed below, took place towards the middle of the eighteenth century. By setting out the basic principles of property law in a lucid manner Blackstone had done much to prepare the way for reform. Blackstone himself had been aware also of some of the absurdities of the system e.g. of fines and recoveries, which are mentioned below. However, no change in the country's medieval and remarkably complex system of land law was mooted seriously until James Humphreys made a critical survey of that system in the 1820s at a time when interest in questions of law reform was increasing.

Humphreys not only offered a number of criticisms of the law of real property but also embodied his suggested reforms within the framework of an overall code. Bentham went so far as to welcome his proposals, a rare accolade for a

---

1 H. Stephen *Commentaries on the Laws of England* (4th edn, 1858) vol I, pp. 168-9.

practising lawyer of nearly 30 years standing! In fact Humphreys had gone rather too far for the liking of some lawyers. Codification was suspect. Similarly, the suggestion that powers were to be given to the tenant for life under a strict settlement — such powers were conferred in fact some 50 years later — appeared to threaten the landed estates upon which the aristocracy based its influence.[2] It was scarcely suprising, therefore, that the real property commissioners, who were appointed as a result of Brougham's famous speech of 1828, took a rather more moderate line.

The commissioners produced four Reports during the period 1829-33.[3] Those Reports cover a fair amount of ground. However, they indicated their approach clearly enough at the beginning of their First Report when they wrote:

'We have the satisfaction to report, that the law of real property seems to us to require very few essential alterations....When the object of transactions respecting land is accomplished, and the estates and interests in it which are recognised are actually created and secured, the law of England, except in a few comparatively unimportant particulars, appears to come almost as near to perfection as can be expected in any human institutions.'[4]

On the other hand the commissioners went on to comment that the law respecting the transfer of real property was 'exceedingly defective' and required 'many important alterations'. The cause of this defective state of affairs was clear enough i.e. 'rules and maxims, which once were suitable and rational, being maintained when the state of society and the modifications of property are changed'.[5] To remedy that state of affairs was a useful enough task. To set it out in any detail would be tedious. Yet some indication must be given of the reforms which appeared to be of importance to the lawyers of the day.

The commissioners believed that a modernisation of conveyancing practice was desirable. They commented that the 'cumbrous and circuitous forms of conveyancing now in use are founded on antiquated doctrines'.[6] Originally the use of conveyancing devices such as the lease and release had served a perfectly useful purpose by reducing the delay and expense which had been involved in conveyancing in accordance with feudal practice. A rationale which had been valid enough in the feudal world no longer seemed valid in the nineteenth century. Now the circuitous device of the lease and release was itself seen as a cause of delay and of expense. Some relief was afforded some years after the commissioners had reported by the Conveyance by Release without Lease Act 1841. More lasting reform still was achieved by the Real Property Act 1845; it had taken 16 years since the publication of the real property commissioners' Report to accomplish that simple reform. Another conveyancing device which had outlived its usefulness was the system of fines and recoveries. In form the fine was a personal action. It secured to the alienee not merely unimpeachable evidence of his title but judicial authority for its validity. Much learning surrounded

---

2 W.S. Holdsworth *History of English Law* vol II, p. 295.
3 First Report made to His Majesty by the Commissioners appointed to inquire into the Law of England respecting Real Property no. 263 (1829), Second Report...no. 575 (1830), Third Report...no. 484 (1832), Fourth Report...no. 226 (1833).
4 First Report...no. 263 (1829) p. 6.
5 First Report (above) p. 7.
6 First Report (above) p. 7.

this conveyancing device which had been born within a living feudal system. A failure to observe that learning could be fatal even in the nineteenth century. The commissioners commented:

> 'Other mischiefs arising from want of due caution in the use of fines are known to every practitioner. In short, the skill and nicety required in levying fines for particular purposes to avoid any of the other effects incident to them, are frequently so great, that irreparable mischiefs are often produced by unskilful or careless practitioners.'[7]

Such difficulties and the very use of what was in practice a collusive device began to appear increasingly anomalous in the modern world. The commissioners criticised the related use of a device known as the common recovery in similar terms. They were 'mere excrescences from the main body of our laws', their abolition 'would relieve both counsel and solicitors from much useless learning'.[8] In the light of the consensus which existed in favour of reform, it was scarcely surprising that reform followed quite quickly. The Fines and Recoveries Act 1833 dispensed with the old learning and established a much more simple system.

Thirdly, there was the whole system of tenure. Tenure was vital to the medieval system of land law. The fundamental principle of tenure was that absolute property in all lands was vested in the Crown. Its origins lay in a desire to provide for the defence of the kingdom, military services being required of many tenants. Ought it to be preserved, then, in the modern world of the 1830s? The commissioners wrote that they felt no hesitation in recommending that it should be retained.

Otherwise, it would be necessary to provide by positive enactment for all the rules deduced from tenure which it was intended to preserve.[9] Even so, the commissioners considered that the variety of tenures which subsisted was 'an unqualified evil; and we think that everything should be done which is consistent with the rights of property, to reduce them all to one simple tenure, stripped of all local customs, and attended by the same rules, as to enjoyment and transmission'. In 1832 when the commissioners wrote, there were eight forms of tenure. No decisive action was taken. A number of Copyhold Acts apart, such action was not taken until the legislation of 1925. Thereafter, all land was held in freehold.

Of course, there was a number of other quite important, although scarcely vital, changes. The Real Property Limitation Act 1833 abolished almost the whole of the real and mixed actions for the recovery of land. The Inheritance Act 1833 and the Wills Act 1837 made notable changes in the law regarding succession. A further useful reform was effected by the Conveyancing and Law of Property Act 1881[10] which shortened the form of deeds. Further, as a result of the Solicitor's Remuneration Act 1881, solicitors who formerly had been remunerated according to the length of the deed, were henceforth to be remunerated in accordance with a sliding scale based upon the value of the property conveyed. These measures facilitated conveyancing; whether they made conveyancing

---

7   First Report (above) p. 21.
8   First Report (above) p. 31.
9   Third Report no. 484 (1832) pp. 4 ff. The Tenures Abolition Act 1660 simplified tenures considerably.
10 Cf. Vendor and Purchaser Act 1874.

correspondingly less expensive to the layman, as could have been done, is less certain.

There was other equally useful legislation. However, the whole of this legislation merits Simpson's stricture that about it there is 'an air of triviality and extreme caution'.[11] Yet it was useful enough in its day. In fairness to the real property commissioners, however, we should bear in mind that the recommendation to which they attached greatest importance was that for registration of titles or assurances. That was a topic which had been mooted in the reign of Henry VIII. Discussion of it continued, as we shall see, throughout the nineteenth century and into the twentieth century.

c) *The political context of reform*

In mid-nineteenth century more radical reform appeared to be possible. At much the same time as the anti-Corn Law campaign both Cobden and Bright established a radical platform which called for 'free land'. By the mid-1850s the steam had gone out of that campaign. Yet as late as 1864 Cobden proclaimed:

> 'I would take Adam Smith in hand...and I would have a league for free trade in land just as we had a league for free trade in corn....If you can apply free trade to land and labour too...then, I say, the men who do that will have done for England probably more than we have been able to do by making free trade in corn.'[12]

In particular Cobden campaigned for the abolition of primogeniture, entails and settlements, and the simplification of land transfers. He met with little success. Indeed, the very vigour of his campaign may have led to the failure of other more modest proposals, as landowners closed their ranks.[13]

The radicals, led this time by Chamberlain, raised the call for free land once again in the 1870s. In 1873 Chamberlain explained that by free land he meant:

> 'I am in favour of freeing the land from all the trammels which press upon its utmost production. I am in favour of promoting by every means its ready sale and transfer. I am in favour of four great reforms. In the first place I would abolish the absurd custom of primogeniture....I am in favour of the repeal of those laws of entail by which more than half of the land in this country is tied up...for the supposed benefit of less than 150 families. I am in favour in the next place of such a revision of the laws which affect the appropriation of commons as shall secure those that remain for the people, and should provide for their tenancy in small plots direct from the state, on fair and reasonable conditions. And I am in favour, lastly, of a full tenant right, for every farmer, in spite of any conditions in his lease, which shall give him property in the unexhausted improvements he may make...'[14]

A number of pressure groups expressed similar aims. For example, in 1869 the objects of the Land Law League, an organisation which included several members of parliament on its committee, were proclaimed as being:

1) To promote the free transfer of land.

11 A.W.B. Simpson *An Introduction to the History of the Land Law* p. 256.
12 Cited by R. Douglas *Land, People and Politics* p. 18.
13 See generally F.M.L. Thompson *English Landed Society in the Nineteenth Century* especially at pp. 283-4.
14 R. Douglas *Land, People and Politics*.

2) To secure the passing of Mr. Locke King's Real Estate Intestacy Bill.
3) To restrict within the narrowest limits the power of tying up land.
4) To preserve the rights of the public over commons, and generally over all lands which require an Act of Parliament to authorise their inclosure: and to oppose the practice of annexing such lands to the estates of the neighbouring landholders.
5) To promote measures by which, without unjust interference with private rights, facilities may be afforded to the workmen and tillers of the soil for acquiring an interest in the land of the country.
6) As one means to the object last proposed:-
    'To endeavour to promote such an administration of landed property owned by public bodies as shall help to carry out such object.'[15]

A number of lawyers joined in the debate with some enthusiasm. Joseph Kay QC denounced the technicality of the land laws which made them 'so difficult even for lawyers to understand, such a vast literature of rubbish has grown up around it...'[16] In particular Kay, in the pursuit of free trade in land, argued against settlements. J.F. Stephen, taking a more formal view of the law, argued that the distinction between real and personal property should be abolished, the law of personal property being made the general law of all property.[17] Clearly, such a change, if implemented successfully, could have simplified the law considerably.

During the period 1909-14 the Liberals were responsible for introducing taxation of land values and for legislating to protect tenants against unreasonable disturbance by landlords. As the twentieth century progressed the Labour Party in particular was of the view that the economic value of land belonged to the community as a whole. Some expression of that view is evident in the Town and Country Planning Act 1947. Indeed, a Ministry of Town and Country Planning had been established in 1943. Little thought had been given to the land question generally. Yet it had long been clear that the country had moved well away from the position that what a man did with his own property, provided it was not unlawful, was of no concern to anybody but himself.

The questions of land transfer, settlements, the enclosure of common lands and questions of landlord and tenant or housing are central to the reform debate in this area. In the first instance we turn to the question of the transfer of real property, a question regarding which the commissioners devoted the whole of their Second Report which was published in 1830.

2 Land transfer

In the whole history of the law of England and Wales few, if any, reforms have been so often proposed, or been so often considered by committees and by commissions, and yet so often ended in failure as proposals to simplify the transfer of land. In 1875 Osborne Morgan QC wrote aptly enough:

'The history of legislation on this subject had been a history of conspicuous, we might say, ignominious, failures. To the present generation of lawyers

15 (1869) 47 LT 336.
16 J. Kay *Free Trade in Land* p. 23. Cf. G.O. Morgan 'Land Law Reform' (1879) 33 Fortnightly Review 803, F.S. Corrance 'The Land Question and Landed Tenures of Possession' (1875) 23 Fortnightly Review 360, W.A. Jevons 'The Land Laws' (1881) 35 Fortnightly Review 385.
17 J.F. Stephen 'The Laws Relating to Land' (1885-6) 6 National Review 729.

the establishment of a system of land registry had been very much what the discovery of a North-west passage was to the last generation of seamen, a thing which everybody thought could be done, but which nobody ever managed to accomplish.'[18]

It had long been accepted that the public registration of all dealings in land would simplify future dealings considerably, with a consequent substantial reduction in delay and expense. Such a suggestion was made during the Commonwealth. During the first half of the eighteenth century the Ridings of Yorkshire moved towards the adoption of such a scheme.

Mr. Sergeant Onslow, in 1815, and Sir Samuel Romilly, in 1816, each sought unsuccessfully to introduce bills for the general registration of deeds.[19] It is not surprising, therefore, that the real property commissioners should have favoured such a scheme for a 'General Registry of Deeds and Instrument relating to Land'. They wrote:

'This has appeared to us to exceed in magnitude and importance all the other subjects within the scope of our Commission: it had excited general interest; and we have found it to be so connected with almost every part of the law of real property, that the nature and details of any improvements to be proposed by us, must greatly depend on the question, whether all deeds and instruments affecting the title to land shall be registered, or whether the security of title is still to rest on other expedients.

It is obvious that a documentary title cannot be complete, unless the party to whom it is produced can be assured, that no document which may defeat or alter the effect of those, which are shown to him, is kept out of sight. It follows, that means should be afforded by the law for the mani-festation of all the documents necessary to complete the title, or for the protection of purchasers against the effect of any documents, which, for want of the use of such means, have not been brought to their knowledge; in other words, that there should be a General Register.'[20]

The commissioners stated that the principal evil under the existing system was insecurity of title. Nor was this evil to be estimated only by cases of actual loss but rather by the lengthy inquiries which it was necessary for a purchaser to institute in order to establish title. Such inquiries inevitably led to expense and delay. They explained that:

'In the process of investigation, which is instituted as to the title, not only every document, the existence of which in any manners appears, and which by any possibility may affect the title, is called for, but various colla-teral sources of information, existing generally or in particular cases, are resorted to. Inquiries are made from the occupiers of the lands and from persons, who have long dwelt in the neighbourhood; county and local histories are examined; searches are instituted for land-tax assessments, awards under Inclosure Bills, grants from the Crown, grants of annuities, records of fines and recoveries, enrolments of deeds, judgments entered up in the several courts of record, securities given to the Crown, probates of

---

18 (1875) 19 Sol Jo 614.
19 For a useful general survey see W.S. Cookson 'Transfer of Land...' *Trans. of the National Association for the Promotion of Social Science* (1859) p. 192.
20 Second Report no. 575 (1830) p. 3.

wills and grants of administration, and various other species of documents. In every case, except where the property is too small to make risk important, as compared with present expense, investigations of this nature, adapted to the circumstances, are prosecuted to a great extent, and they occasion a considerable portion of the delay and expense, which are felt to be the great evils now attending the transfer of real property.'[1]

Accordingly, the commissioners proposed the establishment of a Registry. During the years 1830-34 seven bills were introduced into the Commons with a view to implementing the commissioners' proposals. Lord Campbell made similar attempts in the Lords in 1845 and 1846. All failed. Yet in 1846 a Select Committee of the Lords reported that in their view the marketable value of real property was seriously diminished by the tedious and expensive process which surrounded its transfer. The Committee emphasised that it was necessary to revise thoroughly the whole subject of conveyancing with a view to abandoning a system which was 'prolix, expensive, and vexatious'. They suggested that a registry of title to all real property was essential to the success of any attempt to simplify the system of conveyancing. Thereupon a Registration and Conveyancing Commission was issued in 1847: the Commission reported in 1850. The Commission recommended a system of registration with the aid of a public map. They were not unanimous on all points. Nevertheless, in 1851 Lord Campbell introduced into the Lords a bill which was founded upon the Report. The bill, and the petitions against it, were referred to a select committee. An amended bill was lost in the Commons. In 1853 Lord Cranworth reintroduced the same bill. A select committee was appointed which suggested the appointment of a royal commission. The commission was appointed in 1854 and reported in 1857.[2]

The commissioners stated that the problem was to discover by what means 'consistently with the preservation of existing rights, can we now obtain such a system of land registration as will enable owners to deal with land in as simple and easy a manner, as far as the title is concerned, and the difference in the nature of the subject matter may allow, as they now can deal with moveable chattels or stock'. However, they 'assumed that no plan of registration will be acceptable or desirable unless it leaves, substantially and practically, to the owners of land, powers of disposition and rights of enjoyment of similar extent and facility of exercise with those which they possess under the present system'. The commissioners went on to suggest that a register of title, as distinguished from a register of the various deeds and assurances under which the title had been derived, should be formed. The register was to be formed in such a manner that retrospective inquiry into former dealings and transactions, which was then necessary on a transfer, might be avoided.

In 1859 Cairns, who was then Solicitor-General, introduced two bills which were founded to some extent upon the Report of the Commission. In introducing his Bill for Registration of Title to the Commons in 1859, Cairns quoted the Report of the Commission, as follows:

'When a contract is duly entered into, the investigation of the title often

1   Second Report...no. 575 (1830) p. 3.
2   Report from the Select Committee on the Registration of Assurances Bill no. 889 (1852-53), Report of the Commissioners appointed to consider the subject of the Registration of Title, with reference to the Sale and Transfer of Lands no. 2215 Sess. 2 (1857), Report from the Select Committee of the House of Lords on the Declaration of Title Bill no. 320 (1862).

causes not only expense, but delay and disappointment, sickening both to the buyer and seller. The seller does not receive his money, nor the buyer his land, until the advantage or pleasure of the bargain is lost or has passed away.'[3]

The Bill failed. Lord Westbury's Land Registry Act 1862 was yet another measure which was designed to achieve such a simplication of conveyancing practice. Westbury had said that if his Act were passed every landowner would be able to carry his title deeds in his waistcoat pocket: he pictured a country gentleman in his easy chair after dinner regaling himself with the sight of his muniments of title printed upon a piece of paper about the size of a large visiting card.[4] Indeed, with his customary lack of tact, Westbury had announced that his purpose was to destroy the occupation of conveyancer.[5] The Act, which was passed with little fuss, provided for the establishment of a land registry. The state guaranteed the validity of all titles which appeared on the register. Yet in the first instance the onus was upon the owner to prove his title. Such registration was purely voluntary. In practice many landowners chose not to register. This was due to several factors. In the first instance many landowners' titles were far from being technically perfect at that time: it was scarcely surprising that landowners who suspected that they were in this position were unwilling to volunteer to have this fact made public. In such circumstances there was the possibility also that neighbours might raise the question of boundaries. The conveyancers and attornies also looked with a marked lack of enthusiasm upon an Act avowedly designed to reduce their earnings. Nor was this invariably an unreasonable attitude. For example, in 1875 a Norfolk solicitor regretted a mode of conveyancing which he said could impose upon solicitors 'an infinity of labour and responsibility without a corresponding remuneration'.[6] Finally, the Act's procedures tended to be both cumbrous and expensive. The Act was a failure. Between October 1862 and January 1868 the total number of applications under the Act had been only 507: the total number of titles registered was only 200.[7]

Lord Cairns' Land Transfer Act 1875 was a rather more flexible measure. An attempt was made to make registration compulsory. Indeed, in 1874 the Attorney-General urged that to deprive the Bill of its compulsory character would be to take from it its chief advantage. However, just that was done in the following years — once again the process was to be voluntary. Yet now there was to be no costly, preliminary inquiry. Further, even a possessory title might be registered on the basis that such title was prima facie valid. In respect of subsequent transactions the title which appeared on the Register was to be unimpeachable. Jenks points out that 'as time went on, even a merely possessory title would acquire a tolerable security; for the operation of the Statute of Limitation would gradually eliminate the possibility, or at least the probability, of any claims arising prior to registration being really enforced'.[8] Yet this Act, too, was a failure. It had been optional. It had offered no compensation to those who might suffer as a result of abuse of the register. One would have thought that

3 *Transactions of the Social Science Association* (1872) p. 161.
4 (1875) 19 Sol Jo 614.
5 J.B. Atlay *The Victorian Chancellors* vol II, p. 257.
6 (1875) 58 LT 305.
7 (1875) 19 Sol Jo 614.
8 E. Jenks *A Short History of English Law* p. 263.

such an omission would have made the Act popular with unscrupulous vendors; however, according to Jenks, it made the scheme unpopular. Cairns himself attributed the failure of the Act to its 'being administered through an office and not through a court'.

It was Lord Halsbury, yet another Conservative Lord Chancellor who favoured such a scheme, who carried the more successful Land Transfer Act 1897. This new measure was built upon the 1879 Act. The new Act provided that over the years compulsory registration was to be introduced throughout the country. In addition there was to be compensation for those who suffered as a result of a mistake appearing on the register. The details of the measure were to be drawn up by a committee of experts.[9] Progress was slow, but a start had been made. The Land Registration Act 1925 revised the system, yet even then it appeared to be burdened unduly by unnecessary difficulty and technicality.[10]

The failure of so many proposals upon this question is remarkable, especially in view of the general public agreement with regard to them. Those failures were due to a number of factors. There was the reluctance of the landowners to sanction any changes in the land law which they feared, however irrationally, might threaten the system of strict settlements. In addition they disfavoured any system which appeared to give publicity to matters regarding their land which they felt instinctively was a matter which ought to remain the concern of nobody but the landowners. It was in vain that the commissioners of 1830 urged that publicity would not harm them. In addition the matter was one of considerable technical difficulty. Conveyancers as a group may have been little more than apathetic towards such reforms, yet that would scarcely have thwarted determined political action. At a later date governments may have been unenthusiastic regarding such schemes because of the expense involved — that may have been a factor at least in the slow implementation of the scheme set out in the Land Registration Act 1925. In all it is a tale of good intentions thwarted by irrational fears, apathy and a lack of political will.

3 Settlements

a) *Alienability and family pride*
A legal battle had long been waged with regard to the extent to which land should be freely alienable. On the one hand large landowners had an interest in preserving intact the estates upon which they based their wealth, their dignities and their pride of family. On the other hand there was a strong public interest in making land available to the community as a whole so that it might be worked to good advantage. The Statute De Donis (1285) had rendered land virtually inalienable. 'Infinite were the scruples, suits and inconveniences', wrote Coke in the seventeenth century, 'that the statute...did introduce, which intended to give every man power to create a new-found estate in tail, and to establish a perpetuity of his lands...against a fundamental rule of the common law, that all estates of inheritance were fee simple'. Through the invention of a number of legal devices the conveyancers and the judges defeated the statutory aim. The

9   A. Underhill 'Changes in the Law of Real Property' in *A Century of Law Reform* p. 326.
10   R. Megarry and H.W.R. Wade *The Law of Real Property* (4th edn, 1975) p. 1057.

strict settlement was the medium devised by the conveyancers to tilt the balance once again towards the inalienability of land. In the aftermath of the Civil War they succeeded so well that by the end of the seventeenth century the classical strict settlement, accepted by both lawyers and courts, had been devised, although it reached its final form only in mid-eighteenth century. The nineteenth-century task for the law reformer was to cope with the success and popularity of the strict settlement so as both to ensure that more land came on to the market and so as to allow necessary improvements to be made to the land.

b) *The form of the settlement*

The strict settlement was based upon primogeniture and the concept of estates for life. It was devised especially to ensure that the tenant in tail never came into possession of the land, for, if he did so, he might secure the land to himself and so defeat the whole purpose of the strict settlement. The scheme which was usually followed in the case of the family settlement was along the following lines. Lord A wished to keep the family estate of Blackacre within the family indefinitely, even after his death. Imagine that Lord A was tenant in fee simple of Blackacre. The first task for the conveyancer was to provide that Lord A should become merely a tenant for life and that after his death Lord A's son, B, should become tenant for his life. Next there was a remainder to B's unborn sons successively in tail. Various other possibilities in terms of descent were then listed. Finally, there was usually declared to be a 'remainder' for A's 'right heirs' i.e. 'the person or persons who, at the time when the previous interests have been worked out, may answer the description of A's heir according to the common course of descent of a fee-simple estate'. Upon the death of Lord A, B became both Lord B and tenant for life of Blackacre. At one time Lord B might have had the option at this point, were he childless, of destroying the life estate by a wrongful feoffment in fee: in such a case the contingent remainder to the unborn son would have been defeated. To guard against this possibility, it was necessary to have trustees appointed who might preserve the contingent remainders — in such trustees there was vested an estate in remainder for the life of the tenant for life, to commence when the estate determined.

Let us now imagine that Lord B was not childless but had a son, C. Upon Lord B becoming tenant for life of Blackacre, his son would become tenant in tail in remainder. Upon C coming of age, it would be possible for him to bar the entail in respect of his own issue, even without the consent of his father. Yet C could not bar the entail in respect of those 'in remainder'. The result was that what C had to offer was not worth very much. This restraint upon C was achieved through the medium of the 'common recovery' which might be achieved fully only if the person who was actually in possession of the freehold consented. In 1833 statute abolished fines and recoveries. Now by an ordinary deed of conveyance (if duly enrolled) the tenant in tail i.e. C in this case, might alienate the lands entailed and thereby bar himself and his issue and all persons having any ulterior estate therein. Yet family settlements were protected. The Act provided that where, under the same settlement which created the estate tail, a prior estate of freehold, or for years determinable with life should have been conferred, it would not be possible for the tenant in tail to bar any estate which took effect upon the determination of the estate tail, without the consent of the person to whom such prior estate was given. Accordingly, that person was known as the 'protector of the settlement'. At this point, whether before or after 1833, Lord B would persuade C to join with him in resettling the estate. In return for being provided for throughout the remainder of Lord B's life, a new settlement was drawn up which provided that C was to be merely a tenant for life and for the provision of other successive limited interests, along the lines which his father had agreed at a similar stage of his life. Of course there was no compulsion upon B and C to resettle, other than the contemporary sense of pride in family. The fact that they might choose not to resettle meant that the rules regarding perpetuity were complied with.[11]

Settlements were used also to secure portions for the younger children and a jointure for the widow. In the example given above the settlement would provide for a jointure for the widow of Lord A and portions for B's brothers and sisters. It was the estate itself which met the cost of such provision. Pity poor Lord B if he had numerous brothers and sisters! To meet his financial obligations to them, Lord B might well have to mortgage his estate very heavily indeed. The financial embarrassment was increased by the fact that he was liable for waste, a doctrine which included anything which altered the nature of the property.

Nor might he lease or sell any part of the settled estate. By mid-eighteenth century such debts and restrictions imposed a very real financial burden upon many families. What then saved the great estates 'was the spectacular increase in incomes from land later in the century, when war, industrial revolution and population increase came to their rescue'.[12]

c) *Reform*

As a result the settlement continued to be very popular. After all it was possible for the estate owners themselves to choose how they would have a settlement drawn up. Nor did the public interest appear to require any change. In 1829 real property commissioners commented:

'The owner of the soil is, we think, vested with exactly the dominion and power of disposition over it required for the public good, and landed property in England is admirably made to answer all the purposes to which it is applicable.

Settlements bestow on the present possessor of an estate the benefits of ownership, and secure the property to his posterity. The existing rule respecting perpetuities has happily hit the medium between the strict entails which prevail in the northern part of the Island, and by which the property entailed is for ever abstracted from commerce, and the total prohibition of substitutions and the excessive restriction of the power of devising established in some countries on the Continent of Europe. In England families are preserved, and purchasers always find a supply of land in the market. A testamentary power is given, which stimulates industry and encourages accumulation; and while capricious limitations

11   F. Pollock *The Land Laws* p. 106, A. Underhill 'Changes in the Law of Real Property' in *A Century of Law Reform* p. 282, A.W.B. Simpson *An Introduction to the History of the Land Law* p. 220, H. Stephen *New Commentaries on the Laws of England* (4th edn, 1858) vol I, p. 252.

12   Professor Habbakuk 'Marriage Settlements in the Eighteenth Century' (1950) 32 Trans Roy Hist Soc 30.

are restrained, property is allowed to be moulded according to the cirumstances and wants of every family.'[13]

Brougham had earlier expressed a similar feeling. However, public opinion was about to change. After the repeal of the Corn Laws Cobden became interested in campaigning for free trade in land. In addition there was some desire to enable landowners to contribute to the cost of building railways in agricultural districts. There were also many among the middle classes who disapproved of primogeniture: such people believed that it was wrong for the father to leave the whole of his real property to one child. Above all, there was a very real desire to provide for the improvement of the land.[14] However, the continuing sentiment which favoured strict settlements, is illustrated by the fact that the state chose not to abolish the strict settlement but rather to assist in adapting it to modern needs.

The agricultural reformer, Philip Pusey, believed that the settlement amounted to a barrier to agricultural improvement. Numerous private Acts of Parliament which released an individual tenant for life from the restraints of the settlement support that belief. What Pusey sought 'in effect was a general Act that would allow the tenant for life to borrow', subject to supervision. This was necessary because usually the settlement rarely allowed mortgages for improvements — primarily borrowing was to be undertaken only in order to provide portions. In 1840 Pusey succeeded in securing the enactment of a bill 'to enable the owners of settled estates to defray the expenses of draining the same'. It allowed life tenants to borrow on the security of their estate: Chancery exercised supervision. The Act was a failure. Spring points to two reasons for this failure, First, there was the delay and expense of proceedings in Chancery. Secondly, it was difficult for the lender to ensure that the charge was secure. Later attempts were more successful. The Public Money Drainage Act 1846 provided for the advancement of money to effect improvements in estates. Supervision was to be exercised by the inclosure commissioners; Chancery was to intervene only if there were a disagreement between the tenant for life and the others for whom the settlement provided. Other like Acts followed which culminated in the consolidating Improvement of Land Act 1864 by which landowners might borrow from any source under the supervision of the inclosure commissioners in order to pay for various kinds of improvements. Spring tells us that by 1865 'the inclosure commissioners had reached the height of their powers. They were then filling a large role as guardians of strict settlement. After 1865 they became subject to increasingly criticism, in large part because settlement itself became subject to increasing criticism'.[15]

Meanwhile other legislation had assisted the tenant for life. Some settlements conferred powers of leasing and of sale upon the trustees. Yet even in such cases various safeguards often meant that such powers were not always as useful as the tenant for life would have hoped. The Leases and Sales of Settled Estates Act 1856 empowered Chancery to authorise leases for occupation, mining, or building purposes. It was not a bold measure and a substantial number of consents was needed. The Settled Estates Act 1877 effected a modest improvement by

13   Fourth Report...no. 266 (1833) p. 6.
14   F.M.L. Thompson *English Landed Society in the Nineteenth Century* pp. 65, 69, 257, 283.
15   D. Spring *The English Landed Estate in the Nineteenth Century* pp. 142-171. Note also the Acts which culminated in the Improvement of Land Act 1864.

reducing the number of consents which was required. Yet it, too, was far from being a bold measure.

The Settled Land Act 1882 was a much stronger measure. Simpson has dubbed it 'the only really radical legislative interference with the law of property which the nineteenth century produced'.[16] That is true enough. Yet the Act was by no means as radical as many would have hoped. Accordingly, one critic commented with truth that none of the powers given by Lord Cairns could induce a prudent limited owner to act like a prudent, unlimited, owner for it would still be in his interest to borrow rather than to spend his income. Usually, there was little capital available beyond what was necessary to maintain the estate. If there were capital available, it appeared more fair to allot it to younger children than spend it on an estate which would pass eventually to the favoured eldest son. Such critics believed that Cairns' approach amounted to 'an indulgence of the caprice of present landowners but not a liberation of their land from their power of making capricious restrictions that may last another 40 or 50 years'. In political terms it could hardly have been otherwise. The House of Lords would never have agreed to a measure which deprived landowners of the power to provide for their families after their death.[17] Therefore, the settlement was to remain. So far as was compatible with that basic premise, the tenant for life was to be released from the old constraints. Chitty LJ later summarised the Acts principal effect as follows:

'The scheme adopted is to facilitate the striking off from the land of fetters imposed by settlement; and this is accomplished by conferring on tenants for life in possession, and others considered to stand in a like relation to the land, large powers of dealing with it by way of sale, exchange, lease, and otherwise, and by jealously guarding these powers from attempts to defeat them or to hamper their exercise. At the same time the rights of persons claiming under the settlement are carefully preserved in the case of a sale, by shifting the settlement from the land to the purchase money, which has to be paid into court or into the hands of trustees.'[18]

Therefore, the tenant for life, and not trustees who might delay, enjoyed an unhindered discretion under the Act in the exercise of these powers, except that he might not sell a principal mansion-house or heirlooms or authorise the cutting of timber, except with the consent of the court or the trustees. The life tenant might not divest himself of these powers or restrict their exercise, although he was required to act in a quasi-fiduciary manner for the benefit of all the parties concerned. In addition he might use the purchase money obtained from the sale of land under the Act in order, inter alia, to effect improvements or pay off incumbrances. However, any expenditure on improvements was subject to the control of either the land commissioners or of the court. He might grant building leases for 99 years, mining leases for 60 years, and other leases for 21 years. In addition capital monies which arose under the settlement were to be in the custody not of the tenant for life but of trustees or of the court. It was in such monies that the interest of beneficiaries under a settlement now lay in cases where there had been a sale, rather than in the land itself.

16   A.W.B. Simpson *An Introduction to the History of the Land Law* p. 258.
17   (1880) 33 Fortnightly Review 696. Cf. (1881) 9 Nineteenth Century 258-61.
18   *Re Mundy and Roper* [1899] 1 Ch 288.

There were flaws in the drafting of the Act. It was possible also to argue that to have retained the concept of the settlement at all was to add to the complications of a system which was already too complex. Pollock, writing in 1883, suggested that 'sooner or later the day must come when the system will no longer bear this process, and reconstruction must be faced'.[19] In fact the substance of the legislation of 1882 was to be retained, in an amended form, even in the great legislation of 1925. The decline of the settlement during the twentieth century was due, not to a frontal assault, but to the taxation system.

4 The enclosure of common lands

We have noted already the speed with which the legislature reacted to the demands for enclosure and thereby swept away the long-held legal rights of many villagers in the common land. Yet the process was by no means as high-handed as that bold statement might make it appear. Always there was a concern for due process of law. Often there was consideration that the rights of the poor should not be flouted. On occasion radicals expressed that concern in pointed political terms. As one put it in 1871: 'The question is, for whose benefit are these lands to be cultivated, for the benefit of the territorial aristocracy or of the nation'? By then it was becoming accepted that a man might not invariably do whatever he wished with his own land: the public interest was also to be considered.[20]

In law the common lands of the manor were the freehold waste lands of the lord of a manor. Other men than the lord, who were known as commoners, enjoyed certain rights, which were known as rights of common, in respect of such land. The right of common was an incorporeal hereditament. It enabled the commoners to pasture their beasts, to catch fish, to dig turf, to cut wood, etc. Right of common was by no means unqualified. By the Statute of Merton (1236) and by other later statutes, the lord of the manor might enclose as much of the waste land as he pleased, for tillage or woodground, provided he left common sufficient for those who were entitled to it. Such enclosure was called an 'approving': but it existed only in respect of common of pasture.[1]

There was some enclosure of the common fields during the sixteenth century. However, it was during the second half of the eighteenth century that the enclosure movement gathered momentum. At the beginning of this period the open field system of agriculture was dominant. The common or waste land served the commoners, or villagers, as a valuable source by or from which they might supplement their own small holding in respect of pasture, peat, water etc. Mingay attributes the popularity of enclosures from about 1760 to a quickened growth of agricultural demand and a sustained rise in prices.[2] The French wars and contemporary advances in agricultural techniques contributed to that continuing demand.

19 Pollock *The Land Laws* p. 184.
20 (1871) 3 Fraser's Magazine 301. Contrast *Bradford v Pickles* [1895] AC 587.
1 2 Bl Com (5th edn) 32ff. The lord retained the sole interest in the soil. Consequently, the lord alone held the mineral rights. Both lord and commoner might bring actions for damage done, either against strangers or against each other.
2 G.E. Mingay *English Landed Society in the Eighteenth Century* p. 180. Cf. E.P. Thompson *Whigs and Hunters* (Peregrine, 1977) p. 133.

There were considerable legal difficulties in enclosing lawfully at this time. By virtue of the Statute of Merton the lord could enclose only against common of pasture. Therefore, if the commoners enjoyed rights to catch fish, to dig turf etc. it might not be possible to enclose. In addition the lord was required to leave sufficient pasturage for all persons who had rights of common of pasture. He was required also to leave commoners free ingress and egress to and from their tenements. Such difficulties meant that the lord might well choose to secure the enactment of a private Act of Parliament which would both overcome opposition and secure his title.

A considerable number of private Acts of Parliament were enacted. Such statutory enclosure measures fall into three periods. First, during the eighteenth century there was the wholly private Act of Parliament: there were said to have been 3554 enclosure Acts during the reign of George III (1760-1815).[3] Secondly, after a general measure of 1801 there were said to have been about 2000 Acts before the third period begins with the still more general measure of 1845,[4] and comes to a close in 1875. During that third period 5843 applications for enclosure were confirmed.[5]

During the first period there was often considerable agreement amongst the petitioners for an Act. The private Act appears frequently to have been 'a form of recognising agreements which formerly had been registered in the Court of Chancery or carried out without dispute'.[6] By 1770 there was a considerable degree of uniformity in all statutory enclosure measures. That, together with the delay and expense which were involved in obtaining a private Act of Parliament, as well as the bad methods which had been included in some private Acts lent powerful support to the view that a general enclosure measure should be enacted. Not everybody agreed. In particular there was opposition to a proposal that a majority might compel enclosure. Several committees sat; several bills were lost. Finally, the general Act of 1801 was passed.

There had long been a steadily growing concern that applications for enclosure should be publicised, together with the times and places of meetings at which it would be determined. Other related matters, which were incorporated in the Act of 1801, went to the appointment of commissioners, the method of procedure, and the work of the commission. The powers of commissioners were 'very considerable' and there was no appeal from their decision. There were allegations of mismanagement and of an exercise of arbitrary power. Yet there was to be no appeal to a court of law on the grounds that such a procedure might have been used simply to obstruct enclosure. Gonner's conclusion was:

> 'the claims of the poor were very differently dealt with by different commissioners, principles admitted in some cases being ignored in others. Still, taking the conduct of the inclosures and the awards as a whole, there seems to be no ground for alleging a general partiality on behalf of any particular class. The work appears to have been honestly, if not always well, done, and to have been marked by a rough and ready fairness. The defects lay not so much in the commissioners as in the absence of any general body of

3 F.M.L. Thompson *English Landed Society in the Nineteenth Century* p. 214.
4 (1867) 11 Sol Jo 952.
5 Inclosure Commission: Thirtieth Annual Report of the Commissioners no. C — 1181 (1875) p. 4.
6 E.C.K. Gonner *Common Land and Enclosure* p. 60.

rules to guide them or of uniformity in the acts they had to carry out, a defect more noticeable in the earlier years and cured by the growth of precedent...'[7]

The 1801 Act clearly made for greater uniformity. It had little other effect. The parliamentary expense was reduced thereby; yet the overall expense remained high. By and large, however, procedures remained much the same as before. Thus, in 1843 when Lord Worsley brought forward his bill to facilitate enclosure, there was a familiar ring to his complaint regarding the high cost of enclosure by private Act of Parliament i.e. between £400 and £600. Worsley suggested that a general Act would reduce the parliamentary expenses and the appointment of a board of commissioners would reduce the cost of lengthy proceedings in the localities.[8]

The General Inclosure Act of 1845 established the inclosure commissioners for England and Wales. The Act provided that the expediency of every inclosure and the method of carrying it out should be considered by these commissioners. However, they might do this only upon the application of one-third in value of the persons interested in any lands which were subject to be enclosed under the Act. In addition it was necessary ultimately to obtain the consent of two-thirds in value of the persons interested, and also — in cases where the land in question was waste of the manor — the consent of the lord of the manor. The Act prohibited enclosures within 15 miles of London, or near certain large towns, without the sanction of parliament. In addition village greens were exempt from enclosure and the commissioners might require, as a condition of the enclosure requested, that an allotment should be appropriated for the exercise and recreation of the inhabitants of the neighbourhood. There was also a provision for allotments to the poor. If the application were prima facie valid, an assistant commissioner inspected the land in question and held a meeting in order to hear objections. He reported and a provisional order for enclosure might then be made. Further, section 27 required the commissioners to make a provisional order only if they:

'shall be of opinion, having regard as well to the health, comfort and convenience of the inhabitants of any cities, towns, villages, or populous places'.

It can therefore be asserted with some justice that the 1845 Act amounted to a considerable recognition of a public interest in the common lands. In the light of contemporary attitudes towards property some lords of manors no doubt would have regarded it as a confiscation of their property for the benefit of the public. After all the lord could not obtain an enclosure at all under the Act unless a large majority of the commoners, as well as of the commissioners, assented. Further, parliament could refuse to grant it altogether.

Critics of the commissioners later alleged that the commissioners had not interpreted their powers in a manner beneficial to the public. In 1865 a commissioner lent some weight to this view when he stated that the commissioners did not consider it was for them to determine whether upon public points of view it was right that land should be inclosed because the matter came before parliament afterwards. He went on to say that if the commissioners found the

---

7 *Gonner* pp. 62-63, 76, 77.
8 *Gonner* pp. 90-91, D. Spring *The English Landed Estate in the Nineteenth Century: Its Administration* p. 136.

application right in all its details, they made a provisional order.[9] Had parliament investigated the matter further, that might have been a reasonable approach. In fact parliament did nothing of the kind. One or two comprehensive Enclosure Acts were passed each year as a matter of form with virtually no discussion.

On the other hand it could be argued that the inclosure commissioners were by no means biased in favour of the lord in respect of the amount of land which they allotted to him. Usually the inclosure commissioners compensated the lord by allotting to him no more than one-fifth or one-twelfth of the land enclosed, the remainder being apportioned among the commoners. It could be argued that such an enclosure was more valuable to the commoners than to the lord. Indeed, the lord might not wish the waste lands to be enclosed as he might have lands of his own surrounding the common whose value would be greater, if the common were kept open.[10]

At the same time the allegation was made frequently that insufficient attention was paid to the needs of the poor. Insufficient allotments were made to the labouring poor, the reasons for not granting allotments being 'that the labouring poor have cottage gardens, or that the land to be inclosed is distant from the dwellings of the labourers, is elevated or otherwise unsuitable for the purpose, or that the extent of the inclosure is very small'. That same select committee pointed out in 1869 that it frequently happened that those who attended meetings held by the assistant commissioner to hear objections to the proposed enclosure included those who were claiming profitable rights in the waste land but that the interests of the public and of the labouring poor were not represented.[11] It was by no means a new objection to enclosure procedures. Nor was there any doubt but that the law might be used to counter the wishes of a demanding lord of the manor.

The courts played quite a prominent part in rejecting attemps which lords had made in a number of cases to enclose common land on the basis that they were approving it in terms established by the Statute of Merton. Such attempts had been made in the context of the greatly increased value of building land in the neighbourhood of the big cities, an increase to which easy railway travel had contributed. On occasion, of course, it was the railway itself which required the land. The particular reason why 'approvement' tended to be sought once again was that the inclosure commissioners appeared to be adopting a yardstick of user for the public benefit before they recommended inclosure. It is true that many of their conservationist critics found too little of that approach on the part of the commissioners. Such critics gave powerful support to the Commons Preservation Society. They checked lords who may well have believed that their enclosures were lawful 'approvement' as well as those who were acting unscrupulously.

Early in the century in *Arlett v Ellis* (1827)[12] Queens Bench had rejected the view that a lord might assert as against the copyholders a custom of the manor which was said to authorise him, even without the consent of the homage, to enclose such parts of the waste as he pleased. The court held that such a custom

9   (1877) 21 Sol Jo 435.

10   (1866) 73 Fraser's Magazine 652.

11   Report from the Select Committee on the Inclosure Act no. 304 (1869) p. iii, para. 2 and p. iv. (1870) 1 Fraser's Magazine (n.s.) 185, 191.

12   (1827) 7 B & C 346.

was bad since, if it were good, it would have enabled the lord gradually to annihilate the commons altogether. In the second half of the century such cases became more frequent. In *Smith v Earl Brownlow* (1869) the defendant Earl Brownlow in 1866 had caused 500 acres, part of the common at Berkhamstead, to be inclosed by the erection of two strong fences. One month later workmen in the employ of the plaintiff, one Augustus Smith, a tenant of the manor, removed the fence, albeit taking care to do no unnecessary damage to it. Subsequently, Mr. Smith sought a declaration that he, and the other freehold and copyhold tenants of the manor, were entitled to a right of common over the waste of the manor. He won his case. Other cases followed in which the courts also invariably found for the commoners. In this way several of the London commons were preserved for the public use.[13] Those cases encouraged a contributor to the *Solicitors' Journal* to comment in 1877:

> 'The suits have demonstrated that the difficulty of preventing unjust inclosures has arisen, not from ambiguity or uncertainty in the law but from a shrinking from the expense and labour of litigation. And they have done more than this. For in construing ancient customary rights, and in the difficult application of black letter learning to the altered circumstances of modern civilisation, a court must, to a great extent, be guided by what it considers to be a reasonable view of proprietary rights: and the throwing open of thousands of acres of invaluable building land at the suit of persons whose rights of common would to a casual observer, appear to be at most vague, and almost valueless, cannot fail to have an important bearing on the estimate of what is a reasonable view as to the property in waste lands.'[14]

It was a process which was reflected in the Commons Act 1876 which established a presumption for regulation rather than for enclosure. It was a process which was reflected also in the courts.[15] Finally, the Commons Act 1893 provided that even the lord's right to make a partial enclosure was not to be exercised without the consent of the Board of Agriculture, which was to act upon the criteria established by the Commons Act 1876 in relation to total enclosures. In future there would be few, if any, enclosures.

Certainly the enclosure movement had brought radical change. Yet the concern for due process of law had been impressive. Inevitably, the poor were less likely to be able to press what may have been their legal rights in particular cases. However, even in the eighteenth century, commissioners usually sought to apply the law in an evenhanded manner which suggests that it is over-simplistic to characterise the application of the law as an instance of 'class robbery'. After all, many small men favoured enclosure and, despite the merits of the old style of farming, it is clear that, in the public interest, enclosure was a necessary prelude to the introduction of what was thought to be more efficient methods. When the courts were used in the second half of the nineteenth century, they also proved ready enough to reinterpret traditional assumptions regarding the uses to which a man might put his own land, irrespective of the community interest. Such a change in legal assumptions also amounted to radical change.

13 *Smith v Brownlow* (1870) 9 LR Eq 241, *Warrick v Queen's College, Oxford* (1867) 3 LR Eq 683, *Goodman v Saltash Corpn* (1882) 7 App Cas 633, (1877) 21 Sol Jo 415.
14 (1877) 21 Sol Jo 396.
15 *Robertson v Hartopp* (1888) 43 Ch D 484, A. Underhill 'Changes in the Law of Real Property' in *A Century of Law Reform* pp. 313-14.

5 Housing

Feudal law had no place for the tenant for a term of years, or lease for years. Accordingly, the lease was not subject to feudal rules. Indeed, the relationship between landlord and tenant in those early days was held not to lie in property at all but in contract. By the nineteenth century it was clear that the lessee had an interest in property rather than the right to the performance of a contract. Nevertheless, even then the old distinction lay at the basis of the differences between leasehold tenure and freehold tenure.

During the nineteenth century reformers sought to achieve change in two areas in particular of the law of landlord and tenant. In the first place the common law did not provide for the outgoing tenant to be compensated for improvements which he had made to the land. To many this appeared to be an injustice. Secondly, fear of disease and the related awareness of a continuing housing crisis encouraged parliament to make considerable efforts to regulate by statute the law regarding the letting of buildings for occupation.

The common law held that anything which the tenant affixed to the soil no longer belonged to the tenant but to the landlord. Local custom might qualify that rule. For example, in a suit of trover for ten loads of timber, the facts were that the defendant tenant had erected a barn upon the premises: he had put it upon pattens and blocks of timber lying upon the ground, but not fixed in or to the ground. Upon proof that it was usual in that area to erect barns in that manner, in order to carry them away at the end of the term, a verdict was given for the defendant.[16] However, by the beginning of the nineteenth century there was a tendency to find for the landlord. So in 1822 a classic text suggested that at that time a decision in the above case would have been given in favour of the plaintiff.[17] Statute later reversed that judicial trend. In 1851 it was provided that any tenant who had secured the landlord's consent in writing to putting up farm buildings or machinery at his own cost, might remove them as his own property. The Agricultural Holdings Act 1875 extended this principle, the general principle now being that landlords should pay to their outgoing tenants compensation for unexhausted improvements. In practice the Act was usually negatived by contract — an amending Act of 1883 thwarted that practice. The 1883 Act also provided that agricultural fixtures which the tenant had put up after the commencement of the Act might be removed at, or within a reasonable time after, the expiration of the tenancy. These Acts were the first of a long series of Acts which dealt with agricultural tenancies. Yet agricultural tenants had to await the Agriculture Act 1947 before obtaining some degree of security of tenure.

The nineteenth-century legislation apart, there was no difference in law between the agricultural leasehold and the urban leasehold. However, Pollock pointed out in 1883 that in practice and custom the difference was very great. To a large extent there was often a personal relationship between the tenant farmer and his landlord. This could mean, inter alia, that in a year in which farmers had experienced low profits, the landlord might remit a due proportion of the rent. In return a certain deference was expected of the tenant farmer in matters of

---

16   Bull NP 34 cited by W. Woodfall *The Law of Landlord and Tenant* (6th edn, 1822) p. 213.
17   W. Woodfall *The Law of Landlord and Tenant* p. 213.

game, of hunting, and of voting at elections. It was just such a personal, human-
ising relationship which was lacking in the great, industrial cities of the nineteenth century.

Pollock wrote of the letting of buildings for occupation, whether for business
or as a dwelling house, that the 'transaction and the relations of the parties are
purely a matter of commerce'.[18] Certainly, that reflected the traditional
approach of the law to questions of landlord and tenant. However, it did not
reflect the considerable body of statutory provisions which for a number of years
had impinged upon that traditional approach. A wish to provide adequate
housing for the working classes was the factor which explained this shift in legal
policy. It was a shift which was highly significant in terms of the divergence it
represented from society's laissez-faire principles. It took place over a number
of years.

The courts' traditional approach can be illustrated easily enough. In 1843 a
court held that the law implied no contract on the part of the lessor that a house
was in a reasonably fit state and condition for habitation.[19] Similarly, in 1863
Erle CJ declared that 'fraud apart, there is no law against letting a tumbledown
house' and that the tenant's remedy was upon his contract, 'if any'.[20] Even in
mid-twentieth century the position at common law remained substantially
unchanged in respect of unfurnished lettings.

Yet the nineteenth-century courts were by no means inactive in matters
affecting land. In *Tulk v Moxhay* (1848) the Lord Chancellor established the
modern doctrine of restrictive covenants. He based his decision upon traditional,
equitable principles, saying:

> 'It is said that, the covenant being one which does not run with the land,
> this court cannot enforce it but the question is, not whether the covenant
> runs with the land, but whether a party shall be permitted to use the land
> in a manner inconsistent with the contract entered into by his vendor, and
> with notice of which he purchased. Of course, the price would be affected
> by the covenant, and nothing could be more inequitable than that the
> original purchaser should be able to sell the property the next day for a
> greater price, in consideration of the assignee being allowed to escape from
> the liability which he had himself undertaken.'[1]

The Lord Chancellor had been impressed by the argument that, if the covenant
did not run, 'it would be impossible for an owner of land to sell part of it without
incurring the risk of rendering what he retains worthless'. Therefore, it has been
settled since 1903 that equity will enforce a restrictive covenant against a
purchaser only if it were made for the protection of other land. Thus the restrictive covenant, which was negative in nature, existed over one plot of land for the
benefit of a neighbouring plot of land.[2] It was a bold decision which illustrated
well enough that even in mid-nineteenth century the courts took note of public
policy factors which might govern land use. Still more ample use was made of
the doctrine during the twentieth century. Yet clearly it was difficult, if not

18 F. Pollock *The Land Laws* p. 151.
19 *Hart v Windsor* (1843) 12 M & W 68.
20 *Robbins v Jones* (1863) 15 CB NS 221 at 240.
 1 (1848) 2 Ph 774.
 2 *Formby v Barker* [1903] 2 Ch 539, R. Megarry and H.W.R. Wade *The Law of Real
    Property* (4th edn, 1975) p. 752.

impossible, for the courts themselves to establish new principles which might better working-class housing standards. For that task legislation was necessary. Since mid-nineteenth century numerous Acts of Parliament manifested an ever increasing concern in the matter of the housing of the working classes.

Initially the concern was with public health. There was to be power to compel the owners of dwellings to put them into such a condition as to be fit for habitation and to maintain them in that state. The Public Health Act 1848 charged the local authority or Board of Health with duties in relation to 'sewers, drains, privies, the removal of nuisances, the regulation of slaughter houses, and common lodging houses; the control over streets, water and gas works; the supply of water...; and other matters connected with the sanatory improvement of the place'. In addition the Common Lodging Houses Act 1853 was designed to improve standards in the lodging houses: it even provided quite literally for the policing of those houses in health matters. Just as much to the point the Nuisances Removal Act 1855 provided that:

> 'If the local authorities find a nuisance to exist or to have existed when notice given, and although since removed is likely to recur, they shall cause complaint to be made to a justice, and he shall issue summonses, and, if proved, make order for abatement of discontinuance and prohibition and for costs.'

It was further provided that it was the duty of the local authority 'either by itself or its officers, to make inspection of the district to ascertain what nuisances exist', and to enforce the provisions to abate. In addition, if the local authority did not act, a chief officer of police might, under the direction of the local government board, remove a nuisance where there had been a failure of a local authority and in this case the expenses might be recovered from the defaulting authorities. Unfortunately, the Act was less than precise in defining nuisance. We are told simply that the word 'nuisances' under the Act shall include any 'premises in such a state as to be a nuisance or injurious to health'. Much was to depend, therefore, upon how liberal or restrictive an interpretation was to be accorded to 'nuisance'. On the one hand it was possible to argue in 1883 that 'overcrowding' came quite clearly within the ambit of such a provision and it was overcrowding which was then seen as a great evil.[3] On the other hand it seems that dampness was not necessarily a nuisance and that even a generally ruinous condition need not lead to condemnation as a nuisance. Accordingly, enforcement was uncertain.[4]

Two further waves of legislation gave power to destroy buildings which were incapable of being made to afford proper accommodation. Finally, statutory powers were conferred to replace the buildings thus destroyed by others properly constructed. The principle of the Torrens Act 1869-79 was that the responsibility for maintaining a house in good condition lay with the owner. If the owner failed to exercise that responsibility, the law might intervene, even to the extent of closing or demolishing such house or small group of houses. To that extent officers of health were to have considerable powers, including the power to enter premises on their own initiative. It was seen as a radical measure aimed at improving the housing of the poor, despite the fact that a considerable number of amendments was made to Torrens' original Bill. The Cross Act of 1875,

---

3   (1883) 14 Nineteenth Century 94.
4   E. Gauldie *Cruel Habitations: History of Working Class Housing 1780-1918* p. 254.

together with the Public Health Act of that year, aimed at the clearance of whole slums. Local authorities were given powers of compulsory purchase and the Act stipulated that at least as many persons as were displaced should be rehoused. Thereby provision was made for the third great aim of the reformers i.e. the reconstruction of buildings.

Yet the housing problem was far from solved. The extent of that problem was highlighted in a popular and striking pamphlet — 'The Bitter Cry of Outcast London' — which was published in the early 1880s. Shortly afterwards a royal commission reported that testimony proved 'first, that though there was a great improvement, described by Lord Shaftsbury as "enormous", in the condition of the houses of the poor compared to that of 30 years ago, yet the evils of over-crowding, especially in London, were still a public scandal, and were becoming in certain localities more serious than they ever were; second, that there was much legislation designed to meet these evils, yet that the existing laws were not put in force, some of them having remained a dead letter[5] from the date when they first found a place in the statute book.'

Why, then, had all the foregoing legislation failed, especially in regard to questions of enforcement? Political and social factors were extremely important. Local authorities were reluctant to press property owners, many of whom were of some standing in their community. There still existed a strong belief also in the virtues of individualism and in the capacity of private enterprise — indeed, the Acts of Torrens and of Cross reflected that latter belief. In addition, health officers were reluctant to close down houses when they knew that this might result simply in the family being rendered absolutely homeless. Other factors of a more especially legal nature existed. In 1871 sanitary commissioners reported:

'The number of these statutes and the mode in which they have been framed, render the state of the sanitary laws unusually complex. This complexity has arisen from the progressive and experimental character of modern sanitary legislation which has led to the constant enlargement and extension of existing Acts without any attempt at reconstruction or any regard to arrangement. The fatal result is, that the law is frequently unknown, and, even where studied, is found difficult to be understood ....Intricate legal responsibilities being attached to so many various bodies, or to the same under different names, doubt has often been created as to where the responsibility or power lay, resulting either in inaction, litigation, or frustration of public works already attempted. Boards of guardians, for instance, seldom seem aware that the removal of nuisances in country. places is entrusted to them; and vestries are generally uncon-scious of most important sanitary duties resting on them; nor does the central power seem sufficient to rouse these various bodies to the proper execution of their duties.'[6]

Clearly the housing legislation was confusing. It was scarcely surprising, there-fore, that the commissioners recommended that the law be codified. In fact the Housing of the Working Classes Act 1885 amounted to no more than that: it was a useful enough consolidating measure which introduced no new principle. As

5 First Report of Her Majesty's Commissioners for inquiring into the Housing of the Working Classes no. C-4402 (1885) p. 4.
6 Second Report...Royal Sanitary Commission no. C-281 (1871) pp. 21, 54.

yet the state held back from that greater commitment to itself providing housing which, with hindsight, we can see had been a probable consequence of its actions for some years. In particular, as the Report of 1885 made clear, there was to be no subsidy of working-class housing. There the matter stood at the turn of the century, despite the enactment in 1890 of a Public Health Act and of the Housing of the Working Classes Act which provided, inter alia, for local authorities themselves to provide housing and which gave them powers of compulsory purchase.[7]

Yet it was still the private landlord who was by far the greatest provider of housing for the working classes. That such provision fell far short of what was needed in terms of health alone became evident to a shocked public in the light of the numbers of young men who were found to be physically unfit for the Boer War at the beginning of the twentieth century. There was a public outcry. The Housing of the Working Classes Act 1903, made it illegal for a landlord to let a house which was unfit. After 1909 more local authorities themselves undertook housing. Yet even after the First World War there was a lack of awareness of the extent of the finance which would be required to cope with the housing problem. On the other hand considerable compulsory powers now existed. The Housing, Town Planning & c. Act 1919 (Addison's Act) was designed to provide 'Homes for Heroes'. In many respects it was less successful than had been hoped. However, in Gauldie's words, it did 'set in train a sequence of legislation which was to transform not only the appearance of Britain's towns but the whole framework of her society'.[8]

It capped the legislative trend of well over 100 years. The relationship of landlord and tenant, which had once been determined solely by the parties in terms of freedom of contract was now a relationship whose incidents were determined to a very large extent by statute.

That trend was confirmed especially during the twentieth century by the enactment of successive Rent Restriction Acts which protected for life a tenant who was living in his own home. Nor could a tenant contract out of the protection which the Acts afforded him. Not surprisingly, landlords often sought to create licences rather than tenancies.[9] It was a nice distinction. Yet clearly the law had moved far during the twentieth century in favour of conferring advantages upon the tenant.

6 The legislation of 1925

The legislation of 1925 was a considerable achievement. It contained a number of reforms. It simplified the law. Its quality was demonstrated amply in subsequent years. Indeed, of the 1925 reforms two distinguished commentators have written: 'They are without doubt the greatest single monument of legal wisdom;

---

7 Gauldie *Cruel Habitations: History of Working Class Housing 1780-1918* pp. 284-90, P. Ford *Social Theory and Social Practice* p. 56.

8 *Gauldie* p. 310.

9 *Marcroft Wagons Ltd v Smith* [1951] 2 KB 496, Sir A. Denning *The Changing Law* p. 45. The debates upon the radical Leasehold Reform Act 1967, which granted tenants the right to purchase the freehold, showed that none of the old arguments regarding 'confiscation of property' and 'sanctity of contract' had lost their force.

industry and ingenuity which the statute book can display.'[10]

The nineteenth century knew no major legislation in the field of property until in 1882 the Married Women's Property Act and the Settled Land Act became law. Through the medium of the Land Transfer Act 1897 Lord Cairns sought, as we have seen, to simplify the law by making some provision for registration of title. A royal commission was appointed in 1908 with a view to making further improvements: in 1913 Haldane LC formed a committee with that same end in view. For all his effort there was little to show. However, in 1919 Dr. Addison, the Minister of Reconstruction appointed a departmental sub-committee, whose chairman was Mr. (later Sir Leslie) Scott to report on the question of land transfer. There was widespread agreement upon the existing state of the law. Underhill, a distinguished property lawyer, and no radical, who had a great deal to do with the actual work of reform, even described the then state of the law as 'absurd and scandalous'.[11] With the active political assistance of Lord Birkenhead, the reforming legislation was passed in 1922. Before it came into force, it was repealed in 1925 and re-enacted in the form of seven Acts.

The chief object of the Bill was to assimilate the law of real property with the law of personal property. It was intended also that legislation should render dealings with land safer and easier. Inevitably, such reforms, if they were at all successful, would simplify considerably the law of property. Lord Birkenhead told the House of Lords in 1920 that the Bill was an:

> 'attempt to collect and give effect to the recommendations of commissions and committees of experts who have been labouring in this particular field now for very many years. Indeed, I think I may confidently claim that when the provisions are explained not many of your Lordships will take a very deep interest in it, except those who have to approach this problem on its purely legal side. It is a Bill which has as its object the sweeping away of the distinction between real and personal property, from beginning to end a technical and legal question...'[12]

On the other hand Birkenhead did not doubt the importance of the measure, when, in 1922, he referred to the 'great revolution' which had been effected in the real property system.[13]

Nor is that too generous a judgment. Reforms of this kind had been mooted over many years. It is true also that much of what was enacted amounted to no more than a consolidating simplification of existing law which affected the man in the street hardly at all. The 1925 legislation amounted to a legal, rather than a social, revolution. That did not mean that its enactment was any the less desirable. Nor did its long gestation period mean that its enactment at this time was inevitable. The draftsmen of the legislation laboured hard and well over their work. Lord Birkenhead provided the firm political will which was necessary to push the legislation through parliament. It all added up to a classic piece of reforming legislation: just as important, as much as possible had been done to ensure the success of the new legislation.

---

10   R.E. Megarry and H.W.R. Wade *The Law of Real Property* (4th edn, 1975) p. 1157.
11   A. Underhill 'Property' (1935) 51 LQR 221.
12   39 Official Report (5th series) cols. 154-155.
13   50 Official Report (5th series) col. 1100.

7 Conclusion

Change in this area of law was remarkably slow. The aristocracy's intense feeling for their lands during the nineteenth century was a powerful barrier in the path of change. Their 'passionate, emotional attachment' to the principle of primogeniture was clear whenever proposals were made to make the law regarding real estate upon intestacy the same as that which already provided for equal division in the case of personal property.[14] As a result Dicey, who was no radical, could justly comment in 1905 that, although England had become a democracy, its land law remained that which was appropriate to an aristocratic state.[15] Accordingly, conscious change within this area was usually both piecemeal, cautious and long overdue. One can applaud Lord Birkenhead's property legislation of 1925: it may have amounted to a revolution, as he put it, or at all events to a legal revolution. Yet it had been a revolution which had been an unconscionably long time in the making. Indeed, some aspects of that revolution regarding land transfer, which had been mooted first during the sixteenth century, had still not been implemented fully even by 1950.

When decisive change did come it came rather by stealth. The strict settlement became less prominent not as a result of any frontal assault upon it but because of the effects of new forms of taxation. Changes in the concept of land use arose out of the harsh necessity of improving housing and of preserving in the public interest so scarce a resource as land for the community as a whole. It is fitting, therefore, that the last major legislation during this period should be the Town and Country Planning Act 1947 which sought to regulate the whole future course of land development. Henceforth, no further development of land was to be permitted without the consent of a local planning authority. In many respects the Act was far from successful in practice. Yet, like the first housing Acts of the previous century, it marked a fresh departure.

14   F.M.L. Thompson *English Landed Society in the Nineteenth Century* p. 69.
15   A.V. Dicey 'The Paradox of the Land Law' (1905) 21 LQR 221.

Chapter 14

Labour and capital

1 General introduction

We have no more vivid illustration of the relationship between law and opinion than is provided by a study of the law regarding labour i.e. combinations of workmen and by a study of the law regarding capital i.e. combinations of investors in the joint-stock company.

In its treatment of these combinations the law was influenced by a variety of factors. By mid-twentieth century, however, it was clear that many distrusted the role of the law in the field of labour or industrial conflicts. On the other hand, in the field of capital, of which the joint-stock company is the example taken, the law played a useful, even an indispensable, role.

2 Labour

a) *Introduction*
In mid-eighteenth century statutory provisions regulated the conditions of labour. That approach was soon to give way before the new conventional wisdom which decreed that individuals were to be the best judges of their own interests. The attempts to introduce and then to maintain that individualist position in law, together with the attempts of combinations of workmen first to enforce the old policy of wage regulation etc. and then, especially in the last quarter of the nineteenth century, to secure legal recognition of what they saw as the collective legal rights due to them, made this an area in which rival economic interests met head on. Inevitably, the law reflected that conflict of interests.

b) *The statutory system*
In 1562 the Statute of Artificers set out 'divers orders for artificers, labourers, servants of husbandry, and apprentices'. All persons who were able to work as labourers or artificers and who were not possessed of independent means were compellable by two justices to work as artificers or labourers upon demand. No

master could put away his servant nor could any servant leave his master after being so retained without giving a quarter's warning unless a justice of the peace were to allow him to do so upon reasonable cause. For failure to comply a servant might be committed to prison. Should he have fled into another shire, the justices might issue writs of capias whereby the servant might be put in prison until he should find sufficient surety well and honestly to serve his master. The statute provided also that the justices should have authority to 'limit, rate and appoint the wages'. Finally, provision was made for compulsory apprenticeships of seven years duration with regard to any craft, mystery or occupation. Other statutes made provision for particular trades.[1]

The extent to which such regulations were enforced effectively is uncertain. Very probably there was but little recourse to the wage clauses of the Statute of Artificers during the second half of the eighteenth century. By that time also the courts were unwilling to enforce the apprenticeship clauses strictly.[2] It is quite certain, however, that prosecutions — and the threat of prosecution — for breaches of the contract of service were frequent. It was section 13 of the Statute of Artificers which provided that the workman should not depart from his work before finishing it which caused particular problems. In 1823 one critic complained that in many businesses workmen:

> 'never finish their work, as the nature of the employment is such that they are compelled to begin one before they finish another.... Very few prosecutions have been made to effect under the Combination Acts, but hundreds have been made under this law and the labourer or workman can never be free, unless this law is modified.'[3]

Between 1858 and 1875, 10000 workmen on average were prosecuted each year for breach of contract.

It was the miners who were prosecuted in greater numbers than all other classes of workers put together — very often for refusing, on account of defective safety precautions, to descend the mines.[4] Yet the case which Alexander M'Donald, the President of the Miners Association of England, made against the law in 1865 was essentially moderate. It was unequal, he said, because the penalty of imprisonment was not inflicted upon the employer and imprisonment degraded the workman. He might have added that it was only after 1848 that the practice was adopted in general of summonsing the accused workman rather than arresting him following the complaint of the master.[5]

It was the union campaign for a reform of the master and servant laws which made some employers, especially in the building trade, more keenly aware of their rights under those laws. Accordingly, in the mid-1860s there was an

1   1 Bl Com (5th edn) 425, W. Burn *The Justice of the Peace and Parish Officer* (16th edn, 1788) vol IV, p. 150, J.F. Stephen *History of the Criminal Law of England* vol III, p. 206, R.Y. Hedges and A. Winterbottom *The Legal History of Trade Unionism* p. 11, V.H. Rothschild 2nd 'Government Regulation of Trade Unions in Great Britain' (1938) 38 Col LR 1, 1335.
2   *R v Chase* (1756) 2 Wils 40, *Stephen* pp. 205 ff. On wages see E.P. Thompson *The Making of the English Working Class* chap. 7.
3   S and B. Webb *The History of Trade Unionism* (2nd edn) p. 234.
4   G.D.H. Cole *British Working Class Politics 1832-1914* pp. 30-31, P.S. Bagwell *Industrial Relations: Commentary on British Parliamentary Papers* p. 37.
5   Report from the Select Committee on Masters, Servants, and Workmen, Contracts for Service no. 370 (1865) p. 24, q. 467, S and B. Webb *The History of Trade Unionism* p. 232.

increase in such prosecutions. Especially in the smaller strikes, all strikers might be arrested as being in breach of contract and given the alternative either of returning to work on the employers' terms or of suffering up to three months imprisonment. On the other hand J. Lancaster, a justice of the peace who employed 9000 hands and was Vice-President of the Mining Association of Great Britain, denied that he personally had often been obliged to have recourse to the law. He said that the custom of the magistrates in his district was always to try conciliation: yet the 'moral effect of having the power is often sufficient'.[6] It was a power to which the unions objected with increasing vigour but legislation was not enacted until 1867.

c) *The common law and restraint of trade*

On the one hand there is no reported case, with the possible exception of *R v Journeymen Tailors of Cambridge* (1721) in which any person was convicted of a conspiracy in restraint of trade at common law before 1825 on the ground that he had combined with others to raise wages. On the other hand it was argued that at common law 'every person has individually, and the public also have collectively, a right to require that the course of trade should be kept free from unreasonable obstruction'. In supporting this position Sir William Erle conceded that no grant of this right, nor any prohibition of the violation thereof, was to be found in the direct terms of a law. Yet he cited the judgment of Parker CJ in *Mitchel v Reynolds* (1711) as an authority which illustrated the right to a free course of trade. He maintained that this extended to labour with the result that:

> 'Every person has a right under the law, as between him and his fellow subjects, to full freedom in disposing of his own labour or his own capital, according to his own will. It follows that every other person is subject to the correlative duty arising therefrom, and is prohibited from any obstruction to the fullest exercise of this right which can be made compatible with the exercise of similar rights by others.'[7]

The principal authority upon which Erle relied, which he wrote in 1869, was the judgment of Crompton J in *Hilton v Eckersley* (1855). That judgment, which set out the common law position, wrote Erle, was 'direct to the point that an agreement for any coercion whatever restraining the free will of each party by the will of the whole, is an illegal restraint of trade and indictable at common law'. In that case an agreement by employers to carry on business as the majority should direct had been held to be in restraint of trade at common law. On the other hand, as Cockburn CJ pointed out some years later, it did not follow that because rules might be against public policy, they are therefore criminal.[8]

Restraint of trade remained a vague and uncertain doctrine at both civil law and criminal law. Even after the settlement of many of its difficulties in the

---

6   Report from the Select Committee on Masters, Servants, and Workmen, Contracts for Service no. 370 (1865) p. 64, q. 1441, Select Committee on the Contracts of Service between Master and Servant no. 449 (1866) p. 103.

7   (1721) 8 Mod 10, Sir William Erle 'Memorandum on the Law Relating to Trade Unions' in Eleventh and Final Report of the Royal Commissioners appointed to inquire into the Organisation and Rules of Trades Unions and Other Associations no. 4123 (1869) pp. lxv, lxvii, *Mitchel v Reynolds* (1711) 1 P Wms 181.

8   *Hilton v Eckersley* (1855) 6 E & B 47, *Erle* (above) pp. lxxv-lxxvi, cf. *R v Eccles* (1783) 1 Leach 274, and *R v Turner* (1811) 13 East 228, contrast *Walsby v Anley* (1861) 3 E & E 516, *R v Stainer* (1870) 11 Cox CC 483.

Nordenfelt case (1894)[9] it was still necessary for the court to apply the familiar common law test of 'reasonableness' to the restraint which was alleged to exist in a particular case. Yet, as Campbell LCJ had pointed out in *Hilton v Eckersley*, the case might turn primarily upon the judge's view of political economy and other non-legal topics. Therefore, it was clear during the second half of the nineteenth century that the doctrine's uncertain bounds were a legitimate cause for concern amongst trade unionists, especially as unionists came to believe that all too often trade union aims and methods found little favour with the judges. In practice, however, the equally uncertain bounds of conspiracy[10] provided even greater cause for concern.

d) *Conspiracy*

In 1716 the classic writer, Hawkins, wrote: 'There can be no doubt but that all confederacies whatsoever wrongfully to prejudice a third person, are highly criminal at common law'.[11] It was a doubtful proposition in law. Moreover, it was not clear whether by 'wrongfully' Hawkins meant criminal only or whether he included tortious wrongs also. However, some support was given to his general position in *The King against Journeymen-Taylors of Cambridge* (1721). Several journeymen tailors were indicted for a conspiracy amongst themselves to raise their wages and were found guilty. The report notes that a recent statute had prohibited journeymen tailors from entering into any contract or agreement for advancing their wages but that this had not been included in the indictment; yet this was not a fatal omission as the indictment was for a conspiracy to raise wages. The report states:

> 'it is…for conspiring, that they are indicted, and a conspiracy of any kind is illegal, although the matter about which they conspired might have been lawful for them, or any of them to do, if they had not conspired to do it, as appears in the case of *The Tubwomen v The Brewers of London*'.[12]

In general the later authorities offer no authoritative guidance, although in 1796 Grose J did say obiter that although an individual journeyman might each 'insist on raising his wages, if he can, but if several meet for the same purpose, it is illegal, and the parties may be indicted for a conspiracy'.[13] Clearly the legal position was confused. Certainly it was lawful for workmen to combine if their sole purpose was to seek to enforce, through the appropriate procedure, statutory provisions which governed their particular trade. Any other combination could conceivably have been committing an indictable offence at common law even before the passing of the Combination Act 1799. Erle maintained that the statutes passed for the purpose of adjusting a current rate of wages on some basis other than free competition had tended to prevent a resort to the common law remedy for conspiracy with the result that the records of proceedings under the common law against conspirators for the purpose of restraining freedom for

9   *Nordenfelt v Maxim – Nordenfelt Guns and Ammunition Co* [1894] AC 535.
10 R.S. Wright *The Law of Criminal Conspiracies and Agreements*, F.B. Sayre 'Criminal Conspiracy' (1921-22) 35 HLR 393, J.F. Stephen *History of the Criminal Law of England* vol III, p. 209.
11 *Pleas of the Crown* (6th edn) p. 348.
12 (1721) 8 Mod 10.
13 *R v Mawbey* (1796) 6 Term Rep 619 at 636, cf. *R v Starling* (1665) 1 Sid 174, *R v Edwards* (1724) 8 Mod 320, *R v Eccles* (1783) 1 Leach 274. W.S. Holdsworth *History of English Law* vol II pp. 479 ff.

labour were not numerous.[14] On the other hand Stephen suggested that the inference to be drawn from the existence of a long series of statutes was that, until they were passed, the conduct which they punished was not criminal. It is a view which the lack of convincing authority for any general principle to the contrary tends to support. The result was that the common law of conspiracy regarding combinations was far more vague and uncertain than was warranted by any proper concern for the desirable flexibility of the principles of the common law. That was to lead to controversy in future years. However, in 1799 the legislature enacted a general combination statute.

e) *The Combination Acts 1799 and 1800*
In 1799 the petition of the master millwrights of London to make illegal combinations of their own journeymen only was debated in parliament. It was not unusual for parliament to receive this kind of request. However, Wilberforce commented that, since combinations were 'a general disease in our society', the bill should make all combinations illegal. In June the Prime Minister introduced such a measure. It became law within four weeks. There had been no opposition to the principle of the bill, although there had been some opposition to particular aspects of it. However, in the light of petitions against the Combination Act and other attacks upon it — Sheridan claimed that it was 'pregnant with the foulest injustice' — a fresh Act was carried with similar speed in 1800.[15]

The Combination Act 1800 repealed the Combination Act 1799. The new Act provided at section 1 that all contracts entered into for obtaining an advance of wages, altering the usual time of working, decreasing the usual quantity of work etc. were to be void except that the individual workman might so negotiate with his master. Section 2 provided that any offending workman should be committed to the common gaol or the house of correction for periods of up to three months. Section 3 provided that any workman who entered any such combination or who should endeavour to prevent any workman from hiring himself, or prevail on him to quit his employ, or who should hinder any master from employing any person, or without reasonable cause should refuse to work with any other workman should likewise be guilty of an offence. Section 4 provided that all persons who should attend any meeting for the purpose of making any such contract, or who should summons or endeavour to induce any journeyman to attend any such meeting or who should collect any money etc. would also be guilty of an offence. Section 5 provided that no person should contribute to any expenses incurred for acting contrary to the Act. Section 11 provided that justices might summon witnesses and might commit them for non-appearance or refusal to give evidence. Section 18 declared that it would be a great convenience and advantage both to masters and to workmen that a cheap and summary mode be established for settling all disputes that might arise between them respecting wages and work. Arbitrators were to be appointed: if the arbitrators should not decide the matter within three days after submission to their award, either party might require them to go before and state to a justice

---

14 Sir William Erle 'Memorandum on the Law relating to Trade Unions' in Eleventh and Final
    Report of the Royal Commissioners appointed to inquire into the Organisation and Rules of
    Trade Unions and Other Associations no. 4123 (1869) pp. lxv, lxviii.
15 A. Aspinall *The Early English Trade Unions* pp. ix-xvii.

the points in difference. The justice would then finally determine those points.

To some extent the Act of 1800 met a number of the criticisms which had been made of the Act of 1799. The new section 2 provided that the trial was to be before two justices, not one. No justice who was a master in the trade in which any offence was alleged to have been committed might act judicially. Yet other substantial points were not met. The London journeymen had maintained that the 1799 Act had created 'new crimes of boundless extent' as that Act had made it illegal for any person directly or indirectly to attempt to prevail upon any workman to quit his work. They declared that it would be dangerous thereafter for the petitioners to converse with one another or even with their own families. Yet the new section 3 could hardly have been more sweeping in its stark rejection of any form of combination nor more unhelpful in its failure even to attempt to spell out what limited form of intercourse between workmen with regard to wages and hours etc. might be lawful. However, the primary purpose of the legislation was to provide a speedier mode of justice than was available by preferring an indictment at the sessions or assizes. That, together with the fact that the new offence was general, formed the outstanding features of the Combination Act of 1800.

The Act was not easy to enforce. In particular, satisfactory evidence was difficult to obtain and on occasion the very breadth of the law made the magistrates uncertain of their powers and so unwilling to act. As a result it could be alleged in 1824 that in general the Act had been a 'dead letter'. On the other hand bitter complaints were made of those rigorous prosecutions which did take place from time to time. The Webbs have suggested that the main use of the law to the employers was to checkmate strikes and to ward off demands for better conditions of labour: they believed that it was in the new textile industries that the Act of 1800 was most effective.[16]

The arbitration provisions did not work well in practice. Moreover, quite separate provisions for arbitration e.g. in the cotton industry appear to have fallen foul of the Combination Act. On one occasion when men whose wages had been reduced wished to arbitrate in a body, they were advised that they could only act individually. Accordingly, they submitted 900 applications for arbitration. However, the magistrate regarded this as an attempt to fix wages and held that the Cotton Act gave no such power. This interpretation of the Act, commented the Hammonds, made it 'worthless as a protection to the men against anything but actual fraud or breach of agreement'. Similarly, the Combination Act thwarted the attempts of masters and groups of workmen voluntarily to negotiate with each other.[17]

In fact many workers had wished the old system of regulation of wages to continue. It was not to be: the superior courts showed no enthusiasm for directing the discretion of the justices. In *R v The Justices of Kent* (1811) certain millers stated that their wages had become wholly inadequate to their support and maintenance. Pursuant to section 15 of the Statute of Artificers, they asked the justices to appoint their wages. Lord Ellenborough, in the King's Bench, held

---

16   J.L. and B. Hammond *The Skilled Labourer 1760-1832* pp. 233, 102, S. and B. Webb *The History of Trade Unionism* (2nd edn) pp. 65-72, *Aspinall*, (above) p. xix, cf. R.G. Kirby and A.E. Masson *The Voice of the People, John Doherty 1798-1854* p. 23.

17   J.L. and B. Hammond *The Skilled Labourer 1760-1832* pp. 63-4, 174.

that the justices must hear the case but that 'it rests entirely with them to act or not upon it as they think fit'.[18] Soon afterwards the legislature repealed the wage and apprenticeship clauses of the Statute of Artificers.[19] Laissez faire was on the march.

f) *Reform and counter reform*

The Combination Act 1800 had been introduced for a number of reasons. To some, the new economic theory of laissez faire was important. To others, combinations of workmen appeared to resemble all too closely the recent excesses of revolutionary France. Possibly the government was influenced because it had learned recently of the existence of a powerful combination of Lancashire cotton weavers. Moves to repeal the Act began in 1819. Their inspiration was Francis Place, the radical master tailor. Place persuaded Joseph Hume to lead the parliamentary campaign and he gave Hume the results of his own extensive researches. J.R. McCulloch, the Benthamite economist, was another supporter. Eventually Hume persuaded Huskisson and Peel to grant him a select committee. Choosing not to stress his chief objective, the repeal of the Combination Law, Hume included three subjects within his committee's terms of reference, namely: the emigration of artisans, the exportation of machinery, and combinations of workmen — all of which the law forbade. The committee did not publish a report but instead adopted a number of resolutions. Masters and workmen were to be at perfect liberty to make such agreements as they might mutually think proper: the law, including the common law, was to be amended accordingly. Yet threats, intimidation and acts of violence should be punished efficiently by summary process as they interfered with that perfect freedom which ought to be allowed to each party of employing his labour or capital in the manner he thought best. Hume introduced a bill accordingly which became the Combination Act 1824. This new measure provided that no workman should be

> 'subject or liable to any indictment or prosecution for conspiracy, or to any other criminal information or punishment whatever, under the common or statute law';

for

> 'entering into any combination to obtain an advance, or to fix the rate of wages, or to lessen or alter the hours or duration of the time of working, or to decrease the quantity of work, or to induce another to depart from his service before the end of the time or term for which he is hired, or to quit or return to his work before the same shall be finished, or, not being hired, to refuse to enter into work or employment, or to regulate the mode of carrying on any manufacture, trade, or business, or the management thereof'.

Hume had introduced his bill on 27 May: it received the Royal Assent on 21 June. The Combination Act 1824 had become law so rapidly that some prosecutions were undertaken under the old law,[20] even after its enactment.

18 (1811) 14 East 395 at 400. It was Ellenborough who before being raised to the Bench, offered the interpretation of the Cotton Arbitration Act which is given in the text; *Hammonds* (above) pp. 63-4.
19 In 1813 and 1814. The Combination Act 1824 repealed those powers which existed under individual statutes.
20 Report of the Select Committee on Artisans and Machinery (1824). (1823) 39 Edinburgh Review 317, H. Pelling *A History of British Trade Unionism*.

Place and the Benthamites had believed that it was the combination laws themselves which had encouraged the growth of combinations — repeal the combination laws and combinations 'will cease to exist'. Exactly the opposite occurred. During the economic depression of 1825, combinations pressed their demands hard. To a large section of the public opinion of the day many of those demands appeared to be wholly unjustified. There were demands for a closed shop for union men and for restrictions upon the number of apprentices and the use of machinery. Above all there was violence. Accordingly, in March 1825 Huskisson moved for the appointment of a fresh committee. That committee stated that:

> 'In recommending that liberty of associating and co-operating together, so far as wages or hours of labour are concerned, should be preserved alike to masters and workmen, your committee feel it essential to the regard which is due to the free exercise of individual judgment, to propose that the resolutions of any such association, should be allowed to bind only parties actually present, or personally consenting; not to impose this limitation, would be to afford a dangerous opening to the operation of influence of the most pernicious kind, and by taking away the protection of that competition which arises out of the perfect freedom of individual action, destroy the best defence possessed both by masters and workmen, against the efforts of each other, in support of their conflicting pretensions and interests.
>
> 'This is all the freedom in respect to combination that seems essential for any beneficial purpose; and your committee are of opinion, that all combination beyond this should be at the risk of the parties, and open as heretofore, to the animadversion of the common law, and to be dealt with according to the circumstances of each case.'[1]

Accordingly, the Combination Act 1825 not only repealed the Combination Act 1824, but also provided that no persons should be punished who met together for the sole purpose of consulting upon and determining the rate of wages or prices which the persons present at the meeting, or any of them, shall require or demand for their work; or the hours for which they shall work in any manufacture, trade, or business. And no 'persons shall be punished who enter into any agreement, verbal or written, among themselves, for the purpose of fixing the rate of wages or prices which the parties entering into the agreement, or any of them, shall demand for their work'. There were corresponding provisions with regard to masters. The Act then went on to create a number of offences which were designed to prohibit the use of any form of violence or intimidation in furthering the objects of a combination. Finally, by repealing the Act of 1824, the Combination Act 1825 had revived the common law. That meant that conspiracy was once again part of the law. Further, whereas the 1824 Act had granted the right to combine in wide terms, under the 1825 Act the right lawfully to combine existed only in respect of the limited exemptions regarding wages and hours. Finally, the penal section of the 1825 Act proscribed in the most general terms virtually any act which might coerce the will of another. Yet the 1825 Act did represent a gain on the pre-1824 position so far as workmen were concerned.

---

1   First Report from the Select Committee on the Combination Laws no. 437 (1825) p. 10, N. Gash *Mr. Secretary Peel* p. 349.

A right to collective bargaining had been established, however limited in scope, and this represented a move from a position of status to one of contract. On the other hand the Act's general language, its revival of conspiracy at common law and the individualist philosophy upon which it was based meant that considerable uncertainty remained in law in respect of trade union matters.[2]

g) *Public attitudes and the rise of the trade unions*

The paternal Tudor legislation which governed master and servant may have suited employers and employees well enough in the years before the industrial revolution. It could be argued that there 'are reciprocal duties between masters and servants. From the servant is due obedience and respect; from the master protection and good treatment.'[3] That protection and good treatment which may have been accorded to the servant in a small agricultural community, small business or household was less likely to be accorded in the rapidly growing industrial towns and their large factories. Yet obedience and respect to the master was still expected of the servant. It was all the more shocking, therefore, when workmen combined to press a demand. When 19 printers who had given notice regularly were convicted of conspiring together maliciously to injure their employer in 1810, the judge told them:

> 'Prisoners, you have been convicted of a most wicked conspiracy to injure the most vital interests of those very employers who gave you bread, with intent to impede and injure them in their business, and indeed, as far as in you lay, to effect their ruin. The frequency of such crimes amongst men of your class in life, and their mischievous and dangerous tendency to ruin the fortunes of those employers which a principle of gratitude and self interest should induce you to support, demand of the law, that a severe example should be made of those persons who shall be convicted of such daring and flagitious combinations, in defiance of public justice, and in violation of social order.'[4]

Deference, obedience, respect and a willingness to work for the usual wages would continue to be expected of workmen throughout much of the nineteenth century. Any departure from that norm might appear to be striking at the very foundations of the social order. For example, in *R v Loveless and others*,[5] the case of the Tolpuddle martyrs, the defendants had been charged in 1834 with administering an unlawful oath. In fact it had been the oath required of members of the Grand National Union. Counsel maintained that this statutory offence was confined to mutinous and seditious societies. Baron Williams denied this, holding that the statute extended to all societies of an illegal nature; and all societies were illegal which required their members to take an oath or engagement not required by law. The defendants were found guilty and sentenced to be transported for seven years.

---

2 R.S. Wright *The Law of Criminal Conspiracies and Agreements* p. 13, A.V. Dicey *Law and Public Opinion in England during the Nineteenth Century* (2nd edn) pp. 191 ff., S. and B. Webb *The History of Trade Unionism* p. 97, A. Aspinall *The Early English Trade Unions* p. xxx.

3 *Limland v Stephens* (1801) 3 Esp 269 at 270, per Lord Kenyon.

4 Per Sir J. Sylvester, cited by V.H. Rothschild 2nd 'Government Regulation of Trade Unions in Great Britain' (1938) 38 Col LR 11.

5 (1834) 6 C & P 596.

At the beginning of the nineteenth century the combinations tended to be composed of small, independent groups of workmen which, especially before 1824, stressed the 'friendly society' rather than the industrial aspect of their organisation. During the 1840s unionism advanced upon a craft by craft, town by town basis; despite the fears of the government such unionists probably had little to do with Chartism. Earlier attempts to found a general union, including the ambitious concept of a Grand National Consolidated Trade Union in the 1830s had come to nothing. Accordingly, the formation upon a national basis of the Amalgamated Society of Engineers in 1851 with a membership of almost 12000 marked a step forward in union history. At about this period, too, there was a growing understanding among liberal, middle-class opinion that the unions had a certain amount of justice on their side. Nobody did more to foster that opinion than Robert Applegarth who, at the age of 28, became secretary in 1862 of the Amalgamated Carpenters. He and a number of likeminded colleagues, dubbed the Junta, stood at the head of union affairs during a decisive period of trade union history. On the one hand the unions were pressing their case for reform of the law. Yet opposition to the unions continued to be strong. In 1852 the powerful engineers had lost out in a bitter struggle. In 1859-60 there had been a six month struggle in the building industry during the course of which the employers had sought to require their employees to sign 'the document' which foreswore membership of a union. There was a compromise. The employers withdrew 'the document'; the union dropped the issue of a nine-hour day. However, latent public hostility to the unions was fuelled by allegations of union violence at the time of the Sheffield outrages in 1867. The measure of the Junta's achievement was that by 1875 they had nevertheless secured for the unions much of the legal reform desired by trade unionists. The unions had made considerable progress since 1825.[6]

h) *1825-1875*

Initially there was a tendency to construe the statute narrowly. Yet a much broader view was to prevail. It was held to be an offence to give an employer notice that his workmen would strike unless he dismissed particular workmen, or to tell a workman that he would be struck against or be considered a 'black', or to tell a workman that if he goes to work 'there will be a row', or to use coercion not extending to abusive language or gestures, or for a picket to shout 'Ba-ba, black sheep'.[7] To workmen at least such decisions may have appeared to be an extreme interpretation of the 1825 Act. Then in *R v Rowlands*, Erle J decided in effect that any combination to obtain even a perfectly lawful object e.g. a rise in wages, by means of a strike was an offence at common law. He said that workmen might combine to obtain such wages as they chose to agree to demand but that a combination for the 'purpose of injuring another is a combination of a different nature directed personally against the party to be injured; and the law allowing them to combine for the purpose of obtaining a lawful benefit to themselves gives no sanction to combinations which have for their immediate purpose the hurt of

---

6   S. and B. Webb *The History of Trade Unionism* (2nd edn), H. Pelling *A History of British Trade Unionism*.

7   *R v Selsby* (1847) 5 Cox CC 495. Contrast *Walsby v Anley* (1861) 3 E & E 516, *Wood v Bowron* [1867] 2 QB 21, *Re Perham* 5 H & N 30, *R v Druitt* (1867) 10 Cox CC 592.

another'.[8] An amending statute, the Combination of Workmen Act 1859, did appear impliedly to recognise the right to strike, albeit only in pursuit of an object authorised by sections 4 and 5 of the 1825 Act i.e. wages and hours. Yet the threat of charges of criminal conspiracy in relation to other matters was to hang over the unions for some years.

However, the most shattering legal blow of all to the unions was the decision in *Hornby v Close* in 1867. It was held that a society, one of whose objects was the relief of sick, disabled, and aged members, and the burial of dead members, but of which one of the main objects was that of a trades union, and the support of members when on strike, was not within the protection of the Friendly Societies Act. The result was that the union could not prosecute one of its branch treasurers for larceny or embezzlement of union funds. Blackburn J said:

> 'I do not say the objects of this society are criminal. I do not say they are not. But I am clearly of opinion that the rules referred to are illegal in the sense that they cannot be enforced: and on this ground, also, I think the society not within s.44, as not being "for a purpose not illegal".'[9]

To the unions it seemed that the decision in *Hornby v Close* had equated them with 'something like betting and gambling, public nuisances and immoral considerations — things condemned and suppressed by the law'.[10] Applegarth immediately called a meeting of the Junta. They and their advisers concluded in favour of an inquiry into the unions. Following the Sheffield outrages, during the course of which a number of violent incidents had inflamed public opinion against the unions, opponents of the unions also favoured an inquiry. Accordingly, on 12 February 1867 a royal commission was appointed not only to investigate 'any recent acts of intimidation, outrage or wrong' alleged to have been committed by unions but also to inquire generally into the 'organisation and rules of trades unions', 'the effects produced by such trades unions' on workmen and employers and on the relations between the two and on the trade and industry of the country. The Junta was successful in securing the appointment of Frederic Harrison to the commission as a special representative of the workmen. Thomas Hughes, already a member of parliament, was also a member.

The leaders of the great Friendly Societies, Applegarth especially, made a favourable impact upon public opinion which became more ready to accept trade unions, despite the fact that some evidence concerning restrictive practices in the building trades rattled even Harrison. The unions were helped also by the fact that the committee upon the Sheffield outrages had found that the acts of violence had been limited to a small group of local unions. Even so the commissioners could not agree upon a Report as Harrison and Hughes felt unable to sign even a report which had already been much amended at their instigation. Accordingly, they and Lichfield produced quite an elaborate dissent from the Report which the majority produced.[11] Even the majority recommended the removal of special legislation dealing exclusively with the employment of labour and declared that unions should be lawful, albeit subject to conditions. However, it was the minority report which was to be the more influential. The

8 (1851) 5 Cox CC 437 at 462.
9 (1867) LR 2 QB 153 at 159-60.
10 Per Frederic Harrison, cited by the Webbs in *The History of Trade Unionism* pp. 245-6.
11 Eleventh and Final Report of the Royal Commissioners appointed to inquire into the Organisation and Rules of Trades Unions and Other Associations no. 4123 (1869).

dissenters were careful to ask for no more than bare legal recognition for the unions. They stated:

> 'Trades unions are essentially clubs and not trading companies, and we think that the degree of regulation possible in the case of the latter is not possible in the case of the former. All questions of crime apart, the objects at which they aim, the rights which they claim, and the liabilities which they incur, are for the most part, it seems to us, such as courts of law should neither enforce, nor modify, nor annul. They should rest entirely on consent.
>
> We think the right course is, that they should be left to that spontaneous activity which produced them, and that the state cannot with policy interfere to give them a permanent or systematic character.'[12]

Temporary protection had been given to trade union funds in 1869.[13] Now the Gladstone government dealt further with the unions in two statutory measures. The Trade Union Act 1871 provided at section 2 that:

> 'The purposes of any trade union shall not, by reason merely that they are in restraint of trade, be deemed to be unlawful, so as to render any member of such trade union liable to a criminal prosecution for conspiracy or otherwise.'

The Act further provided that any trade union which registered itself might vest its property in trustees, who might sue and be sued on all matters which touched 'the property, right, or claim to property of the union'. In addition persons who embezzled or who improperly obtained possession of the funds or other movable property of a registered union were liable to a criminal prosecution. On the other hand the Act denied legal personality to a trade union by providing that no union might register as a company under the Companies Acts and that no legal proceeding might be instituted to enforce any agreement entered into for the direct purpose of carrying out any of the objects of the union, or any bond for securing performance of such agreement. In the view of the legal historian Jenks, the Trade Union Act 1871 amounted to the 'most important victory up to that time achieved by the champions of labour organisations'.

The Criminal Law Amendment Act 1871 repealed the Acts of 1825 and 1859. It also provided that no one should be liable to any punishment for doing or conspiring to do any act on the ground that such act restrained or tended to restrain the free course of trade unless one of a number of specified offences had been committed. These included personal violence, and molestation and obstruction.

Some commentators believed that the legislation amounted to a victory for the unions; the ordinary strike was now lawful. The unions took a different view. Their resentment was increased considerably as a result of the decision in *R v Bunn*,[14] a prosecution which arose out of the strike of certain London gas stokers in 1872. It was a case in which, inter alia, Brett J — later Lord Esher — defined 'improper molestation' as:

> 'anything done with an improper intent, which the jury should think was an unjustifiable annoyance and interference with the masters in the conduct of their business, and which in any business would be such

---

12   Report no. 4123 (1869) p. 1x.
13   Trades Union Funds Protection Act 1869.
14   (1872) 12 Cox 316. See also E. Jenks *A Short History of English Law* (3rd edn, 1924) pp. 330-31.

annoyance and interference as would be likely to have a deterring effect upon masters of ordinary nerve'.

Stephen pointed out that the result of the decision was that, although a strike could no longer be punished as a conspiracy in restraint of trade, it might, under certain circumstances, be of such a nature as to amount to a conspiracy at common law to molest, injure, or impoverish an individual, or to prevent him from carrying on his business. It was a decision which appeared to fly in the face of the intention of the legislature. Moreover, although the Master and Servant Act 1867 had modified the old law of master and servant, it was still possible for a workman to be imprisoned for a breach of the contract of service. Indeed, in 1875 it appeared that there had been 204 cases of imprisonment under the 1867 Act.[15]

The trade unions took up the challenge through political means. In the 1874 election two officials of the National Union of Miners were elected to the House of Commons. A fresh royal commission was appointed, but most trade unions refused to co-operate with it on the grounds that it was simply an excuse for delay. Finally, Disraeli's Tory government came out for outright repeal. The Master and Servant Act of 1867 was repealed and replaced by the Employers and Workmen Act 1875 which placed employer and workman upon an equal legal footing. The Criminal Law Amendment Act 1871 was repealed and replaced by the Conspiracy and Protection of Property Act 1875. This new Act provided at section 3 that 'an agreement or combination by two or more persons to do or procure to be done any act in contemplation or furtherance of a trade dispute between employers and workmen shall not be indictable as a conspiracy if such act committed by one person would not be punishable as a crime'. Accordingly, *R v Bunn* was no longer good law, and section 7 appeared to establish the right of peaceful picketing by providing expressly that:

'Attending at or near the house or place where a person resides or works or carries on business or happens to be, or the approach to such house or place, in order merely to obtain or to communicate information shall not be deemed a watching or besetting within the meaning of this section.'

Section 7 provided also that every person who, with a view to compel any other person to abstain from doing or to do any act which such other person has a legal right to do or abstain from doing, wrongfully and without legal authority —

'(1) uses violence to or intimidates such other person or his wife, or children, or injures his property; or

(2) persistently follows such other person about from place to place; or

(3) hides any tools, clothes, or other property owned or used by such other person, or deprives him of or hinders him in the use thereof; or

(4) Watches or besets the house or other place where such other person resides, or works, or carries on business or happens to be, or the approach to such house or place; or

(5) follows such other person with two or more other persons in a disorderly manner in or through any street or road.'

should be subject to penalties. The old language of 'threats', 'molestation' and 'obstruction' had been dropped. On the other hand it was provided that

---

15 Appendix to the Second and Final Report of the Commissioners on Master, Servants, and Workmen no. C-1157 (1875) p. 116.

everyone who wilfully and maliciously breaks a contract to work under a person who is to supply gas or water, or any contract of hiring or service, when he knows or ought to know that such breach of contract is likely to endanger life, cause serious bodily injury, or expose valuable property to destruction or serious injury is liable to punishment. The Webbs concluded that the legalisation of trade unions had been completed by the legal recognition of their methods and that collective bargaining, with all its necessary accompaniments, was, after 50 years of legislative struggle, finally recognised by the law of the land.[16] Events were to prove that to be an over optimistic assessment.

i) *1876-1914*

The courts were asked to interpret the new law on relatively few occasions during the years immediately after 1875. Economic depression meant that for their part the unions were in a weak negotiating position. During the dockers' strike of 1889 there was even considerable public sympathy for the dockers. Yet that year also marks a growing public backlash against some aspects of the new unionism, in particular the boycott. The new unionism, largely of the unskilled and semi-skilled, was challenged by a strong free labour movement, or, as the union members put it, by the use of 'blackleg' labour. The law was to be used in that struggle. Therefore, the stage was set for the unions' opponents both to ask the courts to interpret the legislation of 1875 in a manner hostile to the unions and also to seek through the medium of the civil law fresh means of attacking union methods and the unions themselves. They succeeded so well that in 1903 Asquith could assert that judicial 'intervention in this sphere exposes them [the courts] to suspicion and misapprehension'.[17]

It had been argued, and with some success, that boycotting amounted to intimidation within the meaning of the Conspiracy and Protection of Property Act 1875, s.7 on the ground that any other decision could mean that the 1875 Act could not reach a strong case of boycotting, provided it stopped short of personal violence or direct injury to property.[18] In 1891 the Divisional Court took a different view in *Curran v Treleaven*.[19] In so doing it reversed the courts below. The facts were that upon Treleaven's having refused to comply with the defendant union secretary's demand that he cease to employ non-union men, the defendant called out his members on strike but told them to 'use no violence, use no immoderate language, but quietly cease to work and go home'. Coleridge LCJ held that, although Treleaven may not have unreasonably feared violence, despite the defendant's wishes, yet the defendant's language certainly did not amount to intimidation within any reasonable construction of the statute.

As early as 1876 a judge had warned that picketing was 'a most dangerous

---

16   S. and B. Webb *The History of Trade Unionism* (2nd edn) p. 275, n. 25.
17   122 Official Report (4th series) cols. 235-236. J. Saville 'Trade Unions and Free Labour: The Background to the Taff Vale Decision' in A. Briggs and J. Saville (ed) *Essays in Labour History* vol I, p. 317, H.A. Clegg, A. Fox and A. E. Thompson *A History of British Trade Unions.* During this period there was an increased interest in conciliation. Note the Conciliation Act 1896 and see chap. 6, section 8 (d).
18   (1891) 7 LQR 375, 378.
19   [1891] 2 QB 545 at 562. (1892) See 8 LQR 7. Cf. Appendix to Fifth Report no. C-7421 p. 161.

course to adopt' and seven workmen had been convicted.[20] *Lyons v Wilkins*[1] confirmed that early judicial view. Pickets had sought to persuade workpeople to abstain from working for the plaintiff manufacturer as against whom the defendant trade union officers had ordered a strike. The question for the court was whether this was a 'watching and besetting' within section 7 (4) of the 1875 Act. In February 1896 North J, who accepted that the pickets had done nothing in the shape of intimidation or terrorism, although they had 'carried it rather far', granted an order restraining the defendants from maliciously inducing, or conspiring to induce, persons not to enter into the employment of the plaintiffs. His judgment was upheld in subsequent hearings. In March 1896 Lindley LJ noted that although a strike could be conducted up to a certain point with perfect legality, a strike could not be made effective without doing more than was lawful. Similarly, when final judgment was given in 1898 Chitty LJ commented:

> 'The picketing and the acts done by the pickets were done with a view to compel the plaintiffs to abstain from doing or to do acts which the plaintiffs had a legal right to do or abstain from doing — namely, to compel them to change the mode of conducting their own business. To avoid any possible misapprehension, I state that the strike itself was lawful.'[2]

Chitty LJ went on to say that a watching or besetting was lawful only when it was to obtain or to communicate information — attending in order to persuade was not within the proviso. In real life that was, perhaps, a difference without a distinction. That distinguished contemporary lawyer, Pollock, wondered why persuasion could not be distinguished both in fact and in law from compulsion: if such be the law, he concluded, we are pretty sure it is not the law parliament intended to make.[3]

In the following years the tendency was for the unions to be exposed to civil rather than to criminal actions. Actions for inducing a breach of contract, a new concept of civil conspiracy and the ability to sue the union itself threatened the very existence of the unions.

In 1853 in *Lumley v Gye*[4] the defendant had induced a singer to break her contract to perform in the plaintiff manager's opera house. The plaintiff was successful in suing the defendant for procuring that breach of contract. Once that decision had been affirmed in 1881 in *Bowen v Hall*[5] it was possible to maintain that a contract conferred upon the parties to it rights in rem as well as rights in personam: it not only bound together the parties by an obligation, but it imposed on all the world a duty to respect the contractual tie. Indeed, some lawyers had been surprised that this approach had not been invoked in *Curran v Treleaven*.[6] In *Temperton v Russell*,[7] which was decided in 1893, the plaintiff builder sued the three defendant trade union officials for (1) unlawfully and maliciously procuring certain persons who had entered into contracts with the

---

20 *R v Bauld* (1876) 13 Cox CC 282.
1 [1896] 1 Ch 811.
2 [1899] 1 Ch 255 at 270.
3 (1896) 12 LQR 201. Cf. (1899) 15 LQR 200.
4 (1853) 2 E & B 216.
5 (1881) 6 QB 333.
6 W.R. Anson *Principles of the English Law of Contract* (3rd edn, 1884) p. 206, [1891] 2 QB 545.
7 [1893] 1 QB 715.

plaintiff to break such contracts and (2) for maliciously conspiring to induce certain persons not to enter into contracts with the plaintiff, by reason whereof the plaintiff sustained damage. The defendants had requested the plaintiff to cease dealing with his brother's firm which had refused to abide by an union rule regarding building in Hull. The plaintiff refused the request of the union. Accordingly, the defendants declared that, if any person connected with the building trade in Hull should deal with the plaintiff for materials, the members of the unions should refuse to work for that person upon goods supplied by the plaintiff. Lord Esher accepted that the defendants were not actuated by spite or malice against the plaintiff personally but that they did desire to injure him in his business in order to force him not to do 'what he had a perfect right to do'.[8] For the defendants it was contended that union members had a right to withhold their labour from employers who refused to be bound by their rules. For the plaintiff it was argued that to exercise a lawful right for an unlawful purpose — procuring a breach of contract — was actionable. Lord Esher found for the plaintiff by maintaining that *Bowen v Hall* was binding on the court. In legal terms there can be little quarrel with that ground of the decision, provided it is agreed that there had been a breach of contract in this case. Yet what of the second ground of claim i.e. for conspiring to induce persons not to enter into contracts with the plaintiff? When judgment was given in *Temperton* in April 1893 the judgment of the House of Lords in *Mogul Steamship Co v McGregor, Gow and Co*[9] was long gone. In that case the defendant shipowners had formed an association with a view to securing the carrying trade exclusively for themselves. A rebate of 5 per cent on the freights was to be allowed to all shippers who shipped only with members; agents of members were to be prohibited on pain of dismissal from acting in the interest of competing shipowners. The plaintiffs alleged a conspiracy to injure them. However, the House of Lords held that since the acts of the defendants were done with the lawful object of protecting and extending their trade and increasing their profits, and since they had not employed any unlawful means, the plaintiffs had no cause of action. Surely the *Mogul* decision would afford a sufficient defence on the second count in *Temperton v Russell*? It was not to be, Lord Esher held that:

> 'if there is an agreement to take an unlawful course of action which amounts to a conspiracy, and that conspiracy causes damage to the plaintiff, an action will lie in respect of such conspiracy...the combination here entered into by the defendants was wrongful both in respect of the interference with existing contracts and in respect of the prevention of contracts being entered into in the future'.[10]

Some years later when the House of Lords reversed the two courts below, including Lord Esher's Court of Appeal, in *Allen v Flood*[11] and found for the appellant union delegate, it did appear that the unions had won a notable victory. The facts were that the appellant had informed the employers of the respondents that unless the respondents, who belonged to another union, were discharged, the appellant's men would cease work. Thereupon, the employers

8   [1893] 1 QB 726.
9   [1892] AC 25.
10   [1893] 1 QB 715 at 729-30.
11   [1898] AC 1.

had discharged the respondents who then brought an action against the union delegate for maliciously and wrongfully and with intent to injure the plaintiffs procuring and inducing the company to break their contracts with the plaintiffs and not to enter into new contracts with them. The courts even stated that an act lawful in itself was not converted by a malicious or bad motive into an unlawful act so as to make the doer of the act liable to a civil action. However, the case could also be explained on quite narrow grounds. Indeed, it has been suggested that the only definite conclusion which can safely be extracted from *Allen v Flood* is that it is not tortious for one person to induce or persuade another to do or to abstain from doing some act which he may lawfully do or abstain from doing even though a third person suffers loss or damage thereby, so long as the inducement or persuasion is not effected by illegal means.[12]

Conspiracy was yet another matter. On 5 August 1901 in *Quinn v Leathem*[13] the House of Lords affirmed a doctrine of civil conspiracy. The facts were that the plaintiff, Leathem, conducted a butchers business. One of his regular customers, also a butcher, was Munce; Leathem employed several assistants who were non-union men. A local union of which Quinn was treasurer resolved that its members would not work with non-union men, nor would they cut up meat which came from a place where non-union hands were employed. Leathem told the union that he was ready to pay all fines, debts, and demands against his employees and he asked to have them admitted to the society. The union refused this request. Leathem was to dismiss his men and employ union men. Upon Leathem refusing to do this — one of his employees had nine small children — the union constrained Munce to take no more meat from Leathem upon pain of Munce's own employees being called out on strike. The House of Lords held that the 1875 Act had nothing to do with civil remedies: accordingly, a combination of two or more, without justification or excuse, to injure a man in his trade by inducing his customers or servants to break their contracts with him or continue in his employment was, if it resulted in damage to him, actionable. Unfortunately, there was little clarification of the motive issue i.e. had the defendant been inspired rather by a desire to harm the defendant than to promote his own interest?

In terms of law *Quinn v Leathem* was not novel, it simply reaffirmed *Temperton v Russell*. Yet it came at a particularly unfortunate time for the unions for only a few days previously, on 22 July 1901, the House of Lords in *Taff Vale Railway Company v The Amalgamated Society of Railway Servants* had upheld the decision of Farwell J at first instance that a trade union registered under the Trade Union Acts 1871 and 1876 might be sued in its registered name. There was little authority for such a proposition. Farwell J had said that he based his conclusion upon principle and upon the construction of the Acts. Similarly, Lord MacNaghten said:

> 'The substantial question, therefore, as Farwell J put it, is this: Has the legislature authorised the creation of numerous bodies of men capable of owning great wealth and of acting by agents with absolutely no responsibility for the wrongs they may do to other persons by the use of that

---

12 R.Y. Hedges and A. Winterbottom *The Legal History of Trade Unionism* p. 138.
13 [1901] AC 495.

wealth and the employment of those agents? In my opinion Parliament had done nothing of the kind.'[14]

Union counsel pointed out in vain that the minority report, which had inspired the Act of 1871, had clearly had the intention of avoiding incorporation and the attendant liabilities. Indeed, that had been the understanding of the law which the Royal Commission of 1894 had held.[15] Accordingly, the Amalgamated Society of Railway Servants was required to pay the Taff Vale Railway Company £23000 in damages and costs. The unions were shocked. They sought political influence through the newly founded Labour Party, although many Liberals continued to be sympathetic to their aims. Once a Liberal Government was swept into office in 1906 that influence proved to be highly effective. The Trade Disputes Act 1906 reversed the situation. Brief and to the point it referred to acts done in furtherance of a trade dispute and removed the possibility of any proceedings in conspiracy by providing that:

'An act done in pursuance of an agreement by two or more persons shall, if done in contemplation or furtherance of a trade dispute, not be actionable unless the act, if done without any such agreement or combination, would be actionable.'

Section 2 provided that peaceful picketing should be lawful 'if they so attend merely for the purpose of peacefully obtaining or communicating information or of peacefully persuading any person to work or abstain from working'. Section 3 removed liability for interfering with another person's business or for inducing some other person to break a contract of employment. Section 4 prohibited actions of tort against trade unions. This brief Act had reversed the effects of the recent decisions of the courts. Yet many still rejected both unions and union methods. Accordingly, the legal battle continued, albeit in a much lower key. The *Osborne* judgment, which held that a rule which purported to confer on any trade union registered under the Act of 1871 a power to levy contributions from members for the purpose of securing parliamentary representation was ultra vires and illegal,[16] was followed by the Trade Union Act 1913. This Act enabled a trade union to pursue objects and to exercise powers of any lawful kind, provided it remained a trade union i.e. provided its principal objects were statutory objects as defined by the Act. These legal manoeuvres took place against a steadily worsening background of labour relations.[17] Then came the trauma of the First World War.

j) *1914-1950*

During the War the unions co-operated with the government. However, after the war a period of poor labour relations culminated in the General Strike of 3 May 1926 to 12 May 1926. The aims of the strikers were not revolutionary. Indeed, arrangements were made to continue certain essential services. For its part the government had been able to make contingency arrangements for about a year. Suddenly, and without securing any concessions, the unions called off the strike. A legal consequence of the strike was the Trade Disputes and Trade Unions Act

14 [1901] AC 426 at 438.
15 Labour, Royal Commission no. C-7421 (1894).
16 *Osborne v Amalgamated Society of Railway Servants* [1910] AC 87.
17 For an apocalyptic view see G. Dangerfield *The Strange Death of Liberal England*.

1927 whose aim was to restrict union power. The immediate practical consequences of that Act was that the Labour Party's income from trade-union affiliation fees was reduced by a third, as the new law made it necessary for the contributions of union members to Labour Party funds to be made only if the individual member actually 'contracted in' with a view to paying rather than 'contracted out' of paying. A longer term consequence was a strengthening of union support for the Labour Party because of union resentment at the 1927 Act.[18]

The General Strike itself produced remarkably little litigation. Sir John Simon, a former attorney-general, declared in the House of Commons on 6 May 1926 that the General Strike was illegal and that every trade union leader who had supported that strike was 'liable in damages to the uttermost farthing of his personal possessions'.[19] It was a view with which Astbury J appeared to agree in the National Sailors' and Firemen's Union case on the grounds that the strike was not in furtherance of a trade dispute.[20] In fact the point was not argued before Astbury J and Goodhart has since argued persuasively that the General Strike was indeed in furtherance of a trade dispute — the question of the miners' wages lay at the very heart of the dispute — and so was not criminal; therefore, section 3 of the Trade Disputes Act 1906 applied and the leaders could not be liable at civil law.

One of the first acts of the new Labour Government in 1945 was to repeal the 1927 Act. Upon the Conservative Government rejecting a proposal to re-enact the measure in 1951, there appeared to be a greater measure of tolerance towards the unions. Pelling cites Churchill for the view that: 'a wider spirit of tolerance has grown up, and the question [of such proposals] may well be left to common sense and the British way of doing things'.[1] Yet the unions would continue to have a deep suspicion of the legal process.

k) *Conclusion*

Over the years the workers had rarely found that the courts were sympathetic to union practices. Certainly, there were some instances during the late eighteenth century when skilled groups of workmen resorted successfully to the statutory rating procedures. Yet the Lord Chief Justice's ruling in *R v Justices of Kent* (1811) had shown little enthusiasm for such procedures, an approach which the legislature was soon to endorse by dispensing with them. In subsequent years the judicial interpretation of the Combination Act 1825 had been highly restrictive of union practices. Moreover, both in 1871 and at the turn of the twentieth century it had appeared that the common law could be used to evade the clear will of parliament. To the reformist strike leaders of 1926 it must have appeared a poor law of which it could be claimed that it made that particular general strike illegal and themselves liable in damages. At every turn, it must have seemed to

---

18 H. Pelling *A History of British Trade Unionism* (1974 edn) p. 187. In regard to co-operation note Speaker Whitley's series of committees and the Industrial Courts Act 1919.
19 A.L. Goodhart 'The Legality of The General Strike in England' (1926-27) 36 YLJ 464-5. Cf. F. Pollock (1926) 42 LQR 289.
20 *National Sailors' and Firemens' Union v Reed* [1926] 1 Ch 536.
1   H. Pelling *A History of British Trade Unionism* p. 279. Union gains in terms of employment protection and of working conditions had done much to render work more tolerable for their members.

many unionists that the law had been turned against them in an unjust manner.

This was not necessarily the case. In the late eighteenth century justices had praised the workers who had sought a wage increase through the medium of the statutory procedures rather than by violent means. In the 1840s W.P. Roberts, a solicitor who became known as the 'miners' attorney-general', appears to have achieved considerable success in cases before magistrates. Such examples suggest that the legal system could be made to work in an impartial manner, if the workers' case were presented adequately. All too often lack of means may have prevented that.

In his persuasive memorandum Erle had demonstrated just how strong were the strands of individualism within the common law system. Nor ought this to be a matter of surprise. Baron Bramwell expressed the individualist position in extreme terms in *R v Druitt* (1867) yet his position reflected much of the thinking of the best political economists of the day. Judges are surely not to be criticised for doing that. In the same vein it need cause us no surprise that it was Mr. Justice Brett who was at the centre of so many controversial trade union cases during the closing years of the nineteenth century. For it was Brett (later Lord Esher) who gave a dissenting judgment in the well-known case of *Prince* which concerned the abduction of a girl. In that case the majority found the defendant guilty despite his lack of mens rea. However, Brett, consistent in his individualism, stressed individual responsibility before the criminal law and found for the defendant.[2] As statutes gave some recognition from 1825 onwards to union practices, which were often collective, it was inevitable that clashes would occur with regard to the proper demarcation between the two philosophies of individual freedom and collectivism.

Nor could judges be faulted for seeking to frame a consistent body of law, of which trade union law would form an harmonious, but relatively small part. The rule in *Lumley v Gye* and *Bowen v Hall* originated completely outside the field of labour relations. Similarly, the doctrine of ultra vires, which was used in the *Osborne case*, was familiar enough in the field of company law. Was it all that unreasonable to suggest that all kinds of combination, whether of capital or of labour, should be subject to the same rules? It was in that spirit that Farwell J decided the *Taff Vale case*. Indeed, was it right that large combinations should remain outside the law for some purposes? Perhaps collective bargaining amounted to no more than collective laissez-faire, an outmoded concept in the modern world. Yet the unions' professional advisers had felt that that was the right course for the unions in 1869: employers' organisations had not objected for they were content to see the unions accorded rather less than a wholly lawful status. Those may have been regrettable decisions. Yet Farwell J surely erred in not recognising that this was a requirement which parliament had indeed established. His was a remarkable piece of judicial arrogance which can be excused by no harking back to the basic doctrines of the common law, or resort to more austere forms of statutory interpretation. When groups in society, unionists in this case, believe with some reason that they cannot rely upon the judiciary to carry out the intention of parliament, it is inevitable that the judiciary's impartiality is called into question. Workers could feel equally aggrieved at the decision in *Lyons v Wilkins* which appeared with one hand to recognise a right to

2   (1875) LR 2 CCR 154.

strike and with the other to prevent any steps being taken to make such a strike reasonably effective.

The courts had shown themselves in those decisions especially, despite the decisions in favour of the union position in *Curran v Treleaven* and *Allen v Flood*, to have reacted less quickly than parliament to a changing public attitude towards unionism. Even Dicey, a classic Liberal, recognised that whilst the law of 1800 in effect treated a strike as a crime, and a trade union as little better than a permanent conspiracy, the law of 1875 treated a strike as a perfectly lawful proceeding. Of its very nature the common law was bound to contain authority which reflected the earlier view. For the country and for the law, the tragedy at the beginning of the twentieth century was that the country did not possess enough judges of sufficient stature to recognise that in effect this meant that two policies — the one legislative, the other judicial — existed towards the unions and that the common law view must bow both in letter and spirit to the statutory view.

3 Capital

a) *Introduction*

One of the outstanding features of commercial life during the nineteenth century was the rise of the joint-stock company. The essence of the modern joint-stock company was that the individuals who constituted the company held transferable shares in a common fund and their personal liability was limited to a fixed amount. The joint-stock company itself was a legal person in its own right quite separate from the identity of the individual shareholders or of the persons who managed it. By the second half of the nineteenth century such benefits, although by law they were subject to supervision and regulation, could be obtained quite easily.

In mid-eighteenth century the position had been far different. Incorporation was a privilege which the state was prepared to confer upon few business organisations. The result was that until the mid-nineteenth century the incidents of incorporation remained 'either a dispensation or a favour within the special gift of parliament or a carefully guarded bureaucratic concession'.[3] It was a privilege which the state conferred rather more readily during the second quarter of the nineteenth century as the popularity of this form of business organisation became clear. Many in public life resisted this trend. Individualists opposed corporate action, and especially limited liability, with a fervour and in a style which is reminiscent of some of the arguments which were to be used against nationalisation during the twentieth century. Eventually, those who favoured joint-stock enterprise, including limited liability, won the day. Naturally, their triumph was based upon a sound, laissez-faire approach — individuals were to be allowed to use their property as they pleased. In his speech to the House of Commons in 1856 Robert Lowe traced the legislative landmarks of this story in the following manner:

'It is easy to make anything a privilege. Any right, the exercise of which is denied, becomes a privilege, the very term privilege arising from the

---

3   B.C. Hunt *The Development of the Business Corporation in England 1800-1867* p. 5.

negation of a natural right. The process is this — it begins with a prohibition, then becomes a privilege and last of all is a right. Till 1825 the law prohibited the formation of joint-stock companies. From that time to the present, it has been a privilege; but now we propose to recognise it as a right. So with limited liability; at first it was prohibited. Then came the Statute of 1st Victoria, which gave the Board of Trade power to relax the law in certain cases; and lastly the Act of the last session extended the privileges, but still imposed restrictions. Having thus gone through the first and second stages — prohibition and privilege — we propose now to take our stand upon the only firm foundation on which the law can be placed — the right of individuals to use their own property and make such contracts as they please, to associate in whatever form they think best and to deal with their neighbours on such terms as may be satisfactory to both parties.'[4]

In the following pages we trace this legislative transition from prohibition, to privilege, to right. It is a transition which is completed with the enactment of the Companies' Act 1862.

During medieval times merchants were aware of the possibilities of trading on joint account rather than individually, although there was little recourse to it. It was the merchant adventurers who traded overseas who first made use of the term 'company'. 'Regulated companies', incorporated by royal charter, for the conduct of foreign trade and settlement became quite common during the sixteenth century. However, the primary aim of such companies, as distinct from that of their members, was governmental rather than commercial: they were designed above all to regulate or to govern trade in a particular area. Only at a later stage do we find companies beginning to trade for the profit of their members. In such activity we find the origins of the joint-stock company.

During the second half of the seventeenth century there was a considerable increase in the number of companies which were formed for domestic trade. It was a trend which continued apace during the first years of the eighteenth century. By 1700 the joint-stock organisation had proved its value to the economic life of the country. Yet its very success encouraged the launching of numerous ventures of doubtful validity before an all too eager public which was dazzled by the apparent prospect of acquiring money easily. The confidence of the promoters, and the gullibility of the public, is illustrated well enough by the prospectus of one company which was entitled: 'For an undertaking which shall in due time be revealed'! It was inevitable that many such enterprises would fail. Following the collapse of the South Sea Company in 1720 there were a great many other failures. Now many critics discounted the beneficial uses of joint-stock organisation with the result that a considerable public odium was heaped upon the very concept of joint-stock organisation rather than upon the opportunities for mismanagement and fraud which were possible under the existing system. Joint-stock organisation became a public scapegoat for the financial disaster (the South Sea Bubble) of 1720. In such an atmosphere it was inevitable that the legislature should seek not so much to reform joint-stock organisation as virtually to ban it. That legislative intention was mirrored in the Bubble Act 1720.

4   140 Official Report (3rd series) cols. 129-130.

The Bubble Act referred to:
> 'the growth of dangerous and mischievous undertakings and projects wherein the undertakers and prescribers have presumed to act as if they were corporate bodies and have pretended to make their shares transferable'.

It then enacted that:
> '[the] acting or presuming to act as a corporate body or bodies — the raising or pretending to raise transferable stock or shares; the transferring or pretending to transfer or assign any share or shares in such stock without legal authority either by Act of Parliament or any charter from the Crown, to warrant such acting as a body corporate or to raise such transferable stock or stocks or to transfer shares therein...should be deemed to be illegal and void, and should not be practised or in any wise put in execution, and all such undertakings were to be deemed public nuisances'.

Section 25 went on to provide that nothing 'shall extend...to prohibit or restrain the carrying on of any home or foreign trade in partnership in such manner as hath been hitherto usually and may be lawfully done according to the laws of this Realm now in force'.

Inevitably, the Bubble Act cast a shadow over company organisation during the remainder of the eighteenth century.

b) *Legal forms 1750-1825*

i) *Incorporation by the Crown.* The law had recognised for many years that in some circumstances it was in the public interest that artificial persons might be created who might maintain a perpetual succession and enjoy a kind of legal immortality. Such artificial persons were called bodies politic or corporations and were for the advancement of religion, learning and commerce.

Although a right to incorporation by prescription was recognised, the king's consent to the creation of a corporation was absolutely necessary.[5]. This was conferred in one of two ways. A charter might be granted through the exercise of the prerogative. This was done in the case both of the East India Company (1600) and of the Hudson's Bay Company (1670), although both these companies were later regulated by statute. Alternatively, statute might enable the Crown to grant a charter or equivalent letters patent. This was done in the case of the Bank of England (1694) and the London Assurance (1720).

After a corporation had been formed and named, it acquired the power to:

1)   have perpetual succession;
2)   sue or be sued;
3)   purchase lands, and hold them for the benefit of itself and its successors;
4)   have a common seal;
5)   make by-laws or private statutes for the better government of the corporation.

In addition its liability was limited.

The corporation was then required to act up to the end or design for which it had been created by its founder.[6]

5   1 Bl Com (5th edn) 472.
6   1 Bl Com (5th edn) 467-80, Hunt *The Development of the Business Corporation in England 1800-1867* p.5.

ii) *Private Act of Parliament*. The privileges of incorporation were conferred with increasing frequency during the second half of the eighteenth century through the medium of a private Act of Parliament. Canal and water companies were especially prominent among those incorporated in this way.

iii) *Partnerships and unincorporated companies*. Partnerships were a contract by which two or more persons joined together their money, goods, or labour in order to carry on some business or undertaking in common. It was understood that the gain or loss would be divided proportionably between them. The partners' shares were not required to be equal yet they were required to be joint. Accordingly, each individual partner was jointly and personally liable for the whole of the debts of the partnership.[7]

Clearly this was a legal form which, although appropriate enough for a small business organisation, was scarcely suited to large scale business organisation. Few investors in such an organisation would wish to be personally liable for the whole of the debts of such a large organisation. Similarly, each and every partner might be required to join in the conveyance of the society's property and in the bringing and defending of actions, while the death of a member would necessitate a reorganisation of the whole enterprise. Further, since the membership of a partnership could fluctuate constantly, it would be extremely difficult to know whom to sue. These, and other similar points, were formidable legal obstacles in the path of adapting the partnership to the needs of the modern business organisation.[8] Yet they, and the prohibitions in the Bubble Act, were overcome so effectively, that Maitland could assert with some justice: 'in truth and in deed we made corporations without troubling King or Parliament, though perhaps we said we were doing nothing of the kind'.[9] That result was achieved as follows.

Participants in an enterprise agreed upon the object of the enterprise and the means whereby that object was to be achieved. That agreement was embodied in a deed of settlement. It was this deed of settlement which formed the company. The property of the company was vested in trustees who were required to further the covenants which were set out in the deed of settlement. In this way it was possible to provide both for the company to sue and to be sued and also for the transferability of shares. It was possible even to provide for a form of limited liability, at least as between the partners. Yet there were considerable disadvantages. Above all it was a cumbersome process. DuBois tells us that the forms involved were complicated, the responsibilities of the trustees were great yet their rewards were small, and the question of the succession of trustees was bothersome. In most cases it would have been a relief, DuBois concludes, to turn to the simplicity of the corporation.[10]

c) *The effectiveness of the Bubble Act*
Little effort appears to have been made to enforce the Act. That was a point with

---

7   E. Chitty *The Commercial and General Lawyer* (2nd edn, 1841) p. 436.
8   A.B. DuBois *The English Business Company after the Bubble Act, 1720-1800* p. 217, W.S. Holdsworth *History of English Law* vol 13, pp. 366 ff.
9   F.W. Maitland *Collected Papers* vol III, p. 283. On capital formation see B.L. Anderson 'The Attorney and the Early Capital Market in Lancashire' in F. Crouzet *Capital Formation in the Industrial Revolution* p. 223 and J. Reeder 'Corporate Loan Financing in the Seventeenth and Eighteenth Centuries' (1973) 2 Anglo-American LR 487.
10   DuBois *The English Business Company after the Bubble Act, 1720-1800* p. 221.

which the Attorney-General had to deal in 1808 in *The King v Dodd*.[11] He argued that the reason why this branch of the statute had not been acted upon for so long a time was because it had corrected the evil it was intended to suppress, 'till now of late when it had shown itself again, and it was again necessary, in proportion as schemes of this sort multiplied...to put this wholesome law in force'. Lord Ellenborough said that the law was not obsolete, yet:

> 'the long period which had intervened since the passing of the law, and the little use which appeared to have been made of it, might perhaps afford some excuse for this party, and for others who of late may have been engaged in similar projects, if it should appear that they had fallen unawares into the commission of an offence'.

It was said that it had been 87 years since there had been proceedings under the Act. The facts of the case of *The King v Dodd* were that during 1807 the defendant had published two different schemes. He had proposed to raise by subscription £50000 by 2500 transferable shares of £50 each, payable by instalments not exceeding £10 per cent. The whole was to be under a deed of trust or enrolment in Chancery 'by which no party could be accountable for more than the sum subscribed under the regulations therein stipulated'. Lord Ellenborough said:

> 'But independent of the general tendency of schemes of the nature of the project now before us to occasion prejudice to the public, there is besides in this prospectus a prominent feature of mischief; for it therein appears to be held out that no person is to be accountable beyond the amount of the share for which he shall subscribe, the conditions of which are to be included in a deed of trust to be enrolled. But this is a mischievous delusion, calculated to ensnare the unwary public. As to the subscribers themselves, indeed, they may stipulate with each other for this contracted responsibility; but as to the rest of the world it is clear that each partner is liable to the whole amount of the debts contracted by the partnership.'

Lord Ellenborough's judgment amounted to a clear warning, therefore. Indeed, he concluded by hoping 'that this intimation will prevent others from engaging in the like mischievous and illegal projects'. On the other hand in *R v Webb* (1811) Lord Ellenborough took a more generous view.[12] The facts were that, subsequent to a great increase in the price of bread in 1796, a large number of people in Birmingham covenanted by a deed of co-partnership to raise £20000 by small subscriptions of £1 for each share. Their purpose was to make bread. They were indicted under the Bubble Act as for a public nuisance in that they had raised subscriptions, presumed to act as a corporate body and pretended to raise a transferable and assignable stock. Lord Ellenborough stated that the shares in this Birmingham Flour and Bread Company were not generally transferable in that they were virtually restricted to persons in the neighbourhood and were transferable to no one who would not enter into certain covenants. Lord Ellenborough also queried whether they had presumed unlawfully to act as a body corporate. 'How many unincorporated insurance companies and other descriptions of persons are there that use a common name, and have their committees, general meetings, and by-laws?' he asked. He pointed out that the purpose of the Bubble Act was to suppress certain mischievous and

11 (1808) 9 East 516.
12 (1811) 14 East 406.

dangerous undertakings and commented:

> 'The purpose for which this capital was raised, viz. the buying corn, etc. not manifestly tending to the common grievance, and being in this case expressly found to have been beneficial; the only remaining question is this, whether, as the shares in this institution are, to the extent which has been pointed out, transferable, the defendants have offended against this act in respect of having raised such a description of transferable stock. It may admit of doubt, whether the mere raising of transferable stock is in any case, per se, an offence against the act, unless it has relation to some undertaking or project which has a tendency to the common grievance, prejudice, or inconvenience of his Majesty's subjects, or of great numbers of them...it cannot be said that there has been such a raising of transferable stock as to fall clearly within the scope of the act. It was not the object of the undertaking to raise stock for the purpose of transfer, nor to make such stock a subject of commercial speculation or adventure; it is made expressly transferable to no one individual to a greater amount than 20, and the purchaser is obliged in every case to enter into covenants, and to comply with the condition of taking from the institution a weekly supply of bread and flour.'[13]

Accordingly, judgment was entered for the defendants.

A great deal depended, therefore, upon the facts of the particular case. It would, indeed, have been a strict interpretation of the Act which had found that the self help in these circumstances of the Birmingham men was unlawful. Yet not all corporate objects were so clearly beneficial to the public: nor was the transferability of shares always so restricted. In such cases a company might well be illegal within the meaning of the Bubble Act.[14]

One can only guess at how effective the Bubble Act was in moulding business organisations. Certainly it reflected the conventional wisdom throughout the eighteenth century. Adam Smith wrote that only four trades were suitable for joint-stock operation, namely: banking, fire and marine insurance, making and maintaining canals, and bringing water to a great city. Smith believed that other enterprises by a joint-stock company would be both unsuccessful as businesses and also injurious to the public welfare. However, at the turn of the century the war generated many promotions. It is in the light of that activity that we must place the Attorney-General's action in *R v Dodd* (1808). For some years still the idea of the joint-stock company continued to be linked in the public mind with monopoly. Public hostility to such companies was evident during the burst of promotions which occurred in 1824-25. It was voiced not only by the highly conservative Lord Chancellor, Lord Eldon, but also by Huskisson, of the Board of Trade. The result was that even in 1825, in the view of Hunt, 'the Act of 1720 was still to be reckoned with'. Public criticism focussed not so much upon the object of the Act as upon uncertainty regarding its meaning and likely application in law. Accordingly, in 1825 the Bubble Act was repealed.

d) *The Act of 1825*

The Act of 1825 did little more than repeal the Bubble Act. In the view of the

13   (1811) 14 East 421.
14   *Josephs v Pebrer* (1825) 3 B & C 639.

Attorney-General the common law was perfectly adequate for dealing with fraudulent promotions. Even so, Lord Eldon was responsible for securing a provision to the effect that, despite the repeal of the Bubble Act, 'the several undertakings should be adjudged and dealt with according to common law'. More positively, the 1825 Act did provide that, upon granting charters in future, the Crown might provide that the members of the corporation should be 'individually liable, in their persons and property, for the debts, contracts and engagements of the corporation to such extent, and subject to such regulations and restrictions, as High Majesty...may deem fit and proper'.

i) *The common law position.* In *Duvergier v Fellowes* (1828)[15] Best CJ said that, 'Persons who without the sanction of the legislature, presume to act as a corporation, are guilty of a contempt of the king.' However, this was a case of a 'wild project entered into by speculating persons'. We find that in *Walburn v Ingilby*[16] (1832) Brougham LC, although he tended in public life to be far from friendly to such associations, took a far more charitable view. In *Blundell v Winsor* (1837)[17] the facts were that a joint-stock company had been formed for working gold mines in North America. As the shares might be increased to an unlimited extent and were made assignable at the discretion of the holders, the company was held to be illegal and fraudulent. Shadwell VC said:

> 'this deed is not only illegal because it touches on the prerogative of the king, by attempting to create a body not having the protection of the king's charter, the shares of which might be assigned without any control or restriction whatsoever; but also because it holds out to the public a false and fraudulent representation that the shares could be so assigned.
>
> The undertaking in question appears to have been a wild project, entered into by speculating persons for the purpose of deluding the weak portion of the public of this country...'

With the decision in *Garrard v Hardey* (1843)[18] the law became reasonably clear. Tindal CJ pointed out that *Duvergier v Fellows* had not been a case simply of the formation of a pretended coporate body: it had concerned the formation of such a body for a purpose confessedly illegal. He maintained that the raising and transferring of stock in a company could not be held, in itself, an offence at common law. Since the repeal of the Bubble Act, he went on, transferability of stock alone, without any statement of the mode by which it injured or defrauded the public, could not be an offence at common law.

ii) *Charters.* Relatively few charters were granted under the provisions of the 1825 Act. Probably this was due to public disillusion consequent upon the recession of 1825-26.[19]

e) *A time of change 1834-1845*

There was some modest experimentation during the 1830s. The Trading

15 (1832) 1 CI & Fin 39, Hunt *The Development of the Business Corporation in England 1800-1867*, chap. III.
16 (1832) 1 My & K 61.
17 (1837) 8 Sim 601.
18 (1843) 5 Man & G 471. Cf. *Harrison v Heathorn* (1843) 6 Man & G 81.
19 B.C. Hunt *The Development of the Business Corporation in England 1800-1867* p.41.

Companies Act 1834 was designed to make it rather easier to obtain some of the advantages of incorporation. It provided that the Crown might confer by letters patent those privileges which it might confer either at common law or by virtue of the Act of 1825. In particular, the privilege of bringing and defending actions in the name of a principal officer might be conferred in this way. However, the privilege of limited liability could not be so conferred. In fact the Board of Trade made relatively little use of these powers. Nevertheless, the result of the Act, according to Napier, was that the Crown was empowered 'to create a body or entity which was neither an individual, a corporation, or a partnership, the several members of which might or might not, according to the provisions of the letters patent, be liable for its debts, and which could sue and be sued, not in its own name, but in that of an officer'.[20]

It was a confused situation. However, despite being viewed with suspicion by much of public opinion, joint-stock associations continued to flourish. Accordingly the Board of Trade inaugurated an inquiry in 1837. The report[1] was written by Bellenden Ker whose principal task was to inquire into the expediency of introducing the limited trading partnership which the French knew as the société en commandite. The majority of the witnesses, and the report, did not favour such an innovation. Yet Ker made a number of useful points. Greater uniformity regarding the powers of companies was desirable so that the expense of, and delay in, obtaining letters patent or a charter might be reduced. Such uniformity would also benefit the courts by rendering easier the task of interpreting the powers of the companies. Ker also noted that, as the law then stood, members must be joined as parties to an action. In practice that meant that justice might be denied. However, he could suggest only that the public should know who were the partners liable and have an easy means of suing them. In the event an Act of 1837 provided that the Crown might authorise a restriction of the liability of members of even an unincorporated association to a fixed maximum for each share. However, every association to which this privilege was granted was required to have a registered deed of partnership which divided the capital into a certain number of shares and members were to be liable until transfers of their shares were registered. Further, in its deed of partnership the association named two or more officers by whom it might sue and be sued. In practice the 1837 Act was a failure. Fraudulent companies were not checked thereby. Other companies were less than enthusiastic in rendering it easier for them to be sued. The provisions for a restriction of liability of members were seen as being far from liberal. Not surprisingly, discussion sputtered on with opinion as divided as ever.[2]

A further parliamentary committee, which had originated in the public concern consequent upon a series of frauds of the kind which Dickens sketched so vividly in *Martin Chuzzlewit*, was appointed in 1841. The committee's terms of reference provided that it should 'inquire into the state of the laws respecting joint-stock companies, with a view to the greater security of the public'. With the appointment in 1843 as chairman of Gladstone, who was then President of the

---

20   T.B. Napier 'The History of Joint Stock and Limited Liability Companies' in *A Century of Law Reform* pp. 379, 388, 389.

1   Report on the Law of Partnership no. 530 (1837).

2   Chartered Companies Act 1837, *Hunt* (above) p. 82, W.S. Holdsworth *History of English Law* vol 15, p. 46, E. Jenks *A Short History of English Law* (3rd edn, 1924) pp. 294-5.

Board of Trade, the committee undertook a more comprehensive inquiry. In its report[3] the committee classified 'bubble companies' as follows:

'(1) Those faulty in their nature, founded on unsound calculations and having no possibility of success.'

The committee suggested that the legislature could do little in such instances other than to provide for greater publicity, e.g. in the prospectus.

'(2) Those which, let their objects be good or bad, were so ill constituted as to render it probable that failure incident of mismanagement would attend them.'

Here again the legislature could do little other than to provide for 'periodical meetings and balancing of accounts which would indicate the real condition of the company, and an improvement in the shareholders' remedies against their directors and officers'.

'(3) Those fraudulent in objects.'

The remedy in such cases was said to be easy. It was suggested that the publication of the names of directors, deeds of settlement, the amount of capital etc. would meet attempts at fraud since the public would be provided thereby with the means of knowing with whom they were dealing.

Legislation followed swiftly. In 1844 statute provided for the creation of an office for the registration of joint-stock companies. Before the intention to form a company was made public, the promoters were to give to that office details of the name, the business and the promoters of the company. Other details were to be given after the intention to form a company had been made public. Before the company could obtain complete registration, it was required to be formed 'by a deed or writing under the hands and seals of the shareholders, which must appoint not less than three directors and one or more auditors. The matters to be included in the deed, such as the amount of capital, its division into shares, etc. were prescribed in the Act.'[4]

Provision was made also for returns to be made to the registrar of joint-stock companies, for the machinery for transfers of shares and their registration by the registrar, and for the keeping and auditing of accounts. Moreover all partnerships, with the exception of banking partnerships, which had more than 25 members and freely transferable shares were required by law to be registered.

In the same year a further Act provided for the winding up of insolvent companies under bankruptcy law. Unfortunately this Act, and later legislation, led to a conflict of jurisdiction between the court of bankruptcy and Chancery. Finally the Companies Clauses Consolidation Act 1845 set out standard provisions which in future might be incorporated by reference in private statutes of incorporation. In this way the delay and expense of statutory incorporations were reduced.

f) *The advent of limited liability*

As yet there was no provision for general limited liability. In practice many insurance and trading companies sought limited liability by inserting an appropriate clause in their policies or contracts. In 1853 the manager of the Indemnity

3 First Report on Joint Stock Companies 1844. See *Hunt* (above) pp. 90-93, *Holdsworth* (above) p. 47.
4 Joint Stock Companies Act 1844, *Holdsworth* (above) p. 50.

Marine Assurance Company, which had been founded in 1824 and which in 1853 alone had insured property to the value of over £30m, said that his company's policies had always included the following clause:

> 'no proprietor of the said company...shall be in any wise subject or liable to any claims or demands...beyond the amount of his or her share or shares in the capital stock of the company, it being one of the original or fundamental principles of the company that the responsibility of the individual proprietors, shall, in all cases, be limited to their respective shares in the said capital stock'.[5]

In *Hallett v Dowdall*[6] (1852) the court upheld the old view that, although such a clause was perfectly valid as between the partners themselves, it was of no effect in respect of third parties without notice of it. Increasingly, however, much public opinion began to believe that a general law of limited liability should be enacted.

The Gladstone committee had been told that the existing law was dangerous and unjust towards a man of substance as it required him to put his whole property at the mercy of other persons beyond his control with the result that few men of responsibility could be found to occupy so perilous a position.[7] Others suggested that limited liability would confer benefits upon the small investor.[8] Finally, the Mercantile Law Commission was appointed in 1852.

The commissioners heard a great deal of evidence. Unfortunately, they were 'much embarrassed by the great contrariety of opinion entertained'. Similar divisions were evident in their own ranks. However, the majority came out against change. They reported that:

> 'the question which appeared...of paramount importance was, whether the proposed alteration of the law would operate beneficially on the general trading interests of the country and they have arrived at the conclusion that it would not. They have not been able to discover any evidence of the want of a sufficient amount of capital for the requirements of trade; and the annually increasing wealth of the country, and the difficulty of finding profitable investments for it, seem...sufficient guarantees that an adequate amount will always be devoted to any mercantile enterprise that holds out a reasonable prospect of gain, without any forced action upon capital to determine it in that direction;...many of the opinions in favour of such a system are coupled with a recommendation of more stringent regulations than those now existing for the prevention of fraud. But if such partnerships would increase the danger of fraud, they can hardly be otherwise than prejudicial to our mercantile reputation.'

The benefits had been 'greatly overrated'.

On the other hand the commissioners believed that

> 'many useful enterprises calculated to produce benefit to the public and profit to those who engage in them are of such magnitude that no private

---

5   First Report of the Commissioners appointed to inquire and ascertain how far The Mercantile Laws in the Different Parts of the United Kingdom...may be advantageously Assimilated and also whether any and what alterations and amendments should be made in the Law of Partnership no. 1791 (1854) p. 119.

6   [1852] 18 QB 2, 21 LJQB 98.

7   Hunt *The Development of the Business Corporation in England 1800-1867* p. 98.

8   *Hunt* p. 123.

partnership can be expected to provide the funds necessary...of which docks, railways, and extensive shipping companies may be taken as examples. And there are others of a more limited character, from which benefit to the humbler classes of society may be expected to accrue, such as baths and washhouses, lodging-houses and reading rooms, to the establishment of which by large capitalists there is little inducement. These two classes of undertaking it may therefore be desirable to encourage, by limiting the liability of those who embark in them.'

Yet with regard to both the commissioners believed that there should be some previous inquiry as to the means of carrying them into effect.

The commissioners then recommended that the expense of obtaining private Acts of Parliament should be kept as low as possible. Finally, they suggested that while:

'there is on every side such abundant evidence of satisfactory progress and national prosperity, it would be unwise to interfere with principles which...have proved beneficial to the general industry of the country'.

Of the dissenting commissioners it was Bramwell who, as ever, based his opinion upon first principles:

'If ever there was a rule established by reason, authority and experience it is that the interest of a community is best consulted by leaving to its members, as far as possible, the unrestrained and unfettered exercise of their own talents and industry. Our modern legislation has been founded on this principle, with the sanction of the immense majority of those whose opinions are of any value. The restraint on limited liability partnerships offends against this rule; and I frankly own, that, whatever weight is due to the evidence given us, I attach more value to the operation of that general principle, the extent of the effects of which no one can foretell, and which has done so much where permitted to act. If A and B are desirous of entering into such a partnership, and C of dealing with them on its terms, why should either of them be called on to give a reason for leave to do so, — beyond this, that they deem it for their interest, and that it is their pleasure to do it, and their will?'[9]

In view of the great diversity of opinion which had been revealed, even amongst the commissioners, it was scarcely surprising that the Report failed to settle the question. It was now clear that there had been a considerable shift in favour of limited liability. Virtually all the journals were in favour of limited liability. There was still opposition within parliament. Even the government was not yet in favour of limited liability. Two bills were proposed: there was a further inquiry. Now the government was zealous in proposing limited liability. Lord Palmerston saw the issue as one of free trade against monopoly.[10] Legislation was soon to be enacted with quite remarkable speed.

The Limited Liability Act 1855 provided that, after execution against the company, the shareholder's liability might be limited to the amount which had not been paid up on his shares. Such limitation was subject to the company having fulfilled several conditions of which the best known was to be the addition of the word 'Limited' after the name of the company. The deed of settlement was

9   First Report no. 1791 (1854), above, pp. 23-4.
10 Official Report (3rd series) cols. 1389-1390.

to contain a statement that the company was formed with limited liability, and was to be signed by not less than 25 shareholders who held at least three-quarters of the nominal capital, of which at least 20 per cent was paid up. However, in the following year this measure was replaced by the more comprehensive Joint Stock Companies Act 1856. It was this measure which, in Napier's words, brought us to the 'modern conception of the joint-stock company, with limited liability capable of being established without any special Act of the Crown or legislature, on the mere initiative of a number of private individuals'.

g) *The consolidation of company law*

With the enactment of the consolidating Companies Act 1862 the company was established in its modern form. On the whole the courts worked well in furthering the objects of the new legislation, although it was only in *Ashbury Railway Carriage Co v Riche*(1875)[11] that the House of Lords was compelled to make it clear that in law the shareholders might not ratify a contract which was ultra vires (beyond the powers of) the activities of the company, as established in the company's memorandum of association. The rationale of this rule was clear, said Lord Cairns. The Companies Act had been designed to protect not only the shareholders but also the public and in particular the creditors of a company. Of course, public qualms concerning company activities were evident from time to time. In particular the activities of 'one-man companies' appeared to be an abuse of a system which had established a corporate personality which was quite distinct from that of the individual shareholders and officers.[12] However, the basic principles remained. Supervision and regulation through the Board of Trade made for a consensus of public and commercial opinion.

4 Labour and capital: conclusion

The regulation by law of labour had failed. By contrast the regulation by law of capital, or at all events of the company, had been a success.

Before the triumph of the individualist philosophy in the middle years of the nineteenth century public opinion had looked upon all kinds of combination, whether of labour or of capital, with considerable disfavour. Yet business activity, including combinations of businessmen, invariably possessed a presumption of legitimacy which was denied to combinations of workmen. Accordingly, both the business community and the country as a whole were accustomed to, and even welcomed, the legal regulation of business activities through the courts and through legislation. By contrast the state had withdrawn at the beginning of this period from its traditional, paternal role in labour matters e.g. with regard to the fixing of wages. Subsequently, the presumption arose that, for many purposes at least, combinations of workmen were unlawful and so were subject to legal regulation only in the most negative sense.

When parliament, in the name of the laissez-faire philosophy, finally approved the modern form of company organisation there was a widespread acceptance of the aims of the legislation and a general desire that it should be

---

11 (1875) LR 7 HL 653. See generally C. H.S. Fifoot *Judge and Jurist in the Reign of Victoria* chap. 3.
12 *Salomon v Salomon & Co* [1897] AC 22.

made to work. There was a consensus as to both aims and methods which was invaluable at a later stage when it was necessary to interpret the legislation. Such a consensus did not exist in the field of labour. In the 1870s both unions and employers were content for their differing reasons that unions should remain outside the legal fold to a large extent. Parliament refrained from intervening decisively in the public interest, as it had done in 1855 in the limited liability question. Therefore, the legal position of the trade unions and of the law regarding industrial conflicts was never formulated with the legislative clarity which was achieved in the case of the Companies' Acts. A similar lack of an overall consensus meant that no government department, despite a continuing governmental concern on labour questions could work as constructively and as decisively in this area as could the Board of Trade in the case of the company. That same lack of overall legislative concern meant that, in the field of labour especially, the flotsam of centuries of the common law had laid a minefield which might bury even legislative intentions. Such judicial activity was not necessarily based on class antagonism, as current folk lore would have us believe. On occasion the judges had shown a similar lack of sensitivity to legislative intentions in the field of capital when the common law had appeared to point in a different direction. That had been the case even with so distinguished a judge as Willes J in the *Ashbury case*. Nor does an insistence that all individuals and groups, even trade unions, must be subject to the law, necessarily convey class bias. The fact was that very often the law was less than clear in the industrial conflicts area, especially. That again led to conflict and suspicion.

The dominant fact is that the rate of change had been fantastic. From protectionism to individualism, to laissez-faire, to collectivism had taken relatively few years. A law based on precedents would indeed find it difficult to keep pace with such a rate of change whether the subject matter related to labour or capital.

Chapter 15

The family and the law

1 Introduction

a) Marriage, society and the law

Nineteenth-century society valued marriage highly. 'Nothing could be more striking', wrote even the arch-critic Bentham,[1] 'than the utility of that noble contract, the tie of society and the basis of civilisation.'

The law sought to ensure that sexual relationships occurred only within marriage by providing that fornication and adultery were punishable before the ecclesiastical courts.[2] The monogamous character of marriage was protected by the penal law of bigamy. It was remarkably easy in law to enter into marriage. It was just as difficult in law to dissolve marriage. A further inducement to marry was afforded by the social stigma which attached to the illegitimate child and to the parents of such a child. Indeed, the law treated the child born outside marriage, the bastard, with a remarkable degree of callousness: it was believed that to do otherwise would be to undermine the conventional and desirable concept of marriage and family.

It was recognised that the above principles could lead to great unhappiness for some individuals. That was to be tolerated, however, in the light of the benefit which it was believed that the upholding of the contemporary concept of marriage conferred upon the great majority of marriages. In an age of principles society and the law were at one upon that point during the first half of the nineteenth century.

b) Social change and the family

The fertile and popular concept of equality, together with an increasing emphasis upon the happiness of the individual, meant that some change was

---

1 J. Bentham *Theory of Legislation* chap 5. Cf. 1 Bl Com (5th edn) 440, First Report of the Commissioners into the Law of Divorce no. 1604 (1852-53) p.1.
2 The General Report by the Commissioners...into the Practice and Jurisdiction of the Ecclesiastical Courts no. 199 (1832) p.64.

inevitable during the nineteenth century. Divorce and other matrimonial remedies were made available not only to the rich but also to the middle classes and finally even to the poor. The married woman edged gradually towards a position of greater equality with her husband. Nor could the law remain indifferent to the lot of the child within the family. The law had shown little direct concern for the child as such. In the absence of non parental agencies which might care for the child, that was inevitable. However, from mid-nineteenth century there was an increasing concern at the extent of juvenile delinquency. Later in the nineteenth century there was a greater public awareness of how many children were neglected within, or treated cruelly by, their own families. Greater state intervention in family life resulted. The necessary consequence in law was that parental rights over the child were weakened progressively.

c) *No system of family law*
There was no integrated system of family law even in mid-twentieth century. There were laws of husband and wife, although there was certainly no matrimonial régime on the continental model which might have defined the rights of husband and wife in matrimonial property. There were also laws which governed parent and child. Therefore, although the law of succession may have expressed 'the family in terms of property', a deliberate policy of fostering the interests of the family as such was very much a twentieth-century development.[3] Indeed the first monograph upon 'Family Law' was published only in 1953.[4]

2 Marriage

a) *The formation of marriage*

i) *Introduction.* A sound marriage law 'ought to embrace the maximum of simplicity and the maximum of certainty', a royal commission wrote in 1868.[5] It was an ideal which was never realised in this branch of the law. Before Lord Hardwicke's Act of 1753 there was often a lack of certainty in practice as to whether or not a particular couple was married validly. In the years immediately following the Act of 1753 the rigour with which the Act was applied also led to a degree of uncertainty as to the validity of many marriages. By 1949 the relevant law was contained in as many as 40 statutes. The law was correspondingly complicated. Indeed on some occasions, which were no doubt rare in practice, it was virtually impossible to advise upon the proper practice which a couple intending marriage ought to follow even well into the second half of the twentieth century.[6] By and large, however, the outstanding characteristic of the law in this field was that, in practice, it intervened hardly at all.

3 T.F.T. Plucknett *Concise History of the Common Law* (3rd edn, 1940) p.369, J.Unger 'The Inheritance Act and the Family' (1943) 6 MLR 214, L.N. Brown 'National Assistance and the Liability to Maintain One's Family' (1955) 18 MLR 110, Inheritance (Family Provision) Act 1938, Family Allowances Act 1945, National Insurance Act 1946, National Assistance Act 1948.
4 J. Hamawi *Family Law* (1953), P.M. Bromley *Family Law* (1957).
5 Report of the Royal Commission on the Laws of Marriage no. 1216 (1868) p.xxv.
6 *Chipchase v Chipchase* [1939] 3 All ER 895, *Dancer v Dancer* [1949] P 147, [1948] 2 All ER 731.

ii) *The definition and purpose of marriage.* In his classic treatise, which was published in 1726, Ayliffe wrote:

> 'Marriage is a lawful coupling and joining together of man and woman in one individual state or society of life, during the lifetime of one of the parties; and the society of life is contracted by the consent and mutual good-will of the parties towards each other.'[7]

No express attempt was made further to spell out in legal terms the aims or purpose of marriage. However, since the ecclesiastical courts exercised jurisdiction in matrimonial causes until 1857, the objects of marriage as stated in the *Book of Common Prayer* of the Church of England may be taken as indicative of the underlying policy objectives of the law until 1857 and as being influential until long after 1857. Those objects were threefold, namely, the procreation of children, the avoidance of fornication and the mutual society, help and comfort that each partner to the marriage ought to have of the other both in prosperity and adversity.

Accordingly, as late as 1945 the Court of Appeal was markedly sympathetic to the view that an insistence upon coitus interruptus and the use of contraceptive sheaths could not amount to true consummation of the marriage on the ground that to hold otherwise would frustrate one of the principle ends of marriage. The House of Lords was soon to reject that view.[8] Yet the approach of the Court of Appeal had reflected a continuity of principle in this area of the law, although sterility was never a sufficient ground for a decree of nullity.[9] Equally, it was accepted law during the nineteenth century that in order to consummate the marriage a husband might use such force as, but for the marriage, would have amounted to rape.[10] In addition it was believed, upon the authority of St. Paul, that after consummation a husband had a general right to have intercourse from time to time as pleasure with his wife.[11] The law sought also to enforce cohabitation and a common residence for if either party deserted the other without lawful cause, it was possible to enforce renewed cohabitation by an action for the restitution of conjugal rights.

Only rarely did the courts seek consciously to apply such policy objectives to the facts of particular cases. Accordingly, these principles shaped the law for the most part only in a general rather than in a more precise and legalistic manner. As society's own assumptions concerning marriage shifted, that cautious legal approach proved to be realistic as it enabled the courts to reflect a steadily public opinion in this area. For example, in the later nineteenth century the courts began to reflect society's doubts as to the proper bounds of the husband's dominance over the wife in matters such as his insistence upon sexual intercourse with her at will.[12] At much the same time the action for the restitution of conjugal rights was used not so much for its original avowed purpose but as a useful

---

7   J.Ayliffe *Parergon Juris Canonici Anglicani* p.359. Cf.Lord Penzance: 'marriage...may...be defined as the voluntary union for life of one man and one woman to the exclusion of all others', *Hyde v Hyde* (1866) 1 LRP & D 130 at 139.

8   *Cowen v Cowen* [1946] P 36, *Baxter v Baxter* [1948] AC 274.

9   *B-n v B-n* (1854) 1 Ecc & Ad 248, *L v L* (1922) 38 TLR 697.

10   1 Cor vii 3 at 4. Yet the wife might withdraw occasionally from her husband's bed, *Saunders v S* (1847) 5 N of C 408 at 421, *Rowe v R* (1865) 4 Sw & Tr 162.

11   *S v A* (1878) 3 PD 72, *G v G* (1971) LR 2 P & D 287, *H v P* (1873) LR 3 P & D 126.

12   A.H.Manchester 'A Legal History of Marital Violence' (forthcoming essay).

preliminary to divorce proceedings.[13] A steady, although very slow, liberalisation of society's attitudes towards divorce also necessarily guided the courts in determining the extent to which either partner might insist upon the mutual help and comfort which was implicit in a continuance of the marriage. And, as was noted above, in 1948 the House of Lords felt able even to deny that the procreation of children was an essential aim or purpose of marriage. Nevertheless, the ecclesiastical principles had played a considerable part in shaping the approach of the courts.

iii) *How marriage was contracted.* The element which was essential to a valid marriage in law was the consent of the contracting parties. Consent alone was sufficient to establish a valid marriage,[14] provided only that none of the few grounds existed upon which a marriage might be annulled, e.g. prior marriage or lack of age. The result was that in 1750 a lawful marriage might be contracted in a number of ways.

A spousal or betrothal in words of the present tense (*per verba de praesenti*) e.g. 'I take thee to my wife', 'I take thee to my husband', constituted a valid marriage.[15] Secondly, a promise to marry in the future (*per verba de futuro*) was also deemed to constitute a valid marriage once the union had been consummated. Of such ceremonies Lord Stowell commented:

> 'In the promise or *sponsalia de futuro*, nothing was presumed to be complete or consummate either in substance or ceremony. Mutual consent would release the parties from their engagement; and one party, without the consent of the other, might contract a valid marriage, regularly or irregularly, with another person; but if the parties who had exchanged the promise had carnal intercourse with each other, the effect of that carnal intercourse was to interpose a presumption of present consent at the time of the intercourse, to convert the engagement into an irregular marriage, and to produce all the consequences attributable to that species of matrimonial connection.…In the case of a marriage *per verba de praesenti*, the parties there also deliberately accepted the relation of husband and wife, and consummation was presumed as naturally following the acceptance of that relation, unless controverted in like manner. But a promise *per verba de futuro* looked to a future time; the marriage which it contemplated might perhaps never take place. It was defeasible in various ways…'[16]

The widow of such a union could not claim dower for the ecclesiastical courts, which exercised a matrimonial jurisdiction, had no jurisdiction in such matters. The common law courts, which did exercise such a jurisdiction, required a marriage in church. Church marriages stipulated a number of formalities. For example, by canon law, any clergyman who celebrated marriage without banns or license, or at improper times, i.e. not between 8 am and noon, or at any place other than the church or chapel of the parish where one of the parties lived, was to be suspended from office and benefice. In addition persons under 21 were

---

13 See chap. 15, section 8.

14 Ayliffe *Parergon Juris Canonici Anglicani* p.362.

15 H.Swinburne *A Treatise of Spousals or Matrimonial Contracts* (1686) pp.13, 1.

16 *Dalrymple v Dalrymple* (1811) 2 Hag Con 54 at 65-7. Contrast *The Queen v Millis* (1844) 10 Cl & F 534 — the House of Lords held that a valid marriage at common law could be contracted only *per verba de praesenti* exchanged in the presence of a priest.

prohibited form marrying or contracting themselves without permission of their parents or guardians. Those formalities were to become even more familiar in subsequent years, as we shall see.

The church formalities were scarcely irksome. Yet many couples chose to reject them in favour of an irregular or clandestine, yet legally valid, union. Restoration comedy offers many variations upon the theme. A considerable number of parliamentary attempts were made to reduce the number of clandestine unions. They failed, chiefly because of the large number of unbeneficed clergy who profited from such marriages. London itself was the centre of a thriving trade, especially in the area of the Fleet. Stone tells us that at that time official weddings were heavily taxed while those around the Fleet were both legally valid, very cheap and so very popular. Stone suggests that perhaps not much more than half the population were being married strictly according to the rules of canon law before 1753 and, of those that were, at least half had already entered into full sexual relations.[17]

This overall lack of insistence upon legal formalities did have a number of socially desirable consequences. In a society which purported to frown upon deviant sexual conduct, it offered a certain security at least to some unmarried, pregnant women. It also favoured characterising the children of such unions as legitimate and contributed in general towards characterising any stable union as a lawful marriage, i.e. creating a presumption of marriage. Yet there was also criticism of the law's lack of formality. Fleet marriages in particular attracted considerable criticism.[18]

iv) *Lord Hardwicke's Act 1753.* In 1753 Lord Hardwicke secured the enactment of a measure 'for the better preventing of clandestine marriages'. The Act provided that all marriages must be celebrated in some parish church or public chapel, unless the Archbishop of Canterbury dispensed with that requirement. Persons under 21 could not be married validly unless they had the consent of their parents or guardians. Marriage was to be preceded by the publication of banns or by licence from the spiritual judge. A clergyman who contravened the Act was punishable by transportation for up to 14 years. The Act achieved its objective. Henceforth it was no longer possible in England and Wales validly to marry according to the age-old form of the irregular or clandestine marriage.

The underlying motive of the measure was clear enough. At a time when personal property was becoming more valuable than ever, the Act was designed to confer upon parents greater control over their children's choice of marriage partner. In this way the heiress might be protected from marrying the adventurer who would thereby secure her personal property and also the person who was unsuitable in terms of rank. It was, a wag claimed in later years, a measure which favoured patrimony at the expense of matrimony.

Certainly it was a bill which produced strong emotions during the debates upon it. Mr. Nugent doubted that parliament had the authority to declare a marriage vow void and null. Colonel Halford, who appeared to take the view

17   L.Stone *The Family, Sex and Marriage in England* pp.33-5.
18   For literary examples of such marriages see G.S.Allemann *Matrimonial Law and the Materials of Restoration Comedy.*

that the Act would render marriage less popular, declared that its 'certain consequence will be that of rendering common whoring as frequent among the lower
sort of people, as it is now among those of the better sort'.[19] There was something
in the argument that to make marriage more expensive would undoubtedly lead
to many of the poor avoiding it with a resultant rise both in whoring and in
illegitimate births. It was argued also that it was not in the public interest that
the aristocracy should thereby be allowed to constitute a closed caste, if parents
were to refuse to allow their children to marry outside their own charmed circle.

At least the Act clarified the law. In addition, since the Act required entry of
the marriage in the parish register, proof of marriage was considerably easier.

The courts interpreted the new Act strictly. Any misdescription of the parties
in the banns or in the licence might invalidate the marriage. In *Pouget v
Tomkins*[20] the omission of one Christian name, although it was the one which
had been used most frequently, was held to invalidate the marriage. Increasingly, it appeared to be unduly harsh that a marriage might be annulled in such
circumstances, even though the parties may not have intended to evade the law.
Such rules, it was said, degraded matrimony into concubinage. Accordingly, in
1823 a new Marriage Act provided that a marriage would be invalidated only if
the parties had knowingly and wilfully done or failed to do one of the prescribed
acts. In the wake of all such legislation marriage was seem more than ever as civil
rather than as sacramental in its nature. In its turn that was to make divorce all
the more credible later in the nineteenth century.

v) *The choice of the people.* Yet it was still necessary for all marriages to be celebrated in an Anglican church, save only for Jewish or Quaker marriages and for
the few which were celebrated by special licence. By law, therefore, it was necessary for Nonconformists to marry in a church whose religious practices were
repugnant to them. Granted the religious spirit of the day, it was scarcely
surprising that many such Nonconformists made their unhappiness at their
surroundings known even during the church ceremony itself. To many it
appeared that this particular monopoly of the Church of England had a direct
tendency even to discourage marriage. To others, of course, it appeared that
changes which were mooted in 1836 shook 'the principles of society, and have at
once assailed parentage, marriage, the reverence for the grave, and the religion
of the living'.[1]

The Marriage Act 1836 provided that a couple might choose either as before
to marry in the Anglican parish church, or in a specially registered building
which in practice might well house a non-Anglican religious denomination, or in
a non-religious ceremony in their local civil registry office. In addition those who
chose to marry in the Anglican church might do so not only by banns, licence, or
special licence, as before, but also by a superintendent-registrar's certificate:
and the preliminary to each of the new ways of marrying could be either a
superintendent-registrar's licence, or his certificate. Anderson has reminded us
that so much diversity of choice in the manner of marriage was almost unique
in nineteenth-century Europe. She then comments that if the 'central

19 *Hansards Parl. Hist. of England* (1753) vol 15, pp.13, 39.
20 (1812) 2 Hag Con 142.
1 (1869) 130 Edinburgh Review 262 (1836) 39 Blackwoods Magazine 601.

characteristic of democratic capitalist society were mass choice, then democratic capitalist marriage arrived in England on 1 July 1837'.[2]

vi) *A laxly enforced framework.* The new civil marriage was available to all who wanted it. In nineteenth-century Europe that amounted to a remarkably liberal measure. On the other hand during its early years, a close connection of the registry office with the poor law machinery scarcely recommended it to the population at large. Over the country as a whole, therefore, the civil marriage was relatively unpopular during the nineteenth century. It was during the twentieth century that it became far more popular.

Little provision was made effectively to enforce the marriage laws. Ever since Hardwicke's Act many couples had evaded the law's provisions quite simply by going to Scotland to marry. The blacksmith at Gretna Green just across the border from England became a well known marriage centre as a result. Nor was this a service which was performed only for the occasional romantic young couple. A member of parliament assured the House in 1855 that at fairs and markets in the North of England people met for the first time and then went over the Border by hundreds in order to get married by the blacksmith in Scotland.[3] In 1856, however, that particular practice was lessened very considerably after Brougham secured the enactment of a measure which required there to have been three weeks residence in Scotland before such a marriage would be recognised in England and Wales. Only the carriage trade was able to afford a Gretna marriage thereafter!

No like effective action was taken with regard to enforcement of law regarding the publication of banns. In 1869 it was alleged that, except in thinly-peopled country districts, the publication of banns in church had long ceased to assure effective notice, although this was the most popular mode of marriage.[4] In addition, since a nominal residence for only 15 days was required, it was perfectly possible for couples to avoid virtually all publicity by securing such residence in a parish where they were unknown. In 1868 clergymen told commissioners that this was a common practice. One who described such unions said that they were clandestine marriages and that 'marriages' within the prohibited degrees were frequently so contracted.[5] Other couples no doubt sought relative privacy either because they wished to avoid the teasing of friends or because they had a particular reason, as had many of the numerous domestic servants for whom marriage meant dismissal from service, for avoiding publicity for their marriage. Civil marriage ensured no greater effective publicity. Moreover few breaches of the marriage laws were regarded as being so serious as to justify annulling a marriage. The result was that what were to all intents and purposes clandestine marriages were possible in England and Wales during the second half of the nineteenth century to an extent which was unusual in Western Europe.

vii) *Legal capacity to marry.* Those who in law lacked capacity to marry were

2   O. Anderson 'The Incidence of Civil Marriage in England and Wales' (1975) 69 Past and Present 50.
3   Op. cit. p.68, An Act for Amending the Law of Marriage in Scotland.
4   (1869) 130 Edinburgh Review 264.
5   Report of the Royal Commission on the Laws of Marriage no. 12161 (1868) p.165, q. 1409.

males under the age of 14 and females under the age of 12; persons of unsound mind; persons physically disqualified; persons who were already legally married, and persons who were related to each other within the prohibited degrees of consanguinity and affinity. The question of age and the question of marriage with a deceased wife's sister being included within the prohibited degrees are of particular interest in that they illustrate especially a relationship between public opinion and the law.

In the mid-nineteenth century responsible public opinion recognised that the age of legal capacity to marry had been set at an age which was below that which was either 'prudent or desirable'. However, commissioners recognised that young persons of that age were capable of being parents and suggested that to deny them marriage would be to risk 'introducing more serious evils'. Such early marriages were said to be most common in the cotton districts of Lancashire. A recent census had shown that a considerable number of the male operatives, and a still greater number of female operatives, were married when they were between 15 and 20 years old. Figures in three Lancashire towns with regard to those who married when they were 15 or under were as follows:

	Number of	
Town	*Husbands*	*Wives*
Bolton	45	175
Burnley	51	147
Stockport	59	179[6]

Youthful marriages, and illegitimate births were rather less common during the first quarter of the twentieth century. However, when the law was changed in 1929 — both parties were to be at least 16 years of age — that fact does not appear to have been regarded as being especially significant. What was significant was that the League of Nations was attempting to outlaw child marriages: the reform of 1929 was a contribution by England and Wales to that campaign. In addition it was argued that the marriage law should be made consistent with the criminal law which made it an offence for a man to have sexual intercourse with a girl under 16. Finally, it was argued — falsely, it seems — that the 'age of maturity' was higher than it had been in the previous century.[7]

It all amounted to a remarkable mixture of well meaning, but rather empty moralising, non sequiturs and incorrect assumptions. Yet it remained the law. Perhaps because the numbers involved were relatively small, this was one area of law in which, even in the twentieth century, a concern for principle was allowed to triumph over the reality of how some young people chose to conduct their relationships.

Principle also lay at the heart of the extended discussions regarding the prohibition against marrying a deceased wife's sister. But on this question the discussion was both highly public and prolonged. Finally the law bowed to the reality of how many people chose to conduct their relationships.

Until 1835 marriages within the prohibited degrees were merely voidable. Therefore, if they were not pronounced null and void during the lifetime of both parties to such a union, the validity of the marriage could not be questioned

---

6 Report no. 12161 (1868) p.xxvii.
7 S.M. Cretney *Principles of Family Law* (2nd edn 1976) pp.42 ff. Cretney writes that in the 12 years prior to 1929, only three girls of 13, 28 of 14, and 318 of 15 had married.

thereafter, nor could the legitimacy of the children of the union be impeached. However, in 1835 statute rendered all such marriages in future null and void. It was a prohibition which many members of the community chose either to dispute or even to ignore, despite the consequences which might follow in terms of the illegitimacy of the children of such a union, etc.

A private inquiry, which was limited to a relatively small area, had shown 1364 'marriages' within the prohibited degrees between 1835 and 1868, of which nine-tenths had been contracted with a deceased wife's sister. The commissioners reported that many partners to such 'marriages' were 'persons of station and property, and of unimpeachable character, and religious habits'. Why, then, did such people contract a prohibited union? Naturally enough, in Victorian days, they based themselves upon scripture by asserting that marriage with a deceased wife's sister was not prohibited by scripture. Further, they argued that it was beyond the province of the legislature to prohibit any marriage which was not prohibited by the law of God. They argued also that such marriages ought to be allowed for the benefit of children who had had the misfortune to lose their mother. Finally, they pointed out that the laws of nearly the whole of Europe permitted such marriages. On the other hand those who supported the statutory prohibitions also argued that scripture was on their side. It was argued, too, that, were there to be any possibility at all of future marriage between a husband and his wife's sister, it might lead to 'a criminal intercourse' which would be destructive of the marriage.[8] The controversy, and attempted evasions of the law, continued throughout the second half of the nineteenth century. Ultimately there seemed little point in supporting a prohibition to which so many responsible members of the public had offered principled objection. Accordingly, in 1907 the prohibition was removed by statute.[9]

b) *The respective roles in law of husband and wife*

Blackstone summarised the essence of the wife's position at common law as follows:

'By marriage the husband and wife are one person in law: that is the very being or legal existence of the woman is suspended during the marriage, or at least is incorporated and consolidated into that of the husband: under whose wing, protection, and cover, she performs everything: and is therefore called in our law – french a feme-covert...is said to be covert-baron, or under the protection and influence of her husband, baron, or lord; and her condition during her marriage is called her coverture.'[10]

In law, therefore, husband and wife were one. Yet, as the wags put it, it was the husband who was that one. The husband's dominance within marriage was expressed in a number of ways. The wife took the domicile of her husband. Since the jurisdiction of the courts in matrimonial causes was often to be based upon

8 First Report of the Commissioners into the State and Operation of the Law of Marriage no. 973 (1843) pp.ix-x.
9 Deceased Wife's Sister's Marriage Act. A much more restricted form of incest became punishable at criminal law as a result of the Punishment of Incest Act 1908. On the penal protection of the family generally see L.N. Brown 'The Penal Protection of the Family in English Law' (1968) 42 Estratto dall Annuario di Diritto Comparato e di Studi Legislativi 36.
10 1 Bl Com (5th edn) 442.

the domicile of the petitioner, this could mean that the wife might not be able to obtain matrimonial relief in England or Wales if her husband had acquired an overseas domicile. If she killed her husband then until well into the nineteenth century such killing might be classified not simply as murder but as petit treason — and a guilty wife might suffer death by burning. Other legal principles assumed that she acted under her husband's influence. If a third party beat her, then it was the husband who had available to him in the civil courts an action of trespass *vi et armis*; if her husband were beaten she had no corresponding action since she had no separate interest in anything during her coverture and so in law had suffered no loss or injury. Until close to the beginning of the twentieth century there was even good reason to believe that in law a husband might chastise his wife.[11]

Judicial dicta affirmed the subordinate position of the wife. Sir Herbert Jenner Fust declared roundly in 1847 that:

> 'it is the duty of a wife to conform to the tastes and duties of her husband; to sacrifice much of her own comfort and convenience to his whims and caprices, to submit to his commands and to endeavour if she can, by prudent resistance and remonstrance, to induce a change and alteration'.[12]

Clearly the courts were determined not only to uphold society's respect for marriage but also for the husband's dominance within marriage.

Of course, the common law concept of the unity of husband and wife, when it was allied with the dominance of the husband in that relationship, had considerable implications for property relationships between the spouses.

c) *Property*[13]

i) *Introduction.* The husband's rights in his wife's property depended upon the nature of the property in question. However, at quite an early stage equitable principles mitigated the rigours of a common law doctrine which appeared, to the layman at least, effectively to vest all of the wife's property in her husband. During the final years of the nineteenth century statutory reforms rejected the common law concept of the unity of husband and wife. The new statutory principle was based upon a concept of the separation of property — husband and wife were each to retain the separate property which belonged to them at the time of marriage or which they acquired during the marriage. By mid-twentieth century changing social conditions had rendered that position quite outmoded.

ii) *Freeholds.* All freeholds of which the wife was seised at the time of the marriage, or afterwards, were by law vested in the husband and wife, during the coverture, in right of the wife. During their joint lives the husband was entitled to

---

11   See generally E.Reiss *The Rights and Duties of Englishwomen.* Cf. F.Basch *Relative Creatures*, W.L. Blease *The Emancipation of Englishwomen*, W. Neff *Victorian Working Women*, I. Pinchbeck *Women Workers and the Industrial Revolution 1750-1850*, O.R.McGregor 'The Social Position of Women in England, 1850-1914: A Bibliography' (1955) 6 British Journal of Sociology 48.

12   *Dysart v Dysart* (1847) 1 Rob Ecc 470 at 542.

13   H.Stephen *Commentaries on the Laws of England* (4th edn, 1858) vol 2, pp.273 ff., Reiss *The Rights and Duties of Englishwomen*, A.V.Dicey *Law and Public Opinion in England during the Nineteenth Century* (2nd edn, 1914) pp. 371 ff.

the profits and had the sole control and management. If the husband died before his wife, her right to the freeholds was restored. If the wife died before her husband, her estates of inheritance passed to her heir subject to the husband's right to tenancy by the curtesy of England. That arose in cases where the wife had been seised during the marriage in actual possession of an estate of inheritance, whether in fee simple or fee tail, and there had been a child of the marriage born alive and capable of inheriting the property; then upon the death of his wife, the husband became solely seised of such estate for his life. In such a case he was said to be tenant by the curtesy of England.

iii) *Leaseholds.* The husband became entitled to leaseholds of which his wife had been possessed at the time of the marriage or which accrued to her during coverture. He was entitled not only to the profits and the management during their joint lives but he might also dispose of them as he pleased, by any act during the coverture. They were liable to be taken in execution for his debts and, if he survived her, they were his absolutely: however, he could not dispose of them by will. If he did not dispose of them during his lifetime and she survived him, they became hers by virtue of her original title.

iv) *Other interests.* The personal chattels of the wife, whether they belonged to her at the time of the marriage, or accrued to her during coverture, became in general the absolute property of the husband. Yet choses in action — such as debts due to the wife on bond or otherwise, before her marriage did not in general become the husband's until he recovered them by law, or reduced them into possession. If he died before this was done, they remained to the wife: should she die before he had recovered or reduced them into possession, they were part of her estate.

v) *Paraphernalia, pin-money, dower, protection orders.* If she survived her husband, the wife retained all her paraphernalia — her bed, apparel and personal ornaments suited to her degree — which had not been disposed of in his lifetime. Similarly, there was the wealthy woman's pin-money, for which provision would usually have been made out of her husband's lands or other income. Should she survive her husband, a wife was entitled, provided no act had been done to defeat or abridge her right, to dower. Dower amounted to the third part of all the lands and tenements of which the husband was seised, in fee simple or fee tail, at any time during the coverture, and of which any issue that she might have had could by possibility have been heir, to hold to herself for the term of her natural life.[14]

Statute made a further minor exception in 1857 to the overall dominance of the husband in all matters concerning property by providing that if he deserted her without reasonable cause, she might obtain an order under which any money or property acquired by her lawful industry, or acquired after his desertion, would be protected, and belong to her as if she were a single woman.[15]

14   Provided that the wife consented, it had been possible to bar dower. The Dower Act 1833 provided that a husband might alienate his lands unencumbered by his wife's dower: a wife might claim dower out of her deceased husband's equitable estates.
15   Matrimonial Causes Act 1857, s. 21.

vi) *The wife's additional incapacities.* The wife was incapable, except under special circumstances, of making a will, either of lands or chattels. She was also generally incapable of contracting, or of doing any other act to bind herself or her husband, unless by his authority and as his agent, and any such acts done by her were void. The basis of her contractual incapacity lay in the fact that she had no property which she could bind. Nor was a wife capable of bringing any action at law to obtain redress for an injury sustained in her person and property, unless the action were brought with her husband's concurrence, and in his name as well as her own — for she had no separate interest in anything during her coverture.

vii) *The married woman's rights.* In return the wife received an imperfectly enforced right to maintenance, a right to her husband's consortium, and the right under certain circumstances to withdraw her consortium. They were but a small and inadequately implemented recompense. Accordingly, attempts were made to change the law.

viii) *The role of equity.* Equity mitigated some of the rigours of the common law doctrine by the doctrine of the separate use. Equity recognised any trust created in favour of the wife. This enabled her to have a separate and independent estate in whatever property or interest was secured to her through the medium of a trustee, provided that the intention of the grantor was distinctly declared to the effect that she should have it to her sole and separate use. To prevent a wife nevertheless assigning such a beneficial interest to her husband, equity developed about 1800 the doctrine of the restraint upon anticipation which barred a married woman from anticipating and dealing with any income until it actually fell due. There was also the device of the wife's equity to a settlement. If a husband had failed manifestly to maintain his wife or had been guilty of misconduct, equity would compel him, if he sought its aid, to make due provision for his wife.

Even so, to many contemporary critics it appeared that the wife obtained much the worse of a highly one-sided bargain. In 1856 a committee of the Law Amendment Society urged members to note the evils of the law which affected the property of married women: in 1857 Sir Erskine Perry introduced a reformist bill. Yet traditional attitudes remained constant and the measure was unsuccessful. Incidentally, many women of considerable ability — Mrs. Caroline Norton was one — opposed the 'wild and ridiculous doctrine of equality' between men and women.[16] However, in 1868, at the request of the National Association for the Promotion of Social Science, Shaw Lefevre again brought this issue before parliament. A select committee was appointed. In effect the committee suggested that the equitable solutions amounted only to a partial remedy. Hardship did occur in those cases where a settlement had not been drawn up because of forgetfulness. Numerous cases of hardship also occurred in cases where husbands took their wives earnings in drinking or dissipation for the existing law protected only the deserted wife. The committee also attached 'great weight' to legal changes overseas which had taken place without creating difficulties. Accordingly, the committee concluded that a change in the law was necessary

16 (1868) 34 Westminster Review 374, Reiss *The Rights and Duties of Englishwomen* p.128.

with reference both to the property and to the earnings of married women.[17]

The Married Women's Property Act 1870 was the first hesitant step in that direction. Rather than change the common law principle itself, parliament chose to follow the equitable path of making further inroads into that principle. This much amended Act simply protected the married woman's wages and earnings and extended the range of her separate estate. The Married Women's Property Act 1882[18] was rather more decisive. A married woman was now capable of acquiring, holding and disposing, by will or otherwise, of any real or personal property as her separate property, in the same manner as if she were a feme sole, without the intervention of any trustee. Section 2 provided that:

> 'Every woman who marries after the commencement of this Act shall be entitled to have and to hold as her separate property and to dispose of in manner aforesaid all real and personal property which shall belong to her at the time of the marriage, or shall be acquired by or devolve upon her after marriage, including any wages, earnings, money and property gained or acquired by her in any employment, trade or occupation in which she is engaged, or which she carries on separately from her husband, or by the exercise of any literary, artistic, or scientific skill.'

Now the married woman was freed from all the old disabilities with regard to alienation and to contract and she might protect her rights. In short it was possible to claim that her personal capacity was complete, although her contractual and tortious liabilities could only be enforced against her to the extent of her separate estate, and only to that extent in so far as such estate was not 'restrained from anticipation'. It was still possible in 1930 for a judge to assert that the law governing the husband-wife relationship seemed to be fraught with inconsistency and injustice.[19] However, the Law Reform (Married Women and Tortfeasors) Act 1935 further advanced the cause of the married woman's equality by eliminating the institution of 'separate property'.[20] Now the married woman was in the same position as a man or as an unmarried woman.

The early equitable glosses upon the common law position of the wife may have been due in part to a paternalistic desire to protect the wife who all too frequently, as Lord Chancellor Thurlow put it, was 'kicked or kissed out of her money'. Yet the common law doctrine had become increasingly unacceptable 'as the leasehold grew in importance as a form of investment property and fortunes were made in money, rather than through the ownership of land'. Such valuable monies must be protected from the rapacious husband. Primarily, therefore, equity acted not so much to protect the married woman and certainly not to advance any concept of equality between husband and wife but rather 'to enable married women as individuals to take an active part in business. The purpose of equity was to keep the family (kinship) property intact...'[1] The nineteenth-

17 Special Report from the Select Committee on the Married Women's Property Bill no. 441 (1868).

18 The Act did not affect the married women's status. See *Edwards v Porter* [1925] AC 1.

19 Per McCardie J, *Gotliffe v Edelston* [1930] 2 KB 378 at 381. See O.Kahn-Freund 'Inconsistencies and Injustices in the Law of Husband and Wife (1952) 15 MLR 133.

20 The Married Women (Restraint upon Anticipation) Act 1949 completely abolished the doctrine of restraint upon anticipation.

1 M.Finer and O.R. McGregor 'This History of the Obligation to Maintain' 2 Report of the Committee on One-Parent Families (Cmnd. 5629-1) pp. 97-8. Cf. O.Kahn-Freund in *Matrimonial Property Law* (ed W.Friedmann) p.274.

century legislation can also be seen as a response to a revolution in production.[2] Yet the idea of equality was very much a lively concept during the second half of the nineteenth century: John Stuart Mill's *Essay on the Subjection of Woman* made an important contribution to that debate. Not surprisingly, the concept of greater equality between husband and wife became associated with the idea of extending to all married women that degree of enjoyment of separate property which wealthy married women had already enjoyed in equity for some years. Indeed, the legislation which culminated in the 1882 Act can be regarded as very much a triumph for reformers who were motivated very much by a desire to promote equality. As they achieved their legislative objects in this area, their movement can even be seen as a triumph for law reform.

Nominally the common law basis of the law remained intact. In fact the nineteenth-century legislation had virtually reversed the traditional position at common law, although even in mid-twentieth century traces of the old doctrine lingered on.[3] It is true that at common law the doctrine of the unity of husband and wife had never been applied rigorously. Yet the piecemeal approach to reform, coupled with the illusion that there had been no radical change, helped lawyers to put off the day when they would have to consider adopting a systematic approach to the question of matrimonial property. The result was that the law of matrimonial property may have represented accurately enough the philosophy of an avowedly individualist society. It may also have been an appropriate system for the well-to-do couple who were in possession of investment property which they wished to invest separately. It was very much at odds, however, with the law's traditional concept of the unity of husband and wife. It began also increasingly to be in conflict with the social reality of an increasingly affluent twentieth-century society which questioned the doctrine of the separation of goods between the spouses. Surely it was more desirable, more reasonable, more in accord with everyday usage rather to regard the household goods as being shared in common? Such questions began to come to the fore after the Second World War in respect of the division of family assets such as the matrimonial home and durable consumer goods. The powers granted under section 17 of the 1882 Act offered no sure guide: only in 1969 was the extent of the powers conferred upon the judiciary by this section settled.[4] Lacking any régime matrimonial, the law was about once again to embark upon a long process of revolutionary change: once again such piecemeal change would dwell rather upon the consequences of a dissolution of marriage than upon proprietary rights within marriage.

3 Matrimonial remedies 1750-1857

a) *Parliamentary divorces*
A total dissolution of the marriage or *divortium a vinculo matrimonii* could be obtained by persuading parliament to pass a private Act to dissolve the

---

2 O.Kahn-Freund (1970) 33 MLR 601, 605.
3 G.Williams 'The Legal Unity of Husband and Wife' (1947) 10 MLR 16. Traces of the old doctrine survived especially with regard to questions of income tax, domicile and evidence.
4 *Pettit v Pettit* [1970] AC 777, [1969] 2 All ER 385.

particular marriage. This practice became established only at the beginning of the eighteenth century. It was a means whereby the nobleman with an adulterous wife, who had not yet given birth to an heir, was to be given the opportunity to marry again. There were relatively few such proceedings. Only 60 bills were passed during the period 1715-75. However, their number increased steadily to the extent that 24 of all such Acts, i.e. 76, were passed during the period 1840 to 1856.[5] Above all they were extremely costly; it was estimated that the total cost, under the most favourable circumstances, of obtaining a divorce *a vinculo matrimonii* could hardly be less than £700 or £800. When the matter was much litigated the cost would probably reach some thousands.[6] Clearly divorce *a vinculo* by parliamentary means was available only to the wealthy. Yet it was a form of dissolution upon which modern divorce, which was introduced only in 1857, was based.

Parliamentary divorces could be obtained under ordinary circumstances only at the suit of the husband, but not at the suit of the wife except in cases which were regarded as being of aggravated enormity such as incestuous intercourse with the wife's relations which was held to preclude the possibility of future reconciliation. Therefore the wife could not ask for a divorce *a vinculo* when she was aggrieved by adultery alone: on the other hand the husband, aggrieved by adultery alone, could demand a divorce *a vinculo*, unless his own conduct had been censurable in other respects. Parliament did have a discretion and would mould and adapt its relief as the facts of the case appeared to demand.

In 1798 Lord Loughborough, the Lord Chancellor, framed a series of resolutions which established a stricter and more uniform practice in such proceedings. Henceforth, it was required that a sentence of divorce *a mensa et thoro*, which is discussed below, should have been pronounced before soliciting the bill. Henceforth, all applications for divorce were to be supported also both by a sentence of divorce *a mensa et thoro* and by a verdict at law in respect of criminal conversation with the petitioner's wife: alternatively, all such applications were to be accompanied by circumstances which justified or explained the want of such verdicts. Provision was always made for the divorced wife through the medium of a functionary called 'The Ladies' Friend' whose duty it was to see that the husband petitioning for divorce made some suitable but moderate provision for the divorced wife. The bill itself deprived the divorced wife of any rights that, but for the Act, she might have had as his widow, in the event of her survivorship; the husband was excluded from any rights which he might otherwise have claimed in any property acquired by the wife after the dissolution of the marriage. When the wife obtained a divorce, the property clauses were vice versa substantially the same. After 1840 such proceedings were no longer determined in the whole House — an unseemly and inconvenient practice, in the view of a royal commission — but before a select committee of nine members, of whom three were a quorum. In part at least that change in practice surely amounted to an admission that such proceedings were more properly judicial than legislative and heralded the more radical change that was soon to come.

---

5   *Finer and McGregor* (above) p.92.
6   First Report of the Commissioners…into the Law of Divorce and more particularly into the Mode of Obtaining Divorces *a Vinculo Matrimonii* no. 1604 (1853) p.18.

b) *Nullity of marriage*

The parliamentary divorce dissolved marriage upon a ground which had arisen only after the marriage had taken place. It was possible also to obtain an alternative form of divorce *a vinculo matrimonii* in cases in which the marriage contract was annulled or rescinded on the ground of some antecedent incapacity which rendered it in reality void from the beginning. After 1835 the grounds which would render a marriage void in this manner were relationships within the prohibited degrees, a previous marriage, nonage and mental incompetency. Other disabilities i.e. impotence, and possibly duress, rendered the marriage voidable only. This meant that in law such a marriage was valid until it was actually annulled. Usually these suits were known not as suits for divorce but as suits of nullity. When marriages were set aside, the decree of annulment rendered the marriage void from the very beginning with the result, inter alia, that any issue would be bastardised. Alimony was paid only until decree absolute.

c) *Divorce* a mensa et thoro

The divorce *a mensa et thoro*, or from bed and board, was the equivalent of the modern legal separation. After such a divorce the legal rights of husband and wife remained in most respects what they had been before. The wife was not barred of her dower nor was the husband deprived of his marital rights in respect of her property. Nor were subsequent issue bastardised.

It might be granted for fornication or adultery, for impotency in point of carnal copulation, or for a machination of the wife's death or any other act of cruelty. Usually it was granted at the suit of husband or wife, when the gross misconduct of either of them such as cruelty, adultery, or the like, was held to have rendered it impracticable for them to live together. The commissioners pointed out that the causes of such divorce were 'purposely limited to a few extreme and specific provocations' and were subject to certain rules, namely:

'Divorce will only be granted for the extreme provocations adverted to above; that the law will not suffer it to be obtained on the sole confession of the parties themselves; and thirdly, that it will be refused, even although an offence has been committed which would otherwise justify it, if collusion, connivance, condonation, or recrimination can be pleaded and proved.'[7]

During the separation the court decreed a competent allowance to the wife for the maintenance under the name of alimony. The commissioners explained that this allowance:

'depends on the innocence or delinquency of the parties, and is measured by the means and circumstances of the husband. In cases of elopement or when the wife is living in adultery none will be awarded; but when she is innocent and the delinquency of the husband is clearly established, the law considers that as she is separated by his misconduct from all the comforts of matrimonial society, she ought to be liberally provided for by him. The amount is left to the discretion of the judge; sometimes a moiety of the property has been given, sometimes a third, and sometimes less, regard being had to a variety of circumstances; such as the condition of the

7 First Report no. 1604 (1853) pp.1-2, J.Ayliffe *Parergon Juris Canonici Anglicani* pp.225 ff, 1 Bl Com (5th edn) 441.

husband, his station in life, the support of the children, and especially to the circumstance where the allowance has been a large one, whether the bulk of the fortune came originally from her.'[8]

d) *Restitution of conjugal rights*

Finally, there was the decree of restitution of conjugal rights. In such cases the marriage was pleaded by the party proceeding; it was alleged that the party proceeded against had withdrawn from cohabitation, and the prayer was that the defendant, whether husband or wife, should be compelled to return to cohabitation. In defence, the marriage might be denied or the adultery or cruelty of the plaintiff pleaded in bar.

e) *Incidence of matrimonial causes*

During the three year period 1827 to 1830 the ecclesiastical courts heard a total of only 101 matrimonial causes i.e. suits for restitution of conjugal rights and divorce *a mensa et thoro* as well as suits of nullity.[9] No doubt the ecclesiastical courts were relatively costly, but they were accessible in the sense that they were distributed throughout the country. The public appears to have been making rather less use of the remedies available in the ecclesiastical courts at this time than it was of the much less accessible, far more costly parliamentary divorce. Above all such figures illustrate that for the great majority of citizens the existing matrimonial remedies were irrelevant.

4 Extra-legal remedies

a) *Wife selling*

For many people wife selling appears to have amounted to an acceptable method of dissolving a marriage. For such people wife selling amounted to a poor man's divorce.

A ritual often appears to have surrounded the practice, e.g. the wife might be led into the ring at market by a halter. Often receipts of a kind appear to have been exchanged and tax may even have been paid to an official of the market. Yet the tone of the newspaper reports of such occurrences during the nineteenth century is one of disapproval and even, increasingly, of some wry astonishment. One typical newspaper advertisement in *The Times* of 1797 read as follows:

'On Friday a butcher exposed his wife to sale in Smithfield Market near the Lane Inn, with a halter about her neck, and one about her waist, which tied her to a railing, when a hog-driver was the happy purchaser, who gave the husband three guineas, and a crown, for his departed rib. Pity it is, there is no stop put to such depraved conduct in the lower order of people.'[10]

The fact that newspapers chose to record such instances of wife selling in this way at all suggests that such conduct was relatively unusual during the nineteenth century. Certainly there were no legal grounds for believing that such a

---

8   First Report no. 1604, above, p.2.
9   Reports of the Commissioners on the Practice and Jurisdiction of the Ecclesiastical Courts of England and Wales no. 199 (1832) p.567.
10 G.O.W.Mueller 'Inquiry into the State of a Divorceless Society' (1957) 18 Univ of Pittsburgh Law Rev 545, 568.

ceremony brought the marriage to an end. It was in such circumstances that at Birmingham in 1823 one John Homer was sentenced to be transported for seven years on the grounds of bigamy. Lord Mansfield is also said to have suggested that wife selling might found a criminal prosecution for conspiracy to commit adultery. Yet a case of wife selling was recorded as late as 1887.[11] Clearly numbers of people had chosen, without benefit of law, to terminate their marriage in fact with what appeared to them to be due fomality and in a manner which assured the wife of a fresh protector.

b) *Desertion*

Others simply ran away. How many did so, we cannot tell, although parishes would certainly have been sensitive to incurring the burden of supporting the family of such a runaway. As death might be presumed after an absence of seven years in such cases, it was possible for the deserted partner to remarry after such an interval.

5 Reform

It was unlikely that an expanding, affluent and increasingly influential middle class would be prepared to tolerate a situation in which divorce was available only to the very rich. It seemed especially anomalous that divorce was more readily available in neighbouring Scotland. It was known also that Protestant countries overseas insisted upon no such restriction. Such a restriction appeared increasingly to be both unjust and unequal in that the deserted wife and the poor in general were left without a remedy.

In March 1844 Brougham told a Select Committee of the House of Lords of the sad plight of a mistress of a Ladies' Boarding School. She had separated from her husband 12 years before in consequence of misconduct and repeated acts of adultery on his part. She ran a boarding school with some success and still supported her husband. Yet he remained entitled to the whole of her property. She did not have the means even to apply to Doctors' Commons for a divorce *a mensa et thoro*. The present law afforded her no assistance at all.[12]

Equally the comments which Mr. Justice Maule addressed to a prisoner convicted of bigamy in 1845 aroused considerable public interest. The judge expressed some sympathy for the prisoner. There was one law only for rich and poor, and therefore, the prisoner should have undertaken all the steps which were necessary to obtain a parliamentary divorce. It was true that such a process might have cost him more than £1000 and that his weekly wage was about £1. Yet the law was the law.[13]

Moderate opinion of the day saw the issue of principle as being finely balanced. Dr. Lushington, who was Judge of the Consistory Court of London, expressed it well enough when in 1844 he said:

'On the one hand, by rendering the tie of marriage indissoluble, and

---

11 A.H.Manchester 'A Legal History of Marital Violence' (forthcoming essay).
12 Report from the Select Committee of the House of Lords appointed to consider the Bill...for the better Administration of Justice in His Majesty's Privy Council...no. 34 (1844) p.91, q.923.
13 See *Mueller* (above) p.549.

rendering it utterly impossible that either party can break that tie, you strengthen to a certain degree the motives for the purity both of the husband and of the wife. You produce the effect upon the part of the husband of guarding his wife with greater caution; and on the part of the wife there is presented to her, in case of straying from the path of virtue, nothing but the most desperate prospects to her in society, without a possible chance of being united afterwards to the person who has seduced her. Again, on the other hand, there are mischiefs almost as great; because, supposing the case to occur at an early period of the cohabitation between the husband and the wife, and that they are both of them early in life, it is next to impossible to suppose, in the present state of society, if you deny to them the power of dissolving the marriage tie, but that they will live in the habitual indulgence of practices which are altogether immoral. Therefore, it is a balanced state of circumstances.'[14]

A royal commission was appointed in 1850. In 1853 three commissioners recommended that divorce *a vinculo* should be allowed to a husband for his wife's adultery, but, as a general rule, not to a wife for his adultery, although she might have dissolution of the marriage 'in cases of aggravated enormity, such as incest or bigamy'. In treating the adultery of husband and wife differently, the commissioners were following the practice of the parliamentary divorces. In support they cited Dr. Johnson's comment that 'the difference between the adultery of the husband and the adultery of the wife' (socially speaking) 'is boundless', a reference to the fact that by her adultery the wife might pass off an illegitimate child upon her husband and his family. Above all the commissioners appeared anxious not to encourage divorce. Accordingly, they rejected any extension of the concept of cruelty as a ground of divorce in any form. One commissioner, Lord Redesdale even dissented from the view that divorce *a vinculo* should become a judicial remedy at all. Essentially Redesdale believed that, if facilities for divorce were introduced, a door for escape from marriage would be opened upon every disagreement and that 'the misery and unhappiness which would arise from homes deserted and children abandoned would be bitterly and extensively felt'.[15]

Three bills which Cranworth presented as Lord Chancellor failed. A fourth bill which Cranworth presented on 28 May 1857 succeeded. The Royal Assent was given on 28 August 1857 and it became law on 1 January 1858. The eventual speed of its passage did not reflect any unanimity in parliament. Gladstone especially opposed, even obstructed, the measure. However, in the House of Commons the Attorney-General, Bethell, was a forceful advocate. In the House of Lords Cranworth carried the day, although for the third reading there was a majority of only two votes.

6 Modern divorce 1857

a) *The grounds of divorce*
The new Act[16] deprived the ecclesiastical courts of their matrimonial jurisdiction

14 Report no. 34 (1844) p.5, q.37,
15 First Report...into the Law of Divorce no. 1604 (1853) pp. 22, 16, 13-14, 24.
16 An Act to amend the Law relating to Divorce and Matrimonial Causes in England.

and abolished actions for criminal conversation. Section 27 set out the grounds for the dissolution of marriage:

> 'It shall be lawful for any husband to present a petition to the said court praying that his marriage may be dissolved on the ground that his wife, since the celebration thereof, has been guilty of adultery: and it shall be lawful for any wife to present a petition to the said court praying that her marriage may be dissolved, on the ground that since the celebration thereof her husband has been guilty of incestuous adultery, or of bigamy with adultery, or of rape, or of sodomy or bestiality; or of adultery coupled with such cruelty as without adultery would have entitled her to a divorce *a mensa et thoro*, or of adultery coupled with desertion, without reasonable excuse, for two years or upwards...'

Incestuous adultery meant adultery with a woman with whom, if the husband's wife were dead, he could not lawfully contract marriage by reason of her being within the prohibited degrees of consanguinity or affinity. If the petitioner had been in any way accessory to or had connived at or condoned the adultery, such conduct would be an absolute bar to decree: and the court was under a duty to satisfy itself upon this point. Section 22 provided that in all suits and proceedings, other than proceedings to dissolve any marriage, the court should proceed and act and give relief on principles and rules which were to be as nearly as may be conformable to the principles and rules on which the ecclesiastical courts had heretofore acted and given relief. *Harthan v Harthan*[17] and *Padolecchia v Padolecchia*[18] are recent instances.

b) *Collusion and decrees nisi*

In 1860 an amending statute was passed which authorised the Queen's Proctor, and even strangers, to interpose in cases of collusion. For although the 1857 Act had directed that the court should satisfy itself as to, and inquire into, collusion between the parties, it had failed to provide adequate machinery which would enable the court to perform this duty satisfactorily. The 1860 Act provided also that decrees should not be made absolute until after the passage of three months — the decree nisi procedure — and in 1866 that period was extended to six months.[19]

c) *Judges*

Initially the new court consisted of eight judges. However, by virtue of the amending Act in 1860, the Judge Ordinary was enabled to act alone in those cases in which previously a quorum of three had been thought necessary. Yet the court continued to sit only in London and to frown upon divorce.

d) *Accessibility of the new court*

The government appeared to feel that to make divorce courts less costly would mean making them more accessible: that, in turn, would put temptation before many married people. They wanted divorce accessible, as Bethell put it, but not

---

17 [1948] 2 All ER 639.
18 [1967] 3 All ER 863, [1968] P 314.
19 Report from the Select Committee of the House of Lord appointed to consider the Law respecting the Parties who are entitled or ought to be entitled to sue in the Divorce Court...for a Dissolution of Marriage no.63 (1861) p.4.

too accessible. Indeed, Bethell was at some pains to explain that the new Act had introduced no new principle into the law. The object of the Act was to remove the inconvenience of granting divorce *a vinculo* through the medium of a legislative assembly — in all other respects the law upon divorce was to remain as it was. The one radical proposal which had been made — to put men and women upon a basis of equality — was rejected by Lord Cranworth for all the old reasons.[20] Yet even in 1857 a critic of the bill foresaw that in time there would be further extensions of the jurisdiction to a number of local courts, in order to provide for the equal rights of the poor who could not resort to a metropolitan court.[1]

e) *Recourse to the Act*

By modern standards relatively little use was made of the Act and then, probably, only by the prosperous. The annual average of divorces in the decade after 1859 was 148, during the period 1882-86 it was 349, in the 1890s it was 582, and during the first decade of the twentieth century it was about 620. After 1878 working people resorted in ever increasing numbers to the magistrates' courts. McGregor points out that between 1897 and 1906 magistrates' courts granted over 87000 separation and maintenance orders.[2]

f) *Extension of bounds of cruelty, etc.*

The courts did extend the bounds of cruelty gradually over the years. In 1853 a royal commission stated that in law cruelty, as interpreted by the ecclesiastical judges, amounted 'to a reasonable apprehension of danger to life, limb, or health [which] renders it impossible to discharge the duties of married life'.[3] In *Kelly v Kelly*[4] the Judge Ordinary made it clear that even so a husband was not entitled to place his wife's permanent health in jeopardy. He said:

> 'Without disparaging the just and paramount authority of a husband, it may be safely asserted that a wife is not a domestic slave, to be driven at all cost, short of personal violence, into compliance with her husband's demands. And if force, whether physical or moral, is systematically exerted for this purpose, in such a manner, to such a degree, and during such length of time, as to break down her health and render serious malady imminent, the interference of the law cannot be justly withheld by any court which affects to have charge of the wife's personal safety.'

Yet in 1897 in *Russell v Russell*[5] the House of Lords, by majority, refused to adopt the impossibility of carrying on married life as a criterion of cruelty: for there to be cruelty in law, the conduct complained of had to be such as constituted 'danger to life, limb or health, bodily or mental, or a reasonable apprehension of it...'

That was a narrow approach. However, the courts became ready to adopt a doctrine of constructive cruelty. A course of conduct which was calculated to break the spirit of the sufferer (more usually the wife), and which continued until

---

20   M.K.Woodhouse 'The Marriage and Divorce Bill of 1857' (1959) 3 AJLH 260, 147 Official Report (3rd series) cols. 1194-1195, O.R.McGregor *Divorce in England* p.20.

1   (1857) 102 Quarterly Review 255.

2   O.R.McGregor *Divorce in England* pp.19, 24, W.Lately *The Tide of Divorce* p.99.

3   First Report...into the Law of Divorce...no.1604 (1853) p.13.

4   (1869) LR 2 P & D 31 at 59.

5   [1897] AC 395.

health broke down, or was likely to break down, under the strain was a ground of relief. Mere neglect and want of affection was not a ground for relief.[6] Further, for conduct to be cruel, it had to be grave and substantial. The courts did go some way, however hesitantly, towards relieving the innocent sufferer in cases of alleged cruelty by denying that deliberate intention was necessary to proof of cruelty. At the same time they were not prepared to move towards a wholly objective standard — conduct was required to be aimed in some way at the petitioner.[7] The courts were prepared also to introduce a concept of constructive desertion, although in the 1940s some judges were concerned that such a concept might lead to a new ground of divorce. Lord Greene MR pointed out that incompatibility of temperament or unhappiness in the marital relationship which was not caused by cruelty were not, by themselves, grounds of divorce.[8]

The court's reluctance to liberalise the divorce law is illustrated also by the sparing use which they made of their discretion to grant a decree when the petitioner had also committed adultery. Indeed, the principles upon which that discretion was to be exercised were settled only as late as 1943.[9]

g) *Amendments*

Over the years a number of important statutory amendments was introduced. The Matrimonial Causes Act 1884, by making non-compliance with a decree for the restitution of conjugal rights equivalent to desertion without cause, gave a new significance to this old ecclesiastical remedy. For by virtue of section 27 of the 1857 Act the wife could obtain a decree of divorce on the grounds of her husband's adultery coupled with desertion, without reasonable excuse, for two years or upwards. Accordingly, after 1884 a wife whose husband had committed adultery and who had refused to obey an order for restitution of conjugal rights, might obtain a divorce after 1884 without waiting for two years.[10] The Gorell Commission did propose a further liberalisation of the law.[11] The majority public opinion of the day was not ready for any such move but favoured instead the strongly expressed, and conservative, dissenting view. However, the Matrimonial Causes Act 1923 provided that it should be lawful for any wife to present a petition for divorce on the ground that her husband had been guilty of adultery. The implementation of the Gorell recommendations had to await the passing of a Private Members' Bill in 1937. The member in question was Sir Alan Herbert, the independent member for Oxford University. His most popular critique of divorce, *Holy Deadlock*, had been published in the form of a novel in 1934: in 1948 there were seven editions. Herbert proposed the following additional grounds of divorce, all of which had been recommended by the Gorell Commission:

1) desertion for three years and upwards;
2) cruelty;
3) incurable insanity after five years' confinement;

---

6 Rayden and Mortimer's *Practice and Law in the Divorce Division* (3rd edn, 1932) p.80.
7 D. Lloyd 'Some Recent Developments in Divorce Law' (1951) 4 Current Legal Problems 324.
8 *Buchler v Buchler* [1947] P 25 at 29.
9 *Blunt v Blunt* [1943] AC 517, S.Karminski 'Family Law' in M. Ginsberg (ed) *Law and Opinion in England in the 20th Century* pp.286, 292.
10 An Act to amend the Matrimonial Causes Acts 1884, Judicature (Consolidation) Act 1925.
11 Royal Commission on Divorce and Matrimonial Causes, 1912 (Cd.6478).

4) habitual drunkenness found incurable after three years from first order of separation;

5) imprisonment under commuted death sentence.[12]

With the omissions of the proposals regarding habitual drunkenness and imprisonment under commuted death sentence, the recommendations were adopted and became law on 1 January 1938.

The Matrimonial Causes Act 1950 consolidated the existing legislation. It provided that either husband or wife might obtain a divorce on the ground that the respondent:

'(a) has since the celebration of the marriage committed adultery; or

(b) has deserted the petitioner without cause for a period of at least three years immediately preceding the presentation of the petition; or

(c) has since the celebration of the marriage treated the petitioner with cruelty; or

(d) is incurably of unsound mind and has been continuously under care and treatment for a period of at least five years immediately preceding the presentation of the petition.'

In addition the wife might obtain a divorce on the ground that her husband had, since the celebration of the marriage, been guilty of rape, sodomy or bestiality. Save in exceptional circumstances no petition for divorce might be presented until the marriage had lasted at least three years.

h) *Conclusion*

The most striking feature of the history of divorce law has been the continuity of legal theory and the reluctance to liberalise existing divorce laws or even to make the existing law more accessible to the majority of the population. Yet the increasing public demand for divorce could not be denied. After the Second World War proceedings for divorce were far from being the decorous and austere proceedings which the parliamentarians of 1857 may have had in mind. The Denning Committee heard of one town where at the summer assizes in 1946 no fewer than 320 cases were heard in six and a half days: the scenes outside the courts were described as more reminiscent of the racecourse at Epsom Downs than a court of justice.[13] Accordingly, commissioners were recruited from the ranks of county court judges and king's counsel — they were to hear both defended and undefended cases throughout the country. In addition more extensive grounds of jurisdiction were introduced. Yet no action was taken to implement a recommendation for the institution of a Marriage Welfare Service. Gradually, even unconsciously, the ground was being prepared for an even more radical liberalisation of the divorce laws.

7 Judicial separation

The Act of 1857 provided that there was to be a new remedy of judicial separation for which a decree might be obtained on the petition of either husband or

---

12　See D. Morris *The End of Marriage* p.94.
13　Second Interim Report of the Committee on Procedure in Matrimonial Causes (Cmd.6945) p.8.

wife. This was in lieu of the divorce *a mensa et thoro*. The new decree of judicial separation was to have all the effect which had belonged to the old divorce *a mensa et thoro* and might be granted on the ground of adultery, or cruelty, or desertion without cause for two years and upwards. An order might be made for alimony to the wife and in addition she was to acquire as to property, and many other purposes, the condition of a feme sole. Further, the divorce court, unlike the ecclesiastical courts, might make orders for the custody, maintenance and education of the child.[14]

Judicial separation was of use to wives rather than to husbands and was used quite frequently, despite the disadvantage to which the Gorell Commission pointed, of a decree which did not dissolve the marriage completely. However, after the legislation of 1923 had introduced equality between husband and wife so far as the grounds of divorce were concerned, judicial separation was used in the main only by those who objected to divorce on religious or conscientious grounds.

8 Restitution of conjugal rights

The old remedy of restitution of conjugal rights survived throughout the whole of this period. However, its function had changed dramatically. The 1884 Act had made it a means of establishing statutory desertion. In addition it was brought for financial reasons since the husband's non-compliance with the decree was a ground for ordering him to maintain his wife.

9 Nullity

The old rules continued to be applied in the Divorce Court for the 1857 Act had required that Court to 'give relief on principles and rules which...shall be as nearly as may be conformable to the principles and rules on which the ecclesiastical courts have heretofore acted and given relief'.[15]

In 1913 Sir Samuel Evans[16] noted that the law upon the subject had not stood still but been advanced by judicial decisions so as to be brought into conformity with more modern ideas. In that spirit he held that a wilful, determined, and steadfast refusal to perform the obligations and to carry out the duties which the matrimonial contract involved would ground an action of nullity. He pointed out that the law had always attributed matrimony to the causes which were set out in the *Book of Common Prayer*, and held that the contract of marriage implied the ability to consummate it. In his opinion it also implied the willingness to consummate it. In 1915 the Court of Appeal overruled that decision on the grounds that it was not justified in principle or by the authorities. Pickford LJ said that the decision in *Dickinson* was 'contrary to the principles of the ecclesiastical law as administered in the ecclesiastical courts' and Cozens-Hardy MR declared: 'It is not for us to say whether the wife's conduct has been such as the legislature might properly consider to be a ground for a

---

14   H.Stephen *Commentaries on the Laws of England* (4th edn, 1858) vol 2, pp.287-8, C.E.P. Davies 'Matrimonial Relief in English Law' in R.H.Graveson and F.R.Crane (ed) *A Century of Family Law 1857-1957* pp.311, 347.
15   Section 22.
16   *Dickinson v Dickinson* [1913] P 198.

dissolution of marriage.'[17] The legislature acted in 1937 in response to
A.P.Herbert's criticisms of the existing grounds. Now the wilful refusal of a
spouse to consummate the marriage was to be a ground of relief. In addition
certain other grounds were introduced which had the appearance of concealed
fraud.[18]

10 Maintenance

a) *The duty to maintain*
At common law the husband was under a duty to maintain his wife; the wife
under no corresponding duty to maintain her husband. Yet at common law the
wife was afforded no adequate means of enforcing the husband's legal obligation
to maintain her. It is true that contracts which had been made for the sole
purpose of supplying her with necessaries suitable to her station in life would
usually be binding upon the husband. This was because his consent to such
contracts would ordinarily be presumed, he being under a legal obligation to
maintain her, so long as he and his wife were living together. Such a presumption
might be rebutted e.g. by giving notice to a particular tradesman not to trust
her.[19] In any event that presumption was no great concession to the wife as wife:
the husband's housekeeper also had the benefit of the presumption. Statute
provided for the punishment as a rogue and vagabond of a husband who had
refused or neglected to support his wife so that she became actually chargeable to
a parish or union. However, it was not the wife but the guardians or overseers of
the union or parish who could charge the husband under the Poor Law Amendment Act 1868 and recover from him the cost of maintaining his wife.

b) *Alimony and maintenance after judicial separation or divorce*
After 1857 upon a decree for judicial separation, upon the petition of the wife, or
on a decree for dissolution of the marriage, an order could be made for alimony
or maintenance to the wife. The Act enabled the court to secure to the wife a
gross sum, or an annuity for her life. The usual order was for an annual sum but
sometimes a gross sum was ordered; if so, the wife received it out and out as her
absolute property. An order for permanent maintenance made under this power
was final and could not be varied. Clearly the courts' powers were inadequate in
cases where a husband had no property on which the payment of such gross or
annual sum could be secured but he would be able to make a monthly or weekly
payment to the wife during their joint lives. Accordingly, the Matrimonial
Causes Act 1866,provided that:

> 'in every such case it shall be lawful for the court to make an order on the
> husband for payment to the wife during their joint lives of such monthly or
> weekly sums for her maintenance and support as the court may think
> reasonable; provided always that if the husband shall afterwards, from any
> cause, become unable to make any such payments, it shall be lawful for the

17 *Napier v Napier* [1915] P 184 at 189, 186.
18 Matrimonial Causes Act 1937, Matrimonial Causes Act 1950.
19 H.Stephen *Commentaries on the Laws of England* (4th edn, 1858) vol 2, pp. 278-9, Eversley
    Domestic Relations (3rd edn, 1906) pp.260 ff., J.Barton 'The Enforcement of Financial
    Provisions' in R.H.Graveson and F.R.Crane (ed) *A Century of Family Law 1857-1957*
    pp.311, 347.

court to discharge or modify the order, or temporarily to suspend the same...and again to revive the same order, wholly or in part, as to the court may seem fit'.[20]

If a husband did have property, the wife could not take advantage of this Act. Undoubtedly, this was a severe limitation upon the Act, even though it was possible to make orders under the Act in respect of husbands who enjoyed a considerable income although they had no capital or no capital was available.[1]

So far as guilty wives were concerned, the practice had grown up of not allowing maintenance unless a special case were shown. In *Robertson v R* the Master of the Rolls, Sir George Jessel, appeared to cast some doubt upon that practice. He pointed out that under section 32 the court had a full discretion and was under no obligation to require special circumstances to be shown to entitle the guilty wife to some provision. Such provision was likely to be small, perhaps no more than mere subsistence.[2] The position of the guilty wife remained much the same as late as 1932 i.e. occasionally the court might make the granting of a small allowance a condition precedent to the pronouncing of a decree absolute in favour of a husband. Initially, even innocent wives were treated less than generously. Soon, however, the quantum payable to an innocent wife was usually about one-third of the husband's income, the same principles being applied as in cases of permanent alimony. It was a practice which Lord Merrivale found necessary to dismiss in strong language as late as 1933: in cases of dissolution of marriage, permanent maintenance was to be awarded on principles distinct from those governing the allotment of permanent alimony in cases of judicial separation. The court was guided by its own discretion.[3]

As the court became more ready during the second quarter of the twentieth century to exercise its discretion in favour of a guilty petitioner, it could happen that the conduct of the respondent might have been better than that of the petitioner. Lord Denning in 1950 stated that if, on an investigation of the facts, it appeared that the conduct of the wife had been much less blameworthy than that of the husband then, even though a decree had been pronounced against her and none in her favour, she was entitled to claim maintenance as if a decree had also been pronounced in her favour. The judge who tried a petition for divorce should express his views on the conduct of the spouses to assist those whose duty it was to award maintenance.[4]

c) *Alimony after nullity*

A notable statutory innovation was made in 1907 when it was provided that alimony could be paid on the same footing as in cases of dissolution of marriage.[5]

d) *Maintenance before the justices and the question of marital violence*

A matrimonial jurisdiction was conferred upon justices by the Matrimonial Causes Act 1878. The origins of that legislation lay in an increasing public awareness of the serious assaults to which many wives were subjected by their husbands.

---

20 *Lister v Lister* (1889) 14 PD 175, 15 PD 4, *Rawlins v Rawlins* (1865) 4 Sw & Tr 158.
 1 *Jardine v J* (1881) 6 PD 213.
 2 (1883) 8 PD 94.
 3 *Horniman v Horniman* [1933] P 95.
 4 *Trestain v Trestain* [1950] P 198.
 5 Matrimonial Causes Act 1907.

There had long been an awareness of the weak financial position of the wife who chose to leave her husband. We have noted already the references which Brougham and Lushington made to it during the divorce debates in the 1840s. Similarly, in 1856 Lord Lyndhurst, a former Lord Chancellor, referred to the position of the wife who had obtained a decree of divorce *a mensa et thoro* as follows:

> 'From that moment the wife is almost in a state of outlawry....The law, so far from protecting, oppresses her. She is homeless, helpless, hopeless.'[6]

It could be argued that if a wife chose to leave her husband, she must suffer the unhappy fate which she had brought upon herself — the institution of marriage must be preserved. It became increasingly clear from mid-nineteenth century, however, that many wives were placed in this unfortunate position through no fault of their own. Surely something could be done to help them?

In 1853 an under-secretary of the Home Department told the House of Commons:

> 'No one could read the public journals without being constantly struck with horror and amazement at the numerous reports of cases of brutal and cruel assaults perpetrated upon the weaker sex by men who one blushed to think were Englishmen, and yet were capable of such atrocious acts.'[7]

He secured the enactment of a measure which empowered magistrates to punish more severely in such cases: there might be a sentence of up to six months imprisonment or a fine of £20. Yet the problem did not go away. In 1868 a select committee was told that there was a great deal of brutality on the part of men in their relations with their wives in east London.[8] In 1874 a further inquiry revealed a widespread belief in the existence of such marital violence. However, the judges believed that the existing law was perfectly adequate, although some did suggest that flogging might be introduced as a punishment in such cases. What was essential was to persuade the wife to complain and then to give evidence in court against her husband. In addition one perceptive magistrate was aware that a sentence in such cases might simply result in the family being broken up with the wife and children probably being sent to the workhouse for want of support during the husband's imprisonment.[9] For such wives the choice could be stark — continue to suffer violence or let your children and yourself starve.

It was just the kind of choice which Frances Power Cobbe castigated so persuasively in an article upon 'Wife Torture in England' which was published in April 1878.[10] Meanwhile a Matrimonial Causes Acts Amendment Bill had been read for the first time in the Commons on 14 February 1878. It was a straightforward measure which bore no reference at all to the question of marital violence. However, on 29 March in the Lords, Lord Penzance, a former distinguished matrimonial judge, moved to insert a clause which would afford substantial protection to a wife who had suffered violence at the hands of her

6   142 Official Report (3rd series) cols. 409-410.
7   124 Official Report (3rd series) col. 1414.
8   Special Report from the Select Committee on the Married Women's Property Bill no. 441 (1863) p.63.
9   Reports to the Secretary of State for the Home Department on the State of the Law relating to Brutal Assaults no. C-1138 (1875) 2nd series.
10   F.P.Cobbe 'Wife Torture in England' (1878) Contemporary Review.

husband. Subject to minor amendment, the clause was accepted and the Act to amend the Matrimonial Causes Act received the Royal Assent on 27 May 1878.

The 1878 Act provided that if a husband should be convicted summarily or otherwise of an aggravated assault upon his wife then the court or magistrate, if satisfied that the future safety of the wife was in peril, might order that the wife should be no longer bound to cohabit with her husband. Further, the husband might be required to pay to his wife such weekly sum as the court or magistrate might consider to be in accordance with his means and with any means which the wife might have for her support. In addition it was provided that the legal custody of any children of the marriage who were under the age of ten years should, in the discretion of the court, be given to the wife. No such order for payment or custody was to be made in favour of a wife who had committed adultery unless such adultery had been condoned.

In terms of the method of reform it was no doubt unfortunate that so important an initiative had to be undertaken by a private member during the course of a debate upon a substantially different matter. In terms of legislative clarity it was, perhaps, unfortunate also that what amounted to a matrimonial remedy should attach to criminal proceedings, although it was clearly more convenient and cheaper for the wife to secure an order from the court which had convicted her husband rather than to petition the High Court for a judicial separation. Also an aggravated assault surely should not require also a threat to the future safety of the wife before she could obtain relief. Overall, however, there can be no doubt but that Lord Penzance's clause had given the reformers much of what they wanted.

In the succeeding years the powers of magistrates to grant maintenance and separation orders were increased. In 1895 the Summary Jurisdiction (Married Women) Act, repealed and substantially re-enacted the Act of 1878 while at the same time extending considerably the jurisdiction of the magistrates. This extended jurisdiction did not require the wife, as she had been required under the 1878 Act, to prove that her future safety was in peril. It is possible that that statutory phrase had been omitted with a view to meeting the criticism that all too often under the 1878 Act the court had not granted the wife a non-cohabitation order. What is clear, however, is that the 1895 Act was used extensively. For example, in 1907, 6734 wives obtained separation orders: in 1909, 5009 wives obtained separation orders. It is not clear, however, just how many of these involved cases of marital violence. What is clear is that the remedy was there, if a wife chose to avail herself of it.

Yet objection to the power of summary courts to make non-cohabitation orders continued to be made. Indeed, the Gorell Commission believed[11] that the remedy of judicial separation itself was an unnatural and unsatisfactory remedy, leading to evil consequences and that it was inadequate in cases where married life had become practically impossible. The commission believed also that the general administration of the Acts was not satisfactory where cases were dealt with by lay magistrates: nor were the commissioners happy with the fact that a

---

11 Report of the Royal Commission on Divorce and Matrimonial Causes (the Gorell Commission) 1912 (Cd.6478), O.R.McGregor *Divorce in England* pp.23-4. On the extended jurisdiction of the magistrates' role see also the Maintenance of Wives (Desertion) Act 1886 and the Licensing Act 1902.

court, whose main duties were of a criminal character should entertain such applications.

However, witnesses before the commission pointed out that if a man were guilty of cruelty to his wife, or of neglect to maintain her and the children, she could not obtain an order, without leaving the house as in law the cruelty in question must have caused the wife to leave and live separately from her husband. Yet she might have been carrying on a small trade or business or work of some kind in the house in which she lived with her husband, or for other reasons she might be desirous of continuing to live in the marital home. Protection against cruelty and neglect to maintain was required, said the commissioners, and should be given to her, without enacting the condition that she should abandon her home — in their opinion the condition should be dispensed with. They pointed to a large number of instances of cruelty which had been given to them. For instance, it seemed shocking, they said, that a woman was bound to remain the wife of a man who had been guilty of such gross cruelty towards her that it was absolutely unsafe for her, as regards life or health, to continue to live with him. They gave the example of cases of men compelling their wives to prostitute themselves for the husband's maintenance — cases which they said were by no means uncommon. Accordingly, the majority recommended that cruelty should be a ground for divorce.

Unfortunately, the majority report met with great hostility. That factor, and the advent of the First World War, delayed any immediate implementation of any of the commission's recommendations. Yet over the years the magistrates' powers were extended. An order might be granted to the wife on the ground of her husband's persistent cruelty or wilful neglect to maintain her, even though such cruelty and neglect had not caused her to live separate and apart.[12]

e) *The wife's duty to maintain her husband*

A guilty wife could not be ordered to pay permanent or interim maintenance or alimony to her husband, although her interest under a marriage settlement might be taken away. However, the 1857 Act did provide that:

> 'In any case in which the court shall pronounce a sentence of divorce or judicial separation for the adultery of the wife, if it shall be made to appear the court that the wife is entitled to any property either in possession or reversion, it shall be lawful for the court, if it shall think proper, to order such settlement as it shall think reasonable to be made of such property, or any part thereof, for the benefit of the innocent party, and of the children of the marriage, or either or any of them.'[13]

In fact few cases arose under the statute.[14] However, following the benefits conferred upon the wife by the Married Women's Property Act 1870, the Act provided that where the husband of any woman having separate property became chargeable to any union or parish, the justices who had jurisdiction in such union or parish might, in petty sessions assembled, upon application of the guardians of the poor, issue a summons against the wife, and make and enforce such order against her for the maintenance of her husband.

---

12   See Law Reform (Miscellaneous Provisions) Act 1949.
13   Section 45.
14   Yet see *Bacon v Bacon and Bacon* (1860) 2 Sw & Tr 86, *Milne v M* (1871) LR 2 P & D 295.

11 Parent and child

a) *Introduction*
The relationship between parent and child depended in law upon whether the child were either legitimate or a bastard.

b) *The legitimate child*

i) *Introduction.* The legitimate child was he that was born within lawful wedlock. Just as the husband dominated the legal relationship between husband and wife so at common law the father dominated the relationship in respect of the legitimate children of the marriage. The history of the parental relationship reflects over the years a desire to give the mother a degree of parental right — there is an analogy here with moves for reform in the field of married women's property — a gradual shifting of the legal position from one in which parental right is stressed above all other considerations to one in which the welfare of the child has a role to play, and increasing intervention by the state to protect the child who was neglected or cruelly treated in addition to coping with the age-old problem of juvenile delinquency.

ii) *Parental duties and powers.* The relationship of parent and child was that of a guardian and his ward. The duties which the law imposed upon the parents of legitimate children were threefold i.e. the duty to educate, the duty to maintain and the duty to protect. The powers which were conferred upon parents, invariably the father, were said by Blackstone to be given, 'partly to enable the parent more effectually to perform his duty, and partly as a recompense for his care and trouble in the faithful discharge of it'. Yet by and large the law enforced parental powers rather more effectively than it enforced parental duties.

iii) *The duty to educate.* Parents were under a duty to give their children an education suitable to their station in life. That duty was not enforced. Perhaps, wrote Blackstone, it was thought to be 'punishment enough to leave the parent, who neglects the instruction of his family, to labour under those griefs and inconveniences, which his family, so uninstructed, will be sure to bring upon him'.[15] In 1870 facilities for elementary education were provided by the Elementary Education Act 1870. However, a statutory duty upon parents to cause their children to receive an efficient elementary education was imposed only by the Elementary Education Act 1876.[16] It was a process which culminated in the comprehensive Education Act 1944.

iv) *The duty to maintain.* It was a principle of law that there was a duty on every man to provide for those 'descended from his loins'. However, a person was bound to provide maintenance for his issue only if the children were unable to work, either through infancy, disease or accident. Even then he was obliged only to provide them with necessaries. It was an obligation, first imposed under the

---

15 1 Bl Com (5th edn) 451.
16 Section 4 provided: 'it shall be the duty of the parent of every child to cause such child to receive efficient elementary education in reading, writing, and arithmetic'.

Poor Law, which was gradually strengthened. At the beginning of the twentieth century statute imposed a duty on parents to provide adequate food, clothing, medical aid or lodging for their children in their custody under the age of 14 years for boys, and 16 for girls. The wilful neglect of this duty, which was likely to cause children unnecessary suffering, was a misdemeanour punishable either on indictment or on summary conviction.[17]

v) *The duty to protect.* Blackstone wrote of this duty as being a natural one 'but rather permitted than enjoined by our municipal law; Nature, in this respect, working so strongly as to need rather a check than a spur'.[18] As time went on it became clear that some parents were either incapable of giving such protection or were unwilling to do so. Increasingly, the state began to intervene in such cases.

vi) *Power of parents over children.* The parent might correct his child, being under age, in a reasonable manner. His consent was necessary to the marriage of his under-age children. In cases where the child had any real estate independently of the father, the latter, in his capacity as guardian, usually had charge of it, and might receive the rents and profits during the minority, subject to the liability to account for them on the attainment of full age. A father might also have the benefit of his children's labour while they lived with him and were maintained by him. By will the father might also appoint a guardian to his children. The mother had no legal power over the child in the father's lifetime, at least as against the father. After the father's death she was entitled to the custody of the child until he became 21, yet she could not appoint a guardian by will.[19]

The common law courts could deny the father's right to the possession of his child only in the most flagrant cases of unfitness. If possession of the child were withheld from the father, he might in general regain it by writ of *habeas corpus*. Since the Judicature Act 1873, which provided that the rules of equity in relation to the custody of infants should prevail, and the Custody of Infants Act 1873, the court had a discretion to refuse a father this writ in cases where the father was seeking the writ in order to remove a child of tender years from the custody of the mother. Where the question was simply as to the legality or illegality of the detention of the child, Chancery's powers were identical with those of the common law courts, although by the Custody of Children Act 1891 equitable principles were to be administered in both Chancery and the common law courts in cases of *habeas corpus*. On the other hand where a cause which dealt with an infant's property was before Chancery i.e. the infant was a ward of court, the court had a discretion to award the custody of the infant to one who had no legal right to it. A parent might also petition Chancery whether a cause affecting the infant was pending or not. Eversley wrote that in such cases, in order to give the court more complete power, the infant should be made a ward of court by the parent or some other person constituting himself or herself a trustee for the

17 43 Eliz 1, c.2, 5 Geo 1, c.8. Cf.31 and 32 Vic, c.122 (Poor Law Amendment Act 1868) and 11 & 12 Vic, c.43, 1 Bl Com (5th edn) 448, Eversley *Domestic Relations* (3rd edn, 1906) p.536, 4 Edw 7, c.15, s.1.
18 1 Bl Com (5th edn) 450.
19 1 Bl Com (5th edn) 452, H.Stephen *Commentaries on the Laws of England* (4th edn, 1858) vol 2, pp.300-301.

infant by paying a sum of money (a small sum would suffice) into court, and making an application by summons at chambers for the appointment of a guardian. In such cases the court had power to inquire into all the surrounding circumstances of the case, the claim of the applicant to the custody, and the interests of the ward. Eversley writes:

> 'The Court of Chancery also has the power of summoning witnesses whom it has reason to believe are aware of the whereabouts of the infant who is its ward, and can compel them to disclose their knowledge. This power neither the Kings Bench Division nor the Chancery Division can exercise on *habeas corpus*. If, therefore, there is any doubt or uncertainty as to where the infant is detained out of the custody of the claimant, the most efficacious step is to make it a ward of court and apply to the court for the appointment of a guardian to it.'[20]

After the Custody of Children Act 1891 the court proceeded in a manner which ought to be found in a 'wise, affectionate, and careful parent': The moral welfare of the child was the dominant consideration for the court and the court would act whether the child is under the control of a parent or of some other legal guardian. Eversley went on to warn:

> 'The ideal of what is a "wise, affectionate, and careful parent" may, however, vary from time to time with the composition of the court which is to translate that ideal into practice: and it is not impossible for the courts to vary in the application of that ideal as much as in the construction of the terms of a will.'[1]

vii) *Statutory limitations upon the parental right of the father.* Still more conscious statutory efforts were made further to qualify parental right at common law in three respects. First, efforts were made to offer the mother a right to the custody of her child in certain circumstances. Secondly, courts which exercised a jurisdiction in the expanding field of matrimonial causes were given a jurisdiction in questions of custody. Finally, the state began itself to assume an expanding role in the assumption of parental right.

viii) *The mother and custody.* The right of the father to custody would not be acted upon 'where the enforcement of it would be attended with danger to the child; as where there was an apprehension of cruelty, or of contamination by some exhibition of gross profligacy', said Lord Denman CJ in 1836.[2] That limited exception to the father's right to custody seemed totally inadequate to Mrs. Caroline Norton who was denied even access to her children. As a result largely of her efforts, Sergeant Talfourd introduced a bill in 1837. The Infants Custody Act became law in 1839 but only after considerable opposition, the essence of which was that by conferring a right of independent action upon the mother, the family bond would be weakened.

The new Act, known as Talfourd's Act, provided that the Lord Chancellor and the Master of the Rolls, upon hearing the petition of the mother of a child who was in the custody or control of the father, or any other guardian, might

---

20 Eversley *Domestic Relations* p.517, n.96.
1   *Eversley* p.51.
2   *R v Greenhill* (1836) 4 Ad & El 624 at 640.

make an order for the access of the mother to such child, subject to such regulations as might be deemed convenient and just; if the child were under the age of seven, the court might order that the mother have the custody of it until it reached that age. No order for such access or custody was to be made if the mother was proved to have been guilty of adultery. The object of the Act, said Lord Cottenham, was (1) to obviate the improper and illegitimate use of the husband's rights and authority to put pressure on the wife; (2) to give the court a widened discretion on behalf of the innocent wife and the interests of the children.[3] The Custody of Infants Act 1873 repealed the 1839 Act and provided that the age to which the mother's rights was to be extended was 16, rather than seven, while the mother might retain the care of those children already in her custody until they attained the age of 16. The second section of the 1873 Act made provision for recognition of provisions for the custody of a child in a separation deed. After the Act many deeds of arrangement entered into between husband and wife might be upheld which formerly would have been treated as of no effect. Yet the touchstone of the validity of such an agreement was said to be the benefit of the infant.[4]

The married women's property legislation appeared to have advanced considerably the concept of the wife's equality with her husband. Not surprisingly, therefore, married women made determined attempts during the 1880s to achieve equality with their husbands in questions of custody. It was not to be: once again the old attitudes defeated them. The Guardianship of Infants Act 1886, therefore, represented a useful but only a partial victory for the views of such women. The Act gave the court greater power to deprive a father of the control and custody of his children. Further, upon the death of a father who had not appointed a guardian, she succeeded to the sole guardianship of his infant children; if the father had nominated a guardian, she was co-guardian with such nominee. The mother's disability to appoint testamentary guardians to her children was also removed.

Equality with her husband in questions of custody was conferred upon the wife only in 1925. However, in any dispute relating to a child the first consideration for the court now was not to be any question of parental right. Instead the first and paramount consideration for the court was to be the welfare of the child. Initially, the courts were to show some uncertainty in the application of this concept. Clearly the Guardianship of Infants Act 1925 amounted to a recognition of the view that a child was worthy of consideration in his or her own right rather than as a parental appendage.

ix) *Matrimonial causes.* The Matrimonial Causes Act 1857[5] conferred upon the divorce court a jurisdiction over the control and custody of children in cases of petitions for divorce, judicial separation and — some years later — for the restitution of conjugal rights. The court had a wide and unfettered discretion. Generally, the court considered the interests of the parents and would usually award custody to the parents. Yet by the close of the century, the avowed aim was to do what was best for the interests of the children: the court would look at the

---

3   *Warde v Warde* (1849) 2 Ph 786.
4   *Re Besant* (1879) 11 ChD 508.
5   Section 35.

actual circumstances, the age of the children, and their position in relation to other members of the family. It was an approach which was emphasised by the Guardianship of Infants Act 1925. The following years were to illustrate that the very breadth of the discretion which the courts enjoyed, together with their limited power to make inquiries were to lead both to some uncertainty in the application of this forward-looking principle and to a suspicion that in practice few thoroughgoing attempts were made to determine how the various possibilities open to the court actually might affect the child.[6]

Less affluent mothers were first offered similar relief in questions of custody by the Matrimonial Causes Act 1878[7] which has already been discussed.

c) *The illegitimate child or bastard*

The illegitimate child or bastard was one who was 'not only begotten, but born, out of lawful matrimony'.[8] At common law the bastard was *filius nullius*, that is, in law he had no parent on whom he had any enforceable claim or from whom he could derive any rights. The role of statute over the years has been primarily to mitigate this harsh common law doctrine.

Even in Blackstone's day parents owed a statutory duty of maintenance to their bastard children to the extent that when a woman charged a person before a justice of the peace with having fathered her bastard child, the justice might cause such person to be apprehended and might commit him until he gave security either to maintain the child or to appear at the next quarter sessions to dispute and try the fact. Statute also provided that if 'such putative father or lewd mother, run away from the parish, the overseers by direction of two justices may seize their rents, goods and chattels, in order to bring up the said bastard children'. In Blackstone's day the legal incapacity of a bastard appeared principally to be that he could not be heir to anyone nor could 'he have heirs, but of his own body; for, being *filius nullius*, he is therefore of kin to nobody, and has no ancestor from whom any inheritable blood can be derived'.[9]

The social reality, at which the law only hints, was that the stigma of illegitimacy cast a very real shadow over the lives of many illegitimate children. The very presence of the illegitimate was a reminder of an immorality within society which must be discouraged. Some orphanages were closed to him — although others did sterling work on his behalf — on the ground that the bastard might inherit his parents' weakness and contaminate others; above all he was a charge upon the rates. The latter point was especially important during the second half of the eighteenth century when illegitimate births appear to have been on the increase. It was a period when the overseers placed great pressure upon the putative father to marry the mother, a practice which the Poor Law commissioners condemned in 1832.[10] Accordingly, the illegitimate suffered especially in the administration of the law to an even greater extent than the substantive provisions of the law necessarily warranted. That administrative deterrent was

---

6 *Re Thain* [1926] Ch 676.
7 The Summary Jurisdiction (Married Women) Act 1895 extended the age of the child or children to 16 years.
8 1 Bl Com (5th edn) 454. H.Elisofon 'A Historical and Comparative Study of Bastardy' (1973) 2 Anglo-American Law Review 306.
9 1 Bl Com (5th edn) 458-9.
10 I.Pinchbeck and M.Hewitt *Children in English Society* vol 2, pp. 583-7.

intensified as a result of the severe manner in which the new Poor Law was administered quite deliberately from the 1830s. Despite the considerable public hostility which the new methods introduced overall, the Poor Law commissioners believed that they had succeeded in reducing the number of illegitimate births. As one overseer reported: 'Fear of the new law makes the girls cautious.'[11]

The administrative and social deterrent was to remain, despite fresh legislation which established firmly the bastard's right to support. The Poor Law Amendment Act 1844 provided that the statutory payments should go to the mother of the child and that she should be punishable at criminal law if she failed to maintain her illegitimate child, despite being wholly or partly able to do so. In 1872 an important Act provided for increased support from the father and in 1873 it was provided that the poor law authorities might recover costs which they had incurred in supporting a child.[12] In practice relatively few women chose to make use of the 1872 Act, probably because the social stigma was too great.

Instead children went to the workhouse, died of neglect, or were even killed. Increasingly, the hard lot of mother and child was recognised. Yet many commentators continued to see that hardship as inevitable: it was a necessary support to the morality of the whole community. A contemporary legal magazine commented in typical fashion on a pamphlet 'Infant Mortality' regretting that a father could not be made to contribute more than two shillings and sixpence a week:

> 'The object of the law of bastardy is to keep an infant born out of wedlock from being starved, and from becoming a burden to the parish in which it is born. The law does not presume to encourage immorality: on the contrary, by limiting the sum it evidently does its best to discourage illegitimacy by making the mother also contribute out of the earning something towards the maintenance of her child. Make the bringing up of illegitimate children an easy work, and you will soon find immorality very much on the increase.'[13]

From the beginning of the twentieth century there was increasing medical evidence of the especially disadvantaged position of the illegitimate, even in the context of the lamentable conditions in which many children lived in the slums. The social problem was heightened by the fact that during the First World War there had been a considerable increase in illegitimate births. In 1918 the National Council for the Unmarried Mother and her Child was formed. Soon it was clear that determined attempts were to be made to achieve equality for the illegitimate child.

At this time the legal disabilities of bastards were seen as being principally confined to their incapacity to inherit titles and lands or to succeed *ab intestato* to personal property under the Statute of Distributions. Nor could a bastard avail himself of the benefits conferred by Lord Campbell's Act in compensation for losses sustained by the death of certain relatives.

If a bastard possessed of property, real or personal, died intestate without leaving a widow or legitimate children the Crown took by escheat. In other respects, too, he was treated differently from other children, e.g. the primary

---

11   N.Longmate *The Workhouse* p.71.
12   Bastardy Laws Amendment Act 1872, Bastardy Laws Amendment Act 1873.
13   (1871) 52 LT 152, cf. (1872) 53 LT 170.

right of custody lay with the mother.

In 1926 two statutes went some way towards alleviating the lot of the illegitimate child. The Adoption Act, by recognising the existence of adoption, made it possible for many illegitimate children literally to start life afresh in a new family. The Legitimacy Act provided that a child might be legitimated by the marriage of his parents, a possibility which had first been mooted some seven centuries earlier, provided that neither of the parents had been married to any other person at the time of the birth of the child. The legitimated child was to be entitled to the same rights and to be under the same obligations as if he had been born legitimate. Lord Buckmaster who had first introduced a legitimacy bill in 1924 had hoped for a more radical measure upon the ground that the illegitimate child was suffering for wrongdoing for which he was not responsible. It was not to be. The majority opinion of the day still believed that to equate positions in law of legitimate and illegitimate children might weaken respect for marriage and for the family.

In 1950, therefore, much remained to be done before the illegitimate achieved equality with the legitimate child. Yet some progress had been made. The nineteenth century had established his right to support: the first half of the twentieth century had seen the first hesitant steps taken towards equality. It was scarcely dramatic progress, but there had been a change of public opinion. It has been suggested that the nineteenth-century changes were influenced by the concept of equality and by an increasing humanitarianism. That view must be tempered by the fact that a dominant concern was to reduce the financial demands upon the rates. Accordingly, little attempt was made to make the law accessible to mothers, although poor law authorities were enabled to recover their costs; certainly there were no moves to equalise the status of the illegitimate child with that of the legitimate child. The minor legislative concession which was made in 1926 was long overdue. The groundswell of public opinion which supported it was due principally to the scientifically accumulated evidence of the social disadvantages which the illegitimate child suffered. For most such children the Adoption Act 1926 offered more speedy relief.

d) *Children and the state*

i) *Introduction.* The state made few attempts during the greater part of the nineteenth century to assume parental responsibilities. Yet, throughout the whole of that century there had been a steadily mounting public concern at the high incidence of juvenile delinquency. How was the state to deal with such juveniles, especially if, as some commentators maintained, society was itself partially responsible for a great deal of that delinquency? That approach complemented later in the century a concern for the destitute or neglected child who might not have committed a criminal offence.

ii) *The juvenile delinquent.* The law treated the juvenile delinquent in much the same manner as the adult criminal until early in the twentieth century. From the second half of the eighteenth century, however, there had been some recognition of the desirability of treating him separately, if only to prevent contact with hardened adult criminals which might contaminate him for life. From mid-nineteenth century there was a still more determined attempt even to reform many juvenile delinquents. However, even when the treatment of juvenile delinquents was placed on a separate and national basis in 1908 with the establishment of the juvenile court, there was still some confusion in practice as to the principle upon which such delinquents were to be dealt with: was the court primarily to punish the delinquent or to consider his welfare?

Some four asylums for the treatment of juvenile offenders existed between 1788 and 1830. First in the field was the Philanthropic Society, which was founded in 1788. In those days its views represented the views of only a small number of persons inspired by religious and humanitarian interests. The Society was considered the 'pinnacle of utopianism'. In its First Report Gilbert states that the Society commented:

> 'From the difficulties thrown in the way of obtaining parish relief it happens that thousands of destitute children are left exposed to the worst examples and compelled by hunger to commit depredations on the public.... These deserted people are the class of vagrant and criminal poor. They are a class which belongs to no rank of the civil community; they are excommunicates in police, extra social, extra civil, extra legal; they are links which have fallen off from the chains of society and which, going to decay...obstruct the movement of the whole machine.'[14]

The Society believed that it was not the fault of the individual that he was delinquent: society and parental neglect had contributed to that result. The Society believed also that the education and employment of such children could reform the juvenile delinquent. The Warwick Asylum, which was established by the magistrates of Warwickshire in 1818, is also worthy of note. That asylum, too, was founded upon the belief that a child could be reformed through education and employment, aided by the strong personal relationship which the master of the asylum was able to build up with the 20 or so inmates. Admittedly, however, these institutions were able to deal with only a mere handful of society's multitude of delinquents. Sir E. Wilmot gave further expression to the advanced views of the Warwickshire magistracy which appeared to favour both a far more extensive use of the summary jurisdiction in juvenile cases and even a form of probation. So Wilmot wrote in 1820 'that justices of the peace should act in *loco parentis*, through courts of summary jurisdiction, at which the child would be admonished, flogged, or sent to a special asylum'. Wilmot believed that 'such a trial would prevent the stigmatisation of the offender' and stated that 'some magistrates ignored the law by sending children back to their parents or employers on condition that they behaved in future'. His was a lonely voice. Despite further reports, and such exceptional treatment, the overall picture was that the vast majority of juvenile delinquents continued to be dealt with in much the same way as adults.

The emergence of the Society for Investigating the Causes of the Alarming Increase in Juvenile Delinquency, which was established in 1815, is of interest as an expression of a national concern. It included figures such as Thomas Fowell Buxton on its committee. The Society gave evidence to a select committee in

---

14   First Report of the Philanthropic Society (1789) pp. 28-9, cited by A.Gilbert *Aspects of the Punishment of Juvenile Offenders 1788-1830* (LL.M. Thesis, University of Birmingham, 1976) pp.5, 19.

1817 and may have influenced the committee's conclusions that much of the increase in crime could be attributed to the extreme destitution of working people and that there should be a special reformatory for children.[15] Other committees also considered the question, although the Society appears to have become less ardent in the 1820s.

When change did occur in the trial of juveniles for some criminal offences, the underlying causes of that change were primarily pragmatic. The criminal law commissioners pointed out in 1837 that in cases of larceny:

> 'However small the value of the article stolen, if the offender is above seven
> years of age, and if his offence is a felony, he must be committed to take his
> trial at the assizes or sessions. He must remain for weeks or perhaps months
> in prison without being subject to compulsory discipline.... While it is
> obvious that the adoption of this course in the case of young offenders is, in
> various ways, productive of positive evils, especially in the destruction of
> morals incident to imprisonment before trial, there are no advantages to
> counterbalance them. The formality of a solemn trial adapted to crimes of
> magnitude, when applied to such cases, derogates from the dignity of a
> superior court of justice, and has not the effect of deterring from trans-
> gressions of the law; for the slightness of the offence, and the youth of the
> offender, usually render him more an object of compassion than a fit
> subject of punishment; and if the jury do not, under such feelings, acquit
> him altogether, they recommend him to mercy on account of his youth,
> and the sentence passed upon him by the court is little more than nominal.
> In trivial felonies, therefore, committed without any collateral circum-
> stances of aggravation, a solemn trial by a jury cannot, we think, be of use
> in the way of example; and as to the reformation of the offender the direct
> tendency of the proceeding, by subjecting him to the demoralisation of a
> prison, is the reverse; so that neither of the two great objects of penal laws,
> namely, the prevention of crime and the reformation of the criminal, are
> accomplished by the present mode of trying very young persons for trivial
> offences. Indeed, where the theft results not from any inveterate habit of
> stealing, or settled want of principle, but from sudden temptation or
> childish indiscretion, or the incitement of others, it may often be less
> mischievous to society, to pass over the offence altogether, than to make it
> the subject of prosecution.'[16]

It was not the first time such a suggestion had been made. Both Fielding and the 1819 committee had made similar suggestions.[17] More recently M.D. Hill, the Recorder of Birmingham, who surely knew Wilmot's views, wrote in 1847 that in Birmingham since 1841 magistrates had released juveniles who were not hardened in crime, to their parents or, subject to police supervision, masters on surety.

On the other hand there was still a considerable amount of opposition to any relaxation of the existing rules. However, subsequent to the findings of a further select committee, statute provided in 1847 that offenders below the age of 14 who had been charged with petty larceny could be tried summarily by two justices

15   Select Committee on the Police of the Metropolis no.233 (1817).
16   Third Report from the Commissioners on Criminal Law: Juvenile Offenders no. 79 (1837) p.7.
17   L. Radzinowicz *A History of English Criminal Law* p.551, n.85.

who could discharge the accused if they thought it expedient not to inflict any punishment. The experiment proved successful.[18]

By mid-nineteenth century a substantial section of public opinion was convinced that professional crime by adults could be tackled only by tackling what was seen as the very real problem of juvenile delinquency. Mayhew gives eloquent expression to such views. Indeed, a special prison for boys only was opened at Parkhurst in 1838, although the hulk which had housed children had long had a bad reputation. Certainly, much of the middle of the road liberal opinion of the day saw juvenile delinquency as a product of society: there was a connection, it was thought, between questions of police, sanitation and public health. A conference upon juvenile crime in 1851 appears to have been fruitful in harnessing such feelings in a constructive manner. The Reformatory Schools Act 1854 and the Industrial Schools Act 1857 were a result. For a minority of delinquent children they afforded a welcome and useful alternative to prison. Yet the state remained aloof. The schools were run on a voluntary basis, although by the final quarter of the century there were over 200 of them. The name of Mary Carpenter will always be associated with the distinguished and devoted work which she accomplished in this field. Most children still went to prison — for example, in 1880 Sir William Harcourt, a humane Home Secretary, pointed out that in one year 6000 children between the ages of 12 and 16, and 720 under the age of 12, were sent to prison. Yet even Queen Victoria believed that he was being unduly tender to offenders until he satisfied her that many of the cases in which he was remitting sentences were only for trifling offences and that imprisonment had not a reformatory but a degrading effect.[19]

The concept of the juvenile court was born in the USA. In 1898 Dr. F.W. Wines, an inspiration of the American juvenile court movement, said:

'We make criminals out of children who are not criminals by treating them as if they were criminals. That ought to be stopped. What we should have in our system of criminal jurisprudence is an entirely separate system of courts for children in large cities who commit offences which would be criminal in adults.'[20]

A juvenile court was opened at Birmingham in 1905: similar courts were established elsewhere. The Children Act 1908 required juvenile courts to be established throughout the country. The juvenile court was to be either in a different building or room from that in which other magistrates' work was conducted and only people concerned with the case were to be admitted. The Children Act 1908 together with the Probation Act 1907 and the philosophy which they embodied, amounted to a revolution in the treatment of the young offender. After a further important inquiry,[1] the twentieth-century principles were established in the Children and Young Persons Act 1933. Yet that Act was also deeply concerned with the neglected child as well as with adoption cases etc. A key section provided:

'Every court in dealing with a child or young person who is brought before

18   J.J.Tobias *Crime and Industrial Society in the Nineteenth Century* pp.263 ff.
19   G.S.Cadbury *Young Offenders* pp.68-9.
20   *Cadbury* p.71. A recent study of the American system suggested that a prime function of the juvenile court was to reform children whose behaviour, while not criminal, was repugnant to respectable America: A.M.Platt *The Child Savers: the Invention of Delinquency.*
1   *Young Offenders Committee* (Cmd.2831).

it, either as an offender or otherwise, shall have regard to the welfare of the child or young person and shall in a proper case take steps for removing him from undesirable surroundings and for securing that proper provision is made for his education and training.'[2]

Some juvenile courts took the view this section meant that even in criminal cases the welfare of the juvenile was the paramount, even the sole, factor: other courts took a different view. The result was uncertainty on a key issue. Accordingly, one commentator wrote in 1946 that there was:

> 'not even a universally accepted outlook to provide a common basis on which the juvenile courts can build up their detailed policy. An attitude of mind that one court accepts as axiomatic might be regarded with horror or scorn by another'.[3]

In some areas probation officers were overworked and this led to the dismissal of some cases. Further, over half the probation officers were on a part-time basis and many were neither efficient nor fully trained.[4] Once again the country had diagnosed the problem but had then failed over a number of years either to establish a clear policy guideline upon a vital issue of principle or to make more than minimal resources available. A multitude of fine intentions backed only by the most meagre resources had marked the country's treatment of the juvenile delinquent just as much as it had that of the adult offender. Yet the trend of policy was now clear. Increasingly, it was believed that, as the Philanthropic Society had suggested in 1788, the causes of juvenile crime lay not so much in the criminal nature of the juvenile as in his destitution or neglect.

iii) *The neglected child*. Since the beginning of the nineteenth century a considerable amount of legislation had been designed to protect the moral, physical and social well-being of the child. Invariably, such legislation was enforced in a less than effective manner. A case in point was the Parrish Apprentices Act 1802.[5] Various Factory Acts extended and improved upon the early legislation which sought to protect children who were employed in factories. Other legislation eventually protected the children, the pathetic 'climbing boys', who were engaged in the business of chimney sweeping, or who worked in mines or in shops. Society had sought also to protect the sexual morality of its girls by providing that carnal knowledge of a girl under 13 was to be a felony and by giving justices the power to summon a young girl under 14 who was living with prostitutes with a view to removing her from their company and sending her to an industrial school.

A concern for the neglected or destitute child began rather later. In 1868 the guardians of the union or parish were empowered to prosecute any parent who should wilfully neglect to provide adequate food, clothing, medical aid or lodging for his child under the age of 14 whereby the health of such child should have been or should be likely to be seriously injured. However the statutory aim had been rather to protect the financial interests of the ratepayers than the physical wellbeing of the children — over the years the statute was little used in any event. It was the Poor Law Amendment Act of 1889 which first provided for

2 Section 44 (1).
3 W.A.Elkin 'The Treatment of the Juvenile Delinquent' in L.Radzinowicz and J.W.C.Turner (ed) *Penal Reform in England* pp.106-7.
4 Op.cit. p.112.
5 An Act for the Preservation of the Health and Morals of Apprentices 1802.

the assumption of parental right in such cases. The Act provided that where a child deserted by its parents was maintained by the guardians of any union, the latter might by resolution vest the control of a boy up to 16, and of a girl up to 18, in their body, as though they were the parents of that infant. However, the parent was not thereby relieved from liability to contribute to the maintenance of the child. An Act of 1899 extended the scope of the provisions to include other than deserted children e.g. orphans and the children of parents who were disabled, imprisoned or unfit to have the care of their children.[6] It was the voluntary organisations, whose origins lay largely in an adaptation of American experience, which paved the way for a greater statutory recognition of the child's need to be protected from cruelty. A number of such local societies had been formed during the 1880s. In 1889 The National Society for the Prevention of Cruelty to Children was founded; in that same year a notable Act for the prevention of cruelty to children was passed. Heywood writes[7] that during the five years following the passing of the 1889 Act 5792 persons were prosecuted for cruelty and 5460 of them were convicted: 47000 complaints were examined. The rescue organisations, of which the Barnado Homes was the best known, played a considerable role in protecting, even searching out, the neglected child. They had their legal position in relation to the parents strengthened by the Custody of Children Act 1891 whereby a parental applicant for the production of a child might be deemed by the court to have abandoned or deserted the child, or to have so misconducted himself that the court ought to refuse his right to custody, the court might decline to issue the writ. Where a parent had abandoned or deserted his child, or allowed it to be brought up at another person's or poor law guardians' expense, for so long and under such circumstances as to satisfy the court that he was unmindful of his parental duties, the child was not to be delivered up to him unless the court was satisfied that, having regard to the welfare of the child, he was a fit person to have its custody.

The Children Act 1908 consolidated much of the earlier legislation which was protective of children. Its importance can be seen primarily in that it gathered together into one enactment much of the earlier piecemeal legislation and thereby emphasised the social rights of children. There were also some useful additions to the existing law. For example, the appointment of infant life protection officers would aid the enforcement of the law. Further, the Act showed an awareness that children might be in danger not only from strangers but even from their own parents. Henceforth, the welfare of children was not to be left only to the private philanthropist or to the uncertain benefits of piecemeal legislation, the state, too, was beginning to recognise that it had a duty to ensure that minimum standards were guaranteed for all children.

Governmental responsibility for the provision of such standards was still divided, yet it had long been clear that a divided administrative responsibility encouraged a lack of efficient enforcement of the law. Even as late as 1946 it was necessary to recommend that responsibility for the care of deprived children should be in one department in which should be concentrated the relevant powers under the Poor Law Act, Children and Young Persons Act, Public Health Act and Adoption of Children Acts. Confusion was increased also by the

6   See generally J. Heywood *Children in Care*, Eversley *Domestic Relations* (3rd edn, 1906) pp.833-6.
7   Prevention of Cruelty to Children Act.

fact that the term 'child' was variously defined in the statutes which dealt with different aspects of the problem.[8]

The Children Act 1948 was an attempt to provide a child care service under the Home Office, although it was the local authority which was to carry the immediate responsibility. At the same time there was an attempt to raise the minimum standards. In that respect the 1948 Act benefited from the Curtis Report of 1946 which had highlighted the problem of the deprived child. In particular the Act benefited from the egalitarian spirit which prevailed at the close of the Second World War and which inspired much social legislation. A new meaning was to be given to the concept of equality.

For lawyers this was primarily social legislation which was of little immediate concern to them. Yet the legislation provided for a quite fundamental erosion of parental right to an extent whose bounds were as yet wholly undefined. The question of the independent rights of the child as yet lay in the future.

iv) *Adoption*. In reality many children had been adopted yet the practice went unrecognised in law until 1926. In law it was not possible for a parent to give up his parental rights and duties. Without doubt many children were neglected and some even died as a result of such neglect. In the light of the increased numbers of children, war orphans and unwanted illegitimate children, who became available for adoption during the course of the First World War, the existing arrangements came under some critical scrutiny. One committee concluded that the absence of proper control over adoption resulted in an undesirable traffic in child life and the time had come for the state at least to record such transactions. Despite the considerable experience in such matters of various overseas countries, there was no consensus as to the scheme which should be introduced. However, following the recommendations of Lord Tomlin's Child Adoption Committee the 'cautious and experimental'[9] Adoption of Children Act 1926 was enacted. Applications for adoption orders could be made at the option of the applicant to the High Court, county court, or juvenile court. An adoption order was irrevocable but an adopted child could be readopted either by its parents or by a third party. The effect of an adoption order was to be that 'all rights, duties, obligations and liabilities of the parent or parents, guardian or guardians of the adopted child, in relation to the future custody, maintenance and education of the adopted child' were to be extinguished and vested in the adopting parent as though the adopted child was a child born to be adopter in lawful wedllock.[10] Many of the old anxieties regarding the methods pursued by adoption societies and other agencies remained. After some delay due to the outbreak of the Second World War, legislation introduced in 1943 prohibited any body of persons other than a registered adoption society or local authority from making arrangements for adoptions and provided for the regulation of the work of registered adoption societies. Certainly, considerable use was made of legal adoptions. Between the enactment of the Adoption of Children Act 1926 and the end of 1945 there had been 127 189 such adoptions.[11] The experiment had been a success.

8 Report of the Care of Children Committee (Cmd.6922) pp.178, 5 — the Curtis Committee.
9 I.Pinchbeck and M.Hewitt *Children in English Society* vol 2, p. 602.
10 Section 5 (1).
11 The Curtis Report (above) pp.21-2, S.Karminski 'Family Law' in M.Ginsberg (ed) *Law and Opinion in England in the 20th Century* pp.286, 292. Note also the Adoption Act 1950.

Chapter 16

Conclusion

1 Introduction

a) *Hopes for law reform*

Lord John Russell expressed a commonly accepted aim when he told the National Association for the Promotion of Social Science in 1857 that: 'The laws must be made consistent with the spirit of the times.' It was an aim of which Mansfield and Blackstone would have approved. It was an aim which Henry Brougham had sought to implement with some verve during the course of a long life. The large number of parliamentary committees and of governmental commissions which was appointed during the nineteenth century demonstrates convincingly that many others shared that aim. Similarly, a number of government – inspired law reform committees was appointed during the first half of the twentieth century. It is reasonably clear, therefore, that society has never at any time lacked those who had some desire at least to keep the law abreast of social change or to achieve rather more radical reforms of the law.

b) *Meaning of law reform*

'Law reform' is a phrase which may include changes in the law which vary in their importance from a relatively trivial statutory amendment to the most radical changes in a whole branch of the law or of the legal system. Moreover, much legislative change was directed rather at reform of social institutions than at those areas of the law and of the legal system in which lawyers took a particular interest. Lawyers may be pardoned if, when they attempt to assess the scope and extent of law reform during this period, they focus upon the legal system and upon those areas of law in which they took a particular interest. In addition, when we assess the extent of law reform, it is legitimate to consider not so much the rash of trivial and piecemeal amendments which any system must surely incorporate over a number of years, as major and purposeful reforms.

2 Relevant factors

a) *The overall conservatism of the political and legal systems*

i) *Introduction.* The political and legal systems did not lend themselves readily to change. It is true that radical change was possible. The success of the enclosure movement over a number of years had shown that at an early date. The Combination Act 1824 is an even better example of radical change, swiftly enacted. Another striking example is afforded by the Matrimonial Causes Act 1878 which enhanced the importance of the magistrates' courts. Such instances are relatively rare.

ii) *The political system.* The usual process of inquiry, report and legislation was ponderous. As that process was implemented, public concern upon an issue might wane with the result that legislation was less likely to be introduced. Politicians had other interests which, with some reason, they might regard as more pressing — law reform has rarely been a vote-winner. In addition, parliament was jealous of its legislative powers. Parliament was not to be bypassed. Accordingly, it was only rarely possible to pass through parliament even amending bills of a purely technical character, without running the risks of both parliamentary amendments which might mar the legal quality of the bill and also lengthy parliamentary discussions. The prospect of such discussions could mean that on occasion government departments might be unwilling to put up amending legislation on the ground that this might reopen discussion upon the premises upon which the original legislation had been based. Such parliamentary discussions might mean also that a bill would be lost for lack of parliamentary time. In any event the rules of parliamentary procedure meant that a bill could be lost at the close of a parliamentary session. Alternatively, a sudden change of government could mean the loss of pending legislation.

iii) *The legal system.* Nor did most lawyers lend themselves readily to change. To a certain extent their professional conservatism was not only understandable but even in the public interest. There is a strong and abiding public interest in ensuring that the law shall be as certain as possible. However, professional traditions sometimes encouraged a lack of response to a need for change. For example, lawyers had a perfectly proper and understandable respect for the merits of the common law. On occasion, however, that led the judges to interpret statute in an unduly restrictive manner which in the long term lost both them and the law a certain public respect. Similarly, they refused to simplify the law by way of codification — despite the strong public interest in such codification — because they feared that to do this would be to destroy their beloved common law. To a large extent theirs had been an unthinking, instinctive refusal.

As a politically influential pressure group the lawyers were able successfully either to resist changes of which they disapproved or to shape them to meet their particular demands — at least in those matters in which they were regarded as having a special expertise. They tended to dominate the membership of commissions which were inquiring into what were seen primarily as legal questions. Often they were well represented also upon committees which were dealing with such questions. The majority of such lawyer commissioners and committee men were unlikely to be sympathetic to any proposal which went beyond a minor adjustment of the system. For example, Parke and Stephen were members of the Common Law Commission of 1829. Parke was known to be highly conservative. Both were eminent special pleaders. Yet the excesses of special pleading were already an important factor in contributing to undue expense and delay within the legal system. Not surprisingly, one of the reforms which emerged was the Hilary Rules of 1834 whose most notable effect in the view of the public was that they increased still more the already excessive measure of delay and of expense which existed in the common law system. Members of other commissions were selected upon a similar basis. Even the *Law Times* queried whether the choice of one of the masters of the Court of Exchequer as a member of a commission in 1850 was likely to lead to reform. It was a similar story with the Judicature Commission which, for all practical purposes, was composed entirely of lawyers. Nor was the lawyers' influence less marked even during the first half of the twentieth century. Such an approach had some merit, if the sole scope of the commissions' inquiry was simply to consider the adjustment of a number of legal technicalities. It was upon such a basis that the Master of the Rolls had attempted to reject a proposal in mid-nineteenth century to include lay members on the Chancery Commission. Yet those legal technicalities often had very important social consequences in which the public as a whole had a proper interest. For example, commercial men surely had a proper interest in demanding that commercial litigation should be neither unduly delayed, nor unduly expensive nor lead unnecessarily to hostile feelings between business associates which might mar their future relationship. If that kind of public interest could not be met, then perhaps consideration ought to have been given to a more radical change of the legal technicalities or even of the legal system.

One factor which was highly influential in retarding and cramping the growth of the county court system was the Bar's belief that such a system would destroy the relatively small centralised Bar. The public interest in the continued maintenance of such a small Bar was said to be that it enabled selection to be made of men who would make suitable judges in the superior courts. That was a legitimate ground of public interest, but the case against it tended to go largely by default. Perhaps the valuable traditions of the Bar could have been transferred successfully to local centres. Perhaps judges of the superior courts could have been selected in some other equally satisfactory manner. Perhaps an expanded system of county courts would not only have met the public interest in speedy and inexpensive justice but might also have benefited the self interest of the lawyers by increasing the number of litigants before the ordinary courts of the country. No such inquiry was instituted. The Bar was a proud and powerful profession, which had contributed much that was valuable to public life, but it did not take kindly to any proposals which might alter its own role in any way.

The judges of the superior courts also were influential. On occasion their views were not sought. The Select Committee on Criminal Law of 1819 quite deliberately avoided taking the views of the judges upon the rather specious ground that to do so would be unfair to the judges themselves. In the light of the contemporary judiciary's conservative approach to questions of penal policy, that was an understandable tactic on the part of a reformist committee. By and large, however, it was useful to secure judicial approval of a measure. Judicial disapproval of Cranworth's codification proposals in the early 1850s led to the abandonment of that measure. On the other hand Selborne's wooing of the judges in respect of the Judicature Bill had secured the enactment of that measure.

Of course, fewer lawyers sat upon commissions or committees which dealt with issues which were seen to embrace matters which clearly covered issues broader than legal technicalities. This was true of labour law. Within the field of commercial law both legal and commercial interests worked well together in both the public interest and to their mutual self interest. A measure of codi-fication was one result of that co-operation. Yet the commercial lobby was strong and it had pressed quite hard for a simplification of the sources of the law. In other areas of the law, which were largely technical and where no such influen-tial lobby existed, there was no change. An outstanding example is the criminal law. Criminal law commissioners, who were of considerable academic talent, pointed to a real need for change well before mid-nineteenth century. Other commissioners, who included some of the most distinguished lawyers of the day, made a similar effort later in the century. It was all to no avail. Professional hostility and public apathy saw them off.

This is not to maintain that the lawyers were wholly negative in their approach to law reform — far from it. Individual lawyers contributed a great deal. The passage of the Judicature Acts was due to the political and legal skills of Selborne and of Cairns. Many other examples could be given. The contribution of the lawyers was especially valuable in the reform of technical areas of the law. A good example was the reform of the law of real property which culminated in the legislation of 1925. Similarly, Goodhart has suggested that the increasingly critical tone of academic writing on law during the first half of the twentieth century also contributed to an increased interest in law reform. Yet as a whole the lawyers were less than enthusiastic in their approach to law reform throughout this period whenever proposals for such reform went beyond a limited adjustment to the existing system.

b) *The importance of public opinion*

i) *Introduction.* Clearly public opinion was likely to be a vital factor, if the conservatism of the political and legal systems was to be overcome. Nor is this a matter for surprise. The success of moves to codify the law in Napoleonic France and in Bismarck's Germany may be attributed to a newly found nationhood which found expression in unified systems of law. England and Wales knew no such compulsive force. Yet in mid-nineteenth century there was a considerable public enthusiasm for law reform, as there was for reform in other areas of the national life. The *Morning Chronicle* wanted law reform, the *Law Times* wanted it, *The Times* wanted it — and warned the lawyers not to oppose it. Finally, when Lord Derby announced to parliament his government's intention of introducing measures for simplifying and improving the administration of law and justice, even the government appeared to want law reform. This is not to suggest that the whole country, or even what we might call responsible public opinion, was ablaze with calls for the reform of the law. These were spasmodic announcements which were made over a number of years. Yet taken together such announcements do indicate that the effective public opinion of the day would be receptive to suggestions for law reform. It was not an opportunity which reformers would wish to miss. Certainly it represented an opportunity for reform which had not existed during the period up to 1820. It was an opportunity which was not to occur again until the years after the Second World War.

ii) *The small pressure group.* Of course, public opinion did not go unheard even during such other periods. Several factors ensured this. First, the enthusiasm or influence of a small group might be decisive. This was especially so during the period 1750 to 1830. Then the political and legal worlds were relatively small: personal contact and influence counted for so much more. Even in the latter half of the nineteenth century such an approach could succeed. An example is afforded by the passage in 1878 of Lord Penzance's Matrimonial Causes Act. Possibly the efforts of James Fitzjames Stephen to codify the criminal law, although they were unsuccessful, may also be included in this category. More typical of the period was the pressure group. Bodies such as the Law Amendment Society and the National Association for the Promotion of Social Science sought to influence a wide spectrum of public opinion during the second half of the nineteenth century. Other groups were more specialised still in their interests. The Junta and their advisers, who included Frederic Harrison, a distinguished academic lawyer, exercised some influence upon trade union legislation during the 1870s. The National Council for the Unmarried Mother and her Child was typical of the specialised pressure group in the social field during the first half of the twentieth century. By this time, however, 'lawyers' law' was no longer an area of general public concern, its reform was consigned to a number of specialist ad hoc committees, many of which were government inspired. Yet even at this late period the individual would-be reformer might achieve a notable success. An outstanding example is afforded by A.P. Herbert's successful sponsorship of the Matrimonial Causes Act 1937.

iii) *The jury.* Secondly, the jury represented the authentic voice of the public in many contested civil and criminal trials. By their verdicts in numerous trials juries could amount on occasion to a powerful force for change. During the early nineteenth century the reluctance of juries to convict on many of the lesser criminal charges, which were nevertheless then subject to the death penalty, may have contributed to the eventual success of the attempts which were made to reduce the number of offences which were subject to the death penalty. During the twentieth century a reluctance to convict on motor manslaughter charges, was also a factor of which legislators were increasingly aware. In civil cases also the sympathy of juries with plaintiffs in personal injury cases, especially when the defendant was a railway company, led to some heart searching concerning the continued role of the jury itself in such cases. However, although such decisions on the part of a jury may contribute eventually to reform, they hardly amount to purposeful reform.

iv) *The lay voice on inquiries.* In the third place, therefore, we turn to the lay voice on royal commissions and select committees and as expressed in other ways.

There was a considerable measure of agreement amongst both laymen and lawyers in terms of general principle upon matters such as the necessity of fair trial, of the approval of the principle of equality, and of a desire to avoid undue technicality. In addition there are indications that many members of the public would have preferred in the court system an approach which stressed substantial justice rather than the lawyers' approach which too often, despite a professed dislike by lawyers for undue technicality, stressed the necessity for procedures which resulted in a measure of delay and expense to the litigant which many believed to be unnecessary and even excessive. Lawyers did assent to a simplified form of procedure in the new county courts. The approach of these new courts was demonstrably more popular than that of the superior courts. Yet many lawyers continued to regard the more complex procedure of the superior courts as being invariably the more desirable. Invariably the lawyers, or rather the more influential amongst the barristers, got their way. The lay voice was no match for that of the lawyer when the issue was one of change at the heart of the legal system.

c) *The search for consensus*
An awareness of the difficulties in practice of reconciling such different points of view led often to a consensus approach which stressed how little was being changed. It had nevertheless proved possible on occasion brilliantly to manipulate the system and so achieve a radical solution. Francis Place had shown that with the enactment of the Combination Act 1824. His outright success was relatively short lived. Similarly we find that others who boldly put forward radical schemes were less likely to achieve success. That was true even of many of Brougham's reformist schemes. It was true also of the ambitious codification schemes of both Cranworth and Stephen. By contrast Chalmers succeeded by adopting a more modest approach. Peel had shown the usefulness of such a modest approach which stressed how little was being changed when he succeeded both with his proposals for some consolidation of the criminal law and also with the creation of the new metropolitan police force. It was a lesson which was not lost upon Selborne as he sought to implement the proposals of the Judicature Commission. Substantial agreement already existed; all interest groups were consulted; legislation followed. In the absence of such a consensus other judicature proposals such as those on the county courts failed. It was the difficulty of achieving such a consensus within the profession which was responsible also for the desperately slow progress towards a more satisfactory system of legal education.

d) *The lack of a continuing agency of law reform*
Especially since the mid-nineteenth century the permanent officials in some government departments contributed to reform by knowing when reform was necessary and by encouraging the minister to appoint a committee which could deal with the various problems. By way of illustration of this point Goodhart referred to the regular reforms which had been instituted in the field of company law and also to the contribution which the Home Office had made to prison reform and to penology generally. On the other hand it is true that on occasion a government department might be reluctant to put forward amending

legislation, if it believed that the parliamentary debates upon such amendments might be used in order to reopen a debate regarding the premises upon which the legislation was based. It was true also that the existing government departments tended both to be understaffed for much of this period — this was true especially of the Lord Chancellor's department and of the Home Department during the nineteenth century — and would naturally tend to be reluctant to produce work which might appear to be critical of the efforts of their own department. The result was that no person or body was responsible for the smooth running of the legal system as a whole. Reform of the law and of the legal system continued by and large to depend primarily upon private initiatives and upon the response which might be made to the reports of ad hoc committees and commissions. Opposition to the creation of a Ministry of Justice tended to be as strong in mid-twentieth century as it had been in the mid-nineteenth century.

3   Law reform and the national need of change

To what extent was purposeful reform of the legal system and of those areas of law in which lawyers took a particular interest achieved during this period? Dicey was strongly of the view that much had been achieved, at least during the period 1825-1870. He described those years as the years of Benthamism or individualism and wrote:

> 'The movement of which he, if not the creator, was certainly the prophet, was above all things a movement for the reform of the law. Hence it has affected, though in very different degrees, every part of the law of England. It has stimulated the constant activity of parliament, it has swept away restraints on individual energy, and has exhibited a deliberate hostility to every historical anomaly or survival, which appeared to involve practical inconveniences or in any way to place a check on individual freedom.'

By way of example Dicey referred to the transference of political power to the middle class, to humanitarianism in the form of the mitigation of the criminal law and the emancipation of slaves, to extensions of individual liberty e.g. in the form of the Combination Acts 1824 and 1825, and to the adequate protection of rights e.g. the County Courts Acts 1846-1888. In discussing the 'renovation of English institutions under the influence of Bentham', Dicey concluded:

> 'The efforts of obstructionists or reactionists come to nothing, the toryism of Eldon, the military rigidity of the Duke of Wellington, the intelligent conservatism of Peel, at a later period the far less intelligent conservatism of Lord Palmerston, all appear, though the appearance is in some respects delusive, not in reality to delay for more than periods which are a mere moment in the life of nations, the progress of change. On the other hand, the violence of democrats or the fervour of enthusiasts achieves little in hurrying on innovation.'[1]

Dicey gives us a clear picture of purposeful, albeit measured, change during the period 1825-1870. Can we accept his assessment?

Clearly considerable legislative changes did occur during this period, but

1   A.V. Dicey *Law and Public Opinion in England during the Nineteenth Century* (2nd edn, 1962) pp. 209-10.

many of those changes did not go either to the heart of the legal system or to those areas of law which were closest to lawyers' hearts. This is true of all of Dicey's examples with the important exception of the County Courts Acts and the Combination Acts. However, one cannot help noting both the grudging manner in which the legal profession first bowed to the public demand for the introduction of such courts and then to the constant battle which the Bar waged in order to limit the jurisdiction of those highly popular courts. For their part the Combination Acts 1824-1825 represented a radical change in the law. Yet, although they were important, they did not affect adversely either the community as a whole or the legal system but represented a change which affected only a numerous but politically uninfluential section of the community. Other changes went not so much to legal as to social reform. The new Poor Law, the Factory Acts, the Public Health Acts were all significant measures in terms of the social policies to which they gave expression. They are also of considerable legal interest in that they began to articulate a new approach towards the enforcement of the law. Yet primarily they dealt with issues which were of social rather than of legal reform. In a pragmatic, yet purposeful, manner such Acts grappled with major social problems of the day. No like attempt was made to reform the law and its institutions either during the period 1825-1870 or at any other time during the period 1750-1950.

Reformers had agreed on both philosophical and practical grounds that a simplification of the sources of the law was highly desirable. Their achievement, worthy although it may have been, fell far short of the minimum reforms which would have been necessary to achieve such an aim. Nor had progress in the field of legal education been any more encouraging, despite the fact that the Select Committee of 1846 had analysed the problem so convincingly. Nor had the court system done more than survive more or less adequately. Upon it might be passed the sad judgment which an American scholar passed upon the American system:

> 'The product of a century of law reform, then, is that means are still sought to make the judicial system tolerably efficient in the large centers of population.'[2]

Within the field of substantive law the history of purposeful law reform is no less unhappy. The substantive criminal law during this period is still deserving of Professor Milson's stinging rebuke regarding crime's 'miserable history'. Within the field of commercial law Lord Mansfield's initiative had been welcome. Within the field of civil liability the lawyers created a new branch of law which was suited to the needs of the day. It was scarcely their fault that the pace of social and economic change had quickened so considerably by the beginning of the twentieth century that in its pure form their achievement was relatively short lived. All this scarcely adds up to a picture of purposeful law reform which met the needs of the times.

Perhaps that is too harsh a judgment. The task was both massive and without end. Secondly, we should not equate criticism of a lack of pace in achieving purposeful reform with the view that no purposeful reform was achieved at all. Finally we should bear in mind both the need of stability and the fact that of necessity legal change must often lag behind public opinion to a certain extent.

2 H.E. Yntema 'Legal Science and Reform' (1934) 34 Col LR 206, 217.

Let us consider each of these three points in rather more detail.

First, the task which faced the law reformers was undoubtedly a massive one in terms of both the scope and the extent of the challenge which they faced. In addition the sheer pace of social and economic change throughout the nineteenth century was unparalleled. That alone meant that reforms which were introduced could be soon outdated in terms of their effectiveness. In such circumstances it was perhaps a considerable achievement on the part of all concerned during the nineteenth century to ensure that the legal system and the law managed even to cope with the unique burdens which had been thrust upon them so suddenly. What is regrettable is that during the twentieth century too little was built upon that not inconsiderable achievement.

Secondly, there is the eternal debate concerning both the speed with which it is desirable to introduce change and as to how radical that change should be. That was what lay at the heart of the hostile Benthamite reaction to Brougham's famous speech in 1828. Critical of Brougham's failure to adopt a more radical approach, the *Westminster Review* proclaimed that Brougham was not the Messiah of law reform. In fact even Brougham, the politician, proved to be incurably over-optimistic in terms of what it was politically possible to achieve.

Thirdly, granted the need for certainty within the legal system and the law, together with the fact that the nineteenth century was a period of such rapid change, it was inevitable that reform should lag behind the need of it. Yet reform is not necessarily limited to a mere reactive role. This is true especially of reform of the legal system e.g. the courts, or of questions such as codification. It was surely not beyond the capacity of the lawyers to look ahead to a certain extent in order to determine future demands upon the legal system. The courts are a good example. During the first years of the twentieth century it was as clear as ever that the superior courts, especially King's Bench, were subject to delays of a kind which amounted in many instances to a denial of justice. After so many years of tinkering with the system, it was surely obvious that a quite different approach to reform of these courts was needed if public expectations and the high values upon which the legal profession had always insisted were to be met in a satisfactory manner. It was not to be. Two World Wars may be some excuse for that failure. No doubt a similar ennui also paralysed other areas of national life during these years. Unfortunately, the fact remains that during the first half of the twentieth century the legal system had been allowed to do little more than to lumber and creak along. No lessons had been learned from the past. No science of judicial administration had been formulated. No real attempt was made to bring the benefits of a modern legal system home to all the people. Brougham's vision of 1828 had not been achieved. Yet its ideal remained as valid for the lawyers of the twentieth century as it had been for lawyers in Brougham's time.

For further reference:
F.E. Dowrick 'Lawyers' Values for Law Reform' (1963) 79 LQR 556 and (1966) 82 LQR 497.
A.H. Manchester 'Law Reform in England and Wales 1840-1880' (1977) *Acta Juridica* 189.
A.L. Goodhart *Law Reform* (Holdsworth Lecture, 1952, University of Birmingham).

INDEX

126-7
143-4
174-5
IRP.
P/punitive 326